PRACTICAL GUIDE FOR IMPROVING YOUR METAL FABRICATING SHOP LAYOUT

Richard Budzik
George Kuprianczyk

Practical Publications
6272 W. North Av.
Chicago, IL 60639

*Practical Guide for Improving Your Metal Fabricating
Shop Layout*

© Copyright 1993 by Practical Publications

All rights reserved, including those of translation. This book, or parts thereof, may not be reproduced or transmitted in any form without permission of the copyright owner.

Practical Publications
6272 W. North Av.
Chicago, IL 60639

I.S.B.N. 0-912914-23-8

Printed in the United States of America

Preface

Whether you evaluate alternative layouts for your entire plant or shop or a section of it, you should consider many factors before selecting the most suitable plan. The important factors are condensed and enumerated in this book, along with some details that need consideration.

Each person or company must make decisions concerning the relative importance of these factors--the sequence in which they are presented does not automatically determine their order of importance, as this varies somewhat from one company to another. However, these key factors can be extremely helpful when planning a new layout or when selecting the best layout from several alternatives.

To be kept in mind while reading are the requirements for planning that are necessary for material flow and effective layouts for the physical facilities available, along with inspection and standards.

Depending on your experience in the concepts of layout planning and a knowledge of the specific company's needs, some of the steps featured in this book may require little more than a brief reminder--not pen and paper notations, as would be required for a less experienced person.

Most sections of this book apply to all types of metal fabrication, while a few sections are for close tolerance metal fabrication and a few for the ductwork shops. All sections use a practical approach to solving various layout problems--with suggestions and aids for improving or making a complete new layout.

A special section at the end of the book includes the actual templates for machinery and equipment that has been drawn to 1/4" scale. These can be cut out and placed on the 17x22" graph paper that accompanies each book.

We especially acknowledge **The FABRICATOR®** and **SNIPS** trade publications, both of whom provided outstanding articles. We appreciate their assistance in selecting the most appropriate articles from their many years of devotion to the industry.

Richard S. Budzik

George Kuprianczyk

CONTENTS

1. Shop Layout Considerations — 1

Questions to Ask Yourself
An Efficient Shop Layout--and Its Advantages
Minor Shop Layout Problems
Complete or Partial New Shop Layout
The Shop Layout -- Being Practical
What Makes an Efficient Shop Layout
Taking the Inspection Tour of Your Shop
Analyzing Your Different Shop Layout
Basic Principles of Shop Layout
The "Continuous Flow Line" concept
Basic Methods of Shop Layout
Reluctance of Employees to Change -- Overcoming this Obstacle
Discussion with Your Employees
OSHA and Your Company
Selecting the Best Layout
Implementing the New Layout
The Goal -- an Improved Shop Layout

2. Machinery and Equipment Considerations — 20

Proper Machinery and Tools
Have Enough Smaller Tools
Managing Smaller Tools and Equipment
Ways You Can Prolong the Life of Your Machinery and Equipment
Schedule for Use of Machinery and Equipment
Replacement Policy
Machine Requirements Determined by Volume of Work
Analysis of When to Replace Equipment
Selecting the Right New Equipment -- Comparison of Operating Characteristics
Optional Machine Attachments
Standard or Specially-Built Machinery and Equipment
Getting Price Quotations
New or Used Equipment
Buy, Rent, or Lease Machinery and Equipment
Lease with Option to Buy
Depreciation on Equipment
List of Long-Range Desired Improvements
Keeping Abreast of New Developments

3. **Important Factors to Consider When Determining a New Shop Layout**   **36**

    How Effective Will Be the Flow or Movement?
    Will All Space Be Utilized Well?
    How Effectively are Materials Handled?
    How Can Safety and "Housekeeping" Be Maintained?
    How Effectively Will Supervision and Control Be Maintained?
    Can the Quality of Products or Materials Be Maintained?
    How Will Equipment Be Utilized?
    Will Maintenance Problems Be Affected?
    Can the Expected Capacity Be Achieved?
    How Effective is the Storage?
    How are Security and Theft Considerations?
    Are Working Conditions or Employee Satisfaction Affected?
    Can Supportive Services Be Properly Integrated?
    Does the Layout All Fit with the Company's Overall Organization Structure?
    Is There Flexibility in the Layout?
    Is the Layout Versatile or Adaptable Enough?
    Is it Compatible With Overall Short-range and Long-range Plans?
    Is There Adequate Expansion Capability?
    Does the Layout Use Natural Conditions Economically?
    Is the Layout Compatible for Public and/or Community Relations?

4. **Additional Factors to Consider When Determining a New Shop Layout**   **46**

    Goals of a Facility Design
    Typical Types of Layout Problems
    Steps for a Facility Design
    Why a Master Flow Pattern is Needed
    Typical Flow Patterns
    Basic Flow Pattern Considerations
    Planning Efficient Work Areas
    Material Handling Concerns
    Various Methods of Basic Material Handling

5. **Considerations for Machine and Tool Replacements**   **60**

    Replacement Considerations for Machines and Tools
    Methods for Evaluating Replacement Alternatives
    Economics of Machine Tool Costs

Using the MAPI System for Replacement Decisions (MAPI: Machinery and Allied Products Institute)
Calculating Economic Lot Sizes

6. **Planning the Manufacturing Processes**   **70**

Various Steps for Analysis of Production
Implementing New Techniques and Processes in Manufacturing
Areas of Possible Part Inspection
Considerations for Possible Changes
Controlling Materials and Supplies
Decisions on Space Requirements
Functions of Production Planning

7. **Collection of Articles from THE FABRICATOR® - Official Publication of The Fabricators & Manufacturers Association, Int'l.**   **83**

Maximizing the Return on Your Sheet Metal Equipment
What You Should Know About Leasing Fabricating Equipment
Blueprint for Success: Implementing a Job Shop Software System
The Fabricator's Shop Floor Control Software Chart
Tips for Understanding CAD/CAM Software
How to Purchase a CAD/CAM System
The FABRICATOR'S® Sheet Metal CAD/CAM Software Chart
Fabricating with One-Step NC Controls--Combining CAD/CAM and Shop Floor Programming Techniques
Guidelines for Purchasing Coil Processing Capital Equipment
Using CADD on the Shop Floor
Fabricating Parts from 3-D Drawings--CAD/CAM Can Provide a Strategic Advantage
Short-Run Shearing in Sheet Metal Fabricating
Can Just-in-Time Be Implemented in the Precision Sheet Metal Job Shop?
Keeping Time: The Benefits of a Job Costing System
Measuring Productivity in the Job Shop
Rethinking the Short-to Medium-Run Sheet Metal Process
It's Time to Expand Your Plant--Should You Relocate?
Listing of Articles that Have Been Featured in **The FABRICATOR®**

8. **CAD/CAM Information from Merry Mechanization, Inc.**   **235**

9. **Sample Shop Layouts -- Collection of Articles from SNIPS Magazine**   **254**

    124-Year Old Nashville, Tenn. Sheet Metal firm Noted in the South for Modern Production Equipment
    Z & M Sheet Metal, Fairfax, Va., Use Ingenious Sheet Inventory, Storage System and Production Line for Custom Duct Fabrication
    How Aurora, IL., Sheet Metal Shop Updates Shop Equipment to Keep Competitive
    Modern Asheville, N.C., Sheet Metal Shop Reflects Changeover from Heating-Cooling to Fabrication Work
    L.R.M., Inc., Baltimore, MD., Credits Amazing Growth to Installation of Up-to-Date Sheet Metal Equipment
    Modern Computer Technology Gives Competitive "Edge" to Midland Engineering Co., South Bend, IN.
    Seminole Sheet Metal Co., Tampa, FL., Owes Success to Equipping Shop with Versatile Sheet Metal Machinery
    Charles E. Jarrell & Associates, St. Louis, MO., Opens New Fully Equipped 10,000 Sq. Ft. Sheet Metal Shop
    Successful Sheet Metal Shop Layout Fundamentals Provided by Art Hueur
    H & H Heating & Cooling, Beach Grove, IN., Has Well Organized New Shop for Expanding Business
    Suggested Shop Layout for Brazilian Customer by Lockformer Co., Lisle, IL.
    Richard Voorkees of Vorys Brothers, Submits Ideas on Shop Layouts
    Suggested Shop Layout Submitted by Souther, Inc., St. Louis, MO.
    Profitable Techniques for Handling Coil Stock in Sheet Metal Shops
    Listing of Articles that Have Been Featured in **SNIPS**

10. **Helpful Fabrication Information for the H.V.A.C. Industry**   **297**

    Design Affects Labor
    Listing and Sketching HVAC Ductwork
    Using the Cutting List System (with over 60 sample fittings and their solutions)
    Transitions: Layout Out, Marking & Forming
    Combining Patterns to Save Time
    Making Large Ductwork Economically
    Nesting and Combining Fittings

Determining Blank Sizes for Elbows and Angles
Determining Blank Sizes (Cut Sizes) for Transitions

11. The Role of the Computer in the Sheet Metal Industry -- with Actual Shop Samples   **417**

Cybermation Computer-Controlled Plasma Cutting System
Super-Duct Estimating Software by Wendes (WECS)
Quick Pen for Sheet Metal and Air Conditioning Contractors--
    Computer Aided Estimating
The L-Tech Duct Cutting System
ORCA Sheet Metal Layout System
Pro-Duct Hand-Held Computer System
Bidmaster Estimating Programs
Computer News columns from SNIPS Magazine

12. Materials for Making Your Shop Layout   **479**

1. Factors to Consider
2. Machinery and Equipment Template Cutouts
3. 1/4" Graph Paper

Index   510

The Authors
Richard S. Budzik

Since 1964 Dick has been a teacher at Prosser Vocational School in Chicago. Here he has trained thousands of students, apprentices and mechanics in sheet metal work.

He conducts both day and evening classes. The day sessions are for high school vocational students readying themselves to enter the trade when they graduate. At night, he holds classes for apprentices and also for mechanics wanting to brush-up, advance themselves or simply keep pace with a changing industry.

Also, he has periodically served as a curriculum consultant for the Chicago Public School system. And he has conducted company training programs for several industrial firms.

In his spare time, he has authored a total of 28 books on various phases of sheet metal work, making him one of the most published, if not the most published, author in this field.

Five of these books by Practical Publications are *Today's 40 Most Frequently-Used Fittings (Volumes 1 and 2), Round Fittings Used Today Including Methods and Techniques of Fabricating Round Work, Fittings Used Today That Require Triangulation including The Theory of Triangulation and Specialty Items Used Today.* These volumes cover the sheet metal fittings that are used today, as well as many important facts pertaining to the layout and fabrication of fittings.

Also published by Practical Publications is a 12-volume set containing a textbook, workbook and instructor's guide on each of the following subjects: blueprint reading, shop math, shop theory and shop practices. All of these are geared to precision sheet metal (close tolerance) work. Additional titles include *Practical Sheet Metal Projects* and *Sheet Metal Shop Fabrication Problems.*

Also published by Practical Publications is a textbook titled *Sheet Metal Technology* containing 25 chapters which encompass all facets of the sheet metal industry. To accompany this book, he wrote a student manual and a separate instructor's guide. He also wrote *Careers in Air Conditioning and Refrigeration* published by National Textbook Company.

Dick and his wife Janet co-authored a contractor's business handbook titled *Practical Guide to Increasing Profits for Contractors* which is endorsed by 9 national construction associations and recommended to their members. As of this date, 126 articles taken from this handbook have appeared in construction trade journals.

Before becoming a trade teacher, Dick worked for 10 years as a sheet metal apprentice and mechanic for both large and small shops in the Chicago area.

Aside from his vast trade experience, Dick holds a Bachelor of Science degree in Industrial Education from Chicago State University. He attended evening classes for 14 years, fit into his already busy schedule, to obtain his degree.

He has also co-authored with his wife a mass-market paperback book published by Time/Warner titled *One-Minute Thoughts that Bring Wisdom, Harmony and* Fulfillment.

Other Sheet Metal Books by Richard S. Budzik

Sheet Metal Technology (3rd Edition)
Student's Workbook
Instructor's Guide

Practical Sheet Metal Projects (2nd Edition)

Sheet Metal Shop Fabrication Problems including over 350 Graded Parts

Today's 40 Most Frequently-Used Fittings Including Supplemental Section of 48 Fittings and Items with Over 400 Pages of Shop and Field Information (3rd Edition)

Today's 40 Most Frequently-Used Fittings Including Supplemental Section of 48 Fittings and Items - 296 Pages (4th Edition)

Round Fittings Used Today including Methods and Techniques of Fabricating Round Work (2nd Edition)

Fittings Used Today that Require Triangulation including the Theory of Triangulation (2nd Edition)

Specialty Items Used Today including Methods of Design and Fabrication and Important Trade Topics (3rd Edition)

Instructor's Answer Guide For Practical Sheet Metal Layout Series

Today's Practical Guide to Increasing Profits for Contractors

Sheet Metal Layout Tables for the Heating, Ventilation and Air Conditioning Industry including over 31,000 Practical, Usable, Accurate Mathematical Solutions

Practical Guide For Improving Your Sheet Metal Shop Layout with easy to use Suggestions and Aids

Practical Cost Estimating for Metal Fabrication

Precision Sheet Metal Shop Theory textbook (2nd Edition)
Student's Workbook
Instructor's Guide

Precision Sheet Metal Blueprint Reading textbook (2nd Edition)
Student's Workbook
Instructor's Guide

Precision Sheet Metal Mathematics textbook (2nd Edition)
Student's Workbook
Instructor's Guide

Precision Sheet Shop Practice textbook
Student's Workbook
Instructor's Guide

Opportunities in Refrigeration and Air Conditioning

Third Edition of Sheet Metal Technology Added to the Third Edition are over 100 pages of sheet metal projects–precision parts, assemblies and fittings.

George Kuprianczyk

George is co-author of Practical Cost Estimating for Metal Fabrication; author of numerous computer-aided estimating articles published in several metal fabricating trade magazines; seminar speaker on the subject of computer-aided estimating; metal fabrication trade consultant; sales manager for a large precision sheet metal fabricating company specializing in design and development assistance, proto-type development, short-run fabricating and high-volume production manufacturing of precision sheet metal components and assemblies.

His years of estimating experience in the commercial, industrial, automotive, aerospace and defense industries for both large and small job shops, combined with several years of hands-on shop experience and related industrial engineering studies have helped him bring valuable information and insights to this book.

Part 1
Shop Layout Considerations

The purpose of this Handbook is to suggest ways to make improvements in your shop layout, which will in turn improve production. Changes in a shop layout can result in drastic savings. By having an efficient plant or shop layout, your company will profit in numerous ways, which will be explained throughout this Handbook. Your employees will be able to work more efficiently with less effort, which will result in your company being able to make ductwork much more quickly and more reasonable than before.

Perhaps your shop is set up as efficiently as possible. But after reading this Handbook, you might find that there are still some refinements that could be made in certain areas. As you know, there are all sizes of shops involved in sheet metal work---from a one-man shop to well over 100 employees in a shop.

Sometimes when a company purchases a new machine or equipment, it gets placed anywhere that there is space available in the shop, with the good intention of later "setting up the shop properly." But, as the months go by, somehow this never gets done. However, remember that the time it takes to plan a good shop layout will more than pay for itself due to the time that will be saved over the years.

Having your shop set up as efficiently as possible does not necessarily mean investing a lot of money in new equipment. However, after an analysis of your shop operation and volume of work you do each year, you might find that you will want to purchase some new equipment since it invariably will increase your production. A proper shop layout will result in producing the largest amount with the least amount of time, taking into account the machinery you have available.

When reading and using this Handbook, keep this four-step process in mind:

1. What is the problem?
2. What is the cause of the problem?
3. What are all possible and practical solutions?
4. What is the best solution?

2. Shop Layout Considerations

Each of your shop operations will be critically analyzed individually and coordinated so the work flows from each operation to the next operation in the most logical sequence.

By adapting this system you will do the following:

1. Save time
2. Minimize layout time
3. Reduce scrap or waste to a minimum.

This above system creates a minimum loss of motion and has everyone in the shop working as effortlessly and efficiently as possible.

Many times a huge amount of money is spent on new or additional machinery and equipment, but no thought whatsoever to the logical place to locate it. It takes little effort to purchase a machine, but determining a correct shop layout takes much thought due to all the different alternatives. Another reason might be that we do not want to take the responsibility for making these important decisions.

If not familiar with certain basic principles, planning an efficient shop layout can be real frustrating since it is a constant thought process. You will certainly agree that the greatest production results when each person is given:

- a definite task to be done
- in a definite time
- and in a definite manner.

If a person is earning $15 an hour, he is receiving 25 cents a minute.

If he is earning $18 an hour, he is receiving 30 cents a minute.

If he is earning $20 an hour, he is receiving 33 cents a minute.

So you can see why it is so important that everyone in the shop be kept working as efficiently as possible, which you already know does not necessarily mean working harder; it simply means working smarter. To a large degree, the efficiency of your shop layout conveys to employees the idea that the company is concerned that each one of them is organized and efficient, and doing their job as quickly and efficiently as possible. Having the shop set up in a logical and orderly manner

Shop Layout Considerations

sets a good example to employees. It sets forth in their minds that the company is concerned with the amount of time that can be saved.

What is the most costly activity in your shop? -- most likely movements of any kind, better understood as "hand" or "foot" movements. Throughout this Handbook, each of your shop operations will be analyzed individually and coordinated so that the work flows from each operation to the next operation in the most logical sequence.

As you already know, many large manufacturing companies employ industrial engineers who are directly responsible for plant layout problems. Also there are time-and-motion experts who can study your operations and provide recommendations--but this is very expensive since they have to first devote time to learning your operations and needs (which you already know); then they provide recommendations that you already realize in most cases.

Therefore, unless you find someone who is already familiar with your specific type of operation, people within your company are the ones who can best determine your most advantageous shop layout.

1. Questions to Ask Yourself

Before actually starting to change your shop layout, there are a number of items you must consider especially if your company is considering expanding and purchasing new and additional machinery and equipment. Briefly, they include:

1. What are your company objectives -- current?
 -- long range?

2. What types and volume of work do you handle--
 --currently?
 --anticipate for the future?

3. Where does your company plan to be 2 years, 5 years, 10 years from today?

4. How would an expansion be financed--
 -- from earnings?
 -- from equity?
 -- from debt financing?

4.   Shop Layout Considerations

5. How and where is anticipated business to be generated?

These questions must be answered if new equipment or machinery is going to be purchased. Consider if you will be going into other areas of sheet metal or possibly you are going to expand your present operation so that you can do a larger volume of work.

Another group of good questions concern the details of the specific operations of your shop. These are appropriate whether expanding or not expanding. They are:

1. *Eliminate* - is the operation necessary, or can it be eliminated?
2. *Combine* - Can it be combined with some other operation or activity?
3. *Change Sequence, Place or Person* - Can these be changed or rearranged?
4. *Improve Details* - Can the method of performing the operation or activity or its equipment be improved?

2.   An Efficient Shop Layout--And Its Advantages

An efficient shop layout provides the following advantages:

- production will increase
- reduces labor costs
- improve labor costs
- eliminates or reduces accidents
- produces a better product or workmanship
- could increase floor space
- improve employee morale
- reduces waste of time and materials
- reduces scrap
- improves overall working conditions
- provides insurance benefits
- provides tax benefits

3.   Minor Shop Layout Problems

A problem with your shop layout does not always involve the entire shop. After analyzing a specific current problem, you might decide that its solution only requires one of the following:

Shop Layout Considerations 5.

1. A larger work area for a specific operation.
2. A smaller work area for a specific operation.
3. Relocating the work area for a specific operation.
4. A work area for a new operation.

Frequently it is only necessary to relocate some of the equipment in your plant.

4. Complete or Partial New Plant or Shop Layout

As we had mentioned, sometimes it is not necessary to completely change a shop layout in order to improve it. For example:

- In some instances, a movable table or machine can help solve the problem of limited space. A movable table with several small bench machines attached to it can be moved to the various work areas as necessary.

- Having duplicates of the same tool or machine can save wasted time in looking or waiting for the one tool or machine. For example, having two or three of a specific hand tool can eliminate substantial time that would otherwise be spent looking or waiting to use it.

- Sometimes, purchasing a few extra pieces of equipment can avoid tying up a larger machine.

- You can eliminate carrying finished items to the shipping area by using movable hand trucks or carts. Having a material drop-off rack arranged in an orderly manner near the shearing area can save time, and minimize scrap.

- You can frequently save many steps by making an extra doorway in a wall or completely removing a non-bearing wall.

- Installing additional electrical outlets can sometimes eliminate the need to move from one work area to another.

- Frequently, it is most economical and convenient to have the receiving and shipping areas either next to each other or combined into one. This is especially true for a smaller shop with only one large door, or when only one employee handles both operations. Larger shops generally find it advantageous to have two separate areas due to the volume of work they do.

6. Shop Layout Considerations

These are only examples of a few of the many ways you can economically improve your shop layout without spending a great deal of money. As you examine your present shop layout, you quite possibly will find other improvements you can easily make.

5. The Shop Layout -- Being Practical

A shop layout is a floor plan showing all the machinery, equipment, and materials needed, from receipt of the raw materials to the shipment of the completed products or parts. (See Figs. 1, 2, 3, 4,). The most desirable layout permits the quickest and easiest flow of materials at the lowest cost; this generally means with the least amount of handling.

To arrive at the best shop layout, you must consider numerous factors, including the following:

- the building available
- the machinery and equipment currently available
- the machinery and equipment your company plans to purchase
- the company's employees

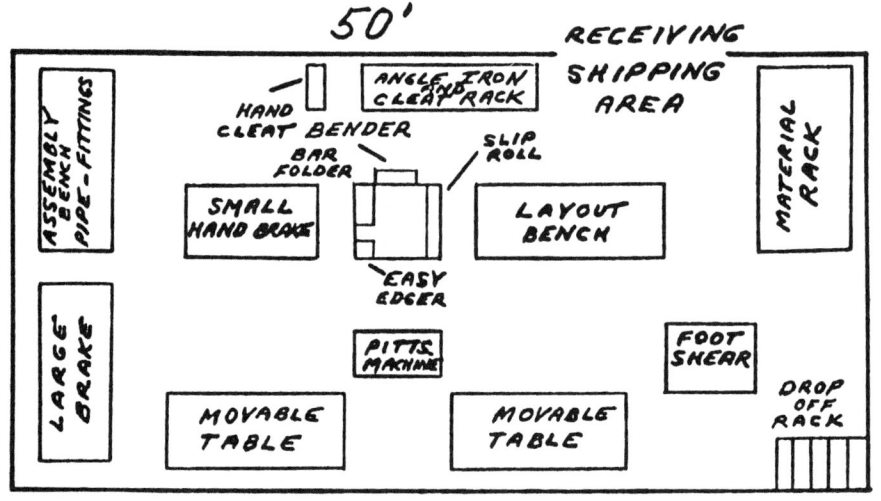

Fig. 1 - Suggested sheet metal shop layout with a minimum of machinery and equipment. Notice the movable tables making the "primary work flow" for pipe move in a continuous manner; also that the angle iron, cleat rack, and material rack are near the shipping-receiving area. Machinery and equipment are located so the movable tables can be easily moved back and forth.

Shop Layout Considerations 7.

If you were in an ideal situation, you could plan the best shop layout for the specific machines, equipment, materials and work areas you need; then you could design the building around this layout. But most companies find that they must plan in the opposite manner: they must fit the best possible work flow into the existing building. This often means working around existing structures and facilities, such as doors, loading areas, beams, columns, and walls.

6. What Makes an Efficient Shop Layout?

A good shop layout should provide the largest column of production with the least amount of time, taking into account the machinery and equipment that is available. For maximum efficiency in production, each operation must be performed in its sequence. The chief objective

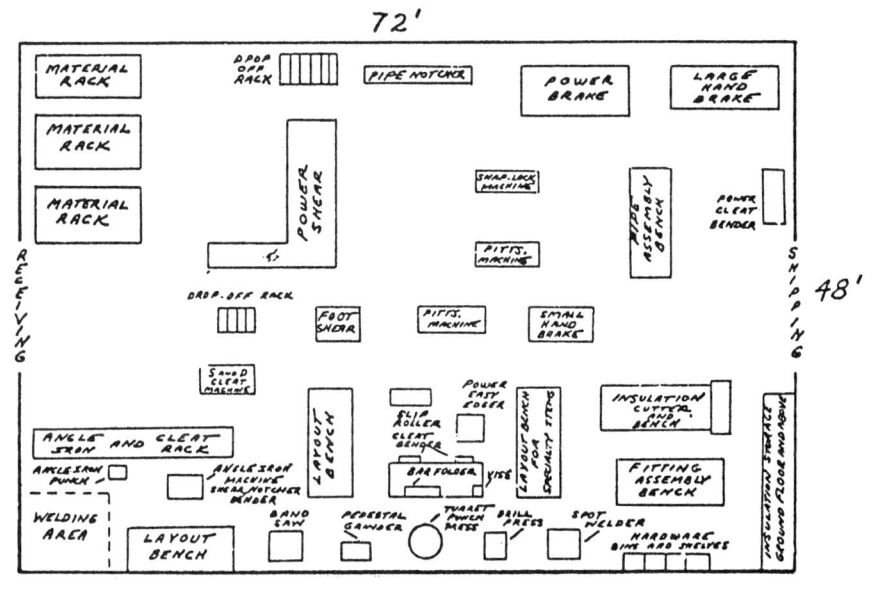

Fig. 2 - Suggested layout with above-average amount of equipment and machinery. Notice the area for the "secondary work flow" which handles fittings and specialty items. Also notice the extra layout bench available for use during the busy season. The hardware bin is near the layout bench for specialty items. Insulation storage is on the ground floor and above. One large drop-off rack is near the power shear; a small one is in the "secondary work "flow" area. All operations start near the receiving area and progress toward the shipping area at the opposite end of the building. Notice the large amount of space in the area for making pipe, which is usually the majority of the work.

8. **Shop Layout Considerations**

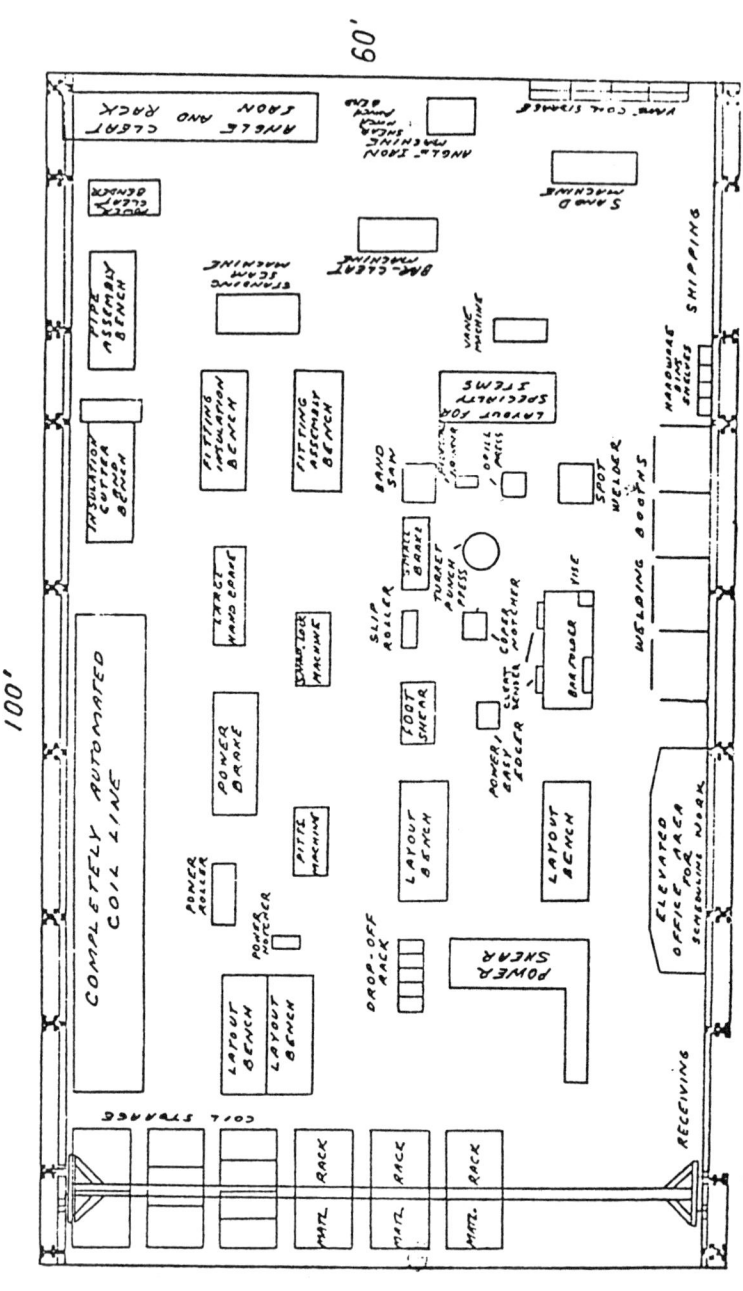

Fig. 3 - Suggested shop layout for a large shop doing a large volume of work. Notice the overhead electric hoist that spans the entire length of the shop, making it convenient to place material in the various storage spaces available in addition to the receiving area. There are 3 completely open aisles between the machinery and equipment, and a large area for shipping. The material rack and 2 layout benches that are back-to-back near the power shear make it ideal when laying out very large fittings. Also notice the large open areas for welding, pipe lining, and pipe assembly; and the uncluttered areas for running cleats and cutting and fabricating angle iron. Not shown is a storage floor for insulation above the insulation cutter and bench. The office area is elevated 4' in order to have a better view of the entire shop.

Shop Layout Considerations 9.

Floor Plan

Fig. 4 - Suggested shop layout for a large sheet metal shop with an above-average amount of equipment and machinery for doing a large volume of work. Notice the number of layout benches for doing large volume work. There are three material racks behind the 10 ft. power shear, with hand trucks, making it convenient for the large volume of work. Notice the locations of the different machines placed strategically among the work benches. Also notice the large area for doing angle iron work, the large welding area, the installation cutter and bench. The foreman's office is placed so he can have a better overall view of the entire shop.

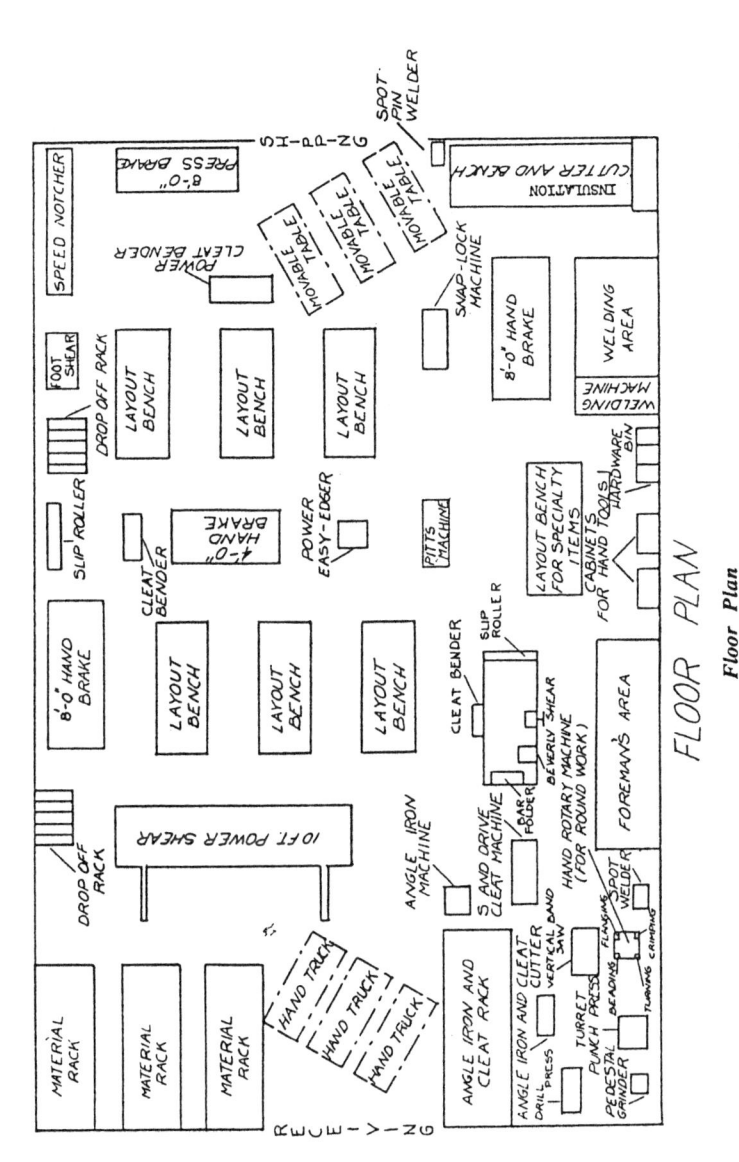

is to eliminate unnecessary movements, keeping to a minimum the movements employees must make.

Remember: Wasted space and wasted time result in wasted money!

7. Taking The Inspection Tour

When you take a physical inspection tour of your shop, write down some notes such as items that need improvement, changes or additions, or even the removal of out-dated, broken and never-used machinery and equipment.

Having a specific place for each item can certainly save time and money. This includes all necessary materials and supplies. In this way, each employee knows where to look when they need a specific item and does not have to go around looking or asking others where it is.

Keep these items in mind when making your plant or shop inspection tour:
1. Is there anything you can do to remove a hazard or to improve safety?
2. Is there unused or infrequently-used space that you can put to better use?
3. Is there anything that is no longer being used that can be disposed?
4. Are there wasted movements that you can economically eliminate or reduce? - - This is one of the most important factors!

8. Analyzing Your Different Shop Operations

After making your inspection tour, analyze each operation separately. Then consider how the work flows from each operation to the next operation. Consider this question:

Does it go in a logical sequence without wasted movements of any kind?

For shops doing sheet metal work, the usual sequence of operations is as follows:

- receiving
- storage of materials and supplies

Shop Layout Considerations

- shearing (blanking)
- layout
- cutting and notching
- punching, drilling, tapping, and reaming
- forming, bending, rolling, and seaming
- finishing (such as painting, plating, insulating, lining, buffing, etc.)
- assembly (riveting, welding--using a variety of fasteners)
- shipping

9. Basic Principles of Shop Layout

The planner needs to consider the following general principles when determining a new or improved plant layout:

1. *Available space.* You can be most economical by using all available space carefully, including any space above-head.

2. *Shortest distance.* You want the materials and people to move the shortest distance possible between operations.

3. *Work flow.* You want to arrange each work area in the most logical sequence in which it is usually performed when making the specific items.

4. *Safety and satisfaction of employees.* Be sure that the layout is basically satisfactory to your employees, and is completely safe for them.

5. *Flexibility.* You need to have a layout in which you can make small changes or adjustments with minimum cost and inconvenience.

6. *Overall integration.* You want to determine the plant layout that takes into consideration each of these five factors in the best manner.

10. The "Continuous Flow Line" Concept

The best shop layouts provide a continuous flow pattern. This means that materials move without interruptions through the various operations from receiving the raw materials to shipping the completed items.

Shop Layout Considerations

The materials or parts are not handled back and forth from one operation to the next, and the paths from operation to operation do not cross each other. Sometimes due to the size and shape of the existing building, this is not entirely possible. But this arrangement is advantageous for fittings as well as pipe. A continuous flow line provides these advantages:

1. increases production.
2. reduces fatigue.
3. minimizes floor space.
4. reduces storage areas.

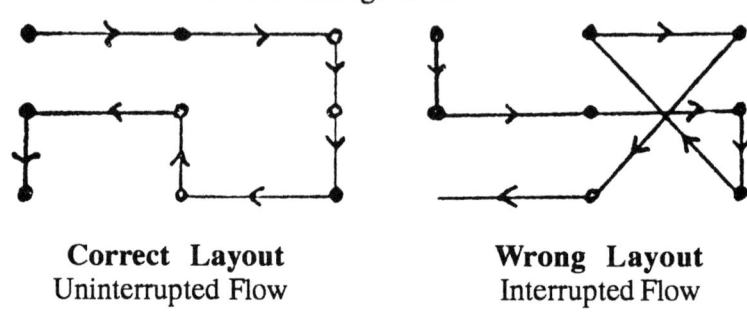

Correct Layout
Uninterrupted Flow

Wrong Layout
Interrupted Flow

Within a continuous flow line, you can have a primary flow line and a secondary flow line. See Fig. 5. The primary flow line can basically handle the standard items, which usually make up the majority of your volume of work. The secondary flow line can be for specially-made or custom items. Regardless of the size or shape of your plant or shop, you quite possibly will be able to draw upon these factors for some ideas and suggestions for improving your existing or new shop layout.

The analysis of materials flow involves determining the most effective sequence of moving materials through the necessary steps of the operations required. An effective flow means that materials move progressively through the operations always advancing toward completion and without excessive detours or back-tracking. The flow-of-materials analysis is the heart of layout planning whenever movement of materials is a major portion of the process or operation.

This is especially true when materials are large, heavy, or many in quantity or when transporting or handling costs are high compared to costs of operation, storage or inspection. Therefore, analyzing the flow of materials is one of the primary steps every person planning a shop layout should understand.

Shop Layout Considerations

RECEIVING

SECONDARY FLOW-LINE

PRIMARY FLOW-LINE

SECONDARY FLOW LINE

SHIPPING

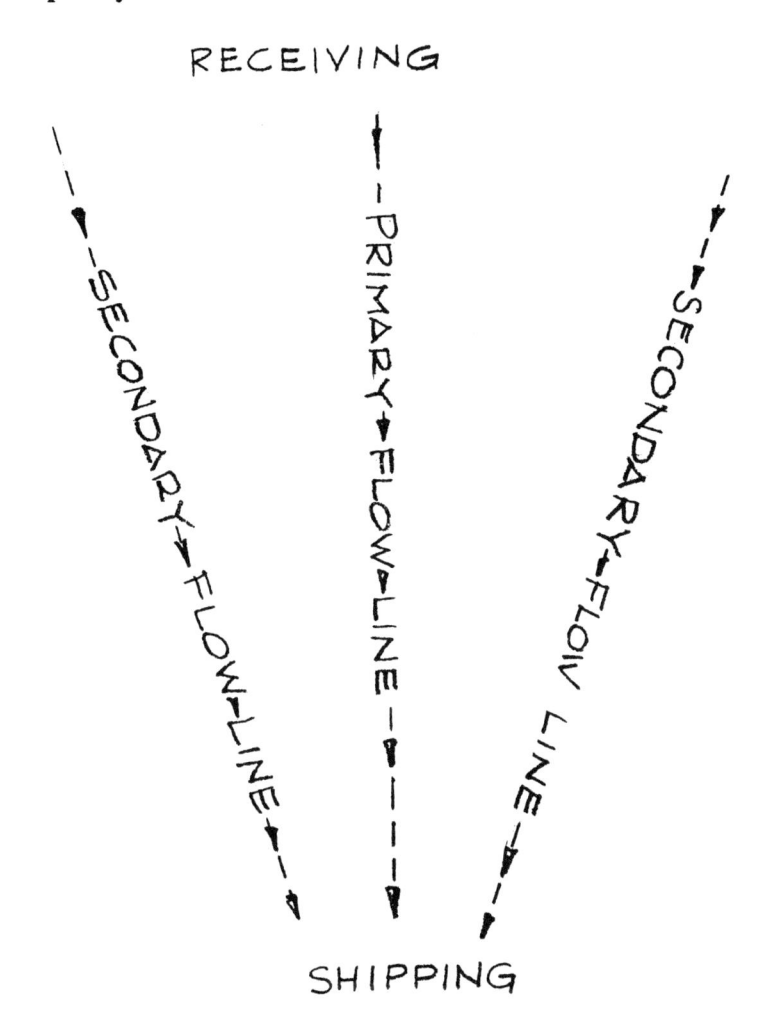

Fig. 5 - A continuous flow line incorporating both a primary flow line and a secondary flow line.

11. Basic Methods of Shop Layout

There are two broad classifications of shop layouts, one with the basic consideration being the products to be made and the other according to the operations through which the products must pass. The operations process layout is generally used when the product is not, and cannot be standardized; or where the volume of the same work is low. These conditions require some flexibility in the sequence of operations.

The product layout is used for standardized products that are made in large quantity for a considerable length of time, or indefinitely. All emphasis is placed on the product, with the machines located in the appropriate sequence for a minimum of handling.

Frequently, the best layout can be obtained by combining the basic features of both these layouts. In this case, each process may be set up as a unit or a department, in order to utilize specialization of labor skills. Then to minimize handling, each unit or department is arranged in the sequence required by the majority of products.

There are various alternatives for arranging machinery and equipment; due to the type of volume of work you do, your specific shop layout would be somewhat different than another shop, even with the same type of equipment, machines and space.

12. Reluctance of Employees to Change -- Overcoming This Obstacle

When you first consider a change in your current shop layout, especially if it is a major change, you might encounter some opposition from the people working in the shop--since most people are reluctant to change. This is natural since most people think of change as meaning one of the following:

- their job will be different.
- their job will be more difficult.
- they will no longer be able to work with the same people.
- fewer employees will be needed.

Before any changes are made, it is a good idea to explain to all the people working in the shop that a new or partially new layout is being installed so that a more efficient operation can be employed. In this way, people do not get overly alarmed that they may not have a job after the new layout is completed.

13. Discussion With Your Employees

Since your shop employees are the ones who are working in the shop every day, get their advice before making any changes in your current

Shop Layout Considerations

layout. They can tell you what current arrangements are convenient and what problems there are, along with being able to suggest improvements. People who have worked in other companies can provide you with additional suggestions due to their past experiences. But you have to ask them, otherwise many times they will not volunteer any information.

When you discuss possible improvements with your shop people, you will probably find surprising results. Each person's suggestions cause the other in the group to think and come up with even more and better suggestions. With this atmosphere, people will feel free to mention their new ideas to you whenever they think of something, not just when you specifically ask them. Depending on the number of people in the shop, your group discussion might be organized in one of these manners:

1. If small enough, meet with all of your shop personnel together as one group.
2. Meet with as many separate groups of shop people as necessary.
3. Meet only with the personnel in supervisory positions.

If you are able to have a group discussion with your shop personnel concerning the improvement of the plant layout, remember these points:

1. *People like to participate in a group activity.* They will be more comfortable being with their co-workers who are also making suggestions. Several heads are better than one if they are working together.

2. *People like to try to improve.* This is a natural tendency and is fostered by encouragement and recognition. Their natural desire to improve continues with confidence when they realize that the improvements are also in their own best interest.

3. *Not all of your peoples' ideas or suggestions will actually be workable.* But the fact of having this discussion with them will open their minds to watching for ways of doing their job better, as well as feeling more comfortable about offering a suggestion or advice on solving a particular problem.

4. Explain to your people that you are looking for more efficient work methods to get more done without actually working harder.

Also consult these same people when you are considering purchasing some new equipment or machinery, since they are the ones who are using it every day. Many can tell you about the advantages and disadvantages of the equipment they are already using, and can tell you what would be desirable in a new machine or equipment. People who have worked for other companies can provide you with valuable information about the various models and brands, as well as production time.

14.   O.S.H.A. And Your Company

Before you begin to make your new or revise your current plant layout, be sure to check the OSHA guidelines and suggestions. They have booklets and pamphlets available.

Details concerning the OSHA are available in Publications #149 titled "The Occupational Safety and Health Act" which is free from: AFL-CIO Committee, 815 Sixteenth St., N.W., Washington, D.C. 20006.

15.   Selecting the Best Layout

You could possibly arrive at 2 or 3 alternative layouts, any one of which seems very advantageous. Any of them can be made to work satisfactorily. However, each has its own advantages and disadvantages. The problem is to decide which of these layouts to select.   You will probably find one of these methods most useful in making this more-or-less final decision:

1. *Balancing advantages against disadvantages.* This does not mean asking yourself which layout has a smaller number of disadvantages, or which one has a larger number of advantages. It means determining which one had the most important advantages and the least important disadvantages. Each shop has different problems.

2. *Cost comparison and justification.* This usually means selecting the layout with the smallest day-to-day operating costs, or the most economical production costs when in use.

Shop Layout Considerations 17.

If you plan to discuss your final layout or several alternative layouts with one or more other people, be sure each plan is clearly labeled. You might still have to make a verbal explanation as the others are probably not as familiar with the new layout as you are.

After selecting the best layout, check it again in one or more of these ways:

1. Challenge the layout with check questions.
2. Ask others to review it.
3. Make further refinements.

The sample check questions you can use include the following:

- Will it increase production?
- Will it reduce costs?
- Will it improve housekeeping?
- Will it eliminate accidents?
- Will it produce a better product?
- Will it increase floor space?
- Will it improve morale?
- Will it reduce waste?
- Will it reduce scrap?
- Will it improve other working conditions?
- Will it increase or decrease maintenance?
- Will it provide insurance benefits?
- Will it provide tax benefits?

Final review with others can be made individually or in joint meetings. You might want to meet with the same people from whom you solicited ideas back in the initial planning stage of this project.

16. Implementing The New Layout

The fact that machinery and equipment are to be moved offers a real opportunity to make other changes and improvements. This is the perfect time to consider steps such as the following:

1. Repair, rebuild, or repaint equipment.

2. Add new fittings, attachments, feeds, deliveries to machines.

3. Initiate new working methods, procedures, controls.
4. Abandon bad operating practices of all kinds.
5. Convert to new materials or new product specifications.
6. Realign the manpower assignments, balancing skills, and time standards.
7. Incorporate better safety practices.
8. Repair the floors, walls, ceilings, and do other major maintenance work.
9. Realign supervisory responsibilities. This is the perfect time since there is an atmosphere of change.

The time chosen and allotted to install the layout may be most important. The person planning the layout should schedule the move during a period of low production or a change in production, process, or equipment. Scheduling moves in this manner helps avoid interruption in shipping schedules, losses in production time, and disrupting effects on employees.

Usually it is impossible to find a time that will completely satisfy everyone. An attempt can be made to maintain production schedules during the move. Or the move can be made on a weekend, holiday, vacation, or during seasonal lulls when production is normally down. It is often advantageous to suspend operations and make the move all at once, rather than to interrupt everyone during the move.

Once the schedule is set, it is often better to go ahead than to hold up if everything is not quite ready. That is, make the installation before being ready with every layout detail. If the installation were postponed until everything was completely ready, the move might never be made. If we tolerate delays, we may find in the future our schedules will never be met.

When the move takes place, the person planning the layout must be on the floor, or at least readily available for consultation with the people doing the moving. No matter how well the layout planning has been done, there are layout adjustments at installation time. Therefore, the planner must be available to answer questions, interpret plans, inspect for completeness, and secure as early a resumption of production as possible. He should not schedule a three-hour meeting during the moving and installation period.

Shop Layout Considerations

Regarding changes, the policy should be firmly established that the installation people cannot deviate from the plans. The person who planned the layout is the only one who can make changes on the plans and must sign and date such changes before the people doing the moving can honor them. If at all possible use your own people to make the move.

17. The Goal - - An Improved Shop Layout

Frequently, it is not possible to have your plant or shop layout in a completely continuous flow sequence, as is naturally desired. You should at least consider this type of arrangement. Try to work toward this desirable layout within the limitations of the building and facilities. Remember that there is not one "ideal" shop layout. But some layouts are better than others.

I am sure we all agree:

> 75% of something is better than 100% of
> nothing, which certainly applies here.

Talking with the people who operate the machines and equipment in your shop is a good step toward improving your production.

Remember that improvements can always be made, but you have to look for problem areas and then determine the best methods of doing the operation. Ideas for improvements do not usually come to you without you looking for them first.

Part 2
Machinery and Equipment Considerations

Changing a shop layout is an excellent time for considering new and additional machines and equipment. To get the most out of your equipment, you must maintain it properly. Consider the suggestions in the next sections for prolonging the useful life of your equipment and for replacing it with new ones. As time goes by and you use the equipment, it deteriorates and becomes less efficient or less accurate (depending on the type). As breakdowns occur more often, the situation becomes more serious due to undependability and repair costs. But new equipment is expensive and you must determine whether the advantages of the new equipment are great enough to justify its investment. This decision should be based on facts and figures which will also be discussed in this Handbook.

1. Proper Machinery and Tools

Good employees who are well-trained cannot do their best work unless they have the proper tools and machinery that are in good condition. From year to year tools change and improve, so it pays to keep well-informed on new developments in order to take advantage of any new tools or machines which must offer some advantage in either speed, efficiency or ease. Materials also change and might require new tools and machines.

Keeping alert to "machine, equipment, and tool news" can certainly be an asset for you, and you can do this by reading your trade publications and consulting with your distributor or attending some conventions or seminars. At least once a year, analyze your tools and machines to determine whether they are in good enough working condition, whether you have an adequate number of them, and whether they do the job they should do.

2. Have Enough Smaller Tools

Have enough duplicates of some of the smaller bench and hand tools. Having three electric drills, rather than one, can save your employees so much time that they pay for themselves over and over again. Otherwise, your employees waste time looking for the one or waiting

Machinery and Equipment Considerations 21.

until someone else finishes using it. Then, when it no longer works, your problems really add up if you only have one, coming back to the idea of 10 cents or 15 cents a minute concept.

3. Managing Smaller Tools, Machines and Equipment

Losses are a big problem with smaller tools and equipment, not only due to the cost but also due to lost time when they are not readily available. In most manufacturing operations, it is best to maintain a Tool Room where employees check out these tools as they need them and are responsible for their return. However, this type of system is generally difficult in smaller operations; it is not economical as it would cost more to maintain a Tool Room than the amount saved due to normal losses. You must weigh the relative cost of the stock room or tool room against the expected savings that would result by having this control.

If you have a large enough company and require a considerable amount of small tools and equipment, you can easily set up a Tool Room and a check-out system. One employee is in charge of it and you might be able to determine some other duties he can perform in his tool room area--minor repairs and maintenance, ordering supplies, etc. When he must leave the Tool Room, he locks it and the other employees know that they must locate him to get the tools they need; unless your shop is very large, finding him should not be very difficult. For example, if he knows that he will be repairing a larger machine, he can leave a note telling where he can be found.

If you have a smaller shop but have experienced rather large losses, you can have the same system. Assign the person in charge of the Tool Room to another duty and your other employees soon learn where to find him when they need tools.

If a tool is broken or damaged while in the possession of an employee, he should be held responsible for reporting that fact to the Tool Room attendant at the time he returns the tool. Occasionally, a broken or damaged tool will be turned in without a damaged tool report. However, the regular inspection of a returned tool prior to its replacement in the storage bin should return that it has been damaged and the attendant should then check with the person who returned it last.

Machinery and Equipment Considerations

If you decide that it is not profitable for you to establish a controlled tool room, you should still consider some steps to help reduce losses. Consider the following suggestions modified as appropriate for your type of operations:

1. Paint the handles of small hand tools all the same identifying bright color. This makes them easier to see, reduces the possibility of leaving them out of place, and reduces the desire to take them home.

2. Stamp the company name wherever possible on each tool so it cannot be easily removed. A good method is to purchase name plates with the company name and securely attach one to each tool, such as by riveting it. Or use a rubber stamp with indelible ink, an engraver, a welding iron, or a branding iron.

3. Number each tool and sign them out to individual employees by number. In this way, tools can be identified when found in the possession of another person or left unattended. Have each new employee sign a receipt for the tools issued to him.

4. Inform personnel, especially supervisors or foremen, of the amount of losses and impress upon them the importance of keeping these losses to a minimum.

5. Have a meeting with your employees emphasizing the importance of having adequate tools of their trade. Provide facts and figures on losses over a specified period of time. This helps point out to them the fact that you are aware of the problem. Then ask for their suggestions on ways to combat the problem; start by making one suggestion such as painting handles and the employees will be able to add other suggestions. Delegate someone to be responsible for keeping track and maintaining tools.

Each of these steps helps to discourage carelessness and theft. You can also control pilferage on jobs. In the case of some types of materials, try to issue the exact amount to each job. Since it is generally a good precaution to have a few extras, issue them separately and place them under the control of the superintendent or foreman so that is will become obvious if anything is missing. Whenever a shortage occurs, bring it to the attention of all the employees who have access to the items, so they will know that the items have been missed.

Machinery and Equipment Considerations

4. Ways You Can Prolong The Life Of Your Machinery And Equipment

To a large extent, prolonging the life of your equipment depends on your employees since they are the ones who use it. You must set a good example in order for your employees to have the proper concern or attitude toward your equipment. Either you or a designated supervisory employee should be responsible for following a definite schedule to see that each item is maintained properly. Depending on the specific machine, this might be checking its adjustments for accuracy, oiling or greasing it. Keeping the entire plant or work area as clean or at least as orderly as possible is a definite step in the right direction. Another is having proper maintenance tools and supplies readily available.

In considering your employees, be sure that each new employee is properly informed about the operation of each machine he will be using. Do not assume he knows about it without asking him--many times various models have distinct features. Always keep the operating instructions or manuals and let your employees know where they are so they can refer to them whenever necessary. Make this easy enough for them to do, or they won't bother and will continue using trial-and-error methods.

If a specific machine is requiring frequent and unnecessary repairs, discuss the situation with all employees who use that specific machine. Tell them how expensive the repairs actually are. Frequently, they are not aware of the seriousness of the situation.

Do not expect some employees to be careful and conscientious when others are not equally concerned. You must consider this problem from an over-all standpoint. When you create the right working atmosphere and most of your employees are careful, the few careless ones will soon feel conspicuous and want to be like the others. When you realize who the careless person is, you can talk with him and explain that both the company and his job depend on the continued operation of the equipment. Remind him that the machine makes his job easier, enables him to get more work done, and therefore earns a higher wage for himself.

You must watch for each employee who is careless and inconsiderate of others when handling materials and equipment; otherwise, other employees will notice this and gradually adopt the same ways.

Machinery and Equipment Considerations

Following these steps will help to make your equipment last longer:

1. Specify definite procedures for the equipment that is difficult to operate, especially if several different employees must use it.

2. Train one or more operators in the proper maintenance of each machine. It is generally best for one specific person to be responsible for its maintenance. Knowing that he is being depended upon makes him more conscientious. If the machine is too complex, specifically instruct your employees to NOT try to repair it, as it requires a specialist.

3. Provide the correct supplies for maintenance. Have all the necessary tools and supplies for cleaning and maintaining the machine.

4. Provide the correct machines so your employees do not have to use a machine for operations it is not equipped to handle. Do not expect them to use materials that are over or under the capacity specified by the manufacturer of the machine.

5. Adjust the equipment to fit your operator. Ask your operator if some small adjustments can be made to improve his job. A small nuisance such as too long of a reach can become very irritating and result in mistreatment of the machine, frequently not even intentional.

6. Keep maintenance records or check lists. Keep a separate record for each machine either on file cards or papers indicating the cost of the machine, when it was purchased, breakdowns with causes, repair costs and other important information. A sample form is shown in Fig. 1. If a machine has required frequent repairs, you can more easily determine whether it is the fault of the operators if you have this record.

7. Assign a specific person as responsible for the care of each machine. When various different people must use the machine, it is more difficult to determine who it is at fault when a machine has been mishandled. But having one person responsible helps in two ways: the other employees know he is conscientiously looking after it and its users; he will be more willing to inform you of those who are not as careful as they should be when using it.

Machinery and Equipment Considerations

ITEM:	MODEL NO.	SERIAL NO.	
DATE PURCH:		PRICE $	
MAINTENANCE CONTRACT:			
Date	Description of repairs		Cost

Fig. 1 - Machine Maintenance Record

5. Schedule For Use of Machinery and Equipment

If you have several jobs in progress at the same time, as most companies do, scheduling the work within the limitations of your equipment can at times become a problem. You might lose considerable time waiting for a machine to be free. For example, be sure that a heavy work schedule for one machine is not required on the same days for work on several different jobs. Getting into the habit of planning ahead can eliminate some of the unnecessary wasted time or difficulty in keeping completion schedules. The advantages to such careful planning include:

1. Helps you determine ahead of time exactly what equipment you need for each job to be completed on schedule.

2. It forces you to more carefully plan and coordinate your jobs.

3. It points out possible problems, such as greater demand than the equipment you have available. So it gives you time to re-schedule some of your jobs or to arrange for rental of the additional equipment, either on a temporary or permanent basis.

6. Replacement Policy

Many companies do not need to have a detailed and scientific replacement policy. In large manufacturing and continuous production line (assembly line) operations, such a replacement policy is very important because when one machine begins to operate slowly or inaccurately, it has an effect on the entire line. We can learn a few points from these larger operations, though, such as:

- Plan ahead; do not wait for an emergency to arise.

- Spread out your replacements so you do not have all the expense at the same time.

7. Machinery & Equipment Requirements Determined By Volume of Work

Try to be sure that all your work is not tied up with one market. When there is a slowdown in one type of work, you still have the other types of work to do since you are also established in the other markets.

List your shop objectives and the type and amount of work you do. Then consider whether you will be going into the other markets in the near future, or possibly you are going to expand your present operations so that you can do a larger volume of the same type of work you already do. To invest a large sum of money in more complex machinery, it is obvious that a large volume of work must be done each year. When your volume increases, you probably can no longer afford to handle many operations by hand, particularly if there are quicker methods available which your competitors are utilizing.

Companies with a larger volume of work are faced with higher overhead--as your volume of work increases, so does your overhead. To remain competitive, you must have as much power equipment as possible, or as much as is available for the type of work you do.

8. Analysis of When To Replace Machinery and Equipment

You should consider numerous factors concerning the machines and equipment you currently have when making the decision of whether or not to purchase a new machine. Some of these can be classified as

Machinery and Equipment Considerations

"technical" factors related to the operation of the machine, and others can be classified as "cost" factors to operate the machine.

"Technical" Factors to Consider:

- Is the present equipment worn out?

- Is the present equipment inadequate due to: its capacity, accuracy, strength, power, speed?

- Is it obsolete?

- Does it lack special features available on newer models that you could advantageously use?

- Would a new machine also do other kinds of operations that the present machine cannot handle?

- Would a new machine replace hand operations?

- Would a new machine be safer or more reliable?

- What are your competitors doing?

"Cost" Factors to Consider:

- Is the cost of repairs too high on the present machine?

- Will ruined work be reduced or eliminated by the new machine?

- Would greater output or faster production result from the new machine?

- Will employees have to be trained to operate the new machine?

- Will the new machine take more or less space, or the same amount of space?

- How many years of effective service may be expected from the new machine?

- Are funds available for the purchase of the machine or can you get financing?

Some of these factors are interrelated--they are both cost and technical factors. You should consider all of them and determine which are the most important to you. Then you will better be able to make the best decision.

9. Selecting the Right New Machinery and Equipment--- Comparison of Operating Characteristics

After you decide to purchase some new equipment, then you have to make the careful analysis of the comparable models of different manufacturers and the varying features and costs. The least expensive or more expensive machine is not always the "right" one for you.

For example, the least expensive one might not have some of the features that would be useful to you, might not have the capacity you need, or might not be sturdy enough for your operations. The most expensive one might have features you do not need and would not even have a use for, it might have a greater capacity than you need, or be of a high quality that you do not need for your operations.

You have to consider how much use this equipment gets and your required output. Also consider these factors:

- Its cost and the capital you have available.

- The quality of work it produces.

- You can obtain a used one in a much shorter time, and need it as soon as possible.

- You cannot afford a new one.

- A company is going out of business and you might be able to get some of their equipment very inexpensively.

10. Optional Machine Attachments

Here are some considerations before deciding whether to purchase the optional machine attachments:

- will you use them often enough to warrant the additonal cost?

- do you have other machines that do the same thing as the attachments can accomplish?

Machinery and Equipment Considerations

- can they be purchased later with no extra charges?
- Are they easy enough to use without excessive time in preparation or setup?

11. Standard or Specially-Built Machinery or Equipment

Specially-built machinery or equipment generally costs substantially more than similar standard machinery. However, if it can handle operations that justify the cost, then it is a worthwhile investment. It might save substantial time in adjusting or setting up attachments to standard machinery. Again, consider the frequency of using these additional features.

12. Getting Price Quotes

When requesting the price and other details for purchasing equipment, be sure to use the word "bid" or "quote" in your request so the equipment dealer or manufacturer gets the impression that you are requesting the price from one or more others at the same time. In this way, they will be more likely to give you the best price and most favorable terms possible.

13. New or Used Equipment?

You might find it advantageous to purchase some used equipment. This is especially true under the following circumstances:

- You only have limited need for the machine, as it will be idle part of the time.
- It is not a very complex machine, so the risks of purchasing a used one are reduced.
- You can obtain a used one in a much shorter time, and need it as soon as possible.
- You cannot afford a new one.
- A company is going out of business and you might be able to get some of their equipment very inexpensively.

14. Buy, Rent, or Lease Machinery and Equipment

Due to more and better machines being available today, the purchase and financing of machinery has become a more important consideration. It is especially important for the types of businesses that require more expensive and a larger amount of equipment. In the past, the only means of obtaining equipment was by purchasing it--either with cash, with a bank loan, or with equity financing. The most common means today is equity financing, especially for more expensive equipment. However, two additional means of obtaining equipment have gained in use in recent years--they are leasing and renting. Both provide the advantage of no capital investment, similar to the concept of leasing or renting a building for your business.

If you use machines which you are confident you will use for their entire useful life, you should probably buy them. You should seriously consider leasing some equipment if your type of business requires larger, more expensive equipment, or if you do not have the required capital for the purchase of some equipment that would be to your advantage to use. The very large manufacturing companies have been leasing some of their equipment for quite some time; in recent years smaller companies have gradually begun to realize the advantages of leasing. What are these advantages?

1. No capital investment is required, saving the need to borrow or allowing these funds to be used to expand your operations in other ways.

2. No borrowing of funds is required, saving your borrowing capacity for when you really need it.

3. You can have the equipment sooner and can be making money from it.

4. Your exact costs can be determined in advance, and you can allocate appropriate costs to each job if necessary.

5. If you have any "cost plus" contracts, you charge rental or leasing costs to the specific contracts.

6. Your operations can be simplified if the leasing company takes care of either insurance or maintenance.

Machinery and Equipment Considerations

Remember that you earn profits by *USING* equipment, not necessarily by *OWNING* equipment. When you find that you no longer need a machine, it is much easier to eliminate its expense if it is rented or leased than if you own it.

Does it cost you more to lease or rent than to purchase equipment? This is a very important question, and you might be surprised to learn that it is frequently less expensive to lease or rent. This depends on the type of business you have and the specific equipment under consideration. One reason that leasing might be less expensive is that these agencies are specialized, so they purchase in volume and have efficient maintenance and repair facilities.

Our recommendation is that the next time you are ready to purchase additional equipment or facilities, evaluate the actual costs of each alternative, especially for larger and more expensive equipment. If your capital investment is out of line with your operating capital, you should consider the "lease-back" option, explained next.

The leasing company generally provides the insurance and maintenance for the equipment. If their service facilities are not convenient to your location, the leasing company makes arrangements with an appropriate local company if it is not economical to provide service by their own mobile service trucks.

If repairs will take a considerable length of time, they will usually provide you with another piece of comparable equipment at no extra charge. This is particularly appropriate for vehicles. Your lease or rental contract can be adjusted so you only pay for the time during which the equipment is actually in service or usable for you.

When you are in the position of needing operating capital, you might be able to use some of the equipment you own to raise these funds. Through a "lease-back" arrangement, you can continue to use the equipment and have the cash at the same time.

Some leasing companies will purchase from you equipment that you currently own (at the fair market value) and lease it back to you. Remember that even when leasing or renting equipment might be more expensive, it can be advantageous to you. It can allow you to use equipment you could not otherwise afford, so you can be more efficient or so you can expand your operations.

In summary, you should consider leasing or renting under these circumstances:

1. When you cannot afford the purchase.
2. When leasing is actually less expensive.
3. When you only need the equipment temporarily.

In the case of some of the very large machines, leasing is the only practical means of obtaining it. You can find leasing companies in the classified section of your telephone directory under "Leasing Services" and "Leasing Agents and Brokers Equipment." If none are listed in your telephone directory, consult the directory of a nearby larger city, or the manufacturer of the equipment under consideration.

The various factors concerning the cost, method of purchase and depreciation increase in importance with higher priced machines. An accountant who is experienced in your field can be helpful in making the best decision for your specific current position and needs.

15. Lease With Option To Buy

A contract to lease equipment can contain a purchase provision with the purchase price stated. This type of arrangement can be advantageous to you if you currently need some type of equipment but aren't quite sure whether or not you will continue to need it, or if you can't immediately obtain the credit necessary to purchase it.

An advantage to this type of lease is that part or all of the monthly rental fee is deducted from the purchase price if and when you decide to purchase it. In the meantime, if your needs change and you have no further use for the item, at the end of the lease you don't own it and don't have to find a purchaser; the leasing company merely takes it back.

16. Depreciation On Machinery and Equipment

Whether you pay cash for a machine or finance it in one of several ways, you cannot list its entire cost as a business expense in the year in which you purchase it. You must spread the expense over the years you will use it; this is referred to as depreciation. You can use one of several methods of depreciation calculations.

Machinery and Equipment Considerations

Calculating the annual amount to depreciate requires two estimates. First, you estimate the salvage value (what you can probably sell it for at the end of its useful life) and subtract this from its cost. Second, you must estimate the number of years you expect to be able to use the machine since different machines have greatly varying useful lives. Then you spread the amount you can depreciate over the expected useful life in one of the ways approved by the Internal Revenue Service.

You do not have to depreciate small machines and hand tools that generally have a useful life of one year or less. You deduct their complete cost when you purchase them.

17. List of Long-Range Desired Improvement

Most companies are not able to make all the desired changes at once in order to improve their shop layout. This is due to a combination of factors. Adequate funds are not available to invest at one time. The employees are busy and don't have time to help make all the desired improvements immediately.

Keeping an "Annual Shop Improvement List" or a "Long-Range Shop Improvement List" can solve this problem. Whenever you or an employee think of something that should be done, write it on your list. In this way, you are able to remember all the good ideas and can read the list occasionally to decide what is most important and should be done next.

You can turn time into profit for the company when a trainee or regular employee finishes a job early, whether an hour or a half day. You can select an item on your improvement list for him to do. Some of the items on this list might be:

1. Organizing an area for miscellaneous materials.

2. Organizing an area for hand tools.

3. Painting the machines light colors.

4. Making a sign: *"Please return all items to their proper places"* or another desirable sign.

5. Putting up some shop safety posters (available from the National Safety Council, 425 Michigan Ave., Chicago, IL 60611).

34. Machinery and Equipment Considerations

Another list to be developed is for the tools and machines you should purchase. Since you usually cannot purchase them all at once, make a list very carefully indicating which ones are most important. In this way, each time you have some extra money to invest, you merely take a glance at this list without making an entire new list each time.

18. Keeping Abreast of New Developments

Years ago, some of the operations that were performed in the shop required a single machine for each separate operation. Today much of this has changed; there are machines that can be arranged in the proper sequence so that they shear, notch, punch, piece, bead, seam and form in one continuous series. Many of these types of machines can be operated by one person.

Regardless of what type of sheet metal machinery you require or what your fabrication problems are, machinery manufacturers are always willing to assist you by demonstrating their machines to you. Some manufacturers even have films to show the complete capabilities of their machinery. Or possibly by showing them your product or piece parts, they can advise you of the best machinery available to produce the product or part.

Forming some of the products and piece parts in sheet metal used to take an extensive amount of forming or series of complicated forming. Today much of this work is handled by roll-forming machines which can be designed to meet your exact needs. Because of this trend, more and more sheet metal fabricators and engineers have become familiar with roll-forming and its capabilities. Each year more parts are produced from the "coil concept" due to its economical advantages which are fast and accurate.

Many parts that at one time required two men to form them, can now be handled by one man due to both the "coil concept" as well as roll-forming.

Trade journals, associations and conventions can help you keep alert to new developments. A definite way to keep yourself informed of any new machinery is to request the various machinery manufacturers to put your company on their permanent mailing list.

Machinery and Equipment Considerations

To determine whether or not the cost of the new machinery is justified, you must consider whether the future savings with the desired new machinery would be large enough to make the change worthwhile. You must take into consideration your company's past, present and future objectives.

Part 3
Important Factors to Consider Before Selecting Any Type of Shop Layout

There are many factors to consider when you plan any change or modification of your present shop layout. The extent of your change helps determine which of the following factors are most important to you. These key factors and their appropriate details are itemized here.

Reading them will help you determine which are most important to you, and might remind you of some factors you might have overlooked. These are especially helpful for shops that do the following general types of work:

1. Metal Stamping
2. Plate Fabricating
3. Sheet Metal Fabrication
4. Manufacturers doing Metal Forming and Stamping
5. Structural Steel Fabricating

1. How Effective Will The Flow Or Movement Be?

This refers to materials, people and/or paper-work. First, consider the sequences of working operations or steps with a minimum of backtracking, transfers, cross-overs and long hauls.

1. Easy access to, away from, and between major areas including receiving, shipping and most important operating areas.
2. Closeness of related areas to each other where movement of material, people, or major paper work is involved; or where frequent personal contact takes place.
3. Largest flow intensities having the minimum distances between them.
4. Regular and consistent flow patterns.
5. Ease of delivery and pick-ups.
6. Accessible for visitors and service people.
7. Easy flow of supplies, tools, scrap or waste and service materials.

Important Factors to Consider

2. Will All Space Be Well Utilized?

This concerns the most effective use of all space or square and cubic footage.

1. Use overhead space in terms of cubic density.
2. Minimum of waste or idle space caused by split, divided, cornered, scattered structures or by too-close columns, too-frequent partitions or walls.
3. Use less desirable or out-of-way spaces for slow or less frequent activities; use convenient spaces for fast and frequent activities.
4. Consideration of sharing space among similar activities.
5. Balancing areas with different seasonal space requirements.
6. Conserve floor space, property and land.
7. Careful location and use of aisle space for these purposes:
    (a) to serve areas adjacent to them
    (b) to lead to areas needing access,
    (c) to handle traffic without wasting space or without excessive aisleways (too few, too many, too wide, too narrow, too cornered or crooked, too angular.)

3. How Effectively Are Materials Handled?

This refers to easily handling all materials, equipment, supplies, containers and waste into, through, and out of the designated areas.

1. Minimum of traffic congestion and interferences other than due to flow pattern.
2. Avoid all re-handling, extra handling, delays, awkward positioning, undue physical effort, undue dependence on urgent moves.
3. Best utilization of handling equipment and containers.
4. Appropriate variety of handling systems, equipment, and containers.
5. Proper tie-in with auxiliary handling methods and equipment such as rail lines, docks, highways, and other access ways.
6. Equipment placed for multiple uses.
7. Ease of using handling devices.
8. Ability to move completely around buildings on own property.
9. Avoid two or more people at same time or place.

10. Combined purposes of handling equipment for storing, sequencing, inspecting, work-holding, weighing, in addition to moving.
11. Minimum need for maintenance, repair and replacement parts for material handling equipment.
12. Take advantage of gravity whenever practical.

4. How Can Safety and Housekeeping Be Maintained?

This point considers the effect the layout has on minimizing safety problems, which incorporate ease of general cleanliness of the areas. It also must consider a step beyond safety of employees and any other people--also consider lack of damage to equipment, products and general facilities.

1. Extent to which all safety codes and regulations can be satisfied.
2. Minimal risk of danger to people or equipment; availability of adequate exits and fire extinguishers.
3. First-aid facilities and fire extinguishers nearby and clearly visible.
4. Adequate protection or separation of dangerous operations.
5. Proper utilization of special safety devices or guards.
6. Ability to clean or clear area of waste, trimmings, trash, etc.
7. Floors free of obstructions, spillage, and mess.
8. No areas overly congested.
9. Ability to keep all areas clean, sanitary and under controlled conditions.
10. Basic straightness and wideness of the aisles and work areas, and freedom from equipment protruding into aisles or work areas.
11. Eliminate congestion and blind corners.
12. Workers and aisles not located under or above unprotected hazards.
13. Workers and aisles not located too near moving parts, unguarded equipment, and other hazards.

5. How Effectively Will Supervision and Control Be Maintained?

This refers to the degree to which each supervisor or manager can observe, direct and control all operations for which he/she is responsible.

Consider these factors:

Important Factors to Consider 39.

1. Ease of seeing all necessary areas fully.
2. Ability to move or reassign workers to other work.
3. Ease of controlling wasted time, lost materials or missing supplies.
4. Ease of controlling quality, quantity counts, schedules, inventories in process, etc.
5. Ability to move around the areas conveniently.

6. Can The Quality Of Products Or Materials Be Maintained?

This refers to the extent to which the layout has an affect on the workmanship and materials--all affecting the quality of the product.

1. Convenience and inter-relationship of quality control activities, which includes: inspection areas, testing facilities, control laboratories, sample room, engineering office, etc.
2. Risk of damage to materials caused by the layout or transports facilities.
3. Possibility of contamination, corrosion, spoilage, or other harm due to the product's nature or condition of the layout.

7. How Will Equipment Be Utilized?

This refers to the extent to which all equipment is used rather than standing idle, but without unnecessary delays waiting for specific machines.

1. Labor-and-machine efficiency planned into the layout.
2. Avoid necessity for duplicating equipment caused by layout; try to use common equipment and services.
3. Degree of efficiently utilizing all equipment including operating, utility, and auxiliary handling.
4. Avoid over-capacity equipment due to the layout.

8. Will Maintenance Problems Be Affected?

Try to have the layout accommodate, without other interferences, frequent or day-to-day service; and, if possible, also accommodate repairs and building machines if frequent enough to warrant consideration.

1. Adequate space for access to machinery and equipment to be lubricated, checked, cleaned, adjusted, on-spot repaired, or otherwise maintained regularly.
2. Adequate janitor and other cleaning facilities.
3. Sufficient space for maintenance and repair work.
4. Adequate space to move a machine without first moving other machines or equipment.

9. Can The Expected Capacity Be Achieved?

This refers to the layout being able to meet the planned needs and output expected.

1. The expected quantities of each variety or item in the operating time planned, without overtime or premium pay.
2. The right products or materials, properly meeting specifications as efficiently as expected.
3. The right output terms of projected quantities and qualities of product.

10. How Effective Is The Storage?

This refers to maintaining proper quantities in stock or materials, parts, products and service items.

1. Easy access to items stored.
2. Adequacy of storage spaces without unnecessarily moving items to get to others.
3. Storage of frequently-used items close to point of delivery and use.
4. Ease of locating or identifying items stored.
5. Ease of stock and inventory control.
6. Maintaining records without excessive time.
7. Ease of making stored items available according to urgency of demand.
8. Protection of material (fire, moisture, dust, dirt, heat, cold, pilferage, deterioration, spoilage, etc.)
9. Including all types of storage-raw, in-process, finished goods, supplies, tools, scrap, or waste, trash and equipment or materials not in current use, repair items, etc.

Important Factors to Consider

11. How Are Security And Theft Considerations?

This point considers how easily you can maintain or safeguard the company's security or classified information, and how well you can control both theft and pilferage of both materials and products.

1. Ease of patrolling buildings and/or grounds.
2. Ease of controlling access to the plant during hours and during off-shift hours.
3. Ease of controlling receiving and shipping functions.
4. Ease of controlling access to and dispensing of tools, materials, supplies and easily pilfered items.
5. Ability to provide guard-controlled traffic access for all pedestrian and vehicular movement for which you are responsible, primarily on your property.
6. Effective control of access to secure areas or information within the plant.
7. Provision of adequate vaults for safe, secure storage of valuable or confidential records and documents.

12. Are Working Conditions Or Employee Satisfaction Affected?

This is a reminder that having relatively pleasant, clean and definitely safe working conditions help to make the atmosphere provide a pleasant place to work. Consider especially being free of awkwardness, disruption and unnecessary inconvenience.

1. Freedom from features causing workers to feel fear, hemmed-in, embarrassed, discouraged, discriminated against.
2. Minimize unnecessary noise, distractions, undue heat, cold, drafts, dirt, glare or vibrations.
3. Working conditions suitable to the type of operation.
4. Convenience for employees--access, distances, interruptions, delays and adequacy and convenience of parking, lockers, rest rooms, food facilities, etc.
5. Utilization of employee know-how and skills.
6. Effect of layout on attitude, performance and general morale of the employees.

13. Can Supportive Services Be Properly Integrated?

This refers to having non-production functions located conveniently for their specific functions. This can include production planning, scheduling, control, time-keeping, material or stock issuing, work count, tool control, personnel records, receiving and shipping systems.

1. Ability of the above functions to handle their procedures and controls to work effectively with the layout.
2. Physical closeness of service areas according to each area's need for the service.
3. Service convenience of baler, salvage equipment, incinerators, filter beds, scrap collection and similar waste control areas or equipment.
4. Ability of engineering and technical advisors to work effectively.
5. Convenient for the utilities, auxiliary service lines and central distribution or collection systems to serve the necessary locations. This might include compressors, steam generators, transformers, chargers and their accompanying pipes, ducts, wiring, etc.
6. Ability of the layout to accommodate desired or effective pay plans, performance measure, cost reports, lot size, order quantities, etc.

14. Does The Layout All Fit With The Company's Overall Organization Structure?

This refers to the degree to which the layout coincides with the overall organization structure.

1. Functions having the same supervisory responsibility are adjacent or close to each other.
2. Assists supervision effectiveness of managerial personnel.

15. Is There Flexibility In The Layout?

This refers to being able to rearrange the layout to handle changes that might become necessary or helpful.

1. Ability to get to some things at more than one point or side.
2. Ability to move machinery and equipment, due to weight, size and/or fixity.
3. Avoid overly dense saturation of space, which makes it harder to move or rearrange.

Important Factors to Consider

4. Standardization of equipment, containers, work places, etc. for visual familiarity and appearance.
5. Freedom from unmarked fixed building features or walls, unmatched floor levels, other barriers or hazards.
6. Easily accessible to service lines, piping, power distribution, heating and ventilating, service holes, etc.

16. Is The Layout Versatile Or Adaptable Enough?

This refers to the ability to make some changes without rearranging the layout drastically. This includes the following types of changes:

1. Quantity or volume
2. Operation Sequence
3. Time-keeping or count system
4. Hours of work
5. Inspection controls
6. Alternate routes
7. Product, materials, or items
8. Frequency of delivery
9. Working methods and operating time
10. Handling or storing methods
11. Material dispatching procedure
12. Additional space for stock
13. Test runs, experimental engineering
14. Standby equipment
15. Utilities or auxiliaries

17. Is It Compatible With Overall Short-Range And Long-Range Plans?

Can the layout accommodate the current plans for short-range and long-range growth projections or changes in the output?

1. The ease of renovation, rehabilitation, modernization or change in function.
2. Effect of the layout on the sale value of the property for other users.
3. Ease of correlation with other buildings, plants or sites of the organization.

4. Ability to fit with the following:
   (a) Long range projections of products and materials.
   (b) Sales or operating quantities
   (c) Working hours
   (d) Operating times
   (e) Process sequence and equipment
   (f) Services

18. Is There Adequate Expansion Capability?

Is there any way the usable space can be increased, still using what is already in the layout?

1. Ability to spread out to adjacent areas---beside, above or below.
2. Ability to use storage or service areas and move them.
3. Ability to add vertical storage equipment, balconies, mezzanines.
4. Freedom from fixed or permanent building features such as divided or honeycombed areas, space blocked-in by physically long equipment, property lines, natural obstructions or limitations.
5. The least amount of disruption or rearrangement of areas other than the one or ones specifically being expanded.
6. Ease of contracting the layout economically, to cut down the size if necessary.
7. Regularity of allocated space amounts in order to readily exchange amounts and types of areas.

19. Does The Layout Use Natural Conditions Economically?

This refers to the degree to which the layout utilizes the natural conditions of the site and physical surroundings, and utilizes the structure of the current building.

1. Rail, line, highway, waterway, bridges, access ways, crossings.
2. Building features, structure, shape, height, construction, docks, door locations, elevator(s), windows, walls, columns.
3. Fitting the work areas into the natural site or into the existing building with minimal extensive changes.
4. Slope, topography, foundation, drainage, direction of sun, prevailing wind.
5. Zoning and restrictions of community or neighborhood.

Important Factors to Consider

20. Is The Layout Compatible For Public And/Or Community Relations?

Does it meet expected appearance, promotional value, or public and community relations if important?

1. Effects on neighbors, both benefits and irritants.
2. Fit with community appearance, tradition, character.
3. Ability to keep exterior relatively neat, clean, and orderly.
4. Regularity, symmetry, clean-lines, and organized appearance.
5. Attractiveness of external or visible features, yards, main structure, extra buildings.
6. Ability to serve as "show-place" or reflect reliability, progressiveness, or other company qualities or images.

Part 4
Additional Factors to Consider When Determining a New Shop Layout

Goals of a Facility Design

The efficiency of a manufacturing process depends on the layout design. The following are the four general goals.

1. Provide efficiency by arranging machines, equipment and work areas so each process can move smoothly along in as straight a line as is possible.

2. Eliminate all possible delays. In some instances, a part is either being stored or moved 80 percent of the time it is in the plant.

3. Plan the flow avoiding any chance of becoming mixed with other parts in adjacent areas.

4. Maintain quality of work by maintaining the conditions that are needed for quality.

Maintain flexibility. There are many instances when it will be necessary to change the production capabilities of a plant or department that was planned for the production of a maximum quantity of a certain item.

Anticipating changes in the original planning can make changes more easily adaptable. A common way to accommodate the rearrangement of equipment is to install utility systems into which service connections can be easily tied when the building is constructed or remodeled. Examples of this are the overhead electrical ducts and the cutting-compound pipe lines. Locating them down the centers of bays allows machines to be unplugged, moved into new locations, and plugged-in again, where needed.

Minimize material handling. A planned layout should have the material handling reduced to a minimum. Wherever beneficial, handling should be done mechanically. All of the movements should be planned to move the parts toward the shipping area. The parts should be "in-process" while in transit, as in painting, baking, degreasing, etc.

Additional Factors - New Shop Layout

Reduce investment in equipment. The quantity of equipment required can be reduced by proper arrangement of machines and departments. Two different parts, both requiring the part-time use of an internal grinder, may be directed through the same machine, thus eliminating the need for a second machine. Planning when selecting the method of processing may sometimes save purchasing a machine. If one part calls for broaching and will use only part of the capacity the machine, a switch to drilling and reaming might be equally effective and the job done on equipment already available.

Maintain high turnover of work-in-process. When the material is moved through the processes in the shortest possible time, the operating efficiency will be the greatest. The time a part spends in the facility adds to its cost, through the tie-up of working capital. The closest to an ideal situation exits in the process-type operation where the material passes from the start to the finish of the process--sometimes without stopping. If in-process storage of material is reduced to a minimum, the amount of work-in-process is reduced, inventory is decreased, and a lower amount of working capital is tied up also. These savings reduce production costs.

Promote effective use of manpower. Poor layout practices may cause a large amount of productive manpower to be wasted. Proper layout may increase the effective use of labor. For example, here are some guidelines to consider:

1. Reduction of manual handling of materials should always be considered.
2. Balance machine cycles so machines and workers are not idle. Consider improved material handling, production control, method engineering and supervision.
3. Limit the need for walking. People walking to and from material supplies and keeping up with the assembly conveyor as it moved along can take as much as 25 percent of the time spent on an assembly line. This time-loss can be reduced considerably by bringing materials closer to the workers with specially-designed racks, hoppers and conveyors.
4. Maintain effective supervision. Keep the closest supervision at the most significant points. A properly laid-out department is easier to supervise. Avoid one that is spread out over too large of an area, or is too congested. Do not let it hinder a supervisor's ability to

handle more employees, keep work moving, and have extra time for other important duties.

Maintain employee convenience, safety and comfort. This includes such basic items as light, heat, ventilation, safety, removal of moisture, dirt, dust, etc. For example, equipment that causes excessive noise can be isolated as much as possible or be placed in an area with sound-deadening walls and ceiling. Reduce the transmission of equipment vibrations with cushions, or special mounting to the floor. Maintain safety by proper planning of the layout. Machines and manufacturing equipment must be positioned to prevent injury to employees and damage to material and to other equipment. Safety may be improved by a careful study of workplace arrangement, material handling methods, storage techniques and other factors involved in an operation.

Make economical use of building space. All the floor area in a plant costs money. You can calculate floor area cost per square foot per month, to include all overhead costs. If each square foot is used to its best advantage, the overhead costs per unit of product is minimized. Floor area that is occupied by equipment in operation is economical; unoccupied, wasted, or idle floor area is an unnecessary cost.

After the necessary allowances for the movement of people and materials have been made, some floor area can probably be used more economically.

General. Often it is impossible to fully achieve these objectives. In fact, some of them are almost in opposition to each other. But, most can be compatible. Nevertheless, each represents an important goal in which the layout is to be designed. An equitable solution must be reached that will be most effective in light of all factors considered.

Typical Types of Layout Problems

Frequently the layout problem involves the revision of an existing process or an alteration in the arrangement of certain equipment.

Design change frequently calls for changes in the process or operation to be performed. this kind of change may require only minor modifications in the existing layout, or it may result in an almost complete re-layout program, depending on the nature of the change.

Additional Factors - New Shop Layout

Enlarging a department - If it becomes necessary to increase the production of a certain part or product, a change in the layout may be needed. This type of problem may only need the addition of a few machines for which room can easily be made, or it may call for a completely new layout if the increase in production necessitates a different process from the one previously used. If parts were being made in hundreds, ordinary toolroom equipment might have been used. But, if the schedule were changed to thousands, it might be appropriate to install a special-purpose machine.

Reducing a department - This problem is the opposite of the previous enlarged department. If production quotas were reduced greatly and permanently, it would be appropriate to consider using a different process than that used for high production. This kind of change would probably require the removal of present equipment and planning for the installation of different types of equipment, especially if the present equipment is adaptable and can more efficiently be used elsewhere.

Adding a new product - If it is similar to the products already being made, the problem is primarily one of enlarging a department. However, if the new product differs greatly from those in production, a different problem presents itself. With a minimum of rearrangement, the present equipment may be used by adding a few new machines here and there in the existing layout. Or it may also be found necessary to set up a completely new department or section.

Moving a department - This may or may not present a difficult layout problem. If the present layout is good, it is only necessary to shift to another location. However, if the present layout has not been efficient, an opportunity presents itself for the correction of past mistakes. This may be the opportunity for a complete re-layout of the department.

Adding a new department - This may arise from a number of different reasons. Such a case would come about if it were decided to make a part which had earlier been purchased from an outside firm, or adding an operation that had been done elsewhere.

Replacing obsolete equipment - This step may require moving equipment if new equipment is larger. It may provide the opportunity for some minor changes that were needed anyway.

Change in production methods - If this results in anything more than a small change in a single workplace, it may also have an effect on nearby workplaces or areas. This usually requires a re-evaluation of the area involved.

Steps for Facility Design

The following steps can be used as a guide for designing an effective layout. They might need some modification.

1. Collecting the basic data is done by the facilities designer, who must rely on several staff activities for the data necessary to design the layout. He should develop a list of data consisting of the following:

- Forecast of sales
- Quantity to be produced
- Production schedule
- Inventory policies
- Production routing
- Percentages of scrap
- Operations to be performed.
- Preliminary methods
- Existing layouts
- Load limits for floor and ceiling
- Building drawing

2. The work of the layout designer starts with analyzing the information to determine the desired interrelationships, and then preparing it for the needed planning steps. One technique that is useful at this early stage is the *Assembly Chart*. This can give a quick and early look at the possible flow of materials.

3. Next, determine the production process for converting the material into the parts and products that are desired. In manufacturing, the process designer examines the blueprints and other data and determines the processes and operations from this gathered information. Then he can figure the necessary route for production. With both the assembly chart and the route for production, the designer can construct an operation process chart.

4. Plan the pattern of material flow. A good material flow pattern will guide the materials. Use the *Assembly Chart* and *Operation Process* as an aid in visualizing a general material flow pattern. Based upon a study of these two items and related data on material movement, the early stages of the material flow pattern should be developed. Then it becomes necessary to consider the other factors that have an

Additional Factors - New Shop Layout 51.

important bearing on the final flow pattern. A well-planned flow pattern should follow certain principles and general methods of material flow in combining material movement with the related factors.

Consider the factors affecting the material flow pattern, and analyze the product itself. Then correlate the methods of processing the various components into a master flow pattern. Expect changes in the layout design as more details are developed. A good layout is flexible and permits future changes without excessive interfering with the existing layout.

5. Examine how the general material handling system changes the inactive flow pattern into an active flow of material through the plant. The ideal system consists of a combination of methods and equipment designed to activate the flow of material. It contains effective methods of performing every handling task -- from the unloading of material delivered by suppliers, to the loading of finished goods into carriers on their way to customers. In between, it handles material into and out of each production or related activity. The system usually involves both manual and mechanical methods, as well as equipment like conveyors, cranes and industrial trucks.

Based on the flow pattern, some decisions should be made regarding general methods of handling material and the type of equipment that may be used. However, do not decide upon detailed handling methods between operations and specific equipment until after individual work stations have been planned.

6. Determine the equipment requirements by determining how many pieces of each type of equipment will be required before continuing the layout process. Although consideration of the number of machines was probably prepared earlier, make final decisions at this point as to the quantity of equipment needed for planning individual work stations and calculating space requirements for each activity area. Also, determine the number of operators needed. If these decisions have not already been made, an estimate is at least helpful before continuing.

7. In the layout design, coordinate the relationships between work areas, related groups of operations, production centers, departments and processes. Then coordinate the flow diagrams of individual processes into the master flow pattern that was originally developed and possibly modified. Records of the major steps in each operation may be made to

force a consideration of the steps (particularly material handling) between the operations. Point out omissions in planning and effectively guide the further integration of operations.

An experienced planner will skillfully go back and forth between these steps as the need for adjustments and coordination becomes apparent.

8. Next, plan the individual work areas. At this point plan each operation, work station, area and process. Determine connections between machines, operators, and auxiliary equipment. Also, give consideration to operator cycling, multiple machine operation, principles of motion economy and material handling to and from the workplace.

Although the flow pattern has established the overall path for material movement, each workplace is a stopping point in the planned flow of a specific item. Therefore, plan the flow through each workplace as an integral part of the overall flow plan. The methods engineer should assist in this portion of the layout design by designing each workplace in detail.

9. Selecting specific material handling equipment is usually a very important factor in layout planning.

10. The service activities and auxiliary functions that assist the production activity must be properly laid out and effectively integrated into the master plan before working further on layout details. Determine the service activities which are needed and work out their details later. For example, determine the contents of locker rooms, tool rooms, first aid and food service areas to permit an estimate of the space requirements for each.

11. Now it is necessary to determine activity relationships to interrelate production activities with auxiliary and service activities. Consider the flow of material and personnel as well as noise, odor and dirt.

12. Determine storage requirements for raw material, goods-in-process and finished products. Calculate square-foot and cubic-foot requirements and carefully design storage area locations conveniently in the layout.

13. After designing the flow pattern and planning the procedures for auxiliary and service activities, estimate the total space required for each activity in the facility then the total area of the proposed facility. At

Additional Factors - New Shop Layout

this stage, space determinations are only estimates that should allow for sufficient area. The final layout will show the total space needs more accurately.

14. Make a preliminary layout which shows areas of activities and the appropriate relationships with planned needs. Allocate activity areas with regard to total space. The relationships between the internal and external flows of materials as well as the relationships with surrounding facilities -- such as the power plant, storage yards, parking areas and adjacent buildings -- will have considerable bearing on the orientation of the proposed building and on the location of the site.

15. Consider building types after the preliminary layout is finished. Although a building may only be a framework around and over a layout, the building may be integral to the production facility. In either case, the layout is still the factor that determines a company's efficiency and should not be altered merely to fit a building. Therefore, consider building type, construction, shape and number of floors to determine some tentative conclusions after completing the layout.

16. Make necessary modifications in the layout and/or the size of the building.

17. Construct the master layout after making adjustments to accommodate the merging of the work area plans, flow diagrams and service and auxiliary activities into a working, composite, flow pattern. Constructing the master layout requires the detailed work and planning done in the preceding steps. Three-dimensional scale models of physical facilities are frequently prepared--commonly to a scale of 1/4" =1 ft--in place of two-dimensional templates.

18. The facility designer and associates now evaluate, adjust and check the master layout with appropriate personnel. Personal factors need to be considered as they are often of greater importance than engineering aspects when final decisions are made. Worthwhile suggestions on matters the layout engineer may have overlooked can also be made by specialists who have contributed to the layout planning and are concerned with methods, production and personnel safety.

19. Depending on plant policies and procedures, plant officials who have special knowledge of phases and relationships between proposed operations must formally approve the layout.

20. The layout designer should closely supervise the installation of the layout to be sure all work is done according to the approved layout plans. As construction work progresses, modifications should be thoroughly investigated and approved by the proper people. The layout designer, architect and construction engineers need to cooperate so the planned layout is properly incorporated into the building.

21. Make continual improvements in the layout. Although the layout has been installed as planned, there is no guarantee that it will work as planned. Equipment may not work properly or employees may not follow approved methods. Material may not move the way expected, so you have to merge operations together as effectively as planned. The layout designer must also observe how the layout affects the production operations. When opportunities for improvement are seen, they should be properly evaluated and put into use.

Why a Master Flow Pattern is Needed

Every production-oriented facility requires a properly labeled master flow pattern for use in current and future planning. It should represent the entire production process and should be consulted each time a facility change is suggested. The proper use and update of a master flow pattern will insure that no department or piece of equipment is located or moved without adequate consideration being given to its relationship to the overall material flow.

A long-range master flow pattern should also be considered to represent expected expansion over 5, or 10, or more years. Facility changes that are contemplated and made with reference to the long-range flow pattern, would permit the gradual transition from a current less-adequate flow pattern to a future flow pattern designed to upgrade the company's overall production capability.

Typical Flow Patterns

The majority of material flow problems fit into one of a small group of general flow patterns. These reflect some of the basic factors in particular flow situations. The following are brief descriptions for the reasoning or application of the patterns:

1. Straight-line--applicable where the production process is short, fairly simple and few components or few pieces of production equipment are used.
2. Serpentine, or zig-zag--applicable where the line is longer than it would be practical to allocate space for a straight line, and therefore bends back on itself to provide a longer flow line in an economically constructed area.
3. U-shaped--applicable where the finished product ends the process near the location where it began for possible reason of external transportation facilities, or use of a common machine.
4. Circular--applicable when a material or product must return to the exact place it started for reasons such as shipping and receiving being at the same location, or a machine used a second time in a series of operations.
5. Odd-angle--this has no recognizable pattern, but it is very common in situations such as: when the primary objective is a short flow line between related area, where handling is mechanized, when space limitations will not permit another pattern, and where permanent location of existing facilities necessitate such a pattern.

Basic Flow Pattern Considerations

The following describe a few flow pattern characteristics to keep in mind when evaluating your current or proposed work flow.

The orderly flow of materials or parts through the work areas should not be interrupted by cross-traffic. Also avoid backtracking and crossing flow lines.

Observe the required flow between work areas to determine the pattern. Interrelated work places should be close together; a part should not go out of line to another area in the course of its processing. Also, avoid backtracking to a machine a second time if providing two identical machines would be uneconomical.

The locations of receiving and shipping activities are usually the beginning and end of the material flow pattern. The receiving activity should orient the flow pattern in relation to the building and also be closely related to the kind of transportation serving the plant.

The shipping activity should also be located in close relation to transportation facilities. Many factors must be considered to determine whether receiving and shipping should be located separately or be combined into one receiving-and-shipping area.

Receiving and shipping are the points where the internal material flow pattern plugs into the external flow of the transportation system. At this point, the overall system flow cycle is completed.

Planning Efficient Work Areas

The work methods design and material flow of each work area should be planned to fit into the overall material flow.

Consider all factors in the work methods design. To successfully integrate work methods into the layout, the facilities designer should carefully question and consider the factors influencing or involved in the work method design process.

To guide your planning of the work area or areas for best efficiency, the designer should consider the principles of motion economy and work place design. Based on experience, these principles are concerned with good practice and reflect the knowledge gained by years of work area planning. Therefore, they should be carefully observed in the work design process and incorporated into the methods when appropriate.

Each work area is a miniature factory with its own receiving, production and shipping area or location for incoming and outgoing materials and finished parts or products. One of the difficulties in planning work areas is properly designing each one for optimum efficiency, and then fitting each one into the overall flow pattern. The following procedure will help to guide this planning process.

1. From the overall flow pattern, determine the flow direction of material and activity through each work area.
2. Make a rough sketch of the major pieces of equipment in their approximate positions in the work area. Then indicate the direction of material flow by an arrow.
3. Determine items to be contained in the work area--such as machines, benches, stock containers and conveying equipment.
4. Indicate the sources of material the work area uses, and the direction in which the material must go.

Additional Factors - New Shop Layout

5. Indicate the destination of the parts or products from the work area, and the direction in which it must go.
6. Sketch any material handling equipment serving the work place or area.
7. Indicate the method and directions for waste and scrap disposal.
8. Indicate the distance between items in the work place on the sketch.
9. Evaluate the sketch considering the principles of motion economy.
10. Have the work area plan drawn to scale and in detail.

Following this procedure should help insure the proper coordination of each work area into the overall material flow pattern. Then begin design efforts to integrate the specific work areas into the overall flow pattern.

Material Handling Concerns

The primary function of material handling is the movement of material, work-in-progress and finished products.

The importance of material handling is becoming more widely recognized since handling activity in the average company easily accounts for 25% to 50% of the production activity, rather than the 10% to 20% frequently estimated. Too many companies are only concerned with direct production and overhead, but do not recognize the economic significance of improper handling methods.

Material handling activities go through these stages of development:
1. conventional
2. contemporary
3. progressive
4. system oriented

In the conventional stage, material handling is considered as the movement of material from one point to another within the facility. Too often, little or no attention is given to interrelationships between the separate steps.

The second or contemporary stage is more desirable. The material handling analyst considers all interrelated plant handling problems and establishes a general material handling plan. This ties each individual work area together and is the desirable approach in modern, well-managed companies today.

In the third or progressive stage, the analyst visualizes all material handling and physical distribution activities as part of one system--the movement of materials from all sources of supply, all handling, and the movement of finished goods to be ready for shipment or distribution.

The systems-oriented approach works toward an integrated solution to the total handling problem in terms of an ideal system. The material handling analyst designs and implements each portion of the system whenever possible, while continuing to work on other phases and gradually implementing them when economically practical.

This approach serves as a worthwhile goal for the design of the most effective material handling system. The degree to which it should be used depends on the importance of material handling to the company.

Various Methods of Basic Material Handling

In addition to the basic types of handling equipment (ranging from pallets to industrial trucks), there are also *basic handling systems*, which consist of a group of related handling devices commonly used in combination. Different companies might use different systems for the same purpose. Differences in plant layout, processes, volume of production, types of products, shipping and receiving procedures, and other factors determine an entirely different system for one plant than for another. The systems described here are rather basic and may be used separately in a plant; or several may be used together as an integrated plant handling system.

1. *Industrial truck systems* include the high-lift platform trucks and the low-lift trucks, pick-up, transport and set down skid-loaded materials. The low-lift trucks are for moving; the high-lift trucks are for stacking, maneuvering and positioning.

2. *Fork truck and pallet systems* are similar to the truck and skid system except the fork truck needs less clearance than the platform truck. The forks permit the use of pallets, which are usually shallower than skids. This saves space in tiering. Several types of powered hand

Additional Factors - New Shop Layout

trucks may be used with either the skid or pallet system. The economic travel distance is about 200 ft.

3. *The tractor-trailer system* is usually more economical for hauling larger quantities of material for distances over 200 feet. Since one inexpensive tractor can tow many loaded trailers at one time, the cost per ton is lower than with lift trucks. Loading and unloading may need to be done by hand, crane, hoist, platform lift or fork lift truck.

4. *Conveyors and conveyor systems* are usually found in operations where items are of uniform size and shape and are repeatedly transported over the same path or for long periods of time. The cost of material handling can be reduced by proper application of control devices, programming systems to conveyors and careful layout. However, conveyors become less economical when they must be loaded and unloaded frequently, especially by people.

5. *Overhead systems* that use cranes and monorail equipment are common in operations where limited floor space, product characteristics or restricted paths, and travel distances hinder the use of lift trucks or conveyors.

Part 5
Considerations for Machine and Tool Replacements

Analyzing costs for manufacturing operations often involve differences in receipts and payments at different dates. A comparison of alternatives having different first costs and annual operating expenses is probable. Using economy studies is generally necessary to recognize the time value of money so that such alternatives may be comparable.

To find the most economical method of solving a given problem, some imagination as well as engineering training and experience may be required. Investigate several alternatives to prevent reaching wrong conclusions by omitting a better solution than those which have been considered. Perfection is not necessarily required for the most economical solution to a problem. Often a careful study will show that a previously rejected alternative gives the most economical solution.

A good economy study should list the differences among the alternatives and give a brief statement about each difference. However, unless differences are reduced to monetary terms, word analysis likely leads to inaccurate conclusions. Frequently, the advantages and disadvantages of a particular alternative are listed so they may be stated more than once with different terminology. Also, even though their monetary value may be different or nonexistent, each item may be rated equal in importance.

Use any advantages or disadvantages that cannot be given a monetary value as judgment factors only.

Information sources of the greatest potential value in making economy studies are accounting records. Many economy studies combine data obtained from the accounting department with data gathered from other sources. The detail in which the accounts are kept and the care with which the actual expenditures have been charged to the appropriate accounts will determine the usefulness of the accounting records. In economy studies, the difference between alternatives is being sought, so the accounting data must first be carefully analyzed.

The cost of maintaining accounting records in adequate detail required by engineers cannot always be justified, so it is not always the fault of the accounting records that the engineer cannot use them. Therefore, the cost information must often be found by analysis rather than from the cost accounting records.

Replacement Considerations for Machines and Tools

A problem frequently encountered by management is whether the existing machines and tools should be replaced with new and more modern equipment. Equipment wears out and is replaced by new developments and improved devices, so many companies are in difficulty both competitively and financially due to incorrect thinking about the replacement problem.

There are many reasons for replacement of machines, tools and equipment. Improved machines are available for performing the same service. Equipment designers work at research and development to find new and more economical ways of completing existing jobs. If the prospective economies from new methods are sufficient, it will pay to replace old assets with new ones or to reserve the old assets for standby purposes or other occasional uses.

There are changes in the type and amount of production requirements. Production expectations from the old equipment may increase or decrease because of an increase or decrease in the demand for its product and service. Changes in the product or service required are also included. Competition among producers in a single industry or competition with a substitute product is what often causes these changes.

Existing machines change. Machines, tools and equipment wear out, corrode and decay due to age and use. Maintenance costs increase; quality and reliability of performance decrease so it pays to replace even the assets still capable of providing continuous service. In some circumstances, wearing out, corrosion, and decay may make replacement totally necessary rather than purely economical.

An old machine might be replaced by a new one that has new automatic features to reduce unit labor costs. This can provide increased capacity to meet an increased demand for the product, and can result in maintenance costs lower than the current high maintenance costs of the old machine.

62. Considerations for Machine & Tool Replacements

Many causes postpone the retirement of machines and equipment beyond economical date. These causes tend to lengthen the actual lives of industrial equipment and property beyond the point where it would be economical to make replacements.

One such factor can be making replacement decisions on a very conservative basis. In such cases, economical replacements are then postponed. In other instances, there may be uncertainty about the continuation of the present demand for the product. Or, the existence of any considerable book value for an existing machine may deter its replacement. Finally, the necessary funds may not be available to purchase the replacement machine.

Methods for Evaluating Replacement Alternatives

Deciding which type of equipment to purchase usually involves choosing between two or more alternatives that have unequal first costs, useful lives and operating costs. Therefore calculations that will produce comparable figures for the alternatives must be made. The annual cost method is frequently used for this purpose.

The annual cost is the sum of the yearly depreciation, interest on salvage value and the annual operating costs. Here, only the recovery factor and straight-line plus average interest methods will be discussed.

The capital recovery factor method is mathematically correct and the straight-line method is only an approximation. Due to much unavoidable inaccuracy of data used in engineering economy studies, the approximate method is generally accurate enough for most manufacturing equipment studies.

Capital recovery factor:
$$A = (C - S)\, crf + Si + O$$

Straight-line plus average interest:
$$A = \frac{(C - S)}{n} + \frac{C(i)(n + 1)}{2n} + S(i) + O$$

A = annual cost
C = first cost
S = salvage value

Considerations for Machine & Tool Replacements

i = interest rate
n = life of asset
$crf = i/[(1 + i)^n - 1]$ this value is taken from compound interest tables
O = operating costs

Economics of Machine Tool Costs

Planning and directing industrial processes means keeping management informed of the plant's current facilities and recommending changes. In order to make such recommendations, the capabilities and costs of the present system must be known. The capabilities of machine tools include their dimensional tolerances, their operating speeds and their scheduling flexibility. The amount of deterioration of the present shop facilities must be known, along with an estimate of possible replacements advisable due to advances in the design of new machines or devices. The associated costs of the present machinery, which include maintenance and setup charges along with direct labor rates, must also be known.

Compare the capabilities and costs of present machinery with the respective estimates of proposed equipment. When these comparisons show economic favor for replacement, recommend such action to management. Use systematic methods to weigh the economic factors in such comparisons.

The MAPI method of equipment replacement analysis is based on a thorough study of the economic life of machinery.

An economic decision concerning capital equipment means choosing to continue as is, to repair or to replace. Constant watching of operating equipment will alert the approach of a repair or replace signal. A major overhaul may partially offset deteriorations, and the inclusion of special auxiliary devices may delay obsolescence. In general, though, deterioration and obsolescence are successfully countered only by replacement.

In the selection of machine tools, auxiliary equipment and small tools, consider the capacity of the machine, its quality capabilities, the number of operations it can perform, and its flexibility, which depends on the variety of parts it can produce, speed, simplicity and reliability.

64. Considerations for Machine & Tool Replacements

Proper timing is one of the important considerations in a replacement analysis. Consider the following:

-the sales outlook for the products
-the current maintenance costs related to past costs
-the approach of a major repair required in the near future
-the length of extended life of the repaired machine
-its economic performance compared with a new machine

Purchasing new equipment often suggests combining present operations or eliminating subsequent operations. For example, a new milling machine may produce such a fine finish that a grinding operation which necessarily followed milling operations on the old machine may no longer be required.

Downtime costs usually rise as a machine ages so a careful analysis of the economic effect of such loss in manpower and scheduling efficiency will indicate replacement.

To some extent, replacement purchases are determined by the company's income tax rate, the depreciation method, the capital mix and the required interest rates for borrowed and equity capital.

Choices among alternative machines should always compare each proposed alternative with the present arrangement. Management usually assumes that equipment analysts have selected the best alternatives. Analysts must be familiar with new developments and maintain close contact with physical equipment in the field to select the best possible alternative for proposed replacement.

Using the MAPI System for Replacement Decisions*

The following pages first explain the MAPI form that has to do with the operational analysis, then the form dealing with investment and return calculations.

---

* MAPI. Machinery and Allied Products Institute, 1200-18th St. NW, Washington, D.C. 20036. For a more detailed explanation, order their book "Business Investment Management, " $30.00 for non-members.

Considerations for Machine & Tool Replacements 65.

This is a suggested form on Page 66. You can develop your own if you prefer or make an enlarged copy of this form for convenient use. It is primarily a list of factors to be considered in the analysis. While it may seem rather long at first glance, it is primarily a memory device or a check-list. Most analyses will require estimates for only a few of the entries. In some specialized cases, you will find it appropriate to add items not shown.

This form is designed for relative-return analysis--the comparison of the project with a stated alternative. For this reason, it calls for estimates of the operating *differences* between two alternatives, usually the current use and a proposed use.

It can also be used for deriving absolute returns mentioned near the end of this section. In spite of the many comments helpful for using these forms, the following merely provides a brief explanation of the least obvious items.

The operating rate called for is the estimated operating rate of the project itself. In estimating the prospective project rate, do not limit your study to the work now done by assets to be replaced by the project. It could be, of course, that the new installation will do no more than take over the work of these assets, but that is unlikely. Include the work it can advantageously divert from assets not slated for retirement. Add any work it will do that is not presently being done at all. In short, figure the operating rate on the maximum beneficial use of the project in the business.

Lines 1-3 relate to revenue (increase or decrease in sales).

Line 1. *Change in Product Quality.* Enter here the effect on sales of changes in product quality resulting from the project (if any).

Line 2. *Increased Output.* The project may expand the output of existing products or may add new ones, or both.

Lines 4-22 relate to operating costs; only enter changes--increases or decreases.

Lines 23, 24 and 25. These require arithmetical computations to derive the result of the analysis, the *annual operating advantage.* Watch the

66. Considerations for Machine & Tool Replacements

PROJECT NO._____ SHEET 1

MAPI SUMMARY FORM
(AVERAGING SHORTCUT)

PROJECT_____
ALTERNATIVE_____
COMPARISON PERIOD (YEARS)_____ (P)_____
ASSUMED OPERATING RATE OF PROJECT (HOURS PER YEAR) _____

I. OPERATING ADVANTAGE
(NEXT-YEAR FOR A 1-YEAR COMPARISON PERIOD,* ANNUAL AVERAGES FOR LONGER PERIODS)

A. EFFECT OF PROJECT ON REVENUE

		INCREASE	DECREASE	
1	FROM CHANGE IN QUALITY OF PRODUCTS	$	$	1
2	FROM CHANGE IN VOLUME OF OUTPUT			2
3	TOTAL	$ X	$ Y	3

B. EFFECT ON OPERATING COSTS

4	DIRECT LABOR	$	$	4
5	INDIRECT LABOR			5
6	FRINGE BENEFITS			6
7	MAINTENANCE			7
8	TOOLING			8
9	MATERIALS AND SUPPLIES			9
10	INSPECTION			10
11	ASSEMBLY			11
12	SCRAP AND REWORK			12
13	DOWN TIME			13
14	POWER			14
15	FLOOR SPACE			15
16	PROPERTY TAXES AND INSURANCE			16
17	SUBCONTRACTING			17
18	INVENTORY			18
19	SAFETY			19
20	FLEXIBILITY			20
21	OTHER			21
22	TOTAL	$ Y	$ X	22

C. COMBINED EFFECT

23	NET INCREASE IN REVENUE (3X−3Y)	$	23
24	NET DECREASE IN OPERATING COSTS (22X−22Y)	$	24
25	ANNUAL OPERATING ADVANTAGE (23+24)	$	25

* Next year means the first year of project operation. For projects with a significant break-in period, use performance after break-in.

Copyright 1967, Machinery and Allied Products Institute

Considerations for Machine & Tool Replacements 67.

signs in this summation. In some cases Line 24 may show a negative figure (expansion projects, for example).

Line 26. *Net Cost of Project.* Add installation to the delivered cost of new facilities. The MAPI system treats tax benefits realizable at the time of installation as reductions of investment. For this explanation, you will need to refer to the complete book footnoted at the beginning of this section.

Line 29. *Retention Value of Project at End of Comparison Period.* It is what the project will be worth to you at that point in time. You may estimate your own retention value since the MAPI charts are not in this book.

Line 30. *Disposal Value of Alternative at End of Period.* The investment in the alternative at the end of the period is its disposal value.

Line 32. *Average Net Capital Consumption.* The symbol P stands for the comparison period specified on the third line of sheet 1.

Line 34. *Before-Tax Return.* While the MAPI system yields an after-tax return (Line 40) as the final test of investment merit, the before-tax return is easier to figure and is often sufficient for trial runs and preliminary testing. If you are going through the after-tax return anyway, you can skip this line.

Line 35. *Increase in Depreciation and Interest Deductions.* To solve for the after-tax return, it is necessary to take account of the increased depreciation and interest deductions brought by the project. What is required is the first-year increase when a one-year comparison period is used and the average annual increase when the period is longer.

Line 37. Use your own income-tax rate (or the rate you expect in the future).

There are a variety of alternative calculations you can use with these forms. Each is explained in MAPI's manual mentioned earlier in this section. They include:

1) Dollar amount of gain
2) Return on equity investment
3) Cash throw-off rate

68. Considerations for Machine & Tool Replacements

SHEET 2

II. INVESTMENT AND RETURN

A. INITIAL INVESTMENT

26 INSTALLED COST OF PROJECT
    MINUS INITIAL TAX BENEFIT OF $_____   (Net Cost) $_____   26
27 INVESTMENT IN ALTERNATIVE
    CAPITAL ADDITIONS MINUS INITIAL TAX BENEFIT $_____
    PLUS: DISPOSAL VALUE OF ASSETS RETIRED
    BY PROJECT * $_____ $_____   27
28 INITIAL NET INVESTMENT (26—27) $_____   28

B. TERMINAL INVESTMENT

29 RETENTION VALUE OF PROJECT AT END OF COMPARISON PERIOD
    (ESTIMATE FOR ASSETS, IF ANY, THAT CANNOT BE DEPRECIATED OR EXPENSED. FOR OTHERS, ESTIMATE OR USE MAPI CHARTS.)

Item or Group	Installed Cost, Minus Initial Tax Benefit (Net Cost) A	Service Life (Years) B	Disposal Value, End of Life (Percent of Net Cost) C	MAPI Chart Number D	Chart Percentage E	Retention Value $\left(\frac{A \times E}{100}\right)$ F
	$					$

    ESTIMATED FROM CHARTS (TOTAL OF COL. F) $_____
    PLUS: OTHERWISE ESTIMATED $_____ $_____   29
30 DISPOSAL VALUE OF ALTERNATIVE AT END OF PERIOD * $_____   30
31 TERMINAL NET INVESTMENT (29—30) $_____   31

C. RETURN

32 AVERAGE NET CAPITAL CONSUMPTION $\left(\frac{28-31}{P}\right)$ $_____   32

33 AVERAGE NET INVESTMENT $\left(\frac{28+31}{2}\right)$ $_____   33

34 BEFORE-TAX RETURN $\left(\frac{25-32}{33} \times 100\right)$ %_____   34
35 INCREASE IN DEPRECIATION AND INTEREST DEDUCTIONS $_____   35
36 TAXABLE OPERATING ADVANTAGE (25—35) $_____   36
37 INCREASE IN INCOME TAX (36 × TAX RATE) $_____   37
38 AFTER-TAX OPERATING ADVANTAGE (25—37) $_____   38
39 AVAILABLE FOR RETURN ON INVESTMENT (38—32) $_____   39
40 AFTER-TAX RETURN $\left(\frac{39}{33} \times 100\right)$ %_____   40

* After terminal tax adjustments.

Copyright 1967, Machinery and Allied Products Institute

Considerations for Machine & Tool Replacements

In addition, there are numerous special situations important in some analyses but not in others:

- Fixed service cutoffs
- Predictable obsolescence
- Predictable changes in the cost of the project
- Anticipated wage increases
- Future capital additions to project assets
- Long break-in periods
- Make or buy considerations

Additional alternatives that justify special considerations are:

- rent or buy analysis
- rent or wait
- alternative leases
- effects of anticipated inflation, with and without income tax considerations
- Absolute return analysis
- Use of marginal returns or total returns when screening projects

Part 6
Planning the Manufacturing Processes

Various Steps for Analysis of Production

In the solution of any engineering problem, pre-production and post-production analyses can be classified into these phases: recognizing, defining, analyzing, synthesizing, evaluating and reporting.

The manufacturing analyst must first *recognize* that a problem exits and must determine what questions should be answered. Select problems which are real, have key value and appear to be solvable within the time available and with the available tools.

Next, *define* the problem in familiar terms and symbols. Identify every aspect of the problem which should be evaluated. Eliminate non-essentials and describe the individual characteristics of the problem.

To properly define the problem, collect all the pertinent facts and classify them into categories applicable to the problem. Some of these are function, reliability, quality, producability, serviceability, tools, machines, materials and skill of operator.

Analyze the data available and study the relationships which exist between the various facts. Use past experiences to find similarities and cause-and-effect relationships. Then prepare a plan which will direct the analysis.

Next, associate the properties and ideas with the problem. *Synthesizing* information provides ideas or solutions to the problem.

Evaluate each alternative solution with the defined problem. Investigate each solution to each subproblem, compare all possible combinations, and then select the best solution to the overall problem.

Prepare a *report* so those concerned can be informed of the solution and the solution may be put into practice efficiently and effectively.

Implementing New Techniques and Processes in Manufacturing

Part of manufacturing analysis includes assisting in the development of new manufacturing processes, techniques and equipment. Introducing any new technique requires the writing of specifications and training of employees.

Two good ways to introduce a new manufacturing technique into production are the laboratory-pilot method and the pilot-factory method.

In the *laboratory-pilot method*, the techniques in the "laboratory" are developed by staff personnel before introducing them into the factory. While some industries build pilot or scale models of the equipment to develop the technique and process, other industries have machines and equipment in the laboratory for experimentation.

This approach is advantageous in several areas. Examples include the chemical milling process; the development of high-energy-rate machining and forming; and the machining, welding and heat treating of new alloys. To develop such processes, precise control by technically qualified personnel is often required so each variable is thoroughly analyzed one at a time. Since the control of each variable is critical to the success, statistical analysis for such process development is not considered practical. The judgment and capability of the engineer are basic to the success of process developments.

The *pilot-factory method* uses factory personnel on a small scale with technical assistance. Choosing the most competent personnel to initiate the process is important to its success as full-scale production is eventually developed around these people. Technical staff assistance in guiding and surveying the initial pilot-factory operation is required. Processes which appear to be simple and straightforward often have hidden problems that cause the introduction of the process to fail. A supervised test of a process in the shop may show that tooling is inadequate, more training is needed, inspection criteria are determined, or there are conflicting, nonexistent production methods.

The advantages and disadvantages of a laboratory-pilot and a pilot-factory operation indicate that both approaches are useful. The proper approach is selected for initiation in the factory by evaluating the processes and machines involved. Coordinating the affected departments is an important step to successfully introduce a new manufacturing method into production. The initiating group must develop a plan in detail and present it to the associated departments.

The plan may include manufacturing, sales, engineering, finance, personnel, quality control and purchasing. Before beginning, clearly determine who is the responsible group --- questions or decisions must be resolved by this group. While technical problems are usually the easiest to resolve, selling the new process to concerned departments is the most difficult. It must be determined when the process development group will let the shop take control of the process.

Another requirement to the successful introduction of a new manufacturing method is the amount of paperwork necessary to record and convey the necessary technical information. Each department is committed to and must comply with a document or specification regarding the manufacturing of the product. Such documents specify equipment, methods, material and controls for the manufacturing process; and they establish an acceptable method for obtaining a specific quality.

First, distribute the process specifications proposal to the following: process planning quality control, tool design, methods engineering, product engineering and manufacturing departments. The proposal should coordinate process requirement, and advise the involved departments in advance. There is a psychological advantage in seeking comments from shop personnel before the introduction of the technique; then they will tend to be more cooperative when their shop receives a new process.

After circulating the proposal, train employees and determine factory facilities and necessary test equipment. Incorporate into the final process specifications all constructive comments that do not interfere with the technical details.

Use a carefully integrated plan to train factory personnel before and during introduction of a new manufacturing technique. The extent of training will depend upon the trainees' previous experience, mechanical aptitude, familiarity with equipment and material to be used, and the new technique's complexity. Sell the operator on the technique's benefits to overcome psychological resistance to change. The technical training can start only after the selling job is accomplished.

Planning the Manufacturing Processes

A good method to introduce a new method is to distribute technical paperwork to affected personnel. With supervision, the operators and lead people can train themselves from the documents. Since technical documents are often difficult to understand, explanatory documents may need to be specially prepared. Although they result in additional costs, this method is usually very productive when previous experience and equipment are similar.

A second way to introduce a new method is to first train key personnel. Costs are easier controlled when personnel are sent to the machine manufacturer for training. Another method is to have a manufacturer's representative provide on-the-job training for the introduction of complex equipment.

Follow-through and education by a service department is a third widely-used way of introducing a new method. This service department means a technical staff which services the line organization; it can consist of laboratory personnel, methods engineering, manufacturing research, materials and process engineering. In most cases, training is on-the-job and is not an additional expense.

Training, technical assistance, documentation and quality control are all needed for the transition of new manufacturing techniques from a prime contractor to a subcontractor.

All subcontracting companies must be in a position to accept new contracts by keeping abreast of the development trend. Free exchange of technical information is vital to the subcontractor. Having acquired information on the development trends, the subcontractor must decide the actions needed to be taken. Problems often force the subcontractor to conduct development and production programs at the same time.

The subcontractor must first obtain all information available on the new process including engineering and quality control aspects. A person or committee may be appointed to visit the prime contractor's plants and obtain the necessary information. This is valuable because it is possible to see the laboratory development results and to talk directly with the personnel most familiar with the process.

An alternate approach is to have prime contractor representatives actually assist the subcontractor in introducing the new process. Committee control helps coordinate the introduction of the process with the required tools and facilities, employee training and the integration of product and manufacturing engineering, quality control and manufacturing. This is handled easiest by the pilot-factory approach. Smaller processes can be controlled by process control policies or other paperwork. When paperwork is not compatible with the subcontractor's process, different approaches are required. Standardizing the more common processes and issuing standardization documentation would benefit all levels of subcontracting.

Areas of Possible Part Inspection

At the receiving inspection, first inspect raw materials for conformance to specifications before being stored or sent to the manufacturing departments. Using drawings or specifications to check individual parts, subassemblies or assemblies before sending them to storage or to the assembly area.

In repetitive manufacturing, inspect the first few parts produced after the operation is completed--for conformance to specifications. To assure the continued production of acceptable work and to prevent scrap, parts are then inspected periodically.

In job lot production, avoid the cost of subsequent operations on a part that is already defective if each group of semi-finished parts is inspected by the operator or inspector to assure quality parts. Set aside defective lots until a decision on their disposition is made. Determine adequate yet economical scrap allowances for different lot sizes to avoid ineffective quality control.

Product-acceptance-sampling inspection uses fixed-limit-type gauges to separate lots into those which can be accepted without inspection and those to be screened to remove defective parts.

Inspection at the assembly area is for either repetitive or job-lot production. Here, inspection of certain quality characteristics prevents the assembly of defective parts which would only slow the assembly operation and cause malfunctioning of the finished product.

Final inspections occur after the final assembly of the unit or product. Here, inspection assures that the product properly functions and has not been damaged during assembly.

Planning the Manufacturing Processes 75.

The manufacturing engineering and quality control departments can select and order the inspection equipment. They also inform the manufacturing department how to use the equipment and when to submit the parts for inspection. The quality control engineer establishes the amount and frequency of inspection as well as methods of control.

Recently, the trend of the inspection function has been to insure and verify product quality before the finished product is prepared for shipment. Inspection is changing from being a subsequent function to becoming a part of the manufacturing process. By performing inspections during the manufacturing process, the process can be modified or stopped before many defective parts are manufactured. Gauges for the operator to use in checking parts are quite often satisfactory for inspecting the output of a manufacturing process. To specify inspection equipment, the process engineer must determine which machines are directly or indirectly controlled.

Patrol inspectors can inspect the process if the operator does not have time to do it. However, placing quality responsibilities in departments where the action is taken improves quality. Regular inspectors are often assigned to tests involving special equipment.

One of the earliest means of statistical quality control is the Shewhart-type control. This chart recognizes that all processes have variation and permits plotting the results of measurements of three or more parts taken periodically as subgroups in the order they are produced. The results from each subgroup are changed into two numbers; the average size is called X-bar; the difference, or range, between the smallest and largest measurement is called R-bar. The average and range point patterns remain within easily-computed boundaries when production variation is stable, but when the process varies or a new variable not characteristic of the process is observed, warnings are given.

Control limits are frequently set at 50% of tolerance of the part so a process can be modified before defective parts are made. After the production run, a check is made to assure that the quantity of defective parts is within the acceptable level.

For the Shewhart-type average and range control chart, compute the control limits for subgroup averages and for subgroup ranges from the variance in the measured results, not with the specification limits. Plans have recently been developed to combine process variability, meeting specification requirements. Three such plans are modified control limit, reject limit and pre-control.

In-process gaging provides some control over the unavoidable variables in the production output of any particular type of machine tool.

Considerations for Possible Changes

Adopting a questioning attitude is necessary for analyzing any operation. Take nothing for granted and subject all operations to change when economically justified.

The most valuable single question that may be asked about any operation is "why." The simplest questioning is "Why are we doing it this way?" Those most familiar with the operation are often the least likely to realize why a particular technique is used. Little will be gained if one merely accepts the first answer given to a question. Only a questioning attitude will obtain the answer to the point under consideration and prove to be as important a tool as any gauge, job, fixture, etc. Here are some other questions that can be asked:

- Where can the operation be done most economically?
- Where can tools and materials be best placed?
- Where can operations best be located relative to each other?
- What is the purpose of the operation?
- What is the operation trying to accomplish?
- What can be done to improve the operation?
- How can this operation be improved?
- When is the best time to do the operation? Certain operations are best done before others, sometimes out of apparent natural sequence. Take all factors into account.
- When can an operation be best scheduled? Sequencing for minimum setup must be considered.
- When must cutting tools be replaced?
- When must fixtures and machines be released for maintenance?

These words of questioning -- "why, what, when, where, who, how" -- should be applied to ay problem and analysis. Specific lists of questions can be made up to aid methods engineers in given areas.

Planning the Manufacturing Processes

The most costly or most troublesome operations should be improved first. An operation that has any of the following characteristics should be given priority and be studied as soon as possible.

1. Operations that are slow.
2. Operations that require fatiguing motions.
3. Operations that represent the bulk of the cost of a product.
4. Operations having long cycle times.
5. Operations with excessive machine downtime.
6. Operations where excessive scrap and rework is generated.
7. Operations that have not been studied for a long time.

The same criteria may be applied to determine which part or parts of an assembly should be studied.

Controlling Materials and Supplies

In most industries, material cost is larger than the cost of labor per unit of product. Therefore, direct adequate attention toward the economic use of materials and supplies in addition to the productivity of labor.

The cost of material is included in the original estimate of the manufacturing cost. Only adequate comparisons determine how closely the manufacturing facilities meet the planned usage.

Control of material must exist on an operational basis. In other words, control should be effective before any serious discrepancies occur. Abnormal trends should be indicated so corrective action can be taken immediately.

Losses are charged to overhead when reporting and record keeping are not adequate to indicate an excessive use of materials or the area where the variance occurs. The significance of overhead is that the burden rates are calculated periodically. Estimates for new work or cost comparisons on existing work reflect these losses in terms of higher costs during any one period. These costs may be higher than planned on existing work as well as the competition's quoted work. It is important to charge material losses to the specific product of which they are a part.

Variances in material usage can result from several causes and have the probability of occurring in any plant:

1. Improper method may be a result of improper instruction or failure to understand the requirements.
2. Poor material handling can result in the damage or destruction of pieces while being moved from one operation to another.
3. Operator carelessness may be due to poor habits or practices of the operator which are not corrected by the supervisor. Another contributing factor can be the attitude of the operator toward the job.
4. Design changes can cause material losses unless provision is made to dispose of parts in process and unusable raw material on hand before the design change.
5. Poor work-area storage facilities may result from using improper containers for finished parts or parts waiting to be processed.
6. Poor records and poor storage facilities can result in parts being hidden behind others, forgotten and re-ordered when not actually required. Good records indicate that enough parts were manufactured and are available in the storage area.
7. Pilfering can cause much loss of material if not kept under close watch.
8. When manufacturing processes have poor quality control, the probability of producing acceptable parts is unlikely. The scrap rate rises above that allowed and results in material loss. Acceptance of parts just bordering the limits of acceptable parts can result in excessive scrap.
9. Hidden scrap occurs often because employees are afraid of the consequences of making unacceptableparts and secretly disposing of the bad units.

A plant with sufficient control to pinpoint all of these problems is unusual. This control should exist on a release-from-storage level. A production item should be released relative to a given production schedule.

Equivalent material releases should accompany a production release issued for a specific lot. These should be posted relative to the amounts purchased to complete a lot or an order. When a lot or job is completed, record the amount of material used and material in inventory. Each plant must plan for its own product, policies and equipment to control material cost.

Planning the Manufacturing Processes

Decisions on Space Requirements

Determine space requirements by using material storage, service areas and the required machine area. Many companies compute the total area used by each type of machine, each area for accessory equipment, stock and operator movement. These data can be used to estimate total area requirements.

Raw material and finished parts storage must be based on customer demand and purchasing policy. Buy raw material in economical quantities and plan the storage area no larger than necessary to store the economical quantity.

Requirements for storage of finished goods are different with each industry. Extensive warehouse space may be needed due to seasonal demand for the product manufactured. If it is not possible to ship the finished parts as they are manufactured, obtain inexpensive warehouse space. If possible, store finished goods in areas that could later be used for manufacturing.

The most serious problem is in-process material storage. In straight-line layouts, minimum space is required because the product moves quickly from operation to operation. When calculating space requirements, allow in-process part banks to balance straight-line layouts. Slower work flow often means more space is required in process departments.

Essential information about the product and process is often obtained from several biased sources which tend to be misleading. Consequently, be relatively familiar with machine capabilities and production processes to assure that the data is complete and accurate.

Calculating Economic Lot Sizes

Calculate economic lot sizes to obtain the minimum unit cost of a part or product. You reach this minimum when the costs of planning, ordering, setting up, handling and tooling total to equal the cost of storage of the finished parts or products. Use mathematical calculations to equal these costs and the lot size. Depending on the number of variables to consider, the formula can range from relatively simple to relatively complex.

The formula for economic lot size is:

$$L = \frac{2NUS}{(T+I)C + 2A[1 - (U/P)]}$$

L = economic lot size
N = days worked per year
U = daily usage, in pieces
S = setup or preparation cost per lot ($)
T = taxes, insurance on inventory (%)
I = minimum desirable rate of return on investment (%)
C = cost per piece including labor, material and overhead ($)
A = storage cost for inventory per piece per year ($)
P = daily production, pieces

Under the following conditions you may simplify the formula:

1. Where the daily production (P) is large in proportion to the daily usage (U) because this will have little effect on the final result.
2. When an entire lot produced is an addition to inventory, it is better to omit the above and the minor item of taxes and insurance on inventory.

Simplified formula becomes:

$$L = \frac{2NUS}{IC + 2A}$$

The formula for calculating the economic lot sizes is seldom exact due to most of these factors being estimated. Therefore, the lot size may vary considerably from the economic lot size without greatly increasing the unit cost.

The fact that the lot size may be reduced below the economic lot size without significantly increasing the unit costs is very important--it enables you to reduce the working capital requirements by reducing the amount of finished inventory.

Planning the Manufacturing Processes

Functions of Production Planning

Production planning activities may include each of the following:

Scheduling is making the timetable for performing particular operations on individual production orders at various machine locations.

Central machine loading means assigning each department's work during a particular time period, such as a week. A central scheduling function of having enough work for the available department machine hours for the week may include sequencing orders on specific machines within the week.

Department machine loading is assigning the exact sequence of work to be performed on specific machines within a specific time period. The foreman or production control clerk may do this in a large department to assure that loading is done or the critical items receive priority.

Giving *special instructions* to the foreman in connection with specific jobs might include special instructions for a particular production method, routing or setup where several options are available. Determine which one is best for overall efficiency.

Dispatching is giving orders and instructions which set production in motion according to routings and production schedules. This includes release of materials to the first operations and work movement from one department to the next.

Expediting means beginning efforts to speed up operations when failure to meet a schedule appears likely. Examples of such efforts include physical tracing of work, contracting of vendors who provide outside parts, and authorization of high-cost production runs and material deliveries.

Following up means determining the current status of a production order in process or a part which is on order.

Production control may be assigned some or all of the responsibility for forecasting production, make-or-buy decisions, timekeeping, purchasing, tool control and traffic.

Unlike the responsibilities of a manufacturing or process engineering group, production control does not develop the operation methods and sequence of operations for producing the product. Also, production control does not supervise the labor personnel who make the product or maintain the quality or the equipment used in making the product. These are responsibilities of quality control, shop supervision and the maintenance group.

Keep inspection and maintenance separate from production control since equipment maintenance and inspection can conflict with meeting the production schedule.

Part 7

Collection of Articles from
The FABRICATOR®

Pages 84-85 describe The **FABRICATOR®** and the Fabricators & Manufacturers Association, International (FMA). Re-prints of articles from The **FABRICATOR®** begin on page 87.

FMA and THE FABRICATOR®

When you need reliable technical information on today's most productive metal forming and fabricating processes, join the Fabricators & Manufacturers Association, International (FMA). This not-for-profit organization serves industry as a resource for metal forming and fabricating technology, as well as management information. FMA serves members in over 25 countries on five continents.

The most important reason to join FMA or one of its technology associations is to receive vital technical and management information that will improve the productivity of your operations. When you join FMA, you automatically receive many informative publications that will keep you up-to-date on the newest techniques, equipment and industry activities.

As a member of FMA, you also have access to the most complete technical library in the fabricating industry. This library is your premier source for useful information that can help you work with suppliers, distributors and potential customers worldwide.

These pages tell you more about FMA's educational benefits and membership services. To receive more information or to join FMA, call the FMA Membership Department at (815) 399-8700.

The FMA staff and educational resources are ready to help you achieve your goals for high quality and productivity in your manufacturing operations.

TECHNICAL DIVISIONS/TECHNOLOGY ASSOCIATIONS

FMA membership allows you to enroll in either the Technical Division or Technology Association of your choice. This member benefit allows FMA to serve your interests more effectively by providing you with specialized technical information in your specific area of activity:

FMA Technical Divisions . . .

FMA Sheet Metal Fabricating Division
FMA Roll Forming Division
FMA Technical Divisions (contd.) . . .
FMA Pressworking Division   (contd.)

FMA and THE FABRICATOR®

FMA Coil Processing Division
FMA Plate and Structural Fabricating Division

FMA Technology Associations . . .

1. American Tube Association/FMA
2. Tube & Pipe Fabricators Association, International/FMA
3. Society for Computer-Aided Engineering/FMA

Educational benefits include:

1. Technical Information Center
2. Technology Conferences, Seminars and Workshops

EXPOSITIONS include:

1. FABTECH Expositions and Conferences
2. PRESSTECH Expositions and Conferences
3. Tube & Pipe International Expositions

PUBLICATIONS include:

1. The **FABRICATOR®**
2. **STAMPING Quarterly®**
3. **TPQ--The Tube & Pipe Quarterly**
4. Quarterly Technology Updates
5. FMA News
6. Member Resource Directory

The **FABRICATOR®** is published 10 times a year. Subscriptions are free to anyone in the metal forming and fabricating industry, and may be obtained by calling the Circulation Department, phone below. You may also write or call for details regarding membership and services available.

Fabricators & Manufacturers Association, Intl.
833 Featherstone Road
Rockford, IL 61107-6302

Phone 815-399-8700   FAX 815-399-7279

MAXIMIZING
the Return on Your Sheet Metal Equipment*

This article describes the actions taken by a metal fabricating company and what it learned by maximizing the use of its fabricating equipment. Instead of buying new equipment, the company increased production and reduced waste by using new methods to expand capacity.

Subcontracting versus Upgrading

The metal fabricating company produces dispensing equipment for the food and beverage industry. Its typical product is made primarily of light-gauge (16 to 24) stainless and galvanized steel.

Starting in the early 1980s as a custom job shop with few products and low volumes, the company grew until it had several product lines with significantly higher volumes. The company achieved rapid growth, partially through a willingness and ability to do custom work and/or ship customized standard product on short notice.

To meet this growth, the bulk of the sheet metal work was subcontracted. While the subcontractor was competent, the frequent design and schedule changes led to missed ship dates and

---

*Reprinted with permission from The FABRICATOR® January/February 1992. Information about this publication and FMA membership on Page 269.

excessive scrap and/or rework costs.

Because of this, and because the volume of subcontracted work had grown so large, it was possible to justify an upgrade to the company's sheet metal shop. The initial investment included a computer numerical control (CNC) rotational punch, a press brake, support hardware and software, and two technicians/programmers.

An implementation plan was developed whereby, after the purchase and start-up of the equipment, parts were to be brought back from the subcontractor based on total dollar volume.

The algorithm used was :

# of parts/year x $/part = $/year

These sums were sorted by order of magnitude, and the part with greatest value was scheduled for first return.

▌ Minimal Additional Equipment

Prior to the purchase of the additional equipment, a waste profile was developed for the sheet metal area. This profile suggested areas of opportunity in waste reduction.

In this case, waste was defined not only as material scrap but also as inefficient production techniques and losses due to improper equipment use.

Based upon the waste profile, the punch was predicted to be incapable of producing all the parts required by the company. Therefore, further increase in production capacity was necessary, yet the purchase of another punch was not practical.

An analysis of the parts produced by the company showed a number of them to be square or rectangular. This suggested that a numerically-controlled shear feed table would be helpful, because much of the punch's time was devoted to slitting hits.

Although the parts needed to be separated, it was determined that a single shear cut could replace dozens of punch hits. Shifting work from a heavily-laden punch to a lightly-laden shear allowed the company to increase production capacity without having to purchase additional equipment.

Using the shear/shear feed table combination to increase production capacity was initially successful. However, as the company gained experience in both programming and the punch, the need for improvement became clear.

▌ Waste Reduction

The greatest opportunity for improvement existed in material scrap reduction and continued equipment use efficiency efforts.

To address this situation, a waste reduction algorithm was developed. This algorithm was designed to develop a part price based on material and machine time for both the punch and the shear/shear feed table combination.

To effectively measure material scrap, this component of the algorithm was divided into two categories. These categories were defined as designed-in or design scrap and process scrap.

Any material within the boundaries of the part was termed "design scrap." The remaining scrap on the sheet was termed "process scrap" and was assigned equally to each of the parts on the sheet.

Next, the hourly dollar value for both the punch and shear/shear feed table combination was determined. Then, for each part the company produced, the amount of design and process scrap and the required machine time was determined.

These figures were converted to dollar values and loaded onto a spreadsheet. Also included were anticipated yearly production quantities from the sales forecast. From this information, an aggregate opportunity cost over the course of a year, by part, was determined.

These parts were then ranked by opportunity cost. The part with the highest cost was first, and that with the least cost was last. The most important thing this did for the company was to show the potential for savings and, based on dollars, to assign priorities.

The algorithm is as follows:

(Units/year) (# of parts/unit) [$ design scrap/part + $ process scrap/part + $ machine time/part] = Opportunity cost part/year

This was no small task. The company produced several hundred unique parts for its product line, and all of these parts went through the same cost analysis.

Several assumptions were built into the algorithm to simplify it. First, if a part required one minute of punch time to produce, all of this time was viewed as opportunity. While this did not give a realistic savings target, it did ensure all parts had a common starting point and that calculations remained relative.

Second, process scrap included the blank border normally reserved for clamping the work. This area was initially viewed as built-in waste.

With this priority system in place, waste reduction proceeded in a systematic manner, and a variety of techniques were used:

1. Where practical, smaller parts were punched out of the designed-in scrap of other larger parts.

2. Dummy moves and clamp shifts were used on the punch to produce parts in the blank border strip normally reserved for clamping. This allowed the throat size of the punch to be increased by 6 inches and parts to be produced in material that was previously considered to be a built-in loss.

3. Whenever possible, irregular shapes or hole patterns were formed using specially-purchased customized tooling.

4. Customized blank lengths in standard rolling mill widths were used to reduce process scrap.

5. Rectangular or square parts were placed immediately adjacent to each other on a blank. All punchinng, with the exception of slitting hits, was performed. The blank was then removed from the punch and transferred to the shear, and the parts were separated using the capabilities of the shear table. With experience, it was possible to hold individual part tolerances to +.010 inch.

6. Whenever practical, the design of the part was changed. These changes were performed to square the part for the shear or reduce the number of tool changes, etc.

7. When the transfer of part separation to the shear was impossible due to its shape, the automatic nesting function in the tooling software was used. This was an inefficient grid nesting function for the company's needs. Therefore, a more efficient method, termed a **true nest**, was later developed.

These methods of approaching waste reduction proved to be very effective. In the first year of its implementation, it reduced controllable costs by 54.65 percent.

Grid Nesting

Grid nesting is the term used to describe the automatic nesting function of the punch's tooling software. After one part was programmed onto a blank and the tool path was established, it was multiplied across the remainder of the blank. This reduced programming time and used the blank's material more efficiently.

While this is good, a standard nesting package is poor at reducing punch time and process scrap. The company was not able to find any nesting packages that would, for example, turn triangular parts to form squares—reducing scrap—and use single slitting hits to separate two parts.

A standard nest appears in **Figure 1** and demonstrates the problems discussed.

the operating system.

The derived knowledge was used to develop what the company refers to as a "true nest." The programming software was manipulated to use as much of the available material as possible through part orientation and to reduce the overall number of tooling hits per part.

This is demonstrated in **Figure 2**,

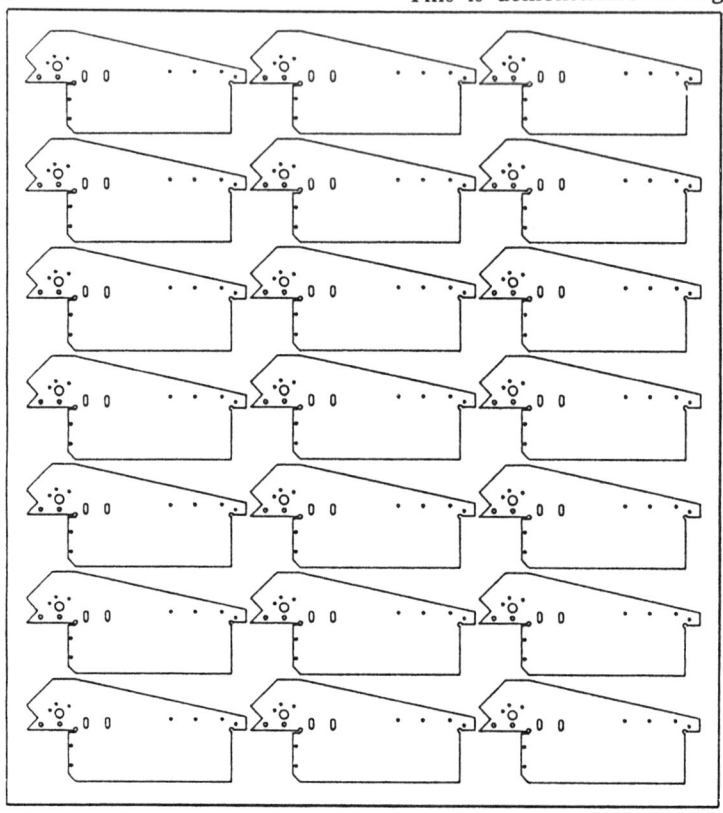

Figure 1
Standard grid nesting is shown here.

▍True Nest

During the initial start-up of the punch and its programming software, the integration of the two proved difficult. Contrary to the supplier claims, the punch and its off-line programming software were incompatible.

Much effort was required from the company to integrate the two. In doing so, it obtained a good understanding of

which shows the same part as in Figure 1, but demonstrates the advantages of a true nest over a grid nest. Parts produced in this manner were then separated using the shake-a-part process.

This type of nesting requires approximately four times the programming time as a grid nest but is worth the effort in the long run. This particular program required four hours of programming

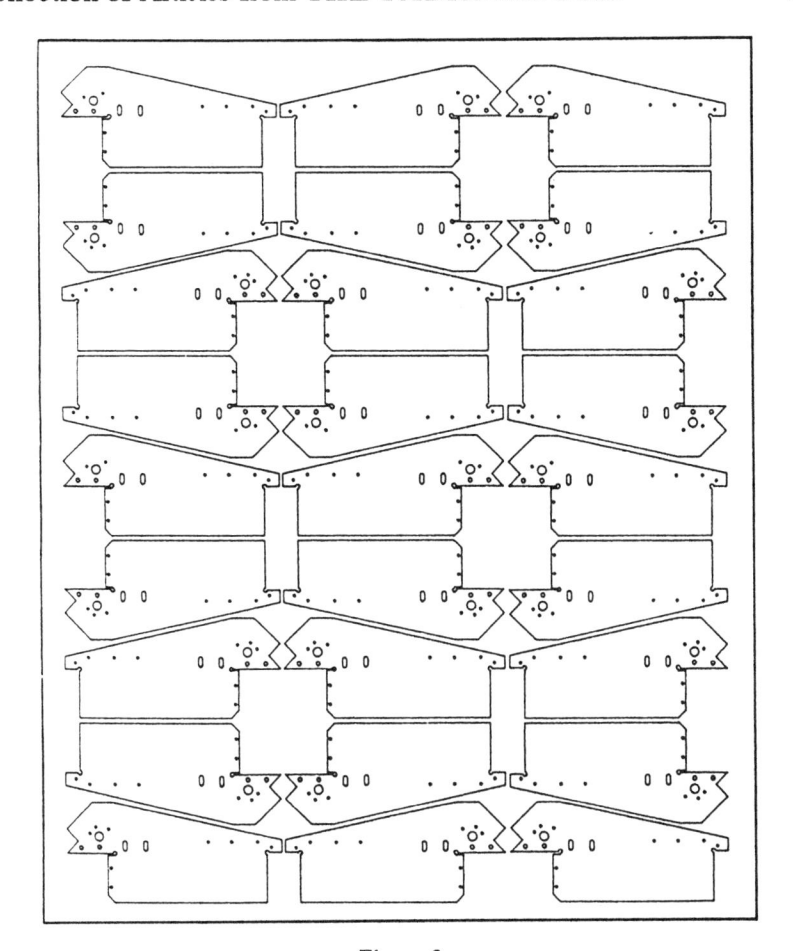

Figure 2

Here, the same parts in Figure 1 are arranged through a "true nest."

time but saved the company $7,488.17 per year.

Operating Procedures

In addition to opportunities in processing efficiencies, there were others to be realized in operating procedures. Production losses from equipment downtime, crashed sheets, and damaged, broken, or lost tooling were significant.

In an effort to track these costs, various elements and attributes of the sheet metal department were monitored using statistical process control (SPC). These elements included throughput of the punch, material losses and machine damage due to crashes, and tooling costs due to loss, neglect, or breakage.

These programs were facilitated by the development of an effective tool accounting and control program and the feedback from operators as to the reasons for sheet crashes.

This program allowed the company to justify a tool sharpener. This resulted in significant reduction in tool turnaround time and cost savings.

Intangible savings also resulted. Because tools could be sharpened quickly in-house, machine operators would turn in tools as soon as they began to dull rather than wait until they had to be

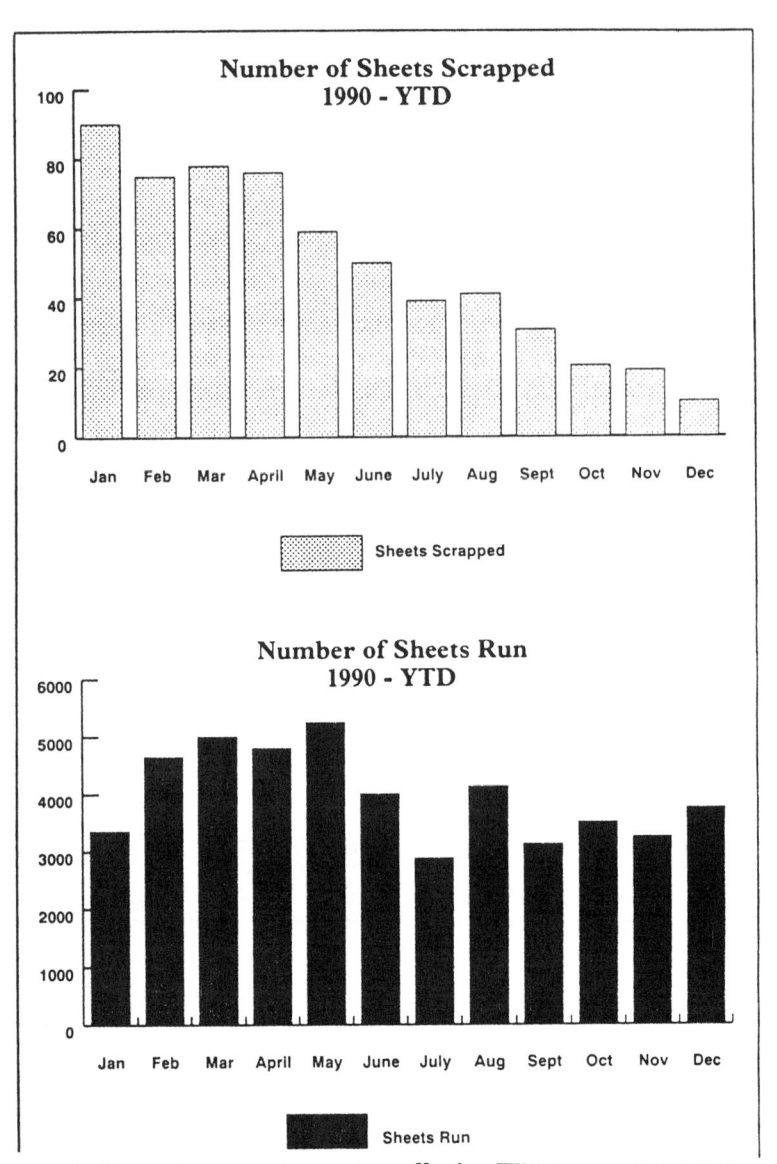

**Number of Sheets Scrapped
1990 - YTD**

**Number of Sheets Run
1990 - YTD**

sharpened. More frequent sharpening resulted in a reduced amount of material to be removed.

The number of sheets crashed as a result of tooling, and subsequent punch downtime, was also reduced. Tool life began to increase, as did the operating speed at which the punch could be run.

▌ Summary

Programs like these and well-defined preventive maintenance were extremely effective. Within one eight-month period, the company went from crashing 1 out of every 56 sheets attempted to 1 out of every 408—an improvement of 728 percent.

The 1990 end-of-year crashed percentage stood at 0.2451 percent and continues to improve. **Figure 3** shows 1990 achievement in histogram form.

While this attention to detail seemed at first to be excessive, the results spoke

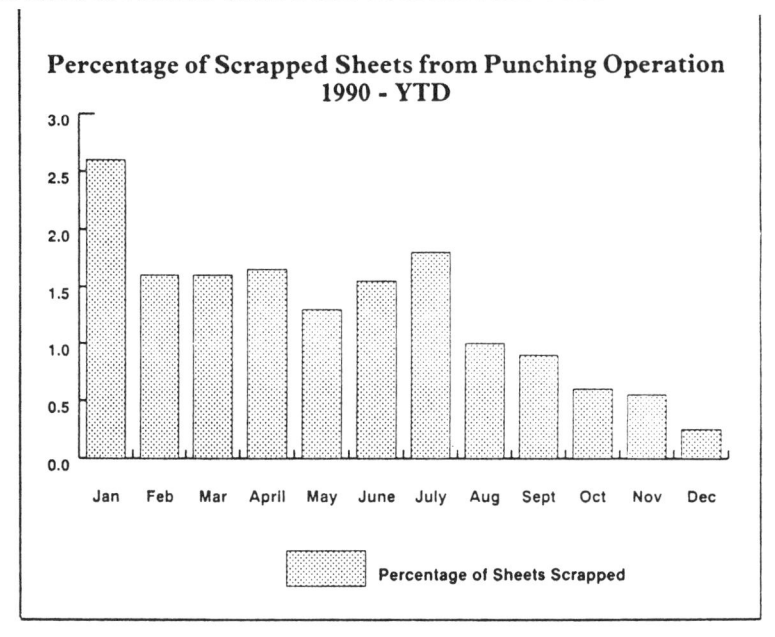

Percentage of Scrapped Sheets from Punching Operation 1990 - YTD

Figure 3

The fabricating company's 1990 improvement in punch scrap waste is illustrated by these three charts, which show the percentage of scrap, the amount of scrap by number of sheets run, and the amount of scrap by a total of sheets scrapped.

for themselves. Fabricators must be "lean and mean" if they intend to survive. Customized equipment, short lead times, and pricing constraints require that all facets of an organization be run as efficiently as possible. ■

The information presented in this article was prepared by Charles Fisher, Process Engineer/Agency Approvals, and Chris Koerber, Engineering Technician, SerVend International, Inc., Sellersburg, Indiana.

What You Should Know About Leasing Fabricating Equipment*

For many small and medium-sized companies, leasing fabricating equipment continues to be a popular way to finance the machinery needed to remain competitive. While equipment leasing has often been thought of as a way for companies without other capital sources to borrow, the reality is that all types of businesses use leasing. This article outlines some areas often overlooked by companies when considering or applying for a lease.

Leasing: An economical alternative

In today's business climate cash flow has become even more critical to a business's success. Leasing fabricating equipment offers you a source for financing long-term debt without spending a lot of cash or tying up lines of liquid credit.

Get to know the leasing company

A quality leasing company will welcome questions about who they are and how they operate. Remember to ask questions like: Is the company a direct funding source, or a broker? Does the company have experience with the fabricating business and equipment?

Tim Brandengburg of Sullivan Mechanical Contractors, Inc., Sullivan, Illinois, signed a leasing agreement with a company who had expert knowledge of fabricating equipment. "The fact that they knew fabricating equipment allowed us to make the whole deal happen in less than a week. We needed to move fast, and our lease let us do that."

Organize your financial information

If you take the initiative to present your financial information in an accurate and professional manner, you will greatly help your chances of approval, and any credit problems should be discussed up front and in detail.

Decide on the equipment and options

As the lessee, you must ask: Is the piece new or used? Is there a short or long delivery schedule from the manufacturer? Is the machine unique in any way (special controls, size, etc.)? Is there more than one vendor involved with the transaction? Once this kind of information is known, the leasing company can provide an accurate quote.

Read the documents you sign

While this is always good advice, it is especially true on documents that involve your fabricating equipment. Make sure you understand what each document represents and what your options are should you pay off early, trade in, or want to add to the lease.

Expect a prompt response

Once you have submitted the financial information requested, you should receive an indication whether or not the application has been approved within a few days. Of course, the larger the dollar amount involved, the longer the process may take. However, any lease application that takes weeks to process (for no legitimate reason) is simply not getting the attention it deserves.

---

* Reprinted with permission from The FABRICATOR® September 1992. Information about this publication and FMA membership on Page 269.

Keep in touch

During the delivery and installation process there may be delays that your leasing company should know about. Do them a service and call first. Throughout the life of the lease, it is always the best policy to let your leasing company know what is happening, especially if there is a problem.

To use leasing to the highest advantage, remember to ask questions and make sure you understand the answers given. By following the suggestions in this article, you can use equipment leasing as a part of your overall financial plan. ■

The information in this article was prepared by FMA member Robert Windoffer, vice-president of sales at Machinery Leasing Company of North America, Inc., Nashville, Tennessee.

Blueprint for Success:
Implementing a Job Shop Software System*

A variety of key factors contribute to the successful implementation of a job shop software system. Although there are no absolute, hard-fast rules that will guarantee success, some suggested guidelines will make the process easier.

■ Key Factors

Have a Plan. Why was the system purchased? This is the first question that a buyer must ask after the purchase. Goals and objectives that are expected to be achieved should be written down upon implementation of the system.

These goals should be shared with the entire staff who will be involved in the implementation. A very important first step is taken when a shop has a clear focus on what it wants to accomplish with the system.

Assign Responsibilities. Someone in the shop must be chosen or appointed to be in charge of the implementation. This person needs to be familiar with all aspects of the business, but does not necessarily have to be an expert in any one area.

In many cases, the office manager assumes this role in a smaller shop, or a DP manager in a larger shop. However, the owner or controller often has filled this role well.

Once an overall coordinator is in place, the major tasks to be performed must be defined, and each task must be delegated to a logical person. For example, the same person doing accounts payable and accounts receivable processing manually should now perform the same functions on the computer.

Whoever writes up the job orders should now enter them into the computer. Whoever types up purchase orders should now process them through the system.

The point is that an integrated system of controls should not interrupt the normal work flow. To the contrary, it should replace the manual system logically, area by area, using the same people responsible for individual tasks before the computer arrived.

Establish Time Frames. An investment in hardware and software may be the equivalent of hiring one, two, or even three employees.

No employer would hire two new employees and let them do nothing for six months. However, some shops purchase a system and let it sit idle for several months with no effort to install.

The prime reason for this idleness is lack of established goals and specific time frames for implementing specific applications.

Once the staff is in place and responsibilities are assigned, it is imperative to take the next step to commit to deadlines for implementing the system. The staff must work with support consultants and an implementation guide to plan activities over a given time frame, and then stick with it.

Use Resources. A software vendor should provide a variety of tools for use during the course of the implementation. Among these tools are:

1. Telephone support
2. Written documentation
3. Classroom training
4. On-site consulting

All too often, shops buy a system which includes all of the above, yet they fail to use what they are entitled to. An implementation guide describes these

---

* Reprinted with permission from The FABRICATOR® April 1991. Information about this publication and FMA membership on Page 269.

services in detail and how to use them most effectively.

Be Realistic. "Rome was not built in a day." This should be kept in mind during computer installation as well. A software system is modular by design, and there are numerous tasks to perform within each module.

A software vendor should provide tools to help the shop each step of the way. However, just as important is the shop's dedication to the project. The system does not get installed by itself, nor can a computer operator get the job done without management commitment.

Companies should plan for a 3- to 12-month implementation. Anything less is probably unrealistic; anything greater most likely means that a shop has not been dedicated to the task.

The Successful Computer Operator

The main computer operator in a shop is a very important cog in the wheel if success is to be achieved. The selection of this role is critical and must have full management support.

If there is weakness on the manufacturing side, the operator will need a high level of support from the plant manager, shop foreman, and president, among others.

Ideally, this person was exposed to the software selection process so there is some orientation before the system arrives. The following should be reviewed and considered as the logical main operator is determined.

Time. This is certainly a critical factor. A common response is, "I did not have time to enter the data." Installation of a system takes time, and there is certainly a learning curve, even if the main operator has installed systems previously.

If the person responsible to implement could be relieved of some other duties, he could better dedicate himself to getting the system up and running. This pays off in the long run.

People who do not have enough time to accomplish their job objectives will eventually succumb to the pressure and fail.

Technical Background. A low-level knowledge of computers and the ability to move around on a keyboard is ideal for an operator. Fear of computers will cripple the installation.

On the other hand, the operator need not be a computer wizard. Too much knowledge sometimes leads to experimentation, which can only take away from the tasks that need to be performed.

If the computer operator has had no computer experience, he should be sent to a hardware training class for some basic computer orientation. The software vendor can also be consulted with to discuss ways of gaining meaningful knowledge.

Brainpower. The operator does not have to be genius level, but it will make for a better installation if he has a thorough, logical, patient, detail-oriented personality. The operator must be mentally prepared for the introduction of a new computer and software applications.

Communication. The computer operator should expect to be in communication with the software vendor fairly often. He should read and reread all written documentation and related material, attend software training classes, receive and circulate newsletters, send enhancement suggestions to the software vendor, and promptly apply software updates.

Written and verbal skills are important. A good working relationship between the operator and his support person is the key to a successful implementation. Good communication is the foundation.

Accounting. Accounting knowledge is essential. The operator does not necessarily have to be a CPA, but there must be a solid bookkeeping background. This knowledge will ensure a rapid implementation.

Patience. Things do not always go as they were planned, whether it is a job within the shop or any aspect of the computer installation.

The computer operator must possess the quality of patience in dealing with adherence to a realistic timetable. He must trust his support person to work through software and hardware issues as they occur.

Shop Knowledge. Above all other characteristics, the most frequent quality found in successful installations is the main computer operator having a good working knowledge of all activities on the shop floor.

With this overall background, the integration between all the software modules makes sense from a business standpoint as opposed to routinely going through the motions.

If the main operator is not shop-oriented at the outset, he must be encouraged with internal training and support. The computer operator can often become an extremely valuable employee for the company.

▮ Summary

Job shop software system implementations are akin to snowflakes and fingerprints—no two are exactly alike. There are, however, a series of fundamental guidelines which will help to ensure the relative success of a computer system.

During the course of this article, these guidelines have been reviewed, and some basic "what to do and what not to do" principles have been pointed out. This is only the beginning of the task, however. The overriding determinant of the computer system's success (or lack of it) will be directly tied to the efforts and internal commitment of the implementing company toward making the system work.

These fundamentals should be reviewed with the implementation team. At the very least, it will refocus implementation efforts in a positive direction, which will lead to a higher satisfaction level and greater return on investment from the integrated manufacturing system.

The information presented in this article was prepared by Rick Borg, Vice President of Marketing, DCD Corporate Headquarters, Minneapolis, Minnesota.

The FABRICATOR's
Shop Floor Control Software Chart*

The FABRICATOR® October issue features this annual Shop Floor Control Software Chart, a new resource for metal forming and fabricating operations.

Shop floor control is vital in today's competitive industry, and the chart is designed to provide information about software that might help fabricators who are looking for such products.

This easy-to-use chart (sample on next page) lists suppliers of software packages; and it itemizes each package's features, hardware requirements, support services and "extra" considerations.

If you subscribe to **The FABRICATOR®** you may obtain more information from any of the suppliers in the chart by using the number assigned to each supplier and mail or fax the Reader Service Card to **The FABRICATOR.** Otherwise, you may contact the suppliers directly to request information.

*Reprinted with permission from The FABRICATOR® October 1992. Information about this publication and FMA membership on Page 269.

The FABRICATOR's 1992 Shop Floor Control Software Chart

Company Name	Software Package Name	Hardware Platform	Estimating	Material Requirements Planning	Quality Control	Job Costing	Materials Management / Inventory Control	Purchasing	Accounting	Infinite Loading	Finite Loading / Scheduling	Forecasting	Bar Coding	Labor Tracking	Serial No. Control	Scheduling Simulation	Order Tracking	Sales Analysis	Telephone Modem	Warranty	Classroom Education	On-Site Training	User Groups	Upgrades / Enhancements	Electronic Data Interface	Proprietary Hardware Required	On-Line Reporting	Source Code Availability	Customization Available	READER SERVICE NUMBER*
ABBA Computer Systems	Manufacturing Partner	PC/Micro and Mini; Unix and Pick OBMS; or Pick O/S Native	x	x	x	x	x	x	x	x	x	x	x	x	x	x	x	x	x	x	x	x	x	x	x		x	x	x	700
Advanced Systems	SPC1+ Network, SPC1+ Professional, SPC1+	IBM PC or equiv., IBM PC or equiv., IBM PC or equiv.			xxx															xxx	xxx	xxx	xxx	xxx	xxx	xx		xxx		xxx	701
Altec, Inc.	Pro-III	Workstation Mini Mainframe	x	x	x	x	x	x	x	x	x		x	x	x	x	x	x	x	x	x	x	x	x	x		x	x	x	702
Applied Statistics	Pro-III-DoD, Applied Stats for Windows, Applied Stats for Macintosh	PC/IBM compatible 386 or higher, Macintosh Classic or higher			x x															x x	x x		x x		x x	x x		x x		x x	703
Armor	Armor Premier Accounting Software	IBM PC XT, AT 386 or compatible	x			x	x	x	x				x	x	x		x	x		x	x	x	x	x	x			x			704
Axis Computer Systems, Inc.	AXIOM/mx™	Digital VAX/VMS SCO Unix RISC/Ultrix	x	x	x	x	x	x	x	x	x	x	x	x	x	x	x	x	x	x	x	x	x	x	x	x		x	x	x	705

Functions: Estimating through Sales Analysis
Support Services: Telephone Modem through Upgrades / Enhancements
Other Features: Electronic Data Interface through Customization Available

Tips for Understanding CAD/CAM Software

Explanations about How the Software Works*

Editor's Note: This article presents tips for understanding various aspects of CAD/CAM software—postprocessing, folding and unfolding, and nesting functions, as well as how the software supports machine tools. It also provides pointers for evaluating software when you are considering a CAD/CAM software purchase.

The sections in this article were written by three CAD/CAM software vendors. For more information on any section in this article, use the number under each section on the Reader Service Card in this issue.

You can also find helpful information on buying software in the article, "How to purchase a CAD/CAM system," starting on page 12 of this issue. In addition, The FABRICATOR®'s new Sheet Metal CAD/CAM Software Chart presents a listing of software vendors and features of their products. This chart begins on page 16 of this issue.

CAD/CAM expert

By Carl Grosso

For fabricators who do not know much about computers or CAD/CAM systems, one point should be understood: Fabricators should not have to become CAD/CAM experts to use the software.

Fabricators can evaluate CAD/CAM software if they understand their applications. Even if a person has never used computers before, knowledge of manufacturing qualifies that person to evaluate the most important aspect of CAD/CAM software.

The question to ask is this: "How well does the CAD/CAM software support my machine tool?"

A mistake many fabricating professionals make when they evaluate CAD/CAM systems is *not asking the vendors to produce NC programs that they can test in the fabricator's machine tools.* Most fabricators will look closely at the NC program to see if it looks familiar, but they do not actually test in their machines. This is usually a major oversight.

Many fabricators do not ask for the NC program generation because it is an inconvenience for the fabricator, involving more time in the evaluation process. However, the NC program is a factor that fabricators need to know.

If CAD/CAM vendors generate NC programs for a fabricator's machine tools, the fabricator will see a demonstration of every facet of the CAD/CAM system. The demonstration will also test the capability to generate DNC programs to the NC control system.

Before your CAD/CAM demonstrations, it is recommended that fabricators tell vendors to test NC programs produced on the CAD/CAM systems. Programs should be generated for every machine tool in the shop, not just one machine—even if they are different types, models, sizes, turret configurations, etc.

Then, if the program is downloaded into your numerical controls successfully, fabricators should watch the machine tools to see how they react to the NC programs.

---

* Reprinted with permission from The FABRICATOR® June 1992. Information about this publication and FMA membership on Page 269.

Punch or cut the parts and check them for accuracy. Be sure the CAD/CAM system supports all of the features the machine tools have. Watch the carriage movement and other functions to verify that the machine tool reacts precisely as it will need to for its applications.

How CAD/CAM software translates computer data for machine tools is an important feature. One method is the traditional *postprocessing*, while the newest technology is *code generation*, sometimes referred to as a *direct driver*.

The primary difference between the two is in how they access the CAD database. A postprocessor translates from a third-party software, which results in longer NC programs. A direct driver utilizes the CAD database, generates shorter NC programs, and minimizes the memory necessary in numerical control.

Drivers also incorporate subroutines for repetitive patterns and machine tool parameter settings, while postprocessors will repeat the NC code each time a pattern is called for, thereby increasing the length of the program and ignoring the capability of the numerical control.

Postprocessors do not use all capabilities of numerical controls. Direct drivers use a higher level of code so they can generate programs that access the sophisticated technology of today's modern NC controls.

CAD/CAM vendors who write their own CAD generally incorporate the code generation (direct drivers) within their software. Postprocessors are usually used in conjunction with third-party CAD software.

Fabricators should ask which postprocessor or direct machine driver will work best for the machines in their shops.

Obviously, how CAD/CAM systems support machine tools is only one criteria to consider. Evaluations of systems should also include thorough dissection of their capability and of service reliability.

However, should a "time crunch" only allow time for a brief evaluation, finding out how CAD/CAM supports the machine tools is the most important criterion.

Carl Grosso is President of Metalsoft, Santa Ana, California.

What is Postprocessing?

By Frank Bakanau

For a particular machine tool to run an NC program created in a CAM system, the program must be delivered to the machine in the proper format for the machine's control to "understand" it.

Many types of machines with different control options and capabilities are available. To run optimally, each machine/control combination requires that the NC code be formatted in a particular way. That's where the postprocessor comes in.

The purpose of a postprocessor is to read a neutral file, commonly called a CL (Cutter Location) file, and create a "tape image" file that will drive the machine tool. The "tape image" is the ASCII equivalent of what would be punched on tape.

Punched tape was an early standard for delivering instructions to the NC machines. Since most of today's CAM system vendors use this type of scheme, the term *postprocessor* is used to describe the function of formatting code for a particular machine/control combination.

Originally, a postprocessor was a custom piece of software that was developed by an APT (Automatically Programmed Tools) vendor, the customer, an outside consultant, or a service bureau. Each "post" was tightly linked to the system on which it was running.

As machining and fabrication standards developed, CAM vendors began developing postprocessors specifically designed to link their individual packages to various machine/control combinations.

Today, the vendor's ability to provide an appropriate postprocessor for a particular machine/control combination is an important consideration when shopping for a CAM package.

A well-written postprocessor will identify fabrication practices that will not work on a given machine, or will automatically generate correct tool change or other important sequences for the machine.

A post can identify whether the requested punching speed is too high, indicate whether the fabricator is trying to manufacture a larger part than the machine's entry into a collision zone. The NC code can then be altered to make the necessary corrections and reprocessed.

The primary drawback to postprocessing is what the term itself describes—**post**processing. The neutral file is converted to machine code **after** the programming has been completed.

Because different machines behave differently, the programmer's idea of what the final tool path will look like may not match what actually happens at the machine.

In the days of language programming such as APT, this limitation was less of an issue. The programmer never really got to see what was going to happen until the actual dry run of the program.

But with today's graphically-oriented CAM systems, the programmer's ability to preview and adjust the final tool path is becoming more and more important in reducing the time needed to match the manufacturing engineer's concept with the reality of how the machine operates.

An alternative to traditional postprocessing is one that combines the machine definition and behavior characteristics into the programming session. Some vendors continue to refer to this new method as "postprocessing"; others believe the term *code generation* is more appropriate.

Code generation actually processes the tool path at the same time the geometry is created—almost **pre**processing. The machine parameters are taken into consideration so that the programmer can view actual machine behavior while creating the geometry.

A simple example of machine behavior that illustrates the difference between postprocessing and code generation might be rapid traverse motion. Some machines have the axes start a traverse at the same time, and travel at a given maximum rate.

This results in a 45-degree motion up to the point where one axis is in position (resolves its move), and the other axis then continues its motion until final position is reached. Other machines will adjust axis feed rates to start and stop both axes simultaneously, resulting in a straight line motion.

The two methods result in different lines of traverse. If the programmer is visualizing a straight line motion to avoid a clamp, while the actual motion at the machine will be a 45-degree move followed by a linear axis move, a potential for crash exists.

By including the machine behavior, code generators allow users to see the actual machine motion before generating CNC code, and thus help avoid possible problems.

Code generators can also provide accurate cycle times during programming sessions, which allows programmers to make better decisions about optimal fabrication processes. Systems using traditional postprocessors *estimate* the travel time, since no knowledge of the final machine is available during the programming process.

This may spark an entire process change. If a machine tool changes tools quickly and on the fly, it might be most efficient to fabricate one part entirely before moving on to the next part. On the other hand, if tool changing takes longer, it might be more efficient to use one tool over as many parts as possible to minimize tool changes.

With code generators, coupled with a flexible programming system, the programmer can try various fabrication approaches to determine the optimal method. In fact, the user can try different *machines* and get feedback on actual motion and cycle times during the programming session.

Due to specialized machine functions, standardized NC code generation is not likely to be available in the near future. However, creating powerful but flexible code-generating tools can reduce the importance of that factor to manufacturing engineers.

Frank Bakanau is Field Sales Manager with Point Control Company, Eugene, Oregon.

Evaluating the fold/unfold function in a CAM software package

By Larry Moran

What differentiates the fold/unfold functions among CAM software products? How can you spot these differences, and other important features to look for, when evaluating CAM software for your shop?

Functions that may be important for your shop's type of fabrication might include tool path optimization, automatic nesting, the ability to define your own custom tools, etc. While all of these factors are important, this segment of this article focuses on the features to consider when reviewing a CAM package's **fold/unfold** functionality.

Creating the geometry necessary to model how a part folds or unfolds is an important function of any CAM software package designed for the metal forming and fabricating industry.

In general, the prime considerations are ease of use and the number of functions the software performs without (or with very little) user interaction. The more automatic the software is, the less time a fabricator will spend generating code, and the faster parts will go out the door.

The size of a part's geometry that is folded is based on the fact that when sheet metal is bent, the material on the inside of the bend is compressed (and thus made shorter), and the material on the outside of the bend is placed under tension (and thus made longer).

The result of this tension/compression is an imaginary line through the approximate middle of the material thickness—called the *neutral axis*—that is under neither tension nor compression. The ratio locating the neutral axis is called the *neutral axis factor* (or *K factor*).

The exact position of the neutral axis varies depending on the type and thickness of the material, amount of bend, type of bend (air bending, bottoming, or coining), and environmental factors such as shop temperature and tool wear. CAM packages with automatic fold/unfold capabilities calculate the compensation for bending the part's geometry using the neutral axis formula that includes an appropriate K factor.

Manually computing flat pattern dimensions that include neutral axis compensations from 3-D part information is a well-defined procedure. However, it is extremely repetitive and time-consuming, and prone to human error.

Being repetitive makes it an ideal process for a computer, which can perform the equations almost instantaneously and with accuracy. Some CAM packages also adjust the geometry of the entire part if the user changes any part of the existing model.

Features to look for in a fold/unfold function include:

1. How the software deals with bend allowances.

2. How part files are imported into the system.

3. The ease with which you can modify geometry.

4. Whether the software automatically repositions features located on unfolded faces.

5. The accuracy of the final tool path of unfolded parts.

6. Whether the package provides hem compensation.

Part Geometry

One of the most critical features is how the software calculates bend allowance—the amount of "extra" material a flat pattern layout needs to compensate for the tension that occurs when it is bent into a 3-D part.

Whether a fabricator will be receiving part information in 2-D or 3-D format, from part prints or directly from a CAD system (via IGES, DXF, or other transfer format), the degree to which the CAM software automatically calculates bend allowances is important to ensure accurate flat patterns in the shortest turnaround time.

If fabricators are working with 2-D part prints or 2-D electronic (CAD) files, the CAM package should combine the 2-D geometry into a folded 3-D part model with as little user interaction as possible. Ideally, the software should calculate bend allowances and repositioning of features on each of the part faces automatically.

Part models that begin in the form of a 3-D print or a 3-D electronic file require some additional considerations when reviewing software capabilities. Will the software automatically unfold 3-D part geometry, calculating for bend allowance and repositioning of features on the part faces, or must the user change the geometry manually?

Typically, systems designed specifically for metal fabrication will automatically determine what geometry is associated with each face of the folded part. Others require the user to identify those relationships or to create the features on each face after the part has been unfolded.

The ease with which part geometry can be modified, and how changes affect the rest of the model, also differs among software packages. If a change is made to one fold, does the software automatically reposition other features on the part face, or must you move those features manually?

If a fabricator changes the geometry on a flat pattern, can he quickly refold the model to check for accuracy and then unfold it again to make more changes?

Other Considerations

Once the flat pattern is completed, the ease and completeness of creating the tool path for cutting the blank is an important consideration.

Some CAM programs create a complete profile automatically, while others require the user to place punch hits or modify the profile where fold lines intersect. Ideally, the software should automatically update the profile of the flat pattern so it reflects any geometry that has been changed.

Along with reviewing how a software package deals with regular bends, consider whether or not it adjusts for hem compensation. When calculating allowance amounts for hems, note that as the bend angle approaches 180 degrees, the bend allowance value increases to infinity. Some CAM systems detect this condition and correct for it automatically, while others require manual adjustments to be made to the hem geometry.

Folding and unfolding geometry is a complex process that can be simplified and automated with the right CAM system.

In addition, a good CAM package will make automatic adjustments for bend allowance, reposition features located on the part faces when the geometry is unfolded, alter the geometry to conform to any changes made by the user, and allow the user to view accurate final tool path throughout the process.

It will also enhance the value of the CAD data by positioning geometry correctly on the part's faces with little or no user interaction. The more automatically the software performs these functions, the easier the programmer's job will be, and the faster parts will get to customers.

Larry Moran is Marketing Communications Coordinator with Point Control Company, Eugene, Oregon.

Matching needs to features in nesting systems

By Andrea Samson

While computer-based nesting is now accepted as an important fabrication technology, not all nesting systems are created exactly alike, any more than all fabricators run their businesses alike.

While this condition makes for lively, free market competition, nesting systems should *solve problems*. Therefore, as with any purchase decision, the prospective technology user must first identify the real problem areas unique to his particular situation.

In a recent Fabricators & Manufacturers Association, International (FMA) automation seminar, a guest speaker reported that typically 75 percent of dollars spent on automation purchases attacked areas that accounted for 10 percent of manufacturing costs. This fact reinforces the importance of self-evaluation. The sidebar to this article presents a Self-Evaluation Checklist which can help fabricators to plan automation of any kind.

In the end, it is more likely that the nesting system a fabricator chooses will be the one with features that work to eliminate the most costly, time-consuming, error-prone, inconsistent, and frustrating problem areas.

Over the years, the definition of a "problem area" has changed. While manufacturers acquired computers and software to eliminate the problem and cost of "direct labor," "indirect labor" to address nesting and programming tasks took its place.

For many manufacturers, the compromise solution was *static nesting*, repeating the same part, or combination of parts. This yielded the least programming and the most material savings, and it kept the machine tool running.

In fact, static nesting, or *grid* nesting, is still the basis of some computer-based nesting systems. This method maximizes the time and effort to develop NC code. When large volumes of the same part are required, it is an appropriate nesting method. However, most fabricators today are not in volume production.

▊ Today's Nesting Systems

The software industry today offers a variety of computer-based systems to solve the new problems. A fabricator can choose from CAM-based systems, graphics-oriented CAM, CAD-based nesting, and hybrids. Built into these systems are software routines that reduce or eliminate many repetitive tasks associated with nesting and programming.

To keep pace with changes in both the business climate and the machine tool's complexity, the functionality of some systems pushes far beyond providing the manufacturer with a material-saving layout. It is now difficult, if not impossible, to totally separate nesting from programming. CAM programming systems offer nesting functions, and nesting systems offer programming functions. In some systems, the nesting function is a relatively isolated task, a menu choice among several discrete part and process development routines that a programmer can choose.

In other systems, nesting is a hub of activity designed to draw in and utilize raw inventory data and order/entry data; support factory floor production and tracking systems; incorporate material handling and part identification devices, etc.

Still other systems offer methods of completely automating the formidable task of programming, including automatic tool selection, repositioning, and clamp avoidance. They also provide automatic tool path and tool change optimization, and more.

Some systems run on PCs and some on workstations. Some systems do all or some of the above, while others do variations. And, while CRTs (Cathode Ray Tubes) introduce a valuable visual assist and have made programming, nesting, and verification much easier, they can tempt a potential buyer to "buy the sizzle instead of the steak."

The primary goal of any nesting and programming system is to electronically assist the development and/or generation of error-free, human-optimized, machine-optimized, material-optimized machine control data. This is the "steak," and it centers around the various tasks accomplished *by the software*, not a computer-literate human.

CAM-Based Systems

CAM-based systems are powerful and offer the freedom to develop any number of nesting/programming solutions. They also depend on the availability of a seasoned programmer who possesses expertise with the software system and a thorough knowledge of materials, machine tools, and cutting tools.

CAM-based systems, particularly stand-alone, machine-directed systems, are typically used when the business fabricates a limited variety of parts, the production volume of each part is relatively high, and engineering changes are infrequent.

It is now difficult, if not impossible, to totally separate nesting from programming.

Graphics-CAM helps to condense many of the programming and nesting tasks by automating repetitive software sequences, machine actions, or predictable variables associated with material composition. As PCs have become increasingly more powerful, these systems are becoming more and more feature-laden. This helps programmers cope with the increasing complexity of the machine tools as well as the "time crunch" imposed by the marketplace.

Typically, these systems are differentiated by "ease of use" methods and file handling methods and procedures. These systems differ also in the number and types of decisions that still involve the participation and expertise of a programmer. They generally feature a semiautomatic, computer-assisted nesting capability.

CAD-Based Systems

CAD-based, fully automatic nesting systems are well suited to fabrication environments that must accommodate frequent design and engineering changes, widely varying lot sizes, and a random-part rapid response. The lack of human intervention in the nesting and programming process is probably the most significant difference between CAD-based systems and other types.

CAD-based systems are frequently found in factories that utilize a variety of machine tools and cutting processes, multiprocess cells, and Flexible Manufacturing Systems (FMSs). The hallmark of this system is its ability to be incorporated seamlessly into a CIM environment. In the past, these systems were concentrated primarily in factories with large mainframe computers.

The typical user profile has changed

dramatically, however, as more processing power and networking capability has become available on workstations and PCs. Increased outsourcing of component processing has also contributed to the changing profile.

▌ Choosing a Nesting System

Beyond those considerations, system integration requirements necessarily impact the type of system chosen. As one software buyer said recently about his nesting requirements, "(it) had to contribute to the factory-wide mandate of creating 'one view of the truth.'"

That statement meant that engineering, design, production, sales, scheduling, accounting, maintenance, shipping, etc., had to share correct data on a timely basis. Their customized product line, operational objectives, and system specifications could not be satisfied by nesting or programming systems based on proprietary, stand-alone, or labor-intensive software applications.

In the past, fabricators have sometimes discovered that their choice of software solutions did not eliminate a specific problem and its cost. Rather, the problem was simply transferred to another department, and the costs appeared elsewhere on the ledger.

To choose a system effectively, fabricators must fully understand that every fabrication-related task that does not directly add value to the product is, in fact, a cost to the business. In that perspective, **costs** include:

1. Unnecessary effort.
2. Inconsistent quality.
3. Machine idle time.
4. Machine time spent cutting parts for inventory.
5. Work-In-Process (WIP) inventories.
6. Scrapped parts.
7. Rework.

In addition, delivery delays may well cost a fabricator a lost order. While material utilization is certainly an important factor, worthwhile systems will provide opportunities to save on other equally important costs.

If the choice of a computer-based nesting and programming system is to come even reasonably close to the ideal solution, the user should try to identify and prioritize all the tasks and functions that represent unacceptable costs or bottlenecks. Choosing then becomes a matter of determining a budget and proving that the system being considered can eliminate that cost.

The evaluation of a particular system should include hands-on interaction with the system features. It is important to understand clearly what the humans have to do to accomplish the desired result—in essence, benchmarking system flexibility or indirect labor efficiency just as you would benchmark material efficiency.

CAM-based nesting and programming, graphics-based CAM, or CAD-based/automatic nesting and programming systems will all get fabricators from original geometry to cut part. How efficiently or cost-effectively they get fabricators "from art to part" depends on system capabilities. Match the real needs to the capabilities. ■

Andrea Samson is Marketing and Public Relations Manager with Precision Nesting Systems, Inc., Cresskill, New Jersey.

Self-Evaluation Checklist for Automating Sheet Metal Operations

What information do I currently collect? What do I want to collect? Who needs or should have the information? Where is it in the organization? How will I collect and pass the information?

Assessing the information flow helps define the interfaces and the products that need to be in place. And, it is not an easy task.

The following are some, but not all, of the questions that are typically part of any automation planning effort:

1. How are part orders generated?

2. How is raw inventory tracked? Is it reliable? How is the information communicated? To whom?

3. How are engineering change orders, "hot parts," or prototype parts getting into production?

4. Are there off-site locations that require integration to the system? If so, what data needs to be shared?

5. How are parts tracked through production and assembly? How is that data transferred back to the active production schedule?

6. Is part data available in graphic format? If so, where does the information reside? In a CAD database?

7. Is there a large library of NC tapes? Do the tapes need to be converted in a format so that it is usable by another model, make, or type of machine tool? How will you accomplish that conversion?

8. What production feedback should be made available to various departments? Which department? Examples: cutting time, tool and machine maintenance, material utilization, rework, plate weight and kerf weight, etc.

9. How are parts identified? Bar code? Label? Etching?

10. Will you need to support a plotter? Any other peripheral device?

11. What computers are currently in use? What other departments are using them? Are existing computer resources underutilized? How will it fit into the new automation plan? Can it be upgraded? Is there a special platform required for new technologies?

12. How is the machine tool being programmed?

13. How much memory is available in the NC controller? Enough for the output from the new technology?

Source: July/August 1989 The FABRICATOR®, "The reality of factory automation," Precision Nesting Systems.

How to Purchase a CAD/CAM System*

Making the right choice through company surveys and vendor comparisons

By Dan Justen

Computer-aided design/computer-aided manufacturing (CAD/CAM) is a vital part of most successful metal fabrication facilities. It is the link between the product requirements and the manufacturing process that is used to fabricate a product.

The proper software package can either help a company's bottom-line performance or be a hindrance. When purchasing any element that can have such an impact on operations, extreme care should be taken.

The first priority of a machine programming system is, of course, to program the machine. However, a company should be aware of other objectives of the purchase, such as reduced lead times, machine use, and reduced waste.

A commonsense approach to purchasing a machine programming system or any CAD/CAM product is to perform a company survey (see **Figure 1**).

Too often, a company selects a system and later finds there is a problem integrating with another area of the business. The survey takes into account the overall needs of the company, focusing on products, personnel, equipment, and the current CAM program. It identifies the needs of a company and helps make the decision process easier.

A company should share this information with its software vendors. The vendors should be asked to demonstrate the specific features of their product that will meet the needs found in the survey.

A competent software professional should be able to walk through a shop and explain what features will be used to create the parts.

After the company survey is complete, the same method is used to determine which software system to purchase.

Company Survey, Step 1: Products

As shown in Figure 1, the first step for a company is to identify its products and put them into categories. Even a contract shop making constantly-changing products can identify the type of parts it most often produces.

Separate the parts into categories, all of which pertain to some feature of a CAM system.

For example, if a product has a high number of holes, perhaps with repeating patterns, a company would want to investigate how each software package deals with patterns. Whether a shop can nest parts or run them as "families" will have an effect on the type of system to purchase.

Identify what operations are performed on the parts. If a high percentage of the product is formed in the press brake, consider a fold/unfold package in the software.

The quantity of lot sizes and the repeatability of jobs should be taken into account. A prototype shop will not be interested in the extra cost of a package that heavily features nesting.

---

* Reprinted with permission from The FABRICATOR® June 1992. Information about this publication and FMA membership on Page 269.

```
Company Survey - Products

PRODUCTS:       _____
                _____
                _____

CATEGORY: Feature                    % of Total Parts
         ☐ Low Number of Holes       _____
         ☐ High Number of Holes      _____
         ☐ Flat Parts                _____
         ☐ Formed Parts              _____
         ☐ Contours                  _____
         ☐ Straight Perimeter Cuts   _____
         ☐ Parts Can Be Nested       _____
         ☐ Parts Cannot Be Nested    _____
         ☐ Parts Can Be Run As Families _____

OPERATIONS: Feature                  % of Total Parts
         ☐ Punching                  _____
         ☐ Shearing                  _____
         ☐ Thermal Cutting           _____
         ☐ Forming -  press brake    _____
                      other press    _____
         ☐ Hardware Insertion        _____
         ☐ Finishing                 _____

QUANTITY:  Product        Lot Size    Repeat Jobs
           _____      _____     _____
           _____      _____     _____
           _____      _____     _____

MATERIAL:     Type           Size         Quantity
☐ Use Stock Sizes  _____    _____      _____
☐ Use Blanks       _____    _____      _____

                        PERSONNEL
Experience          Employee   Employee   Employee
Mach. Programming   _____    _____    _____
Computer            _____    _____    _____
CAD                 _____    _____    _____
Education           _____    _____    _____
Software Products   _____    _____    _____
```

Figure 1
This is a sample company survey sheet for software products.

Material type and sizes should be identified. A fabricator of stainless steel parts will be keenly interested in material use. A product shop using mild steel blanks will have different needs.

Company Survey, Step 2: Personnel

The quality of the personnel involved is crucial to any operation. Identify the individuals involved and their skill levels. CAD/CAM systems vary in ease of use and complexity. The system must match the qualifications of a company's personnel or the operation will not be successful.

Using a programming system reduces the requirements for in-house knowledge of numerical control (NC) codes. A designer can now become more involved in the manufacturing process and thus develop a better design for the manufacturing environment

Company Survey, Step 3: Equipment

A survey of equipment as shown in **Figure 2** may seem the easy part, but it should not be taken lightly. For example, if a company's control has the ability to do subroutines, bolt hole circles, etc., then the software should take advantage of them when it is practical for machine optimization.

Also, older machines may have a memory problem necessitating the use of subroutines. An older machine may not have an RS 232 port to use to download the program. If a company is not going to download, it should not pay for a direct numerical control (DNC) link in its software package.

Company Survey - Equipment

TURRET PRESSES	Machine	Machine	Machine
Model			
Size Limitations			
Control			
Subroutines			
Serial No./Yr.Manuf.			
Special Functions			
Tool Indexing			
Laser			
Plasma			
Shear			
Tapping			

THERMAL CUTTING MACHINE			
Model			
Size Limitations			
Control			
Subroutines			
Serial No./Yr. Manuf.			

COMPUTER AIDED MANUFACTURING PROGRAM

MACHINE PROGRAMMING SYSTEMS

Machine	System Used	No. of Workstations	Location

Data Transmission To Machine	Paper Tape __	DNC Link __
Receives Input From	Drawings __	CAD Program __
Transmit Data Back To CAD Program	Yes __	No __

COMPUTER AIDED DRAFTING PROGRAM

System Used	Dedicated To	No. of Stations	Location

COMPUTER HARDWARE

Model	Description	Dedicated To	Location

Figure 2

This company survey sheet focuses on equipment, both equipment for fabricating operations and computer equipment.

Combination machines, such as punch and laser or plasma, have special needs. A company should be able to program both the punch and laser/plasma option easily from the same program and not have to merge files together.

Company Survey, Step 4: CAM Program

The present and future needs of a CAM program must be addressed by the programming system (see Figure 2).

When considering buying a machine for the first time, keep in mind that a software system purchased from a machine manufacturer may only be able to program that manufacturer's equipment. In that case, if a machine was later purchased from a different vendor, another programming system would have to be purchased, too.

Data transmission is a key element for a smooth flow of information. If an operator is using information from a CAD file and makes a change to the part, the operator would want the ability to transfer that information back to the CAD program.

Not all programs have two-way CAD links. The needs of the CAD program should be a primary concern.

The use of CAD programs is increasing in popularity for both product and contract shops. Many fabricators use their CAD programs for all types of drafting, sheet metal, machined parts, weldments, etc., and personnel are comfortable with them.

Some programming systems are very intense in the use of their own CAD program. The use of this type of internal CAD program is limited to the sheet metal programming package, and the purchaser must pay for it, whether or not it is used.

The programming system must match a company's current or future CAD program. Some companies have several different CAD programs used in different locations. Many contract shops are now receiving CAD drawings on computer disk rather than conventional paper drawings from their customers.

Computer hardware used in the plant should be identified. The majority of a company's computers may be a certain type. If the company stays with that same type of computer, personnel will have an easier time learning a new program. A company may also be able to use an existing computer, eliminating the need to purchase a new one.

Software Comparison, Step 1: System Requirements

Now that the survey has been completed, the collected information must be used. As shown in **Figure 3**, a software comparison profile is a good format to use to compare selected vendors. On one sheet of paper, vendors can be compared, and justification can be shown for the selection.

The information from the company survey is used to configure the required system and the features that are most important to a company.

For example, a company may want a punch press program with DNC and CAD links and reverse engineering features. Reverse engineering processes old programs into the new system so entirely new programs do not have to be made.

Software Comparison, Step 2: System Profile

After sharing the survey information with the vendor, get recommendations from the vendor. Their product should satisfy the needs of a company's product, personnel, equipment, and the needs of the existing CAM program according to the survey.

Software Comparison, Step 3: Software Profile

Naturally, to compare the software, a company must first see a product demonstration with all concerned parties.

To be assured that a vendor's software will meet a fabricator's requirements, the fabricator should take the time to sit down and program several parts, not "canned" demonstration parts. In this way, the fabricator will discover how easy it is to use and how long it takes to make a program.

Regardless of the vendor, all of the software will have some common areas on which to base a decision.

As shown in Figure 3, key areas are selected and each software rated on a 1 to 10 basis. An area in which a vendor is weak may be offset by another feature, or perhaps the price.

A primary selection criteria should be how easy the system is to use. A programming system does not have to be complicated to be good. Actually, the simpler it is, the better. Employees will learn it faster, and their everyday use of the product will be more enjoyable.

The time it takes to make a program is a direct result of how easy it is to use. The system should prompt the operator as to what action to take. For example, when making an array pattern, the text screen should prompt the user to enter X and Y coordinates along with pattern spacing information.

Whether it is a single- or dual-screen system, the graphics should be of the highest quality and easy to manipulate. The picture should be large enough for easy viewing with good "zoom in" features. Graphics should always be in view and never be hidden while performing any operation, such as pull-down menus.

Information regarding any item should be readily available. For example, a user should be able to click on a hole and have its X and Y coordinates instantly appear.

All text information should be in clear

Software Comparison Profile

VENDOR

Software Price
Hardware Price
Total Price

SYSTEM REQUIREMENTS

☐ Punch Press Program
☐ Thermal Machine Program
☐ DNC Link Software
☐ CAD Link Software
☐ Folding
☐ Unfolding
☐ Reverse Engineering

SYSTEM PROFILE

Supports Existing Equipment
Meets System Requirements
Compatible W/ Existing CAD
Hardware Compatibility
Match Personnel Qualifications

SOFTWARE PROFILE
(Rate on a scale of 1-10)

Meets Our Needs
Ease Of Use
Time To Make A Program
Graphics
Text
Create Tools
Tool Library
Parts Library
Nest Parts
Ease of Use For
  Combination Machines
Tool Path Optimization
CAD Data Transfer
DNC Transfer
On Line Help

COMPANY

Support
Training
Upgrade Policy

Figure 3
A sheet like this can be helpful when comparing software vendors.

terms that are easily understood. Look for universal command terms such as profile, array, and nibble. Text information should be available to generate reports.

A tool library should be used with the tools easily created. New tools should be generated from simple commands and standard shapes, such as rounds, squares, single D, and obrounds.

Special shape tools should be easily drawn from an internal CAD program. These special shapes should be able to be displayed on the graphic screen displaying the part. For example, a clover-leaf-shaped punch should be displayed on the part as a clover leaf.

How a nest of parts is created is a priority to a production shop. Their method should be clearly understood. Terminology varies widely between vendors.

There are many different levels and forms of automatic nesting. Investigate the different processes used to manipulate parts and manually create a nest. The "ease of use" varies greatly between software developers.

Tool path optimization should be scrutinized. Does the program work the way the machine was intended to operate? The system should allow for user-defined parameters and manual override of the program. Transfer of information should be smooth, whether it is to download to a machine or a CAD system.

Price levels cover a broad range. Software packages that have their own sheet metal CAD system are more expensive than others that are used in combination with any of the popular CAD packages.

A separate CAD/CAM system can be more flexible. A combined system allows only one operator to use it at a time. Using a separate CAD program on another computer allows one person on CAD and another on CAM simultaneously, thus increasing production.

Some packages combine everything—CAD, DNC link, CAD link, etc.—and the purchaser is charged for the whole package. If a company is not on a CAD program or does not want to download to its machine, it should select a vendor that will supply only the portion the company will use and charge it accordingly.

Using this survey method can help a fabricating company, as well as its vendor, in addressing its needs in a thorough, professional manner. The software professional should become a part of the team and work for the continued success of both companies. ■

Dan Justen is National Sales Manager with Bowin Technology, Cleveland, Ohio.

THE FABRICATOR'S®
SHEET METAL CAD/CAM SOFTWARE CHART

A Buyer's Guide for Sheet Metal Fabricators*

The FABRICATOR® June issue features this Annual Sheet Metal CAD/ CAM Software Chart, a new technical resource for the metal forming and fabricating industry. This one-of-a-kind listing of CAD/ CAM vendors and their software specifications is designed to help you find out what CAD/CAM software is available and identify which products would best suit your operations.

The software presented in this chart (sample of chart on the next page) is specifically for sheet metal forming and fabricating operations. This includes press brakes, punch presses, lasers, right angle shears, waterjet cutters and laser/thermal cutters.

In addition to the vendors listed in this chart, many machine tool manufacturers provide CAD/CAM software with their equipment and may not be listed in this chart. However, the equipment manufacturers can also be considered in purchasing decisions. To identify various equipment manufacturers, you can refer to **The FABRICATOR's** annual equipment charts, which include: Precision Punching Chart, Right Angle Shear Chart, Press Brake Chart, Shear Chart Precision Laser Cutting Chart for Sheet Metal, and Multiaxis Laser Cutting & Welding Chart.

Each vendor listed in the chart also has a paragraph description, like the one shown with the sample chart on the next pages.

If you subscribe to **The FABRICATOR**, you may obtain more information from any of the vendors in the chart, by using the number assigned to each vendor and mail or fax the Reader Service Card to **The FABRICATOR.** Otherwise, you may contact the vendors directly to request information.

* Reprinted with permission from The FABRICATOR® June 1992. Information about this publication and FMA membership on Page 269.

The FABRICATOR®'s Sheet Metal CAD/CAM Software Chart

■ U.S. AMADA, LTD.

Amada CAD/CAM lets you design a part, assign tooling, and have a postprocessor generate the G-code for Amada turret punch presses or laser cutting systems. This software can be adapted for use on other manufacturers' equipment. The postprocessor optimizer automatically does tool sort, tool path, multiples, clamp zone, and sheet length repositioning, and can optimize programs in either G-code or X-Y coordinates, to cut run times by 10 to 50 percent.

Amada also offers a 3-D CAD/unfold program that converts 3-D drawings to 2-D layouts in seconds. Data can be entered manually, downloaded from a host computer, or fed in by a floppy disk.

Amada's newest program, AUTONEST, will automatically lay out parts on a sheet or series of sheets.

Fabricating with One-Step NC Controls

Combining CAD/CAM and shop floor programming techniques*

By David Neman

The field of numerical control (NC) has seen some dramatic advances since the days of paper tape, with the evolution basically occurring in three phases.

The early advances tended to be concentrated among the computer programs and hardware auxiliary to NC controllers, rather than on the controllers themselves.

Computer-aided design (CAD) and computer-aided manufacturing (CAM)

---

* Reprinted with permission from The FABRICATOR® October 1992. Information about this publication and FMA membership on Page 269.

vendors increased the sophistication and functionality of their products, while others developed distributed numerical control (DNC) and otherwise improved the linkage between CAD/CAM workstations and NC controllers.

The next phase of NC advancement brought the introduction of more intelligent computer numerical control (CNC) controllers, giving the machine operator substantial shop floor programming (SFP) capabilities. Program edit capabilities were enhanced, new canned cycle commands were added, and graphic console screen display and screen prototyping capabilities were introduced.

The most recent advance in the NC field is the advent of one-step NC, sometimes called direct numerical control. This latest development is the focus of this article.

One-Step NC

The methodology used to produce a part on a one-step system reflects a fusion of conventional CAD-CAM-download-NC part programming techniques and standard SFP techniques (see **Figure 1**).

In conventional part programming, a graphically-oriented CAD system is used to generate a part file in DXF, IGES, or comparable format. This file—together with tooling information—is fed through a CAM program and postprocessor, and a toolpath specified in G codes or other tool tip motion language is generated.

The G codes are loaded into the conventional NC controller, where the only functions performed are those which can be performed only at the machine, such as indexing.

CNC controllers with SFP capabilities allow the part designer to avoid using a CAD/CAM workstation by facilitating the generation of G codes or other toolpath language directly at the machine console.

The capabilities of these controllers vary widely, with the more expensive controllers providing the more sophisticated features. However, almost all of these controllers provide a means of editing the stored program before it is run.

While many provide features that facilitate program entry (command prompting, special function keys), others provide a graphic representation of the part, and others allow one program to run while another program is being edited.

While standard SFP-capable CNC controllers have evolved from the old-style "download, index, and run" NC controllers, one-step controllers are basically extensions of CAD workstations.

How It Works

A one-step system is essentially a CAD system capable of generating cutter motion. Like SFP systems, one-step systems can fabricate a part in stages while it is being designed, or they can fabricate the part after the design is complete.

The one-step console has a graphic user interface typical of CAD systems. A mounted trak-ball or mouse allows the user to manipulate a pointer on the monitor screen, which always shows a representation of the part under design. With the pointer, the operator selects a shape primitive (or "entity") from a toolbox appearing on the screen, then "draws" the shape on the screen.

After the shape is drawn, its shape and placement can be corrected by clicking on "edit blocks," in the manner seen in PC-based drawing and simple CAD packages. The user also has the option of typing the entity's coordinates on the console keyboard.

At this point, the one-step user interface begins to diverge from CAD. Since one-step gives the user the ability to fabricate the stock on an entity-by-entity basis, two restrictions are placed on one-step entities:

1. They must define areas that are cut from the stock.
2. They must have tooling information associated with them.

To help the user comply with the first restriction, special entities are provided that allow the user to define rectangular, circular, and elliptical island profiles, as well as contour profiles with interconnected lines and arcs.

The screen always displays the appearance of the part after all confirmed entities have been fabricated, so any unintended extrusions can be visually identified and eliminated.

To identify the tooling used with an entity, the user selects the desired tool from a list maintained on the screen's menu. The last tool specified is used by default. The screen changes immediately to reflect the effect of the new tooling, and the pocket-filling toolpath is automatically corrected.

Attributes such as feed rate, cutting direction, and coolant use may also be specified for each entity, as well as tool selection.

When the entity is defined as desired, the operator confirms the entity selection. This incorporates the entity into the part definition and, if fabricating is enabled, causes the entity to be fabricated either immediately or after all previously confirmed entities have been fabricated.

Entities and their attributes may be changed after confirmation, but the changes will not be reflected in the part being fabricated.

The machine control characteristics of a one-step system are similar to those found in most NC controllers. A digital readout appears in a box superimposed on the screen while the machine is moving. This box can be moved if the user wishes to work on a design while fabricating is in progress, or the DRO can be suppressed entirely.

Machine operator messages (such as tool change requests) similarly appear in boxes on the screen—as does a jogging control panel—when indexing is required, or when jogging control is requested.

DXF Files and Stand-Alone Software

In many cases, parts are best designed away from the shop floor. A fabricating shop often does not provide an optimum work environment for programming parts, especially complicated parts. Furthermore, customers who do their own CAD work and submit a DXF file on diskette instead of a drawing need to be supported.

One-step developers have taken some steps to address these issues. Some one-step controllers currently accept part designs in the DXF format. In others, DXF file support should be available shortly.

When a DXF file is loaded into a one-step system, the user is prompted to specify the tooling used for each entity. The part design can subsequently be transferred to and from diskettte files written in the system's proprietary format.

One-step stand-alone systems provide another way to use a one-step system without having to do all of the design entry at the machine console. A one-step stand-alone software package runs on a personal computer that has a one-step user interface and all of the part design features found in a one-step controller.

The user can design a part with the stand-alone software, write the part file on diskette, and subsequently load the part file into the controller and machine the part.

Applications

Under which circumstances is one-step technology most useful, and where is it best to stick with conventional CAD/CAM/NC or SFP techniques?

Clearly, one-step controllers can only

be used with the manufacturing technology for which they are designed. One-step controllers are available for fabricating machinery working in the XY plane, such as punch presses and laser cutters. They are not available for press brakes, shears, or similar machinery.

Some shops have little need for the special capabilities of one-step design and are thus best served by conventional technology.

For instance, a shop with large staff of trained part programmers producing large runs of parts has little use for one-step's rapid artwork-to-prototype cycle and ease of operation. Such a shop would probably have a greater need for maximal toolpath optimization and part file compatibility—areas in which one-step systems do not excel.

On the other hand, a prototyping shop that is in the process of upgrading machines to NC is a prime candidate for one-step technology. One-step's machine-while-you-design prototyping capability, short training time, and economical cost are all advantageous here.

Many shops fall between the two described above. **Figure 2** provides a table that can help these shops weigh the relative merits of CAD/CAM/NC, SFP, and one-step design.

A shop should not be deterred from one-step technology simply because it already has all the NC machines it needs. One-step design control systems are available that tie into many kinds of conventional NC controllers, giving the user one-step design capabilities.

	CAD/CAM/NC	Stand-Alone Shop Floor Programming	One-Step System
Complexity of Parts Supported	Low-High	Low-Moderate	Moderate
Elapsed Time: Drawing To Prototype	Higher	Lower	Lower
Display During Part Design	Generally color, graphic view of part	Generally monochrome display of part program	Color, graphic view of part
Design Data Entry Method	Usually by drawing with a mouse or digitizer	Normally through the console keypad	Via trak-ball drawing or coordinate key-in
Smallest Machineable Unit	Part (without shop floor intervention)	G code block (or equivalent)	Shape primitive
Major Advantages	Handles the most sophisticated designs; interoperability among machines; tool path optimization	Control over individual tool motions; can correct part at machine; SFP present in most new controls.	Ease of use and training; art-to-part time; user interface natural for a machinist; error tolerance; cost.
Major Disadvantages	Complexity; training time and specialized personnel needed; art-to-part time; cost.	Training required; difficulty in making all but the simplest changes at the machine.	Lack of interoperability; subtractive design method unfamiliar to CAD users.

Figure 2

This table compares different aspects of CAD/CAM/NC, SFP, and one-step design.

Such a design control console, cabled to the RS-232 serial input port of an NC controller, sends postprocessed G codes to the controller whenever fabricating is to be performed. If the NC controller is capable of conversational programming through its serial port, the system behaves in exactly the same manner as a one-step retrofit controller.

If the serial port does not have a conversational mode, the operator will need to command the NC controller to accept a download every time a new part, or group of entities, is set for fabricating.

The design control system can be a ready-to-mount console or a software package run from personal computers.

Summary

One-step control, derived from elements of both CAD and SFP technology, provides a new method of converting a drawing to a fabricated part in a minimal amount of time, with a minimal amount of training. ■

David Neman is Chairman and Co-founder of BCD Engineering, Reston, Virginia.

124. Collection of Articles from **THE FABRICATOR**®

Purchasing any major piece of capital equipment, such as a slitter or cut-to-length line, can benefit a fabricating company by improving the product and increasing production.

Today, new lines have state-of-the-art electronic controls with increased line speed and production rates, and improved tolerances. With computer-generated setup programs, much of the guesswork has been eliminated.

If a fabricator is considering the purchase of a new piece of coil processing equipment, the following guidelines will help purchase the correct equipment at the best price.

General Specifications

The general specifications require the fabricator to decide what type of product will be processed, such as aluminum, stainless, hot rolled, cold rolled, etc. Then the coil size, inside diameter (ID), outside diameter (OD), weight, width, thickness, and shear stress must be determined.

The volume of coils per day, month, and year is important. The finished product condition required, including thickness, finished coil size, packaging, flatness, length and width tolerances, and edge conditioning is also important.

Check with the mill suppliers to see if the suppliers are planning any size or weight changes. A list of individual components, such as coil car, uncoiler, peeler, breaker rolls, crop shear, slitter edge trimmer, and recoiler, should be made and reviewed.

When this general specification is prepared, begin selecting vendors for bidding on the particular line.

Preliminary Selection of Vendors to Bid

A list of manufacturers who make the type of coil processing equipment needed should include manufacturers which the fabricator has purchased from previously, customers who have purchased from the fabricator, companies contacted at trade shows, etc. Eliminate manufacturers who usually build lighter-duty equipment than needed; it is easier to reduce capacity than to increase capacity.

A request for quotation should be sent to the various manufacturers, or a verbal request can be made and confirmed with a follow-up letter. The number of requests should range from three to five. This will provide a good cross section; more than five is too many to consider and time-consuming to evaluate.

Type of Quotation

Decide on the *type* of quotation you want. It takes significant time and expense for bidders to prepare a complete, detailed proposal.

An option is to ask for a preliminary **ball-park** estimate, which can be provided by the bidder when they review the bidder's past projects and prorate cost increases.

A **budgeting** estimate is a more accurate cost figure for the basic components, with the bidders doing little or no engineering calculations for the estimate.

Another type of quotation is the **detailed formal proposal**. This would include all components, some engineering calculations, and an accurate cost estimate.

Quotation Evaluation

Once you have received three to five proposals, make a spreadsheet analysis. The spreadsheet (see **Figure 1**) includes vendor names, proposal numbers, date of proposal, and a list of all major components in the proposal.

Important individual items to include would be motor horsepower, line speed, type of controls, capacity bearing size, lubrication, weight of equipment, and standards such as J.I.C. and NEMA.

This is an example of a summary sheet that can be used to make spreadsheet analyses of proposals for coil processing equipment manufacturers.

Figure 1

After each item, note any special features the manufacturer has included.

The final page should list delivery details, engineering drawings, service and installation services, training services, terms, F.O.B. shipping point, spare parts, and price.

It will probably be necessary to call some of the bidders to obtain certain details that some vendors included in their proposal that the others did not include.

Once the spreadsheet is made, decide on the two or three suppliers to be interviewed by eliminating bidders if they meet any of the following criteria:

1. Specifications are too general.
2. The price is too high or too low.
3. Delivery terms are not satisfactory.

Next, contact the vendors to schedule interviews and formal presentations. If needed, have the vendors revise their proposals to add any specification changes or additional features which you have discovered you will need since first submitting the original request for bid.

Try to schedule two or three vendors so they can be interviewed on the same day. Have key people in the meeting, including the plant manager, sales manager, engineering staff, and any other decision-making people.

Ideally, a specific meeting time for each vendor should be set up so that no more than one hour is allotted between meetings for discussion and general business.

The vendor should bring to the presentation the salesman, a local representative if one is in the area, engineering backup, and possibly a major subcontractor of electrical controls or special items not built by the vendor. Data supplied by the vendor should include:

1. Production data based on previous lines they have built.
2. An estimate of the number of people needed to run the equipment.
3. Photos of existing installations.
4. A customer list.
5. A slide or video presentation.

Also, the vendor should provide general information about his company. This may include number of employees, number of years in business, sales volume and percent of sales in this particular line, any litigation pending on past orders, patent and royalties related to the equipment, how they test their equipment, and their credit rating.

Proposal Review

During the formal presentation, each major component should be reviewed item by item. Discussion should include the uniqueness of your product and any features about the vendor's equipment that can improve your ability to sell your product.

Most vendors are familiar with your competition, and they may know information that is helpful. For example, your biggest competitor has a 72-inch slitter and you are thinking about buying a 60-inch slitter—so should you buy a 72-inch slitter?

In addition to the individual components of the proposal, you should discuss the following items:

1. Does the vendor have his own installation crew, or do they subcontract to local firms?

2. Does the vendor provide supervision during installation?

3. Will the vendor do a turnkey project, including foundations, equipment, installation, and debugging?

4. Is there a warranty on parts only or for parts and labor, and for how long?

5. Does the vendor include training, and what are the costs?

6. Does the vendor assign a project engineer who you can contact during the project?

7. Are engineering drawings and spare parts list included?

Insurance for installation and product liability, permits, and state and city codes are also important items that should be discussed.

Vendor Selection to Bid Again

After the formal presentations, narrow the field down to two bidders. If the quotations for the identical equipment and price for all three to five bidders is within 5 percent of each other, eliminate the vendors with the least experience, poor engineering, poor service, or slower delivery.

Ask your final two selections to provide another rebid based on final specification and list of equipment. At this point, most vendors will know who they are competing with in the rebid process, but if not, you can tell the vendor. However, do not give either vendor a copy of the other's proposals.

During this rebid period, visit one or two similar installations built by each vendor. Based on the spreadsheet analysis, formal presentations, and visits to installations, you can determine the preferred vendor and the secondary vendor.

Before the vendors complete their new bids, ask both to come in for a final review so that you can tell them when the order will be placed. Make the first review with the secondary vendor, and the last review with the primary. Tell both to submit their best price, realistic delivery date, terms, warranty, and any other extras not included in their original proposal.

Final Selection

The final selection should be made through a roundtable discussion will all members of your selection committee. If anyone missed part of the previous presentations, have the rest of the group bring him up to date.

Once the vendor is selected, a formal purchase order should be written, including a complete description of the equipment with reference to final proposal number and any revisions. A deposit check should be prepared and sent with the order if required. Communicate your decision to the vendor you did not choose.

Acceptance of Equipment

During the fabrication of the new equipment, your engineering representatives should make one or more trips to the vendor's plant to review the drawings and inspect fabrications.

Any modification can be discussed and changes made at the manufacturer's plant, not at your site. Many small details, such as control location and push-button sequence, can be decided before the equipment is sent to your site for installation. You may need to add some extra items, but it is much less expensive to do it at the manufacturer's plant than at your plant.

After the equipment installation, training, and start-up has been completed at your plant, prepare a "punch" list for the vendor to complete. Once the punch list is completed, your engineering staff can use the list to review the installation and all equipment and authorize final payment.

How to Get What You Paid For and Maybe More

Negotiate the down payment required; 10 percent is normal, and it should never be more than 20 percent.

You can require that warranties for both parts and labor begin the day production levels are met. Training at your plant and service schools should be included.

Many equipment manufacturers will do joint advertising with the fabricator. This can be cost-efficient and beneficial for both parties.

Also, some manufacturers will assist in leasing long-term financing. Ask your manufacturer if his company does this.

With careful planning and attention to detail, you can purchase the coil processing equipment that fits your specific needs and helps increase production of high-quality parts. ■

The information presented in this article was prepared by Arthur Helt, President, Helt Industries, Lake Forest, Illinois. Originally presented at the "Coil Processing" conference, May 14-15, 1991, Oak Brook, Illinois, sponsored by the Fabricators & Manufacturers Association, International (FMA).

USING CADD ON THE SHOP FLOOR

A powerful tool for fabricators*

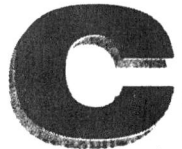

Computer-Assisted Design and Drafting (CADD) software, as the name implies, is most commonly used in design or drafting departments. What is not commonly known, however, is that CADD can also be a powerful tool on the shop floor.

Shop personnel spend a great deal of time with pencil, paper, and calculator producing shop sketches, laying out work, deriving dimensions, determining tool offsets, planning the location of workpiece clamps, and designing jigs and fixtures.

Each of these tasks can be accomplished more quickly and accurately with a CADD system.

A shop-floor system does not need to be an expensive, full-featured CADD system. There is little need for three dimensions, solid modeling, engineering analysis, or other sophisticated features.

Many inexpensive CADD packages are powerful shop tools. High processor speeds, high-resolution monitors, and large amounts of memory and disk space are not required for these applications. They perform well even on slower PCs, as well as on laptops and portables.

Case Study

One place where CADD is being used effectively in the shop environment is at the Goddard Space Flight Center (GSFC) in Greenbelt, Maryland.

One of the National Aeronautics and Space Administration's nine field centers, Goddard was established in 1959 as the first major scientific laboratory devoted entirely to the exploration of space. Its primary mission is to expand human knowledge of Earth, its environment, the solar system, and the universe through the use of near-Earth orbiting spacecraft.

At the space center, scientists, engineers, and technicians design, develop, fabricate, test, and launch spacecraft.

Some of the fabrication and assembly of spacecraft structures, scientific instruments, astronaut tools and training aids, and ground support equipment is the task of GSFC's Spacecraft Assembly Section. The section first acquired a portable computer to serve as a storage and input device for a numerically-controlled (NC) punching machine.

CADD software was purchased to make shop sketches and to serve as a training aid to introduce technician apprentices to CADD. Section personnel quickly discovered other applications for the software.

Applications for CADD Software

Suppose that the operator of a manual punching machine needs to punch a row of holes at an angle to the edge of a sheet. The operator would normally use a calculator to derive the Cartesian coordinates of each hole, hand draw and dimension a shop sketch, then punch the part (see **Figure 1**).

Further, suppose that instead of single holes, the part required shapes to be cut

---

*Reprinted with permission from The FABRICATOR® September 1991. Information about this publication and FMA membership on Page 269.

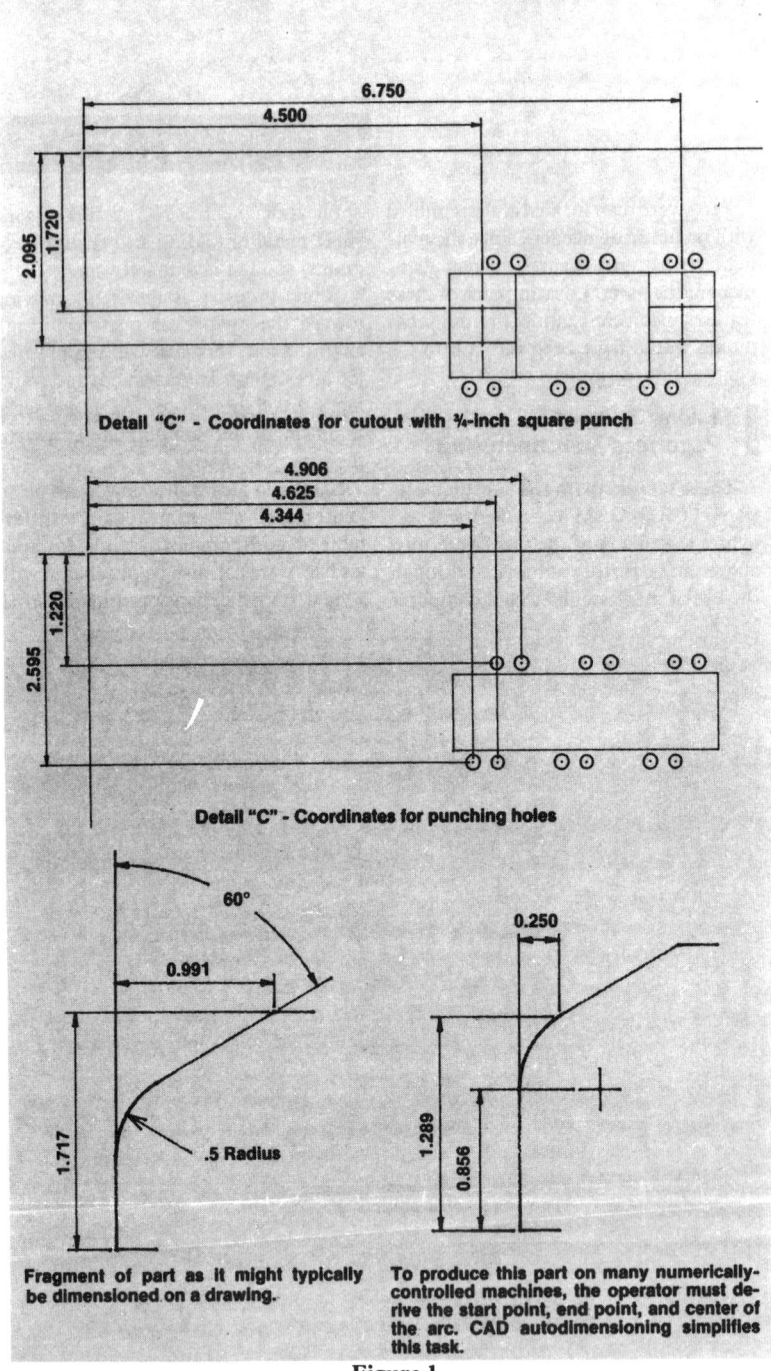

Detail "C" - Coordinates for cutout with ¾-inch square punch

Detail "C" - Coordinates for punching holes

.5 Radius

Fragment of part as it might typically be dimensioned on a drawing.

To produce this part on many numerically-controlled machines, the operator must derive the start point, end point, and center of the arc. CAD autodimensioning simplifies this task.

Figure 1
Without CADD software, a manual punching machine operator must use a calculator to derive hole coordinates and hand draw and dimension a shop sketch before punching the part.

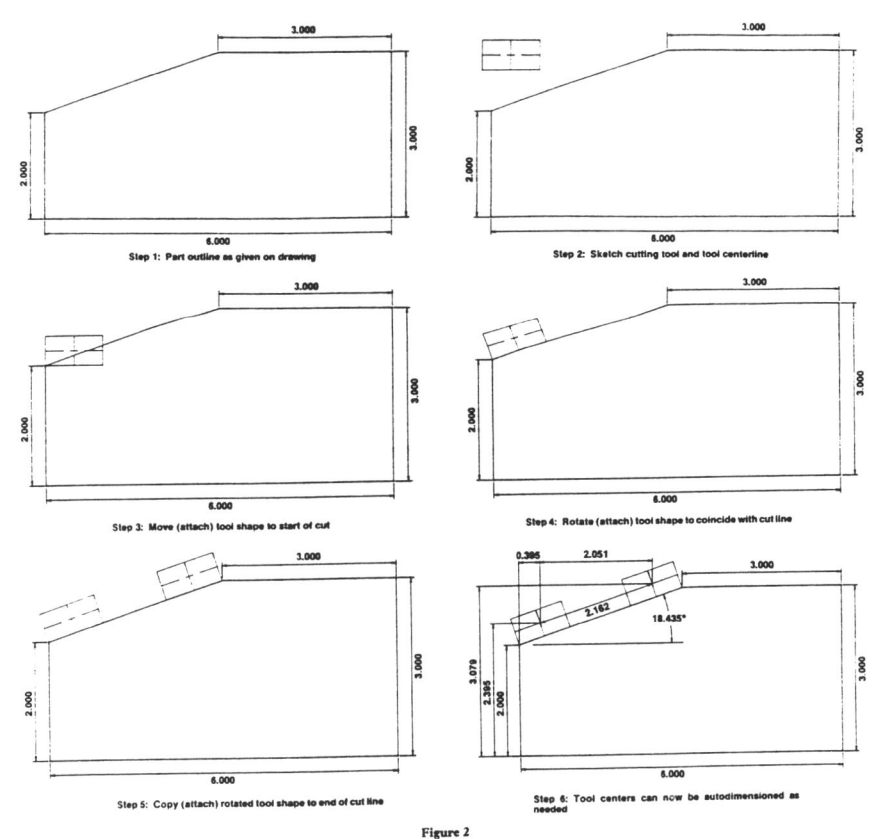

Figure 2
Six steps are involved when determining tool offset with CADD software.

out using a number of different punches. The operator would then have to calculate tool offsets and the coordinates of the center of each punch stroke. These are tedious and time-consuming operations, full of opportunities for error.

With a CADD system, the operator can quickly and accurately sketch the part directly, using whatever dimensions are given on the blueprint. He can then add tool shapes and paths, rotating tool shapes to the required angle, and automatically obtain the coordinates needed to produce the part. The steps involved in determining tool offset with CADD software are shown in **Figure 2**.

Machine operators must plan their work. When studying a blueprint, the technician must determine how to fixture the part at every phase of production. The location of machine tool clamps and potential interference between the workpiece and the tool must be considered.

The success of this operation is heavily dependent on the technician's judgment and skill in interpreting blueprints and on his ability to mentally visualize complex shapes.

A CADD system can facilitate this work. The shape of machine parts, tools, and clamps can be superimposed directly on the part drawing. They can then be positioned and moved to emulate production requirements, and locations can be accurately measured.

Techniques in Action

A current GSFC project provides a good example of these techniques. An instrument canister structure for a telescope is fabricated entirely of 12-gauge sheet titanium, punched and cold formed.

Due to the difficulty of drilling titanium, each of more than 2,000 rivet holes and hundreds of mounting holes for machine parts had to be accurately punched in the parts prior to forming.

Personnel used their shop CADD system to read the designer's AutoCAD® drawings of the structure. Adjacent views were then clipped and combined, factoring in bend allowances, and working drawings of the laid-out piece parts were dimensioned and plotted.

These drawings provided the NC punch programmer with all of the information needed to produce the parts in a format compatible with his requirements.

Parts were then formed and assembled with no fixturing needed, since the mating rivet patterns ensured correct alignment of the parts. Locating each of these features using conventional layout techniques would have been difficult to the point of impracticality.

Moving Toward "Paperless Manufacturing"

Those familiar with the latest innovations in CAD/CAM technology will recognize that many of the tasks described above can be further automated through the use of more sophisticated computer applications, such as NC postprocessors, sheet metal unfolding and nesting programs, and flat layout software.

While industry is inevitably moving toward the "paperless manufacturing" environment, this goal will require major investments in equipment and training. A basic shop-floor CADD can serve as an important stepping stone toward the paperless shop.

Skills and techniques developed on an "entry level" system are readily transferrable to more complex systems. Computer hardware can also be purchased with a view toward expansion. For the small job shop or prototyping operation, a basic system may be all that is ever required.

Even when additional hardware and CADD software is acquired, the original basic system often remains one of the most often-used programs because of its ease of use. For strictly two-dimensional drawings, it will probably remain the application of choice.

Think of an inexpensive CADD system as a "smart pencil." Anything that can be done with a pencil can be done with a CADD system, but in less time and with perfect form. The sketch has perfect dimensions that can be easily accessed, is permanent, yet easily edited, and can be reproduced at will.

A basic CADD system can also be used to perform many of the same tasks, such as printing signs, graphs, and charts, as more expensive and hard-to-use graphics software. It is a good training aid for plane geometry and trigonometry and can serve as an introduction to more advanced CADD systems. ∎

The information presented in this article was prepared by David Clark, Aerospace Engineering Technician, Goddard Space Flight Center, Greenbelt, Maryland. Lead-in photo courtesy Intergraph Corporation, Huntsville, Alabama.

FABRICATING PARTS FROM 3-D DRAWINGS

CAD/CAM can provide a strategic advantage*

Fabricating prototype sheet metal parts from two-dimensional drawings used to be a time-consuming, labor-intensive process fraught with the dangers—and associated costs—of human error. This is no longer true.

Thanks to advances in computer-aided design and computer-aided manufacturing (CAD/CAM) tools, prototype sheet metal parts can be fabricated from 3-D "sketches" and shipped to designers in days instead of weeks with an accuracy and quality previously impossible.

Because the parts are fabricated using standard production processes, tooling, and hardware, the cost of implementing such technology is competitive with most high-ranking external suppliers.

Quick turnaround and direct communication with manufacturing result in higher-quality, lower-cost products being brought to market in record time.

▌Benefits in Action

All of these benefits and more are being realized at two sheet metal technology centers in California. The two fabrication shops produce aluminum and steel sheet metal assemblies that are used as structural and cosmetic components in the packaging of electronic test equipment.

The shops are flexible in nature, producing lot sizes ranging from 1 to 1,000 and having process capabilities of numerical control (NC) punches, NC brakes, chromate conversion protective finishing, welding, Class A painting and screen painting, and hardware assembly.

The parts produced range from chassis that support printed circuit assemblies, microwave packages, power supplies, and displays, to vinyl-clad or painted exterior covers, to painted and screen-printed display models.

The gains at both sheet metal fabrication sites are achieved through the use of several tools: solid modeling, design, and drafting software; UNIX networking; fabrication software; and standardized sheet metal production processes.

Since implementing these processes, turnaround time on prototype sheet metal parts from 3-D drawings has been cut by two to eight weeks, depending on the complexity of the part. Average turnaround is now seven days, with three-day turnaround available upon request.

Nearly half the prototype jobs being handled at the sites are from 3-D files, and the percentage of 3-D parts is growing rapidly. By October, 1991, the company expects that 90 percent of prototype jobs will be 3-D.

After creating an unannotated 3-D drawing, files can be electronically transmitted over a UNIX network in minutes to the shop. There, a sheet-metal programmer runs the fabrication software to unfold the 3-D image and program the NC punch presses.

Unfolding and programming averages 1.5 hours. A process routing is then created, and the part is ready to be fabricated.

The following is a brief look at each of the key steps in fabricating prototype sheet metal parts from 3-D files.

*Reprinted with permission from The FABRICATOR® June 1991. Information about this publication and FMA membership on Page 269.

Unannotated Drawings

When laying out new designs using the software's 3-D capability, a mechanical engineer does not have to annotate a drawing. That saves weeks in the product development cycle. Using standard tolerances and processes means that dimensions and datums are not required on the 3-D prototype drawings.

Instead, all of the geometric information required to fabricate the part is contained in the 3-D solid body file. The result is that lengthy drafting queues and actual drafting time are eliminated in the prototype phase.

Electronic Data Transfer

The phrase "paperless factory" applies to this step in the creation of sheet metal prototypes.

During 1990, the fabricating shops demonstrated the capability to receive CAD files from various locations within the U.S. and abroad. Transfer times are less than 10 minutes.

Not only does an electronic data transfer save days in paper transit on prototype builds, but it also makes design for manufacturability feedback and quoting much faster.

Computer-Aided Unfolding and Programming

The fabrication program "reads" the geometry of the 3-D file created with the solid modeling, design, and drafting software. After reading the geometry, the part is unfolded into a flat sheet. The fabrication program suggests the tools necessary to punch out the part, and a programmer approves tool selections and calls up special application tools when required.

The fabrication program's flat layout and NC programming, which can take from 30 minutes to 4 hours (and averages 1.5 hours) is at least eight times faster than doing layouts on a drafting table and programming by conventional tape prep methods.

In addition to the time savings, accuracy is enhanced at least tenfold. The reason is that all of the geometry is automatically translated from the design software to the unfolding and programming package. This eliminates tedious, error-prone hand calculations and the delays and manual entry of such programs.

The result is that there is now improved flexibility in programming, resulting in an average turnaround time through programming of one day. The fabrication shops average more than 1,200 prototype jobs a year.

Standard Sheet Metal Processes

The use of standard tolerances, fold allowances, hole sizes, raw materials, hardware, and finishes allows prototype parts to be completely processed in the shop.

The processing of prototype sheet metal parts can be accomplished quickly because of the shop's range of processing capabilities. The shop runs small lots and has a reserve capacity for prototypes, too.

Having such capabilities as NC punches and brakes and chromeric coating in-house eliminates the time-consuming process of subcontracting that work.

Since parts are produced using standard processes, design for manufacturability feedback is an automatic part of the prototype service.

The investment in CAM has more than paid for itself through increased productivity, quality, responsiveness, and customer satisfaction. The success of this CAM application is proof that leading-edge manufacturing technology need not come at the expense of competitively-priced parts.

The combination of the solid modeling, drafting, and design software, UNIX networking, fabrication software, and standard production processes has provided a strategic capability to the fabrication shops. That capability is unavailable through any subcontractor.

In the future, these CAD/CAM tools might be used to allow a designer to get a prototype part produced as soon as he or she has conceived it, by the exact manufacturing process to be used for volume production, and at the same cost as volume production units.

Being so close to the production process, a designer could not only optimize designs for function, but also for manufacturability. The ultimate goal is to bring products to market faster with superior designs and lower costs. ■

The information presented in this article was prepared by Tom Alexander, Manufacturing Engineering Manager, Hewlett-Packard Company, Fort Collins, Colorado.

SHORT-RUN SHEARING IN SHEET METAL FABRICATING
A matter of material handling*

By Joseph M. Fowler

Shearing sheet material with a squaring shear is the fundamental first step with most short-run metal fabricating. To many fabricators, shearing is a burdensome chore resistant to the higher-tech material handling methods that are part of the computer numerical control (CNC) punch press and laser.

Computer-controlled shearing machines, resembling large corner-notching presses, have had some success. However, their initial cost, required programming, and factors associated with the repeated cycling of a short cutting knife have not yet led to the wholesale replacement of the guillotine shear.

The general use of a 10-foot (3-meter) long knife to trim a 10-foot long sheet in one stroke will not be replaced anytime soon. This article discusses several methods of material handling that are available to users of conventional shears.

A guillotine squaring shear is a special form of power press. It has a weighty ram carrying a long upper knife nearly the width of the ram. This upper knife is carried at an angle or **rake** to a horizontal lower knife.

As the ram descends, the upper knife passes close behind the lower knife, parting the sheet material placed in between. The shear cuts like a scissors in the sense that the actual cutting point moves from one end of the part to the other. However, the lower knife does not move, and the angle between the knives does not change during the cutting stroke.

Traditionally, most power-operated shears for sheet metal use a mechanical drive. Energy stored in a rotating flywheel is transferred to the ram through a mechanical clutch. Hydraulically-driven or partially hydraulic shears have become more popular in recent years because they are less expensive for equivalent cutting capacity and have easily adjustable "rake" features.

A squaring shear is called that because a **squaring arm** or side guide is attached to the front of the shear. It is mounted perpendicular to the shear knives.

When the lengthwise edge of a sheet is placed along the squaring arm and the front portion is inserted between the knives, the cut that results should be precisely perpendicular (90 degrees) to the side of the sheet resting along the squaring arm. This is what is meant by a "square" corner, and a rectangle with four precisely squared corners is said to have been squared.

In many metal service centers and other high-production shearing operations, it is commonly thought that mechanical squaring shears are faster and more reliable. But reliance on the 55 or 65 strokes per minute (SPM) specification in the manufacturer's catalog tells only a small part of the story.

A basic analysis of the time spent shearing reveals that most of the time is spent handling material, as in:

1. Getting the material into the shear.
2. Maneuvering the material while it is in process.

---

*Reprinted with permission from The FABRICATOR® December 1992. Information about this publication and FMA membership on Page 269.

3. Separating the good parts from the scrap.

4. Rehandling material when a second dimension is cut from the primary rectangle.

5. Checking dimensions (quality assurance).

The typical one-second cycle time is largely irrelevant except in cases where narrow strips are being sheared in an automatic cycle mode, such as 1-inch strips derived from the full dimension of a 10-foot sheet, over and over again.

Front-to-Back Shearing

Most shearing is done front-to-back. Typically, a 4-foot by 10-foot sheet is brought to the shear and rested on front support arms extending out toward the operator. A single operator, if the weight of the sheet is not too heavy, maneuvers the longest edge of the sheet under the knives for an initial trim cut.

The operator rotates the sheet 90 degrees and places the cleanly trimmed edge flush against the squaring arm. The operator then trims the leading edge of the sheet, which is now the shorter width, creating a square corner. The procedure is usually repeated until the sheet is trimmed all around or at least on three sides.

A trimmed rectangle is often recut to a smaller size against a backgauge set to the desired finished dimension. The operator pushes the trimmed edge of the sheet squarely against the backgauge and cycles the shear.

Presumably, the blank that is cut away and falls behind the shear will be a precisely squared rectangle, dimensionally identical to the setting on the backgauge readout.

Sheet Droop and Sheet Supporters

The drawbacks of front-to-back shearing occur in several areas.

First, light-gauge material tends to droop and not hit the backgauge bar squarely. Droop is a serious problem when accurate shearing is required.

The amount of droop is directly a function of the thickness and stiffness of a particular material and the ratio of the width of material to the length overhanging the knife. For example, in mild steel of 20 gauge and thinner, sheet droop usually becomes a problem when the backgauge is set to 12 inches or more.

The first attempt to combat droop, no doubt, was a person with a broomstick. Unfortunately, it is still not an unfamiliar sight in many otherwise sophisticated metal fabricating operations to see a helper around a shear with a broomstick (or similar apparatus) pushing a drooping sheet up against a backgauge bar.

Many shears have contact probes or switches embedded into the surface of the backgauge bar to ensure a certain degree of accuracy in the cut. The shear cannot be cycled until these probes are engaged by the edge of the workpiece.

However, if the backgauge is deeper than the far edge of the drooping material, then the person with the broomstick may still be called upon.

Of course, more respectable mechanical solutions to droop have been available for more than 50 years. One early approach, which works only for ferromagnetic material, employs a series of permanent magnets.

The magnets, in roller form, are mounted in nonmagnetic steel channels and attached to the underside of the shear ram. Notches for the channels are cut into the backgauge about 1 foot apart, permitting the backgauge bar to move unimpeded forward and back. As the sheet material is slid over the back of the shear table, it is attracted to the underside of the permanent magnet rollers which guide it squarely against the gauge bar.

Unfortunately, in most of the designs using permanent magnets, the rails are attached directly to the shear ram. And although each rail is spring-loaded to yield vertically, it absorbs a tremendous physical pounding which causes the springs to quickly come out of adjustment. In high-production applications, these devices are difficult to maintain.

Electromagnetic Sheet Support

A modern embodiment of magnetic sheet support is the electromagnetic sheet supporter (see **Figure 1**). This type is more powerful and more easily controlled.

Electromagnetic sheet supporters may differ in basic design, but they use similar methods of attachment to the shear. They are supported by the side frame of the machine instead of by the movable ram. Therefore, they are not subject to the same level of violent motion as many of the predecessor devices. Also, electromagnets do not lose magnetic pull due to aging.

Pneumatic and Hydraulic Sheet Support

Pneumatic or hydraulically-operated sheet support devices have been part of shear conveyor/stackers since the 1940s.

In the most familiar design, an air cylinder is connected to an upwardly rotated arm. In raised position, the top of the arm sits directly below the pass line of the sheet. The sheet slides along the top of the arms until it meets the backgauge. When the shear is cycled, the air cylinders pull the arms down out of the way of the ram. Many shear conveyors were sold only because they provided sheet support.

Now, various shear manufacturers offer pneumatic sheet supports separate from a shear conveyor. Two manufacturers offer a pneumatic sheet support comprised of boomerang-shaped links that are rotated up into notches cut into the backgauge of the shear. In raised position, each arm forms a horizontal support surface for the sheet.

Pneumatic sheet supports offer effective and reliable sheet support when they are built into the shear backgauge from inception. Sheet supporters designed to duck under the backgauge bar, such as those built into shear conveyor/stackers, tend to be less reliable.

The newer electromagnetic systems are more elegant, quieter, and ready and in position as fast as material can be moved through the shear. However, they are the most expensive and only operate with magnetic materials.

Separating the Trims from the Good Parts

Perhaps the most prevalent headache associated with front-to-back shearing is separation of the trim from the good cutoffs—the usable blanks.

As the sheet is sheared, each part falls down below the ram in back of the shear. A chute attached to the shear directs the cutoff material toward the back. Narrow trims also end up in back mixed in with

Collection of Articles from THE FABRICATOR®   139.

Electromagnetic Rollers

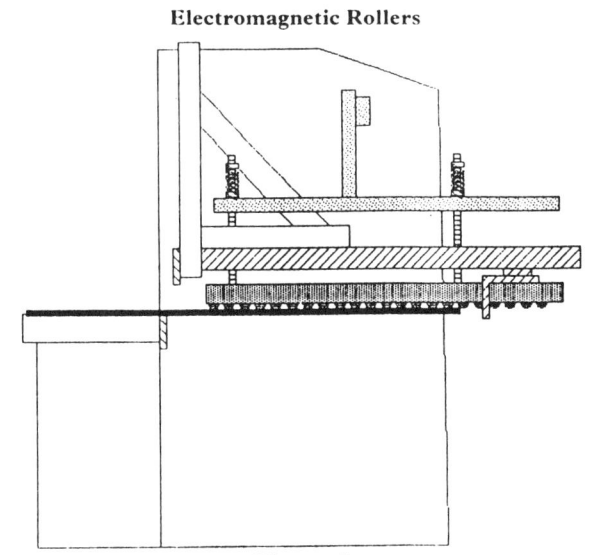

Figure 1

Electromagnetic rollers, as shown here, keep material from drooping.

Power-Shearing 24- to 10-Gauge Sheet Metal

A: Setup Time: 1: .3 standard hours per job lot, for both with and without shear feedback system.
*Note: without CNC gauging on the shear
B: Unit Standard (Allow once per occurrence)

Area of Finished Piece Part (in Sq. Ins.)	Shear WITH Shear Feedback System 24-18 ga. 16-14 ga. Standard Hours		Shear WITHOUT Shear Feedback System 24-18 ga. 16-10 ga. Standard Hours		Area in Sq. Ft.
To - 28.8			.0015	.0020	To - .2
28.9 - 86.4			.0035	.0040	.21 - .6
86.5 - 144.0			.0050	.0060	.61 - 1.0
144.1 - 216.0			.0060	.0080	1.01 - 1.5
216.1 - 360.0	.0038	.0049	.0080	.0100	1.51 - 2.5
360.1 - 576.0	.0049	.0063	.0130	.0160	2.51 - 4.0
576.1 - 864.0	.0064	.0083	.0180	.0220	4.01 - 6.0
864.1 - 1,152.0	.0081	.0105	.0230	.0280	6.01 - 8.0
1,152.1 - 1,440.0	.0099	.0128	.0280	.0330	8.01 - 10.0
1,440.1 - 1,800.0	.0118	.0153	.0320	.0380	10.01 - 12.5
1,800.1 - 2,160.0	.0140	.0181	.0340	.0400	12.51 - 15.0
2,160.1 - 2,520.0	.0162	.0210	.0350	.0420	15.51 - 17.5
2,520.1 - 2,880.0	.0184	.0238	.0360	.0430	17.51 - 20.0
2,880.1 - 3,456.0			.0420	.0500	20.01 - 24.0
3,456.1 - 4,032.0			.0440	.0530	24.01 - 28.0
4,032.1 - 4,320.0			.0460	.0550	28.01 - 30.0

Figure 2

This chart shows standard time data gathered from a manufacturer of stainless steel tanks for commercial photographic processing, comparing two standard 10-foot mechanical shears, one equipped with a feedback conveyor and one without a feedback conveyor.

the good parts.

The remedy for this problem is a scrap or trim separator. The trim separator is a movable chute or door located above a scrap bin. Ordinarily, the operator presses a button before cutting the trim piece. This button opens the scrap door and permits the trim to fall into the catch bin.

When a good part is cut off, the trim door remains closed and the good part slides down over the chute covering the scrap bin.

In its most popular configuration, the scrap door is located at the exit end of a conventional shear conveyor/stacker which moves the cutoff parts away from the back of the shear. Eventually, the shearing operation must be stopped so that the scrap bin can be emptied.

A difficulty associated with this style of scrap separation is that long, narrow trims often twist and bow to such a degree that they are not conveyed successfully. They can become entangled in the conveyor belts and even cause conveyor chains to break.

Shear conveyor scrap bins have been eliminated at Central Steel & Wire Company in Chicago. At this high-production steel service center, squaring shears are located in a line next to one another. The backs of the shears project over a trough, and a long conveyor belt parallel to and directly below the knives of the shears runs in the bottom of the trough.

Trim scrap drops into a gap over the trough between the shear knives and the shear conveyor/stacker (or feedback conveyor) located behind each shear. Trim scrap from all the shears is conveyed simultaneously along the trough through a scrap chopper and is automatically deposited into a haul-away container.

▌Back-to-Front Shearing

One way to avoid many problems associated with front-to-back shearing is to do the opposite thing—push the sheet in from the back of the shear to the front.

This method is required when parts are to be sheared to very high accuracy—without the help of CNC feeding devices—and when large blanks of delicate or scratch-prone material are sheared. Then, the cutting dimension is determined by gauges located on support arms in front of the shear where the operator is normally stationed.

There are several advantages to this method:

1. The part derived from the larger sheet is fully supported by the table of the shear or by support arms projecting out in front of the shear. Droop is not a problem.

2. Accuracy is enhanced because the operator can be certain that the part is in true contact with the gauging points.

3. The cutoff blank is already in the operator's hands, ready for secondary handling—effectively eliminating the need to rehandle cutoff parts.

4. Trim scrap does not mix with the good cutoffs since it falls behind the shear.

The chief disadvantages of back-to-front shearing are:

1. The requirements for additional personnel to feed the sheet from the back of the shear.

2. The apparent loss of speed in push-

ing a sheet quickly against the backgauge.

To overcome these disadvantages, another technique was developed.

Front-to-Back-to-Front Shearing: The Shear Feedback Concept

In 1959, a special reversible conveyor was developed for an office furniture manufacturing company in Brooklyn, New York, where large light-gauge steel blanks were required to make desks and filing cabinets.

Further refinement of this machine led to what is today an alternative material handling technique, the feedback conveyor or shear feedback system. While a number of feedback conveyors will deliver a cutoff sheet back to the operator under certain circumstances, the one developed in New York was the first that primarily acted in this "feedback" mode.

One of the problems associated with bringing a sheet into the narrow opening between the shear knives was waviness or **bow** in the sheet. For that reason, an electromagnetic roller was adapted to flatten magnetic material as it is delivered into the opening. For nonmagnetic material, a pinch roller was provided to help feed the sheet.

Now, in a preferred format, the feedback conveyor is used in conjunction with a shear that has CNC front gauging devices. Programmability enables front gauges to be set and changed as quickly as backgauges, and thus makes the technique even more competitive than it was in the past.

The chart in **Figure 2** shows standard time data gathered from a manufacturer of stainless steel tanks for commercial photographic processing. It shows a comparison of one standard 10-foot mechanical shear equipped with a feedback conveyor, and one without.

As shown in the chart, the feedback conveyor has been applied to a 10-foot shear which has had a portion of the backgauge removed to permit room for the feedback conveyor. The data generated compares standard hour units to a given size blank. Area is considered in the dominant characteristics; material thickness is divided into two categories.

The chart indicates that the variation in standards with and without the feedback conveyor is due to savings in personnel and faster generation of finished parts.

As shown in **Figure 3**, the sheet material is introduced through the shear knives from the operator's station in front of the shear. It travels back onto the conveyor table and is delivered back-to-front, to the front gauges. Thus, the primary sizing is accomplished using front gauges.

However, the secondary cutting of the first blank is often cut to a backgauge, especially where the parts are 12 inches or less when measuring the longest dimension—in other words, where droop or marring of material is not a consideration.

In conventional front-to-back shearing, the material is handled in a roundabout manner—the material that is first cut must be returned to the front of the shear for recutting. Using the feedback conveyor, material is delivered in a straighter path—between the knives. Shortening the path of material flow nat-

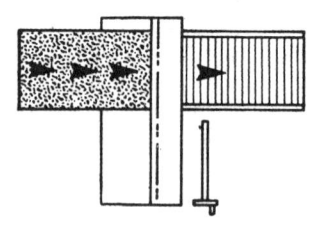

1. The sheet moves between knives away from the operator. The operator places the edge of the sheet between the shear knives. The sheet is taken away from the operator onto feedback rolls by electromagnetic pinch rolls.

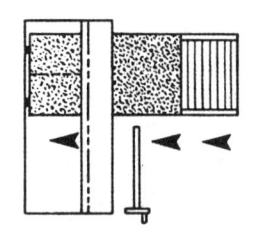

2. The sheet feeds back to front gauges on the shear bed. The leading edge of the sheet trips a limit switch on the feedback system which causes sheet to feed back to the operator.

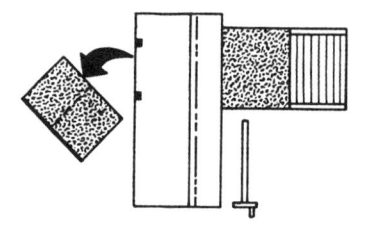

3. The first blank is parted from the full sheet. The operator places the edge of sheet against the gauges mounted in front of the shear, cycles the ram, and parts a first blank.

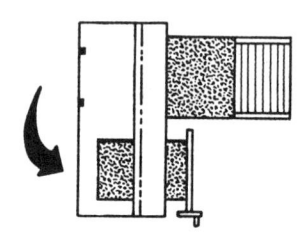

4. The blank is trimmed and recut to finished dimension. With this first parted blank in hand, the operator makes trim cuts or additional parting cuts until the blank is completely sheared. Finished parts may be stacked in front or allowed to fall behind the shear if the final dimension is backgauged.

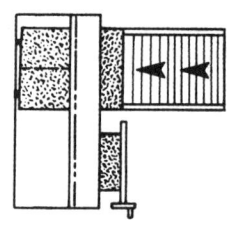

5. The remainder of the sheet feeds back to the front gauges. Operations are repeated until the sheet is completely sheared. The next portion of the sheet remaining on the feedback system is then automatically delivered to front gauges, and the sequence of operations is repeated until sheet is entirely sheared.

Figure 3

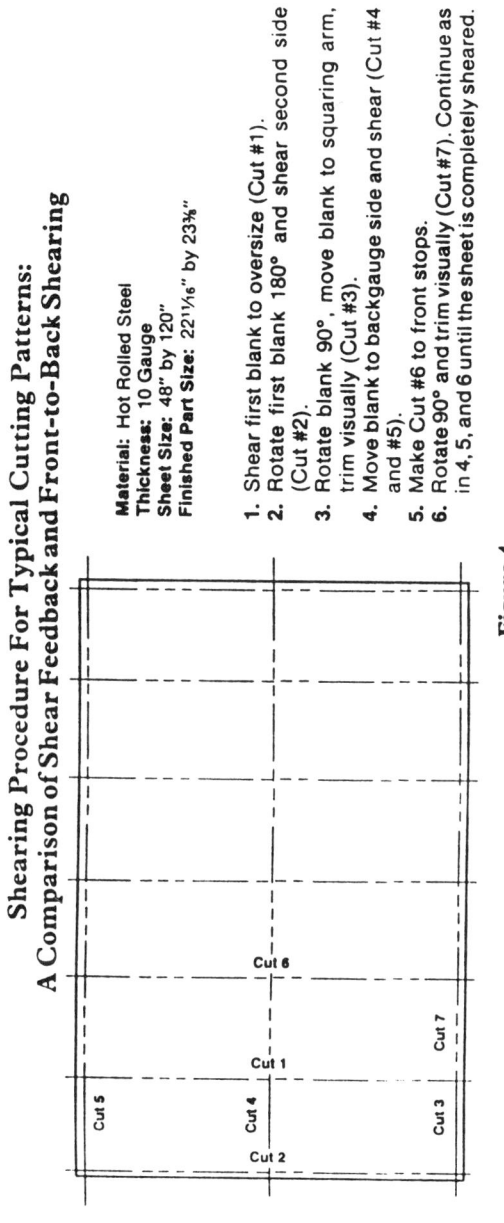

Shearing Procedure For Typical Cutting Patterns:
A Comparison of Shear Feedback and Front-to-Back Shearing

Material: Hot Rolled Steel
Thickness: 10 Gauge
Sheet Size: 48" by 120"
Finished Part Size: 22 1/16" by 23 5/8"

1. Shear first blank to oversize (Cut #1).
2. Rotate first blank 180° and shear second side (Cut #2).
3. Rotate blank 90°, move blank to squaring arm, trim visually (Cut #3).
4. Move blank to backgauge side and shear (Cut #4 and #5).
5. Make Cut #6 to front stops.
6. Rotate 90° and trim visually (Cut #7). Continue as in 4, 5, and 6 until the sheet is completely sheared.

Figure 4

urally has a more positive effect the more often multiple handling is required.

As another illustration of this feedback conveyor technique, one food service equipment manufacturer derives six blanks from each 12-gauge, 48-inch by 96-inch sheet. Each sheet weighs 140 pounds. The finished size of each blank is 19¾ inches by 24⅜ inches.

Using a conventional, front-to-back approach to shearing, the standard hour figures would be:

.0031 std. hours for shear to length
.0053 std. hours for shear to width
.0084
.0016 std. hours for rehandling material for secondary cutting
.0100 Total

When using the same shear equipped with the feedback conveyor and a combination of front and backgauges, the handling time was reduced to .0054 standard hours per piece. **Figure 4** shows an example of the shearing process.

▮ Other Shearing Techniques

In cases where one cutoff from the primary sheet will finish the part, the advantage of the feedback conveyor is lost. In such cases, some form of CNC front-to-back feeding device may be justified.

These systems push a sheet through a shear in precise increments. The trailing edge of the sheet is clamped by feeder grips which incrementally push the sheet into the shear. A backgauge is not required because the feed dimension is controlled by an accurate lead screw usually driven by a computer-controlled servo drive.

These systems are more suited for cutting small parts that have already been fabricated on a CNC punching machine. Frequently, one of two cutting dimensions has already been "sheared" on the punch press. Consequently, a single cut on a family of punched parts will free a whole group of parts.

This is not an appropriate system where large, unfinished blanks must be cut and then squared or resquared.

CNC front gauges and backgauges for shears are now widely available. As these systems decrease in cost, they will be incorporated into more factories and fabricating cells.

A marriage of CNC gauging techniques with the appropriate material handling equipment and improved part stacking apparatus may characterize many future square shearing installations for short- and medium-run fabricating. ▮

Joseph M. Fowler is President of American Actuator Corporation, Stamford, Connecticut. Lead-in photo by Tony Riffel, Hobart/PMI, Troy, Ohio.

CAN JUST-IN-TIME BE IMPLEMENTED IN THE PRECISION SHEET METAL JOB SHOP?

One company shows how job shops can benefit*

Over half of America's precision metal forming is produced by job shops. Therefore, much of the future of U.S. manufacturing rests with the job shop and their ability to implement Just-In-Time (JIT) manufacturing.

But implementing JIT is tough and certainly not as easy for a job shop as it is for an original equipment manufacturer (OEM). There are probably less than a dozen precision sheet metal job shops in the U.S. that have actually implemented all of the major JIT manufacturing technologies.

Many in the industry feel that JIT is impossible to implement at the job shop level. These perceptions and the old ways of doing business are going to be hard to shake. But there are a few companies, such as Everest Electronic Equipment, that are shaking out the old ways and proving that JIT is not only *possible* at the job shop level, but can be highly profitable as well.

Everest Electronic Equipment, Anaheim, California, is a precision sheet metal job shop that is an exception to this stereotype and is proof that JIT technologies do have a place in the job shop. The company's custom sheet metal operation is one of the largest in southern California, with close to 135 employees.

The company is made up of three profit centers: the Plastic Molding Division, the Electronic Enclosure Division, and its Custom Sheet Metal Division. The plastic and electronic enclosure divisions are physically and organizationally separate from the custom sheet metal business and will only be addressed in this article as an aside.

Poor Profits Force Rethinking of Manufacturing Philosophy

Four years ago, amidst a rapidly changing market, Everest found it increasingly difficult to remain profitable. Terry Wells, president of the company, realized he had to find some way of rapidly improving the company's manufacturing efficiency. After attending a workshop on JIT, he decided to convert the Electronic Enclosure Division to JIT.

The Enclosure Division manufactured a standard product line for the telecommunications industry. Wells' efforts at the enclosure division proved very successful and were a springboard to a more ambitious undertaking—converting the job shop division to JIT.

"If it had not been for our proprietary line, I am not sure we would have ever implemented JIT in the job shop," he commented. His success with the Enclosure Division gave him the experience and confidence necessary to implement JIT in the custom job shop division. This effort proved to be much more formidable than converting the product line to JIT.

There was resistance from everyone, including the owners of the business who were not involved on a day-to-day basis at the company. Because of his confidence in the JIT approach, Wells persisted in its implementation. Within a year, his efforts began to show remark-

---

*Reprinted with permission from The FABRICATOR® June 1991. Information about this publication and FMA membership on Page 269.

able results.

At the end of a year, the company had freed up more than $1,000,000 in inventory, reduced employees by 20 percent, and cut floor space by almost one-third. This was achieved while maintaining the same sales volume.

Key Elements of JIT

The company has incorporated many JIT technologies in its manufacturing. However, the three most important of these technologies were:

1. Statistical Process Control (SPC)
2. Machine cells
3. Kanban

In manufacturing circles, **Kanban** refers to a production control system that *pulls* work through a shop rather than pushing it through, as is done with the traditional production schedule.

At the heart of the company's JIT operation is the **machine cell**. A machine cell is a tight grouping of machines that are arranged to process raw material into a complete assembly or as close to a complete assembly as possible. It has been described by some as a factory within a factory.

Prior to implementing the machine cell concept, the company was arranged functionally. Press brakes were in one area, turret punch presses in another, and shears in still another area.

Under the old layout one particular assembly component, a tubular frame, traveled a quarter of a mile back and forth through the shop. After the cellular concept was implemented, travel distance was reduced to about 40 yards.

Everest's quality assurance manager claims that the new layout reduced the distance a typical part travels to one-tenth the former distance.

Research has shown that a strong link exists between the distance that a part travels and the amount of Work-In-Process (WIP). The greater the travel, the greater the WIP.

In Everest's case, reducing the part travel distance, along with the implementation of other JIT technologies, resulted in the reduction of WIP, elimination of hundreds of material storage racks, and all the personnel once needed to keep track of that inventory.

When is a Cell Set Up in the Custom Division?

At the company, a specific machine cell is established whenever a JIT partnership is developed with a customer, and the business from that relationship represents a minimum of $100,000 per month. The cell is set up incorporating all of the equipment required to process that particular company's business. The partnership allows machine layouts to be reconfigured and products redesigned with the intent of eliminating setup time.

This goal has been totally achieved on the turret punch press, which is set up with a standard tool load of 58 tools that never require a tool change or a work clamp adjustment. Programs are downloaded directly into the control driving a 58-station turret punch press. Direct Numeric Control (DNC) eliminates the manual input of tapes.

The adoption of a standard sheet size of 48 inches by 72 inches eliminates shearing as a separate process and further simplifies the operation. Even in the brake area, which is stubbornly resistant to JIT efforts, permanently configured die rails that can handle up to five bends have slashed setup time from hours to minutes.

What Makes up a Machine Cell?

In the traditional job shop, fastening brake tooling permanently to a die rail for a particular job is prohibitively expensive, but it makes eminent sense in a JIT operation where partnering provides a long-term commitment and forecast. The extra tooling costs can be amortized over a job that is known to be a recurring one throughout the year.

Initially, a typical cell at the company was comprised of a turret press, one to two press brakes, a hardware insertion machine, two spot welders, TIG (Tungsten Inert Gas) welders, and a cleanup booth.

The company had four turret machines driving four cells. Today they have 70 percent of all their work, over 700 parts, going through one new turret punch press which feeds three different cells.

This was accomplished by making the following changes:

1. Eliminating shearing as a separate operation by using only one standardized sheet size (48 inches x 72 inches) processed in the turret press.

2. Incorporating an automated load and unload device into the turret press.

3. Standardizing on one turret load so that tool changes were completely eliminated.

4. Nesting up to 20 different piece part programs at a time on one sheet.

Statistical Process Control

Although many would not view a job shop as a likely candidate for SPC, the company uses machine operators to monitor machine processes by using SPC on a daily basis. SPC is performed on the turret punch press by checking a test pattern that uses every punch in the turret.

A few critical dimensions are checked, then each hole is checked for burr. Even a small burr will result in the insertion of a freshly-sharpened tool.

If the test pattern indicates that the process is within the SPC control limits, then no other parts are checked that day, including no first article inspections. First article inspection would not be possible if the machine had to be set up for each new job.

Through SPC and a simplified, streamlined operation, the inspection department was virtually eliminated at Everest. Yet, despite the elimination of over five inspectors, the company's reject rate has dropped from 1.5 percent to less than .1 percent since the change in manufacturing methods.

Machine Cells and Setup Reduction Slash Lot Size

By reducing setup time and clustering all the processes close together in a machine cell layout, small batches have finally become economical for the company. There was a time when Everest worked on lot sizes so large that it took up to three to four months to complete a job, resulting in inventory turns of only three per year.

Today their lot sizes, normally 15 to 20 units, are shipped out weekly and sometimes daily. The smaller lot size has pushed the company's inventory turns to more than 13 per year.

Reduction in Forklifts

Through their JIT efforts, which have led to small, easy-to-move batches, the fleet of forklifts at the company has been reduced 50 percent. Special material handling carts designed for moving small batches can be seen everywhere. Machine operators or laborers pushing these small carts have replaced the remaining forklifts and forklift drivers.

The Cell Determines Work Force Organization

Work and workers are organized around the cell concept. The goal is for all machine operators in a cell to be cross-trained and knowledgeable in the operation, setup, and maintenance of all machines in that cell. This includes the ability to perform SPC checks on each process.

It is the cross-training combined with cell layout economics that allows operator productivity to explode.

The cell concept improves morale by enriching the work environment. There are two reasons for this. The first is that cross-training results in a greater sense of accomplishment for the operator. Second, through the development of a cell team, camaraderie, pride, and motivation improve. It is not surprising that absenteeism has dropped at the company.

JIT and the Precision Sheet Metal Job Shop

When asked about the feasibility of smaller job shops adopting the techniques which have worked so well at the company, Wells noted that many aspects of JIT can easily be incorporated in any size job shop.

The reason is that most job shops specialize in a certain area of the market, narrowing the processes, material sizes, and product geometries done by the job shop. This specialization makes JIT easier to bring about.

Furthermore, most job shop business conforms to the 80/20 rule; 80 percent of the business comes from 20 percent of the customers.

According to Wells, most job shops with less than $1,000,000 in annual sales get 70 to 80 percent of their work from one to three customers. Combine this with the fact that most jobs follow a set processing sequence, and the stage is set for JIT.

What are the biggest obstacles to JIT implementation?

Paint vendors and the lack of internal engineering capability were mentioned as the primary obstacles. Many paint shops have pricing policies and quality problems that work against JIT. In addition, many job shops do not have the engineering expertise to help customers design products for manufacturability.

There are two implications of these observations. One is that new relationships will have to be established between painters and the smaller job shops that they serve or job shops will have to learn how to paint as well as fabricate. The second is that engineering talent will have to be developed and used more than in the past.

The company was fortunate in that its ability to establish and finance its engineering group through monies released from inventory reductions. But these same monies are available to many shops that have thousands of dollars locked up in raw material and WIP.

Vendor Customer Relationships

After being asked what he liked most about JIT, Wells responded, "From a personal standpoint, JIT means not having to argue with customers. Prior to JIT there were always two potential areas of conflict: Depending on the needs of the moment, a customer would call up and say, 'Where are my parts?' or 'Do not ship our parts!'

"With the quick response that machine cells provide, plus the implementation of Kanban, our customers always have exactly what they need to sell when they need to sell it! And our use of SPC also ensures that our customers and the customer's customer will be satisfied with the product.

"JIT will not work unless the customer is committed to JIT also."

One of these commitments requires the adherence to a *frozen schedule*. The word "frozen" does not seem to be consistent with the flexibility that JIT implies. However, JIT does require better planning, and much of the flexibility gained from JIT results from a better orchestration of events.

There is a long-term forecast that is flexible, but within that forecast period a frozen schedule is required so that the job shop and its vendors can get ready for the order. A small change in a frozen schedule can cause large disruptions in the job shop. This is actually an everyday occurrence in the traditional manufacturing operation, but the constant "fire-fighting" allows no time for the smooth running of the operation.

For the JIT operation, a frozen schedule, however, is usually short in duration. It normally approximates the lead time for that assembly or part, and may only be a week or so.

It goes without saying that JIT commitments are in the interest of both the customer and vendor. The customer benefits by getting on-time deliveries of product that requires no inspection. The job shop benefits by getting predictable, long-term business in much higher quantities.

The information presented in this article was prepared by Jerry Rush, Director of Marketing and Sales Support, U.S. Amada, Ltd., Buena Park, California.

KEEPING TIME:

The benefits of a job costing system*

Accurate job costing is crucial to the financial success of a job shop. It is even more important than accurate estimating, if only because the accuracy of estimating cannot be determined unless the costing is accurate.

Furthermore, most job shops do a fair number of repeat orders, so it is particularly important to gauge the profit or loss on a job before taking on a repeat order. Consequently, automating the labor portion of job costing by installing a computerized timekeeping system is quite attractive to manufacturers, particularly to job shops.

A timekeeping system can also assist expediting job routing and scheduling, job billing and invoicing, estimating and so on. In addition, timekeeping can also be used in the traditional ways, to keep track of employee attendance, to serve as the basis for a payroll system and to calculate employee productivity.

To understand how so many different types of information can be extracted from a timekeeping system, it is helpful to understand something about how a computer works, and what sort of information is stored in a timekeeping data base.

A typical job time slip, whether recorded on paper or on computer disk, consists of seven essential items of information: employee identification (who did the work); job or contract number (for whom was the work done); task identification (what sort of work was done); starting time, ending time, date (when was the work done and how long did it take); and production quantity (how much work was done).

Not every item is strictly necessary in every instance. For example, overhead work is not assigned to a contract. But these seven items include all the fundamental data required for a great variety of different applications.

Computers are inherently good at a number of basic tasks. Foremost among these tasks are searching, sorting, calculating, and printing.

Here is how a typical computer program works. Suppose the program is asked to print the hours worked for each employee for the week of January 11, 1988. The program steps are as follows:

1. **Search** the time slips for all slips dated on or after January 11, 1988 and on or before January 17, 1988.

2. **Sort** the time slips by date and by employee.

3. **Calculate,** for each day and for each employee, the number of hours worked.

4. **Print** a report showing the number of hours worked for each employee on each day.

This type of program is at the heart of systems that are designed to do time and attendance, hours and wages, job costing and so on.

■ Payroll

Now consider a program designed to do payroll. Starting with the information just printed, the program multiplies the number of hours worked each day by the employee's hourly wage, calculates the local, state, federal, and social security taxes, as well as other withholdings, and finally prints the checks along with the withholding statements and various accounting reports.

In an integrated accounting system, the hours worked by each employee are taken directly from the

---

*Reprinted with permission from The FABRICATOR® January/February 1988. Information about this publication and FMA membership on Page 269.

timekeeping data base. This saves work, since the report of daily hours worked does not have to be typed out separately by a clerk or secretary.

However, such a procedure is not nearly as simple as it seems. First, vacation time and sick pay must be dealt with separately, since this time does not appear on the job slips. Second, procedures must be developed for lateness, minor overtime, weekend work, lunch and dinner breaks, etc.

These considerations often outweigh the convenience and savings of a fully-integrated accounting system. Indeed, it is sometimes better to use an outside payroll service, which can keep up with changing tax codes and rates, than to try to do payroll inhouse. An integrated accounting system should not be viewed as an end in itself.

■ Shipping

Including shipping records in the timekeeping data base requires some additional explanation. The standard type of job time slip, discussed above, can also be used to record shipping information.

"Task identification" is used to specify shipping, and "production quantity" is used to specify the number of pieces shipped. However, it is also useful to record where the pieces are being shipped. Usually, they are shipped to the customer who ordered them, but pieces may also be shipped to other vendors for intermediate processing (painting, plating, etc.)

For this reason, a shipping record must have an extra field—"vendor"—to record where the pieces have gone. When the pieces are returned from a vendor after intermediate processing, this can also be recorded on a shipping slip, so that the information is readily available on the computer.

With this sort of information available in a computer file, it is easy to see how an expediting program can be constructed. When a customer calls to ask "where's my job," the expediter asks the computer to search for all job slips that refer to the job, sort them in a time-sequential order, and print them out (usually on the screen).

The shop that has this information in a computer file can immediately give the customer an accurate story: "That job was shipped to the painter on the eleventh. He usually takes a week, so we should have it back by the eighteenth. We should be able to ship it by the nineteenth."

■ Real-time Data Collection

Only a "real-time" system can provide the expediter with completely up-to-date information. But that is not the main reason for entering data on an immediate basis. The use of "remote" or "on-line" terminals for data entry will dramatically improve the accuracy of the data collected.

First of all, an on-line data entry terminal can screen out illegal entries, so that only real jobs and real task information is collected. (In systems in which data are collected only at the end of the day, errors are not corrected until the next morning—and sometimes not until three or four days later—if they are corrected at all.)

Second, time entries are recorded automatically by the computer, and are less subject to fudging. And third, real time data entry eliminates an entire step in the data entry process, thus improving accuracy and reducing costs.

Of course, a real time system is more expensive than a manual-entry system. But the improvement in accuracy is generally worth the extra cost.

■ Work Center Utilization

A timekeeping program can also monitor work center use. The program simply searches the job slips for labor under a particular work center, sorts the slips in order of date, and reports the number of hours worked on each work center for each day of the month.

In this way, at a glance, one can see which centers are underutilized, and which are overworked. This is particularly useful if a piece of high-cost capital equipment is defined as a single work center. With the computer, company's can make sure the equipment is getting optimal use.

■ Job Costing

Job costing is the main reason for installing a timekeeping system. The computer program searches the job slips for all records belonging to a particular job, sorts them according to work center, calculates the hours worked at each center, multiplies the hours worked by the rate for the work center, and adds up the dollars.

The printed report can be extremely detailed or can simply be a single number, the job labor cost. Furthermore, the actual job cost can be compared with the estimated cost at almost any level of detail, so the estimating program ("integrated" or "stand alone"—it does not really matter) can be cross-checked against the real world.

Job cost summaries can be used as input data for job profit and loss accounting programs. Clearly, some additional information will be needed at this stage, such as the cost of materials, outside vendor processing, sales commissions, etc.

Still, it is useful if the job costing program is "integrated" with the job profit and loss accounting program in some way, so that retyping of the same data in several different programs is minimized. The integration must be done with great care, so that occasional errors in the timekeeping data do not seriously affect the accounting data bases.

By their very nature, accounting programs make it hard to correct errors. Simply erasing and writing over data is not permitted. Instead, an "audit trail" of the changes must be kept.

For this reason, it is very important to "shield" accounting programs from data entry errors. This is best done inside the timekeeping data base, where error correction can be done quite easily.

When a job is shipped to the customer, a timekeeping program can also inform the accounting program of the fact that the shipment has taken place. The quantity shipped can also be transferred to the accounting data base.

In this way, the accounting program can be instructed to generate an invoice as soon as a job is shipped, thus reducing paperwork and also shortening the time lag between shipment and payment. Once again, there are dangers in "integrating" the timekeeping and accounting programs too closely, since errors in the accounting data base are difficult and expensive to correct.

Job scheduling and routing can be additional benefits of a timekeeping system, especially for jobs that are frequently repeated. If the same job has been run in several different ways, according to different routes, a glance at the job summary information can indicate the most efficient way to do the job in the future.

Furthermore, given the ability of a computer to sort information quickly, job lists can be sorted in order of scheduled delivery date or start date, so that work can be prioritized quite easily.

In manufacturing facilities that

make one or more standard products (as opposed to job shops, in which the product changes from day to day), it is possible to use timekeeping data to produce summaries on employee productivity, to pay piecework bonuses, and to determine the most efficient way to assign workers to various tasks.

When timekeeping programs are pushed in this direction, they can become part of an MRP package. As a rule, MRP and small business are rarely a good match, and MRP and the job shop can be a disastrous match. Still, employee productivity reports, used by themselves, can help any business that makes a standard product.

Purchasing a Job Costing Software Package

Learning to use a new software package is never as easy as the salesman says. Usually, the more complex or "integrated" the package is, the more difficult it will be to learn.

With a really difficult package, you may end up in a situation in which only one person in your company really understands how to operate it. What happens if that one person is ill, or quits?

To avoid this sort of problem, insist on guarantees. Expect to pay for some employee training, either directly or indirectly. Use an independent consultant to help you choose both hardware and software.

Above all, avoid buying "fully-integrated" software packages unless you can get them in "modules," purchased one at a time, which helps limit your risk and minimize the problems that occur during the training period. Do not try to do everything in one swift step, but instead proceed cautiously, starting with the modules that seem to give you the most rapid return on investment.

In other words, start by skimming off the cream. Do not try to computerize your entire business right away, but just those parts of your business where the payoff is best. To "fully" computerize your business can take a year. You may want to pause somewhere along the way to re-evaluate.

Output and Input

Another important consideration in choosing a software package is the input/output ratio: How much time and data must be put into the program in order to get it to run, and how much information is then output.

In some classes of programs (for example, scheduling), a large amount of data must be entered into the program in order to get any meaningful results. Having the data typed in on a daily basis is expensive, and this expense must be paid for from improved efficiency. The payback is not always clear.

In a timekeeping system, by contrast, there is very little new data entry. On the shop floor, employees punch in and out at a job shop clock instead of filling out time sheets. There is very little change in the level of effort required. In the office, jobs are entered into the computer when the purchase order is received. Very little data entry is involved. Thus, in a timekeeping system, the output/input ratio" is exceptionally high—you get a lot of information for very little additional work.

If a company employs fewer than one hundred people, its first move into the world of microcomputers should involve timekeeping, which gives job shops a bigger return on investment than any other kind of software.

Timekeeping is easy to use, easy to understand, and extraordinarily informative. In a small job shop, computerizing timekeeping should be the first step taken to computerize the business.

MEASURING PRODUCTIVITY IN THE JOB SHOP

There's got to be a better way*

For more than 20 years, manufacturing companies, worried about productivity, have been spending liberally and working sincerely in what has often proven to be a continuing and frustrating failure. Productivity in America has become what many consider a national disgrace.

In the world and domestic markets, the U.S. keeps losing. Losing is not the historic American way. There is confusion because, in general, things are being done better, but still America loses. Certainly, people think they are doing the right things.

The fact is that some things being done are wrong, so wrong that they negate many of the good things most fabricators do in their plants.

After more than 20 years, it is time the message is sent out clearly to executive America, "There's got to be a better way!"

True, a tiny percentage of plants, characterized as "repetitive manufacturing," have gained much from the Japanese method called "Just-In-Time" (JIT). There may be 100 or more of such plants. The majority of American plants, tens of thousands of all sizes, however, have spent their money on all sorts of expensive systems but have failed to budge productivity.

Technically speaking, these are "job shops." Job shops are "different." They are little understood and tend to react adversely to certain management actions and control methods which virtually everyone uses and accepts as conventional.

This article urges fabricators to look analytically at their own plants, and the accompanying sidebar suggests a specific way to do this. The methodology should lead to success in productivity and profit through a better understanding of their job shop.

▍Typical Job Shops

Job shops are plants which manufacture a variety of products using general-purpose machines, not machines dedicated to a single product. The variety makes each job order differ from the next in its sequence of processing steps (routing) and/or processing times at each routing point.

The paths of orders criss-cross and backtrack over and around one another so there is no clear pattern as is found in repetitive manufacturing. In this "helter-skelter" job shop world, jobs compete for processing time at almost every step in their routings. Competition often causes serious time-wasting traffic jams.

The queued-up idle work creates a management nightmare, which math scientists and economists call "The Job Shop Problem." Orders are completed later than promised. Tension runs high. Control efforts made in desperation, like priorities, give way to hot lists, which give way to red-hot lists and "drop everything" lists. An honest appraisal is such shops are out of control.

In plants with this queuing characteristic, the productivity issue is entirely different from ones without, and the problem is resilient to most shop control methods. The chaotic symptoms are well

*Reprinted with permission from The FABRICATOR® October 1991. Information about this publication and FMA membership on Page 269.

known, but little is understood about the cause and the cure.

Although not the only causes, two things, which managers perform with righteousness in running these shops, are wrong. These actions deepen the queues so they are massively counterproductive and wasteful of profit. These two actions are:

1. Using priorities to get stuck jobs moving.
2. Filling the shop with an overabundance of orders.

The unseen results in the typical job shop are that the cash flow cycle "flows" only about 24 minutes a day[1], and the average order falls uncontrollably idle for 19 days out of every 20 days that it is in the shop. Virtually every order is shipped late. This equals only a 5 percent efficiency rate—this, after 20 years of "productivity improvement."

There has got to be a better way.

▮ What is the Better Way?

The "better way" starts with making the cash flow and queue factor visible with measurements, using the technique described in this article's sidebar. The size and nature of the problem comes clear only with measurement, but nobody seems to measure productivity. Accountants and consultants don't. Therefore, fabricators should be doing it themselves.

Surely, fabricators would like to know how much productivity they have gained and how much more is still available month to month. They need to know what the values are in added profit and reduced working capital.

To see these as practical values, the method of measurement is crucial. It must provide clear data for managing productivity specifically in the fabricator's own job shop environment. It must identify and quantify both what is wrong and the benefits of making it right.

Like strong medicine, this may not go down smoothly. Some managers and executives might be disturbed by the measurement looking like an admission that they have been thwarting the operations and conveniently blaming labor. Their fears may be eased to know that everyone has been doing the same thing for the past 200 years.

Easing these fears is a good reason for the sensitive CEO to originate and participate daily in the productivity effort. The CEO, better than anyone else, is positioned to maximize the benefits by coordinating the efforts of his vice presidents and managers.

With a clear and accurate measurement, the definition of the problem and the "better way" solution become obvious. Start by using the measuring method presented here, and begin tomorrow to make substantial productivity gains.

Use the manual, no-cost methods described in the sidebar to jump productivity about 20 percent. Gains of 100 percent are a certainty for every business using any queue-reducing computer system backed up by this kind of measuring. Gains of 300 to 600 percent should generally be expected.

For complex shops, gains often reach 900 percent. For the most complex shops, like those which remanufacture jet engine parts, 1,143 percent has been attained.

These are actual numbers achieved in a variety of plants. Similar opportunities exist for other fabricators using the measurement method shown in the sidebar. The method works for the "Mom and Pop" shops, as well as for the giant 10,000-person shipyards, repair depots, or oil refineries.

Is Labor the Cause of Productivity Problems?

The real problem causing the failure of productivity is obscured by a false one. The flawed opinion that always puts labor at blame will be disproved by measuring productivity.

A practical measurement will reveal that productivity suffers from underutilization of all resources. In the shop, this shows vividly as idle Work-In-Process (WIP) inventory, which tends to stack up around many work centers. In the financial activity, productivity is usually unseen because accountants do not report it.

Yet, once measured, it appears as such a significant underutilization of capital that no executive, having seen it, will allow it to continue. WIP inventory clogging the shop and sluggish capital utilization are management, not labor, responsibilities. Because productivity is a management problem, it can be solved quickly with improvements which will be seen instantly.

This measurement will prove that "Work Flow equals Cash Flow," and the flow cycles of each are dominated by a productivity-eating waste called "queuing."

Executives who do not want to perform the measurement themselves should have their accountants recalculate this "Productivity Accounting" as part of their regular monthly *internal* operating statement. Managers need this information because they ought to pay closer attention to cash flow in their everyday decisions.

Caution: Do not let Productivity Accounting become part of the *external* accounting reports. Lending banks and stockholders will not approve, for example, that a fabricator is using capital only 24 minutes a day, if that is the case. This is a real number for most manufacturers, but none can know it until it is measured.

The false blame on labor can be set aside with a "scientific test." Observe the Department of Labor's monthly pronouncement of productivity's rise and fall referred to as "the productivity of America's labor." This is as harmful as it is wrong.

Workers do not whimsically flip a national productivity "Up-Down" switch. They perform the same month to month, yet productivity fluctuates. There must be another reason.

Labor is only one of three elements which go into production—labor, materials, and overhead. The labor portion of the product price generally ranges from 5 to 10 percent, and, generally, labor does what management sets out for it to do.

Neither labor's cost nor influence on management could be so great as to explain the low level a fabricator will find in measuring his own plant. It is, instead, how well these three elements are coordinated and managed which makes for productivity.

Proof that labor is not the major contributor to productivity fluctuations is in the Input/Output Balancing "scientific test" in this article's sidebar. This is a technique by which a fabricator reduces the quantity of orders input to the shop until output surges. Then the order load is stabilized by keeping the input equal to the output.

Less "in," more "out" is what will result, and that is what productive efficiency is all about. This *management* step causes about a 20 percent increase in productive output in the first month with *no* change in labor.

This author's observation is that U.S. labor does its job well, but labor and the other resources are managed to keep them busy, not to maximize productivity.

The Measuring Method

The productivity measuring method shown in the sidebar does the following:

1. Measures a typical order for how many total days it spends in the shop. The method uses the shop calendar, normally five days a week, 241 workdays in a shop year (fabricators using the method can adjust the calendar to their times).

2. Measures how many days the typical order was actually being worked on out of the total days.

3. Measures the difference between total time and working time, which is queuing, time spent idly waiting the next turn for further processing. If this time is excessive, a fabricator has a productivity problem.

4. Evaluates and equates the work flow cycle and the cash flow cycle—*work flow* for its effect on shop efficiency and competitiveness of order completion times, and *cash flow* for its effect on the amount of capital actually needed to run the manufacturing function and for the profit contribution of improved productivity (work flow) which cycles the cash flow faster.

It is suggested that you follow the worked example in the sidebar for understanding, then carefully substitute very accurate data for your own shop analysis. If the subject is a job shop, be forewarned. Productivity probably will be between 1 and 12.5 percent. If it is higher, the chances are that:

1. The processes are simple (fewer than five steps).

2. Inaccurate data was used or a mistake made.

3. The order load stands at about five orders. Scheduling five or fewer orders for productivity can be done flawlessly. Six orders can be scheduled 720 different ways, 10 orders 3,628,800 ways—only one of which may be both practical and productive. Many shops could have hundreds or thousands of orders, which is a challenging task.

4. The shop is already operating with a queue measuring and queue controlling computer system for scheduling.

5. The shop is not a job shop, so productivity is not a problem.

To get a quick answer to the size of a fabricator's productivity problem before taking the time to understand the example in the sidebar, use the "back of an envelope" formula shown in **Figure 1**. The formula will provide the ratio of average queue-time to work-time in your shop.[2]

Conclusion

Measuring method for productivity analysis

The following example[3] of Productivity Analysis is excerpted from an actual case. It was selected for its similarities to most job shop manufacturing activities.

It is suggested that after reading through the analysis for understanding, fabricators substitute their own plant's figures and recalculate the formulas to analyze their own shop productivity. Although this method uses simple arithmetic, it demands absolute accuracy of data. Do not approximate any numbers. Use accounting and shop records for all data.

If you have a job shop, you may find that your productivity measures very low. This is to be expected of shops having characteristic queuing of work in process. For a quick verification of the low measurement, compare the calculated average delivery time with your known delivery experience. If these match, it indicates that the input data is sound. If not, recheck the data.

If your final result does not fall within the norm of 1 percent to 12.5 percent productivity, or if you feel confused about any aspect, circle the main article's Reader Service Number to contact the author for free help.

The following analysis is for a fictitious job shop called *Sample Specialty Company*.

Q-CONTROL® Productivity Analyst

Data for Year Ending: 12/31/89	FOR: Sample Specialty Co.
SHEET METAL	Shop Name
87	Direct Labor Employees
163,976.4	Direct Labor Hours in 12 Months
932	Shop Orders Available For Work
1,665	Shop Orders Completed in 12 Months
241	Workdays in Shop Year
N/A	Value of WIP Inventory
$ 8,640,814	Sales Volume—same period
12	Hours Per Day (unequal shifts taken as a single shift)
25	% Cost of WIP Ownership
25	% Expected Sales Growth Rate
Percentage To Sales Of: —	
12.59 %	Direct Labor (DL)
28.31 %	Direct Material (DM)
7.66 %	Variable Overhead (VOH)
21.21 %	Fixed Overhead (FOH)
30.23 %	Profit
100 %	Total (100%) Percent

An estimated 1.4 people work on an order as a team on average.

IDLE TIME IN JOBS (Shop Orders)

This data allows analysis of the idle time in the average job process.

How long jobs are active is a function of labor skills, attitudes, machine technology, and manufacturing design. We need not examine these now since changes in these areas take considerable time to influence. Instead, we examine the idle queue time which can be controlled by managing, with immediate profit and productivity gains.

To find the idle time, we measure how long an average job works, compared with its total time in the shop. The difference is how long it waits in queue.

These are time measurements. We use them to measure productivity, then relate productivity to: dollars of profit, working capital needs, cash flow, and effect on profit.

Time Calculations

Working Time Per Hypothetical "Average" Order is 5.86 days. Calculation:

$$\text{Working Days Per Order} = \frac{\text{Total DL Hours In 12 Months}}{\text{Orders} \times \text{Hrs.} \times \text{People} \atop \text{Completed} \quad \text{Per Day} \quad \text{Per Order}}$$

$$\frac{163,976.4}{1,665 \times 12 \times 1.4} = 5.86 \text{ Working Days Per Order}$$

Order Completion Rate is 6.90 per day. Calculation:

$$\text{Completion Rate} = \frac{\text{Orders Completed in 12 Months}}{\text{Workdays in Shop Year}} = \frac{1,665}{241}$$

= 6.9 Orders Per Day

Total Time of Orders in the shop is 134.90 Days Flow Time. Calculation:

$$\text{Flow Time} = \frac{\text{Shop Orders "Live"}}{\text{Order Completion Rate}} = \frac{932}{6.9} = 134.90 \text{ Total Days}$$

Waiting Time In Queues is 129.04 Q-Days. Calculation:

Q-Days = Days Flow Time - Working Days Per Order
= 134.90 - 5.86
= 129.04 Days

Saving half this waiting time, 64.52 days, is a reasonable management goal. As a result, we propose reducing flow time to 70.38 days. Calculation:

Proposed Days = Q-Days divided by 2 plus Workdays
= (129.04 / 2) + 5.86
= 70.38 Days

RESULTS: Quicker completions = Improved Deliveries, More Billings.
Less In-Process Inventory = Lower Cost, More Cash, Less Shop Confusion, More Profit.

PRODUCTIVITY EFFECT PROPOSED

Present Utilization of WIP = 4.35%. Calculation:

$$= \frac{\text{Working Days Per Order}}{\text{Present Days Flow Time}} \times 100$$

$$= \left(\frac{5.86}{134.90}\right) \times 100$$

= 4.35% Present WIP Utilization

Proposed Utilization of WIP is 8.33% (Easy first goal). Calculation:

$$\text{Proposed WIP Utilization} = \frac{\text{Working Days Per Order}}{\text{Proposed Days Flow Time}} \times 100$$

$$= \left(\frac{5.86}{70.38}\right) \times 100$$

= 8.33% Proposed WIP Utilization

Present flow time of orders averages 134.90 workdays or 26.98 weeks.

Propoosed flow time will average 70.38 workdays or 14.08 weeks. (Easy goal begins to look better in practical results.)

FINANCIAL ANALYSIS

Overview:

In manufacturing, cash and work flows are almost identical because working capital spends most of its life as WIP. Thus, analyzing WIP utilization in the work flow cycle provides a practical, parallel analysis of capital utilization in the cash flow cycle.

Present Work Flow Cycles are 1.79 per year. Calculation:

Present Flow Cycles = $\dfrac{\text{Workdays in Shop Year}}{\text{Present Days Flow Time Per Job}}$

= 241 / 134.90

= 1.79 Per Year

Proposed Work Flow Cycles = 3.42 Per Year. Calculation:

Proposed Flow Cycles = $\dfrac{\text{Workdays in Shop Year}}{\text{Proposed Days Flow Time Per Job}}$

= 241 / 70.38

= 3.42 Per Year

Effect Of Proposed Cycles With Present Sales Level

With STATIC SALES of............... $8,640,814
Increasing Cycles:
  Reduces WIP by $1,613,989
  Reduces Overhead by .... $ 403,497
  Reduces Required Working
    Capital by $2,017,486
  Increases Profit by .... $ 403,497
                                (Big bucks from
                                  a little goal)

Calculation:

WIP Value With Present Cycles = $\dfrac{\text{Sales - Profit}}{\text{Present Work Flow Cycles}}$

= $\dfrac{8{,}640{,}814 - \left(8{,}640{,}814 \times \dfrac{30.23}{100}\right)}{1.79}$

= $3,374,621 Present Average WIP

WIP Value With Proposed Cycles = $\dfrac{\text{Sales - Profit}}{\text{Proposed Work Flow Cycles}}$

= $\dfrac{8{,}640{,}814 - \left(8{,}640{,}814 \times \dfrac{30.23}{100}\right)}{3.42}$

= $1,760,633 Proposed Average WIP

Reducing WIP Frees Up Funds, Reduces Overhead And Adds Profit.

Calculation:

Freed Up Funds Value = Present WIP Value - Proposed WIP Value

= $ 3,374,621 - $1,760,633

= $ 1,613,989 Freed Up

Reduced Overhead = Freed Up Funds x Cost of WIP Ownership

= $1{,}613{,}989 \times \left(\dfrac{25}{100}\right)$

= $403,497 Overhead Savings

Reduced costs are increased profits, shown here as a percentage of sales.

%Profit Added = $\dfrac{\text{Reduced Overhead}}{\text{Static Sales Volume}}$

= $\left(\dfrac{403{,}497}{8{,}640{,}814}\right) \times 100$

= 4.67 % Added Profit

Total Value With Static Sales:

Reduced Capital Required = WIP Funds Freed Up + Reduced Overhead

= $ 1,613,989 + $403,497

= $ 2,017,486 Capital Savings

Effect Of Proposed Cycles With 25% Increase In Sales

With Increased Sales of 25%

Proposed Increase = Proposed Sales - Present Sales

= [8,650,814 + (8,640,814 x .25)] - 8,640,814

= $ 2,160,204

Even with increasing cycles from 1.79 to 3.42, assuming no other improvements, the WIP required is lower. Calculation:

Proposed WIP = $\dfrac{\text{Proposed Sales - Profit}}{\text{Proposed Work Flow Cycles}}$

= $\dfrac{[(8{,}640{,}814 \times 1.25) - [(8{,}640{,}814 \times 1.25) \times .3023]}{3.42}$

= $2,200,791 Proposed

Which is a $ 1,173,831 savings from the Present WIP.

= $ 3,374,621 - $2,200,791

= $ 1,173,831

But the greatest benefit comes from the contribution to profit from the sales increase, provided controls can pass the increase through substantially unchanged overheads. Then the costs are only the direct costs, and gross margin becomes contribution to profit.

Direct costs for increased sales are: DL 12.59 %
                                            DM 28.31 %
                                            VOH 7.66 %
                    Total Direct Costs 48.56 %
                    Leaving Gross Margin 51.44 %

FINANCIAL SUMMARY

Contribution To Profit = Gross Margin x Proposed Increase

= 51.44 % x 2,160,204

= $ 1,111,209

Savings Of WIP OH   = $ 293,458

CTP Plus WIP Savings = $ 1,404,666

With 25 % increase to sales:

Total Profitability   = $ 4,016,785 Calculation:

Profit Achieved On Prior Sales   = $ 2,612,118
Contribution To Profit On Sales Increase = $ 1,111,209
WIP Overhead Savings   = $ 293,458
Profit From Queue Reduction   = $ 1,404,666
Total Profit   = $ 4,016,785
Plus, Freed Up Capital From WIP   = $ 1,173,831
Total Value Of Queue Reduction   = $ 5,190,615

Based on this conservative view of time savings, each day of the proposed 64.51 days reduction in Queue Time contributes $21,771.03 to your profit. Calculation:

Contribution = $\dfrac{\text{Contribution To Profit On Increased Sales} + \text{WIP Ownership Cost Savings}}{\text{Average Queue Days Saved}}$

= $\dfrac{\$ 1{,}111{,}209 \;+\; 293{,}458}{64.52}$

= $ 21,771 Per Day

Note: This is the opportunity value of a Cash Flow Day saved.

Small improvement goals are easy to reach. Repeat them as many times as possible in your shop. Every shop gets at least 100 percent gains. Most get between 300 and 600 percent. Some have reached 900 percent. One gained 1,140 percent, but that was a very complex, almost uncontrollable shop before the productivity effort was started.

It is recommended that fabricators now measure their own manufacturing, carefully substituting very accurate numbers for the data used in the example.

$$\text{Q-factor} = \frac{(Q \times I \times T \times E) - M}{M}$$

Where **Q** = Quantity of orders in the shop on an average day during the period to be measured.

T = Workdays during the period. (For most shops there are 241 workdays in a year.)

I = Work hours per shop day. (Prorate unequal shifts as if they were extensions of the primary shift.)

M = Manhours of total direct labor during the period. (Use the actual payroll hours.)

E = Employees working simultaneously as a team on a single order on average.)

Figure 1

Shown here is a "back-of-the-envelope" formula for calculating the ratio of average queue-time to work-time in a job shop.

The information presented in this article was prepared by Wm. E. Sandman, Wm. E. Sandman, Inc., Boca Raton, Florida. The following references were used in the article:

1. About 2,000 job shops were measured. These averaged 5 percent for both the utilization of capital and productivity. For an eight-hour business day, 5 percent is 24 minutes.

*2. Reference **How To Win Productivity In Manufacturing**, Wm. E. Sandman, AMACOM, American Management Associations, 1981.*

From this analysis it is clear that queuing is the major cause for low productivity. All other reasons combined are relatively insignificant.

This provides management with a focal direction, reduction of queues, which is both manageable and measurable. It should, likewise, be clear that any shop decision or management system which fails to control the natural proliferation of queues is missing the main point. ■

RETHINKING THE SHORT-TO MEDIUM-RUN SHEET METAL PROCESS *

Would most fabricators like to punch, shear, and bend anywhere from 1 to 500 finished sheet metal parts profitably?

Would they like to get those orders out the door before competitors can even submit their quotes?

Would most fabricators like to make new products or accommodate product design changes in hours or days without need for special tooling?

These and other benefits are possible for some fabricators, using application-proven technology, if they are willing to rethink their short-to medium-run sheet metal processes.

Rethink? Today's fax machine shortens negotiations between buyers and sellers by weeks. Its payback in time savings makes it a relatively low cost, valuable investment. That kind of rational approach is what is being suggested in sheet metal processing.

■ Competition—The Driving Force

The reasons users may want to rethink their sheet metal processes are much like the two sides of a single coin. On the one side is the need to enhance the fabricator's competitive stance by being able to respond faster to customer requirements. On the other side is the possible limitation of traditional fabricating technology.

With conventional sheet metal processes, response time can be slow because part-specific tooling needs to be changed to run different parts, especially when bending parts on press brakes.

There is another fundamental problem: there are too many links in a typical fabricating chain (see **Figure 1**), as opposed to a streamlined process. Multiple operations require more in-process inventory buffers and repetitive parts handling. These can eat away at manufacturing time, personnel time, floor space, and profits.

Shortcomings can be overcome if fabricators apply a different processing method that reduces throughput and job setup time, making small lot sizes economical to produce by employing fewer machine operations with flexible tooling systems.

■ Punch and Shear Together

Reducing manufacturing time and costs begins with the punching operation. With turret presses, all tools must be rotated to a single striking position. By contrast, live head punching/shearing technology uses an independent press head for each of its 23 punches, expandable to 28 punches, including auto-indexing. Not only does it eliminate turret-indexing time, but the live head machine also needs only ½ to ⅓ as much part-positioning time.

On a CNC turret-type machine, it is common to use a given punch's shape over the entire sheet before indexing the next punch to the single striking position. The multiple striking positions on a live head machine permit concurrent and rapid punching, so up to ⅔ of part-positioning time can be saved.

The live head machine is also capable of shearing, normally a separate operation, to reduce overall part throughput time. The built-in right-angle shear eliminates the need for multiple part handling and in-process inventory buffers with before-and-after shearing machine stagings.

*Reprinted with permission from The FABRICATOR® August 1990. Information about this publication and FMA membership on Page 269.

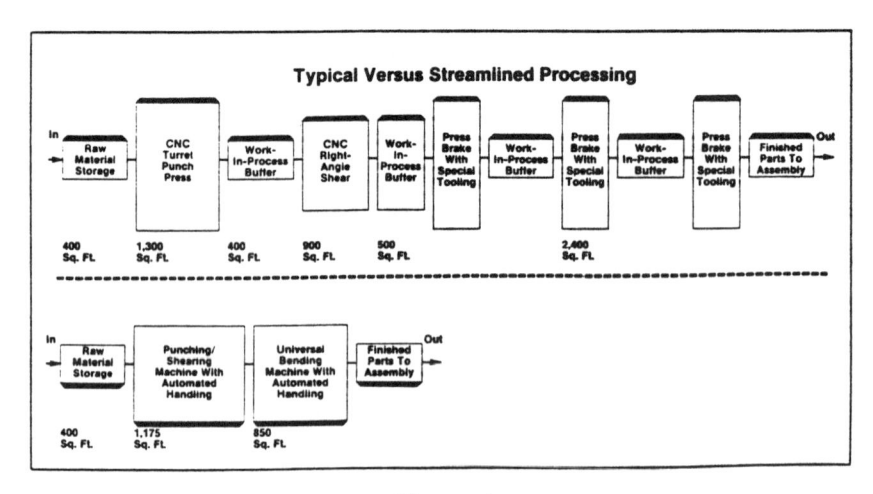

Figure 1

With only one setup and referencing instead of two, part accuracy is higher. The live head machine's right-angle shear is used to trim the incoming sheet, separate multiple parts of the same part, or separate multiple parts of dissimilar parts in a dynamic nest.

Figure 2 compares features of the live head CNC punching/shearing machine with the corresponding features of conventional CNC turret punch presses.

Universal Bending Machine

The distinctive aspect of the universal CNC bending machine lies in its integral tooling. The tooling can produce all bends, ± 180 degrees with varying radii, for any shape panel.

Press brakes may be equipped with standard tools and require high operator skill levels, or may use multiple sets of dedicated tooling with multiple machine operations to form finished parts.

The universal bending machine allows forming of different-shaped parts in one operation without the need to design, build, maintain, store, or changeover special tooling. When equipped with predesigned material handling interfaces, it can run untended, with two-minute changeovers between part runs.

How A Universal Bending Machine Works

Figure 3 shows a universal bending machine employing the panel bending method. It also shows a sequence of part bends to demonstrate how this method works.

This panel forming method uses a combination of air bending and wiping techniques to form all ± 180-degree part bends using a single, universal blankholder tooling system. Each incoming prepunched, notched blank arrives flat and remains flat on the worktable throughout the forming process.

The blank's inside corner notch provides the NC reference location. Bends are seldom gauged from outside edges. Therefore, any over/under or out-of-square material condition appears in the outermost flanges instead of accumulating in the panel's center.

A CNC-directed manipulator moves the part to the universal blankholder, a compact arrangement of ½-inch-

Comparison of Live Head CNC Punching/Shearing Machine to Conventional CNC Turret Punch Press

Live Head CNC Punching/Shearing Machine	CNC Turret Press
1. 23 stations, every station is live. 2. 20 stations have tools in 5-tool, quick-change chartridges. 3. Punch and die positions are fixed with respect to each other, allowing tighter die clearances. Tool lives can be up to 50 percent longer. 4. Positioning referenced to workpiece centers, not to edges or flanges subject to distortion. 5. Stand-alone or capable of interfacing with companion forming machine tool in a pre-engineered automated system. 6. Right-angle shear is built-in standard feature. Punching and shearing can be done on a single machine. 7. Suitable for up to 11-GA steel.	1. Turret indexes tools to one striking position, located with a shot pin. 2. Individual tools only. 3. Relative positions of punch and die subjects to tolerances that may vary from station-to-station and with machine age. Tool lives may be shortened by punch-and-die sets not being exactly aligned. 4. Workpiece positioning referenced to back of workholder and side of table. Camber/bow induced in workpiece from punching or shearing may shift workpiece away from initial positioning. 5. Designed as stand-alone unit. Interfacing with other units in a cell or system may be difficult. 6. Most with punching only. Other operations require one or more separate machines, in-process buffer storage, additional setup time, and loss of initial positioning accuracy. More floor space required for equivalent throughput. 7. Some models can handle heavier gauges.

Figure 2

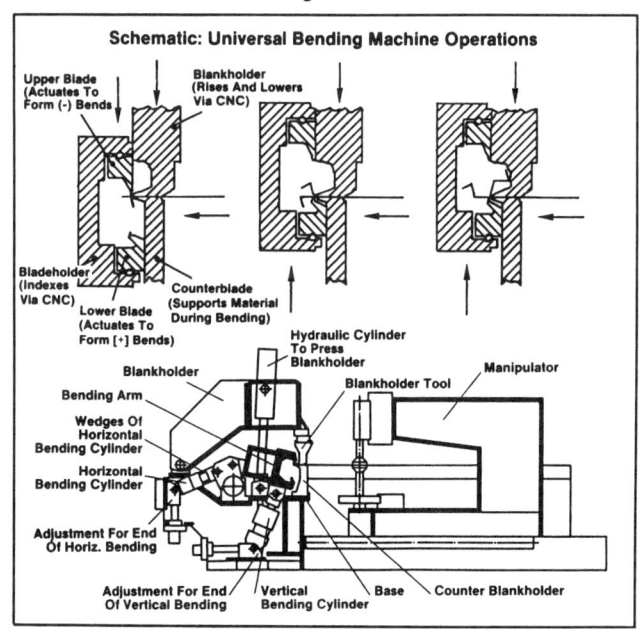

Figure 3
Universal bending technology uses a combination of air bending and wiping techniques to produce up to ± 180-degree part bends in one operation with varying radii on all four sides of sheet metal panels.

wide die segments and incremental end blocks. The blankholder rises to allow the blank to extend over the table's edge and lowers to firmly hold the workpiece in position during the wiping/forming process.

The manipulator moves the blank to each position. When the blank is positioned over the table's edge, an upper or lower wiping blade is CNC actuated to produce the desired bend. Then the blankholder releases its grip, allowing the manipulator to index the part for additional up or down bends.

The manipulator can bring the part back out of the forming area, rotate it 90 degrees, 180 degrees, or 270 degrees, and align it to form other sides of the panel with this up/down forming technique.

The bending blades control the bend angle and radius. The distance of the blade to the die set is set by CNC, and determines the bend radius. The closer the blade, the smaller the resulting radius. The overall stroke of the blade, programmed and controlled by CNC, determines the angle.

Many configurations of angles and radii can be produced with the two standard forming blades and standard die segments. Radii can be programmed to vary from bend to bend and part to part, an advantage when forming prepainted and vinyl-clad materials.

Multiple and complex bends can be made with wiping/forming technology. **Figure 4** shows some of the bends that can be made in the same operation. Users have applied this bending capability to avoid adding secondary operations such as spot welds and product stiffeners.

▌Quick Changeover

Part changeover requires activating a part program from computer memory and automatically grouping the proper number of die segments. Fabricators can feed the machine material manually or with pre-engineered automated material handling equipment.

Part changeovers take from 90 to 120 seconds or less, because each part-specific bend is contained in the software, not in special-built die sets.

Metals that can be processed include cold rolled steel (CRS) aluminum, stainless steel, galvanized galvanealed, prepainted, vinyl clad, and more. Material thicknesses from 11 to 24 gauge with bend lengths up to 157 inches are possible. Maximum bend heights are 8 inches.

▌Cutting Processing Costs

As a stand-alone unit, a live head CNC punching/shearing machine avoids tool indexing time, reduces part positioning time, and combines operations to cut the overall manufacturing time required to punch and shear parts. One universal bending machine can form finished parts faster than multiple press brake operations, according to the manufacturer.

Integrating the two machines in an automated, streamlined operation enables users to cut processing costs. Integration does not limit the ability to operate either machine independently on different jobs. Comparisons with traditional processes are shown in **Figure 5**.

▌Applying Fewer Operations

Computer Integrated Manufacturing (CIM) is a strategy to gain an edge over competitors with:

1. Faster throughput or door-to-door time, from raw material to high quality finished parts ready for shipment

2. Less in-process inventories, including tooling, partially fabricated parts, and idle capital equipment

3. Quicker response to current and

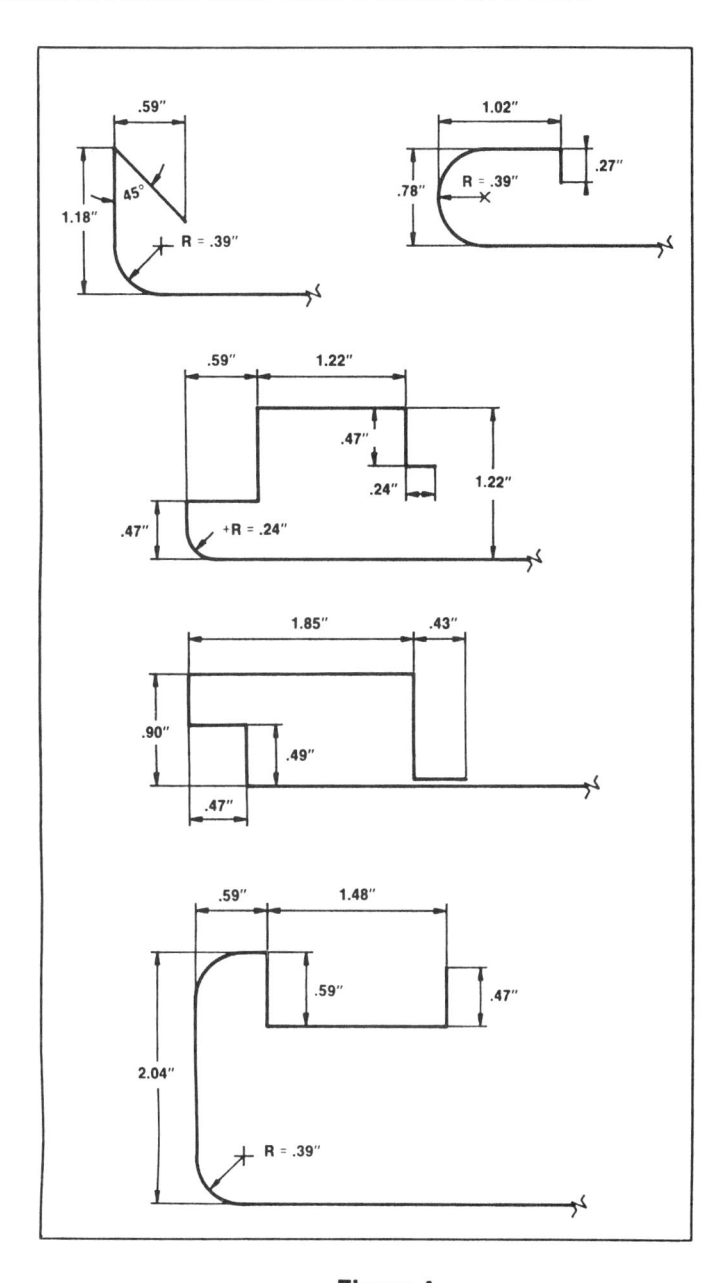

Figure 4
Cross-section of typical bends that can be formed on a universal bending machine in one operation.

Comparison Of Part Processing Methods

	Typical Method Average Requirements With Typical Method (Turret Punch Press, Shears, And Press Brakes)	Streamlined Method Average Requirements With Steamlined Method (Live Head Punching/Shearing Machine And Universal Bending Machine)
Number Of Machines	6	2
Total Setup Time Required For Changeover To New Run Of Parts	3 Hours (½ Hour x 6 Machines)	5 Minutes
Typical Part Throughput Time, From Start To Finish	3 Days	3 Minutes
Annual Cost Of In-Process and Post-Process Part Inventories	Usually Substantial	Negligible
Special Tooling	Always Required	Seldom Required
Floor Space Requirements (Includes Machinery And Finished Part Inventories)	10,000 Square Feet	4,000 Square Feet
Forklifts	2 Full-Time Lift Trucks With 2 Full-Time Drivers	1 Stand-By Lift Truck With No Assigned Driver
Number Of Part Handlings	6	1
Number Of Operators	6 (Plus 2 Lift Truck Drivers)	1

Figure 5

future customer requirements, including product modifications and new products

Given these objectives, the practical places for fabricators to start applying CIM are in areas that yield the highest rewards with the least amount of risk.

A strategy employing fewer operations to punch, shear, and bend finished parts may fit this initial CIM investment classification for some fabricators. With fewer operations required, fabricators can gain:

1. Closer accuracy with fewer machine setups and part referencings
2. Faster door-to-door throughput time
3. Less in-process inventory with fewer before-and-after machine stagings
4. Fewer material handlings and less material handling equipment
5. Less floor space
6. Fewer machines to buy, maintain, and staff with operators
7. Fewer machines to program for changeovers to different part runs
8. Fewer machine/part programs to alter for product design changes or new products

Significance for Flexible Automation

These streamlined machines are modular units that do not use special tooling. Users can apply units and interface them with material handling equipment because they are designed for these interfaces.

Most conventional punching, shearing, and bending equipment were originally designed for stand-alone rather than system applications. Accordingly, as appealing as automated cells or other aspects of CIM might be, it can be challenging to integrate conventional machine tools, material handling equipment, and software.

Manufacturers invest in automation to improve their long-term competitive stance, not just for immediate gain. Current Manufacturing Resource Planning (MRP) systems depend on sales forecasts rather than actual orders-in-hand.

The reliance on forecasts is not surprising, given the flexibility limitations of production equipment available when MRP software was written. Now, the capability of today's equipment makes flexible order-driven MRP more feasible.

Importance of "Time-to-Market"

"Time-to-market" has become a major strategic issue among top executives of small, medium, and large companies. Why? Because supplying customers what they want as fast or faster than competitors provides profitable advantages.

For example, consider the experience of a commercial lighting manufacturer. The company learned of a special type of lighting system, including a unique sheet metal housing, that was desired quickly by a major airport in Florida.

The company won the project for two reasons: time and cost. Using a dual-machine fabricating system, they were able to create NC part programs and begin running production parts in two weeks because there was no need to design or build any special tooling for forming operations.

Time-to-market, using conventional fabricating methods, may have been up to one year or longer. This lighting company's manufacturing advantage permitted them to beat competitors and win another project.

Time-to-market is also a "hot" issue due to today's global competition. U.S. markets are vulnerable, as competition now extends beyond the

States. While at first this may seem to be a problem, U.S. fabricators have more domestic and global opportunities if they apply smart manufacturing strategies.

Another reason for the importance of time-to-market is shorter product life cycles. Product technology and improvements are occurring so rapidly that new products become obsolete faster. This necessitates an ability to respond fast with new products or modifications if fabricators are to survive and prosper in the global market.

Many Japanese, European, and U.S. companies have invested heavily in tools that pay off with improvements in their design engineering and production flexibility. Remember, the primary purpose of CIM is to gain a competitive advantage with shorter time-to-market for current products, new products, and product modifications.

Customer contacts and market research keep fabricators abreast of what customers want. When shifts in customer requirements are detected, fabricators go to work with flexible, practical tools that enable them to design, build, sell, and profit more than competitors who cannot respond as quickly.

Even if a few customers prefer a special type of product, these requirements are affordable to meet because of the flexibility and productivity of their manufacturing equipment and systems. The objective is to make lot sizes as few as one economical to produce quickly in response to actual orders, instead of sales forecast-driven production that ends up in inventory waiting for customer orders.

The strategic time-to-market capability of flexible manufacturing equipment has now become a significant factor in the evaluation of capital equipment for all businesses, including fabricators.

The sidebar on page 35, a cost justification worksheet, has two parts. The first part deals with strategic marketing issues from a cost-savings perspective, while the second half focuses solely on manufacturing cost savings.

▌Fabricating with Faster Market Response

Consider the impact on sales and profits of being able to modify or improve products or offer customers new products without having to design, build, procure, or maintain special tooling. Meeting new customer requirements with new products can be accomplished in hours or days with live head punching/shearing technology and universal bending technology.

Also, prototypes can be made on actual production tools, rather than relying on personal craftsmanship that may not always be repeatable on the shop floor. Converting a handcrafted prototype to the first production part often requires costly and time-consuming reworking/debugging of tooling before acceptable parts can be manufactured dependably in production.

Today's fabricating, like the fax machine, uses practical technology to reduce operations, shorten throughput time, and lower in-process inventories.

And, today's fabricating is earning more profits through lower manufacturing costs and improved customer satisfaction with faster response to their requirements—including product specials. Streamlined processing is being used by job shops and original equipment manufacturers to gain competitive advantages.

The information presented in this article was prepared by Russell Branton, Vice President, Salvagnini America, Inc., Hamilton, Ohio.

IT'S TIME TO EXPAND YOUR PLANT

Should you relocate?*

By Kent E. Crippin

Once the question has been answered about relocating your existing operations, several economic issues should be reviewed to determine the most appropriate location. Naturally, while site requirements and transportation linkages are important, the issues of economic advantage and disadvantage are paramount to selecting the most appropriate location.

Each company has its own requirements and criteria. The criteria should address several issues that may impact the bottom line, thus determining the economic or financial advantages and disadvantages to relocation.

Analyzing these issues and the results will provide the opportunity to gain a perspective of how relocation might be able to contribute to the bottom line. Thus, management should determine whether or not they should relocate their company. Relocation then might not be such a remote consideration.

■ Relocation Factors

Factors that often influence the economics of relocation generally fall into one of four categories. However, when each of the categories are combined, they can generate considerable economic advantage to the company. Those advantages are:

1. Economic incentives
2. State manufacturing climate
3. Taxes – inventory/merchants – manufacturing
4. Employee taxes/benefits

Each of the factors has its own characteristics and varies from location to location. The combination of state and local level factors will indicate opportunities that can be achieved at the time of relocation.

However, there is an extensive negotiation period that may need to occur between the owner and local and state officials to obtain the greatest economic advantage possible. Seeking the appropriate location with the right benefits is a significant task.

Therefore, it is necessary to have a good understanding of the factors that can influence relocation.

■ Economic Incentives

Economic incentives include a variety of tools that local government may use depending upon its desire to attract industry. The incentives usually focus on:

Incentive	Government
Property Tax Abatement	City/County
New Job Tax Credits	State
Investment Tax Credits	State
Sales Tax Exemptions	City/County
Utility Co. Incentive Plans	City/County
Enterprise Zones	City/State
CDBG Grants	City/State
Loan Programs	State
Waiver of Building Permits and Fees	City
Corporate Tax Benefits	State

Each of these incentive programs and community benefits should be understood by the owner in order to

*Reprinted with permission from The FABRICATOR® June 1993. Information about this publication and FMA membership on Page 269.

obtain a perspective of the economic benefit for locating in a community and state. A description of the incentives is as follows:

Property Tax Abatement. The abatement of real estate property taxes is generally for a period of 10 years. The abatement can be for a greater period or up to 25 years, but extension is only in specific cases and in accordance with a specific type of program.

Abatement is generally governed by state statute for local government.

The tax issue becomes relatively significant when considering the amount of real estate property tax paid by industry. Many local communities have the authority to abate either all or a certain portion of the real estate taxes.

Many areas, while they allow real estate taxes to be abated, omit property taxes generated for school districts. In any event, each area is different and should be reviewed to determine how to maximize the respective real estate property tax abatement.

Commercial personal property tax in some instances can also be abated. This is not as common a practice, but is one that should be reviewed by the company owner. When considering a new plant and the purchase of new equipment or even using existing equipment, the taxes can be significant. If they can possibly be abated, it results in a significant advantage to the bottom line.

The abatement of taxes is an effective program used to generate and attract new development to a community. Tax abatements are generally agreed to in the form of a schedule of tax payments or payment in lieu of taxes during the abatement period.

New Job Tax Credits. A corporate tax credit is provided for each new job created at the relocation site. Job credits are often provided in an Enterprise Zone and as a state incentive.

Investment Tax Credits. This is a corporate tax credit based upon the value of the facility at the time of construction. The tax credit is generally carried for a 10-year period as a credit against the corporation's state taxes.

Sales Tax Exemption. A sales tax exemption is provided on construction materials used to construct the new facility and for the purchase of plant manufacturing equipment and machinery. The exemption is a one-time exemption.

Utility Company Incentive Plans. The providers of electrical power each have incentive plans to attract companies to new sites. Usage costs are generally discounted over a five-year period by each of the providers.

Enterprise Zone. The Enterprise Zones differ in their benefits. Each state and zone has its own schedule of benefits.

Community Development Block Grant (CDBG). This is a grant from a state that passes through the community to finance construction of public infrastructure.

State Loan. Very often, state economic development agencies will provide short-term loans for interim construction financing and other uses at a very low interest rate. Sometimes the borrower may receive a zero percent interest rate. Depending on the situation, the loan may be for as much as 10 or 20 years.

Building Permits and Fees. It is possible for a community to waive these fees. Such fees can be extensive if plans call for a multimillion-dollar building.

Corporate Tax Benefit. Tax credits are applied to the annual corporate tax payment in the respective state where the facility is located.

These ten economic incentives represent incentives that are generally available. Note that the use of any one incentive is negotiable with the governmental entity responsible for its administration.

In some states and localities, additional incentives may be available. Serious candidates for relocation should keep abreast of both state and local incentives.

Very often, a competition develops when a city or state learns of the potential relocation. The competition for a significant industry such as a metal fabricator is understandable from the perspective of the additional jobs that would be provided in the community and the economic benefit associated with those jobs.

The real meaning of the impact cannot be appreciated without reviewing the dollars associated with that impact in the community.

Manufacturing Climate by State

States are generally divided into two groups: states with high manufacturing intensity, and those with low manufacturing intensity. For a state to be a manufacturing-intense state, it must meet one or both of the following criteria averaged over the last four years:

1. The state must contribute more than two percent of the value of manufacturing shipments in the country. Two percent is the average value of manufacturing shipments per state in the U.S.

2. The state must have 16.15 percent or more of its work force engaged in manufacturing. This percentage was the national average in 1986-1989.

This author's company recommends 16 factors (see **Figure 1**) for owners to consider when reviewing a relocation site. These factors serve only as an indicator of the relative importance for selecting a state in which to locate a manufacturing plant.

Inventory/Merchants – Manufacturers Tax

This is a tax on inventory. The designations vary by state. Some states have done away with this tax, but there are many that still impose it. Such taxes can be significant depending on the size of a metal fabricator's inventory.

This would probably only be significant in the event of stock items, but since most fabricators perform work on bid or custom-oriented basis and immediately ship to the customer, these taxes may not be a major issue for fabricators.

Employee Taxes/Benefits

Many owners, when considering relocation, take into consideration the impact upon their employees and key management. Since taxes vary from state to state, it is pertinent to deter-

State Relocation Factors	
Rank	Factor
1	Average Hourly Wage
2	Education
3	Workers' Compensation Insurance Levels
4	Statutory Average Workers' Compensation Cost per Case
5	Percentage of Manufacturing Workers Unionized
6	Expenditure Growth vs. Personal Income Growth over 5 Years
7	Value Added
8	Fuel and Electric Energy Costs
9	Tax Effort
10	Change in Average Hourly Wage over 5 Years
11	Unemployment Compensation Trust Fund Net Worth
12	Average Unemployment Compensation Benefits
13	Change in Tax Effort over 5 Years
14	Change in Unionization over 5 Years
15	Debt Growth vs. Personal Income Growth over 5 Years
16	Man-hours Lost

Figure 1
These are 16 factors recommended for metal forming and fabricating company owners to consider when reviewing a relocation site.

mine how the relocation may affect employee taxes.

In some instances, there is very little difference from one state to another. It could be that an employer would have to pay additional salary and wages to coerce current management and employees to move to the new location. This also applies to benefits from one state to another.

Economic Advantage & Disadvantage

When determining the economic advantage or disadvantage in a relocation consideration, the analysis should focus upon the tax structure of the respective community and state.

The basis for economic incentives and considerations for relocation generally focus upon the tax structure of the community and to what degree the community is willing to abate the tax revenues.

Therefore, when analyzing a potential relocation site, the incentive can be quantified and measures can be established for comparing one location to another. The community should further be reviewed to determine if there is a "match" between the community and the industry when there are no incentives.

The economic incentives and the resulting analysis should be viewed as an indicator of the community's willingness to work with the fabricator, thus providing the amenities to locate in their community.

As an example of considering the impact of economic incentives, examine in **Figure 2** the 10-year summary of economic incentives for a manufacturer who is currently considering relocation at one of five sites.

It is interesting to note that each community in Figure 2 did not approach the subject in the same manner. Consequently, because of the capabilities of the respective cities and their authority, the total incentive could impact the location by a range from $1.3 million to more than $13

Collection of Articles from THE FABRICATOR® 173.

10-Year Summary - Economic Incentives Analysis Plant Relocation					
Economic Incentives	Community 1	Community 2	Community 3	Community 4	Community 5
Tax Credits	$ 0 [1]	$ 387,750	$ 387,750	$ 387,750	$ 0
Enterprise Zone	476,000	0	0	0	8,444,185
Sales Tax Exemption	884,000	0	0 [2]	0 [2]	0 [2]
Utility Company Incentives	336,225	448,044	447,324	320,868	320,868
Property Tax Abatement	7,472,909	0	0 [3]	0 [3]	0 [3]
Special Bonds	0	0	8,302,340	5,885,487	6,822,760
Economic Incentive	9,169,134	835,794	9,137,414	6,594,105	13,979,568
CDBG Grant	500,000	500,000	500,000	500,000	0
Total 10-Year Benefit	$9,669,134	$1,335,794	$9,637,414	$7,094,105	$13,797,568

[1] Tax credits included in Enterprise Zone total
[2] Sales tax exemption included in Special Bond total
[3] Property tax abatement in Special Bond total

Figure 2
This is a 10-year summary of economic incentives for a manufacturer who is currently considering relocation at one of five sites. Note that each community did not approach the subject in the same manner. In each community, tax abatement is a major issue.

million.

In each community illustrated in Figure 2, tax abatement is the major issue. However, even without tax abatement, there are significant dollars that can be achieved over a 10-year period.

Is Relocation A Remote Consideration?

Yes, relocation is a major decision. However, because of the cost associated with relocation, the metal fabricator should be looking for every economic advantage.

It becomes obvious that regardless of the issues of lease, buy, or build, the location within the respective community and state must be a carefully thought-out decision to gain the economic advantage.

The issues are significant and require considerable attention as an owner or CEO enters into the relocation arena. It can be a very rewarding experience if the owner and his/her team does their homework and gains a perspective of the economic advantage and impact on the bottom line. ■

Kent E. Crippin is Director of Management Consulting for Grant Thornton, Kansas City, Missouri.

Collection of Articles from THE FABRICATOR®

Listing of Articles That Have Been Featured in THE FABRICATOR®

The following pages list the articles that have been featured in THE FABRICATOR®. Information about THE FABRICATOR® and FMA (Fabricators and Manufacturers Association, International) is on pages 84-85.

January/February 1980

"High frequency contact and induction welding of tube"
Cliff Hubbard, Thermatool Corp.

"Bending sheet metal by the multiform process"
W.T. Smith, Keeton Sons & Co., Ltd.

"Automated pipe processing system currently under construction"
Ollie Gatlin, Avondale Shipyards, Inc.

"A material alternative: Stampable nylon sheet"

"Fundamentals of solid state welding: Understanding solid state components"
Jack Fulcer, Miller Electric Mfg. Co.

"Understanding production machines and their elements: Servo setup"
Jim Swanson, Dricoline

"Partners in productivity"
John Kensey, Eaton Leonard Corp.

"Moving to metric: Metals industry conversion plan released"

"Director's platform: Is the U.S. foreign trade deficit necessary"
Herbert Rudolph, C-R-O, Inc.

"Welding tips and techniques: MIG aluminum welding"
John Shaputis

"Tax forum: Fighting inflation with LIFO"
David Stafseth, Peat, Marwick, Mitchell & Co.

March/April 1980

"Comparing spiral with U & O press pipe"
Ben Dolphin, Ben Dolphin Consulting Service

"A new understanding of sheet metal formability"
Stuart P. Keeler, National Steel Corp.

"How to weigh the cost of new equipment"
Donald W. Mikesell, McCullagh Leasing Inc.

"Understanding production machines and their elements: Maintenance and troubleshooting of DC motors"
Jim Swanson, Dricoline

"Fundamentals of solid state welding: Who uses solid state and why?"
Jack Fulcer, Miller Electric Mfg. Co.

"High frequency contact and induction welding of tube - Part II"
Cliff Hubbard, Thermatool Corp.

"Moving to metrics: Machine tool conversion options"

"Tax forum: Inventory valuation after the Thor Power Case"
David Stafseth, Peat, Marwick, Mitchell & Co.

"Director's platform: Increased productivity - A fight against inflation"
Kenneth L. Slawson, Strippit Division, Houdaille Industries

"Welding tips & techniques: The basics come first"
John Shaputis

May/June 1980

"New coil slitting system may revolutionize industry"

"What's happening in finishes for steel appliances"

"How to produce sheared parts without a shear"
Chris Bergerson, Strippit Division, Houdaille Industries, Inc.

"Fundamentals of solid state welding: How a solid state circuit works"
Jack Fulcer, Miller Electric Mfg. Co.

"Custom roll forming: Combining a versatile process and excellence in design"
Robert Boeddener, Custom Roll Forming Institute

"Transporting heavy fabrications requires extensive preparations"

"1001 questions about plate & structurals: Beam measurement"
Jim Swanson, Dricoline

"Moving to metrics: Don't overlook you measuring tools"

"Tax forum: Update on current developments"
David Stafseth, Peat, Marwick, Mitchell & Co.

"Director's platform: Whatever happened to management by objectives?"
William L. Aldridge, Brothers, Inc.

July/August 1980

"Formed-steel panel line produces industrial panels in continuous process"

"Nuclear power plant pipes at Tubeco undergo radiographic regimen"

"General press lubrication"
Donald R. Hixson, IRMCO

"Specifying & buying coated coil"
George Liebrock, National Coil Coaters Association

"Cutting machine yields fourfold production capacity boost"

Collection of Articles from THE FABRICATOR®

September/October 1980

"Principles of coil feeding methods: Times are changing"
Jerry Finn, P/A Industries, Inc.

"Understanding the brazing process of nonferrous tube fabrications"
Larry Shanks, Bohn Heat Transfer Division

"New welding process increases production in joining, cladding"

"Are strikes avoidable?"
Woodruff Imberman, Imberman and DeForest

"1001 questions about plate & structurals: Beam gauging systems"
Jim Swanson, Dricoline

"Smoke problems at stamping plant eliminated"

"Tax forum; Proposed regulations defining debt, equity"
David Stafseth, Peat, Marwick, Mitchell & Co.

"Productivity (Paradise) lost - Part I"
William E. Sandman, Wm. E. Sandman Associates Co.

"Director's platform: Productivity - or poverty"
George Goudreault, AP Parts Co.

November/December 1980

"Properly designed piping system conserves energy and reduces costs"
F.R. Olegar, PPG Industries, Inc.

"The need for pollution and contamination control of tube mill lubricants"
Edward Heidenreich, Hyde Products, Inc.

"Tax forum: New depreciation and investment tax credit rules are coming"
David Stafseth, Peat, Marwick, Mitchell & Co.

"1001 questions about plate & structurals: Plate bowing"
Jim Swanson, Dricoline

"Productivity (Paradise) regained - Part II"
William E. Sandman, Wm. E. Sandman Associates Co.

January/February 1981

"Advancements in the design, use and techniques of coil slitting lines - Part I"
John Madachy, Loopco Industries, Inc.

"Cold roll forming material of varying thicknesses: A practical and economical process"
The Yoder Co., Cleveland, OH.

"Protecting profits and jobs with automatic cost reduction"
Robert G. Scott, Eddy-Rucker-Nickels Co., Cambridge, MA.

"Combination cradle/feeders/straighteners cut time, labor and floor space in half"

"New machine or used: The $100,000 dilemma"
John Gillanders, Bending Services, Inc., Houston, TX.

"1001 questions about plate and structural fabricating: Reducing noise levels in your shop - It can be done"
Jim Swanson, Dricoline

March/April 1981

"Successful job shop triples size in 18 months"

"Proper selection of welding processes saves time"
Jack Fulcer, Miller Electric Mfg. Co.

"Leadership through marketing: Foundations for marketing success"
William Kramp, W.A. Kramp & Associates

"Pipe bending tips and techniques: Non-slip tooling and the quick-change mandrel"
John Gillanders, Bending Services, Inc, Houston, TX.

"Press brake light curtain increases worker visibility, mobility"

"Advancements in the design, use and techniques of coil slitting lines - Part II"
John Madachy, Loopco Industries, Inc.

"1001 questions about plate and structural fabricating: Punch and die manufacture - When you need one immediately!"
Jim Swanson, Dricoline

May/June 1981

"What you don't know about resistance welding can cost you"
David R. Mitchell, Falstrom Welding Products, Inc.

"How to choose the proper plate bending roll - Part II"
H. Merrit Kinsey, Bertsch and Co, Inc.

"Advancements in the design, use and techniques of coil slitting lines - Part III"
John Madachy, Loopco Industries, Inc.

"Leadership through marketing: Setting goals for marketing success"
William Kramp, W.A. Kramp & Associates

"Pipe bending tips and techniques: Pipe bending capabilities expanded through innovation"
John Gillanders, Bending Services, Inc, Houston, TX.

"Solving problems in the preparation of plate edges for welding"
Erwin H. Roessle, American SMT-Pullmax, Inc.

"1001 questions about plate and structural fabricating: Buying that electronic control"
Jim Swanson, Dricoline

"Survey examines productivity problems: Are government and industry working together?"

September/October 1981

"Robots: How they can be efficiently utilized in metal stamping - Part I"
Douglas E. Booth, Livernois Automation Co.

Collection of Articles from **THE FABRICATOR®** 179.

"A powerful bending machine, accurate tooling, and a well-trained operator add up to good tube bending - Part I"
Fred Costello, Coast Iron & Machine Works

"1001 questions about plate and structural fabricating: An evaluation of machine builders"
Jim Swanson, Dricoline

"Multiplexing comes of age"
David F. Bechtol, Eaton Corp., Cutler-Hammer Sales

"How to choose the proper plate bending roll - Part II"
H. Merrit Kinsey, Bertsch and Co, Inc.

"Pipe bending tips and techniques: 'Off the rack' or 'tailor made'"
John Gillanders, Bending Services, Inc, Houston, TX.

"Leadership through marketing: Finding needs and fending off competition"
William Kramp, W.A. Kramp & Associates

November/December 1981

"Designing a plant layout for efficient roll forming operations"
George Halmos, Delta Engineering Ltd.

"A powerful bending machine, accurate tooling and a well-trained operator add up to good tube bending - Part II"
Fred Costello, Coast Iron & Machine Works

"Robots: How they can be efficiently utilized in metal stamping - Part II"
Douglas E. Booth, Livernois Automation Co.

"Pipe bending tips and techniques: The missing element in cost effective bending - maintenance!"
John Gillanders, Bending Services, Inc, Houston, TX.

"1001 questions about plate and structural fabricating: Teeter-totter economics"
Jim Swanson, Dricoline

"Leadership through marketing: Looking at your product - A new perspective"
William Kramp, W.A. Kramp & Associates

January/February 1982

"New press wraps up folded panel process"

"Use of synthetic lubricants growing in metal forming operations - Part I"
Joseph Ivaska, Tower Oil & Technology, Chicago, IL.

"What's better than a right-to-work law?"

"Pipe bending tips and techniques: Plan now for the economic upturn in the future"
John Gillanders, Bending Services Inc., Houston, TX.

"Leadership through marketing: Sales - Making the connection"
William A. Kramp, Palos Machinery Co.

"Director's Platform: Cost saving - Overlooked in industry"
Robert H. Brinker, Brinker Machinery Sales Co.

March 1982

"Utilizing computer design engineering for piping systems"
James Madden, Isopipe Texas, Inc.

"Tips & techniques for fineblanking - Part I"
Michigan Precision Industries, Inc.

"New punch portal riveting system may spell new era for fastening"

"Temperature monitor label helps trailer manufacturer weld flat bed trucks"

"Use of synthetic lubricants growing in metal forming operations - Part II"
Joseph Ivaska, Tower Oil & Technology, Inc.

"Pipe bending tips and techniques: Tooling & die storage - One shop's approach"
John Gillanders, Bending Services, Inc., Houston, TX.

April 1982

"How to apply water injection plasma cutting to a CNC punching and nibbling machine"
Joseph Troiani, Trumpf America, Inc.

"The servo controlled flying cutoff reduces scrap and downtime"
Jeffrey M. McGinnis, Tallyrand Industrial Systems

"Pipe bending tips and techniques: Buying a new bending machine"
John Gillanders, Bending Services, Inc., Houston, TX.

"A unique welding wire dispensing system saves time and money at Steelcase"

"STRIP: A computer system for coil slitting"
Walter Johnson, Sigma Tech

"Tips and techniques for fineblanking - Part II"
Michigan Precision Industries, Inc.

"1001 questions about plate and structurals: Machine justification"
Jim Swanson, Dricoline

May/June 1982

"The practical application of eddy-current techniques to the production testing of seam welded tube"
Frank McGinn and Vern Mace, Barkley & Dexter Laboratories, Inc.

"Practical design guide for brake and roll formed products"
George T. Halmos, Delta Engineering Ltd.

"Press isolators: Their function and effectiveness"
Sheldon E. Young, Vibro/Dynamics Corp.

"New steel research findings spotlight causes and prevention of lamellar tearing"

"Director's Platform: Why are we not competitive?
William Watt, Bloomer-Fiske, Inc.

Collection of Articles from **THE FABRICATOR®** 181.

"Pipe bending tips and techniques: Competition in small diameter pipe bending is heating up"
John Gillanders, Bending Services, Inc., Houston, TX.

July/August 1982

"Integrated roll forming lines boost productivity for office furniture manufacturer"

"How Bergstrom keeps its 10-year-old plant 'like new'"

"Eyeing the assembly line"
Rajarshi Ray, *Phototonics Spectra*.

"Pipe bending tips and techniques: Taking a look at some recent developments"
John Gillanders, Bending Services, Inc., Houston, TX.

"Accumulator supports coil strip vertically to minimize downtime"
Jacek Gajda, Sendzimir Engineering Corp.

"Practical design guide for brake and roll formed products - Part II"
George T. Halmos, Delta Engineering Ltd.

September 1982

"Pre-coated steel tube brings color to the world"

"Success may depend on selecting the correct stamping press"
Heinz Becker, Canada Clutch, Inc.

"AWS codes, standards and specifications prove extremely helpful to the fabricator"
Robert L. Harris, American Welding Society

"Pipe bending tips and techniques: A major breakthrough in pipe bending?"
John Gillanders, Bending Services, Inc., Houston, TX.

"Welded steel tubing gets more attention in auto use"
Ralph Hennie, Steel & Tubes Division, Republic Steel Corp.

"Solvent switch solves 'warm weather' cleaning problem at Cabot operation"

"Tailor-made training courses designed for workers at new Mississippi plant"

October 1982

"Rotary bending offers a new approach to press brake bending"
Robert L. Foley, Accurate Mfg. Co.

"Material handling systems help automate the operation of power squaring shears"
Merlyn A. Jarman, Continental M.D.M., Inc.

"Pipe bending: Who-What-When-Where-Why? Can a central database answer these questions?"
John Gillanders, Bending Services, Inc., Houston, TX

"Innovations in fabrication yield tax benefits"
Robert Feinschreiber, Feinschreiber & Associates

"Tips for working with expanded metal in the fabrication shop"

"Advanced fabricating techniques for sheet metal and plate working"
Richard E. Rinehart, W.A. Whitney Corp.

"All about welding wire: The do's and don'ts of wire selection"

November/December 1982

"The laser: How is 'tomorrow's technology' being used today?"
Fred Vezina, Strippit Division, Houdaille Industries, Inc.

"Fulfilling your shop requirements with the right plate bending machine - Part I"
A.H. Krieg, Widder Corp.

"Export methods of payment: When? How?"
Leon Cohan, Jr., Liebert Corp.

"Lift on wheels connects coil storage to processing line"

"How to select the correct central coolant system for your tube mill"
Edward Heidenreich, Hyde Products, Inc.

"Solving slug pull back problems on punch presses"

"Custom-formulated electrode welds electrostatic precipitator"

January/February 1983

"High frequency welded beams offer new structural design versatility"
Larry Lamphier, Welded Beam Co., and Cliff Hubbard, Thermatool Corp.

"Die designing with a modern day alternative - nitrogen die springs"
Richard A. Wallis, Forward Industries

"Laser system designs offer increased flexibility"
Coherent, Inc.

"Fulfilling your shop requirements with the right plate bending machine - Part II"
A.H. Krieg, Widder Corp.

"Welding wire: Its role grows as MIG process zooms"
Reprinted from Canadian Welder & Fabricator

March 1983

"Metal embossing with engraved rolls"
C. Van Kouwenberg, Roehlen Engraving, Division of Standex International

"Hydraulic fluid line tubing finds many applications in industry today"
Ralph Hennie, Steel & Tubes Division, Republic Steel Corp.

Collection of Articles from THE FABRICATOR®

"The human side of engineering: A problem too often overlooked"
Dr. James J. Renier, Honeywell, Inc.

"Cutting with lasers opens the door to new business for fabricator"
Strippit/Houdaille

"A simplified method to determine and compare welding costs"

April 1983

"Automatic tool changing solves special tube bending problems"
Michael Ball, Eaton Leonard Corp.

"Welding techniques simplify joining of dissimilar metals - Part I"
Dr. S. Elliott and S.B. Dunkerton, The Welding Institute, Cambridge, England.

"Using the air-carbon arc process to prepare economical j-grooves"
Lance Soisson and Jeff Henderson, The Arcair Co.

"Laser surface treatment affords increased controllability"
David A. Belforte, Belforte Associates

"Spotting accounts receivables danger signals helps firms survive"
Charles T. Brown, American Credit Indemnity Collection Services, Inc.

"Cold drawn special sections: Little known part shaping process holds big promise"

May/June 1983

"How to bend pipe without bending the rules"
Alan Williamson, Conrac Machine Tool

"New concept in punching more than doubles productivity"
Ronald E. Van Wieringen, Wiedemann Division, Warner & Swasey Co., A Bendix subsidiary.

"Panel forming line increases productivity, reduces inventory"

"Gauging improvements for increased productivity from power press brakes"
Tim Gravenstreter, Hurco Manufacturing Co., Inc.

"Welding techniques simplify joining of dissimilar metals - Part II"
Dr. S. Elliott and S.B. Dunkerton, The Welding Institute, Cambridge, England.

"Coil coating: The way to apply organic finishing"
Robert Surface, Armco, Inc., Middletown, OH.

"Welding with lasers offers increased flexibility of applications"
Coherent, Inc.

September 1983

"Three manufactures combine expertise to produce a fast, dimple-free tube cutoff system"

"Structural fabricator expands market, modernizes plant to survive slow economic times"

"Oscillating shear and dual stackers reduce material loss in coil handling systems"

October 1983

"How metal forming lubricants affect the finishing process"
Joseph Ivaska, Tower Oil & Technology Co.

"Coordinating drives by applying microprocessors to tube and pipe mills"
Bruce A. Finch, Reliance Electric Co.

"Working with 'The Metal That's Mostly Air'"
John Hibel, Keene Corp., Metal Products Division

"Portable machine cuts titanium plate beveling costs"

"Alloy steel wire: Product needs spur interest in its attributes and advantages"

"The proper application of equipment is the key to a successful laser operation"
James G. Moore, Eddco, Inc., Bridgeport, CT.

November/December 1983

"Bending on an angle roll: How to make the correct calculations required"
Goran Kajrup, Roundo A.B., Hasselholm, Sweden, and Allan Flamholz, COMEQ, Inc., Baltimore, MD.

"Pipe bending costs cut by utilizing today's technology"
Alan B. Williamson, Conrac Corp., Greenville, SC.

"Rotary embossing: Understanding the options and benefits"
Gordon Osbeck, Contour Roll Co., Grand Haven, MI.

"Coil coated steel: How to store, handle, form and fasten it"

January/February 1984

"Innovative methods of cold roll forming produce complex parts more efficiently"
Harold A. Williamson, Dahlstrom Industries, Inc., Schiller Park, IL.

"Computer technology and the sheet metal industry"
Donald Prill, The LVD Corp., Plainville, CT.

"Flexible manufacturing systems: The ultimate in technology for sheet metal fabrication"
Carl Grosso, U.S. Amada Ltd., Buena Park, CA.

"New bending brake concept tackles conventional and complex bending with ease"
Bernie Blomquist, Roper Whitney Co., Rockford, IL.

"Correct selection of cut-to-length system maximizes roll form productivity"
George Halmos, Delta Engineering Ltd., Willowdale, Ontario, Canada.

"A systems approach to coil storage and handling"
Marv Miller, Southwestern Ohio Steel, Inc., Hamilton, OH.

Collection of Articles from **THE FABRICATOR®**

"New generation of press systems simplifies cold forming"
Kimikazu Aida, Aida Engineering Co., Columbus, IN.

March 1984

"Automated system produces aluminum radiator tubes at 600 FPM"

"Machine vision performs noncontact dimensional inspection of stampings an stamping assemblies"
Gary Johnson, Perceptron, Inc., Farmington Hills, MI.

"Tube and pipe branch forming method eliminates the need for fittings"
William Holyoak, T-Drill, Norcross, GA.

"Point of operation safeguarding: Does your press comply with OSHA requirements?"
Roger Harrison, Rockford Systems, Inc., Rockford, IL.

"NC tape preparation system reduces errors and eliminates tape proofing"

"Clustercoil proves its versatility in coil slitting applications"
Jack Born, Clustercoil Corp, Pittsburgh, PA, and J.C.W. Perkins, Wyko Equipment Ltd., Dudley, West Midlands, United Kingdom.

April 1984

"Innovations in material handling systems increase plate bending productivity"
H. Merritt Kinsey, Bertsch and Co., Inc., Cambridge City, IN.

"High frequency heating offers more versatility to selective surface hardening"
Cliff Hubbard, Thermatool Corp., Stamford, CT.

"New slit coil tension unit provides finishing touch for light gauge slitting line"

"A grasp of resistance welding fundamentals insures an improved finished product"
Lauri John Murto, Teledyne Peer, Benton Harbor, MI.

May/June 1984

"Robotic welding systems are growing up"

"What is involved in implementing a Just-In-Time production program?"
AP Parts Co. and Rath & Strong, Inc.

"Increasing slitting line productivity with the proper slitter tooling system"
S. A. Jacoby, ASKO, Inc., Homestead, PA.

"CNC right angle shearing provides a competitive edge for today's fabricator"
Richard Metzger, Strippit Division, Houdaille Industries, Akron, NY.

"Small assembly plants can profit from pollution abatement process"
William Blankenship and Robert L. Allen, U.S. Environmental Protection Agency, Region III, Philadelphia, PA.

"Selecting welding wire for HSLA steels"

"Cutting costs with sparks"
R.A. Arthur, London Press Service. Reprinted from Spectrum, Central Office of Information, London, England.

"Mechanical power press 'self tripping' may soon be approved by OSHA"
Roger Harrison, Rockford Systems, Inc., Rockford, IL.

July/August 1984

"Induction pipe bending vs. conventional techniques"
Peter Hartley, Engineering, London, England.

"Optimizing productivity through computerized structural steel process"
Homer E. Livingston, McNally Pittsburg, Inc., Pittsburg, KS.

"Lasers: New light on old processes"
Tech Tran Corp., Naperville, IL.

"Roll forming: Use of HSLA steels increases"
George Halmos, Delta Engineering Ltd., Willowdale, Ontario, Canada.

"Upgrading tube mill cutoffs"
Frank Canda, Yoder Division, Intercole Bolling Corp., Cleveland, OH.

"Flexible manufacturing systems: Fabricating's future"
Strippit/Houdaille Industries, Akron, NY.

"CNC retrofit improves punch press performance: A case history"

"Shape cutting steel: Comparing three methods"
Jerry Karow, MG Industries, Menomonee Falls, WI.

September 1984

"Measuring press force the modern way"
Donald Wilhelm, Helm Instrument Co., Inc., Maumee, OH.

"Press brake control: The challenging choices"
Richard Pozzo, Dynamics Research Corp., Wilmington, MA.

"Steel wire: Introduction to a versatile material"

"Short run tooling saves in the long run"
Ronald W. Phillips, Midbrook Products, Inc., Jackson, MI.

"Future shock for pipe fabrication?"
John Gillanders, International Piping Systems, Ltd., Baton Rouge, LA.

"Single universal press replaces three machines"

October 1984

"Robotic unit simplifies arc welding of hospital bed frame"
David Elovich, G.E. Robot Systems, Peoria, IL.

"Automated and programmable equipment yields arc welding productivity"
James A. Hoffman, Bancroft Corp., Waukesha, WI.

"New approaches improve high speed metal stamping"
Dennis Boergfer and Donald Hemmelgarn, Minster Machine Co., Minster, OH.

"A purchasing manager's guide to self-clinching fasteners"
John O'Brien, Penn Engineering & Manufacturing Corp., Danboro, PA.

"Achieving the best utilization of cyanoacrylate adhesives"
William G. Repensek, Permabond International Corp., Elm Grove, WI.

"Switching to synchronous belt drives on steel strip grinders, polishers saves"

"Electron beam welding reduces rejects on jet engine blades"

November/December 1984

"A first-hand look at Italian metal fabricating"
John Nandzik, The FABRICATOR, Rockford, IL.

"Realizing energy and cost savings from a properly-designed pipe bending system"
Peter R. Olegar

"Automatic weld temperature control system improves pipe, tube mill productivity"
C.N. Hubbard, Thermatool Co., Division of Inductotherm Corp., Stamford, CT.

"Manufacturing with the use of transfer systems"
Robert Rice, Tooling Division of M.S. Willett, Inc., Cockeysville, MD.

"Achieving cost savings in hydrostatic testing of pipe"

"Investigating the strength of a welding elbow versus an induction bend"
Shumpei Kawanami, Yukimitsu Hanamoto, and Nobuyoshi Kitayama, Tokyo, Japan, and Yoshio Takeuchi, Ikutoku Technical University.

"The knuckle-joint press takes a leadership role in forming technology"
Winfried Beisel, Graebener Press Systems, Inc., Providence, RI.

"Induction heating advances the processing of tube and pipe"
Trevor Savage, Electroheating International, Ltd., London, England.

"Swivel-armed sander/grinder smooths out rough areas for fabricator"

January/February 1985

"Company increases tubing production capacity by 60 percent without adding another mill"
C.V. Loznak, Eugene Welding Co., Marysville, MI.

"Custom roll forming offers fabricators an alternative"
Custom Roll Form Institute, Cleveland, OH.

"Tube end finishing: Effectively utilizing equipment, methods and tooling"
Alan Williamson, Tubetech, Inc., Greenville, SC.

"Pressroom pick and place robots offer fast payback"
American Monarch Machine Co, Metamora, IL.

"Integrating coil end joiners in tube mills, roll formers and coil processing lines"
Steve Shaffer, Northeast Machinery Sales, Inc., Munroe Falls, OH.

"New tax benefits for exporters"
Robert Feinschreiber, Feinschreiber and Associates, Key Biscayne, FL.

"Correct use of impeders makes big difference in high frequency welding"
Harold J. Dreckmann, Permag Corp., Hicksville, NY.

"New trends in roll forming"
Productivity and Quality Center, Pittsburgh, PA.

"Use of CIM in fabrication used to be unique: That's not the case anymore"
Don Ewaldz, Ingersoll Engineers Inc., Rockford, IL.

"Eliminating the risk of industrial automation using real time simulation"
Max W. Hitchens, HEI Corp., Carol Stream, IL.

"Robots do make work: Clearing up the misinformation"
Robotic Industries Association, Dearborn, MI.

September 1985

"Implementing process control with machine vision in stamping and assembly environment"
David H. Benner, Perceptron, Farmington Hills, MI.

"Metal container assembly produced at 350 parts per minute"
Robert R. Rice, M.S. Willett, Inc., Cockeysville, MD.

"Laser proves valuable tool in fabrication of metal stamping die sets"
Thomas Culkin, Photon Sources, Inc., Livonia, MI.

"Sheet steel makers report on quality-upgrading"
AISI's Transportation Dept.

"NC tape system drives FMS cell for Wisconsin company"

October 1985

"Precision tooling for American-style press brakes promises productivity gains"
Edward Malloy, Accurate Manufacturing Co., Chicago, IL.

"Automated sheet metal cell reduces lead times by 68% at Deere's Harvester Works"
William J. VandeVoorde, John Deere Harvestor Works, East Moline, IL

"Recent developments in high precision tube straightening - Part I"
Mike Owens, WYKO Equipment, Ltd., Dudley, England, and Bill Wagner, WYKO, Inc., Knoxville, TN.

"Temperature indicating crayons ease body repair of new cars"

"Tax reform and its consequences"
Robert Feinscreiber, Feinscreiber & Associates, Key Biscayne, FL.

1985 Welding Issue

"New developments in fabricated filler metals"
J. Caprarola, Jr., Alloy Rods Corp., Hanover, PA.

"Lasers solve many welding problems"
Pat Harris, Coherent General, Inc., Sturbridge, MA.

"Gas Metal Arc Welding: Versatility in process and application"
Raymond T. Hemzacek, Argonne National Laboratory, Argonne, IL.

"Can you benefit from a welding robot?"
Nicholas P. Sikich, Bancroft Corp., Waukesha, WI.

"Recent trends and developments increase use of resistance welding"
R.D. McCreery, Jr., McCreery Corp., Cleveland, OH.

"Common sense strategic planning for the welder/fabricator"
Boris M. Krantz, Krantz Associates, Inc., Watchung, NJ.

"Low voltage EB welding comes of age"
Preston Macy, EBTEC, Agawam, MA.

"Utilize arc welding to hardface metal surfaces"
Richard S. Sabo, The Lincoln Electric Co., Cleveland, OH.

"Working with tantalum and columbium"
Louis E. Huber and Sherwood Goldstein, Cabot Corp., Reading, PA.

November/December 1985

"Roll forming: Choosing the right system for your needs"
John Toben, Artos Engineering Co, Roll Forming Division, Milwaukee, WI.

"Recent developments in high precision tube straightening - Part II"
Mike Owens, WYKO Equipment, Ltd., Dudley, England, and Bill Wagner, WYKO, Inc., Knoxville, TN.

"TiN coating comes to the punching industry"
James Mishek, Thomas Emery, and John Morehead, Wilson Tool International, White Bear Lake, MN.

"Computerized optimization program advances coil slitting"
Mike Maguire, AKV Products, Ruesch Machine Co., Subsidiary of Met-Coil Systems Corp., Chicago, IL.

"Computer-aided roll design: An art or a science?"
George T. Halmos, Delta Engineering Ltd, Willowdale, Ontario, Canada.

"Critical decisions to consider before implementing CAD/CAM/CAE - Part I"
William G. Beazley, William G. Beazley & Associates, Houston, TX.

"Defining tube and pipe: What are the differences?"
John Gillanders, Bendak, Inc., Houston, TX., and Ralph Hennie, Pepper Pike, OH.

January/February 1986

"European tube makers capitalize on U.S. cutoff technology"
John Borzym, Alpha Industries, Inc., Novi, MI.

"Improving quality with silt coil tensioning"
Fred Bresnahan, Loopco Sales, Inc., Amherst, NY.

"New inspection instrument solves wide range of product-quality problems"
W.R. Hain, Nondestructive Testing Systems, AT&T, Springfield, NJ.

"Critical decisions to consider before implementing CAD/CAM/CAE - Part II"
William G. Beazley, William G. Beazley & Associates, Houston, TX.

"Cutting torch increases oxyfuel cutting speeds"
John Lowrey, AGA Gas, Inc., Cleveland, OH.

"Shared FSCs: An innovative benefit for small and medium size exporters"
John J. Korbel, Price Waterhouse, Office of Government Services, Washington, D.C., and Charles M. Bruce, Cole & Corette, P.C., Washington, D.C.

March 1986

"Integrating CNC fabricating machine tools into flexible manufacturing systems"
Dirk Naessens, LVD Co., Wevelgem-Gullegem, Belgium.

"Laser cutting specialist is on the leading edge"
John T. Winship, Wordsmith Enterprises, Allendale, NJ.

"Update on CAD/CAM hardware and software'
Harris Corp., Computer Systems Division, Fort Lauderdale, FL.

"Tube fabrication improved with flying cutoff control system"

"Computer-assisted shimless slitting improves coil processing productivity"
AKSO, Inc., Homestead, PA.

"Critical decisions to consider before implementing CAD/CAM/CAE - Part III"
William G. Beazley, William G. Beazley & Associates, Houston, TX.

"NC part programming for metal fabricators ready for the future"

April 1986

"Laser robots provide increased manufacturing flexibility"
David A. Belforte, Belforte Associates, Sturbridge, MA.

"Quick die change systems integrate with today's JIT concepts"
William P. Murphy, M & S Birmingham Corp., Birmingham, MI.

"Just-In-Time: A revolution in management"
Robert E. Sessions, General Electric Co., Bridgeport, CT.

"Leveraged buyouts of metal fabricating companies: What's involved?"
Richard L. Fausett and James W. Fox, Arthur Young & Co., Los Angeles, CA.

"Applications growing for use of tin mil steels"

"Thermal incineration provides pollution control"

May/June 1986

"Micro CAD/CAM and the tube fabricator"
Cone & Cone, West Bloomfield, MI.

"Skelp slit width calculations for electric weld pipe mills"
Walter M. Stage, Tubular Services, Inc., Division of Pipeco, Inc., Houston, TX

"Induction heating: An evolving technology for pipe fabrication"
John Gillanders, Bendak, Houston, TX.

"Cost effective precision tube bending"
Ronald R. Stange, Tools For Bending, Denver, CO.

"Induction bends meet ANSI burst test requirements"
Dorothy Hill, Johnson Controls, Inc., Clearfield, Utah.

"The promising possibilities of cellular manufacturing"
Glenn Kline, U.S. Amada, Ltd., Buena Park, CA.

"Corrective sheet metal leveling: Science, art, or black magic?"
Henry E. Theis, Herr-Voss Corp., Callery, PA.

"New system provides continuous coil without accumulators"

"Successful Tampa slitter shows fabricators how to improve productivity"

"Federal 'Right To Know' law to impact thousands of U.S. companies"
Council for Materials Safety in Manufacturing, Pittsburgh, PA.

"First laser welding of cans"

"Industrial America can recover: Commitment to automated production needed"
Mark W. Lowell, TRUMPF, Inc., Farmington, CT.

July/August 1986

"CNC coping enters the structural steel fabricating industry"
Lyle Menke, Peddinghaus Corp., Bradley, IL.

"Manufacturing technology: How much is flash?"

"Fineblanking applications increase as technology advances"
Heinz Heller, Feintool, Cincinnati, OH.

"Improving press brake productivity with combined clutch/brakes"
Victor P. Kovacik, Orttech, Inc., Willoughby, OH.

"How to bring small business efficiency to Pentagon buying"
Jay Cooper, Northrop Corp., Los Angeles, CA.

"HVAC company realizes near-zero percent errors with NC tape programming system"

September 1986

"Interactive processing and graphics improves sheet metal parts programming"
Larry Higgins, American Channels, Inc., Lexington, MA.

"CIM-Tools: How a small manufacturer can make effective use of them"
D. John R. Richardson, Ontario CAD/CAM Centre, Cambridge, Ontario, Canada.

"Industrial robots: What are the best applications?"
Excerpted from *Industrial Robots: A Summary and Forecast*, Tech Tran Consultants, Inc., Lake Geneva, WI.

"Data transfer strategy gives die design shop an edge"
John M. Martin, Binghamton, NY, for Harris Corp., Fort Lauderdale, FL.

"Investigating the uses of shear knives"
Albert W. Winterman, The Wapakoneta Machine Co., Wapakoneta, OH.

October 1986

"Critical factors in automating metal stamping operations using robots"
Chris Reed, Prab Robots, Inc., Kalamazoo, MI.

"Cutting, marking, and processing structural sections automatically"
Gunter C. Wilkens, Osytechnik, Eschborne, West Germany, and John M. Kalogerakis, Swan Hunters Shipbuilders Ltd., Tyne and Wear, Great Britain.

"Implementing an advanced pressworking system"
Charles J. Gregorovich, Thee Minster Machine Co., Minster, OH.

"A versatile manufacturer needs a versatile computing system"

"Stand-alone laser provides its value in New Hampshire job shop"

November 1986

"Designing weld-fabricated products efficiently"
John P. Stewart, LaSalle, Quebec, Canada

"Taking advantage of the industrial robot as a welder"
E. Christopher Forland, General Electric Co., Oak Brook, IL.

"High frequency welding impeders: Their use, position, and construction"
William Humber, Neosid (Canada) Ltd., Toronto, Ontario, Canada.

"Maintenance welding of precision parts for construction equipment"
Don Yarnell, Binder Machinery Co., South Plainfield, NJ.

"Borescope offered as alternative to traditional x-ray tube inspection"

December 1986

"Myths and misconceptions of cold bending process piping"
Anthony Granelli, 600 Machinery, Inc., Clute, TX.

"Presence sensing: The productive solution to machine guarding"
Lloyd Pillsbury, Data instruments, Inc., Acton, MA.

"Producing quality tube and pipe branches and fittings by extrusion"
Warwick A. Johnston, Kaltek, Inc., Atlanta, GA.

"CAD/CAM for sheet metal fabrication"
Carl Grosso, Metalsoft, Inc., Santa Ana, CA.

"Managing the change process"
Frank Petrock, General Systems Consulting Group, Ann Arbor, MI.

"Update on can-making steels: Trends and developments in can stock and containers"

January/February 1987

"SPC: Statistical process control and automation"
Hans J. Bajaria, Multiface Inc., Dearborn Heights, MI.

"Scheduling coil in the computer age: Are we able to get results from all the bells and whistles that we design into today's equipment?"
Barry A. Hengstler, Metro Metals, Northbrook, IL.

"Flying dies: Their design and economic impact"
Donald R. Hill, Hill Engineering, Inc., Villa Park, IL.

"Synergistic coatings solve NASA's problem"

"Import quotas on NC turret punch presses"
Carl Grosso, Metalsoft, Inc., Santa Ana, CA.

"Does concession bargaining really cut labor costs?"
Matthew Goodfellow, University Research Center, Inc., Chicago, IL.

"New tax law: What's hiding in there for fabricators?"
Robert Feinschreiber and Margaret Kent, Key Biscayne, FL.

March 1987

"Choosing the right tube welding process"
Frank W. Canda, Yoder Manufacturing, Bedford Heights, OH.

"Flying dies: Their design and economic impact - Part II"
Donald R. Hill, Hill Engineering, Inc., Villa Park, IL.

"Rotary bending: Successful applications prove new forming concept"
Robert L. Foley, Accurate Manufacturing Co., Alsip, IL.

"Which tube cutoff method is the right choice for your production needs?"
Harrison C. Berkeley, Production Tube Cutting, Inc., Dayton, OH.

"Statistical process control: A key to Japanese quality"
Carl Grosso, Metalsoft, Inc., Santa Ana, CA.

"Solving precision circular welding problems"
Keith J. Futter, Risley, Bedford, England, and Peter J. Farrow, Progressive Product Marketing, Inc, Houston, TX.

April 1987

"Computer language aids sheet metal CAD/CAM"
Joseph Troiani, TRUMPF, Inc., Farmington, CT.

"Automated stretcher leveling increases coil quality"
Red Bud Industries, Red Bud, IL

"Shop floor control: Is it an impossible dream?"
William E. Sandman, Sandman Associates Co., Huntingdon Valley, PA.

"Fastener developed for installation into stainless steel sheets"
Leon M. Atarian, Penn Engineering & Manufacturing Corp., Danboro, PA.

"Small factory of the future"
Carl Grosso, Metalsoft, Inc., Santa Ana, CA.

"Manual estimating methods give way to computer-aided systems"
Steven Murray, Mellish & Murray, Chicago, IL.

May/June 1987

"The case for bend fittings"
John Gillanders, Bendak, Inc., Houston, TX

"Tension testing of drawn aluminum alloy tubing"
Dr. J.P. Faunce and R.L. Harrell, EASCO Aluminum, Winton Division, Winton, NC.

"Voluntary standards developed for the bending of pipe"
Drew Kershaw, Sunland Services, Inc., Baton Rouge, LA, and Frank Corgiat, Dynamic Products, Inc., Houston, TX.

"Skelp cost savings for electric weld tube mills:
Walter M. Stage, Tubular Services, Inc., Houston, TX.

"Expanded eddy current inspection of tubular products provided by computer analysis"
Don Bugden, Magnetic Analysis Corp., Mount Vernon, NY.

"Managing heavy plate welding: Many managers stop managing too far up the ladder away from the welding operation"
Jack Barckhoff and Walter R. Edwards, Barckhoff and Associates, Inc. Excelsior, MN.

"It's not what the Japanese do, it's what we don't do"
Ingersoll Engineers Inc.

"Computers control production of steel and plate"
Reprinted from *Sheet Metal Industries*, Surrey, England.

"Fabricating centers: Versatile solution to plate, structural fabricating"

"Getting the best deal when you buy or sell your plant"

Alan Scharfstein, DAK Corporate Investors, Orangeburg, NY.

"How to benefit from export incentives"
Robert Feinschreiber and Margaret Kent, Biscayne, FL.

"Reader emulator replaces paper tape reader"
Edmond T. Mignogna, ETM Services, Inc., Port Chester, NY.

"Vision inspection: Promising technology for NC punching"
Carl Grosso, Metalsoft, Inc., Santa Ana, CA.

"The quality of being predictable and on time"
John Richardson, Ontario Centre for Advanced Manufacturing, Cambridge, Ontario, Canada.

"Methods of sheet metal punch press programming"
Robert Jones, Techware Computing Co., Clearwater, FL.

July/August 1987

"Quoting metal parts with a computer"
Carl Grosso, Metalsoft, Inc., Santa Ana, CA.

"Quality: The MRP/JIT fit"
Dr. J.R. Richardson, OCAM's CAD/CAM Centre, Cambridge, Ontario, Canada.

"Programming software offers new opportunities to contract fabricating shop"
Carl Watkins, Product Development, Point Control Co., Eugene, OR.

September 1987

"Automation trends in high-speed press operations"
Paul Pfundtner, Red Stag, Inc., New London, WI.

"Pressforming superplastic sheet for aerospace components"
Reprinted from Sheet Metal Industries, Surrey, England.

"Target makes change its advantage"

"Computerized press monitoring system: The essential management tool"
Robert Storer, Toledo Transducers, Toledo, OH.

"Supplying metal formed parts to the automotive industry"

"New generation laser cutters provide practicality"
Mike Palmer, Mazak Nissho Iwai Corp., Schaumburg, IL.

"Solid stat tube welding has arrived"
Humfrey Udall, Thermatool Corp., Stanford, CT, and Jean Lovens, Inducto Elphiac, Belgium.

"Programmable curving offers flexibility in design changes"
Maynard Carlson, The Tinker Shop, Inc., West Salem, WI.

"If a strike is expensive, why have it?"
Woodruff Imberman, Imberman and DeForest, Chicago, IL.

"Managing heavy plate welding: Many managers stop managing too far up the ladder away from the welding operation - Part II"
Jack Barckhoff and Walter R. Edwards, Barckhoff and Associates, Inc., Minneapolis, MN.

Spreadsheet software: An indispensable electronic tool"
Carl Grosso, Metalsoft, Inc., Santa Ana, CA.

"Quality: Computers manage the variables in pre-manufacturing"
John Richardson, Ontario Centre for Advanced Manufacturing, CAD/CAM Centre, Cambridge, Ontario, Canada.

October 1987

"How a flat strip becomes a welded tube: The purpose of every roll and stand on a tube mill"
Joseph Olson, Chicago Roll Co., Elk Grove Village, IL.

"Automation trends in high speed, straight side press operations - Part II"
Paul Pfundtner, Red Stag Inc., New London, WI.

"How U.S. manufacturing can thrive"
Excerpted from Manufacturing Automation Series, Datapro Research Corp, Delran, NJ.

"Flexible stamping system: Productive adaptation, not compromise, for changing press room requirements"
Atlas Automation Division, Automated Manufacturing Systems, Inc., Fenton, MI.

"Relocating your plant?: One company's moving story"
Chief Industries, Inc., Grand Island, NE.

"Custom machine builder relies on programmable controllers"
Omron Electronics, Inc., Schaumburg, IL.

"Automated accounting offers financial control"
Carl Grosso, Metalsoft, Inc., Santa Ana, CA.

"Automatic nesting supports punch, plasma machinery"
Deere Tech Services, a division of Deere and Co., Moline, IL, and Precision Nesting Systems, Inc., Closter, NJ.

November 1987

"Providing the welder/fitter with an accountability instrument"
John P. Stewart.

"Control manufacturers lead resistance welding into new era"
Resistance Welder Manufacturers' Association (RWMA), Philadelphia, PA.

"Profitability through weldment quality improvement: The goal is to eliminate the rework"
Walter R. Edwards, Barckhoff and Associates, Inc., Minneapolis, MN.

"Ownership, motivation, and corporate performance: Putting an ESOP to work"

"Resistance brazing processes create a new twist on an old idea"
Roger Hirsch, Unitrol Electronics Inc., Northbrook, IL.

"Self-contained spot welding gun improves weld quality, productivity for stainless steel fabricator"
J. Gerard Doneski, LORS Machinery Inc., Union, NJ.

Collection of Articles from THE FABRICATOR®

December 1987

"Abrasive blast finishing: An evaluation of current blasting technologies"
Richard Woodfield, Empire Abrasive Equipment Corp., Langhorne, PA.

"Product design for finished quality: What design engineers need to consider about finishing"
J.L. Stauffer, Townley Engineering Inc., Livonia, MI.

"Grinding, blending, and finishing flat stainless steel surfaces"
Walter N. Welsch, Dynabrade Inc., Tonawanda, NY.

"New technology for water wash paint booth operations"
Benjamin D. Ravitz, Rave Industrial Service and Supply Corp., Sylvan Lake, MI.

"Process removal of overspray presents unique problems for seamed can manufacturer"
Harbridge Inc., Fond du Lac, WI.

"Practical testing of submerged arc welded pipe"
A. Palynchuk, Western Instruments, Inc., Edmonton, Alberta, Canada.

"Designing for hard tooling"
Lawrence Curtis, Jr., North American Tool & Die, San Leandro, CA.

"Use of CVD/PVD coatings in metal forming applications"
R.H. Horsfall, Multi-Arc, Division of Andal Corp.

"Using microcomputers to facilitate tube inspection"
Michael Cone, Cone & Cone, Pontiac, MI.

"Straightening circular saw blades with roll straightening machines: Automate the straightening of saw blades in single workpieces or large quantities"
A.R. Juen, Georg Fischer, Ltd., Brugg, Switzerland.

January/February 1988

"Computers ease slitter tool setup"
Albert W. Winterman and John R. Gosnell, The Wapakoneta Machine Co., Wapakoneta, OH.

"The evolution of hydraulic press brakes: A review of different hydraulic press brake systems"
Jose Pacheco, A. Dias Ramos-Maquinas-Ferramentas, Lda., and Stephen A. Lazinsky, COMEQ, Inc., Baltimore, MD.

"Servo drives: The AC solution"
Robert P. Brennan, The Rexroth Corp., Indramat Division, Wood Dale, IL.

"Making America competitive again: What is it going to cost?"
Gerald Greenwald, Chrysler Motors Corp.

"Coil handling equipment options"
Sam Phillips, Bushman Equipment Inc., Milwaukee, WI.

"Motorized grip feed upgrades coil processing line"
Red Bud Industries, Red Bud, IL.

"Coil processing FFS reduces inventory, labor"
Cecil Moore, Iowa Precision Industries, Cedar Rapids, IA.

"Investing in microcomputer-based CADD"
Howard Singer, Grant Thorton International, Miami, FL.

"Keeping time: The benefits of a job costing system"
Peter O'Donnell Offenhartz, Software Tailors, Inc., parent company of MATTimekeeping Sytems, Wellesley, MA.

March 1988

"The selection and use of roll forming lubricants in integrated systems - Part I"
Joseph Ivaska, Jr., Tower Oil & Technology, Chicago, IL.

"Roll forming to tight tolerances - Part I"
George T. Halmos, Delta Engineering, Inc., Willowdale, Ontario, Canada.

"New automated welding techniques establish torch-to-work relationships"
Randall M. Folkmann, Melton Machine & Control Co., Washington, MO.

"New die change methods increase press uptime"
Daniel R. Leighton, Atlas Automation Division, Automated Manufacturing Sytems, Inc., Fenton, MI.

April 1988

"Is an FFS a viable option for your manufacturing process?: tips for decision makers and guidelines for implementation"
Loretta A. Degasperi and Mark Barszcz, Strippit Inc., A Unit of IDEX Corp., Akron, NY.

"Roll forming to tight tolerances - Part II"
George T. Halmos, Delta Engineering, Inc., Willowdale, Ontario, Canada.

"The selection and use of roll forming lubricants in integrated systems - Part II"
Joseph Ivaska, Jr., Tower Oil & Technology, Chicago, IL.

"Incentives: Figuring in the human factor"
Billy R. Thomas, Ferris State College, Big Rapids, MI.

"New standard broadens OSHA regulations"
J. Norman Stark and M.C.D. Stark, J. Norman Stark Co., L.P.A., Cleveland, OH.

"Achieving a CIM concept"
Howard B. Singer, Grant Thornton International, Miami, FL.

May/June 1988

"Reshaping tube in line"
Joseph Olson, Chicago Roll Co., Elk Grove Village, IL.

"Typical ERW defects"
Alex Palynchuk, Western Instruments, Inc., Edmonton, Alberta, Canada.

"New bending technology eliminates mandrels, wiper dies"
Ron Stange, Tools for Bending, Inc., Denver, CO.

Collection of Articles from **THE FABRICATOR®**

"SPC for tube fabrication"
David A. Marker and David R. Morganstein, Westat Inc., Rockville, MD.

"TiN coating solves tube production problem"
Roger D. Bollier, Balzers Tool Coating Inc., Tonawanda, NY.

"AS/RS expedites sheet metal fabrication"
Don Nikolai, Webb-Triax Co., subsidiary of Jervis B. Webb Co., Cleveland, OH.

"Automated tube handing options"
Herbert J. Amster, Krasney-Kaplan Corp., Cleveland, OH.

"Sensor technology launches robotic arc welding"
Arthur Fryatt, London, England.

"Fertile turf for a sheet metal FMS: Two West German companies collaborate to achieve CIM"
John T. Winship, Wordsmith Enterprises, Allendale, NJ.

"Innovative fabricating line produces steel pallets"
Groko Pallets North America, Inc., Romeoville, IL.

"Computer-aided slitting system eliminates shims"
ASKO, Inc., Homestead, PA.

"Finite dynamic scheduling for make-to-order job shops"
John Wicker, MICROSS Manufacturing Systems Inc., Montville, NJ.

"Computer-aided storage retrieval system"
Kishan Bagadia, Spacesaver Software Systems, Inc., Brookfield, WI.

"Outdated marketing focus restricts microcomputer industry"
Roberta Graves, Qualitative Marketing, San Jose, CA.

July/August 1988

"Industrial lasers: Practical cutting applications"
Brian Urban, International Laser Machines Corp., Indianapolis, IN.

"What's new in waterjet/hydroabrasive cutting?"
David F. Wightman, Ingersoll-Rand Waterjet Cutting Systems, Elmhurst, IL.

"Improvements advance plasma arc cutting applications"
Jerry Karow, MG Industries Systems Division, Menomonee Falls, WI.

"Robotic deburring workcell meets new demands in the aerospace industry: A series of tools and brushes permits an automatic, programmed system"
Glen Carlson, Acme Manufacturing, Madison Heights, MI.

"Computerized cutting layouts slash waste"
Robert A. Gowen, Pattern Systems International, Inc., Parsippany, NJ.

"Expert system provides diagnostics for cutting systems"
Pat Harris and Richard Saunders, Laser Expert, Inc., Portola Valley, CA.

September 1988

"Integrating the 'invisible factory': CIM must achieve business objectives and have a strategic focus in order to work"
Roger Peterson, The FABRICATOR, Rockford, IL.

"High-tech revisited: On automating America - What have we learned so far?"
Jack R. Barckhoff, Barckhoff and Associates Inc., Minneapolis, MN

"Robots in the pressroom: Success factors for robotic press tending applications"
GMF Robotics, Auburn Hills, MI.

"How to select and apply PLS technology"
John Lindsey, Gemco Electric of MagneTek Controls, Clawson, MI.

"Trade tour: A lesson in foreign business"
Met-Coil Systems Corp., Cedar Rapids, IA.

"Fastener insertion presses adapt to the marketplace: A wider range of end-uses requires more versatile machines"
Leon Attarian, Penn Engineering & Manufacturing Corp., Danboro, PA.

"Current CAD and CAM trends for sheet metal punching and profiling"
Tony Billet, Radan Computational Ltd., England.

"Automating with transfer technology: Guidelines and instructions for selecting a transfer press and automation"
Donald J. Hemmelgarn, The Minster Machine Co., Minster, OH.

"Monitoring the production of formed parts: Electronic tools that foster efficiency"
David Skinner, Toledo Transducers Inc., Toledo, OH.

"A new threshold for nesting: Automatic nesting technology applied to the die design process"
Precision Nesting Systems, Inc., Cresskill, NJ.

"PSDI: It's been a long time coming"
Wayne Groenstein, Interlake Stamping of Ohio, Inc., Willoughby, OH.

October 1988

"CNC burning technology for structural members: Automated burning systems recognize and react to mill tolerance deviations"
Tom Boyer, Peddinghaus Corp., Bradley, IL.

"The shape of things to come: the changing scene of structural shape distribution"
William K. Hughes, The Levinson Steel Co., Pittsburgh, PA.

"Systems reduce handling of structural shapes: Fabricate in the same way, in the same amount of time and with the same quality every time"
W.A. Whitney Corp., Rockford, IL.

"Gainsharing: How to achieve the payoff"
Matthew Goodfellow, University Research Center, Inc., Chicago, IL.

"Essentials for quick roll changeover in roll form systems: A discussion of the elements of repeatable setup"
John Toben, Met-Coil Systems Corp., Cedar Rapids, IA.

"Computer-aided drafting: More than an electronic pencil - much more"
James E. Jackson, Compudron, Inc., Roswell, GA.

"Passing the baton in an industry in transition"
Thomas C. Smedley, Structural Software Co., Roanoke, VA.

November 1988

"Monitoring the weld process"
CRC Evans Automatic Welding, Houston, TX.

"Fabrication by welding: Process selection and application"
Timothy E. Gittens, Linde Division of Union Carbide, Somerset, NJ.

"New methods for comparing welding costs: A tool for determining the impact of deposited metal costs on fabrication costs"
Alloy Rods Corp., Hanover, PA.

"Specialty fabricators benefit from dedicated resistance welders: manufacturers achieve greater productivity and cut welding costs"
John J. Speranza, LORS Machinery, Inc., Union, NJ.

"Intelligent automated welding techniques: A presentation of some British automation developments for spot, electron beam, and laser welding applications"
Arthur Fryatt, British Consulate General, Chicago, IL.

"Lasers capture critical welding jobs: Laser systems have secured precision welding jobs where high reliability sealing is essential"
Laurence S. Derose, TEXCEL, Inc., Westfield, MA.

"Brazing beryllium copper: Concrete data on brazing techniques or an increasingly popular family of materials"
Frank Dunlevey, Brush Wellman Inc., Cleveland, OH.

"Distortion control in the drawing office"
John P. Stewart, South LaSalle, Quebec, Canada.

"Resistance welding: Helping design engineers meet the quality crunch"
Resistance Welder Manufacturers' Association, Philadelphia, PA.

December 1988

"Dispelling the myths of induction bending: Factors for evaluating the piping industry's most misunderstood process"
John A. Gillanders

"Controlling cutoff for accurate tube lengths: An overview of accuracy problems and solutions for tube cutoff"
Richard Schach, Robonex, Inc., Solon, OH.

"Manufacturing tube bending tools for today's market: CNC technology allows more flexibility in tool design"
Bill TIngley, Bend Tooling, Inc., Grand Rapids, MI.

"Enhancing press brake productivity in small to medium batch processing"
Arthur Johnson, Accurate Manufacturing Co., Alsip, IL.

"Production systems for welding tube: A total system approach to high frequency welding of tube and pipe"
Humfrey N. Udal, Thermatool Corp., Stamford, CT.

"Affordable graphics for punch press programming"
Jim Vincent, Merry Mechanization, Forest Lake, MN.

"How to implement a software project: Addressing employees' fears with consideration to the bottom line"
Kishan Bagadia, Spacesaver Software Systems, Inc., Brookfield, WI.

"Developing quality surfaces with dry process mass finishing"
David A. Davidson, PEGCO Process laboratories, Bartlett, NH.

"Edge cleaning, deburring, and surface conditioning"
Alfred F. Scheider, Osborn Manufacturing, Inc., Cleveland, OH.

"High performance grains offer greater grinding efficiency"
Joseph G. Cietek, Norton Co., Troy, NY.

"Getting a handle on dirty solvents: Long term liabilities make on-site recycling an attractive option"
Rufus M.G. Williams, Jr., Recyclene Products, Inc., San Francisco, CA.

January/February 1989

"Slit coil tensioning: Working toward perfect coils - An overview of slit coil defects"
Henry E. Theis, Herr-Voss Corp., Callery, PA.

"How to select the proper plate bending roll: A guide for determining the capacity requirements and proper design for specific applications"
Bertsch, Division of Park Corp., Cambridge City, IN.

"Multicut blanking: Increase production on cut-to-length lines"
Dean Linders, Red Bud Industries, Red Bud, IL.

"Guarding personnel from machinery-related injury: Examining the advantages and disadvantages of various safety systems"
R.J. Newhouse, Weldotron, Piscataway, NJ.

"Initiating innovation: A multidisciplinary approach"
David Covucci, Innovation Partners, Inc., Princeton, NJ.

"Control of variables crucial to laser performance: A discussion of the factors affecting laser cut quality"
Howard S. Abbott, C. Behrens Machinery Co., Danvers, MA.

"The latest microprocessor-based control technology: New controls provide multiaxis part production flexibility"
Robert P. Brennan, Indramat, Division of Rexroth Corp., Wood Dale, IL.

March 1989

"Curving and straightening roll formed parts: Part I"
George T. Halmos, Delta Engineering, Inc., Willowdale, Ontario, Canada.

"Pulse welding: Closing the gap between cost and quality"
Impulsphysik GmbH, O.W. Sailor & Associates, Bishop, CA.

"Successful TiN coating. applications in roll forming"
Jodie Alexander, Multi-Arc Scientific Coatings, West Chicago, IL.

"Curved panels create 'space station on Earth': Space camp facility mimics design of 1990s space station"
Jack van Breukelen, Curveline, Inc., Ontario, CA, and Ed St. Martin, George D. Widman, Inc., Gardena, CA.

"Disposing of hazardous wastes: Important considerations for management"
John Licks, Safety Kleen Corp., Elgin, IL.

"A tool for making tools: Advances in machine motion move lasers into die making applications"
Donald J. Hoffman and Leonard R. Migliore, Amada Laser Systems, Buena Park, CA.

"A case for CIM: J. Tracy O'Rourke, President and CEO of Allen-Bradley Company, makes his case for CIM"
J. Tracy O'Rourke, Allen-Bradley Co., Inc., Milwaukee, WI.

April 1989

"The tooling of a punch press: Advancements in machine tooling"
Richard M. Eckert, Strippit, Inc., Akron, NY.

"Fundamentals of waterjet technology: A discussion of high pressure waterjet equipment selection for cutting and surface cleaning applications"
Jay K. Guha, Monaken Technologies, Inc. Pittsburgh, PA.

"Forming applications for CNC punch presses"
Glenn Cole, C.E. Tooling Inc., Las Vegas, NV.

"The benefits of FMS technology in a sheet metal system: The profitability of a sample system is examined"
Jack Rosa, Wiedemann Division of Warner & Swasey Co., King of Prussia, PA.

"Curving and straightening roll formed parts: Part II"
George T. Halmos, Delta Engineering, Inc. Willowdale, Ontario, Canada.

"Achieving laser technology's potential for accuracy and quality"
Mazak Nissho Iwai Corp., Schaumburg, IL.

May/June 1989

"Attracting attention: Magnets in material handling"
Don Dennen, Eriez Magnetics, Erie, PA.

"AS/RS application in flexible systems"
James Wolf, Wolf Automation, Inc., Oxnard, CA.

"Exporting - It's growing importance: A survey of exporting options"
Robert Hodam, Robert Hodam Technologies, Inc., Sacramento, CA.

"Improving warehouse profitability: Four important considerations for operating warehouses at a profit"
Dennis D. Wagner, American Handing Equipment Co., Cleveland, OH.

"Principles of circular cold sawing: A guide to circular sawing with tips for selecting blades, speeds, and cutting angles"
Fred Hales, Kaltenbach, Inc., Columbus, IN.

"Accident prevention tag compliance: A discussion of OSHA specifications for the design, application, and use of accident prevention tags"
Bud Cohan, Guhana, OH.

"How to buy a used lift truck: A step-by-step guide to locating a good buy"
Lawrence F. Thompson, Caterpillar Industrial Inc., Mentor, OH.

"Slit coil tensioning: Working toward perfect coil - Part II"
Henry E. Theis, Herr-Voss Corp., Callery, PA.

"Laser cutting special materials and shapes: Defining unsuitable areas for laser processing"
Mazak Nissho Iwai Corp., Schaumburg, IL.

"Process and art for forming components from tubular shapes"
Robert Friedman, American Machine & Hydraulics Inc., Newberry Park, CA.

"The economics of rotary draw bending"
Tony Granelli, TOGR Inc., Lake Jackson, TX.

"Selecting and applying lubricants for tube fabrication"
Joseph Ivaska, Tower Oil & Technology, Chicago, IL.

"On-line inside trim monitoring for welded tubulars"
Alex Palynchuk, Western Instruments, Edmonton, Alberta, Canada.

"Rapid arc: A unique mode of GMAW transfer"
Ed Craig, Airgas Inc., Radnor, PA.

"Moving toward fully mechanized pipe welding"
Helmut K. Hahn, SIM-PAC Systems Corp., Victoria, British Columbia, Canada.

"Bar coding: Providing the key to greater productivity - Developments in automatic identification technology"
William P. Hakanson, AIM USA, Pittsburgh, PA.

July/August 1989

"New CD welding technology joins precoated sheet metal: Developments in capacitor discharge welders allow precoated appliance housings to be welded without surface marring"
Panasonic Factory Automation Co., Franklin Park, IL.

"The reality of factory automation: Integrate and add to the 'islands of automation' you already have"
Precision Nesting Systems, Inc., Cresskill, NJ.

"Modern brush deburring: A survey of wire brush deburring methods - from manual to completely automated systems"
Bruce Garvin, Accurate Equipment Co., Cincinnati, OH.

"Exporting: Costs and caveats - Determining costs and understanding geopolitics"
Robert Hodam, Robert Hodam Technologies, Sacramento, CA.

"System allows wastewater discharge into open streams"
Lancy International, Inc., Warrendale, PA.

Collection of Articles from THE FABRICATOR®

"Laser technology from the U.K.: An update from The Welding Institute on CO2 and YAG developments in the United Kingdom"
Derek Russell, The Welding Institute, Cambridge, England.

"Laser processing: Time and costs"
Mazak Nissho Iwai Corp., Schaumburg, IL.

"Preparing NC programs with graphics-based systems"
Brian Dockter, Anderson O'Brien, Inc., St. Paul, MN.

"PC-based cost estimating technology boosts accuracy and efficiency"
John Moore, Precision Machining and Metal Fabricating, Inc.

"CAM system keeps the turret presses humming: How AT&T's Little Rock facility's CAM system acts as the intermediary between design and manufacturing functions"
Point Control Co., Eugene, OR.

"How to cost justify computerized job control: A survey to help managers identify areas where savings and increased sales can be realized with tighter job control"
Lori Pappas Sweningson, Job Boss Software, Inc., Minneapolis, MN.

September 1989

"Statistical data collection for welded pipe mills: A system for controlling the production and quality of welded tube and pipe"
A.K. Hofmeister, Abbey Etna Machine Co., Perrysburg, OH.

"What went wrong?: A study of 48 fabricating firms that failed"
Matthew Goodfellow, University Research Center, Inc., Chicago, IL.

"Exporting: How it's done - A step-by-step procedure for successful exporting"
Robert Hodam, Robert Hodam Technologies, Inc., Sacramento, CA.

"Latest tube cutoffs break the downtime barrier: Advances minimize size changeover and maintenance time"
Richard Hartmann, Jr., Alpha Industries, Inc., an affiliate of Thermatool Corp., Novi, MI.

"Laser welding of stainless steel tube: A viable alternative when HF induction and TIG welding are not"
David Havrilla, Rofin-Sinar, Inc., San Jose, CA.

"Automating roll form layout"
Dick Baranowski, Baran Computer Services, Phoenix, AZ.

October 1989

"Precision sawing adds value for end users: How to precision cut plate and extrusions for a profit"
Kenneth E. Forman, Metl-Saw Systems, Inc., Benicia, CA.

"Versatility in today's ironworkers"
Paul DeRamo, The Hill Acme Co., Cleveland, OH.

"Retrofits upgrade shape cutting capabilities: A hydroelectric equipment manufacturer modernizes with retrofits"
Burny Division of Cleveland Machine Controls, Cleveland, OH.

"Safety and the metal fabricator: Guidelines for putting a safety program into practice"
Harry Borowka, The Merrit Co., and Mary Ann Giorgio, editor of OSHA Reference Manual.

"Reducing heat affect: How to lessen thermal damage in laser cut parts"
Strippit, Inc., A Unit of IDEX, Akron, NY.

"Computerization yields control during growth and change"
Tom Smedley, Structural Software Co., Roanoke, VA.

November 1989

"Calculating heat input with shielded metal pulsed arc welding: Transistorized power sources provide adjustable pulse frequency"
Dr. Ulrich Dilthey, Haiger, West Germany, and Robert Killing, Duisburg, West Germany.

"Welding repair at the Indy 500: A behind the scenes look at the greatest spectacle in racing"
Richard Smith, The Lincoln Electric Co., Cleveland, OH.

"420 Hz high frequency resistance spot welding control: Improving weld quality and process productivity"
Dr. Chyng Hua Shiou and Michael DeFalco, Weltronic/Technitron Corporation, Carol Stream, IL.

"Resistance welding scheduling with neural networks: 'Thinking' computers help determine weld parameters"
Jordan Stojanovski, James Osborne, and Nancy Martin, C.M. Smillie Group, Ferndale, MI.

"Laser strip welding: Achieving minimum excess for thin strips in short cycle times"
Lee Cooper, Oxytechnik Systems Engineering, Dover, DE.

"Temperature indicators: Useful tools in high-tech welding"
Alfred Fleury, Tempil Division of Big Three Industries, Inc., South Plainfield, NJ.

December 1989

"Using common hand-held tools in an automated system: Deburring with brushes, milling cutters, a nd other tools"
Dr. Klaus Przyklenk, Robert Bosch GmbH, Stuttgart, West Germany.

"Case Study - From postpaint to prepaint: How one company updated its paint line to meet EPA regulations"
Leo Manta, Manta VIN-COR Steel Corp., Chicago, IL.

"Selecting electric immersion heaters: Choosing the right equipment for plating, anodizing, and other finishing processes"
Dennis Rezabek, Process Technology, Inc., Mentor, OH.

"Finishing: Where do you start? - An introduction and review of the metal finishing process"
G. Lowell Tupper, Coral International, Waukegan, IL.

"The bureaucracy of the EC"
Brian Pallasch, the American Society of Association Executives.

"EC 1992: A European perspective"
Sir Jack Stewart Clark, A.T. Kearney London Board of Directors.

Collection of Articles from THE FABRICATOR®

"Forming metal with precision and economy"
Faculty of Engineering and Computer Technology, Birmingham Polytechnic, Birmingham, U.K., and Lerche Engineering Ltd., U.K.

"Robot welding at BMW: High-tech application of welding cells in West Germany"
Axel Glocker and Jurgen Ritterhaus, BMW, Dingolfing, West Germany.

"Streamlining Work-In-Progress with material flow: Minimizing production times for sheet metal parts"
Dr. Joachim Sahm, C. Behrens Machinery, Danvers, MA.

"The growth of the Spanish machine tool sector"
Theresa Olmsted, The FABRICATOR, Rockford, IL.

"Soviet oil tank production rates rise: Prefabricated coiled strips reduce assembly time"
Reprinted from Machinoexport, Moscow, Russia.

"Factory on wheels concept applied to roll forming"
Heinz Blass, Rolltech, Stafford, Queensland, Australia.

"Computer integrated cost estimating: Taking advantage of computers for quoting efficiency"
Daniel Eremenchuk, E-Z Systems, Inc., Addison, IL.

"Lasers share in Danish success: One company uses cutting lasers for photographic reproduction equipment"
Olle Appelberg, AGA AB, Sweden.

January/February 1990

"New developments in sheet metal flexible fabrication systems: How to plan cost-effective automation"
Howard Abbott, C. Behrens Machinery Co., Danvers Park, MA.

"A new way to do Just-In-Time: One view on how to revolutionize traditional JIT operations"
Dennis Butt, JIT II Corp., Wadsworth, IL.

"Optimized force measurement: Improving the effectiveness of stamping presses and other forming machines"
Don Wilhelm, Helm Instrument Co., Maumee, OH.

"Service centers: More than just steel"
Andrew Sharkey, Steel Service Center Institute, Cleveland, OH.

"Case Study - How a British sheet metal fabricator obtains efficiency: Tooling enhancements increase quality and service"
Bob Ballard, Wilson Tool International, Swindon, Wiltshire, U.K.

"The bureaucracy of the EC: How policy is made"
Brian Pallasch, the American Society of Association Executives.

"Fabricating washing machines in China: A Chinese factory makes the most of automation"
Feldmann, Inc., Rockford, IL.

"New laser system to reduce processing time: Using computer control to improve productivity"
Jeff Adams, Mitsubishi International Laser division, Bensenville, IL.

"Economic aspects of laser welding"
G. Marconi, A. Maccagno, and E. Rabino.

"Latest advancements in CNC punching technology: New controls feature improved productivity"
Jerry Rush, U.S. Amada Ltd., Buena Park, CA.

"Shop floor control in real time: How a real-time computer system helped increase a job shop's revenue"
James Pond, Exton, PA.

March 1990

"Automatic roll forming and assembly: How one company reduced setup time and significantly increased production"
Thomas Richter, Frantz Manufacturing Co., Sterling, IL.

"Open loop flying die punch and cutoff presses: Improving performance with microprocessors"
Richard Allman, Applied Microsystems, Inc., St. Louis, MO.

"Advances in coil processing: Cut-to-length line performs multiple operations"
Dean Linders, Red Bud Industries, Red Bud, IL.

"Improve the marketing of your industrial products: The common elements in successful marketing strategies"
Matthew Goodfellow, University Research Center, Inc., Chicago, IL.

"Roll forming systems: Precut versus postcut concepts"
Richard Pearson, The Bradbury Co., Inc., Moundridge, KS.

"The design of a new coil coating line"
William Cochrane, The Bronx Engineering Co., Ltd., Lye, Stourbridge, West Midlands, U.K.

"Standards, testing, and certification"
Reprinted from *Europe 1992: The Facts*, United Kingdom Department of Trade and Industry.

"Improving press formability of precoated sheet steels with lubricants: Part I"
Motohiro Nakayama, Tatsuya Kanamaru, Yukio Numakura, and Masato Yamada, Nippon Steel Corp., Tokai-shi, Japan.

"Programmable controllers in fabrication and flexible manufacturing systems: Improving consistency and quality through high-speed communication"
Joseph Tenhagen, Allen-Bradley Co., Inc., Highland, Heights, OH.

"Can CAD/CAM be customized?"
Ibraham Zeid and Nicholas Katis, Northeastern University, Boston, MA, and Theodore Bardasz, Computervision Corp., Bedford, MA.

"Laser selection and implementation: How to choose the correct laser for specific applications"
Reprinted from *Lasers in Materials Processing*, Tech Tran Consultants, Inc., Lake Geneva, WI.

April 1990

"Circular cold sawing: When and why to choose a cold saw for cutting applications"
Keith Monarch, Dake, Grand Haven, MI.

Collection of Articles from THE FABRICATOR®

"Waterjet cutting systems: Using high pressure for clean cutting"
Mick Corcoran, Ingersoll-Rand Waterjet Cutting Systems, Baxter Springs, KS.

"Cutting steel for quality and safety"
Thomas Joos, Broco, Inc., Rialto, CA.

"Levelers are not for leveling - At least not when used by roll formers"
Eric Theis, Herr-Voss Corp., Callery, PA.

"Latest developments in tube inspection machines: How vector measuring machines can provide tube inspection accuracy"
Don Kinley, Eaton Leonard Technologies, Inc., Carlsbad, CA.

"Flexible notching of motor laminations"
Alfred Bareis, Herbert Plocher, and Bernd Wannenwetsch, Schuler, Inc., Columbus, OH.

"EC 92: What can business expect?"
Mary Saunders and Don Wright, Office of European Community Affairs, Washington, D.C.

"Improving press formability of precoated sheet steels with lubricants: Part II"
Motohiro Nakayama, Tatsuya Kanamaru, Yukio Numakura, and Masato Yamada, Nippon Steel Corp., Tokai-shi, Japan.

"Laser cutting of nested parts: A method for achieving total process efficiency"
James Rutt, Coherent General, Inc., Sturbridge, MA, and Andrea Samson, Precision Nesting Systems, Inc., Cresskill, NJ.

"Laser cutting: Examining system components that affect laser applications"
Gregg Simpson, Peerless Saw Co., Groveport, OH, and Thomas Culkin, Lumonics Materials Processing Corp., Livonia, MI.

"How to evaluate CNC controls for thermal cutting: Design features and comparisons"
George Stelmaschuk, Burny Division of Cleveland Machine Controls, Cleveland, OH.

"Integrating automatic ID and EDI: Simplifying production application systems"
Jim Grosso, Fel-Pro, Inc., Skokie, IL.

"Spinning applications in the stamping process: How metal spinning helps form circular hollow parts"
Eric Fankhauser, Toledo Metal Spinning Co., Toledo, OH.

"Slide out-of-parallel problems: Why they affect part quality and available tonnage"
David Smith, Smith & Associates, Monroe, MI.

"Quick Die Change: Making the transition"
Michael Moran, Hilma Corp. of America, Brookfield, CT.

"On-stream deburring of strip material: One way to improve profits in stamping and related industries"
Austen Barnes, Barnes Advanced Technology Inc.

"Fully automatic take-up winders: Maintaining continuous press operation"
Bob Roskuski, Automated Control Systems, Inc., New Haven, IN.

"Lasers in stamping: One way the automotive industry benefits from laser processing"
John Ruselowski, Raycon Corp., Ann Arbor, MI.

May/June 1990

"Computer solutions for steel fabrication: A glimpse at what is available in structural steel software"
Edmund Bruening, Design Data, Lincoln, NE.

"Designing & constructing steel bulk storage tanks"
Bernard Zwirn for the American Iron and Steel Institute, Washington, D.C., and the Steel Plate Fabricators Association, Westchester, IL.

"Section modulus test protects against beam failure: What fabricators should know about how producers assure that a beam will hold its weight"
Gerald Shinville, Northwestern Steel & Wire Co., Sterling, IL.

"Using shot blast technology: Applications for effective structural surface preparation"
Jody Slocum, Slocum Industrial Equipment, Snellville, GA.

"Sheet metal joining method combines drawing and forming: An alternative to conventional methods"
Siegfried Naumann, TOX Corp., Addison, IL.

"How to assure success with MRP II"
Larry Pentak, Business Education Associates, Saratoga Springs, NY.

"Examining electric resistance weld tube mills for small to medium size carbon steel tubing"
Walter Krenz, Rafter Equipment Corp., Cleveland, OH.

"Setting free the automatic guided vehicle"
Dr. Brian Rooks, *FMS Magazine*.

"Improving press formability of precoated sheet steels with lubricants: Part III"
Motohiro Nakayama, Tatsuya Kanamaru, Yukio Numakura, and Masato Yamada, Nippon Steel Corp., Tokai-shi, Japan.

"Marketing in Europe in 1992"
Don Linville, U.S. Department of Commerce, Washington, D.C.

"Reaching the potential for kilowatt-level Nd:YAG lasers: An alternative for high-power density welding"
Steven Llewellyn and Thomas Kugler, Lumonics Laser Systems Group, Livonia, MI.

"Laser marking for fabricators"
John Kaminski, Laser Marking Services Inc., Smithfield, RI.

"Selecting a laser processing system: How one company reduces costs by using a five-axis laser"
Tom Paquin, Laser Specialists, Inc., Fraser, MI.

"Computer-Integrated Manufacturing in the 1990s: Competing in the world market"
Robert Collins, GE Fanuc Automation North America, Inc., Charlottesville, VA.

"Should CAM stand alone? A review of CAD and CAM interaction for fabrication"
John Baker, Machine Tool Specialists Ltd., Australia.

Collection of Articles from **THE FABRICATOR®** 211.

July/August 1990

"Fundamentals of resistance welding: How metal stampers can provide complete assemblies to their customers"
Bill Williamson, Teledyne Peer, Benton Harbor, MI.

"Examining the spot weldability of Galfan: Performing electrode life tests for efficient welding"
Ed Adamczyk, Weirton Steel Corp., Weirton, WV.

"A new approach to gas mixing for pulsed arc welding: Expanding boundaries for cost efficiency"
Don Viri, Viri Manufacturing, Inc., Fairfield, CA.

"Applications for electron beam welding: How the process works & how fabricators can use it"
David Huntley and John Leveille, EBTEC Corporation, Agawan, MA.

"Major changes are coming for fabricators who use degreasers"
William Tancig and Alisa Wickliff, Illinois Hazardous Waste Research and Information Center (HWRIC)), Champaign, IL.

"Dual-blade, dimple-free shear cutting of tube: An update on cutoff technology for high technology"
Klaus Schonfeld, Haven Manufacturing Brunswick, GA.

"Rethinking the short- to medium-run sheet metal process: Alternatives for profitable punching, shearing, and bending"
Russell Branton, Salvagnini America, Inc., Hamilton, OH.

"How to change without chaos: Weathering the storm of transition"
Monni Ryan, Sherman & Associates, Warren, OH.

"Communication and technology for punching and other hole-making processes: Tips for fabricators doing business in Israel"
Ray Noam, Rynan Ltd Industrial Representatives.

"EC 1992: Commerce Department leads programs for U.S. Business"
Reprinted from *Focus*, National Center for Manufacturing Sciences, Ann Arbor, MI.

"Fabricators can get international tax benefits"
Robert Feinschreiber, Feinscreiber & Associates, Key Biscayne, FL.

"CO2 lasers function as job shop workhorses: Dependable profitability in sheet metal industry"
Glenn Berkhahn, Mazak Nissho Iwai Corp., Schaumburg, IL.

"Justifying CO2 laser cutting: Reviewing machine configurations and machine purchasing criteria"
Bill Kramp, TRUMPF, Inc., Farmington, CT.

"Reaping the rewards of retrofits: How a company fine-tuned two Flexible Manufacturing Systems"
Sam Torrisi, Automation Intelligence, Inc., Orlando, FL.

"CIM in metal fabrication: Finding out what CIM really means"
Kevin Lotz, Intergraph Corp., Huntsville, AL.

September 1990

"Design considerations for roll forming rolls: Facts to help roll formers get the right tooling for their needs"
Milton Carder, Jasco Tools, Rochester, NY.

"What every fabricator should know about punch press tooling"
Paul Baker, and Richard Eckert, Strippit, Inc., A Unit of IDEX Corp., Akron, NY.

"New NC turret tooling considerations for automated fabricating: Eliminating wear, slug pulling, and punch galling"
Andrew Hornberger, Wilson Tool International Inc., White Bear Lake, MN.

"How to choose abrasive cutoff wheels for steel fabrication"
Peter Johnson, Norton Co., Worcester, MA.

"Guidelines for successful installation of a turret punch press with plasma"
Phil Schenk, Peterbilt Motors, Denton, TX.

"Steel surface hardening process helps extend tooling life: A method for improving production while reducing costs"
James Smith, Jr., Indianapolis, IN.

"Versatility means effectiveness for Flexible Manufacturing Systems"
A.H. (Sandy) Cherry, The Bradbury Co., Moundridge, KS.

"EC 1992: How to identify joint venture partners"
Richard Porter, KPMG Peat Marwick McLintock, London, England.

"Staying competitive using five-axis laser clean cutting: How to improve the quality of three-dimensional parts"
Shareen Foster, Laser Industries, Orange, CA.

"Laser cutting and welding systems for JIT production"
Zami Aberman, Robomatix, Novi, MI.

"How to purchase a design and programming system for sheet metal fabrication"
Michael Boggs, Striker Systems, Inc., White House, TN.

"A new approach to mechanical design automation: Solids-based design and analysis"
Bradford Morely, SDRC, Milford, OH.

October 1990

"Solving common slitting problems: How operators and management can help solve problems"
Ronald Paquin, Alcan Rolled Products, Kingston, Ontario, Canada.

"Implementing high production double roll forming lines: Examining roles of buyers and vendors in acquiring and activating equipment"
Bruce Burnside, Knapp & Vogt Manufacturing Co., Grand Rapids, MI.

"Using robots for GTAW and plasma arc welding: Achieving cost-effectiveness with robotic welding tools"
Steve Sulc, GMFanuc Robotics Corp., Auburn Hills, MI.

"Improving pipe shop efficiency: Following one company's example and learning from their experience"
James Scott, Dow Chemical Co. Pipe Shop, Texas Division, Freeport, TX.

"Case Study - Achieving integrated material handling: How a smaller company evolved into a flexible factory, and how other fabricators can benefit"
Arden Zink, Millard Manufacturing Corp., Omaha, NE.

Collection of Articles from THE FABRICATOR® 213.

"Combining tubing with pressure-stress forming: Alternatives in closed-lop cross sections"
John Hendricks, Steelcase, Inc., Grand Rapids, MI.

"Waterjet and laser methods offer alternatives for different applications: Factors to consider when choosing a cutting method"
Chip Burnham, Flow International, Kent, WA.

"hat opportunities are down the road?: Finding the hidden benefits of 'soft' issues in manufacturing"
Thomas Blunt, T.O. Blunt & Associates - Manufacturing Management consultants, Louisville, KY.

"Shimless tooling: Achieving burr-free slitting"
Raymond Wiemer, R.F. Wiemer & Associates, Rocky River, OH, and Belmont Steel Corp, Franklin Park, IL.

"Reviewing basic roll forming processes"
Werner Wasmer, Dreistern Inc., Hatfield, PA.

"European standards for nonferrous metals"
H.J. Fischer, FNNE: Nonferrous Metals Committee of the Deutsches Institute fur Normung (DIN), Cologne, West Germany.

"Using personal computers to record shop time: How one job shop replaced time clock and manual labor tracking system with bar codes and PCs"
Jim Slater, National Metal Fabricators, Elk Grove Village, IL.

"Guidelines to successful CO2 laser welding"
Paul Salvo and Derek Daly, TRUMPF Industrial Lasers Inc., Wilmington, MA.

"Understanding state-of-the-art industrial lasers: The components of productive fabricating tools"
Arthur Fryatt, Production Equipment Digest, London, England.

"Why isn't there a laser in every sheet metal job shop?: Why European and Japanese shops buy more laser cutters than the U.S."
Leonard Migliore and Donald Hoffman, Amada Laser Systems, Buena Park, CA.

"How CO2 lasers can reduce costs: job shop efficiency in metal cutting"
Glenn Berkhahn, Mazak Nissho Iwai Corp, Schaumburg, IL.

"Laser versus conventional drilling for ceramic-coated metals"
Thomas J. McDonald, Laser Fare Ltd., Smithfield, RI.

"Viewing the 3-D CAD design of automotive tooling"
Jim Susor, Waltonen Engineering Service, Inc., Madison Heights, MI.

November 1990

"Eliminating welding fumes and gases: Important safety considerations in gas and arc welding"
A.H. Krieg, A. Kreig Consulting & Trading Inc., Woodbridge, CT.

"How to optimize fabrication costs with welding"
Dr. Al Lesnewich, Severna Park, MD.

"A fabricator's guide to resistance welder selection"
John Speranza and J. Gerard Doneski, LORS Machinery, Inc., Union, NJ.

"A quick guide to welding hazards: Reviewing some of the most common dangers"
Pascal Dennis.

"How to implement a robotic welding system"
Zane Michael and Chris Anderson, Motoman, Inc., Troy, OH.

"Using pulsed arc MIG welding on copper: Reviewing the MIG welding process and looking at possible transformer applications"
Jena Howard, ESAB Welding Products, Florence, SC.

"Personal protective equipment for welding: Helping to make the shop safe"
Robert Ennamorato, The Fibre-Metal products Co., Concordville, PA.

"Applications of industrial robotic systems for arc welding: Studying a systems design for robots, positioners, welding equipment, and safety measures"
Carl Eberhard Cloos and Ulrich Dilthey, Carl Cloos Schweiβtechnik, GmbH, Halger, West Germany.

"Linear friction welding creates new design opportunities"
Richard Smith, The Welding Institute, Cambridge, U.K.

"Robotic seam finding sensor systems: A new technology for precision welding"
Sven Johansson, Selective Electronic, Inc. (Selcom), Southfield, MI, and Bjorn Back, Selcom AB, Partille, Sweden.

"The new EC merger control regulation"
Reprinted from Update on EC-92, National Association of Manufacturers.

"Roll leveling of flat parts for welding: Design makes the difference in quality part welding"
A.R. Juen, Haemmerle, Brugg, Switzerland.

"Investigating industrial applications of high-energy electron beam welding: Exploring new possibilities for fabricators"
A. Ducrot and R. Braley, Framatome Technical Center, Chalon-Sur-Saone, St. Marcel, France.

"Beam material interactions in CO2 laser spot welding of steel: Considering possible economic benefits"
Charles Albright, The Ohio State University, Columbus, OH.

"EC 1992 and common standards for welding sotware"
Andy Churley, The Welding Institute, Cambridge, U.K.

"Examining a new method for nondestructive testing of welds"
W.A. Graeme and A.C. Eizembe, Du Pont NDT Systems Group, Wilmington, DE.

"Using controls in resistance welding operations: The effects on variable welding conditions"
Robert Cohen, WeldComputer Corp., Albany, NY.

December 1990

"Forming metal with press brakes: Reviewing theory of operation and types of machines"
Bob Tillotson and Ron Carr, Wysong & Miles Co., Greensboro, NC.

Collection of Articles from **THE FABRICATOR®**

"How to select the correct press brake control technology: The decision-making process for practical productivity"
Joe Loudenback, Autobend Systems Division, Hurco Companies, Inc., Indianapolis, IN.

"Examining equipment setup controls for optimizing shearing processes: process parameters that affect sheared part quality"
Steve Hill, Pacific Press & Shear Inc., Mt. Carmel, IL.

"Using urethane tooling for press brakes"
Govind Lakshman, Polyurethane Products Corp./Press Brake Tooling Corp., Addison, IL.

"Reviewing the components of shears: Basic machine construction and operation"
Reprinted from <u>An Introduction to Metalforming Theory & Practice (Second Edition)</u>, compiled by Edward Lloyd, International Business and Technical Magazines, Redhill, Surrey, England.

"Retrofitting hydraulic clutch-brakes for turret punch presses: A possible alternative for cost savings"
John Nesheim, Slicer Controls Inc., Minneapolis, MN.

"Dry-ice cleaning can replace solvents in industrial cleaning: An alternative for traditional methods"
Alex Cheng, Noetic Systems, Los Altos, CA.

"Fabricating structural steel with CNC-controlled machines"
Rolf Klein, Peddinghaus Corp, West Germany.

"European Monetary Union"
Stephen Cooney, National Association of Manufacturers, Washington, D.C.

"What to consider when purchasing a high-tech CO2 laser"
Dick LeBlanc, ASI Robotics Sytems, Inc., Jeffersonville, IN, and H. Max Pugh, Tigart Laser Systems, In., Indianapolis, IN.

"Using the 'slab' laser: productivity and processing advantages in industrial applications"
William Dobbins, MLS Laser Systems Inc., Rockaway, NJ, and Hanspeter von Arb, MLS Laser Systems AG, Cham, Switzerland.

"Simulation technology: Scheduling and controlling the shop floor"
Douglas MacFarland, Pritsker Corp., Indianapolis, IN.

January/February 1991

"Cost estimating and economics of thermal cutting: A down-to-earth look at plasma arc and oxyfuel cutting costs"
Jerry Karow, MG Industries, Menomonee Falls, WI.

"Understanding plasma arc cutting: An option for nonferrous metals"
Peter Schreiner, The Lincoln Electric Co., Cleveland, OH.

"Solving tooling problems for JIT manufacturing: Getting the most from a punch press"
John Deegan, TRUMPF, Inc., Farmington, CT.

"Marketing industrial products: Changes in strategy can carry significant benefits"
Matthew Goodfellow, University Research Center, Inc., Chicago, IL.

"Preparing to sell a company: Taking early action also helps improve ongoing business"
George Stevenson, Stevenson & Company, Chicago, IL.

"Is the sun setting on your company's competitive edge?: A new study indicates the future of the U.S. metal forming & fabricating industry depends on worker training"
John Nandzik, Fabricators & Manufacturers Association, International, Rockford, IL.

"Developing a quality workforce: Investments in training programs"
Mary Roberts, Oregon Bureau of Labor and Industries, Portland, OR.

"Investigating the causes & cures for wing wave on roll formed parts"
Li Hanhui, Baoshan Iron & Steel Complex, Shanghai, Peoples Republic of China.

"New developments in Automatic Guided Vehicles"
Darren Taylor, Frog Systems B.V., Utrecht, The Netherlands, a subsidiary of Industrial Contractors Holland B.V.

"The torn curtain: Working with Eastern Europe"
Gregory Asbee, Met-Coil Systems Corp., Cedar Rapids, IA.

"Choosing a laser cutter: Advice for the confused buyer"
John Nobles, Rhodes Pierce-All Ltd., Slough, Berkshire, U.K.

"Computers and material handling: Spreadsheets help planners compare and justify system alternatives"
Roy Freas, Rapistan Corp., Grand Rapids, MI, and Howard Zollinger, Zollinger Associates, Inc., Grand Rapids, MI.

"Choosing the right lubricant: Stamping and drawing compounds"
Robert Rauth, Pillsbury Chemical & Oil, Inc., Detroit, MI.

"Reducing die maintenance costs through product design"
David Smith, Smith & Associates, Monroe, MI.

"The straight facts: What stampers should know about coil straighteners"
J. Douglas Plank, The Minster Machine Co., Minster, OH.

"Monitoring presses in real time: A tool for quality"
John Blumberg, Production Process, Londonderry, NH.

March 1991

"Welding dissimilar metals: Beyond the abilities of traditional resistance welding"
Del Laudel, D.L. Laudel & Associates, Mercer Island, WA.

"How power brushes can improve welding operations"
John McGinnis, Weiler Brush Co., Inc. Cresco, PA.

"Exploring application economics of welding inverters: New arc welding power source offers multiprocess welding"
Joy Strazisar, Kemppi, Inc., Mentor, OH.

"New bending technology offers alternative to press brakes: Sequential bending can be used for any volume of forming work"
Roger Benedict, Roper Whitney Co., Rockford, IL.

"Can you restructure executives?"
Matthew Goodfellow, University Research Center, Inc., Chicago, IL.

"Environmental cube system helps eliminate tolerance errors: A technique for higher quality in the automotive industry"
Bud Reno, Visioneering, Inc., Fraser, MI.

"Assessing training needs: Is it really a skills problem?"
Brian Murphy, The HRD Department, Inc., St. Paul, MN.

"Avoiding tool damage by using PVD and CVD coatings: Test results in punching and flanging"
E. Grosset, P. Peyre, P. Cherry, J. Gasnier, and C. Tournier, Centre Technique des Industries Mechaniques (CETIM), Senlis, France.

"EC 1992 growth markets: Export opportunities in Europe"
Edited by Ann Corro and Maryanne Lyons, Office of Western Europe, U.S. Department of Commerce International Trade Administration.

"Cutting and welding with lasers: The influence of material thickness on efficiency"
John Powell, Laser Expertise Ltd., Nottingham, U.K.

"Find the right CO2 laser: Matching the laser to the application"
Phillip Anthony, Rofin-Sinar Inc., Plymouth, MI.

"Monitoring the ERW pipe weld profile: High-resolution ultrasonic B-scan systems"
Shelagh Fitz and Tony Richardson, Inspectech Ltd., Scarborough, Ontario, Canada.

April 1991

"New technology for fabricating structural steel: Helping fabricators remain competitive into the 21st century"
John J. Holland, Peddinghaus Corp., Bradley, IL.

"Designing a safe robotic work cell: Fundamentals for meeting safety standards"
Vernon Mangold, Jr., Kohol Systems, Inc., Dayton, OH.

"Rewarding productivity with bonuses: Beating the competition through an employee incentive program"
Jon Wehrenberg, Jamestown Advanced Products, Inc., Jamestown, NY.

"Case Study - Air-to-air recovery units eliminate weld smoke: How one company found a different solution to a common problem"
William Hood, Hood Energy Systems Co., Rockford, IL.

"The basics of sheet metal fabricating"
Richard Budzik, Prosser Vocational High School, Chicago, IL.

"Putting lasers to work in fabricating applications: Developing a laser processing system"
Hadi A. Akeel, GMFanuc Robotics Corp., Auburn Hills, MI.

"Combining laser cutting & punching: Is it better than individual machines?"
Joachim Sahm, C. Behrens Machinery Co., Danvers, MA.

"Selecting structural steel detailing software: Guidelines for fabricators"
Gene Todd, Computer Detailing Corp., Southampton, PA.

"Blueprint for success: Implementing a job shop software system"
Rick Borg, DCD Corporate Headquarters, Minneapolis, MN.

May 1991

"Benefitting from the proper use of cut-to-length lines: Gaining a competitive edge in a depressed market"
Den Linders, Red Bud Industries, Red Bud, IL.

"Slitting: Art or technology - Part I: Planing for slitting operations"
George Ziverts and Andrew Ziverts, Metcon, Inc., Wilmette, IL.

"Reliable feeding of coiled and sheared strip: Techniques for feeding stamping presses and punching machines"
H.A. Lubbertsmeier, ALBA Vorschubtechnik GmbH, Wuppertal, Germany.

"Roll forming troubleshooting and trouble prevention"
George Halmos, Delta Engineering Inc., Willowdale, Ontario, Canada.

"New forming process uses cycloidal principle: Applications for high production and complex components"
R.S. (Bob) Burnett, Bulcan Industries, Aurora, Ontario, Canada.

"finding the hidden treasure: How to choose a scrap processing service"
Albert Cozzi, Cozzi Iron & Metal, Inc., Chicago, IL

"Up against a wall: Managing in an economic downturn"
Donald Ewaldz, BayResearch Technologies, Rockford, IL.

"Thin-wall tube mill uses new technologies: Incorporates new accumulation, roll forming, and cutoff"
Bob Stockton, Livernois Engineering Co., Dearborn, MI.

"The basics of roll forming: Examining fundamental kinds of roll formers and how they work"
Zain Ali, The Bradbury Co., Inc., Moundridge, KS.

"Spray equipment for environmental compliance: Helping fabricators meet requirements in finishing"
Jack Adams, Binks Manufacturing Co., Franklin Park, IL.

"Finishing and the environment: How to prepare for the clean air act amendments"
Dinesh Bhushan, Durr Industries, Inc., Plymouth, MI.

"New flexible abrasive deburring tools: An update on advancements in technology"
Alfred Scheider, Osborn Manufacturing/Jason Incorporated, Cleveland, OH.

"Infrared: A hot alternative for industrial finishers"
Nick Fusilli, Thermal Innovations Corp., Manasquan, NJ.

"California amendments lean toward HVLP spray: Recent regulations could impact entire coating industry"
John B. Darroch, Apollo Sprayers International, Inc., Vista, CA.

"Meeting CO2 laser system safety laws and guidelines: Requirements for the builder and the user"
Glenn Berkhahn, Mazak Nissho Iwai Corp., Schaumburg, IL.

"Keeping automated systems running with maintenance software: Programmable controllers and personal computers lend a hand"
Phil Jarvis, Jervis B. Webb Co, Farmington Hills, MI.

Collection of Articles from THE FABRICATOR®

June 1991

"Can JIT be implemented in the precision sheet metal job shop?"
Jerry Rush, U.S. Amada, Ltd., Buena Park, CA.

"A comparison of alternatives: Reshearing on a CNC punch press"
James Ofria, Automec, Inc., Waltham, MA.

"Slitting: Art or technology - Part II: Manual planning method"
George Ziverts and Andrew Ziverts, Metcon, Inc., Wilmette, IL.

"New storm water requirements impact all fabricators: Permits could be required for facility drainage"
Joanne Johnson, Environmental Science & Engineering, Inc., Chicago, IL.

"The ABCs of strike avoidance: Establishing business and labor practices for happier employees"
Woodruff Imberman, Imberman and DeForest, Chicago, IL.

"Using patterns and cutting metal: A basic description of correct use and the types of tools"
Leo A. Meyer

"Managing training costs: Know what you want and use common business practices"
Brian Murphy, The HRD Department, St. Paul, MN

"Producing prototypes through laser modeling: A more cost-effective trial-and-error method"
Tim Heller, Quadrax Laser Technologies, Inc., Portsmouth, Rhode Island.

"Fabricating parts from 3-D drawings: CAD/CAM can provide a strategic advantage"
Tom Alexander, Hewlett-Packard Co., Fort Collins, CO.

July/August 1991

"Increasing productivity on non-CNC controlled press brakes"
Robert Foley, Accurate Manufacturing Co., Alsip, IL.

"Choosing dies for press brakes: Considerations for different angle types"
Excerpted from the *Verson Die Manual*, by Verson - A Division of Allied Products Corp., Chicago, IL.

"Keeping pace with 'state of the art' punching technology: One fabricator switched to automation to stay competitive"
Theresa Olmsted, The FABRICATOR, Rockford, IL.

"Slitting: Art or technology - Part III: Computer-aided planning for savings realization"
George Ziverts and Andrew Ziverts, Metcon, Inc., Wilmette, IL.

"How to choose the correct service center: Guidelines for holes per dollar'"
Michael A. Koporc, Cleveland Punch and Die Co., Ravenna, OH.

"Using press brakes for punching and tube forming: A look at dies and special applications"
Excerpted from *Verson Die Manual*, by Verson - A Division of Allied Products Corp., Chicago, IL.

"Throwing a punch for better tooling performance: Developments in punch designs in the United Kingdom"
Eric Ford, **Engineering Gazette**, London, England.

"Setting up for tube bending: Preventive maintenance tips for increased productivity"
Jeffrey Tapper, Tube Fab Systems, Inc., Division of Tube Fab Tooling, Inc., Grand Rapids, MI.

"Solving problems using direct drive technology for punching operations"
Michael Aiken, Superior Electric, Bristol, CT, and Richard Butler, rain Systems, In., Assumption, IL.

"Measuring productivity in the job shop: There's got to be a better way"
Wm. E. Sandman, Wm. E. Sandman, Inc., Boca Raton, FL.

"Another new approach: The EC once again takes ont he standards-making process"
Adriadne Montare, Crowell & Moring, Washington, D.C.

"The fundamentals of sharing: Examining the principles of shearing, with an emphasis on guillotine shears"
LVD Co. n.v., Wevelgem-Gullegem, Belgium.

"Finding the best employee training method: Options for meeting the employees' and company's needs"
Brian Murphy, The HRD Department, St. Paul, MN.

"Preparing for the arrival of your first CO2 laser"
Derek Lumley, Avebury Circle Ltd., Berkshire, U.K.

"Exploring the benefits of laser/turret cells: Examining productivity and cost justification"
Donald Hoffman, U.S. Amada, Ltd., Buena Park, CA.

"Eliminating the fear factor of lasers: How to increase laser acceptance through education"
Gary B. Conner, Oregon Advanced Technology Center (OATC), Wilsonville, OR.

"Lasers and automatic nesting systems: A total process solution"
Gregory MacLean and Andrea Samson, Precision Nesting Systems, Inc., Cresskill, NJ.

"Estimating tool and die costs: Using parametric estimating and Group Technology"
J.E. Nicks, MiCAPP, Inc., Big Rapids, MI.

November 1991

"Joining dissimilar metals: Bimetal welding of aluminum using inertia welding"
Al Wadleigh, Interface Welding, Carson, CA.

"How new OSHA regulations for personal protective equipment will impact welders: Company management is given sole responsibility for employee safety"
Robert Ennamorato, The Fibre-Metal Products Co., Concordsville, PA.

"Examining the resistance weld interior with the contained half-weld technique: Measuring without disturbing the actual weld"
W.V. Alcini, General Motors Research Laboratories, Warren, MI.

"Welding stainless steel: Selecting the steel, designing the weld, and choosing the process"
John Gerken and Damian Kotecki, The Lincoln Electric Co., Cleveland, OH.

"What fabricators should know about weld metal cooling rates: Distinguishing thick and thin plates"
Excerpted from *Welding Handbook*, 8th edition, Volume I, American Welding Society. Adapted by Hallock C. Campbell.

"Understanding shielding gases for metal arc welding - Part I: Evaluating their effects on productivity and metallurgical properties"
N. Stenbacka and K.A. Persson, AGA AB Innovation, Lidingo, Sweden.

"Overcoming magnetic field problems in welding: Eliminating welding disruption for pipe and other applications"
Eric Ford, *Engineering Gazette*, London, England.

"Special pallets aid robotic welding"
Chris Gill, Autotech Robotics, Mentor, OH.

"The basics of butt and flash/butt welding"
Bill Keiler, Micro Products Co., Chicago, IL.

"Fundamentals of robotic arc welding: A review of procedures and applications"
Bill Heller, MG Industries, Monomonee Falls, WI.

"Reducing cost and weight with laser blank welding: Achieving an important goal for automotive manufacturers"
John Baysore, Utilase Blank Welding Technologies, Detroit, MI.

"Flexible gas tungsten arc welding systems: Using multiple TIG torch selector techniques"
Craig Srba, Stainless Design, Inc., Westerville, OH.

December 1991

"Guidelines for purchasing coil processing capital equipment: How to work with vendors to get the best value"
Arthur Helt, Helt Industries, Lake Forest, IL.

"Achieving reliable, repeatable roll form setups: How to maintain machine accuracy and product quality"
Don Botting, Steelcase Inc., Grand Rapids, MI.

"Understanding shielding gases for metal arc welding - Part II: Evaluating their effects on productivity and metallurgical properties"
N. Stenbacka and K.A. Persson, AGA AB Innovation, Lidingo, Sweden.

"Punch press material handing in the U.S. and Europe: How does it differ?"
Ray E. Hundsdoerfer, TRUMPF Inc., Farmington, CT.

"10 tips for choosing a supplier: Making the best precision metal stamping purchase"
Charles Edwards, Micro Stamping Corporation, Somerset, NJ.

"Getting the thumbs up: Successfully justifying advanced technology"
Donald Ewaldz, BayResearch Technologies, Rockford, IL.

"The skillful art of coil joining: A review of the basics helps us understand the newest technology"
Lee Kothera, Guild International Inc., Bedford, OH.

"Welding with lasers: Examining basic equipment, performance, economics, and safety"
Tim Webber, Applications Manager, Martek Lasers Inc., Livermore, CA.

"What's new in welding environments? New OSHA revisions may spark changes in safety procedures"
August Manz, A.F. Manz Associates, Union, NJ.

"Taking the strategic approach to electronic safeguarding: An in-depth look at requirements, alternatives, and applications"
Dwight Brass, Sick Optic-Electronic, Inc., Eden Prairie, MN.

"Electronic floor mats provide safety while enhancing productivity"
Craig Kochsiek, Larco, Brainerd, MN.

"Looking at hydraulic press brake & shear safety: Factors beyond OSHA requirements"
Robin Wissing, Hydrapower Machinery Corp., Palmetto, GA.

January/February 1992

"Maximizing the return on your sheet metal equipment: Benefitting from what one company learned"
Charles Fisher and Chris Koerber, SerVend International, Inc., Sellersburg, IN.

"Operating a modern right angle shear: Understanding CNC operations and the justification process"
Hal Olson, Murata Wiedemann, Inc., Downers Grove, IL.

"Making hardware installation part of the turret punch press operation: New tool technology installs self-clinching nuts"
John O'Brien, Penn Engineering & Manufacturing Co., Danboro, PA.

"Using capital equipment to stay competitive: Observations from a sheet metal shop owner"
Robert Sobocinski, Raskin USA/Balliu Lasers, Buford, GA, and Sherry Picklesimer, Tri-State Advertising Co., Warsaw, IN.

"Fabricating with zirconium: Properties and applications for an alternative metal"
Teledyne Wah Chang Albany, Albany, OR.

"Operating a fabricating plant in Indonesia: Tips on working in a developing country and an Asian culture"
Bernard Zwirn, Hill and Knowlton, Inc., New York, NY.

"Finishing with brushes: A review of available materials and designs"
Jim Henderson, The Milwaukee Brush Manufacturing Co., Monomonee Falls, WI.

"Making the best laser cutter purchase: What's available and what to look for"
Brian Finn, Laser Lab Limited, Cheltenham, Victoria, Australia.

"Converting from a manual to a computerized information system: management information systems that work for fabricators"
Rick A. Costello, Kent Corporation, North Royalton, OH.

Collection of Articles from THE FABRICATOR®

"Using robots in painting applications: New software tools aid painting robot programmers"
Avi Elliassaf, Tecnomatix Technologies, Novi, MI.

March 1992

"How to overcome problems in automated welding: Painful mistakes that could be avoided"
Terry Raymond, T.N. Raymond Consulting, White River Junction, Vermont.

"Joining metal with dip brazing: How dip brazing can provide benefits over standard welding"
Bill Bonneau, Precision Brazing Industries, Inc., Pompano Beach, FL.

"Welding in Computer Integrated manufacturing"
John Weston, The Welding Institute, Abington, Cambridge, U.K.

"Hot dip galvanizing after fabrication: Considering the potential for fabricators"
Geoff Mann, Norandal Sales Corp., Toronto, Ontario, Canada.

"Gainsharing for metal fabricating companies: Eliminating the balance sheet in benefit programs"
Matthew Goodfellow, University Research Center, Chicago, IL.

"The basic elements of a press brake: A review of bending methods and machine types"
T.E.C. Orest, M-F Industries, Inc., St. Croix Falls, WI.

"Education and training in welding technology: An essential tool to help Africa survive"
Christopher Smallbone, South African Institute of Welding, Johannesburg, South Africa.

"Measuring tube and pipe with laser sensors: Producing products closer to final specifications"
Ray Butow and Brian Boley, Aromat Corp., New Providence, NJ, and Steve June, ProTec, Cedar Lake, IN.

"CAM moves into the sheet metal shop: Gauging the benefits of direct integration with cutting equipment"
Bill Belanger, Cybermation Cutting Systems, Inc., Medford, MA.

April 1992

"CNC shearing and slitting: Following the trend toward easy operation, high productivity"
Teesing Machines B.V., Rijswijk-Z.H., The Netherlands

"Common questions and misconceptions about cut-to-length lines"
Dean Linders, Red Bud Industries, Red Bud, IL.

"Service centers provide option or flat-rolled processing"
Andrew G. Sharkey, Steel Service Center Institute.

"On a roll toward Just-In-Time manufacturing"
Zain Ali, The Bradbury Co., Inc., Moundridge, KS.

"What is coil coating?: Looking at applications and benefits"
Robert W. Moorman, Glidden Co., Westlake, OH.

"Measuring and inspecting tube assemblies: A difficult but

important process"
Homer Eaton, Supraporte Inc., Carlsbad, CA.

"Following one metal fabricator's steps on the path to success"
Woodruff Imberman, Imberman and DeForest, Chicago, IL

"An overview of roll forming systems"
David Voth, Contour Roll Co., Grand Haven, MI.

"Laser marking aluminum in full color: A fabricator's introduction to the technology"
Peter Laakmann, Synrad, Inc., Bothell, WA.

"A new in-die process inserts contacts: This one-operation stamping process uses progressive dies"
Mitchell Zaleski and Ronald Malinowski, Pylon Tool Corp., Northbrook, IL.

"A new consideration for implementing and strengthening Quick Die Change"
O. (Sam) Oishi, JIT Automation Inc., Scarborough, Ontario, Canada.

"Using ion implantation to improve forming tool life: Low-temperature process reduces wear and galling without dimensional change"
Dr. Ralph Alexander, consultant to Implant Sciences Corp., Wakefield, MA.

"Using a 'shop floor simulator' in stamping"
Medhat Karima, Forming Technologies Inc., Oakville, Ontario, Canada.

"Comparing stand-alone and integrated estimating systems: The additional functions performed in integrated systems"
Phillip Rhodes, NOVA Software Development Corp., North Easton, MA.

"Case Study - Expanding a manufacturing business through automation"
Lyn Lammert, JMAS Corp., Aurora, CO.

May 1992

"Selecting a metal cutting saw: How to avoid buying the wrong machine"
John Stong, Dake, Grand Haven, MI.

"Cutting & drilling with CO2 lasers: Applications in aerospace fabricating"
Madi Rathinavelu, Corry Laser Technology, Inc., Cory, PA.

"ID scarfing: Removing the inside weld bead of welded tube & pipe"
Michael Nelson, Nelson Tool Corp., Sunbury, OH.

"Alternatives to vapor degreasing offer pros and cons: Difficult choices are coming for metal finishers"
Felipe Donate, The Dow Chemical Co., Midland, MI.

"The art of welding"
Theresa Olmsted, The FABRICATOR®, Rockford, IL.

"Understanding new resistance welding technology"
Larry E. Moss, Automation International Inc., Danville, IL.

"Increasing your laser system's lifetime: How to prevent problems through routine maintenance"
Dr. Russell Kurtz, LIWA and Co., Monterey Park, CA.

"Profile cutting with CNC software: Gaining productivity through computer technology"
John W. Rosenberg, Microcomputer Technology Consultants (MTC) Ltd., Lockport, NY.

"Examining the CIM equation: What is missing in the implementation of CIM?"
Don P. Williams, Rock Valley College, Rockford, IL.

"Operating a robot system safely: Safe procedures start with the operator"
William Meier, IGM Robotics, Milwaukee, WI.

"Making ergonomic changes in production methods: One company improved efficiency and worker health"
Daniel Grippo, Atlas Copco Industrial Tools, Farmington Hills, MI.

"The essentials of stamping press safety"
Williams, White, & Co., Moline, IL.

"Now hear this!: Protecting your employees' hearing"
MaryBeth Iannaconne, A.M. Best Co., Inc., Oldwick, NJ.

June 1992

"How to purchase a CAD/CAM system: Making the right choice through company surveys and vendor comparisons"
Dan Justen, Bowin Technology, Cleveland, OH.

"Increasing tool performance using PVD coatings: Fighting wear, abrasion, and corrosion in forming and punching"
Frederick Teeter, Balzers Tool Coating Inc., North Tonawanda, NY, and Rainer Wild, Balzers AG, Lichtenstein, Germany.

"Tips for punch press tooling maintenance: Helpful hints to prevent galling, wear, material warp, and other problems"
Dennis Lowry and Jerry McCann, Mate Punch and Die Co., Anoka, MN.

"The countdown to Ten: The U.S. government moves toward the metric system. How does this affect you?"
Theresa Olmsted, The FABRICATOR, Rockford, IL.

"The hidden keys to good welds: Unlocking secrets to high-quality welding"
Philip Flynn, United Technologies Corp., Windsor Locks, CT.

"Introduction to laser technology and material processing"
David R. Whitehouse, Whitehouse Associates, Weston, MA.

"Metal forming with lasers: New technology allows bending of brittle metals"
Dr. Henryk Frackiewicz, Polish Academy of Sciences, Warsaw, Poland.

"Tips for understanding CAD/CAM software: Explanations about how the software works"
Carl Grosso, Metalsoft, Santa Ana, CA; Frank Bakanau and Larry Moran, Point Control Co., Eugene, OR; and Andrea Samson, Precision Nesting Systems, Inc., Cresskill, NJ.

"JIT manufacturing with automatic nesting systems: Meeting today's fabricating requirements with new technology"
Greg Canouse, Machine Tool Programming, Columbia, PA.

July/August 1992

"Analyzing press brake deflection characteristics: A review of available systems"
Robert Wonsetler, Pacific Press & Shear, Inc., Mount Carmel, IL.

"The basics of air bending and bottoming"
Excerpted from An Introduction to Metal-Forming Theory, Principles, and Practice, compiled by Edward Lloyd.

"A quality review of lubricant alternatives: Methods for screening and testing potential lubricants for metal forming"
James E. Dyla, American Charcoal Co., Division of AMCOL Corp., Dearborn, MI.

"New technologies for fabricating medium-thickness plate in Germany: How one company implemented a stand-alone manufacturing center"
Heinrich Bidmon and Edmund Beuche, Carl Schenck AG, Darmstadt, Germany.

"Selecting and using lubricants in sheet metal forming: The basics of lubricant types and applications"
Elliot S. Nachtman, Tower Oil & Technology Co., Chicago, IL.

"Examining new CO2 laser technology: The pulsed slab discharge laser"
Peter Allen, Coherent General, Inc., Sturbridge, MA.

"Marking tubular or roll formed products: Manual and programmable methods for product identification"
Frank Stephens, Telesis Marking Systems, Chillicothe, OH.

"Creating prototypes from solids data: Five primary steps toward implementing the process"
Dave Frei, Hewlett-Packard Co., Fort Collins, CO.

September 1992

"Laser welding of structural components: Tests show how it can help reduce construction costs"
Conrad Banas, United Technologies Industrial Lasers, South Windsor, CT.

"Using CNC drills to make holes in large metal parts: Staying competitive by using automation"
Donald Wright, Compustep Products Corp., Peterborough Ontario, Canada.

"Understanding tangent bending: An alternative forming method for preformed and prepainted metal"
Thomas Orwig, Sales Manager, The Taylor-Winfield Corp., Warren, OH.

"Metal forming with explosives: Underwater explosions present an alternative for fabricators"
Prem R. Hingorany, Explosive Fabricators, Inc., Louisville, CO.

"What is the true cost of maintenance?"
Terry Wireman, Wireman & Associates, Eaton, OH.

"FMSs prepare fabricators for the future: What's in a flexible system & how it's set up"
Rick Wester, Finn-Power International, Schaumburg, IL.

"Marketing for smaller fabricating companies: Figuring out what 'marketing' really means"
Matthew Goodfellow, University Research Center, Inc., Chicago, IL.

"Finding the right plate bending roll machine: How to work with the machine builder to meet your application requirements"
Francesco Massa, Malco S.P.A., Chiari (Brescia), Italy.

"Bending tube with a dedicated bender: Uses of the machine in high-volume bent tube production"
Frederick E. Avery, Wauseon Machine and Manufacturing, Inc., Wauseon, OH.

"Problem solving and team building: Training strategies and methods for a stronger workforce"
Brian Murphy, HRD Department, St. Paul, MN.

"How to choose the right steel detailing software system and accessories"
Gene F. Todd, Gene F. Todd Drafting Service, Souderton, PA.

"Implementing CAD/CAM software: Learning from one company's implementation experience"
Gary Fulton, TekSoft CAD/CAM Systems, Phoenix, AZ, and Kevin Booth, West Jordan Facility Natter Manufacturing, Inc., West Jordan, UT.

October 1992

"Roll forming heavy gauge and high-strength steels: An overview of equipment needs"
Robert Jackson, Yoder Manufacturing, Bedford Heights, OH.

"Improving roll forming performance: A study of electronic length measurement"
Robert Pickering, Applied Microsystems, St. Louis, MO.

"How to purchase or build a coil tracking system: An important factor for service centers & larger fabricators"
Barry Hengstler, Visions in Metal, Merriville, IN.

"Maintaining roll forming lines: Achieving better performance through training and preventive maintenance"
Donald Penick, Kirsch Co., Sturgis, MI.

"Examining material handling and JIT manufacturing trends: A look at two important actors in today's fabricating market"
Louis Giust, Litton Industrial Automation.

"Making the most of consulting services for small fabricating companies"
Don Aufderheide, Work Measurement Systems, Inc., Indianapolis, IN.

"Establishing a subsidiary overseas: How one company has benefitted from expanding into Israel"
Hill & Knowlton, Inc.

"Coating with urethane: VOC compliance does not necessarily mean lower quality"
Phil Moeller, Crystal Coatings, Inc., Sugar Grove, IL.

"Selecting and justifying a laser cutting system: Examining the benefits of lasers"
Michael Pellecchia, U.S. Amada Ltd. Laser Division, Buena Park, CA.

"Reducing scrap and inventory with coil optimization software: Eight steps of implementation"
Lloyd I. Wolf III, Wolf Consulting, Inc., Pittsburgh, PA.

"Computer-aided die estimating in stamping and punching: Taking steps toward accuracy and consistency"
Jim Chain, CGE Technologies, North Canton, OH.

"Retrofitting older flame cutting machinery: An alternative to purchasing new equipment"
Joseph F. Zak, Zak and Associates, Sunderland, MA.

"Monitoring design progress in a concurrent engineering environment: A design assessment tool prototype"
Daniel M. Nichols, Concurrent Engineering Research Center (CERC), Morgantown, WV.

"Intelligent process control and its potential impact on deep drawing"
Dennis N. Harvey, MTS System, Eden Prairie, MN.

"Fabricating with one-step NC controls: Combining CAD/CAM and shop floor programming techniques"
David Neman, BCD Engineering, Reston, VA.

November 1992

"Developing quality systems for welding: Understanding the key elements needed to meet ISO 9000 and other quality standards"
John M. Menhart and Gary G. Wittstock, Technical Professional Alliance, Pittsburgh, PA and Wheaton, IL.

"Using MIG welding guns: Answers to some common questions"
Cathy Walbridge, Bernard Welding Equipment Co., Beecher, IL.

"Designing a robotic welding system"
Jim Morris, Genesis Systems Group, Davenport, IA.

"Using electrodes in gas metal arc welding: The importance of diameter, feed speed, and current"
Ed Craig

"Preventive maintenance for resistance welders"
James Dally, Standard Resistance Welder Co., Winston, GA.

"Why the growing interest in gas tungsten arc welding? A brief glance at its origins and applications"
Tom Myers, Weldcraft Products, Inc., Burbank, CA.

"Flame straightening plate: How to use techniques safely and effectively"
John P. Stewart

"MIG gun designed to eliminate repetitive motion injuries: Rotating conductor tube designed for ergonomics"
Dale Bervig, Tweco Products, Inc., Wichita, KS.

"Welding with cast-iron tables: A review of tables, tooling, & recent developments"
Paul D. Cunningham, Weldsale Co., Philadelphia, PA.

"The basics of resistance spot welding"
J. Gerard Doneski, Lors Machinery, Inc., Union, NJ.

"Fiber-optic delivery of Nd:YAG lasers: Welding with nonconventional beam delivery"
Thomas R. Kugler, Lumonics Corp., Livonia, MI.

"Choosing a computerized maintenance management system for welding machines"
Kishan Bagadia, UNIK Associates, Brookfield, WI.

December 1992

"Using robots for bending with press brakes: Expert systems help bring automation to bending"
Jerry Rush, RACE Industries, Inc., La Mirada, CA.

"Improving part quality and productivity: How advanced press brake technology can help"
Ben Rapien, Cincinnati, Incorporated, Cincinnati, OH.

"Primary considerations for press brake operations: Basic safety, quality, and production techniques"
Terry Hays, Standard Industrial Corp., Clarksdale, MS.

"Short-run shearing in sheet metal fabricating: A matter of material handling"
Joseph M. Fowler, American Actuator Corp., Stamford, CT.

Case Study - Fabricating vending machines in Japan: Remaining flexible with ever-changing customer demands"
Excerpted from Sheet Metal magazine

"Using new-configuration coil slitting lines: An explanation from the ground up - Part I"
Eric Theis, Herr-Voss Corp., Callery, PA.

"Safe operation, maintenance, and service of fabricating lasers: A technical training approach"
Phillip Hoffman, General Motors Corp., North American Operations, Warren, MI.

"Cutting 3-D parts with lasers: CO2 and Nd:YAG lasers in five-axis configurations"
Tim Webber, Hobart Laser Products, Livermore, CA.

"Implementing an automated shop floor control system: Three steps for success"
Lynn A. Dumais and Sal Rebecchi, Industrial Software Companies, East Providence, RI.

"Using estimating software for fabricators: Should it be developed in-house or purchased?"
Betsy Engstrom, Fab/Trol Systems, Inc., Eugene, OR.

January/February 1993

"Keeping up with current turret punch press innovations: Punching with servo-controlled hydraulic ram presses"
Mark Brownhill, U.S. Amada, Ltd., Buena Park, CA.

"Automating the fabricating shop with computer power: An important tool for the sheet metal industry"
Charles van Sorgen, The Sorba Group, Holland.

"Case Study - Tool installs self-clinching nuts in turret punch presses: Automated hardware insertion helps this fabricator increase productivity"
John O'Brien, Penn Engineering & Manufacturing Corp., Danboro, PA.

"ISO 9000 and the metal fabricating industry: The quest for world-class quality in a global marketplace"
Kathy S. Attebery and Serge E. Gaudry, FED-PRO, Inc., Rockford, IL.

"Witnessing the transition of a company: Learning from an honest description of a company's tough times"
D. Greg Cummins, Roper Whitney Co., Rockford, IL.

"Using a tensioning device in slitting systems: Benefits of loop slitting"
Bill McMahon, Kent Corporation, North Royalton, OH.

"Using new-configuration coil slitting lines: An explanation from the ground up - Part II"
Eric Theis, Herr-Voss Corp., Callery, PA.

"Forming and fabricating round fittings - Part I: A fundamental review of pattern development & use"
Richard S. Budzik

"Building a back-to-basics marketing strategy: Encouraging the marketing and sales staffs to help each other"
Mike Quinn, McGuiness + Quinn, Manchester, NH.

"Operating a laser machine safely: OSHA standards for construction and general industry"
Robert A. Curtis, U.S. Department of Labor - OSHA, Salt Lake City, UT.

"Talking shop: An overview of voice data collection technology"
Kerry P. Lamson, Daxus Corp., Pittsburgh, PA.

"Choosing manufacturing resources planning software: Which product meets fabricators' and stampers special needs?"
W. Maclay Schmick, AXIS Computer Systems, Inc., Marlborough, MA.

"CAD design & detailing stamping dies for replaceability: Helping job shops improve cost-effectiveness and communication with vendors"
Carl Meyer, Progressive Tool Co., Waterloo, IA.

"Using modular tooling to make sheet metal components: Short-run stamping gone high-tech"
Ernie Chapman, Chapman Engineering, Santa Ana, CA.

"Controlling blank holder force and pressure: A way to improve part quality"
Mustafa A. Ahmetoglu, Taylan Altan, and Gary Kinzel, The Ohio State University, Columbus, OH.

"Using visual indicators in world-class pressworking: How to encourage employee teamwork and contribution"
David A. Smith, Smith and Associates, Monroe, MI.

"Employee ownership plan boosts stamping company's growth: Investment in employees pays of with higher quality and profits"
Corey Rosen, National Center for Employee Ownership, Oakland, CA.

Collection of Articles from THE FABRICATOR®

March 1993

"Welding process fundamentals - Part I: Understanding shielding & fluxing, SMAW, and FCAW"
Duane K. Miller, The Lincoln Electric Company's Welding Technology Center, Cleveland, OH.

"Purchasing personal protective equipment for welders and other fabricating employees: How this affects loss control, productivity, and quality of work life"
Robert J. Ennamorato, The Fibre-Metal Products Co., Concordville, PA.

"Evaluating required welding code certification tests: Are they are burden, or an opportunity?"
Russ McCubbin, ProTech Support Services, Rochester Hills, MI.

"The employee empowerment process: A hands-on review for creating value-added management with employee ideas"
Roger Stroh, FMC Corp., Agricultural Machinery Division, Jonesboro, AR.

"Secrets to operating in Mexico"
Mariah E. deForest, Imberman and DeForest, Chicago, IL.

"Forming and fabricating round fittings - Part II: A fundamental review of pattern development & use"
Richard S. Budzik

"Laser welding with robots: Comparing CO2, Nd:YAG, and continuous wave Nd:YAG technologies"
Gary Keller, Motoman Inc., West Carollton, OH.

"Answers to frequently-asked questions about ISO 9000"
American Society for Quality Control (ASQC), Milwaukee, WI.

"Using concurrent engineering to develop and produce parts: The computer-integrated product development environment"
Gary Bonadies, Westinghouse Electronic Systems Group, Baltimore, MD, and Michael Pecht, University of Maryland, College Park, MD.

April 1993

"Examining the differences in coil slitting techniques between Europe and the U.S.: A look at what we an learn and future trends"
Rudolph Witt, Messerfabrik Neuenkamp, Reimscheid, Germany, and Harold Harwood, Dienes Corp., Spencer, MA.

"Getting economic and environmental dividends in coil coating: Benefits of prepainting metal"
David A. Cocuzzi and George R. Pilcher, Akzo Coatings Inc., Columbus, OH.

"Choosing the correct lubricant for modern roll forming operations: Three key points for making the right selection"
Joseph Ivaska, Jr., Tower Oil and Technology, Chicago, IL.

"How to evaluate and choose shop floor control software: Advice from fabricators and software vendors to help clear up confusion"
Theresa Olmsted, The FABRICATOR, Rockford, IL.

"Advances in CAD/CAM systems for lasers: A glance at recent trends and criteria for evaluating systems"
Brian Dockter, N/Cell Systems, Inc., Minneapolis, MN.

"Bridging the gap in automated data collection: The impact of systems integration, radio frequency, and EDI"
Kimberly Lombard, Intermec Corp., Everett, WA.

"Welding process fundamentals - Part II: Understanding SAW, GMAW, ESW, and EGW"
Duane K. Miller, The Lincoln Electric Company's Welding Technology Center, Cleveland, OH.

"Finding the right laser job shop: What to look for in an outsourcing partner"
John Butterly, Laser Industries Inc., Orange, CA.

"Welding thick metal with CO2 lasers: High-power lasers present new capabilities"
Iain Ross, Laser Ecosse Limited, Dundee, Scotland.

"Solving laser-optic problems: Solutions for industrial CO2 lasers"
E.J. Danielewicz and G.H. Sherman, Laser Power Optics, San Diego, CA.

"Developing successful laser marking applications: Marking with a beam-steered Nd:YAG laser"
Richard L. Stevenson, Control Laser Corp., Orlando, FL.

"Case Study - Examining plate steel manufacturability for heavy equipment applications: The quality of plate from steelmakers affects the fabricator's application abilities"
Tom Majewski, Caterpillar, Inc., East Peoria, IL.

"Prepainting strip edges for tube and pipe mills: Skiving on-stream improves edges for better welds"
Austen B. Barnes, Barnes Advanced Technology, Inc., Buffalo, NY.

"Why ISO 9000?"
Walter J. Schuelke, Robodyne Corp., Minneapolis, MN.

May 1993

"Cutting with precision plasma technology: Stabilized jet helps improve cut quality"
James White, Komatsu-Cybermation, Medford, MA.

"Factors affecting band saw cutting performance: Making your sawing operation a profit-making function"
HE & M Inc., Pryor, OK.

"Cutting metal with abrasive waterjets: A comparison to other beam-cutting technologies"
Chip Burnham and Glenda Podesta, Flow International Corp., Kent, WA.

"An option for doubling drilling productivity: Cutting drilling costs in half by changing point geometry"
Fritz Fiesselmann, Evergreen Engineering Associates, Troy, MI.

"It's time to expand your plant - what should you do?: Should you lease, buy, or build?"
Kent E. Crippin, Grant Thornton, Kansas City, MO.

"Intelligently using public utilities in your expansion plans: Getting information about areas you're considering for new or existing plant expansion"
Gary Owens and John Schissel, Midwest Resources, Des Moines, IA.

Collection of Articles from THE FABRICATOR® 233.

"Using drills for structural hole making: Hole integrity and flexibility play increasingly important roles"
Larry Spengler, Pacific/Vernet, Mt. Carmel, IL.

"Stamping with hydraulic presses: An in-depth look at their characteristics and applications"
Robert G. Lown, Greenerd Press and Machine, Nashua, NH.

"Organizing your plant into cells - yes or no: Why some cells success and others don't"
Donald B. Ewaldz, Bay Technologies Inc., Rockford, IL.

"Point-of-operation safeguarding mechanical power presses: How to choose the proper guards and devices"
Roger Harrison, Rockford Systems, Rockford, IL.

"Maintaining safety in laser facilities: Safety audits reveal widespread unsafe practices"
James R. Johnson, Rockwell Laser Industries, Orlando, FL.

"European ergonomics focuses on people: U.S. companies can learn from their view"
Ake Hedman, Airfloat Systems, Decatur, IL.

"The ergonomic perspective on repetitive strain injury, cumulative trauma disorder: What exactly is Carpal Tunnel Syndrome?"
Andrew Marcotte, The Joyce Institute, Seattle, WA.

"Selecting industrial hand protection: Taking a serious look at the role gloves play"
Charles Davis, Broner Glove & Safety Co., Troy, MI.

"Welding process fundamentals - Part III: Understanding GTAW, oxyfuel cutting, plasma arc cutting, and gouging"
Duane K. Miller, The Lincoln Electric Company's Welding Technology Center, Cleveland, OH.

"Designing industrial laser beam delivery: Transmissive and reflective systems"
William Lawson, Laser Machining, Inc., Somerset, WI.

"Interaction between light and matter during laser processing"
Leonard R. Migliore, Consulting in Laser Material Processing.

"Getting started on ISO 9000"
Walter J. Schuelke, Robodyne Corp., Minneapolis, MN.

"A strategy for implementing new manufacturing management systems: Using a team approach"
Joseph Bielawski, TekSyn, Inc., Indianapolis, IN.

June 1993

"How to improve the utilization of your turret punch press: Suggestions for tracking and maintaining machine productivity"
David Young, Strippit, Inc., A Unit of IDEX Corp., Akron, NY.

"Implementing flexible manufacturing: How these systems can improve JIT capabilities"
Joachim Sahm, C. Behrens Machinery Co.,Inc., Danvers, MA.

"Special tooling applications for turret punch presses: Achieving flexibility and cost savings"
Ed Day and Mike Nissly, Wilson Tool Corporation, White Bear Lake, MN.

"Innovations in CNC punching: How do they affect fabricating techniques?"
Norm Williamson, TRUMPF Inc., Farmington, CT.

"Understanding the functions of tube drawing tools: How to get the most from your processes"
William Schultz and Jeffrey Sever, Plymouth Tube Co., Aluminum Division, Chandler, AZ.

"It's time to expand your plant: Should you relocate?"
Kent E. Crippin, Grant Thornton, Kansas City, MO.

"How to control and reduce your litigation risks"
James K. Horstman, Williams & Montgomery Ltd., Chicago, IL.

"Which is the best choice?: Punch/laser cells or combination machines"
Mark Brownhill, U.S. Amada, Buena Park, CA

"Designing industrial laser beam delivery: Transmissive and reflective systems - Part II"
William Lawson, Laser Machining, Inc., Somerset, WI.

"Developing implementation plans and quality manuals"
Walter J. Schuelke, Robodyne Corp., Minneapolis, MN.

"A knowledge-based system to facilitate concurrent engineering"
Rajiv Kohli and Guisseppi A. Forgionne, University of Maryland, Baltimore Co. (UMBC), Cantonsville, MD.

Part 8

Sheet Metal CAD/CAM Package from Merry Mechanization, Inc.*

The Merry Mech Gold Series™ is for a wide range of sheet metal fabrication needs. It is a combination and expansion of their former SMP81 software and SMP 3D Modeling and NC Programming Package. The SMP81 Factory illustration on the next page graphically depicts the relationships and compatibility of their software, described and illustrated on the following pages. MMI (Merry Mechanization, Inc.) also provides operator manuals, training programs and engineering services. Call or write to either location:

Merry Mechanization, Inc.
333A S. Indiana Avenue
Englewood, FL 34223
813-475-1788

Merry Mechanization, Inc.
1068 S. Lake Street
Forest Lake, MN 55025
612-464-8910
800-264-8910

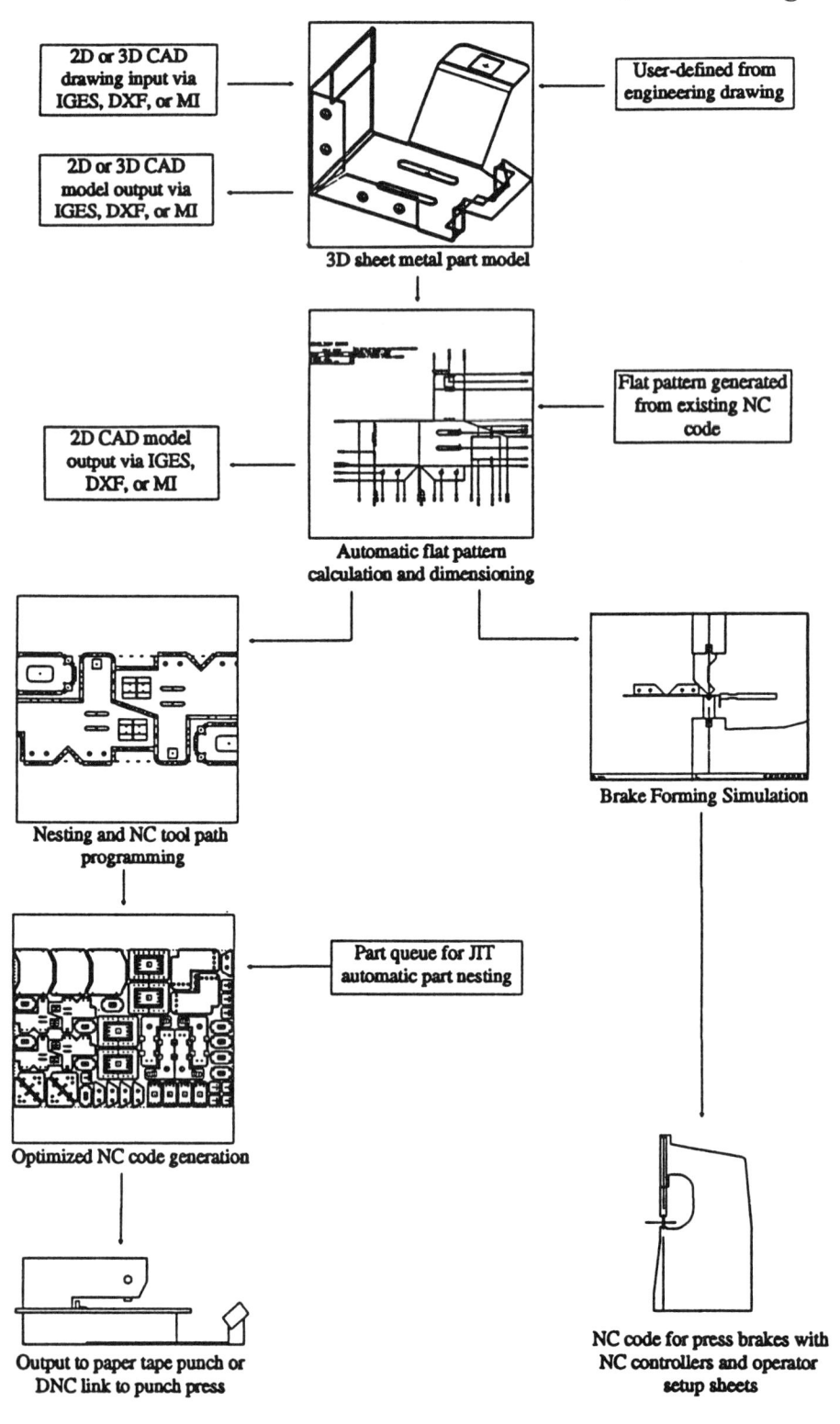

Sheet Metal CAD/CAM Package

- 2D or 3D CAD drawing input via IGES, DXF, or MI
- 2D or 3D CAD model output via IGES, DXF, or MI

→ 3D sheet metal part model ← User-defined from engineering drawing

- 2D CAD model output via IGES, DXF, or MI

→ Automatic flat pattern calculation and dimensioning ← Flat pattern generated from existing NC code

→ Nesting and NC tool path programming

→ Brake Forming Simulation

→ Optimized NC code generation ← Part queue for JIT automatic part nesting

→ Output to paper tape punch or DNC link to punch press

→ NC code for press brakes with NC controllers and operator setup sheets

Sheet Metal CAD/CAM Package

237.

The SMP-81 Factory

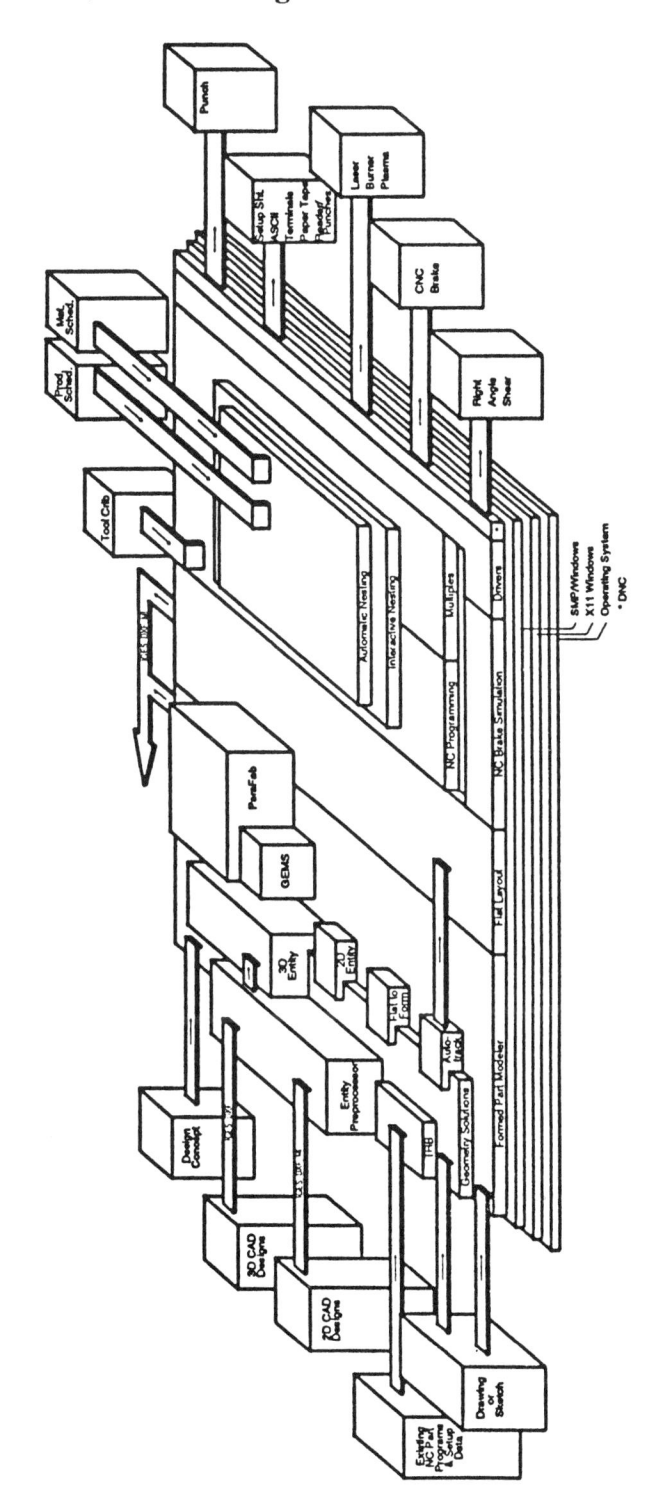

Formed Part Modeler*

This unique, feature-based sheet metal modeler underlies all of SMP-81's part definition and automatic flat layout capabilities. Parts are modeled by sheet metal features and attributes such as corners, holes, bends and thickness which may be input directly or from a variety of other sources.

Figure 1

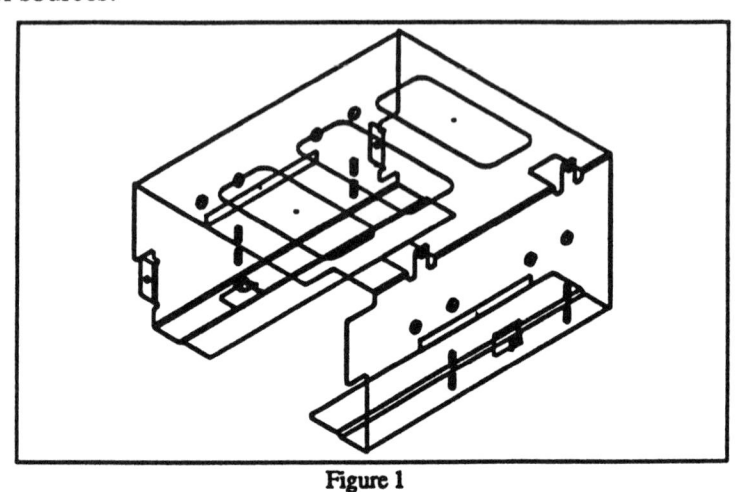

Figure 1:
This hard drive chassis has several different sheet metal features.

Figure 2:
SMP-81 software can handle up to 200 bends and 6,000 holes on a single part.

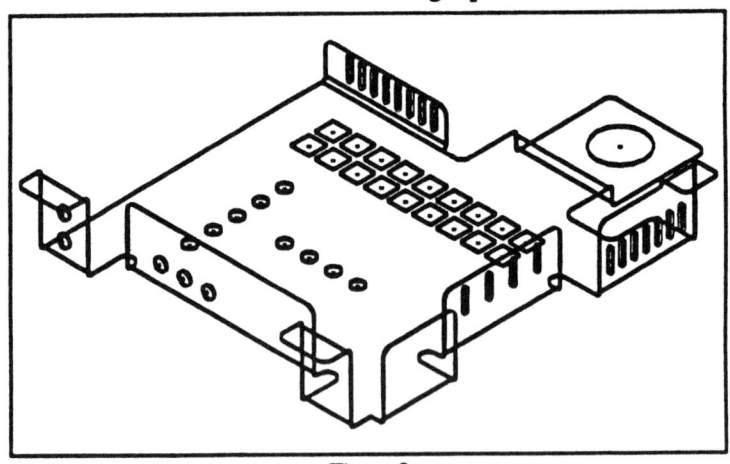

Figure 2

*CAD/CAM Information, Merry Mechanization, Inc. See Page 235 for further information.

Sheet Metal CAD/CAM Package

Graphical Editor for Modeling Sheet Metal (GEMS)

Provides parametric pattern and dynamic model editing capabilities for faster creation of parts with common or repetitive sets of features. GEMS provides the basis for automated family of parts functionality. Both the formed and flat views of the sheet metal part are displayed simultaneously, and editing either view instantly updates the other.

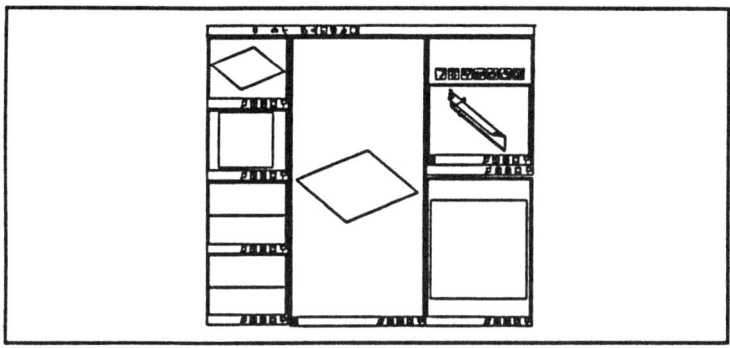

Figure 1

Figure 1:
To begin using GEMS, simply start out with a base plate. It can be of any shape or a previously-defined part.

Figure 2:
Notice that a GEM has been attached to two edges. The GEM consists of two bends and two holes.

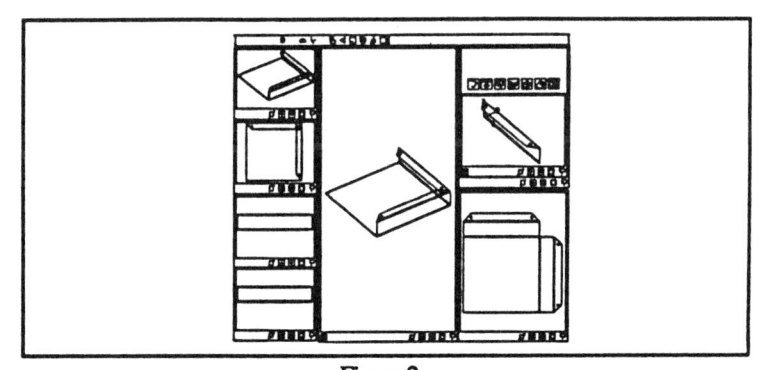

Figure 2

*CAD/CAM Information, Merry Mechanization, Inc. See Page 235 for further information.

Geometry Solutions

Integral 2D drawing package solves geometric problems when the source drawing is poorly dimensioned. It also allows editing of 2D data from CAD or TRB as well as defining special tool geometry for punching and forming.

Figure 1

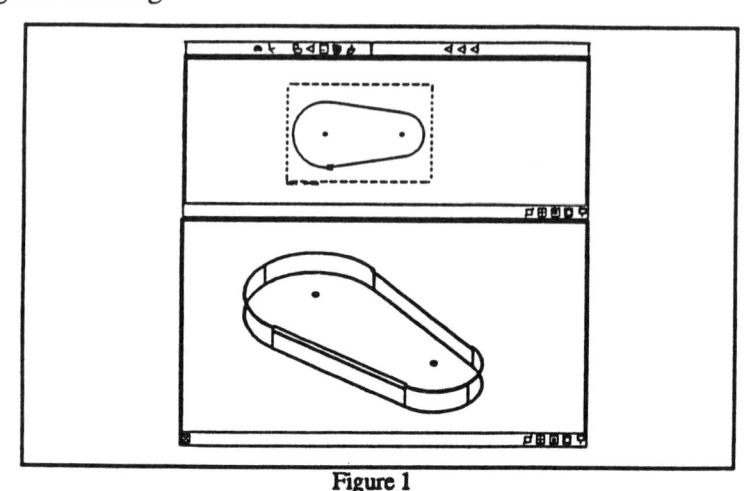

Figure 1:
This is a fan guard. Tangencies were used to describe the top surface in Geometry Solutions.

Figure 2:
Any special tool can be defined with Geometry Solutions. For example, this louver.

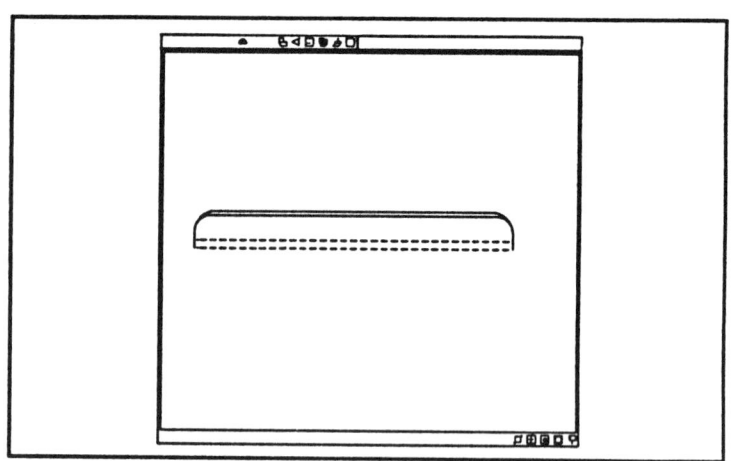

Figure 2

*CAD/CAM Information, Merry Mechanization, Inc. See Page 235 for further information.

Sheet Metal CAD/CAM Package

Tape Read Back (TRB)

Converts existing NC code and tooling data to 2D geometry of the part currently being manufactured. TRB facilitates reprogramming, cross posting, or re-creating design data from existing NC code.

```
G92X50000Y39370
G98X750Y3750I0J0P0K0
G72X265Y807
G66I375J4500P250T216C4500
G72X530Y1072
G66I742J13500P250T216C4500
X512Y2000T108
G72X1512Y2375
G66I1500J0P1000T235
G72X2262Y2875
...
```

Figure 1

Figure 1:
This is an example of a previously-generated partial ASCII file which was read by SMP-81's Tape Read Back.

Figure 2:
This is an example of regenerated part geometry that was created by SMP-81's Tape Read Back feature. It shows the original NC programming for the part.

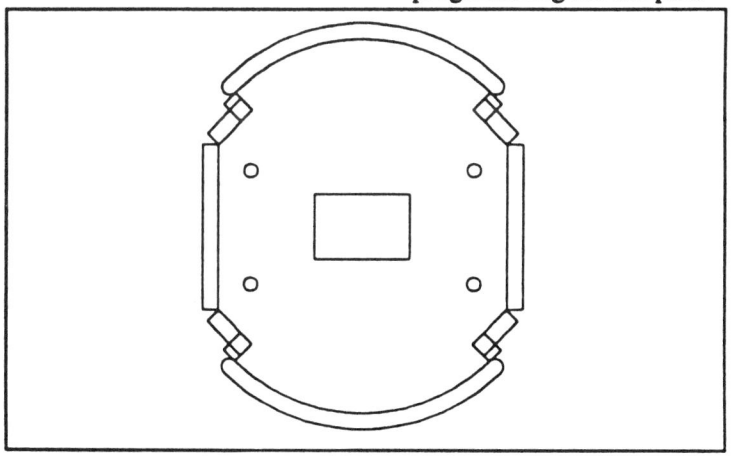

Figure 2

*CAD/CAM Information, Merry Mechanization, Inc. See Page 235 for further information.

Flat to Form

Autoprocesses flat 2D geometry to SMP-81's feature based model. It recognizes bends and inserts them into the model which creates an accurate formed part from the flat drawing.

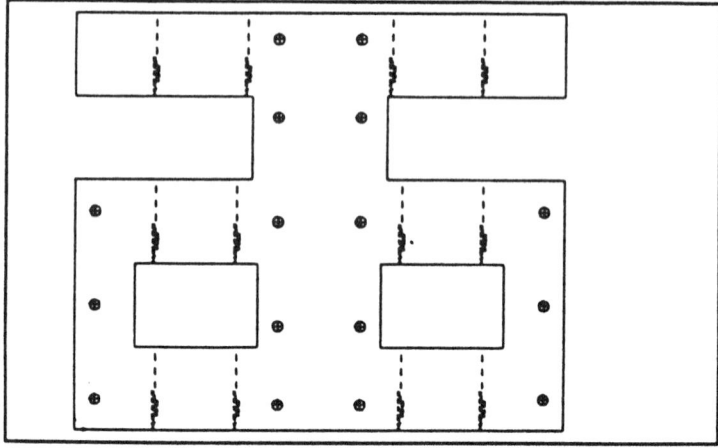

Figure 1

Figure 1:
This illustrates how the bend lines are labeled on a flat in SMP-81's Flat to Form.

Figure 2:
This is an enlargement of one of the labeled bend lines.

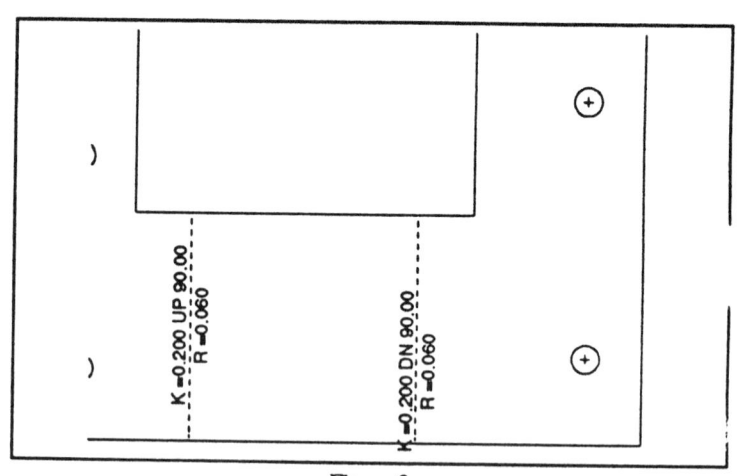

Figure 2

*CAD/CAM Information, Merry Mechanization, Inc. See Page 235 for further information.

Sheet Metal CAD/CAM Package 243.

2D Entity Input

Allows creation of the 3D feature-based model from multiple 2D views. Provides for digitizing true spacial coordinates from multiple non-true views.

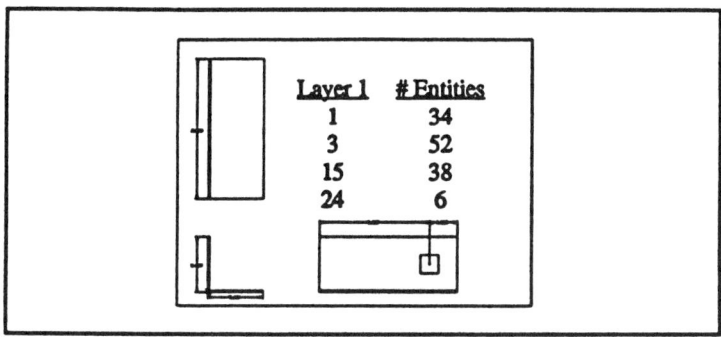

Figure 1

Figure 1:
This is an example of a 2D CAD file displaying all of the layers.

Figure 2:
SMP-81's 2D CAD Interface easily handles non-true views and compound bend angles.

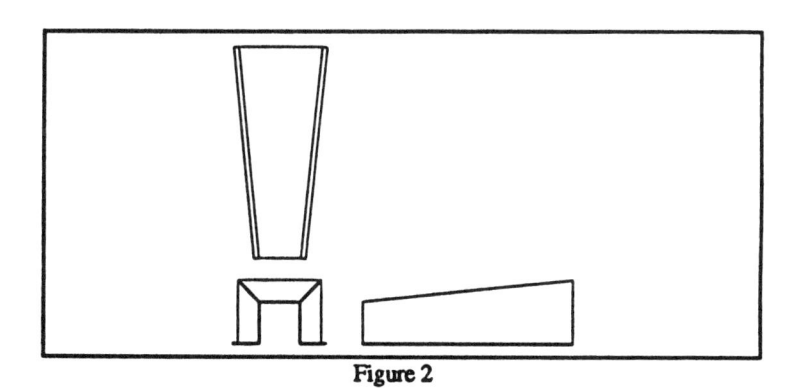

Figure 2

*CAD/CAM Information, Merry Mechanization, Inc. See Page 235 for further information.

Sheet Metal CAD/CAM Package

3D Entity Input

Quickly and accurately translates 3D entity data into SMP-81's feature based representation. Highly-automated edge tracking and mass hole selection functions are complemented by user interaction to facilitate working with less than perfect data received from CAD systems.

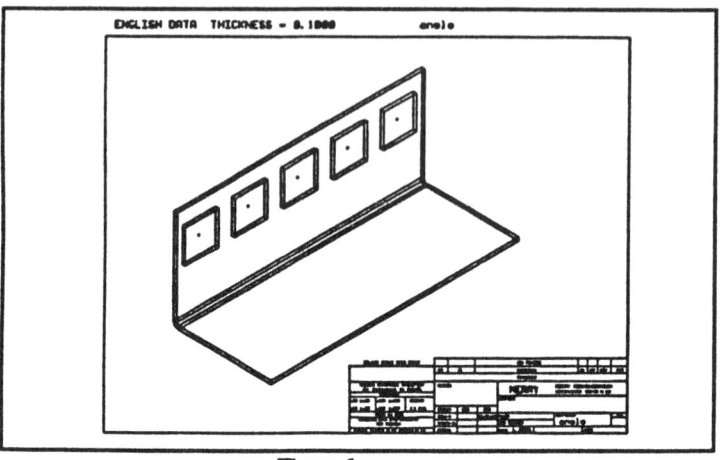

Figure 1

Figure 1:
This is an example of a 3D part that was brought into the SMP-81 program using several different layers. It also displays a title block in the lower right hand corner.

Figure 2:
Entire flanges can be brought into the SMP-81 program from your CAD system by our Autotracking capabilities.

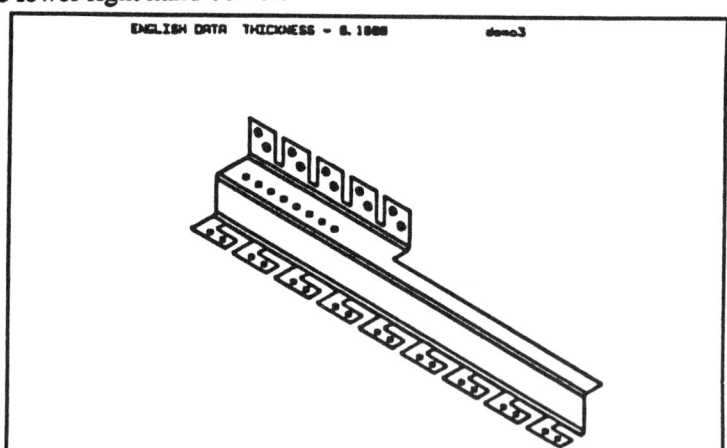

Figure 2

*CAD/CAM Information, Merry Mechanization, Inc. See Page 235 for further information.

Sheet Metal CAD/CAM Package 245.

Entity Preprocessor

Converts industry standard CAD data formats (IGES, DXF, and MI) into SMP-81's internal representation for lines, arcs, and other drawing entities. Allows viewing of the CAD data and separating of parts from assemblies.

AutoTrack

Automatically converts flat 2D geometry (single view, no bends) into SMP-81's 3D model. The part passes directly to the flat layout dimensioning routine and NC programming modules.

ParaFab

Offers complete automation for both design and manufacturing of single parts or families of assemblies.

Machine Driver

Converts graphic part program data to machine ready data and setup sheets. It also supports most NC punch presses, lasers, and plasma cutters as well as a range of flame cutters, wire EDMs, right angle shears, and CNC brake presses. Customization of non-supported machines is available.

Operating Systems

The SMP-81 program can be run on both DOS or UNIX. It is supported on a broad range of engineering workstations and high-end PCs.

*CAD/CAM Information, Merry Mechanization, Inc. See Page 235 for further information.

Flat Layout

Automatically generates a fully dimensioned flat drawing in seconds with many user formatting options. It is instantly updated when the formed part model changes and may be plotted or output to CAD via IGES, DXF, or MI formats.

Figure 1

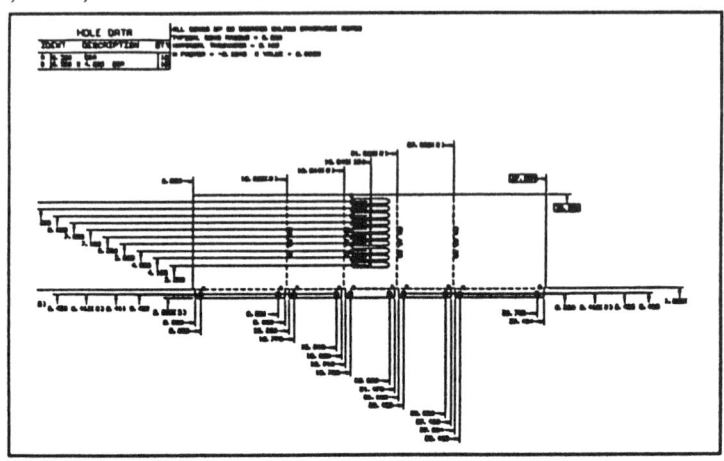

Figure 1:
This flat layout was produced automatically with the SMP-81 software and displays horizontal text and fully-dimensioned features.

Figure 2:
This 100% accurate flat layout displays vertical text and a hole chart listing all of the holes, their identification number, style, and quantity.

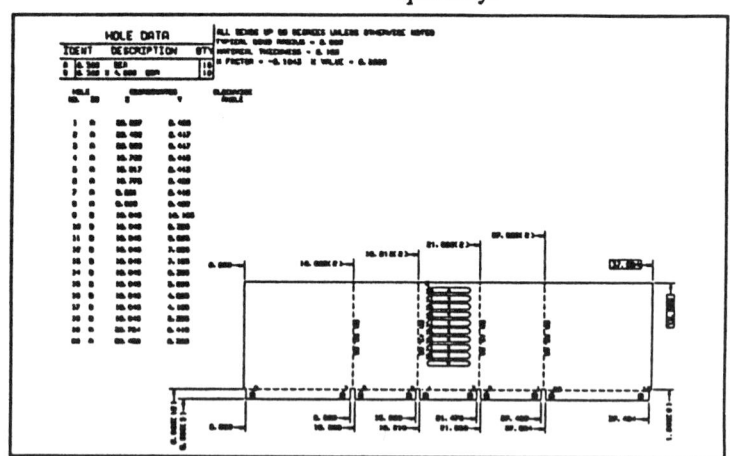

Figure 2

*CAD/CAM Information, Merry Mechanization, Inc. See Page 235 for further information.

Sheet Metal CAD/CAM Package

Graphic NC Programming

Provides automatic part programming for punching and laser contouring, with visual editing and instant verification. Supports a wide range of machine functions including auto-indexing, special tool shapes, trap doors, loaders, unloaders, right angles shears, and combination punch/laser operations. Tool paths are associative to the part model and are automatically updated when the formed model changes.

Figure 1

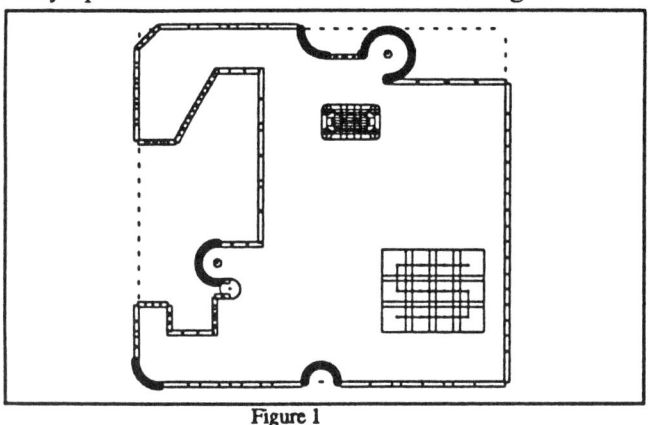

Figure 1:
AutoPunch selects appropriate tooling and automatically punches all holes, cutouts, and edges within seconds.

Figure 2:
The NC Programmer added and moved tabs, changed the tool selection, and altered the hit sequences without affecting other aspects of the part program.

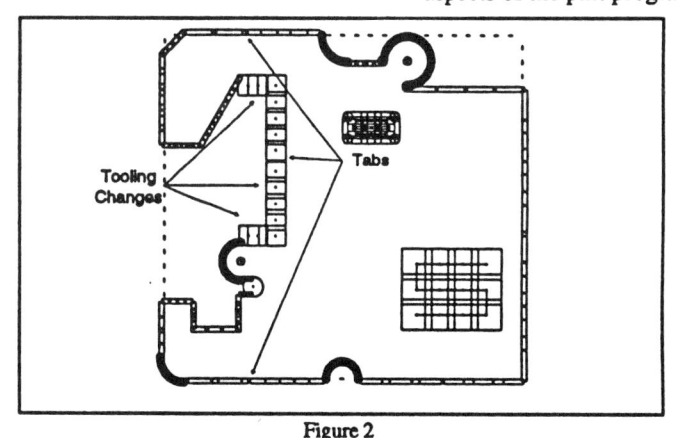

Figure 2

*CAD/CAM Information, Merry Mechanization, Inc. See Page 235 for further information.

Sheet Metal CAD/CAM Package

Multiples

This grids multiple parts on a sheet. It also performs safety checks, sequences and optimizes the tool path, supports repositioning and flips or rotates the sheet when machine travel limits are exceeded.

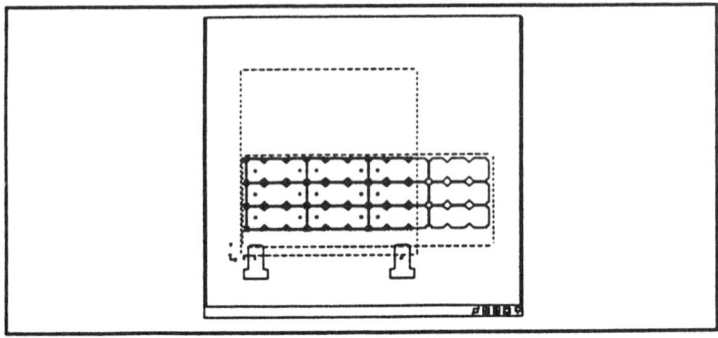

Figure 1

Figure 1:
A part can be gridded on a given size sheet or the SMP-81 program will calculate the sheet size for you.

Figure 2:
Safety zones are automatically checked, displayed, warned.

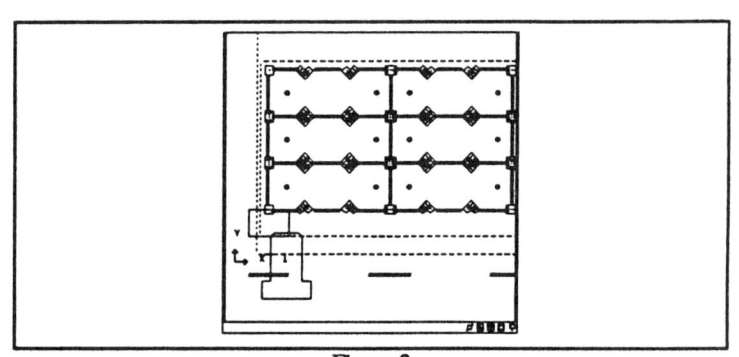

Figure 2

*CAD/CAM Information, Merry Mechanization, Inc. See Page 235 for further information.

Sheet Metal CAD/CAM Package

Interactive Nesting

Provides a fast, easy method of minimizing material usage, and groups multiple different parts to be produced on the same sheet or as a kit for the AutoNester.

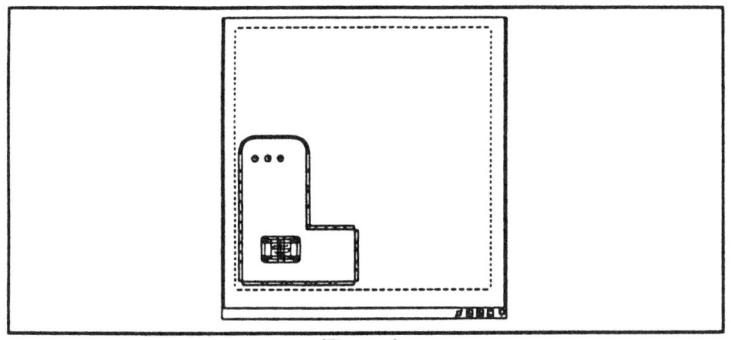

Figure 1

Figure 1:
This is a single part that was brought into interactive nesting.

Figure 2:
A part can be rotated at any angle or flipped.

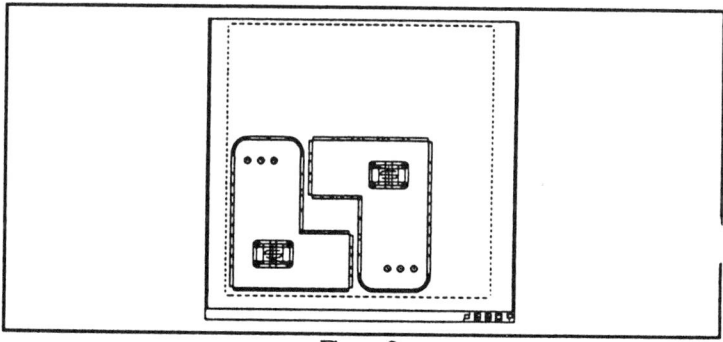

Figure 2

*CAD/CAM Information, Merry Mechanization, Inc. See Page 235 for further information.

Automatic Nesting

Schedule-based automatic nesting routine to support JIT requirements. Generates nests of parts to satisfy the production requirement, with or without user interaction.

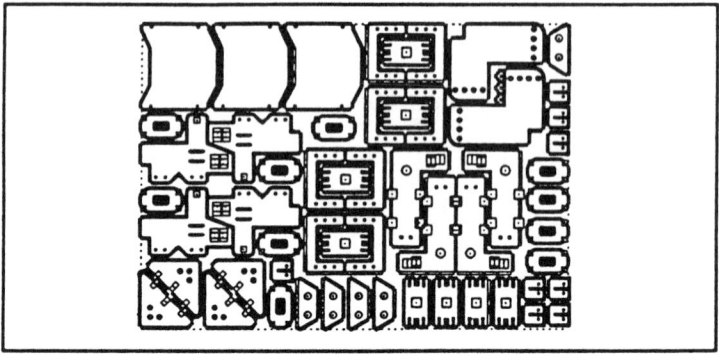

Figure 1

Figure 1:
This is an example of an SMP-81 nest for punching.

Figure 2:
This illustrates an automatically generated nest for lasering.

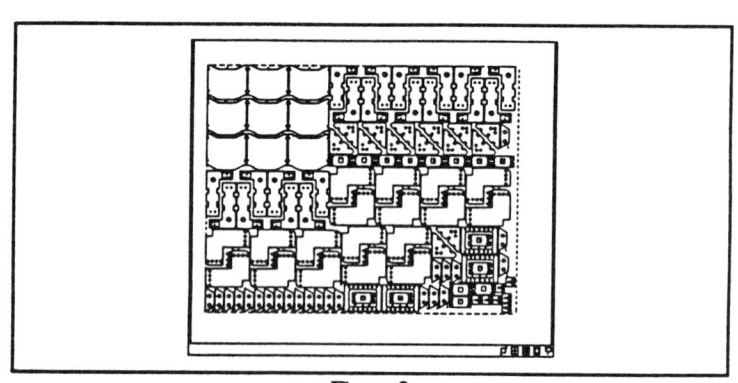

Figure 2

*CAD/CAM Information, Merry Mechanization, Inc. See Page 235 for further information.

Sheet Metal CAD/CAM Package   251.

Brake Forming Simulation

Graphically simulates bending operations. This allows brake setup and bend sequencing to be determined in the office rather than on the shop floor. Output suitable to both CNC and conventional brakes is generated.

Figure 1

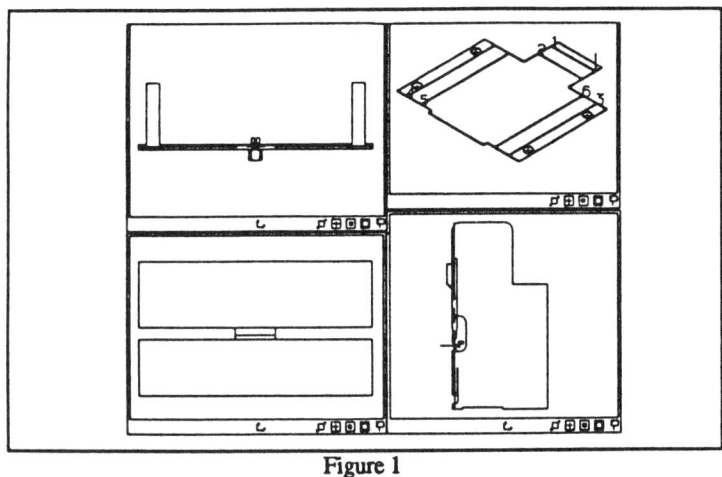

Figure 1:
A part is initially put into the brake as a flat, and the bend sequence can be defined or altered.

Figure 2:
This is an enlarged view of the side of the brake.

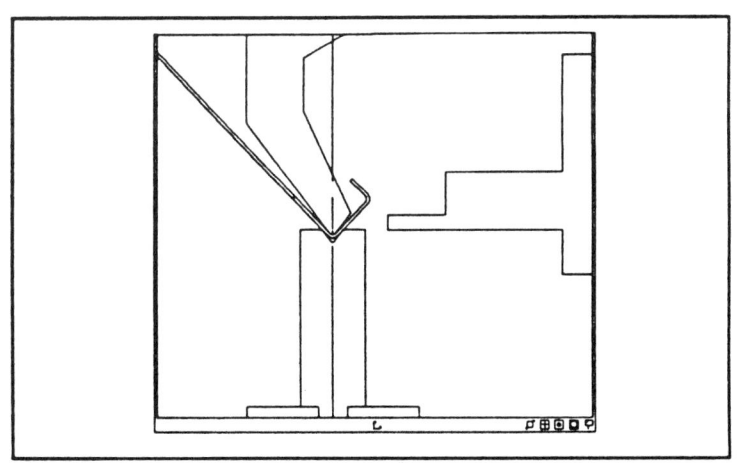

Figure 2

*CAD/CAM Information, Merry Mechanization, Inc. See Page 235 for further information.

SMP/Windows

Fast, consistent and easy-to-use multi-window user interface to all SMP-81 graphic application modules. It provides quick display manipulation and can be customized to individual preferences.

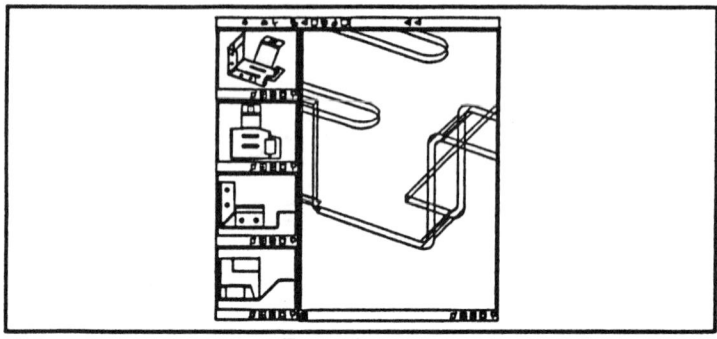

Figure 1

Figure 1:
This is a windowed-in view of the isometric view.

Figure 2:
The flat pattern can be viewed simultaneously.

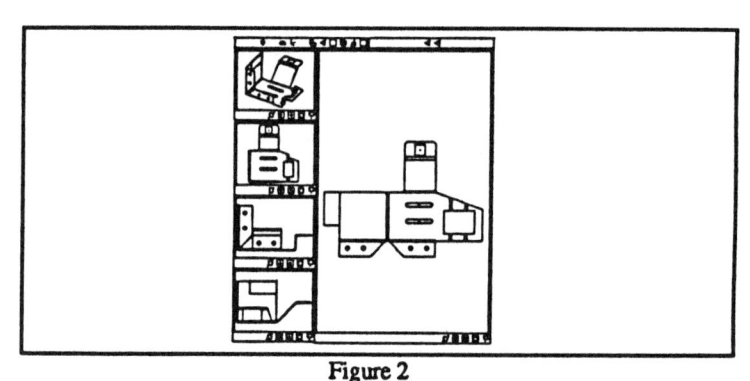

Figure 2

*CAD/CAM Information, Merry Mechanization, Inc. See Page 235 for further information.

Sheet Metal CAD/CAM Package

Distributed Numerical Control

Communicates with machine controls, shop floor terminals, tape readers/punches and text printers to initiate the production process.

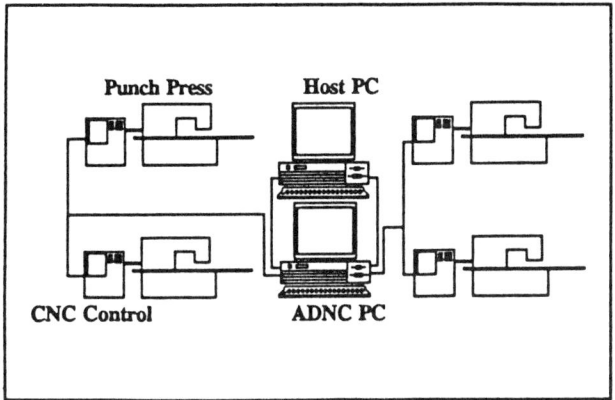

Advanced Distributed Numerical Control (ADNC)

Advanced DNC (ADNC):
ADNC acts as an NC file server by pulling NC data from the host/programming system and distributing the data to as many as 16 shop floor machine controls. ADNC gives the operator the ability to save and edit NC data with the ADNC full screen editor and view setup sheets without leaving the shop floor. In addition, ADNC increases productivity and efficiency by downloading files quickly and easily.

Host-Based DNC (HDNC):
HDNC utilizes the multi-tasking/multi-user capabilities of the computer running SMP-81 to initiate and control DNC operations. HDNC was designed to accelerate the transfer of NC data between the host/programming system and the machine controls in operation by transporting information through high speed RS-232 lines. By using the optional ASCII terminal, the operator can control the downloading of NC data and view setup information at any time directly from the shop floor.

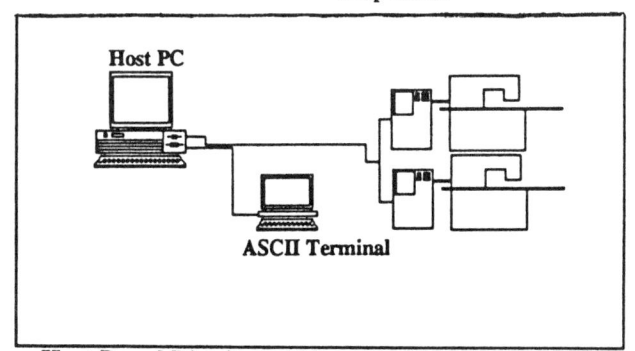

Host-Based Distributed Numerical Control (HDNC)

*CAD/CAM Information, Merry Mechanization, Inc. See Page 235 for further information.

Part 9

Sample Shop Layouts
Collection of Articles From
Snips Magazine

Page 255 describes SNIPS Magazine. Reprints of articles from SNIPS Magazine begin on Page 256.

SNIPS MAGAZINE

SNIPS is published monthly and is a journal of constructive help for the air conditioning, warm air heating, sheet metal and ventilation trades, and those who do roofing work in connection.

SNIPS is a friendly, close-to-the-reader, newsy periodical, long established as the "Bible" of the industry. Stories feature work done by readers, plus numerous new product reviews and reports of local, state and national trade association activities on an almost exclusive basis.

In addition to the feature articles, **SNIPS** regular "Department News" sections include:

Advertisers Index
Book News
Coming Conventions
Computer News
Editor's Page
Estimating, Credits and Collections
HVACR Service Information
Heating Problem Discussions
Hydronics News
Industry Educational News
Insurance and Safety Matters
Letters From Readers
Little Journeys to Interesting Places
Machine, Tool and Shop News
Management Matters
Market Matters
National Association News
Obituaries
Rambling With Reps
Refrigeration News
Roofing, Siding and Insulation News
Solar Heating News
Solid Fuel Heating News
Successful Sales Ideas
Supply Trade and New Product News
Supply Trade Personnel News
Truck News
Ventilation News
Want Ads

SNIPS features local and regional events in the "Sectional News" including the US in 14 sections, Canada and other foreign countries.

A special service provided by **SNIPS** is its Book Department which carries a wide selection of trade and related books.

Write for subscription information and for a Book Catalog:

SNIPS Magazine
1949 Cornell
Melrose Park, IL 60160   FAX 708-544-3884

124-Year-Old Nashville, Tenn., Sheet Metal Firm Noted in the South for Modern Production Equipment

R. D. Herbert & Sons Co., Nashville, Tenn., Utilizes Sheet Metal Facilities Recognized as the Finest in the South ... Welty-Way Duct Production Line Operated ... Spiral Pipe Machine Makes Pipe from Several Metals ... Dodge Scan Machine Saves Time, Labor and Shoe Leather ... Instimate Computer Cuts Estimating Chores by 10% ... Two Gigantic Liquid Asphalt Tanks Keep "Hot Stuff" at 300°

In 1850, before the Civil War divided the North and the South, a man of enterprise, T. L. Herbert, founded Herbert Materials Co. in Nashville, Tenn.

Today his great grandson, Robert D. Herbert III and Frank D. Wilk, Jr., operate a sheet metal and roofing contracting firm which is considered as one of the finest equipped in the South.

We refer to R. D. Herbert & Sons Co., 601 Harrison St., Nashville, Tenn., 37219, which is considered as a big, old company with young aggressive management.

SNIPS Tours R. D. Herbert & Sons Co.

It was a pleasure for SNIPS to visit this fine Nashville, Tenn., firm and to accompany "Bobby" Herbert, the 40-year-old professional engineer who received his degree from Massachusetts Institute of Technology and who is the president of the company. Young Herbert works closely with Frank Wilk, a Vanderbilt graduate who is executive vice president of R. D. Herbert & Sons Co.

$300,000 Invested in Mechanization

In looking about the R. D. Herbert & Sons Co. establishment, it was easy to understand the firm's success story. Employees, in their teens when they joined the company decades ago, have stayed "in the family" and have contributed stability to the firm with their experience and maturity.

To meet the demands of business expansion and possible competition from other ambitious sheet metal contractors, R. D. Herbert & Sons Co. has invested well over $300,000 in modern fabrication equipment.

Thomas Levins Herbert, Sr., Great-Grandfather of R. D. Herbert, III, President of R. D. Herbert & Sons, Nashville, Who Founded Firm at Close of Civil War. Previously, the Operation Was a Hardware Store

Sheet Metal — Roofing Share Spotlight at R. D. Herbert

It was about 50 years ago when the firm became involved in roofing work which now represents about half of the company's activities. E. L. Bass has been the backbone of roofing operations for over 40 years.

In the late 40's the firm became involved with the production of ductwork and later branched into stainless steel custom kitchen work for which they have achieved a reputation of expert craftsmanship.

Sheet Metal Operations Divided Between Job Shop and HVAC Work

We call our readers' attention to the shop layout sketch which accompanies this story. This sketch illustrates the fact that the 100-foot by 200-foot sheet metal shop houses two distinct and separate operations ... the job shop, fabricating custom sheet metal work and the production shop involving fabrication of spiral pipe and ductwork for other area air conditioning contractors.

Combined sheet metal and roofing contracting activities now produce an estimated three million dollars of gross sales.

Welty-Way Duct Line Purchased from Cardinal Machinery, Memphis

R. D. Herbert & Sons Co. points with pride to its Welty-Way duct production line which receives coil stock, straightens it, shears it to required blank size, notches and beads it. Snaplock edges are applied by Lockformer Co. Pittsburgh machines.

L-shaped duct sections, formed on the firm's Dreis & Krump press brake, are nested and stacked on wooden skids to await loading on trucks with fork lifts.

A 5-ton overhead traveling crane is employed to handle 10,000 lb. coil stock for use by the Welty-Way duct line and the spiral pipe machine.

Spiral Pipe Machine Produces Pipe From Galvanized, Stainless, Aluminum

This machine, provided by Spiro U.S.A., Inc., 450 S. Wheeling Rd., Wheeling, Ill., 60090, can produce 3" to 48" diameter galvanized, aluminum and stainless steel spiral pipe from coil stock. Change-over to new diameters can be accomplished in less than five minutes.

R. D. Herbert & Sons also provide their customers with quality Spiro-Vent reducers and other fittings produced by Spiro, U.S.A.

Insulation Center Features Gripnail Air Powered Fastening System

Because insulated ductwork is much in demand, R. D. Herbert & Sons maintains a special insulation center in the shop.

R. D. Herbert Mechanics David Pursley, Left; and Wallace Jones, Right, Flank Pattern Master which Projects Layout Pattern Onto Metal and Is Traced with Felt Pen (SNIPS Photo)

Featured in the Center is a Lockformer Co. insulation shear which cuts insulation to size from an overhead shop-made straightener set-up.

After being cut to size, insulation is "glued" with an adhesive made by a Nashville firm which specializes in shoe repair adhesive sprayed on to duct blank. Insulation is mechanically fastened with a Gripnail air powered gun which stands up well under stress of large volume production.

(Continued on Next Page)

R. D. Herbert III, Left, President of R. D. Herbert & Sons Co., Nashville; and Frank A. Wilk, Jr., Right, Exec. Vice Pres., Display SMACNA Membership Plaque which Hangs in Office
(SNIPS Photo)

Picturing the Exterior of the Building Housing R. D. Herbert & Sons Co. in Nashville, Tenn. Sheet Metal Shop Measures 100' x 200'

Sheet Metal Draftsman Jim Lowe Pictured Next To Instimate Computer which Features an Electronic Scanning Probe which Feeds Blueprint Data into Memory Bank for Estimating Purposes
(SNIPS Photo)

---

*Used with permission from SNIPS Magazine. Complete information about SNIPS Magazine is on Page 255.

Collection of Articles from SNIPS

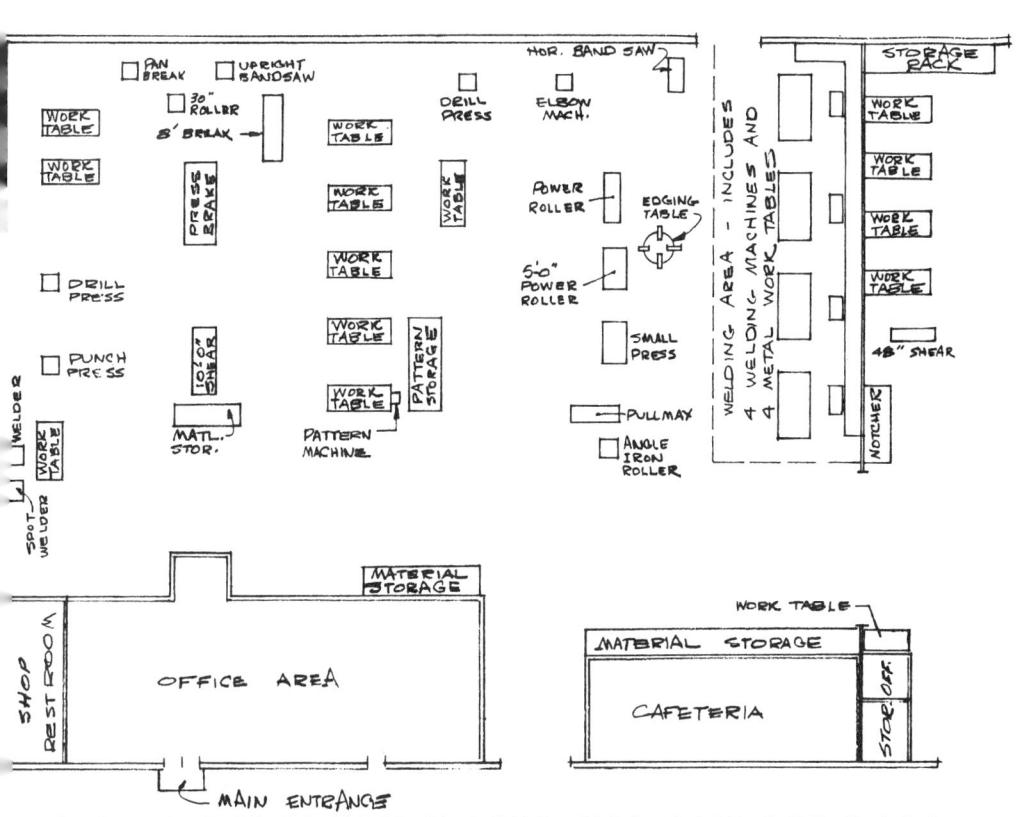

Above Shop Layout Shows the Job Shop Section of R. D. Herbert & Sons Co. Metal Shop which Employes About 15 Men. The Welding Shop in the Upper Right Hand Corner Employes 6 to 8 Welders. Cafeteria in Lower Right Hand Corner Was Result of OSHA Inspection When Inspector Saw Men Eating Lunch at their Benches. Now the Attractive Cafeteria Is Enjoyed by All Employees

(Continued from Preceding Page)
Pattern Master Saves Time
In Pattern Development Work

Another space-age machine which the firm employs to reduce costly pattern lay-out time is the Pattern Master produced by Pattern Projection Co., 2303 Dillow Rd., West Linn, Ore., 97068. Over 175,000 variations of the most difficult patterns used in sheet metal work are available on film and stored in less-than 1 cubic foot of space.

The patterns may be enlarged up to 48" in diameter and transferred to metal within three minutes.

Dodge Scan Machine Saves Shoe Leather

The R. D. Herbert organization receives five sets of plans in the office every day via their F. W. Dodge Scan machine which projects plans reduced to micro-film and made available to subscribers by McGraw-Hill Information Systems Co., 1221 Avenue of The Americas, New York, N. Y. Instead of R. D. Herbert personnel running down to architects' offices to pick up plans, they look over five sets of plans a day in the firm's drafting offices; and they figure one job each day from the micro-filmed plans which are enlarged to standard size by a projector.

In the words of Bobby Herbert, "this is one machine that we couldn't do without."

Intimate Computer Features Scanner
For Taking Over Estimating Figures

R. D. Herbert & Sons Co. utilizes the NCR 399 computer which itemizes phases of work according to an activity such as sheet metal, HVAC, roofing, etc.

R. D. Herbert Mechanics Lift Section of Sheet Metal Duct Work which Just Came Off Welty-Way Duct Machine to a Rolling Cart which Will Transport Section for Insulating or Braking

A highly valued piece of equipment which has saved 10% of the firm's estimating chores is the Instimate machine produced by Diversified Electronics, 720 E. Evelyn Ave., Sunnydale, Cal., 94086.

This unique computer is equipped with a scanning probe which the operator runs over the blueprint, taking off totals of the poundage of ductwork and fittings.

The Instimate also computes manhours of labor which the job will take.

It was interesting to learn that the R. D. Herbert & Sons Co., was able to increase its business volume from one million dollars to three million dollars without need for expanding its three-man estimator staff.

Welding Work Handled for Smaller
Sheet Metal Contractors

R. D. Herbert & Sons maintains a welding shop within its general sheet metal shop, employing from six to eight welders. They are able to provide heliarc and MIG welders for their own requirements, as well as for smaller sheet metal contractors not equipped to do welding work. Half of the firm's welding is for other companies.

Much Stainless Steel Kitchen Work
Handled for Nashville Restaurants

The R. D. Herbert job shop which employs 15 men handles stainless steel up to 10 ga. It also fabricates custom sheet metal

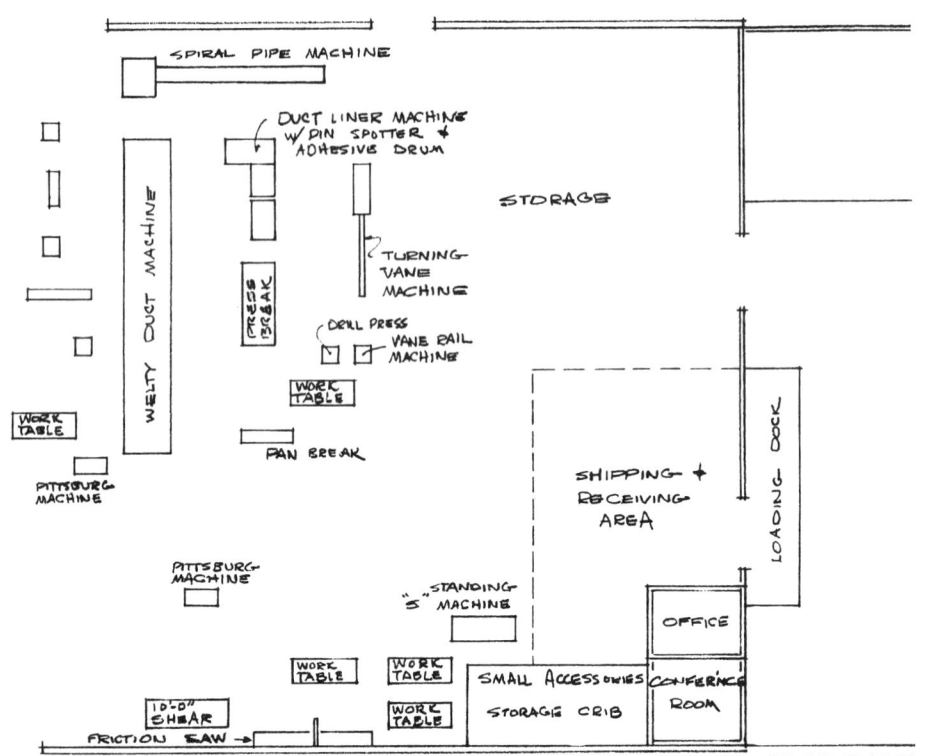

Above Segment of Shop Layout Shows the Area of the Sheet Metal Shop which Is Devoted to HVAC Work. A Work Force of from 10 to 12 Men Work in this Section. Most Notable in this Area Are the Welty-Way/Lockformer Duct Line, the Spiro U.S.A. Spiral Pipe Machnie and Harper Turning Vane Machine. Next to the Welty-Way/Lockformer Duct Machine Is the Area Where Ducts Are Lined with Insulation

R. D. Herbert & Sons Mechanic Pictured at the Console which Programs Production of Ductwork on Welty-Way Products, Inc., Coil Line which Straightens Coil Stock, Shears to Length, Notches and Beads Blank. Lockformer Co. Duplex Attachment Forms the Pittsburgh Lock Seams Permitting L-Shaped Duct Section to "Snap" Together

Collection of Articles from SNIPS

Red Shockley, Left, Foreman of R. D. Herbert & Sons Co.'s Job Shop, and Burton Wilson, Right, Pictured Next to the Spiro U.S.A. Spiral Pipe Machine which Uses Coil Stock to Fabricate Galvanized, Aluminum, Stainless Steel and Plastic-Coated Steel Spiral Pipe from 3" to 48" in Diameter

R. D. Herbert, III, Pictured Next to the Firm's Stocks of Spiro U.S.A. Fittings. In the Foreground Is Several Lengths of Spiral Pipe Manufactured in the Shop
(SNIPS Photo)

items such as tanks, belt guards and blow pipes.

They also fabricate and hang vent hoods for kitchens in restaurants and institutions. Although these establishments can buy prefabricated stainless steel sinks and bowls from restaurant equipment manufacturers, back orders and uncertain deliveries has prompted these firms to order custom made sinks from R. D. Herbert & Sons Co.

As a service to these customers a special truck has been fitted with grinding and polishing equipment for jobsite finishing of stainless steel trim.

R. D. Herbert & Sons Relieves Restaurant Chef's Fainting Spells

Bobby Herbert told us an interesting story about the chef at the new Nashville gourmet restaurant, Julians, who was fainting because of excessive kitchen heat. The Herbert firm installed an adequate kitchen hood and fan to pull out 4000 cfm of heated air. A shop-made make up air unit provided 3500 cfm of tempered make-up air to replace the exhausted air.

Kitchen Work Handled in 15 Restaurants In Opryland Amusement Center

In Nashville, a popular tourist attraction is the Opryland Amusement Center which includes restaurants featuring ethnic food. R. D. Herbert & Sons Co. handled kitchen work in 15 Opryland restaurants.

Innovations Found in Roofing Department Include R.I.G. Materials Spray System

A labor-saving machine which cuts labor on a built-up roofing job from six men to two men is owned and operated by the R. D. Herbert Roofing Department. We refer to the RIG machine being marketed by Midland Engineering Corp., South Bend, Ind., which blows roofing adhesive and granules through a ¾" vinyl hose to roofs as high as 30 feet, powered by a 10 HP compressor.

The machine is housed in an expanded metal "cage" reinforced with angle iron and mounted on a trailer for trailing to the jobsite.

Two Asphalt Road Tankers Converted Into Stationary "Hot Stuff" Tanks

R. D. Herbert's Roofing Department has built their own stationary "Hot Stuff" tanks from two 10,000 gallon asphalt tanks. One tank contains asphalt for flat roofing; the other tank has "hot" for steep roofing.

The tankers were sprayed with three inches of urethane foam insulation with a Gusmer spray gun. The insulation was reinforced by 3" wire mesh, and the tanks were covered with 26 ga. aluminum on the outside.

Asphalt in the two tanks is kept at a constant temperaure of 300°F. with LP-Gas burners.

Roofing Department Also Handles Architectural Sheet Metal Work

An example of the architectural sheet metal work handled by R. D. Herbert & Sons' roofing department can be illustrated by a $100,000 standing seam 16 oz. copper roof applied on the residence of a local department store tycoon which included a complete copper rain drainage system.

R. D. Herbert & Sons Supports SMACNA and NRCA Industry Work

R. D. Herbert & Sons keeps abreast with the latest industry developments and trends through its membership in Sheet Metal and Air Conditioning Conractors National Association (SMACNA) and National Roofing Contractors Ass'n (NRCA). We are indeed proud, also, to number this fine firm among our SNIPS long-time subscribers.

R. D. Herbert, Welder, Shown Welding Stainless Steel Restaurant Sink for which Firm Is Famous in Nashville

Z & M Sheet Metal, Fairfax, Va., Use Ingenious Sheet Inventory, Storage System and Production Line For Custom Duct Fabrication

Telling How An Integrated Lockformer Production Line Can Produce 36 Sizes of Duct From Only 10 Sizes of Sheared Blanks . . . Joe Zivic and Harry McCauley Tell of Flexibility and Ease of Set-Up of the Lockformer Production Line . . . Cantilevered Storage Rack Is Integral Part of System . . . Firm Does No Installation Work — Only Duct Fabrication for Washington Area Dealer-Contractors

One of the fastest growing sheet metal firms on the Middle Atlantic coast has experienced a phenomenal growth in six short years by putting on a production basis, custom-made heating and air conditioning duct and fittings for a special segment of the residential market.

Joe Zivic and Harry McCauley of Z & M Sheet Metal Inc., Fairfax, Va., decided a few years ago to become the best and biggest supplier of "packaged" custom-made duct systems to large tract builders of homes. Their success is apparent in their current customer list of over 96 active accounts. At the moment, they are supplying between 50 and 60 housing projects in the Washington area alone.

But this success is not by happen-stance. It is part of a master plan Joe Zivic and Harry McCauley began to develop back in 1967 when the Z & M firm was first organized. Both men, in the sheet metal business since 1946, recognized a growing need for a firm to meet the unique requirements of the large-scale housing market.

Geared Production Operations to Market Demands

So they geared their production operations to the demands of the market with a unique concept seldom employed in producing short run custom duct work. The conventional approach in the industry was to produce duct and fittings in advance, inventory them, and ship from this inventory as ordered.

Z & M felt this was a costly way to do it. They knew that the large production shops used duct fabrication lines and systems to achieve maximum production at the lowest possible cost. So they were determined to find a way to adapt production line methods to short run custom jobs.

Z & M found the answer to their needs in a combination of an ingenious sheet inventory and storage system and an integrated Lockformer production line. With this new concept of a preplanned inventory, Z & M can produce thirty-six sizes of duct from only ten sizes of blanks.

Maintain 10 Sizes of Sheared Blanks In 2" Increments

To produce the various sizes of duct as needed by their customers, Z & M maintains sheared blanks in ten sizes varying in width by two-inch increments from 96" x 17½" to 96" x 35½". These ten sizes, three in 28 gauge and seven in 26 gauge, will produce 36 different sizes of duct sections with a minimum of 8" x 8" up to a maximum of 26" x 8". (See chart 1.)

Chart 1
SHEARED STOCK FOR DUCT RACK

SHEET SIZE	DUCT SIZE	DUCT SIZE	DUCT SIZE	DUCT SIZE
96 x 17½	8 x 8	10 x 6	12 x 4	
96 x 19½	10 x 8	12 x 6	14 x 4	
96 x 21½	12 x 8	14 x 6	10 x 10	
96 x 23½	14 x 8	16 x 6	12 x 10	
96 x 25½	16 x 8	18 x 6	14 x 10	12 x 12
96 x 27½	18 x 8	20 x 6	16 x 10	14 x 12
96 x 29½	20 x 8	22 x 6	18 x 10	16 x 12
96 x 31½	22 x 8	24 x 6	20 x 10	18 x 12
96 x 33½	24 x 8	26 x 6	22 x 10	20 x 12
96 x 35½	26 x 8	28 x 6	24 x 10	22 x 12

Only 1½ Minutes to Change from One Size to Another With Lockformer Production Line

The major factor that makes this method practical and feasible is the flexibility and ease of set-up of the Lockformer production line. It takes only about 1½ minutes to change over from one size duct to another.

That's less time than it would take in the conventional way to put a pre-finished duct section into inventory, remove it when needed, and do the necessary paper work for inventory control.

Z & M Turn to Lockformer For Suitable System

For help in determining the most suitable system for their needs, they turned to the Lockformer Co., 711 Ogden Ave., Lisle, Ill., as they had so many times before for roll forming equipment.

The answer was a Lockformer engineered line consisting of a Lockformer 20-gauge Notcher, a Duplex Roll Former, Lockformer Beader and a special Lockformer Bending Machine to make a 90° bend to form the "L" section. This line produces three 8 foot "L" sections per minute with two men.

Showing Cantilevered Storage Rack which Is Integral Part of Z & M Sheet Metal Production Duct Fabrication System. Rack Has 10 Shelves, Each with A Capacity of 5,000 Pounds. From 10 Sizes of Sheared Blanks, Firm Can Produce 36 Sizes of Duct

Z & M Sheet Metal Workman Feeds Sheared Blank Thru Start of Production Line — the Lockformer Residential 20 Ga. Notcher

After Notching and Forming of Male and Female Locks, Semi-Formed Sheet Continues Thru Lockformer Beader, Shown Here

Collection of Articles from SNIPS

How Lockformer Production Line Works

Here's how the line works: The proper size sheared blank for the scheduled job is taken from the storage rack and sheared to length, then notched by one man on the Lockformer Residential Notcher at the beginning of the line. The notched blank is then fed into the Lockformer Duplex where both male and female sections for the button punch snap lock are formed simultaneously.

The material automatically continues through the Lockformer Beader onto a powered roller conveyor where it is carried into a special Lockformer Bending Machine which bends it 90° into a finished "L" section, then to a conveyor where a man turns drives on a hydraulic cleat bender.

New Cross Over System Results in 25-30% Added Production

The method formerly used in the Z & M plant was a crossover system requiring two men, a power brake with one operator, a powered cleat bender with one operator and one man on the notcher for a total of five men. The new system has eliminated three men and results in 25 to 30% more production.

ABOVE: An Overall View of the Lockformer Engineered Production Line in Shop of Z & M Sheet Metal, Inc., Fairfax, Va. The System (Feeding Right to Left) Consists of Lockformer Notcher, Duplex Roll Former, Lockformer Beader, and A Special Lockformer Bending Machine to Make a 90° Bend to Form "L" Sections. BELOW: Showing A Finished "L" Section. Two Z & M Men Can Produce Three 8 Ft. "L" Sections Per Minute

Sketch Showing the Layout of the Shop of Z & M Sheet Metal, Inc., Identification of All Sheet Metal Machinery in Shop Is Described in Left Column. The Lockformer Engineered Production Duct Line is Shown As No. 5 In Sketch

1—Rack
2—Maplewood Round Pipe Machine
3—Smith Cleat Bender
4—Lockformer 20 Ga. Button Punch Snap Lock Machine
5—Lockformer Duct Pipe Machine
6—Lockformer Notcher
7—Layout Tables
8—Lockformer Bandsaw
9—10—11—Shears
12—Steel Stock Rack
13—Slitter
14—Brake
15—Lockformer 8900 with 3-in-1 Rolls
16—Assembling Table
17—Lockformer Flanger
18—Lockformer 20 Ga. Pittsburgh Machine
19—Conveyor Table
20—Steel Rack
21—Cleat Bender
22—Riveter
23—Lockformer Insulation Cutter
24—Insulation Table
25—Lockformer "S" & Drive Machine
26—Coil-Line
27—Lockformer Bandsaw
28—Rack
29—30—Presses
31—Table 32—Brake
33—Press 34—Rack
35—Hole Puncher
36—Elbow Machine
37—Riveter
38—Compressor
39—16 Ga. Lockformer
40—Elbow Machine
41—Boot Machine
42—Shear
43—Storage Bin
44—Duct Rack
45—Pipe Storage

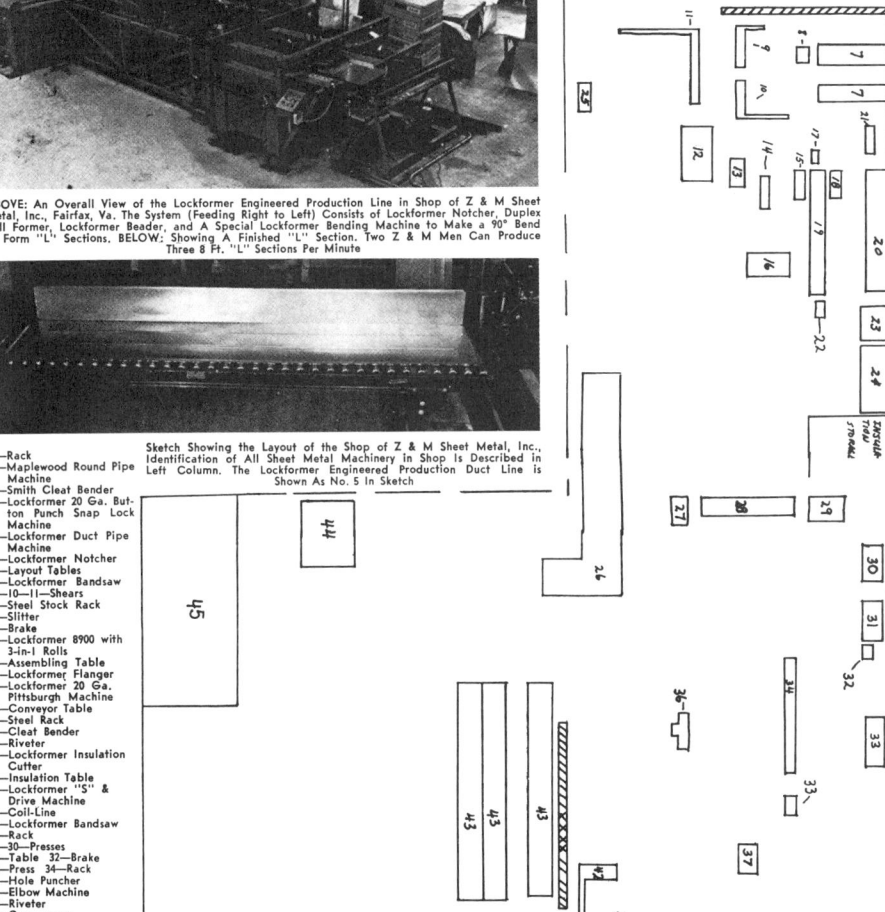

AT LEFT: Reading from Top to Bottom of the Z & M Sheet Metal Production Line. At Top, Lockformer Notcher. In Center, Sheared Blank Is Going Thru Lockformer Duplex, Forming Male/Female Locks. Bottom, Sheet Continues Thru Lockformer Beader to Conveyor. AT RIGHT: Sheet with Locks, and Beaded, Continues On Conveyor Into the Special Lockformer Bending Machine (Bottom) which Is Shown Roll Forming "L" Section

Z & M Sheet Metal

There is less waste due to operator error. In fact, Joe Zivic reports that he has not received one complaint of twisted duct since he installed the system. He also points out that beading gives a more rigid and stronger duct than cross-braking.

Report Savings of 30-40¢ per 8 Foot Duct Section

Z & M estimates the present system results in a saving of 30¢ to 40¢ per 8 foot section and this does not include warehousing and inventory costs incurred with previous methods. That means a $60 to $70 saving per day based upon a $10 to $11 per hour direct labor rate.

How the Cantilevered Storage Rack Is Integral Part of System

The cantilevered storage rack which is an integral part of the system has 10 shelves each with a capacity of 5,000 lbs. Additional material savings are possible because the storage system as Z & M has set it up, permits them to buy at full truck load prices.

Z & M also point out that without this sysem, they would have to maintain approximately three and a half times their present inventory to meet the varying requirements of their customers. With the present set-up, Z & M saves the cost of valuable shop space that would normally be required for both raw material and finished duct inventory.

Other savings result from reduced scrap waste because of being able to make maximum use of blanks. What little scrap that is left, is largely utilized in making cleats.

Steps Taken By Zivic and McCauley In Handling Duct Fabrication for Project Work

It is interesting to note the very efficient and business-like way that Joe Zivic and Harry McCauley have set up to handle so many active customers. Take an example of a builder planning to construct 200 houses of five different models.

The first step at Z & M is to get a take-off of the plans for each model and then run sample samples. The sample ductwork is delivered to the jobsite where the heating and air conditioning contractor will install it and then check the material list and make any necessary changes.

A final master list for each model is then prepared and the customer orders duct and fittings for each house as he needs them. An order will come through for so many Model A, so many Model B, etc.

Z & M will then make the complete duct package for each house and deliver by truck to the basement of the house under construction. Harry McCauley estimates that average delivery time is three days after receiving the go ahead from the heating and air conditioning contractor. Deliveries range from six to 15 units at a time.

One of the ways that Z & M's operation can be described is that it offers "one-stop shopping" for the installation contractor.

He gets a complete package of rectangular duct or round pipe with all necessary fittings at a flat pre-quoted cost per house.

Incidentally, Z & M does not provide hardware, flues, registers, grilles or other necessary components for the heating and air conditioning system. Nor does Z & M do any installation work.

Great Strides In 5½ Years of Operation By Z & M

The Z & M firm was started in May 1967 by Joe Zivic, president and Harry McCauley, secretary. Like most beginning shops it was small, only 3,000 sq. ft. of space and three employees in addition to Joe and Harry. Today the company operates with an average of 30 employees, in a 17,000 sq. ft. plant. In 1972 the firm fabricated over 4,000,000 pounds of steel. The firm has been one of SNIPS' lifetime subscribers for several years.

Shop Built Around Lockformer Equipment

Joe Zivic says, "Perhaps the major factor in our rapid growth is our equipment which keeps us ahead of competition, both from the standpoint of lower labor costs and total output per shift. We built our shop around Lockformer equipment because we know Lockformer to be the pace setter when it comes to labor saving machines."

Lockformer machines in the Z & M shop, other than the production line, include Models 20 and 24 Pittsburgh Lock Machines, Super Speed Cleatformer, 20-gauge Button Punch Snap Lock Machine, 20-gauge Residential Notcher, 20-gauge Auto-Guide Power Flanger, Cheek Benders, Easy-Edger and Band Saws."

The subject of labor saving equipment is extremely important to Z & M because as they point out, "Labor costs have become such a large portion of the total cost of a job that the only way that we can maintain an acceptable profit level is to increase productivity. Back in the 40's sheet metal shops were more concerned with material costs and less with labor costs because hourly rates were so much lower.

"Then followed a period of rising labor rates and material then became a minor cost factor. Today, however, the picture has changed. Material is both scarce and expensive and, of course, labor costs continue to rise. In other words both material and labor costs are now factors in the profitability of any size shop."

Z & M Type of Operation Easily Adapted Elsewhere

This unique duct fabrication approach used so successfully by the Z & M company, is equally adaptable to any shop handling a volume of residential and/or light commercial jobs. A Lockformer Production Line is so fast, so flexible, that it eliminates the need to produce and inventory duct in advance. The shop simply runs duct as needed.

As Joe Zivic says, "Any shop turning out 100 or more duct sections per day could pay for this system in a short time just in labor savings alone".

Information on any of the pieces of Lockformer equipment referred to above can be obtained upon request from The Lockformer Co., 711 Ogden Ave., Dept. S, Lisle, Ill., 60532.

Collection of Articles from SNIPS 263.

How Aurora, Ill., Sheet Metal Shop Updates Shop Equipment to Keep Competitive

Harry Gengler Sheet Metal, Aurora, Ill., Adds New Lockformer Super Cleatformer ... Attachments Produce Flat "S" Cleat, Drive Cleat and Tap-in Collars ... New Machine Eliminates Costly Manual Shop Labor ... Lockformer Pittsburgh Machine Still Giving Good Service After 27 Years ... Gengler Shop Also Includes Unique "Tig" Welder ... Unique Welding Operations Permit Gengler Shop to Handle Many Versatile Welding Jobs in Specialty Sheet Metal Situations

Sophisticated machinery you might expect to find only in a larger shop, has been behind the success story of the Harry J. Gengler sheet metal firm in Aurora, Ill., which has just completed its fourth equipment expansion program.

"We have always tried to operate on the principle that initial outlay for useful machinery will eventually be recouped by more customers and less man hours on the payroll," said Harry Gengler, Sr., who has been in the sheet metal business for 26 years in Aurora.

He started in a small shop of less than 1,000 square feet, working only on residential jobs. Now the growing Gengler operation has an 8,000 sq. ft. shop, six sturdy trucks and specializes in big commercial and industrial work.

Practical for Modest Size Shops to Use Modern Production Sheet Metal Machinery

There is frequently a great debate among modest size sheet metal men on the economics of buying a new fast production machine versus paying out for man hours to do the job the slow way. Few shops of this size have the assortment of machinery which is found at Gengler's. In the past such equipment was thought to be too much money in one big chunk for the "little guy" to swallow. Even Gengler's capital expenditure has been spread over quite a few years.

But with today's rising labor costs, the argument becomes more easily won by the machine and the smart owner buys as much sophistication as he can possibly afford.

(Continued on Next Page)

ABOVE: An Interior View of the Gengler Sheet Metal Co. Shop Which Is Well Lighted, Kept Immaculately Clean, With Machinery Well Spaced So Each Man Has Adequate Working Area

AT RIGHT: An Exterior View of the Gengler Sheet Metal Co. Shop In Aurora, Ill., Which Still Carries Sign of Firm's Original Name, Gengler's Tin Shop

A Layout of the Well Equipped Gengler Sheet Metal Co., Aurora, Ill., Showing Position of Various Machines and the Material Flow Thru the Shop. The Numbered Machines Are Identified Correspondingly, Below. Our Thanks to Dale Wolf, Shop Foreman For This Layout

1 — Lockformer Super Speed Cleatformer
2 — Lockformer Snap Lock Machine
3 — Lockformer Pittsburgh Machine
4 — Layout Bench
5 — Peerless Spot Welder
6 — Drill Press
7 — 60" Power Roll
8 — 120" Engel Power Bendall
9 — Layout Bench
10 — 96" Chicago Hand Brake
11 — Engel Drive Bender
12 — Hossfeld Bender
13 — 54" Pexto Power Shear
14 — Lockformer Power Edger
15 — Lockformer Duct Liner Cutter
16 — Duct Liner Glue Table
17 — Gripnail Bench
18 — Lockformer 18 Ga. Pittsburgh Machine
19 — Lincoln Welder
20 — NCG - TIG Welder
21 — Welding Layout Bench
22 — 10 Ft. 16 Ga. Chicago Brake
23 — Lockformer Standing Cleat & Standing Seam Machine
24 — Angle Iron Notcher and Bender
25 — Layout and Gutter Bench
26 — Lockformer Band Saw
27 — Roper Whitney 19 Ton Punch

Two Generations of Men and Machinery Share the Responsibility and Work Load at the Harry J. Gengler Sheet Metal Shop, Aurora, Ill. At Left is an Old, But Sturdy Lockformer Pittsburgh Machine, Still in Constant Use After 27 Years of Service. Standing Beside It Is Harry Gengler, Sr. and Next is Jack, His Son, Who Is Attending the Newer Lockformer Snap Lock Machine

Dale Wolf, Left, Shop Foreman at the Harry J. Gengler Sheet Metal Shop, Aurora, Ill., and Harry Gengler, Sr., Right, Inspect the Newest Equipment Addition, In the Firm's Expanding Business. The Machine is a Lockformer Super Speed Cleatformer with Power Slitter

(*Continued from Preceding Page*)
New Lockformer Super-Cleatformer Saves Valuable Shop Time

Their first machine, a compact Lockformer 22 gauge Pittsburgh lock roll former with acme pipe and top edger was purchased in 1944. It has plenty of company now in the wide array of equipment that has spawned more jobs and required an on-going expansion program.

The newest machine recently delivered by Lockformer is a combination flat S cleat, drive cleat and tap-in collar maker. The Super Speed Cleatformer machine replaced an older Lockformer S cleat model and has welcome additions, including a power slitter.

"One big advantage of the new Lockformer equipment," said Gengler, "is the 'three-in-one' rolls with the perforating notcher arrangement. This allows us to notch and tap in the collar in one run instead of two, cutting time and equipment use in half."

Gengler Adds Unique "Tig Welder"

"Naturally," said Gengler, "it would be sheer stupidity to have an expensive machine for infrequent usage. But sometime you have to look ahead. We saw the opportunity about 10 years ago to do some heavy work in stainless steel. We had already been into commercial and industrial work for about eight years. Now a big door was opening into the multi-use of steel fabrication. We bought a 'Tig Welder', which permits fine precision welding of all metals, including stainless steel and aluminum."

Tig Welder Opened Door to Specialty Sheet Metal Work

"The Tig Welder is necessary for fabrication of all food processing equipment such as portable food holding bins, hoppers and conveyors. It also allows us to fabricate highly diverse material transfer equipment. Without this machine, we would not be so heavily involved in all kinds of steel fabrication that represents a healthy income to the business."

How New Machinery Benefits Customers

"Our machines have many other fringe benefits," continued Gengler. "For instance, the new Lockformer equipment enables us to utilize our drop off material to fabricate S cleats by virtue of its scrap cutting device. However, an even more important consideration is that we don't have to buy or farm out much of our fabrication. This way, we not only save money on man hours, we control the quality of fabrication and cut down on the time a customer waits for a finished job."

Welding Section Isolated in Shop

The most recent shop remodeling program allowed Gengler to isolate most welding in one separate area. Not only is this a more organized way of arranging equipment, it has a built-in safety factor by eliminating the dangerous flashes to the eyes of passersby. Separation also keeps the fine metal dust resulting from grinding operations from getting into nearby machines.

Heavy Duty Manual Punch Purchased for Special Job

In addition to the new Lockformer machine, Gengler has recently acquired a 14 gauge hand brake and a heavy duty manual punch. The latter is a good example of Gengler philosophy in action. The costly equipment was purchased for a special job when the firm was awarded the contract to make 12 gauge stainless steel test benches. "The cost would have been exorbitant to have had the holes drilled," he said, "and just as pointless to pay three times more for a hydraulic punch for minimal usage. We bought what the job warranted — and expect to find plenty of use for it in the future."

Gengler's Work is in Western Suburbs of Chicago

Gengler has worked mostly in the west suburban area where recent jobs include the East Aurora High School, the Y.M.C.A., a big job for Caterpillar Tractor, Marmion Abbey and the Hilton Inn. The firm does much work for General Mills and recently was awarded the intriguing job of working on a big AT&T underground facility in Plano, Illinois. Gengler did the fabrication work for a building originally built for Northern Ill. Gas in Aurora, which is now the City Hall. He also did the high school in Wheaton. One of his favorite jobs is the administration building for the Loyal Order of Moose in Mooseheart, Ill., a school for underprivileged children.

Plans Call for Addition of Hydraulic-Operated Shear

The roomy uncluttered Gengler operation abounds with equipment normally found in much bigger operations. There is a 10 foot shear, a Lockformer Model 18 gauge Pittsburgh machine with one inch standing seam rolls, a Speed Notcher with 16 gauge capacity, a Lockformer 20 gauge snap lock, Button Punch, a drive bender and two more Lockformer machines — a power edger and an insulation cutter.

And what is the newest piece of machinery slated for the enterprising Gengler firm? A brand new hydraulic operated shear. Gengler feels this will eliminate a lot of waiting time as there are many periods when this machine will be in constant use.

27-Year-Old Lockformer Pittsburgh Machine Still Giving Good Service

The theory that spending money on sophisticated machinery pays off for even the comparatively small operator has certainly been proven by Harry Gengler. Looking fondly at the neat little Lockformer 22 gauge Pittsburgh machine, he said, "This machine still serves us well after 27 years — and we expect to get the same kind of service from our new Lockformer Super Speed Cleatformer. We buy for the future — and the future pays us back — or at least, it has up to now."

With positive thinker Harry Gengler and his son Jack at the helm, it looks like a sure bet that the future will be a lucrative one for the Gengler firm.

Write for Super Cleatformer Literature from Lockformer

Readers wanting details on the Lockformer Super Cleatformer and the available options may obtain literature and prices from the Lockformer Co., Dept. "S", 711 Ogden Ave., Lisle, Ill., 60532.

Gengler's New Lockformer Super Speed Cleatformer Pictured as it Forms Button Punch Snap Lock on Galvanized Duct Section at Bottom Left. Other Formed Material is Also Shown Coming From Machine

Modern Asheville, N.C., Sheet Metal Shop Reflects Changeover From Heating-Cooling to Fabrication Work

Telling How Metal Fabricators of Asheville, N.C., Moved from an Old Multi-Story Building to a Modern Single-Level Structure . . . Firm which Formerly Handled Heating and Air Conditioning Switches to Commercial-Industrial Sheet Metal Fabrication . . . Shop Layout Shows How Modern Sheet Metal Machinery Is Arranged

The old adage, "The Only Sure Thing is Change", is particularly true in Asheville, N.C., where Metal Fabricators of Asheville, Inc., is opperated by B. J. Haynie. The firm has seen many changes in its 33 years of operation. For example, the company was formerly called Bishop's, Inc., and originally, specialized in central heating and air conditioning installation until high labor costs forced a change to industrial and commercial sheet metal fabrication.

In 1968, another important change took place: they moved from an old multi-story building. The new location, just inside the city limits, two miles from the old place, provided lower insurance rates, city trash pick-up, police and fire protection, etc.

Firm Designs And Builds New Sheet Metal Shop

Haynie notes the unique nature of his firm's sheet metal specialty work made it more practical for him and his staff to custom design the building with the help of the sub-contractors. The open-span building utilizes steel, concrete block and brick. The sheet metal shop has an area measuring 70 ft. x 120 ft.

About the Provisions Made For Simplified Materials Handling

The building has a 12 ft. wide by 14 ft. high overhead door in each end of the shop area. A 12-foot space is kept clear from end to end in the center of the shop to simplify the movements of materials, before, during and after fabrication.

A loading dock is located at one end of the building; a trailer and tractor can be driven into the other end. Sheets are unloaded from the trailer onto a four-wheeled truck, two wheels in the center, one on each end, which has the capacity of 8,000 pounds, then rolled in front of the sheet racks for storing.

Metal Sheets Of All Kinds Racked Near Loading Dock

To understand the way Metal Fabricators of Asheville has arranged its shop, refer to the left portion of the accompanying shop layout. No. 46 identifies the loading dock. No. 24 indicates sheet racks on each side of the dock entrance. No. 8 shows vertical sheet racks. No. 9 locates the racks for stainless steel sheets. Racks for sheets 3 ft. x 4 ft. or less are shown in No. 26.

Wide Variety Of Metal Sheets Stored

Aluminum sheets are stacked, .025 through ¼ in. plate; Types 304 and 316 stainless steel sheets, 26 ga. through 11 ga.; hot rolled sheets, 18 ga. through 3/16 in.; galvanized 28 ga. through 10 ga.; also copper and brass sheets. Angles, rod, flats, channels, pipe and tubing are stocked in aluminum, stainless steel and carbon steel. Pipe and angle are in racks at No. 23.

Telling How Scrap Metal Is Handled

A metal rack 30-feet long is divided into 50 sections and is labeled as to metal and gauge for storing droppings from the shear (No. 1). Their "Dumpster" (No. 42), mounted on casters, is used for handling small scrap and trash, which is picked up by the City of Asheville. Saleable scrap (aluminum, stainless steel, brass and copper) is stored in portable wagons or carts (No. 43 & No. 44) which can be easily loaded at the firm's loading dock.

About the Sheet Metal Work Handled

Metal Fabricators of Asheville, Inc., is a sheet metal company, which custom-designs and fabricates specialty items such as sinks, tanks, hoods, machine guards, blow-pipe and ventilating systems on an individual or production basis. The firm specializes in working with stainless steel, aluminum, copper, brass, hot rolled and galvanized iron.

About the Sheet Metal Equipment

The sheet metal fabrication equipment includes a 225-ton Dreis & Krump Chicago press brake with a 3/16 in. capacity which is a real work-horse in the realm of industrial sheet metal requirements. A Wysong & Miles 10 ft., 3/16 in. power shear is another plus machine, as well as the 5/16 in. American Pullmax Universal Shearing and Forming Machine (No. 3).

Extensive Welding Operations Feature Five Heliarc Welders

An important specialty of "Metal Fabricators" is the Heliarc welding of stainless steel and aluminum. Refer to the upper righthand corner of the shop layout. (Welders are indicated in No. 12 — Miller Electric 300 amp. Heliarc; No. 13 — Lincoln 250 amp.; No. 14 — Lincoln 300 amp.; and No. 15 — Lincoln 400 amp. Spot welders are shown in No. 16.) The Welding Department takes up approximately 20% of the floor space. The area was selected because it was near incoming power lines; also, it is in an area which could be curtained off to prevent eye damage.

The firm's emphasis is centered on not only doing a competent job, but also one, which when completed, has a pleasing appearance. For this finishing operation a Haskins portable polisher (No. 47) and a pedestal grinder (No. 45) are employed.

A welding bench (No. 33) with a ½-inch steel top and a soldering bench (No. 32) are conveniently located close to the welding department.

Layout and Work Benches Clustered

The shop layout shows a cluster of five layout and work benches adjacent to an 18 ga. Pittsburgh machine (No. 5) and a 20 ga. Pittsburgh machine (No. 7) and a foot-operated shear (No. 27); the bench with the rolls and folder (No. 28) and the edgers, flangers and crimpers are together on one bench (No. 29).

Across the main aisle an 8 ft. hand brake (No. 34) and a box brake (No. 35) are located together. The benches were located so that power, electric and compressed air would be easily available. When concrete was poured for the floor 3/16 in. steel troughs were installed in the floor with removable covers flush with the top surface of the floor to accommodate power lines, with outlets, as required.

Power Saws Grouped Together Near The Welding Department

An area has been set aside for sawing operations, including a vertical band-saw (No. 17), a table model saw (No. 19), a horizontal band saw (No. 20) and a cut-off saw (No. 21). The saws and power threader were located near the angle, bar

Picturing Mechanics Working on Dreis & Krump "Chicago" Press Brake, Right. At Left Can Be Seen Wheeled Cart for Transporting Sheets for Forming by Press Brake

Mechanic at Right Center Shown at Work on Wysong & Miles 10 Ft. 3/16 in. Power Shear. Mechanic at Left Operates Pullmax No. 8 Combination Machine with 5/16 in. Capacity

In the Welding Department Sheet Metal Mechanic Uses Lincoln Idealarc Arc Welder. Note Breech Pipe and Fittings in Left Foreground

Close-up Picture Shows Welding of Sheet Metal Cone and Flange with Lincolnarc Arc Welder. Typical Examples of Sheet Metal Fabrication Work Handled By Metal Fabricators of Asheville, Inc.

and pipe racks to facilitate the handling of materials.

An Attractive Mailer Celebrates Firm's 33rd Year In Business

We are grateful to B. J. Haynie for providing us with the shop layout and the photographs which accompany this story. The pictures were used in an attractive self-mailer brochure which Metal Fabricators of Asheville, Inc. has prepared to mark the firm's plus 33 years of sheet metal craftsmanship.

SNIPS adds its congratulations to the firm which has combined the skill of experienced craftsmen with the latest sheet metal equipment to achieve a reputation for "a job well done."

Picture Shows Vertical Sheet Metal Storage Rack in Foreground and Stainless Steel Scrap Bin in the Back

Mechanic Shown Buffing Stainless Steel Weld. Dreis & Krump "Chicago" Press Brake Serves as Background

Shop Sketch Showing Positions of Various Machines and Benches at Metal Fabricators of Asheville, Inc. Numbers Indicate Equipment which Is Identified As Follows

1 — 10 Ft. 3/16" Power Shear
2 — 12 Ft. 225 Ton Press Brake
3 — No. 8 — 5/16" Pullmax Machine
4 — 4 Ft. Power Rolls
5 — 18 Ga. Lockformer
6 — Rail
7 — 20 Ga. Lockformer
8 — Vertical Storage Metal Sheet Rack
9 — Vertical Storage Stainless Steel Rack
10 — Layout and Work Benches
11 — Welding Rod Storage Cabinet
12 — Miller 300 Amp. Welding Unit
13 — Lincoln 250 Amp. Welding Unit
14 — Lincoln 300 Amp. Welding Unit
15 — Lincoln 400 Amp. Welding Unit
16 — Spot Welders
17 — Vertical Band Saw
18 — 20 H.P. Air Compressor
19 — Table Model Saw
20 — Horizontal Band Saw
21 — Cut-Off Saw.
22 — Storage Shelving
23 — Pipe and Angle Racks
24 — Sheet Racks
25 — Powered Pipe Threader
26 — Vertical Storage Racks for Sheets 3 Ft. or 4 Ft. or Less
27 — Foot Operated Shear
28 — Rolls and Folder Bench
29 — Edgers, Flangers and Crimpers on Bench
30 — Drill Press
31 — Punch
32 — Soldering Bench
33 — Welding Bench (½" Steel Top)
34 — 8 Ft. Brake
35 — Box Brake
36 — 7 Ft. x 12 Ft. Portable Welding Bench
37 — Die and Punch Rack
38 — Blower for Ventilating Shop
39 — Ladder Racks
40 — Water Cooler
41 — Coke Machine
42 — Scrap Dumpster
43 — Stainless Steel Scrap Wagon
44 — Aluminum Scrap Wagon
45 — Pedestal Mounted Grinder
46 — Loading Dock
47 — Portable Mounted Polisher

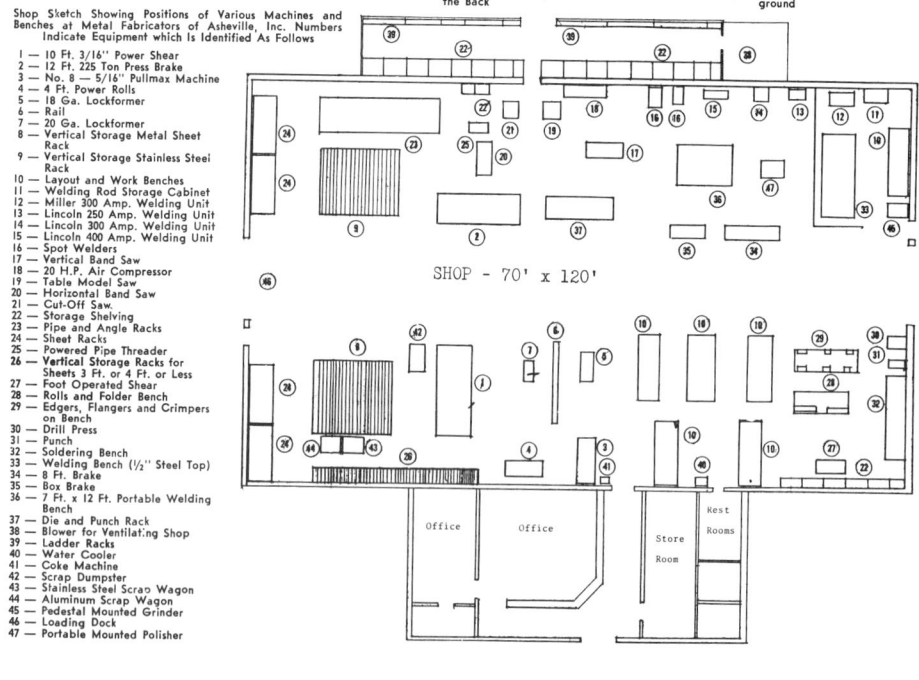

SHOP - 70' x 120'

Collection of Articles from SNIPS

267.

L.R.M. Sheet Metal Mechanic Is Pictured at Console Controlling Operation of Welty-Way "Feedie" Machine (See Sheet Metal Layout Sketch)

Shop-Made Mobile Carts, Loaded with Duct Work and Fittings, Are Shown in Staging Area Where L.R.M. Vehicles Pull in for Loading and Transport to Job the Next Morning

L.R.M., Inc., Baltimore, Md., Credits Amazing Growth To Installation of Up-to-Date Sheet Metal Equipment

Telling How Luke R. Mask, President of L.R.M. Inc., Baltimore, Md., Parlayed 23 Years Working in All Phases of Heating and Air Conditioning to a Successful $1.5 Million Annual Business in Just Four Years . . . Welty-Way Econo Shear Coil Line Turns out 25 Feet of Duct Work Per Minute . . . Olivetti Computer Saves Time in Calculating Heat Losses and Heat Gains . . . Two-Way Radios on Six of Eleven Trucks Stretch Territory Covered by Installation and Service Crews . . . Mask Depends on NESCA to Keep Technical Know-How Current . . . Rheem Heating & Air Conditioning Supplied L.R.M., Inc. by United Supply & Distributing Co., Baltimore

Picturing the Welty-Way Econo Shear Coil Line Machine which Produces 25 Ft. of Duct Work Per Minute. Future Plans of L.R.M., Inc. Call for Complete Automation of Duct Line which Will Then Be Operated by One Man

Success stories in the heating and air conditioning industry are being written every day, but few are as spectacular as that of Luke R. Mask, president of L.R.M., Inc., 2-6 Alco Place, Baltimore, Md., 21227. It was four years ago when Mask established his own business. Since then Mask has built the firm up to an annual sales volume of $1.5 million.

Mechanization of Operations Helps L.R.M., Inc. Spurt

Modern methods and equipment together with Mask's determination to make good, are very much responsible for L.R.M., Inc.'s surge to the top. In this connection it is interesting to learn of Mask's use of coil stock instead of conventional flat galvanized sheet in the fabrication of sheet metal duct work for heating and cooling air distribution systems.

There were several good reasons for using coil stock, he said. First, scrap waste is 80% less as compared to flat sheets; coil stock is easier to store and to handle with L.R.M., Inc.'s fork lift truck.

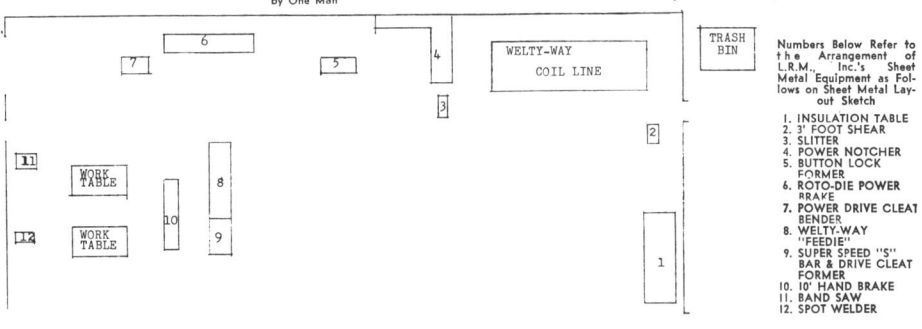

Numbers Below Refer to the Arrangement of L.R.M., Inc.'s Sheet Metal Equipment as Follows on Sheet Metal Layout Sketch

1. INSULATION TABLE
2. 3' FOOT SHEAR
3. SLITTER
4. POWER NOTCHER
5. BUTTON LOCK FORMER
6. ROTO-DIE POWER BRAKE
7. POWER DRIVE CLEAT BENDER
8. WELTY-WAY "FEEDIE"
9. SUPER SPEED "S" BAR & DRIVE CLEAT FORMER
10. 10' HAND BRAKE
11. BAND SAW
12. SPOT WELDER

Collection of Articles from SNIPS

Mrs. Luke R. Mask, Secretary-Treasurer of L.R.M., Inc. Who Heads the Office Staff

Luke R. Mask, President of L.R.M., Inc., Left, Is Shown Consulting with Carl Hellwig, United Supply & Distributing Co., Baltimore, Md., Wholesale Distributor of Rheem Heating and Air Conditioning which is Sold and Installed in L.R.M.'s New Home and Apartment Heating and Cooling Work

To utilize the advantages of coil stock, Mask purchased a Welty-Way Econo Shear coil line manufactured by Welty-Way Products, Inc., Cedar Rapids, Iowa. This duct fabrication system which had the capability of producing 25 feet of duct work per minute used 24, 26 and 28 gauge galvanized coil stock. Two giant "spools" of coil stock, only one of which can be used at a time, are the beginning point of the duct fabrication process.

From the coil the metal is uncoiled, and a power straightener takes the "curl" away from the stock. The metal is then sheared to size and number of pieces dictated by a programmed console which automatically determines duct blank production.

About the Various Other Machines Used In the Process of Fabricating Duct Work

The accompanying layout sketch of the L.R.M., Inc. sheet metal shop shows the various steps which the duct blanks take after they leave the Welty-Way coil line system. First, the sheared section is routed to Lockformer Co. power notcher where the blanks are notched at all four corners and moved to the Lockformer Co. Button Lock machine for application of the locks; the section continues to the Roto Die power brake and the power drive cleat bender where the finishing touches are applied to the ducts.

Shop Made Carts Store Finished Duct Work

The finished duct sections for each job are stacked in a shop made mobile cart ready to load on installation trucks at night which are ready for an early start the next morning. The carts are eight feet long, three feet wide and constructed from 22

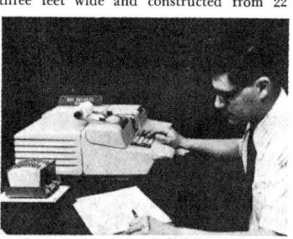

L.R.M., Inc. Sheet Metal Mechanic Pictured Running Duct Blank Through Lockformer Button Lock Machine where Lock Is Applied to Duct Section

Showing Some of the Coil Stock which Is Stored in L.R.M. Warehouse and Clark Fork Lift Truck which Moves Coil Stock to Welty-Way Coil Line

Ray DeLooze, Estimator and Designer, Pictured at Olivetti Underwood Programma 101 which Is Used to Figure Heat Losses, Heat Gains and Pricing of Jobs

ga. galvanized sheets reinforced by 2" by 2" angle iron spot welded into a sturdy framework.

Motorola Two-Way Radios Installed on Six Trucks

Another utilization of modern technology by L.R.M., Inc. was in the employment of two-way radios to dispatch the service and installation crews. The Motorola communications equipment permits a dispatcher to route the nearest truck to emergency calls and provides an opportunity for service parts sharing by the nearest L.R.M., Inc. trucks in the field. This is a valuable, money-saving and time-saving competitive tool, since it cashes in on quantity parts price advantages; and it eliminates wasted time shopping for parts at a supplier or returning to headquarters.

Utilizing the two-way radio to good advantage are L.R.M., Inc.'s two servicemen who handle all in-warranty service calls as well as a considerable number of charge service calls.

Olivetti Computer Calculates Heat Loss, Heat Gain

Luke R. Mask handles much of the firm's heating and air conditioning engineering work with the assistance of Ray DeLooze. Their work in figuring heat losses and heat gains for the heating and air conditioning estimates they submit to customers is greatly simplified through the use of an Olivetti Programma 101, a small computer which also is utilized for job cost analysis.

Picturing the Mountains of Rheem Gas Heating Units which Are Stored in L.R.M. Warehouse. Equipment Is Supplied by United Supply & Distributing Co., Baltimore

Company Specializes in New Home and Apartment Heating-Cooling Work

L.R.M., Inc. has a work force of 53 employees. The firm operates from a 90 ft. x 100 ft. building. 90% of the heating-cooling work is residential, 87% of which is done in new construction. L.R.M., Inc.'s market area is defined as Baltimore and surrounding counties.

They have recently completed Heritage Woods Apartments for Hess Realty; Town & Country West Apts. for Monumental Properties; Cinnamon Ridge Apts. for Robert & Harry Meyerhoff and Rich Mar Apartments for Joseph Schwartz.

Mask Relies on NESCA for Keeping in Touch with Technical Data

Luke R. Mask is a member of National Environmental Systems Contractors Ass'n (NESCA) and relies upon that group to keep him in touch with technical advancements in the industry. This year SNIPS met Luke and Mrs. Mask at the annual NESCA convention at Disneyland near Anaheim, Calif.

Mask also claims membership in the National Ass'n of Home Builders, Home Builders Ass'n of Maryland and the AHACC of Maryland.

Rheem Heating and Air Conditioning Supplied By United Supply & Distributing Co., Baltimore, Md.

L.R.M., Inc. relies upon United Supply & Distributing Co., Baltimore, Md., for its supply of Rheem warm air furnaces and companion central air conditioning equipment and accessories. Luke Mask works closely with Carl Hellwig, vice president of "United Supply" for assistance in arranging inventory deliveries.

We are grateful to Rheem Mfg. Co. for providing us with many of the photographs which illustrate this story and for much of the information about the L.R.M., Inc. success story.

Collection of Articles from SNIPS 269.

Picturing the Attractive and Modern Building which Houses the Headquarters of Midland Engineering Co., Inc. in South Bend, Ind. The Firm, Headed by William R. Steinmetz, Specializes in Sheet Metal for HVAC Systems, Roofing, Partitions and Floors, Ceiling and Walls in Commercial Buildings

Modern Computer Technology Gives Competitive "Edge" To Midland Engineering Co., Inc., South Bend Ind.

Telling How the Sheet Metal Div. of Midland Engrg. Co., South Bend, Ind., Utilizes the Time and Labor-Saving Compuduct System for Shop Fabrication and Control As Well As for Take-Off, Estimating and Costing for HVAC Duct Work and Architectural Sheet Metal . . . Midland Engrg. Enters 51st Year In Business . . . William Steinmetz, Who Heads Firm, Is Current President of National Roofing Contractors Ass'n and Vice President of Midwest Roofing Contractors Ass'n

When William J. Steinmetz founded Midland Engineering Co., Inc., in South Bend, Ind., his motto was "Integrity and Responsibility". Today, 51 years later this business philosophy is being carried on by the son of the founder, William R. Steinmetz, here pictured, who has been president of the company since 1961.

The willingness to use advances in technology in operation of sheet metal, roofing and interior finishing sub-contracting has contributed largely to Midland Engineering Co.'s success for over 50 years.

William L. Steinmetz, President of Midland Engineering Co., Inc., the Current President of National Roofing Contractors Ass'n

LEFT PICTURE — Brian T. Simms, who Heads Sheet Metal and HVAC Operation, Shown Operating Compuduct Teletype wrich Prepares Data for Computer. RIGHT PICTURE — Charles W. Frazier, Sheet Metal Project Engineer, Shown Inserting "Mode" into Compuduct Computer. Blinking Lights on Machine Indicate Information Being Processed Back and Forth to the Teletype

(SNIPS Photos)

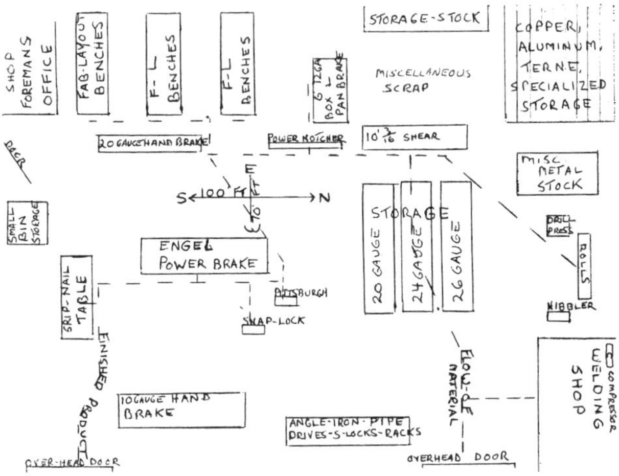

Higher Production Cancels Out Inflationary Wage Levels

In these days of upward spiraling wage levels in the construction industry, sheet metal, air conditioning and ventilating contractors are hard pressed to bid job contracts at a profit. In the final analysis the answer seems to be finding ways to increase manpower production to keep pace with rising wages.

According to Brian Simms, manager of Midland Engineering Co.'s sheet metal department, the South Bend firm's answer to the need for a competitive edge in winning contracts in its area is the Compuduct System developed by Construction Technology, Fairfield, N.J. Simms told SNIPS that the unique Compuduct system was purchased at the Construction Technology booth during the recent ASHRAE Show in Chicago after learning about the system in SNIPS.

(Continued on Next Page)

Presenting a Layout of Midland Engineering Co.'s Sheet Metal Machinery as Situated in the 100' x 70' Insulated Butler Steel Building Provided SNIPS by Brian Simms. Also Shown In Broken Line Is "Flow of Material" ➤

Midland Engineering Mechanics Pictured At Firm's 14 Ga., 10 Ft. Engel Power Press Brake

(Continued from Preceding Page)

Manual Take-Off Procedures Consume Valuable Time

Simms revealed that on many occasions in the past estimates for HVAC work had to be prepared at a moment's notice. Simms and two aids often would work 14 hours a day taking off fittings from blueprints and extending figures onto a take-off sheet. Information provided included weight of metal in fittings and all specialty items, the lineal footage of duct work and the estimated manhours for fabrication and field installation.

In the frenzy to meet the deadline, not only was there margin for error working the long hours, but the routine clerical work tied up valuable executive time which could be better employed in sales or market analysis activities.

Describing the Machines Making up Compuduct System

The Compuduct System is made up of two units. One unit resembling an electric typewriter is the teletype thru which the computer requests information from the operator. In the "fabrication mode" it requests duct dimensions which the operator can enter directly from the drawings. It then produces a complete fabrication data sheet along with the other shop paperwork. As it is doing this, it automatically applies specifications while selecting the fabrication method based upon sheet equipment and sheet sizes.

In the estimating mode, it requests only the basic take-off data such as width, depth, lineal feet, etc. and automatically applies specifications and "Midland's" cost factors; specialties as well as duct work are entered. If the computer doesn't know the cost factors, it asks the operator for them!

Simms and Frazier Had No Previous Computer Experience

The second unit which looks like a modern vending machine is the computer itself. The only visible activity during operation is the blinking of its many lights as information is processed back and forth to the teletype.

An interesting aspect is that, should the computer find the dimensions for a fitting "impossible", it will come back and advise the operator before producing a fabrication sheet. Gross errors are automatically rejected by the computer, since the unit knows more or less what to expect. The computer "rotates" any fitting entered to represent it as one of the standard 15 types.

Though having no previous computer experience, both Simms and Charles W. Frazier, sheet metal project engineer, were able to operate the computer from the day that it was installed.

Construction Technology, Inc. Programs Computer To Individual Requirements of "Midland Engineering"

Brian Simms notes that following delivery of the Compuduct System, he has been working closely with Dick Levine of Construction Technology, Inc., 12 Industrial Rd., Fairfield, N. J. 07006. The machine has been programmed to correlate on a job estimate all of the factors which individually tie in with the sheet metal set-up at Midland Engineering Co., Inc.

It is interesting to learn from Simms that the computer estimates faster and more accurately than could ever be done manually. When furnished with Midland Engineering Co.'s costs for fittings and joints of different gauges, the computer furnishes a read-out giving a breakdown by weight, accordingly. When furnished with the number of fittings in each run, the computer applies a different labor factor for the percentage — pounds of fittings against straight labor.

Illustrated 50th Anniversary Seal Was Issued In 1972 by Midland Engineering Co.

The thoroughness of this process is accentuated by the fact that it is at least seven times faster than previous methods using calculators and adding machines. Simms revealed that over 40 hours a week of paperwork alone has been saved since the installation, freeing a man for other work!

Jobs in Process Can Be Checked for Profitability

A vital phase of any business is the determination of whether or not the jobs being handled are actually profitable. Simms revealed that Compuduct also checks and corrects fabrication data and estimates to the pound, the blanks used for each job, categorized by gauge, pounds of fittings and pounds of straight duct. This information, combined with manhour records, indicate to Simms which jobs in progress must be watched with regards to profitability.

Computer's Memory Recalls Important Elements of Job Details

Simms revealed that Compuduct has the ability to "remember" job specifications, shop machinery capabilities and eliminates the constant training of every new employee in the firm's methods and equipment.

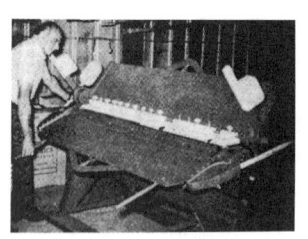

Sheet Metal Shop Foreman Warren Drews Pictured Operating the New GripNail, Air-Operated Insulation Fastening Tool

Doyle Downey Shown Bending Metal Sheet On New Dreis & Krump 6 Ft., 12 Ga. Box and Pan Brake

Warner Drews, the sheet metal shop foreman, is particularly devoted to Compuduct because it allows him to supervise the mechanics under him and releases him from routine bookkeeping and training chores. Since Drews is responsible for maintaining OSHA safety standards in the shop, the elimination of duties connected with the preparation of numerous lists required for work distribution and controls is assured — thanks to Compuduct.

Long Range Plans Call for Using Compuduct for Other Divisions

Simms said that Midland Engineering Co. is set up so that the firm's various divisions handling roofing, floors, ceilings, lighting, partitions have access to materials handling and warehousing equipment maintained for the common use of every activity. In this connection, Simms said that long range plans at Midland Engineering Co. call for using Compuduct in the firm's other divisions.

Simms also adds that, while the Compuduct System and estimating were already programmed by Construction Technology, plans call for Midland Engineering Co. undertaking its own programming chores, utilizing a self-programming language provided with the system.

About the Modern Sheet Metal Equipment In Midland Engineering Co. Shop

It was our pleasure to accompany Simms on a tour of Midland Engineering Co.'s 100' by 70' sheet metal shop which is housed in a Butler metal building. Modern sheet metal equipment in the shop includes an air operated GripNail "gun" for the setting of mechanical insulation fasteners, a 10 ft., 14 ga. Engel press brake and a new 6 ft., 12 ga. Dreis & Krump box and pan brake. The accompanying shop layout provided by Brian Simms shows the arrangement of sheet metal machines and the flow of the work.

Chet Ruszkowski Pictured in Operation of 10 Ga., 3/16" Columbia Power Shear

(All SNIPS Photos)

Collection of Articles from SNIPS

Seminole Sheet Metal Co., Tampa Fla., Owes Success To Equipping Shop with Versatile Sheet Metal Machinery

SNIPS Tours Seminole Sheet Metal Co. Operated by Glen McNabb in Tampa, Fla. . . . 50,000 Sq. Ft. Sheet Metal Shop Described as the Largest in State of Florida . . . Building Also Houses McNabb's Companion Business, Florida Mechanical Systems, Inc. . . . Welty-Way Duct Line Produces L-Shaped Duct Sections Automatically . . . Illustrated Sheet Metal Shop Layout Sketch Shows Location of Various Machinery McNabb Utilizes to Provide Versatile Sheet Metal Fabrication Service . . . McNabb Honored by Many Trade Groups for His Service to the Sheet Metal Industry

What is the measure of a man? This question was answered when SNIPS visited Glen McNabb recently at Seminole Sheet Metal Co., the Tampa, Florida sheet metal business which he founded more than 25 years ago.

McNabb has built his firm in just a quarter of a century to a position of prominence in the State of Florida. But, he was never too busy to give of himself to the industry from which he took his livelihood. His plaque honors listed elsewhere in this story pinpoint the esteem which his fellows in the industry have for him.

Seminole Sheet Metal Co.'s New Location Occupies 50,000 Sq. Ft.

When SNIPS visited Seminole Sheet Metal Co. at 4811 W. Sligh Ave., in Tampa, it was interesting to learn that the firm is housed in 50,000 sq. ft. building which has 2,000 sq. ft. of office space. This compares to the 17,600 sq. ft. structure which the firm occupied at its original location, which was roughly 2½ times smaller than the new facility.

Mechanical Contracting Div. Housed Under Same Roof as Industrial Div.

Florida Mechanical Systems, Inc. is a mechanical contracting firm also operated by McNabb which is housed in the same building as Seminole Sheet Metal Co. This organization sub-contracts every portion of the job except the piping.

Many times, McNabb admits, other Tampa sheet metal contractors are more competitive than Seminole Sheet Metal Co. and are awarded the contract for the ductwork. When the job is let for bid, the sub-contractor with the lowest bid gets the job, regardless of the possibility that Seminole Sheet Metal may not successfully bid the contract.

Welty-Way Coil Line Includes Automatic Duct Fabrication Machinery

On our tour of McNabb's sheet metal shop, the dominant section of fabrication machinery was the duct line manufactured by Welty-Way Products, Inc., Cedar Rapids, Iowa. The automatic duct production line utilized coil stock which was straightened, sheared, beaded, notched and broken.

If specifications call for cross-braking of ducts, the Welty-Way Bruct is bypassed and duct blanks go to the Dreis & Krump Speedi-Bender for cross-braking and "L"-shaped forming.

Duct Lining Center Located Adjacent to Duct Fabrication

As a matter of practical logistics, the duct lining center was located near the Welty-Way duct line so that this operation could be achieved with a minimum of handling. Seminole Sheet Metal Co. operates two Lockformer insulation machines — one 60" wide, and the other 48" wide.

Two Binks spray units spray 3-M, Benjamin Foster and St. Clair adhesives, preliminary to mechanical "pinning" with either a KLM welding system or a similar system manufactured by the H. A. Jones Co., of Dayton, Ohio.

Lincoln and Hobart Welders Featured In Seminole's Welding Department

Since a well-equipped welding department is a "must" for sheet metal shops handling industrial work, Seminole Sheet Metal Co. operates 22 welding machines, mostly Lincoln and Hobart units. Of these, three were automatic wire feed welders.

Unusual Two-Story Structure Within Shop Serves as Foreman's Office

An accompanying photograph shows the unusual super-structure which was part of the original building interior. The 16-foot by 24 foot two-story structure is used for a foreman's office on the second floor, and also provides space for a draftsman.

This 50,000 Sq. Ft. Building Houses the Tampa, Fla., Headquarters of Seminole Sheet Metal Co. (Right Side) and Florida Mechanical Systems, Inc. (Left Side)

The Focal Point of Seminole Sheet Metal Co. is the Welty-Way Products, Inc.'s Duct Production Line which Combines Feeding, Straightening, Shearing, Beading and Notching of a Coil Stock Blank Preliminary to Forming into a Section of an "L"-Shaped Duct by a Dreis & Krump Speedi-Bender Machine, Not Pictured

Glen McNabb, President of Seminole Sheet Metal Co., Pictured with Plaque Honors Displayed in Reception Room. He Holds Florida Construction Industry License Permitting Him to Work Anywhere in the State

(All SNIPS Photos)

Glen McNabb Pictured Next to Impressive Array of Turning Vanes Produced on Harper Vane Machine for Use by Seminole S.M. Co. and for Sale to Area Sub-Contractors

Collection of Articles from SNIPS

On the ground floor, there are toilets, showers and lockers for employees, as well as some storage space.

Inventory Clerk Keeps Track of Parts; Checks Out Portable Electric Tools

An area of the shop measuring 24 ft. x 60 ft. is enclosed with an eight-foot chain link fence. This space is used for the storage of miscellaneous material stocks, including small shop items such as fasteners, repair parts, etc. An inventory clerk who also makes repairs of hand tools and portable electric tools is responsible for checking out tools to mechanics or the job. When the job is finished, he checks back and determines where the tools are and

(Page of Shop Photos on Next Page)

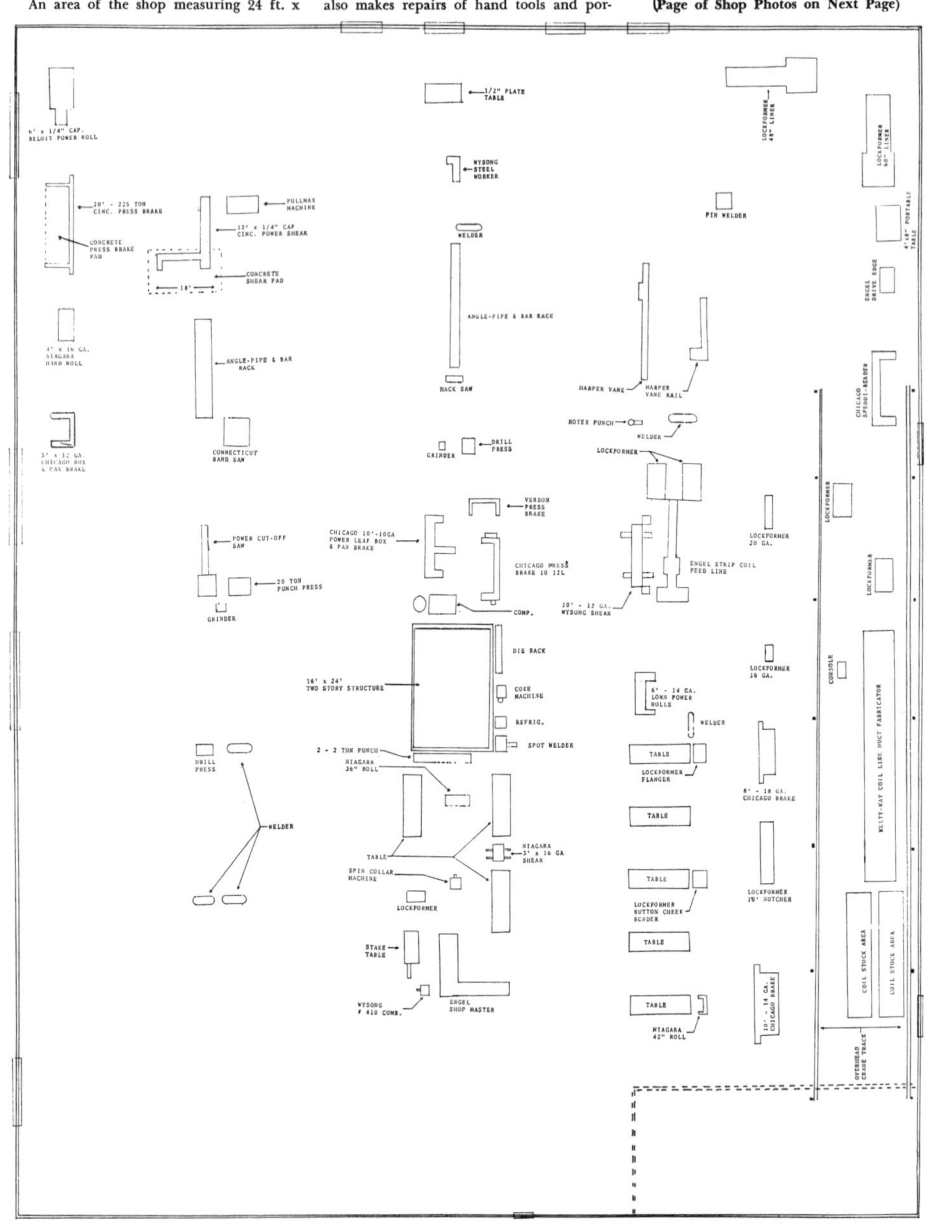

Sheet Metal Shop Sketch of Seminole Sheet Metal Co., Tampa, Fla., Shows Arrangement of the Wide Variety of Sheet Metal Machines Employed by Glen McNabb to Handle the Various Sheet Metal Fabrication Services Provided Industrial Firms. Other Machinery Produces HVAC Components for Use in Own Jobs and for Sale to Other Area Sub-Contractors

Collection of Articles from SNIPS   273.

Picturing the 16-Ft. by 24-Ft. Two-Story Building which Housed Foreman's Office and Draftsman's Space on Second Floor and Toilets, Showers and Lockers on Ground Floor.

This Everett Industries' Abrasive Cut-Off Saw Cuts I-Beams up to 6" and Channel Beams from 8" to 10"

Picturing an Unusual Material Handling System Consisting of 2" Pipe Posts Welded into 3/16" Plate Base, Each Topped with a Ball Bearing Swivel. Sheets Slide Easily into Cutting Bed of 12' 1/4" Cincinnati Power Shear

This Harper's Machinery Set-up Produced Turning Vanes, Vane Rails and Spin Collars for Shop Use and for Sale to Other Sub-Contractors
(All SNIPS Photos)

This Trio of Lockformer Machines, Each Equipped with Casters for Easy Movement Around the Shop, Produces Reinforced "S" Locks, Government Pocket Locks, 2½" Standing "S" Locks and 1" "S" Locks.

This Hendley-Whittemore ¼" Power Roller Machine Can Roll ⅜" Steel 48" Wide, as Well as Companion Flanges and Angle Rings

Glen McNabb Is Pictured Next to Heavy Capacity Dreis & Krump "Chicago" Power Press Brake

Picturing the 180° Curved Sections of ⅜" Steel which Were Rolled on Hendley-Whittemore Co. Power Roller Machine for Use in Vat Made For Local Schlitz Brewery

This Picture Shows the Base of ⅜" Steel Vat Fabricated for Local Schlitz Brewery. Sections of Steel Welded Together Will Receive Other Sections on Top Until Required Height is Reached.

gets them back. They are checked and repaired, if necessary.

McNabb explains that the system cuts down on losses of tools, parts and fasteners which happen when loose inventory controls are prevalent.

Rolling Tables Used for Handling Of Fabricated Sheet Metal

A basic form of materials handling in Seminole Sheet Metal Co. is the use of ten 4-foot by 8-foot rolling tables. The tables, reinforced with welded angle iron bracing, are equipped with 8" swivel casters and have a 3,000 pound capacity. One man can easily roll a table carrying sheets or completed work to a desired location.

Overhead Crane Handles Coil Stock

Seminole Sheet Metal Co. utilizes a 10,000 pound capacity overhead crane for the handling of coil stocks from delivery trucks, dropping them to a storage area or to the cradle of the coil line.

Shop-Made Racks Store Metal Sheets

Another innovation which McNabb instituted in his shop is a pair of shop designed

Picture Shows Ingenious Shop-Made 9-Tier Material Storage Rack which Has a 70,000 Pound Capacity. Adjacent to Rack at the Right Is One of 10 Rolling Tables, Each with 3000 Pound Capacity, which Is Used to Move Finished Work in Shop

Picturing the Engel Coil Feed Line (Model CSF-5) with 9" Width For Production Roll Forming of Government Locks and Standard "S" Locks
(All SNIPS Photos)

and shop fabricated sheet storage racks. When the racks were designed, provision was made for the deposit and withdrawal of sheets by fork lift trucks.

Each rack had five tiers capable of storing 5,000 pounds each and four tiers, each with a 1,000-1,500 pound capacity, with a total capacity of 70,000 pounds when completely filled.

Posts with Ball Bearing Swivels Provide Method for Sheet Handling

Another intriguing shop-made system for simplifying the handling of sheet metal sheets was in evidence near the throat of the 12' ¼" Cincinnati power shear (The firm was awaiting delivery of a 20 ft. 225 ton Cincinnati press brake, and we may assume that the same systems are to be employed with the new machine.).

Sheets to be sheared are lifted by fork lift truck onto a unique shop made materials handling system which consists of a number of holes high 2" pipe posts welded into the floor base. Ball bearing swivels on the top of each post permit the effortless movement of sheets into the cutting bed of the shear.

Hendley & Whittemore Power Rolls with Angle Roll Forming Handles Plate Work For Big Vat

An interesting shop project which McNabb showed SNIPS was a vat which the firm was fabricating for the local Schlitz brewery to store residues of ingredients remaining from the brewing process. For this work a ¼" capacity power roller manufactured by Hendley & Whittemore Co., Beloit, Wis., rolled out four-feet wide sections of ⅜" plate. The curved segments were welded together until the vat reached the specified height.

Companion flanges and angle rings were also rolled out on the machine by Seminole Sheet Metal Co.

About the Function of Various Machines in Seminole S.M. Co. Shop

In our tour of Seminole Sheet Metal Co.'s shop it was interesting to note the wide variety of machinery the firm has at its disposal to take care of the various demands which its customers have for metal fabrication requirements. Following, it is our pleasure to list these machines with a brief explanation of their use:

Wysong Model 100 Steel Worker, shears angle, flat bar, round or square rod; copes, notches and punches 2" x 2" x ¼" stock.

Pullmax Machine, 7/32" capacity, makes circle louvers and inside and outside circles.

Engel (Model CSF-5 — 9" width) coil feed line, cut-off station and electronic console for production roll forming of government locks and 1" — 1½" — 2" standing "S" locks.

It also provides blank stock for the Harper turning vane and rail fabrication system.

Universal shearing and forming machine.

Everett Industries' Abrasive Cut-Off Saw-handles I-beam up to 6"; and 8" to 10" channel iron.

Machines Permit Sale of Sheet Metal Items to Other Sub-Contractors

Besides permitting Seminole Sheet Metal Co. to fabricate many components for HVAC system applications, the machines provide an opportunity for the firm to sell turning vanes, rails, spin collars and "S" locks to sub-contractors.

Scan System Used to Estimate Mechanical Contracting Jobs

An interesting piece of equipment which Florida Mechanical Systems utilizes to save time and labor is the Dodge/SCAN Microfilm System. The area McGraw-Hill Information Systems Co. micro-films drawings and specifications of jobs to be let. As a subscriber, McNabb's estimator is furnished with micro-films of jobs being let which his estimator can project to original size thus saving time and travel in obtaining bidding documents.

Honors Heaped Upon McNabb for Time He Has Given Industry

Glen McNabb's success is particularly significant because of the time and energy he has plowed into the sheet metal industry. For this work he has been recognized with numerous awards and tributes expressed in plaques displayed in his reception room.

Following are McNabb's awards and the sentiments expressed on them:

BOB CAMPANELLA MEMORIAL AWARD — 1966

Selected as the individual member of the State Ass'n who contributed the most towards the betterment of the Ass'n during the year.

SMACNA — FLORIDA WEST COAST CHAPTER — January, 1968

In grateful appreciation of his dedication and service in the development and promotion of the sheet metal industry.

ROOFING & SHEET METAL CONTRACTORS OF FLORIDA, INC.

President — 1968-1969 With appreciation for his contribution of time and effort to improve the roofing and sheet metal industry of the state.

SHEET METAL & AIR CONDITIONING CONTRACTORS NAT'L ASS'N

An expression of appreciation for outstanding service as Chairman, Council of Chapter Representatives, May 1968 — May, 1969.

FLORIDA CONSTRUCTION LICENSING BUREAU, CONSTRUCTION INDUSTRY LICENSE

Be it known by all men that Glen McNabb being duly qualified by written examination and thorough investigation of character, is hereby certified to practice Sheet Metal Contracting throughout the State of Florida — Issued July, 1974.

Collection of Articles from SNIPS   275.

Charles E. Jarrell & Associates, St. Louis, Mo., Opens New Fully Equipped 10,000 Sq. Ft. Sheet Metal Shop

Information Provided by Arthur B. Heuer, Vice President, Sales, Engel Industries, St. Louis, Mo., Tells How Local Mechanical Contractor Opened a Fully Equipped Sheet Metal Shop . . . Telling How Charles E. Jarrell & Associates, St. Louis, Mo., Hired Vincent Novak to Operate Sheet Metal Shop . . . Sheet Metal Shop Layout Accompanying Story Shows Flow of Metal Sheets to Various Sheet Metal Machines . . . Thirteen Sheet Metal Machines Serve as Nucleus of Jarrell Sheet Metal Fabrication Operation . . . If HVAC Volume Warrants It, Sheet Metal Duct Production Line Will Be Purchased and Operated in Larger Building

Back in 1960, Charles E. Jerrell established a mechanical contracting business which he now operates with his son, Michael C. Jarrell, at 11551 Adie Rd., St. Louis Mo., 63043. During the 19 years which this mechanical contracting firm has been in business, ductwork for the heating, ventilating and air conditioning systems handled by the firm had been purchased from local sub-contractors some of which were operating automatic duct production lines.

Sub-contracting for the ductwork on a per pound basis freed the mechanical contracting firm from the necessity of maintaining a sheet metal operation and involvement in labor matters related to sheet metal journeymen. An added advantage was in the estimating factor which maximized materials and minimized labor factors.

In recent years, mechanical contractors, very much like roofing contractors who formerly "subbed" out all of their sheet metal work, found that sheet metal contractors often had to put their own needs first, holding up important HVAC work until production time was available. In addition, sheet metal contractors producing their own duct are able to underbid mechanical contractors who have to pay "drugstore prices" for sub-contracting HVAC ductwork and components.

Charles E. Jarrell & Associates, Inc. Hired Manager of Sheet Metal Department

When the decision was made to form a sheet metal department, the firm hired Vincent Novak as manager. Novak has 29 years in the sheet metal industry, 28 of them being spent with Mound Rose Cornice & Sheet Metal Works, St. Louis, which had been one of Jarrell's HVAC ductwork sub-contractors.

Novak was given 10,000 sq. ft. of floor space in which a sheet metal shop would be established. The mission of the shop would be to fabricate all of the HVAC ductwork which Charles E. Jarrell & Associates would require in its various design and build projects.

Art Heuer of Engel Industries Has Become Shop Layout Expert

Over the years, Arthur B. Heuer, vice president—sales, Engel Industries, Inc., 8122 Reilly Ave., St. Louis, Mo., 63111, has established for himself a nationwide reputation as an expert in the effective layout of sheet

An Overall View of the Sheet Metal Shop Shows the Engel Roll Formers at the Bottom of the Picture, the Shopmaster Units at the Right Center and the Rolls of Duct Liner at the Upper Right Hand Corner

machinery to provide the smooth and efficient flow of materials from the metal sheet to the finished duct or fitting.

Heuer has collaborated with other sheet metal machinery manufacturers to produce a booklet on suggested sheet metal shop layout planning and has contributed editorial material to SNIPS on the subject which will be incorporated into SNIPS Sheet Metal Layout booklet when it is reprinted.

Novak Appreciated Availability, Quick Delivery of Machinery By Engel Industries, Inc.

When the time came for creating an efficient shop layout format, Vince Novak relied upon his many years in the sheet metal industry to guide him. Novak readily identifies with Engel Industries and was acquainted with Charlie Engel, who designed the Shopmaster sheet metal system. In fact, Novak purchased Shopmaster No. 6 from the St. Louis company.

Besides knowing about the capability of Engel sheet metal machinery Novak said that it was important to him that the machinery was available when he needed

Pictured Next to Two Engel Shopmaster Machines which Perform Blanking, Notching and Slitting Functions Are Tim Shockleg, Left, Shop Supt.; and Elmer Self, Right, Sheet Metal Mechanic

Art Heuer, Left, Vice Pres. - Sales, Engel Industries, Inc., St. Louis, Mo., Pictured with Vincent Novak, Right, Mgr. of Charles E. Jarrell & Assoc., Sheet Metal Dept. at Front Entrance of Building

Sheet Metal Shop Layout of Charles E. Jarrell & Associates, St. Louis, Mo., on Page 17 Was Provided by Vincent Novak, General Mgr. of the Sheet Metal Department.

Sheet Metal Machinery Is Represented by Numbers on the Layout, Showing How Sheet Metal Sheets Moved Through Various Stages of Fabrication Until They Become the Finished HVAC Duct Section or Fitting.
1. Engel 18 Ga. Shopmaster which Produces HVAC Fittings
2. Engel 16 Ga. Shopmaster which Produces Straight Duct
3. Engel Beading Unit
4. Engel Roll Former (Snaplock, S & DC)
5. Engel Roll Former (Standing "S" Slip Snaplock)
6. Engel Bendall — Power Brake
7. Engel Cleat Bender (Table Model)
8. Duro Dyne Model FG-1 Pinspotter
9. Engel Slit-O-Matic for Shearing Fiber Glass Insulation Liner
10. Cincinnati Power Shear — Model 1010 (10 Ga.-10 Ft.
11. Angle Iron Worker
12. Engel 24" Open End Flanger
13. Engel 750 Edgenotcher
14. Engel Edgemaster Flanger
15. Hand Brake (8-Foot)
16. Wysong Foot Shear (#1652)
17. Power Slp-Roll (To Be Added in the Future)

Collection of Articles from SNIPS

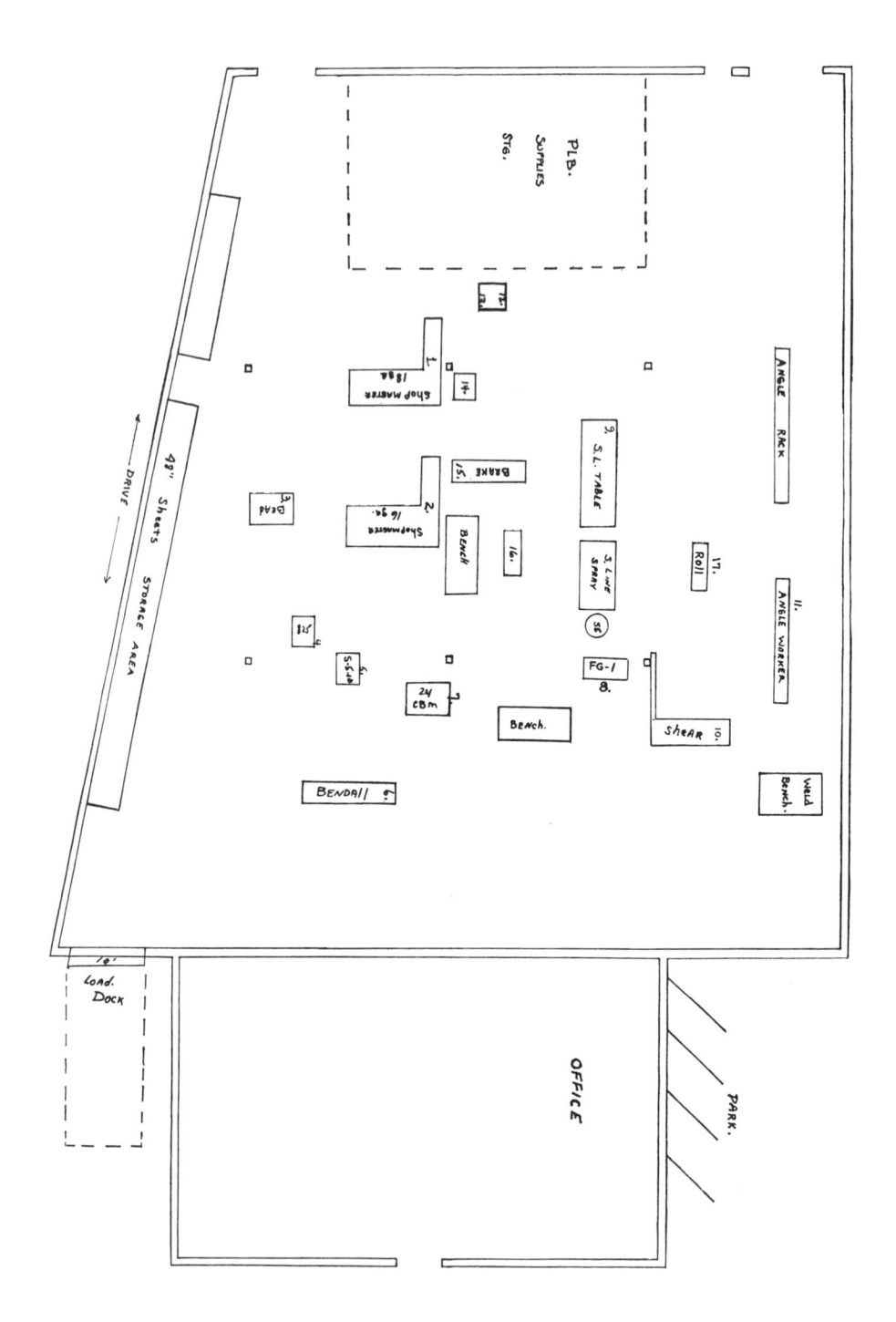

Collection of Articles from SNIPS

277.

Engel Industries V.P.-Sales Art Heuer, Left, Shows Film on Shopmaster System to Field Installer Roger Blackwell, Center; and Mechanic Elmer Self, Right

▶ *In the Picture at Right, Shop Supt. Elmer Shockleg Operates Engel Slit-O-Matic Machine which Shears Fiber Glass Duct Liner to Size. Note Rolls of Duct Liner Stored on Shelf Above Machine*

it, since quick delivery was offered by Art Heuer. Another advantage was the accessibility to service from the St. Louis based manufacturer.

Engel Industries Receives Order For 13 Sheet Metal Machines

In March, 1979, Engel Industries agreed to supply 13 sheet metal machines to be delivered to the new sheet metal machinery department, as follows:

Engel 18 ga. Shopmaster for fabricating fittings; Engel 16 ga. Shopmaster for fabricating straight duct; Engel beading unit; Engel Roll Former, Snaplock S & DC; Engel Roll Former, Standing "S" Slip Snaplock; Engel Bendall power brake; Engel Cleat Bender—table model; Engel Slit-O-Matic insulation slitter; Engel 24" Open End Flanger; Engel 750 Edgenotcher; and Engel Edgemaster Flanger.

In addition, the shop was fitted with a Duro Dyne FG-1 Pinspotter, a Model 1010, 10 ga.. 10 ft. Cincinnati power shear, an angle iron worker, an 8 ft. hand brake and a Wysong Model 1652 foot shear.

Novak Tells SNIPS How Sheet Metal Blanks Are Routed to Machinery

Vincent Novak estimated that the Charles E. Jarrell & Assoc. Sheet Metal Dept. would use approximately 500,000 pounds of metal sheets annually. To insure an adequate supply the firm uses four St. Louis, Mo., suppliers; Souther, Inc.; Hammond Sheet Metal; Hubbell Metals Div. (National Steel Corp.) ; and Reynolds Metals.

Novak said that the 48" x 120" galvanized steel sheets are handled by two mechanics who move the flat sheets with a rented forklift truck in four working hours.

Briefly, the sheets are routed to the shop beginning with either model Shopmaster where they are notched and slit to size; next, the blank is sent to the beader which takes place of cross braking, then they travel to the roll forming machines where the male or female snaplock or Pittsburgh

Shop Supt. Tim Shockleg Pictured Demonstrating Engel Motor-Powered Cleat Bender

lock is formed. Next, the cleat bender turns the cap strip on the side of the duct.

The last step takes place at the Bendall machine where the blank is formed into an L-shaped half section of duct.

Tim Shockleg, Sheet Metal Shop Supt., Left; and Sheet Metal Mechanic Elmer Self, Right, Pictured at Right in Front of Engel Beading Machine which Does Job Formerly Handled by Cross Braking Operation

Duro Dyne Pinspotter, Adhesive Used to Secure Duct Liner

If the ductwork requires acoustical or thermal liner, the fiber glass insulation is cut to size by the Engel Slit-O-Matic. The liner is secured to either the duct or the fitting with Duro Dyne WS (water soluable) adhesive and mechanically fastened with the Duro Dyne Model FG-1 Pinspotter.

Finished Duct Work Loaded on Skid

When the duct work or fittings reach the last production station in the shop, they are loaded on a wooden skid after being coded for the job with a rubber stamp. The skid is loaded onto the company truck with a small, company-owned fork lift truck.

At the present time, 15 mechanics are kept busy in the field with the HVAC ductwork and fittings produced by a 2-3 man work force in the sheet metal shop.

About the Projects Handled By Charles E. Jarrell & Assoc.

Charles E. Jarrell & Associates has handled the mechanical contracting work in several large projects in the St. Louis, Mo., area. Some of the larger jobs include:
• Sheraton Hotel in downtown St. Louis
• The J. C. Penney, Stix-Baer and Fuller department stores (in Fairview Heights, Ill.)
• The Gold Tower Building
• Sheraton Hotel
• Westport Plaza in St. Louis County

Currently, Charles E. Jarrell & Associates is an active member of the Mechanical Contractors Association of American (MCCA). As the future unfolds, plans call for its sheet metal arm to become affiliated with the Sheet Metal and Air Conditioning Contractors National Ass'n (SMACNA).

Another eventuality for the future is the possible addition of an automatic duct production line. This will take place when and if the volume of HVAC work warrants it, and it will require larger quarters than are available in the present set-up.

Next to the Sheet Metal Bench at the Left Can Be Seen the Engel Model 1010 Bendall which Formed L-Shaped Duct Sections Pictured at the Right

Model 1010 Cincinnati Power Shear (No. 10 on Sheet Metal Shop Layout) Is Located Near Engel Shopmaster Machines

Successful Sheet Metal Shop Layout Fundamentals
Provided by Art Heuer

Information on Sheet Metal Production Planning and Layout Essentials Gleaned from Talk Delivered by Art Heuer, Souther, Inc., St. Louis, Mo., at 1975 Annual Convention of Florida Roofing, Sheet Metal Air Conditionng Contractors Ass'n at Orlando, Fla., ... Basic Layout Steps Provided ... Heuer Refers to SNIPS Layout Book Available for $1.00 ... Heuer Tells when Revised Sheet Metal Layout Is Needed and How To Make the Sheet Metal Layout Sketch

One of the areas in the sheet metal field about which there is a shortage of published information is that concerning sheet metal shop layout. Therefore, we are pleased this month to present information on this important subject which has been gleaned from a talk before the annual convention of the Florida Roofing, Sheet Metal & Air Conditioning Contractors Ass'n (FRSA) at Orlando.

The information was presented by Art Heuer of Souther, Inc., 1952 Kienlen Ave., St. Louis, Mo., who for many years was sales manager for Engel Industries, Inc., St. Louis, Mo., manufacturer of sheet metal machinery.

Heuer Explains When a Sheet Metal Shop Layout Is Necessary

Many sheet metal contractors ask, "When should I prepare a shop layout for my business?" To this question, I submit for consideration the following six elements which should be present, either single or combined, because of current business conditions:

1. When starting a new contracting business.
2. New or additional plant space is required as a result of production volume increases.
3. The sheet metal shop changes emphasis from residential to commercial work, etc.
4. Shop is moved from one building to another.
5. When adding a major new sheet metal machine, such as a 10' power shear, 10' power brake or a coil handling system.
6. When use of raw material, such as steel changes from flat sheets to coil stock, as well as flat sheet stock.

Production Planning Reflected in Shop Layout

The secret of successful and profitable sheet metal fabrication lies in proper production planning — the right kind of tools used in the right way.

The sheet metal shop should be an integrated efficient production line that will turn out the greatest amount of work with the least amount of time, effort, and cost. Sheet metal fabrication involves:

1. Preparation of metal in the flat; cutting metal to the required size and notching it to a pattern.
2. Forming metal, either a lock seam, cross breaking or beading, bending, or shaping metal to a radius.
3. Final assembly, including final seaming, forming cleat edges and completion of the sheet metal product.

Material Handling Must be Reduced to a Minimum

For most efficient operation the shop must be planned so that production operations can be performed in the proper sequence. Tools should be arranged systematically to keep material handling to a minimum. Cut down the amount of space through which materials or sheet metal mechanics must travel. Avoid the re-handling and piling of material and back tracking from one operation to another.

Art Heuer, Right — Standing, Souther, Inc., St. Louis, Mo., who Conducted Shop Layout Discussion; Chats With Ted Sulak, Left. Sales Mgr. for Feco Div., Bangor Punta Corp. Cleveland, Ohio. Picturing Some of the "Students" who Remained for Our Picture, Left to Right, Morris Whidden, Reliable Sheet Metal, Tampa; Skeet Goldman, E. C. Goldman, Winter Park; Larry Shimkus, Southern Regional Representative for Lockformer Co.; Nels Frid, N. E. Frid Sheet Metal, Winter Park; Ralph Walker, Tropical Sheet Metal, Tampa; Vince Walker, J. B. Wallis Co., Jacksonville; and Jim Falkner, Falkner, Inc., Orlando

(SNIPS Photo)

Set Up Two Flow Lines for Materials

The most efficient production is obtained from the setting up of two flow lines; one primary, and the other, secondary. The primary line should handle the standardized types of components which comprise the bulk of the shop's work. The secondary line should handle the special or tailormade items. Plan the production so that as much work as possible moves through primary or standard flow lines. The secondary flow line should be for special fittings and other types of work not adapted to the primary line.

Listing Objectives for Production Planning

In order to implement sound planning practices, it is necessary to constructively and creatively strive for simplicity in shop production. In this respect the following objectives are relevant:

1. Simplify and mechanize all operations.
2. Gain full value from money invested in production tools and shop equipment.
3. Stress flexibility in production by planning and selecting the means and methods used so that capacity can be increased when required.
4. Effect versatility in production so that many different types of operations can be accomplished.
5. Work toward reducing space required; effect good housekeeping practices and work toward a systematic production area.

Getting Down to Actually Making Shop Layout

Considering the basic steps to take when making an individualized shop layout, begin with a scale drawing of the shop floor plan, omitting from the plan moveable items such as machinery or material racks in the intial plan.

These basic steps can be considered when making the rough plan:

1. Locate all existing walls, columns, power sources, doors and loading areas, and include in the plan stairways, windows and drive areas.

2. List all equipment in the shop and draw to scale the equipment or machinery to be considered in the layout, such as mobile tables, benches, A-frames, steel storage racks, vertical racks, brakes, notchers, roll formers, etc.

Draw symbols for these items on cardboard or colored paper; cut them out and label them. Also cut out aluminum samples or make use of miniature tool samples.

3. Place symbols in the best possible order, keeping in mind the above mentioned practices in production planning.

Use ¼" to Equal One Foot as Scale

The scale of a shop layout is always an important consideration. The best scale to use in preparing the shop layout is with ¼" to equal one foot. In this way, it is large enough for adequate detail, yet not so large as to be difficult to work with.

If shop dimensions are over 200 x 200 feet, use a smaller scale of ⅛" equal to one foot. The size of the paper to be used and the work surface where the layout is prepared will help control the scale used.

SNIPS Layout Booklet Recommended by Heuer

In order to assist the sheet metal contractor in the preparation of a suitable shop layout, it is suggested that one or more of the following resource materials be used.

1. Shop Layouts, a 44-page booklet published by SNIPS Book Dept., 407 Mannheim Rd., Bellwood, Ill., 60104.

2. Planning for Profit, a 6-page booklet offered by The Lockformer Co., 711 Ogden Ave., Lisle. Ill., 60532.

3. Production Efficiency in Sheet Metal Fabrication, a complete production kit complete with grid and template sheet, available from Engel Industries, Inc., 8122 Reilly Ave., St. Louis, Mo. 63111.

H&H Heating & Cooling, Beech Grove, Ind., Has Well Organized New Shop For Expanding Business

Firm, Established By James Harris In 1947, Now Operated with His Three Sons and Daughter . . . Firm Engages Primarily In New House Heating-Cooling Installations . . . Nearly 350 General Electric Heat Pumps Installed In Past Year . . . Our Thanks to Triangle Sheet Metal Supply, Indianapolis, For Pictures and Sketch of Well Planned New Shop of H & H Heating & Cooling

Back in 1947, 31 years ago, James "Big Jim" Harris and his wife, Loretta, co-founded a sheet metal and heating shop in Beech Grove, Ind., a suburb of Indianapolis. When he originally started, his work was pretty much confined to roofing and gutter installations.

Jim had three sons, Gary, Ron and Tim, who literally grew up in the business, working in the shop after school and during the summer vacations. They are now part of the management team along with their father. Harris also had a daughter, who assisted in the office after school and during the summer. She is now Mrs. Marleah Garrett and continues to assist in the office work of the establishment. Her husband, Wally Garrett, is part of the firm's installation division.

Gary Harris, the oldest son, now is handling all of the firm's crews. He is also involved in organizing and setting up jobs, plans the scheduling as well as doing the bidding and performing other chores.

H & H Moves Into New Building, Doubling Previous Size

All during the 31-year history of H & H Heating & Cooling, the firm operated in a building in Beech Grove, comprising about 3,500 sq. ft. This had been adequate in the growing years of the concern. However, as the business expanded to the installation of more and more warm air heating and air conditioning systems, the need for more space to handle the increased volume also became necessary.

So, construction was started on a new shop and office building. This was completed and the move to the new quarters in late June. H & H Heating & Cooling, Inc., is now headquartered in a most attractive new 7,000 sq. ft. building at 875 Bethel Ave., Beech Grove, Ind., 46102.

The building is located on two acres and 1½ acres are black-top paved. There is also an area 64 ft. x 84 ft. that is surrounded by an 8 ft. high chain link fence for company vehicle storage.

New Shop Well Planned For Fast, Smooth Fabrication

The new H & H building is spacious and well lighted, as can be seen in a couple of the accompanying shop photos. In addition, sufficient windows were provided to give supplemental natural lighting. The entire shop and office is air conditioned, and shop and warehouse doors are truckbed high to allow for easy loading of equipment and accessories.

When the new shop was planned, allowances were made for the placement of the firm's sheet metal fabrication machinery to obtain smooth and fast production. All of the ideas that Jim Harris gained from his 30 years experience were incorporated in the new plant. He also had some assistance from the folks at Triangle Sheet Metal Supply Co., Indianapolis, from whom he has purchased all of his sheet metal fabricating machinery.

As can be seen by the accompanying sketch of the shop in the new H & H building, there is adequate room for workmen to move around while fabricating duct work and fittings. Readers will also note how heating, cooling and heat pumps are stored in one general area while furnace pipe, fittings, registers and other accessories are stored separately, elsewhere.

Plans Under Way For Additional Sheet Metal Machines

Since H & H Heating & Cooling is continuing to expand, plans are also under way to acquire some additional sheet metal fabricating equipment, so that the continued increased volume of work will be able to be handled smoothly.

The most recent item acquired by H & H from Triangle, was a Lockformer Super Speed Cleatformer, which replaced an old Lockformer.

The Lockformer Super Speed Cleatformer saves time because with its 3-in-1 rolls with the perforating notcher arrangement, it quickly makes flat "S" cleats, drive cleats and tap-in collars.

Among the new items under consideration is a Lockformer Triplex machine which provides reinforced "S" drives, drive cleats, button punch snaplock pipe and combination "S" and drive cleats.

Another Lockformer machine being given

Picturing the Attractive New 7,000 Sq. Ft. Building which Houses H & H Heating & Cooling In Beech Grove, Ind., A Suburb of Indianapolis. The Well Lighted Structure Also Has Plenty of Window Area For Natural Light

James "Big Jim" Harris, Seated, Co-Founder, in 1947, of H & H Heating & Cooling, Inc., Beech Grove, Ind., Shown with His Three Sons, Now Involved in the Operation of the Business. L to R, Tim Harris; Gary Harris; and Ron Harris. Harris' Daughter and Son-In-Law Are Also Part of Firm. Harris Co-Founded Firm with His Wife, Loretta

Wendell F. Phillips, Left, Pres. of Triangle Sheet Metal Supply Co., Indianapolis, Pictured with Jim Harris, Rght, Head of H & H Heating & Cooling, Inc., In Front of New Shop Building. Phillips Provided Much Information and the Pictures For This Story, while His Son, Scott Phillips, Drew For Us, the Sketch of the New Shop which Appears On Opposite Page

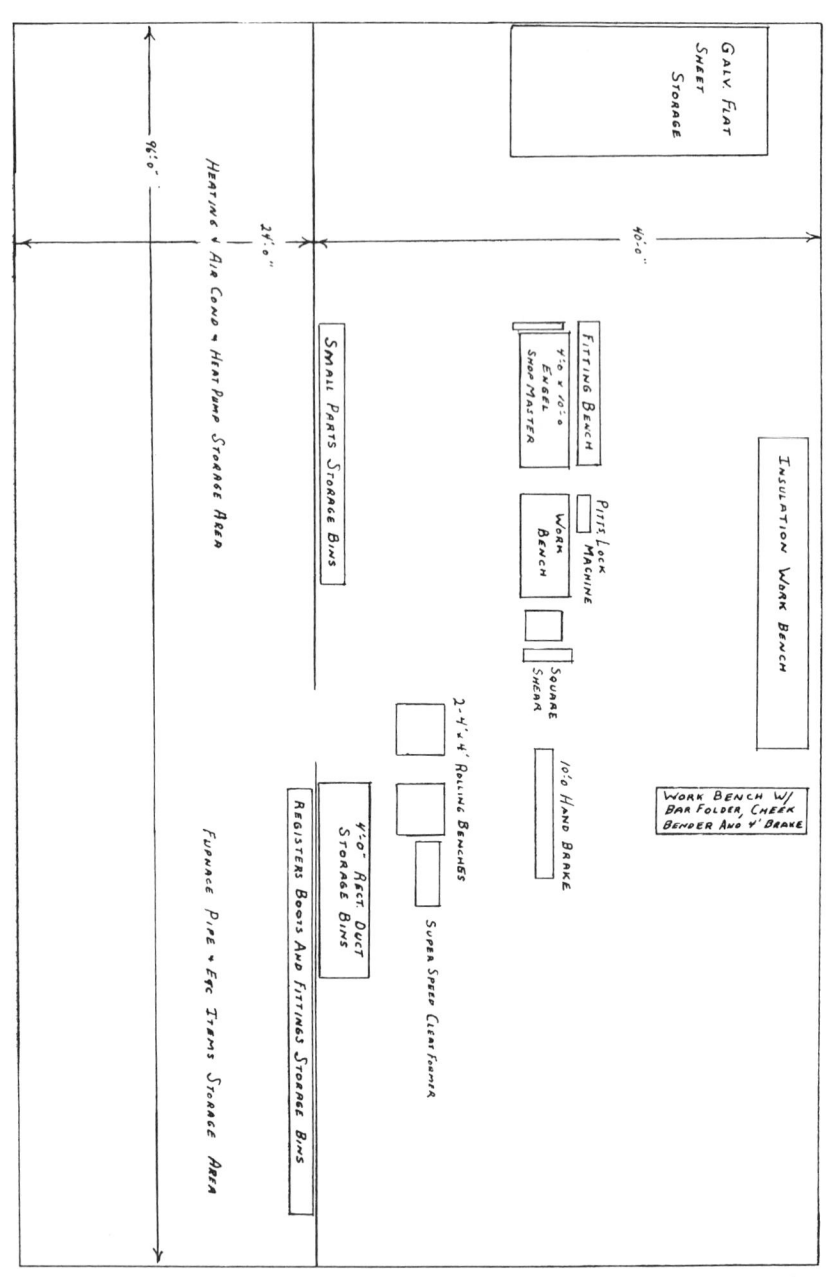

Sketch Showing the Placement of Sheet Metal Machinery in the New H & H Heating & Cooling Shop In Beech Grove, Ind. Equipment Was Positioned For Fast and Smooth Flow of Materials As They Are Fabricated. There Is Adequate Room To Move Around, So Workmen Won't Be Bumping Into Each Other As They Go About Their Work. Note How Equipment and Accessories Are Stored In Warehouse Area for Quick Removal to Job Sites. Entire Shop Is Air Conditioned Along with Offices

Collection of Articles from SNIPS

A View of the Spacious Shop of H & H Heating & Cooling, Inc., Beech Grove, Ind., Showing Placement of Machinery For Quick and Easy Movement of Materials. Lockformer Super Speed Cleatformer Is Shown In Foreground and Tim Harris Is In Background At Work On Bench

Another View of the New H & H Heating & Cooling Sheet Metal Shop. Building Is Well Lighted and Has Ample Door and Window Areas For Entrance of Natural Light. In Background Is the Firm's Small Parts Storage Bins. All Machinery in the H & H Shop Has Been Acquired from Triangle Sheet Metal Supply

thought to is the new Lockformer "Shear-N-Notch" duct fabrication and layout system for making rectangular ducts, fittings, elbows and transitions.

Reasons For Planned Machinery Additions

In an interview with Ron Harris, he stated that one of the reasons for contemplating adding to the shop equipment is that the firm fabricates in the shop all of the rectangular duct and fittings used on its jobs. These are made from Empire-Detroit steel sheets which are acquired from Triangle.

Ron Harris also stated that the firm buys all of its round duct and fittings, prefabricated from Triangle Sheet Metal Supply. The H & H firm uses 100% metal on all ducting systems.

H & H Heating & Cooling Concentrates On New House Work

Ron Harris stated that H & H Heating & Cooling concentrates 90% to 95% of its heating and air conditioning installations to the new house market in Beech Grove, and other suburbs of Indianapolis.

For this work, they use General Electric equipment which is acquired from the local GE Indianapolis warehouse. The firm has also pretty well standardized on Hart & Cooley registers and grilles for these installations, as well as the Hart & Cooley line of Metlvent. These Hart & Cooley products are also purchased from the Triangle firm.

Picturing the Center of the H & H Shop and the Engel Shop Master Machine which Is One of the Work-Horses in Fabricating Duct Work

Heat Pumps Installations Have Surpassed Conventional Heating-Cooling Units

Ron Harris reported further to us that they have been concentrating on the installation of heat pumps in these new homes. From June 1, 1977, through May 31, 1978, the company installed a total of 348 GE heat pumps.

In addition, some $50,000 worth of gas and oil fired combination General Electric heating-cooling was sold and installed by H & H, with a ratio of roughly 3 to 2, of gas over oil.

A small amount of custom sheet metal work is also still handled by the Harris firm, but they have phased out the roofing and gutter work which was the mainstay in the early years.

H & H Now Has 25 Employees and Operates 13 Trucks

From its rather humble beginning, 31 years ago, H & H Heating & Cooling has grown where today there are around 25 employees. Some 13 trucks are used in conjunction with its installation and service work.

Open House Held

When the move to the new building was completed, H & H Heating & Cooling held an open house for its employees, customers and suppliers. More than 150 attended and were treated to a buffet of food and fruit. Those attending the open house were greeted by the Harris' as well as Mrs. Dorothy Jackson, who has been with the firm many years, and is secretary and in charge of the office.

We were informed of the new H & H shop and office, as well as the open house by Wendell F. Phillips, president of Triangle Sheet Metal Supply Co., Inc. When we found it was impossible for someone from SNIPS to attend the affair and to look over the big new shop,

One Portion of New H & H Building Has Been Set Aside for Heating-Cooling and Heat Pump Warehousing, As Shown Here. Firm Specializes In New House Work, Installing Nearly 350 General Electric Heat Pumps In Past Year

A View of the Furnace, Pipe and Fittings Area In New H & H Building. Company Buys All Round Duct and Fittings from "Triangle" and Fabricates All Rectangular Duct In the Shop. All Duct Work on H & H Jobs are of Metal

Suggested Shop Layout for Brazilian Customer
By Lockformer Co., Lisle, Illinois

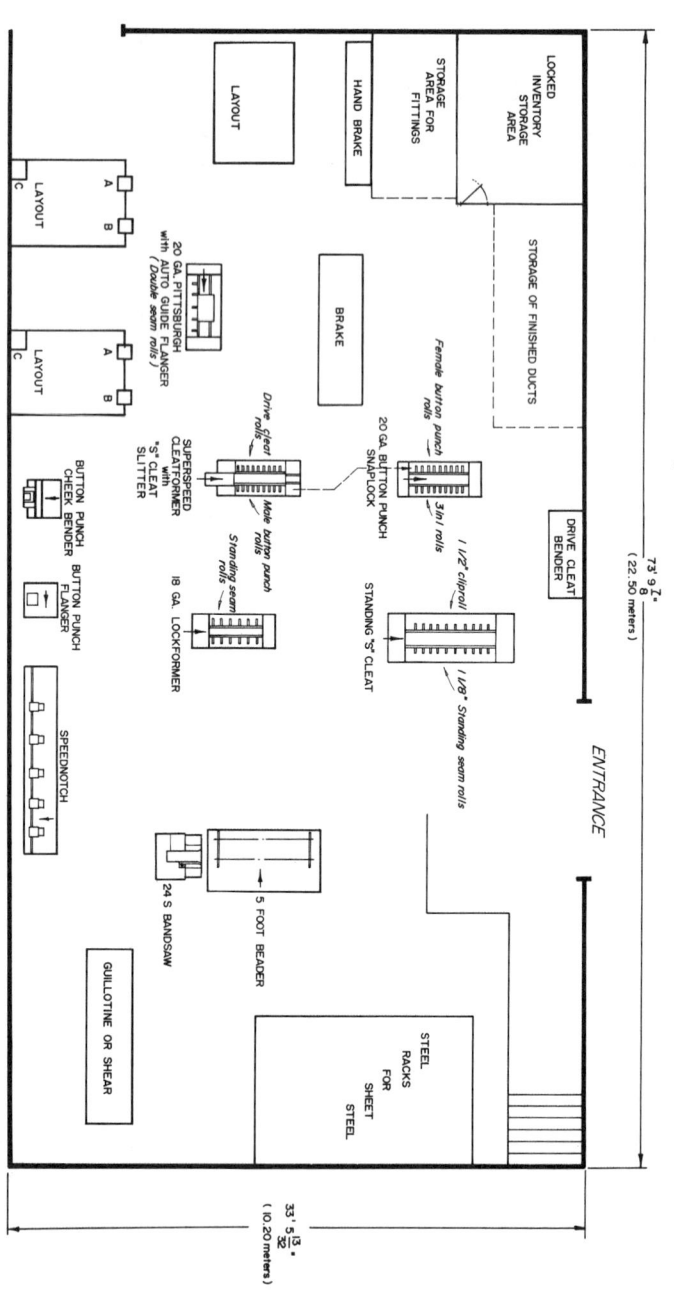

TYPICAL LIGHT COMMERCIAL & INDUSTRIAL SHOP LAYOUT

HAND TOOLS
A — EASY EDGER
B — 24 CHEEK BENDER
C — AIR OPERATED BENCH NOTCHER

# Richard Voorhees of Vorys Brothers, Submits Ideas on Shop Layouts

One of the country's foremost wholesalers of sheet metal working machinery is Vorys Brothers, Inc., Columbus, Ohio. Richard S. Voorhees is manager of the machinery division.

When he heard that we were putting together some information on shop layouts, he kindly submitted for inclusion in this booklet, some very helpful information. Voorhees has assisted many shops in his trading area with their shop layout problems. He says:

"In doing shop layouts, we learned early, that no two shops are alike in terms of physical layout, or what the owner/foreman expects in the way of production. In order to simplify our work in assisting customers, and customers helping themselves, we felt that the idea of "work centers" should be detailed.

"The various "work centers" could be added together in straight line, or "U" type of flow to fit the equipment, space and production needs of the user. Therefore, by using a "shear-notcher center", a "lock center", and a "duct forming center", the customer could come up with a wide variety of shop layouts for the basic volume in his shop.

"In addition to this basic requirement, we have had such areas as "layout/small parts centers", "cleat forming centers", "angle and bar centers", etc. This idea has been interesting and presumably helpful to several of our customers."

The sketches on the opposite page, as furnished by Voorhees, show typical examples of the "duct forming center", "lock center", and "shear-notch center".

Voorhees Also Presents Ideas On the Amount of Time That Can Be Saved Avoiding Unnecessary Walking

Another idea that Voorhees feels strongly influences cost and is likewise, concerned with shop layout, as well as machine selection, is the idea of "walking". Voorhees has sent us the following information about walking:

-- A man walks 40 ft. per minute
-- His step is about 2 ft.
-- 40 divided by 2 = 20 steps per minute
-- Man-hour cost (@$6.00 hr.) = 10¢ per minute
-- 20 steps = 10¢
-- 1 step = ½¢
-- 20 steps per minute x 60 minutes x 2,000 hours per year = 2,400,000 STEPS PER YEAR
-- How Much Time Should a Man Walk???

Voorhees offers duct shop considerations to minimize walking, as follows:

(A) - Use castered tables to transport sheets between operations.
(B) - Consider the use of wrap-around duct, so that the duct is cut-to-length only.
(C) - Use a "job ticket" to list all fabrication -- combine gauges and sizes in logical order to minimize changing. "Pre-Think" the work.
(D) - Do as many operations as possible (within a range of 4 to 6 steps) without laying the sheet down, i.e., shear and notch.
(E) - Use "cross-over" system to form male and female snaplock -- it saves about one-third of the steps.
(F) - Use 3 or 4 pre-sheared square or rectangular BLANKS, such as 12x18, 24x24, 36x36, to make all fittings at the layout bench and store them under the bench. The steps saved will more than pay for any additional scrap, and material cost will be directly accounted for.

Another matter reviewed by Voorhees is giving thought to taking a look at the small repeat operations in the shop. He says, that often, by changing the order of operations, or mounting a tool differently, a considerable amount of time can be saved.

Some ideas provided by him are as follows:

(A) - Two short pieces (in form of a gravity conveyor) attached to the top-back of the hand brake allows getting rid of formed duct without extra steps.
(B) - Mount Cleatbender - vertically, or use two, rather than one.
(C) - Locate shear and notcher together in the form of a try-"square".

Another sketch provided us by Voorhees appears on the following page. It illustrates a generalized layout (not to scale) for the "medium volume duct shop". This layout was made to work in a reasonably confined space to minimize walking.

1. Duct Forming Center

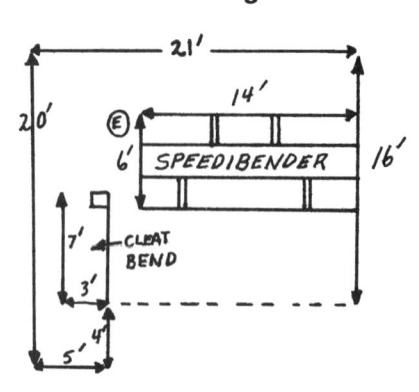

2. Lock Center/Snap-Pitts

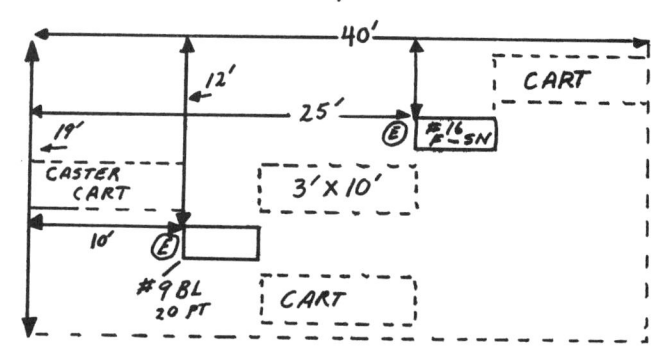

3. Shear- Notch Center

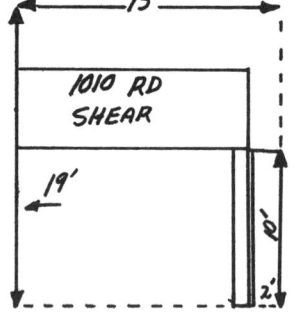

1, 2, & 3 can be arranged in different patterns to suit shop size & configuration.

The sketches on this page, as furnished by Richard Voorhees, show typical examples of the "duct forming center", "lock center", and "shear-notch center".

Collection of Articles from SNIPS

285.

The Medium Volume Duct Shop

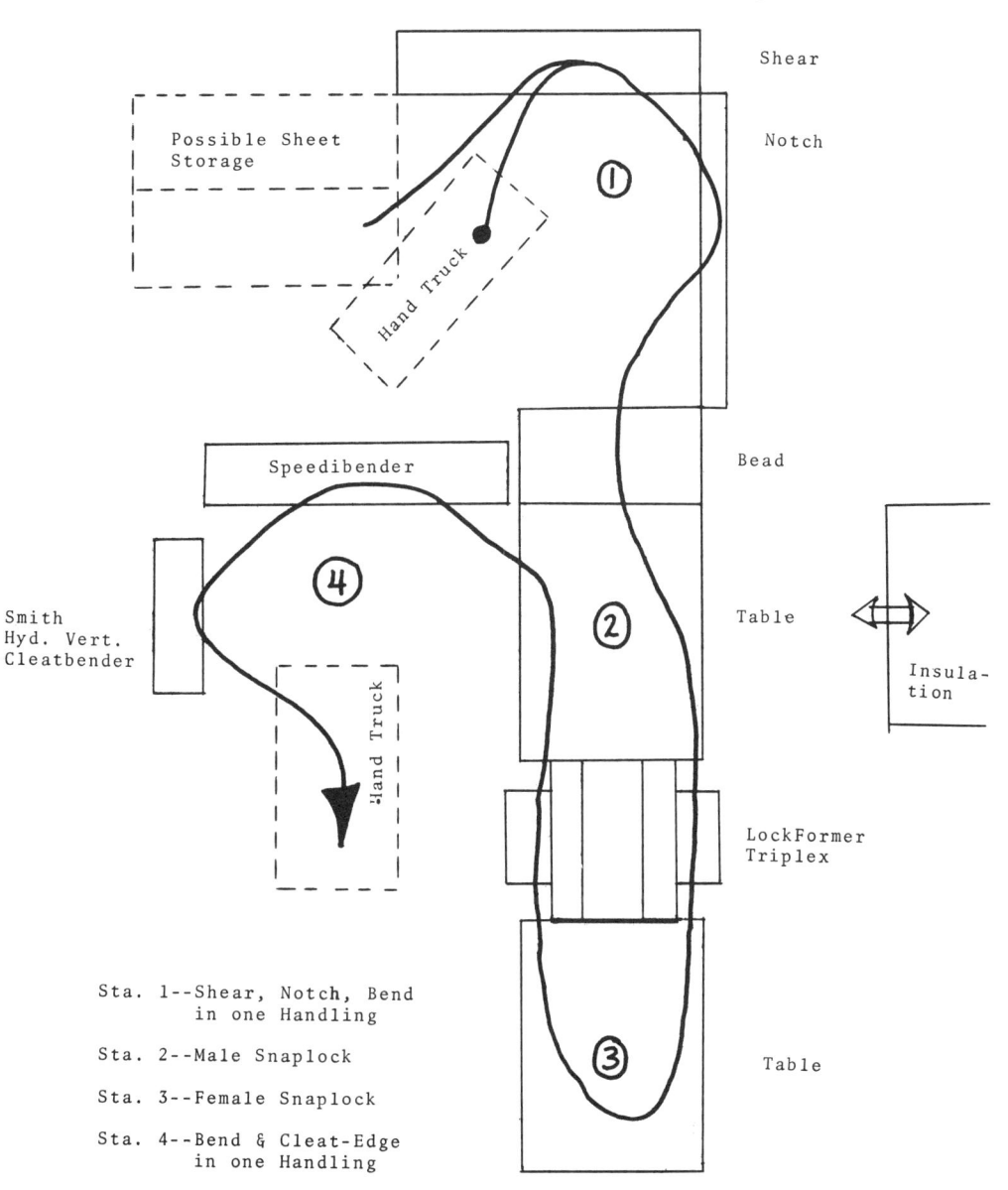

Shear

Notch

Possible Sheet Storage

Hand Truck

①

Speedibender

Bead

Smith Hyd. Vert. Cleatbender

④

②

Table

Insulation

Hand Truck

LockFormer Triplex

③

Table

Sta. 1--Shear, Notch, Bend in one Handling

Sta. 2--Male Snaplock

Sta. 3--Female Snaplock

Sta. 4--Bend & Cleat-Edge in one Handling

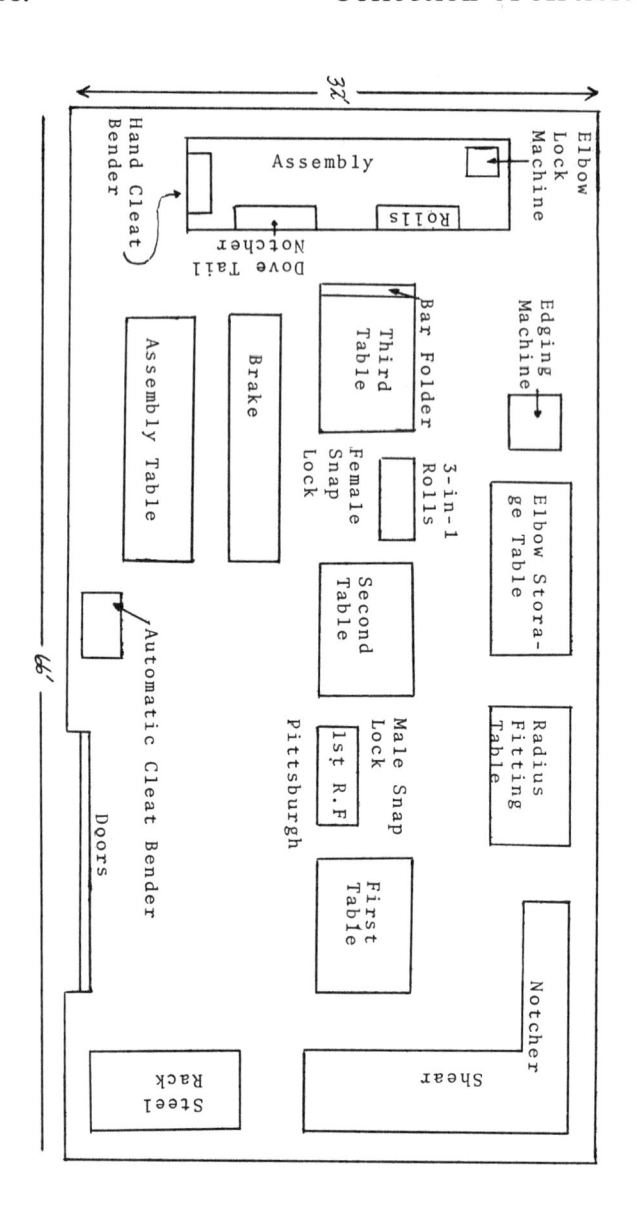

Suggested Shop Layout Submitted By Souther, Inc., St. Louis, Mo.

Collection of Articles from SNIPS 287.

Sheet Metal Fabrication News

Profitable Techniques For Handling Coil Stock In Sheet Metal Shops

In A Talk Before the Florida Ass'n Annual Convention, Art Heuer, Vice Pres.- Sales, Engel Industries, Inc., St. Louis, Mo., Discusses Equipment and Components Used In Handling Coil Stock, Cradles Used to Decoil the Material and Products That Can Profitably Be Fabricated From Coils Rather than Sheet Stock

A View of the Engel Model 1200-B Mini-Cleat Roll Former. It Forms ½" Mini-Cleats from Coil Stock or Flat Blanks

Picturing An Engel Model CFS-6 Coil Strip Feed Line for Drive Cleat, Flat "S" Cleat and Standing "S" Cleat Production

A 6,000 lb. Expanding Mandrel for Use with Narrow Coils for Starting Collars, Turning Vanes and Standing "S" Cleats

Over the years, Art Heuer, shown here, vice president-sales, Engel Industries, Inc., 8122 Reilly Ave., St. Louis, Mo., 63111, has regularly attended the annual conventions of the Florida Roofing & Sheet Metal Contractors Ass'n (FRSA).

About every other year he is asked to participate on the program to disperse his vast knowledge of information for the Florida trade on sheet metal fabrication tricks and on improved machinery to perform this fabrication work.

It has been the pleasure of the SNIPS staff to sit in on many of Heuer's presentations at these Florida gatherings and to have follow-up stories in these editorial columns on some of them.

When FRSA held its 58th annual convention a short time ago, they asked Heuer to present some information on handling coil stock, since so many firms are switching over to the use of metal coils, as opposed to utilizing sheet stock. Once again, Heuer did an able job in presenting some valuable information on "Profitable Techniques for Handling Coil Stock in Sheet Metal Shops."

We are selecting portions of Heuer's talk to present to our readers since there is such a vast and continuing growing interest in this subject. Heuer's talk was accompanied with numerous slides of actual use of coil handling equipment and he has shared some of these with us for illustrations in connection with this news.

Since Heuer broke his talk down into three distinct categories, we likewise are following this pattern. They were:

1—Equipment and components as used in transporting, handling and loading of coils.

2—Cradles used to decoil the material.

3—A summary of products that may be profitably fabricated from coils rather than from sheet stock.

About Equipment Used To Transport, Load and Unload Coil Stock

Heuer started off describing equipment and components that are used in transporting, handling and loading coils from 2⅛" wide to 60" wide, whose weights may vary from as little as 250 lbs. to 15,000 lbs.

Bridge Crane and Mono-Rail System

The bridge crane which has a capacity of from 5 to 7½ tons allows the most flexibility in handling coils. This type of crane allows the shop to store 60" wide coils as well as load and unload floor mounted cradles or stands.

The mono-rail appears to be the most popular method now in use with coil handling systems for rectangular and L-shape duct lines. Electric hoists offer a large range of available capacities, lifts, speeds, types of mounting and controls.

Low head-room hoists in 5 to 10 ton capacities are generally used with a single speed motor trolley. Two types recommended by Heuer are P & H electric hoists and the Lodestar electric hoist with motor driven low head-room trolley.

Smaller Components Are Utilized with Bridge Cranes of Mono-Rails

In order to utilize the bridge crane or mono-rail system, other smaller components are required. These are the yoke and C-frame holder to unload and mount coils on the shaft and flange ends with adjustable I.D. A number of types of web slings are also used to transport coils.

Types offered are nylon web slings and 4" wide wire mesh slings. Wire mesh slings are widely used in metal working shops where loads tend to cut the slings. Unlike nylon and wire rope, wire mesh slings will resist abrasion and cutting.

A-Frame Used By Smaller Shops

The A-frame is used by smaller shops where coil loads may be 3,000 lbs. or less. The A-frame is usually moveable on floor casters and equipped with a simple chain fall.

Showing a 6,000 lb. Coil Up-Ender with 180° Rotation. It Features Hydraulic Operation

Pictured In the Engel Plant In St. Louis Is a 10,000 lb. Coil Car in the Rear with An Engel Shopmaster in the Foreground

Showing Part of a Mono-Rail System with Coil Handling Yoke for Raising and Loading 15,000 lb. Coils for L-Shape Duct Production. Finished L-Shape Duct Sections Are Shown In Foreground

A 10,000-12,000 lb. Expanding Mandrel For A Coiline with Coil In Position, for 48" and 60" Duct Fabrication

An Engel Coil Strip Feed Line and Model S-S-10 Roll Former with Digital Controller That Is Utilized for Forming 1⅛" Standing "S" Slips

(Continued from Page 38)

The fork lift is the second most commonly used piece of equipment in the movement of coils. Capacities of fork lifts range from 5,000 to 10,000 lbs. The fork lift can perform a variety of jobs in loading and unloading coils, pallets and smaller coils.

The fork lift requires a fairly large space to maneuver, however. Electric 12 volt battery-type fork lifts are often used to transport coils of up to 1,000 lbs.

Various Types of Cradles Used to Decoil Stock and Feed Next Operation

There are various types of cradles available that can be used to decoil stock and feed the next operation. The open-end expanding mandrel uncoiler has the greatest flexibility.

The arbor expansion is usually from 19" to 23". The coil expanders have a capacity from 6,000 to 20,000 lbs. with a maximum coil lift of 60" and maximum coil O.D. of 64". A coil car and lift may be used with coil expanders for coil loading capabilities. An up-ender may become an integral part of a coil car and lift and it tilts coils to 90°.

Strip feed lines require smaller coils in widths of 2⅛" to 8". Single and double stock reels are available and two manufacturers are Durant Tool Co., Providence, R.I., and Cooper-Weymouth Co., Clinton, Me. Double stock reels allow the operator to load stock on one side as the other unwinds. Features of double stock reels include quick adjustment for stock width, self-centralizing, standard drag, and magnetic brake models.

Versatile double-head reels are offered for coil weights in the range of 600 to 1,200 lbs. each. These are made by Engel, as well as by Welty-Way (Iowa Precision Industries), Cedar Rapids, Iowa. Non-powered double reels are offered by Harper Metal Products Inc., San Bruno, Cal., for use with their 4" vane maker and 4" rail former.

Floor mounted cradles are most commonly used with L-shape duct fabrication lines. They are available in both 48" and 60" width capacity, and up to 15,000 lbs. per cradle position. The contractor can choose from single, 2-1 and 3-1 floor mounted cradles.

Duct lines have a maximum capacity of 14 ga. galvanized and often go to 28 and 30 ga. stock. As many as six cradles are placed one behind the other and the coils are fed up to a coil selector station either mounted at shear level or floor mounted.

About Finished Products That Can Be Profitably Formed from Coils

The final portion of Heuer's talk showed examples of various finished products that he has come across in his travels that are now being formed from either galvanized or aluminum coil stock, and which were formerly fabricated from sheet stock. These applications include:

1 — L-shaped duct production from 48" and 60" wide coils.

2 — Spiral pipe production — 4" to 60" finished diameters in 10' to 20' lengths.

3 — Flexible spiral duct — 3" dia. duct in 8' lengths in seven seconds from aluminum coils.

4 — Turning-vane production of both 2" and 4" double vane and 2" and 4" rail from coils. These coils are shipped five per skid with 20" I.D. and 49" O.D. maximums.

5 — Flat reinforced "S" slips using 3⅝" wide coils and drive cleats using 2⅛" wide coils. Also, two sizes of government or pocket locks.

6 — Bar cleat and variable standing "S" cleat lines.

7 — Special applications — including filter frames, receiver or register boxes, louver and damper frames as well as 10 ga. reinforcing for commercial ducts. The angles vary in size from 1"x1" to 1½"x1½" to 2"x2" in 20' lengths with hole punches with these units usually programmed by a digital controller.

Several of the accompanying photos are of Engel machines used in connection with coils for fabrication. Additional information on them can be obtained from Art Heuer at Engel Industries, at the address noted above.

Collection of Articles from SNIPS   289.

Listing of Articles That Have Been Featured in SNIPS Magazine

The following pages list articles that have been featured in selected issues of **SNIPS** Magazine in recent years. Information about SNIPS Magazine is on page 255.

APRIL, 1990

Air Conditioning Contractors of America Elects Isaac, Rochester, N. Y., President At 22nd Convention 22

Builders Heating Supply Co., Hosts Big Product Show In Lansing, Mich. 116

California SMACNA Names Hoppe of Fremont, President At 24th Annual Convention 106

Canadian Environmental Exposition Attracts Record Crowd In Toronto .. 90

Colorado SMACNA and Rocky Mountain ASHRAE Chapter Put On 9th Annual Trade Show In Denver........... 112

Chicago Furnace Supply Stages Open House and Product Show In Lisle, Ill..................... 126

Chicago SMACNA Chapter Holds 13th Annual Trade Show, Attracting Over 2,300.................... 122

Gas Appliance Manufacturers Ass'n 55th Annual Meeting Report 36

Gladwin Machinery & Supply of Illinois Has Open House and Machinery Show In Elk Grove, Ill... 128

Huge Stainless Steel Exhaust Duct System Goes Into Dallas Area Automobile Plant 32

Indiana PHCC Convention and Expo Attracts 3,000 to Indianapolis 96

Malco Products Announces Winners of Fiber Glass Duct Tool Kits From ASHRAE/ARI Show Visitors . 140

Metal Distributing Co. Alexandria, Va., Settled In New Quarters 139

More Photos From the National Rfg. Contractors Ass'n Convention 89

Northwest Mechanical, Seattle, Completes Unique Job For Bellevue, Wash., Swim Club 108

Robertson Htg. Supply, Alliance, Ohio, Presents 1989 Sales Achievement Awards 110

Smith of Elite Software, Covers Light Commercial Load Calculation . 64

Solar Observatories In Indianapolis, Ind., and Madison, Wis., Get Copper Domed Roofs 16

Stainless Steel Tin Man Fabricated By Dee Cramer, Inc., Flint, Mich. .. 118

Three States Supply Hosts Machinery Show In Little Rock, Ark. 120

Visit to Aaron York's Quality Air Cond. & Heating In Indianapolis, Ind................ 60

Wisconsin Sheet Metal/Mechanical Ass'ns Hold 7th Annual Joint Convention 92

Wrongful Discharge of Employees Is Major Causes of Employer Problems 12

MAY, 1990

Augusta Roofing & Metal Works, Augusta, Ga., More Than 75 Years Old, Is Second Oldest Industry Firm In That State 72

Behler-Young Co., Puts On Open House At Kalamazoo, Mich., Branch 98

Excelsior Mfg. & Supply Had Big, Windy Open House In Joliet, Ill. 90

Florida Air Conditioning Contractors Ass'n Stages Annual Conference And Trade Show 76

Harrington Bros., Randolph, Mass., Specializes In Duct Fabrication For Hospitals and High Rises 108

Indiana Sheet Metal Council Holds Successful Mini-Convention 84

Mid-Way Supply Puts On Open Houses At Two Illinois Branch Locations 86

Mina Corp., San Francisco, Cal., Fabricates Fiber Glass Duct Work For Big Office Building In San Jose, Cal.................. 22

National Capital Chapter of ACCA Sponsors 8th Annual Trade Show In Greenbelt, Md 106

National Sheet Metal Apprentice Contest Held For 18th Time In St. Paul, Minn 16

Northern Indiana Sheet Metal Contractors Ass'n Hosts 22nd Annual Plant Engineers Night 82

Rafoth Sheet Metal, Dubuque, Iowa, Applies New Roof to Davenport Stadium 103

Sheet Metal Products Co., Holds 14th Customer Appreciation Day In Peoria, Ill 88

Sheriff of Pro/Duct Discusses, "Working At Home — Telecommuting" 62

Shuster of PaineWebber Gives ABC's Of Investments 12

SMACNA Of Pennsylvania Holds 19th Annual Convention In Allentown ... 110

Souther, Inc., St. Louis, Mo., Celebrates 125th Year In Business with Machinery Show 120

Tampa, Fla., Office Building Gets Waterproofing Retrofit 66

Worcester Air Conditioning, Ashland, Mass., Adds Much New Machinery To Its Shop 26

JUNE, 1990

Bryant Entertains Nearly 600 Dealers At Indianapolis 500 Race 74

Electric Motor Seminars Held By Dreisilker Electric Motors, Glen Ellyn, Ill. 93

Energy Administration, Inc., Hicksville, N.Y., Offers HVAC Commercial/Industrial Design and Mechanical Management 56

Excelsior Mfg. & Supply Holds Open House In Itasca, Ill. 90

Dick Friday, Rochester, N.Y., Announces Sale of Business Which He Founded In 1928 79

G & T Supply, Liverpool, N.Y., Hosts Williamson Dealer Meeting 80

Gantler Co., Pittsburgh, Pa., Applies Terne Coated Stainless Roof On Incline Building 70

Handling The Angry Customer 13

N. B. Handy Co., Stages Big Machinery Show In Norfork, Va..94

Information On the Opportunities For Education of the HVACR/Sheet Metal Contractor/Wholesaler and Employees 22

Kalamazoo Heating & Air Cond. Ass'n Has Successful Golf Outing 102

Langford Service Co., Moves Into Modern New Building In Jackson, Mo. 105

Lawrence Air Systems, Barrington, R.I., Handles Space-Pak Installation In Providence 77

Met-Coil Exhibits At Machinery Show In Japan 44

NAPHCC Educational Foundation Launches New Contractor Educational Program 34

North Carolina PHCC Elects New Officers At 80th Convention 97

Northern Illinois ACCA Chapter Has Program On Refrigeration Recovery and Collections 84

Over 5,000 Attend Big Trade Show Held By Milwaukee Stove & Furnace Supply Co., Milwaukee, Wis. 99

R & M Heating & Cooling, Coloma, Mich., Installs Dual Water Source Heat Pumps In Big Residence 16

Shop of Daytons Bluff Sheet Metal, Maplewood, Minn., Visited 30

Trane Chicago Sales District Puts On Big Dealer Meeting 88

Vendome Copper & Brass, Louisville, Ky., Specializes In Intricate Copper Work 83

Whipps Supply Co., Holds 3rd Trade Show In Croydon, Pa. 78

JULY, 1990

Acme Sheet Metal, Kansas City, Mo., Does Retrofit Work On Area Office Building 102

Advice To Business Owners To Update Wills To Save Taxes 8

Air Distribution Institute Holds Spring Meeting In Scottsdale, Ariz. 36

Auer Steel & Heating Supply Celebrates 50th Anniversary With Open House and Trade Show In Milwaukee, Wis............ 98

Central States Conference On Sheet Metal Apprenticeship Held In Detroit, Mich. 22

Collection of Articles from SNIPS

Gilley's Sheet Metal, Rockford,
Heats and Cools Parts Warehouse
In Marengo, Ill. 85
Greater Chicago Chapter of RSES
Stages Second Annual
Awards Banquet 88, 90
Kentucky Sheet Metal Ass'n Holds
Annual Convention.....................127
Large DuroZone Damper Installed
In Rhode Island Post Office 117
Midwest Roofing Contractors Ass'n
Slates 41st Annual Convention
In San Antonio, Texas 82
More Photos from ACCA Convention
In San Francisco, Cal....................40
More Pictures From Sheet Metal
Contractors of Iowa
Convention 111
NHAW Announces Quality
Improvement Colleges At
Spring Meeting 16
National Machine Tool Show,
Chicago, Sept. 5-13, Features
1,200+ Exhibitors 34
Presenting Balance of Photos From
Canadian Environmental
Exposition (CEX) In Toronto......130
Sheriff Discusses "Computers
As Appliances" 78
SMACNA of Michiana Holds 16th
Annual Golf Outing....................108
Valley Controls & Supply Hosts
Second Annual Open House In
Grand Junction, Colo.................128
Year Old Triad Roofing, Inc.,
Winston-Salem, N.C., Invests
In Sheet Metal Equipment.........121

OCTOBER, 1990

Air Conditioning Contractors of Ohio
14th Annual Convention Report 84
Business Problems Encountered By
Contractor Proprietors Explored
By Dougherty of PROOF 48
Columbia Pipe & Supply, Chicago, and
Weil-McLain Co-Sponsor
Lake Cruise 88
Florida Roofing & Sheet Metal
Contractors Ass'n 68th Annual
Convention Report............................98
Glenwood Comfort, Itasca, Ill., Hosts
Comfortmaker Dealer Meeting...........90
How Centrifugal Chillers Should
Contain CFC-11 Refrigerant...............40
How the Thermostatic Expansion
Valve Works 44

How to Save On Worker's
Compensation Insurance 108
Joint Apprentice Training Center
Opened In Evansville, Ind. 114
Karl, Wyandotte, Mich., Named
"SMACNA Contractor of the Year"..14
Michigan ACCA 6th Annual
Convention Report 80
NAPHCC 108th Annual Convention
Report 32
Northern Indiana Apprentices Feted
At Graduation In Gary......................112
SMACNA 47th Annual Convention
Report 18
Spiral Pipe of Texas Expands
Fort Worth Facilities.........................126

NOVEMBER, 1990

Air Distribution Institute Stages
Annual Meeting In Chicago 52
Air Flow, Milwaukee, Wis., Conducts
Successful Product Show 64
HRAI of Canada Holds 22nd Meeting
In Quebec City................................102
How to Find the Right Money Manager
For HVAC Plan...................................32
Indianapolis Wholesaler Recommends
Needed Service Instruments 54
Oklahoma City Apprentices Honored
At Awards Banquet............................86
Procon, Inc., Greensboro, N.C.,
Installs Metal Roof On
Bank Building 80
Quality Sheet Metals, Carbondale, Ill.,
Uses Spiral and Flat Oval Pipe
On University Job 22
RSES 53rd Annual Convention Report...28
Roper Whitney Holds "Distinguished
Dozen" Awards Dinner 38
Sheriff Comments On "Fast Information"
That Is Now Available........................34
State-of-the-Art HVAC Systems Goes
Into $ Million-Plus Home In
Fairfield, Conn....................................16

MARCH, 1991

Air Conditioning Contractors of
America (ACCA) Convention Report .22
Corn-Fueled Furnace Installed By
Persons Heating, Rodney, Mich.. 98
Dolco Aluminum, Springfield, Va.,
Adds Machinery to Handle Increased
Metal Roofing Market......................116
How Kirk & Blum Designed Ventilation
System For Saturn's Powertrain
Plant In Spring Hill, Tenn. 36

Collection of Articles from SNIPS

How to Make the Perfect Investment 8
Lennox Dealer Marketing Advisory Meeting Attracts Over 200 to Dallas, Texas 62
National Roofing Contractors Ass'n (NRCA) Convention Report 70
Nelco Mechanical Ltd., Kitchener, Ont., Canada, Fabricates Unique Stainless Steel Star 103
New Delta Airlines Hangar At Atlanta Airport Gets On-Site Duct Fabrication For Huge Vent System .. 18
Northeastern Illinois SMACNA Chapter Holds Annual Dinner-Dance 108
Northern Illinois SMACNA Chapter Hosts Annual Apprentice Graduation Dinner In Rockford 104
Over 27,000 Attend ASHRAE-ARI Exposition In New York City 30
Sample Estimating Programs Offers 47
Sheriff Discusses Project Management Software 66
Sheet Metal Contractors of Iowa Holds 22nd Annual Convention 90
SMARCA Stages Winter Meeting In Bloomington, Minn 88
SNIPS Begins Its 60th Year 14

APRIL, 1991

ADDCO In New Refurbished Quarters In Harvey, Ill. 26
Alternative Refrigerants and Recovery/Recycling Equipment Makes For Smoother CFC Phase-Out 30
Bremer Sheet Metal, Glen Ellyn, Ill., Installs Unique HVAC System In Local Church 16
Chicago Roofing Contractors Ass'n Stages 8th Annual Trade Show 78
Chicagoland Sheet Metal Contractors Ass'n Holds 14th Trade Show 82
Fidelity Engrg., Hunt Valley, Md., Automates Sheet Metal Shop 97
Illinois-SMACNA Holds Annual Meeting, Reelect Officers 76
Indiana PHCC Convention-Expo Attracts Over 3,000 66
Kelley of Dean Witter Reynolds Discusses "Perfect Investment" 6
King of E.L. King & Associates, Des Moines, Iowa, Covers Selling Commercial Service Contracts 39
Long Bros., Dallas, N.C., Applies Metal Roof System On Area Church 92
MCAA Convention Report From Hawaii. 64
Midwest Roofing-Sheet Metal, Evansville, Ind., Fabricates 43 Ft. Aluminum Spire For Local Church 22
More Photos From NHAW Convention 110
SMACNA Colorado and Rocky Mountain ASHRAE Host Annual Trade Show 74
Smith of Elite Software Asks, "Do You Get What You Pay For?" 44
Volpone of H.J. Ziegler Heating, Ashtabula, Ohio, Discusses Residential Service Contracts 36
Wisconsin Sheet Metal Ass'n and Mechanical Contractors Ass'n Hold 8th Joint Convention 70

JUNE, 1991

Able Distributors, Chicago, Puts On Open House At New Location 68
Ace Supply Open House In St. Paul, Minn., Attracts Over 350 78
Air Distribution Institute Gets Encouraging News At Spring Meeting In Florida 46
Badger Metals, Appleton, Wis., Has Open House For Its New Facility 74
Disastrous Fire Strikes E.H. Gustafson & Co., Skokie, Ill 64
Gas Appliance Manufacturers Ass'n Holds 56th Annual Meeting 34
How Waste Chiller Oil Could Be Classified As Hazardous Waste 38
Kelley Tells Advantages of Maintaining A Central Assets Account 10
Many Opportunities Available For Education and Training In the HVACR/Sheet Metal Industry 30
Metalmaster, Crystal Lake, Ill., Applies Metal Roof On Shopping Center In St. Charles 26
Mid-Way Supply, Burr Ridge, Ill., Holds Spring Open House 66
National Restaurant Ass'n Expo Reveals New Products For SNIPS Readers 22
SMACNA of Pennsylvania Stages Its 20th Annual Convention 58
Sullivan, Greensboro, N.C., Elected New President of the North Carolina PHCC 95
Top Sheet Metal Apprentice Winners Selected At 19th Annual Contest 16

JULY, 1991

Amber Mechanical Contractors Host Open House In New Alsip, Ill., Headquarters 92
American Engineering, Arlington Heights, Ill., Handles Huge HVAC/Sheet Metal Job In New Gurnee Mills Outlet Mall 16
Chicago Town Home Exteriors Feature Much Terne Coated Stainless For Window Bays 24
Greater Chicago Chapter of RSES Stages Annual Awards Dinner 96

Collection of Articles from SNIPS 293.

Kentucky Sheet Metal Contractors
 Ass'n Holds Annual Meeting............105
Markus Industries, Des Plaines, Ill.,
 Replaces Gas Air Conditioners In
 Chicago Townhouses.........................98
NAPHCC Readies Its 109th Annual
 Convention In San Francisco..............90
National Ass'n of Oil Heating
 Service Managers Holds 38th
 Convention and Trade Show..............88
SMACNA of Michiana Hosts 17th
 Annual Golf Outing...........................102
Segroves of Shop Data Systems Puts
 On Seminar For Tweet-Garot,
 Green Bay, Wis...................................10
Sheet Metal and HVAC Training
 Provided At Vienna, Ill.,
 Correctional Center............................95
Sheriff Discusses Computer
 Instruction Manual Jargon..................82
Trinity Contractors, Arlington,
 Texas, Retrofits Their Plasma
 Cutting Machine................................127
Fred Vogt & Co., St. Louis Park,
 Minn., Visited......................................30

AUGUST, 1991

Eastern States Sheet Metal
 Apprentice Contest Participants
 Presented..95
Energy Efficient HCFC's Help
 Limit Global Warming.........................74
E. H Gustafson & Co., Skokie, Ill.
 Rebuilding After Big May Fire............86
Illinois Sheet Metal Apprentice
 Winners Presented.............................85
Mid-Lakes Distributing, Chicago
 Hosts Open House to Introduce
 Well-McLain Boiler Line.....................84
Milwaukee Sheet Metal Ass'n Holds
 Successful Annual Golf Outing..........80
"Money Improves Productivity"
 Is Myth..126
Plans Available For Fabricating
 Copper Hurricane Lantern.................101
Quality Heating & Sheet Metal,
 Brookfield, Wis., Heats/Cools
 1,400 New Homes In 1991, Many
 With Zone Controls.............................82
SMACNA Convention and Trade Show
 All Set For San Antonio, Texas...........16
Smith of Elite Software Says,
 "DOS 5.0 — Good to Go!"...................52
South Seminole Sheet Metal,
 Longwood, Fla., Handles Big Duct
 System Job In Orlando City Hall........30
Stromberg Sheet Metal, Washington
 D.C., Implements Tech Changes........34

SEPTEMBER, 1991

Columbia Pipe & Supply, Gurnee, Ill.,
 Stages Customer Appreciation Day.100
Eastern Oklahoma Sheet Metal
 Apprentices Honored with Dinner......81
Fiber Glass Industry Contests
 CBS New Story...................................14
Gupton Sheet Metal, South Boston,
 Va., Applies Metal Roof System
 To Area Retirement Complex.............16
HRAI Of Canada Elects New Officers
 At Annual Meeting............................109
Importance Of Customer Appreciation
 Discussed By Tom Davies..................12
Many Products From National Hardware
 Show of Interest To Readers
 Reviewed.....................................34, 36
R.E. Michel Co. Personnel Create
 Unusual Objects From Acme Pipe,
 Duct and Fittings................................72
Northern Illinois ACCA Chapter
 Puts On Annual Golf Tournament......94
Northern Indiana Sheet Metal Ass'n
 Hosts 23rd Annual Golf Outing..........68
Professional Company Assists Owners
 To Reorganize Outside Of
 Bankruptcy Court................................28
Sheriff Comments On "Personal
 Computer: 10 Years Old"....................56
Taxon-Blackhawk, Rockford, Ill.,
 Installs 98 Tons of Cooling On
 New Area Restaurant..........................22
Tolin of Denver, Colo., Discovers
 Refrigeration Recovery Is
 Costly Proposition..............................60
Utah Court Finds That Water Heater/
 Space Heating Systems Are
 Not Boilers..65
Visit to AMPCO Production Facilities
 In Olive Branch, Miss.........................26

NOVEMBER, 1991

G. W. Berkheimer Co., Tinley Park,
 Ill., Holds Big Dealer Meeting
 On Gas Venting...................................78
Chicagoland Sheet Metal Contractors
 Ass'n Install New Officers..................72
EPA Says Contractors Must Comply
 With Prohibition Against
 Venting Refrigerants..........................14
Fabtech Show Features Many Products
 Of Interest to SNIPS Readers............36
Florida Roofing & Sheet Metal Ass'n
 Holds 69th Convention.......................56
Kreutzer, Garden City, Kans., Is
 New President of NAPHCC.................52

Midland Engineering, South Bend, Ind., Applies Terne-Coated Stainless Steel Roof On Church.........16
Midwest Roofing Contractors Ass'n Holds Convention In Indianapolis.......46
Northern Indiana Joint Apprentice Committee Dinner-Dance Held............64
Oklahoma City, Okla., Apprentices and Journeymen Honored At Dinner ..91
RSES Hold 54th Educational Conference In Birmingham, Ala. 22
Retirement Party Held For Aschliman of A to Z Sales, Elmhurst, Ill. 82
Sheriff Points Out Ease of Use of Macintosh Computer 42
York International, Elmhurst, Ill., Stages Dealer Meeting.........................76

FEBRUARY, 1992

ASHRAE-ARI Exposition Attracts Over 17,000 To Anaheim, Cal. 16
Area Sheet Metal, Hobart, Ind., Hosts Open House For Its 20th Anniversary 76
DiversiTech Honors Manufacturers Reps At Sales and Awards Meeting..64
Ferris State University, Big Rapids, Mich., Gets Equipment Donations...................................88, 89
HVAC Dealer-Contractors Urged to Branch Into Lucrative Indoor Air Quality Work 28
Mechanical Contractors Ass'n of America Holds 103rd Convention..30
More Pictures From Michigan ACCA Chapter Convention 90
Northeast Illinois ACCA Chapter Meeting Draws Big Crowd For Jim Norris Talk..................................67
Northern Illinois SMACNA Chapter Holds Apprenticeship Dinner.........68
Peerless Enterprises, Rexdale, Ont., Handles Big Metal Roofing And Wall Panel Project 100
Refrigerant Recovery-Recycling Equipment Manufacturers Offer Variety of Options............................34
Seven Questions to Ask Computer Software Vendors Offered By FMI Corp.......................................36
Southern Illinois Group Forms Alliance to Fight Utility Incursion....70
ZM Sheet Metal, Chantilly, Va., Employs Innovative Manufacturing, Distribution and Sales Techniques...........................24

APRIL, 1992

Air Conditioning Contractors of America (ACCA) Holds 24th Convention In Honolulu, Hawaii......16
California SMACNA Holds 26th Convention In Phoenix, Ariz. 104
Chicagoland Sheet Metal Contractors Ass'n 15th Annual 1-Day Trade Show Draws Nearly 2,300 72
How to "Unstick" Reversing Valve Explained By Kuhn, Hedback Distributing, Indianapolis, Ind. 32
Illinois-SMACNA Elects Randles, Decatur, President At Annual Meeting...68
Indiana PHCC Ass'n and Other Groups Co-Sponsor Expo/Convention, Attracting Over 4,000 79
Kimbrel Rfg. & Sheet Metal, Elk Grove Village, Ill., Adds Copper Roof and Gutters to DePaul University Library, Chicago................................24
Meloling of Carrier Tells How to Prepare For Making the Big Sale 28
Mosby Mechanical, Longview, Texas, Reduces Noise In College Fitness Center 108
North/East Roofing Contrs. Ass'n Holds 66th Annual Convention And Trade Show In Boston 88
No$_x$ Control Equipment Options For Boiler Owners 64
Prolonging Equipment Life Protects Profit...................................110
St. Louis ACCA and SMACNA Chapters Announce Officers 100

NOVEMBER, 1992

Air Conditioning & Refrigeration Institute Elects Tambornino At 39th Annual Meeting.........................30
Air Distribution Institute Unveils Video Plans At Annual Meeting.......28
Basi Outlines New Rules On Retirement Plans 9
42nd Industrial Ventilation Conference Set For Feb. 14-19 46
How Mechanical Interiors, Inc., Dallas, Texas, Beefed Up Its Sheet Metal Operation 22
Midland Engineering, South Bend, Applies Standing Seam Metal Replacement Roof On Amoco Whiting, Ind., Plant..........................79

Collection of Articles from SNIPS 295.

Neumann Co., Wheeling, W. Va., Becomes Part of LINC Service Network...............92
Office Building Columns In Aurora, Ill., Covered with Metal...............85
Photos From Two Recent Eastern

DECEMBER, 1992

B & M Sheet Metal, Roanoke, Va. Reaps Much Publicity with River Race Raft Entry...............34
FMI Management Comments On Need For On-Going Service To Capture Long-Term Business...............44
E. H. Gustafson & Co., Holds Open House At New Skokie, Ill., Manufacturing Facility...............90
How Benoist Bros., Mt. Vernon, Ill., HVAC Wholesaler, Uses Load Calculation Software As Marketing Tool...............36
How To Deal with Cracked Heat Exchangers...............42
Illinois Supply Hosts Open House At New Branch Location In Countryside, Ill....................88
Income Tax Suggestions For 1992 Provided By Bart Basi...............10
International Heating, Refrigerating & Air Conditioning Exposition All Set to Open In Chicago, January 25...............16
Mader Roofing Co., Oak Park, Ill., Reroofs Wright Museum with Wood Shakes...............87
Michigan IAQ Seminar Urges Improved Filter Systems...............40
Northamerican Heating & Airconditioning Wholesalers Ass'n Stage 46th Convention...............26
Refrigerant Recovery Equipment Sources Seen At RSES Conference, Reviewed...............78
Smith Mechanical Contractors, Kingsport, Tenn., Upgrades Sheet Metal Shop Equipment...............96
Washburne Trade School, Chicago, Ill., Holds Open House...............86
York Chicago Branch Announces Several Customer Awards...............94

APRIL, 1993

ACCA Publishes New Manual Covering Commercial Applications...............35
Abbott & Associates, Bloomingdale, Ill., Holds 24th Anniversary Celebration Honoring Employees...............68

Basi Explains 1993 Changes In Social Security...............59
Brill of Acme Mfg. Co., Sends Report And Photos of the National Capital ACCA Trade Show...............86
Chicagoland Sheet Metal Contractors Ass'n 16th Annual Trade Show Attracts Over 2,100...............75
Creative Direct Mail Can Generate Good Leads...............18
Final Rule Summary On Recycling Refrigerants Issued By the Environmental Protection Agency...............24
Indiana Mechanical/Engineering and Contracting Expo Attracts Over 3,200 To Indianapolis...............60
Iowa Sheet Metal Apprentices Sweep All Four First Place Positions At Regional Contest...............94
Modern Heating & Cooling, Indianapolis, Ind., Retrofits Church HVAC System...............16
NHAW Hosts Successful Midwest Zone Meeting In Oak Brook, Ill...............70
Presenting 19 Products of Interest From the Plant Engineers and Maintenance Show...............32
Schnelle of Northern Weathermakers, Northbrook, Ill., Discusses Commercial HVAC Service In the 90's...............21
Sheet Metal Products, Peoria, Ill., Puts On 17th Customer Appreciation Day Trade Show...............72
SMACNA and MCA of Wisconsin Hold Their 10th Annual Joint Meeting and Trade Show...............64
Tevebaugh, Indianapolis Mechanical Inspector, Comments On Chimney Liner Installations...............52

JUNE, 1993

Basi Tells IRS Views on Reimbursing Expenses Advanced By Employers...............33
Chicago Furnace Supply, Lisle, Ill., Holds Dealer Meeting On the New Coleman Lines It's Handling...............66
Chicago Metal Rolled Products And Florida Welding Firm Fabricate Large Metal Dome For TV Show...............10
Coastal Supply Co., Knoxville, Tenn., Trade Show Draws Over 1,000...............80
Comfortmaker Branch, Elmhurst, Ill., Stages Annual Dealer Meeting...............69

**Dodge Reports Construction
   Contracting Down In May** 6
**DuPage Htg. & Air Cond., Lombard,
   Ill., Installing 267 Combination
   Heating-Cooling Units In Area
   Retirement Complex** 24
**Eastern Sales, Lowellville, Ohio,
   Holds Unique Trailer Days In
   Alliance, Ohio** 88
**Excelsior Mfg. & Supply Corp.,
   Itasca, Ill., Puts On
   Successful Open House and
   Trade Show** 71
**Florida Ass'n (FRSA) Readies For
   Its 71st Annual Convention** 76
**Georgia SMACNA Hosts 2nd Annual
   Trade Show** 76
**Many Readers Write Bob Murphy
   Regarding His 40th Anniversary
   with SNIPS** 8
**More Pictures from Several
   Events Attended By the
   SNIPS Staff** 83, 87, 90, 93
**National Ass'n of Oil Heating
   Service Managers Trade Show and
   Convention Attracts Over 3,000** 58
**Sheet Metal Training Facilities
   In Farmingdale, N.J., Operating
   From Modern New Quarters** 60
**SNIPS Visits "Hands-On" Copper
   Roofing Installer Training
   School In Colorado** 16
**Three States Supply, Memphis,
   Tenn., Gives Awards to Its Top
   Branch and Top Sales Rep** 56
**Wide Variety of HVAC/Sheet Metal/
   Roofing Training Opportunities
   Available** 18

Part 10
Helpful Fabrication Information For The HVAC Industry

#1 - *Design Affects Labor*

This section will discuss and illustrate suggestions that can save time regardless of whether designing a complete or partial ductrun system, or redesigning the system that was drawn up by the engineer or architect.

Generally in commercial and industrial work, the HVAC engineer is responsible for the system design, the equipment selection, and is concerned about static pressure and velocities. Often what appears as excellent air flow design on paper is very costly to fabricate in the shop; and quite often another design can minimize shop fabricating costs.

The sheet metal contractor is responsible for installation as per design drawings. However, due to field conditions and changes, it sometimes becomes necessary to make up a re-designed drawing, working from and adhering to the engineer's general design and dimensions. This is commonly referred to as a shop drawing.

If you are responsible for design, you should consider whether to use all rectangular, round, or oblong duct, or all three types. (There is limited performance data available on rectangular fittings as compared to round fittings.) Keep your mind open to other methods and to innovations.

The three main factors for planning the ductrun system:

1. Labor cost in fabricating and installing ductwork.
2. Fan and equipment requirements.
3. Noise or sound factor.

Much more design consideration must be used when designing high velocity ductrun systems over low velocity systems.

Helpful Fabrication Information

Labor Rates Outweigh Material

Years ago system designers were concerned with using the least amount of material and consequently used more fittings per system. Today material cost is of little concern compared with wages paid to a sheet metal worker. As a result, today fewer fittings are used in the system since people concerned with planning use as much straight duct as possible, due to cost reduction machinery available for producing straight duct.

It is far more important to be concerned with simplifying a ductrun system in regards to using as few fittings as possible and increasing the total weight as opposed to trying to reduce the poundage by using more fittings.

Design Trend: Simplify!

The number of different fittings required has been reduced to the simplest and most practical fittings that will do the job. This is why there is much new sheet metal machinery introduced--the most important single factor affecting the sheet metal industry.

Generally speaking, in commercial and industrial work the percentage of shop fabrication time, compared to installation and erection time, is about 25 percent: approximately 25 men in the shop and 75 in the field. This can vary considerably, depending on the type of machinery the contractor is using. There are some shops that only require 10 men in the shop to keep 90 men going in the field. This depends on the amount and type of machinery and how efficiently the shop is laid out.

To reduce shop fabrication time to a minimum, eliminate fittings wherever possible. The easiest and most practical way of eliminating fabrication time is to eliminate the fitting if at all possible.

Various Designs Within a Fitting

There are often a variety of different styles or types of fittings within a certain category that you can sometimes use. However, depending on where the fitting is going to be used, it may not have to be as efficient. Example: If it were for a return run, it would not have to be as efficient as in a supply run.

Just because a fitting takes more time to make does not mean it is the most efficient one to use; however, generally speaking, this is true. The single most important rule to adhere to is to use as much straight ductwork as possible; however, this is not always acceptable due to design characteristics. But being constantly aware of this one rule can reduce shop fabrication costs considerably and sometimes even material.

Answer these questions:
1. Is it a residential, commercial or industrial application?
2. Is it a low or high velocity system?

These two answers alone can help to determine the amount of design consideration you must give the system.

Unusual Fittings

An "unusual" fitting is sometimes referred to as a "radical" fitting. Sometimes due to job or field changes that could not be foreseen, it becomes necessary to design a fitting that is considered unusual, which in the majority of cases is an increased cost over the conventional fitting you would have chosen. Developing a skill for visualizing the unusual fitting that needs to be designed is a valuable asset. This is often very difficult for people to develop since many times they are in the constant habit of thinking and visualizing standard or conventional types of fittings.

Sometimes this problem of designing an unconventional fitting can be solved by designing several standard simple types of fittings and hooking them together. Developing this skill takes practice and is increased by the amount of experience in certain types of work--such as remodeling or repair or replacement of ductrun systems, full or partial.

Two factors to consider when designing an unusual fitting are:
1. Proper air flow.
2. Velocity factor.

There is usually an absence of any of these unusual types of fittings in new construction since better initial planning is done from the very beginning of the job. However, there sometimes are exceptions to the rule. Two of the most common reasons for designing an unusual fitting are extreme obstruction and space limitations. Sometimes, due to space limitations, it becomes necessary to combine two fittings within one; this is much like combining patterns.

Helpful Fabrication Information 300.

Combining Patterns

Combining patterns is the responsibility of the shop person making the fitting. These two questions should be answered when combining of patterns is considered:

1. Is it possible to combine patterns of the fitting to be made?
2. Is it practical to combine patterns?

Although many fittings can have their patterns combined, it is not always practical due to the extensive amount of layout time required. Listed below is other important information that has to be taken into consideration:

1. Size of the fitting--if the fitting is large, it is not practical to combine patterns.
2. Time to be saved--compared to additional layout time required.
3. Quantity required--more than one is required and it is going to be used again in the near future.
4. Lined (insulated fitting)--depending on the method of securing the insulation.

If the person who is planning the ductrun system is able to determine the probability of combining patterns and definitely knows that it would save time, he can simply note this on the shop or listing ticket. The person who is able to make the right decision is in a key position to save the contractor time and money.

Nesting and Combining Fittings

Both nesting and combining fittings can be advantageously used in solving ductrun problems.

The term "nesting" means that two or more fittings are next to each other, whereas "combining" fittings refers to using one fitting in the place of two or more fittings. Many sheet metal contractors prefer nesting over combining fittings for these reasons:

1. Layout is usually simplified.
2. Standard fittings can sometimes be purchased or made inexpensively.

Helpful Fabrication Information

3. If there are any changes in the field or job site, you can take care of them more easily.

Many contractors would rather have their employees use one fitting to nest or combine several fittings, but they do not have the skilled shop manager to layout the combined fittings which can be more complex. When nesting fittings, extra field time is required in hooking the fittings together and reinforcing them. Some contractors who do heavy commercial and industrial work have them joined and reinforced in the shop. This is particularly true when high pressure systems are being installed.

Large Fittings

When making large fittings, the single most important factor is to try to utilize the full width of the sheet of metal. This results in a saving in material because there is a minimum of scrap.

Another approach is to divide the fitting equally and use the same amount in each pattern. The disadvantage is that the scrap is not very usable; the advantage is that when using standard seams, it is not necessary to place additional pieces of angle iron on the fitting to insure its rigidity. Here the saving is in reducing shop or field labor that would be required to attach the angle iron. It also eliminates the cost of additional angle iron. However, it takes more skill to make up this type of fitting.

Housings

Intelligent location of seams can save many hours in the field when installing the access doors.

The person who plans the seam layout carefully can save all the time that it would take to cut holes for the access doors that would be installed later on the job site after the housing has been erected and secured into position. A scale drawing should be made of the front and top views, or sometimes referred to as the plan and elevation views, so that seam locations can best be determined. Use a scale 1 1/2" equals 1'0"; this is 1/8 scale.

Helpful Fabrication Information

Specialty Items and Components

The residential sheet metal contractor can now purchase much of the ductrun system from a manufacturer or a supplier. These manufacturers specialize in certain items that are used in heating, ventilating and air conditioning systems. They make these items available through wholesalers or directly to individual contractors.

Today when a ductrun system is to be made up of round ductwork, the sheet metal contractor can merely select the standard fittings from a catalog. The 12-ft. lengths now available in round spiral pipe and 10-ft. lengths in round pipe, greatly reduce and field connection time previously required when round pipe came only in shorter lengths.

In addition to solving space and ductrun problems, the use of flexible pipe also reduces field connection time by eliminating many connections.

Many times it is not possible or practical to purchase certain components you will need in a job you are installing depending whether it is residential, commercial or industrial. However, there are jobs for which many components can be purchased.

Numerous specialty items are manufactured in standard shapes and sizes; some of these items are available in several types of material. Some of these items are purchased in quantities and stocked by the sheet metal contractor, but the majority are purchased as needed.

Due to increasing costs, buildings now being contracted, both residential and commercial, have limited space. Therefore, to convey the necessary volume of air within limited space, high pressure ductwork is needed. High pressure ductwork can be made in round, rectangular or flat oval (oblong) shapes. Because of the spiral machines, round duct has become the most economical to fabricate and the easiest to erect.

However, because of extreme space limitations in some buildings, it is sometimes necessary to use flat oval duct. Because of the high cost of the spiral machines, many shops purchase their round or flat oval duct from distributors or manufacturers who can provide a variety of sizes.

Also as a result of increased material costs, ceiling heights are much lower today than they were years ago, which has led to many construction changes.

Helpful Fabrication Information

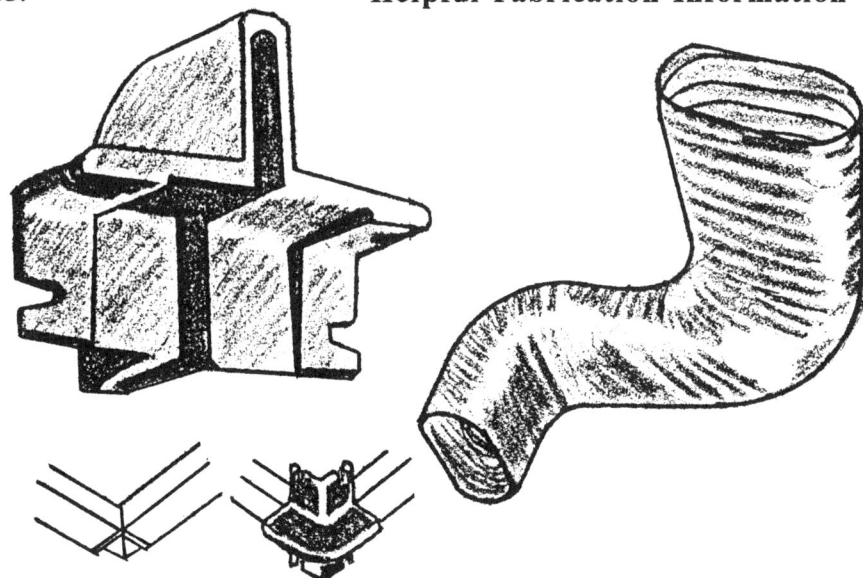

Fig. 1 - Corner Cleat caps eliminate costly mitering, welding and are easily installed by using four sheet metal screws.

Fig. 2 - Flat-oval ducts are often necessary in newer buildings where extreme space limitations exist. As shown here, the duct is now available in flexible form.

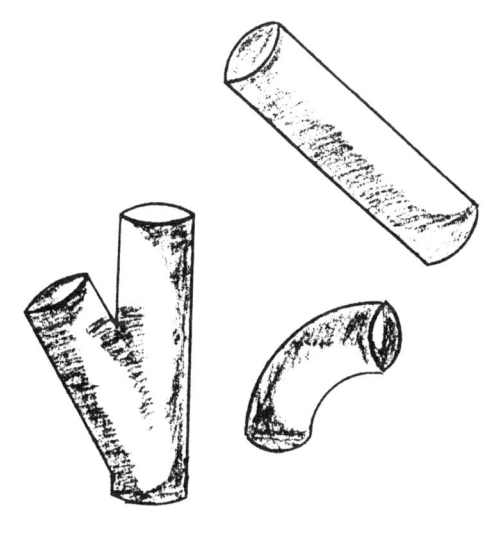

Fig. 3 - Fittings and stacks that are used for exhausting harmful fumes. PVC products that are growing in acceptance.

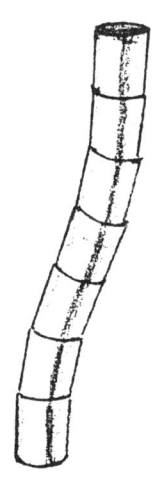

Fig. 4 - Flexible snake sections that can be purchased ready-to-install are useful when installing a chimney liner that requires an offset.

Helpful Fabrication Information

Fig. 5 - Available in coil form, flexible duct connectors come in a carton ready to complete fabrication. They are pre-assembled, with the sheet metal permanently secured to the fabric by seam locks.

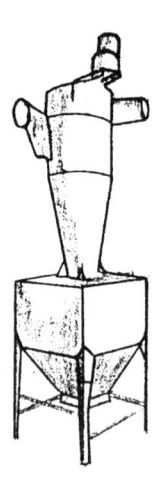

Fig. 6 - Most fittings, pipe used in blow pipe systems are available in a variety of sizes. Collectors are seldom made in the shop. They are instead purchased as complete units such as the one shown above.

Revolution in Machinery

In the past, round pipe was available in 2-ft. lengths, and even then it was more economical for the sheet metal contractor to purchase it rather than to make it. Even greater economy became available when round pipe could be purchased in 10-ft. lengths, thus greatly reducing field connection time. This availability is a result of the development of the spiral machine which first appeared on the market in the middle 1950's.

Helpful Fabrication Information

The advantages of spiral duct over rectangular duct which provide overall economy are as follows:

1. Longer lengths, which require less connection time.
2. Slip type coupling for fast and easy field connections.
3. Minimum friction loss.
4. Stronger and more rigid, requiring less duct stiffeners.
5. Lighter weight.

Flat oval spiral duct is available in 160 different sizes. Now, round pipe (not spiral) is also available in 10-ft. lengths with snap lock seams which can be used when it is not necessary for them to be completely airtight in residential work or commercial work where the system is low velocity.

Time-Saving Suggestions

1. When drawing or listing any pipe or fittings, consider the sizes of the sheets you have in the shop--the length and width. When drawing a fitting, try to dimension it in such a way that the patterns can be cut out from a sheet without making the pattern in two pieces. This is not always possible, but whenever possible it should be adhered to.

2. Ask yourself: Can this fitting, duct or component item be purchased ahead of time; and if so, will it be practical to have it there ahead of time? Many times it is not practical. Sometimes a standard fitting is used extensively throughout the job and a little pre-planning could save much additional shop labor cost.

3. Wherever practical, use as much straight pipe and fittings as possible, so long as it does not affect the system's efficiency and performance.

4. If at all possible, try to avoid using duct-turns; if space allows use curved elbows. Determine for yourself: If return elbows did not have duct-turns, would you encounter problems in obtaining architect's approval? In some parts of the country and on certain jobs, it has been a known fact that duct-turns are not used in the return elbows. Sometimes we are not governed by space limitations; and by being alert to this, we do not need to use elbows with duct-turns. We merely use curved elbows.

Helpful Fabrication Information   306.

5. Decide the amount, location, and quality of dampers required. Be sure you do not have more than what is adequate but have enough to be adequate.

6. Get into the habit of asking yourself if there is an alternative fitting that would be easier than the first one you visualized.

Avoid Over-Compensation

Some contractors, due to inadequate technical knowledge, over-design some of their jobs. For example: since they are not absolutely sure where to place some of the dampers in a system, they over-compensate by placing an abundance of dampers in the entire system, which is very costly as well as oftentimes not necessary and even placed in the wrong locations where they serve no purpose whatever.

This concept is also being used in selecting equipment in the system. Due to the energy costs we are faced with, there is some equipment that could be a smaller capacity if the system had been designed correctly in the first place. ACCA Education Council is working with the National Bureau of Standards and the National Science Foundation to develop better types of systems and to investigate alternative fuel sources.

The Energy Task force is already marshalling the necessary forces to help ACCA contractors meet the challenges imposed by fuel shortages. Their technical manual committees will be providing members with the data they need to design better systems and to upgrade existing systems to reduce energy waste.

Balancing and Adjustment

To be able to balance and adjust any ductrun system, it is absolutely necessary that certain standards be maintained throughout the entire system. Not adhering to certain standards in duct design makes it almost impossible to balance and adjust some ductrun systems that have been installed. The point to remember here is that everything has a price; if you want or have to guarantee that the system will be properly balanced, you must plan early in the initial stage of designing so that the system is able to be balanced. If this planning is going to take place after the installation, this can be quite expensive, if it is even possible.

Helpful Fabrication Information

For specific information on designing ductrun systems, contact your National or Local Sheet Metal Association such as ACCA, SMACNA or MCAA. Many of them have developed their own manuals with standards and practices accepted by architects and engineers throughout the country.

Responsibility for determining certain standards and practices to be followed must be explained and spelled out to the person or persons who are responsible not only for the design of ductruns and fittings, but also to the people who are going to be making them up.

Contractors try to send straight duct to the job unassembled or knock down (K.D.) and have all their pipes made in L-shaped sections for this main reason--because of the advantage when shipping it on the truck to the job site. Another important decision is to determine who is going to be responsible for making other types of decisions--such as how to make the fitting, or what type of fitting to design.

Here again, it is up to someone to determine standards and practices to be followed in the shop when dealing with the following concerns:

> --Combining patterns, making large fittings, making a housing. To the person planning or designing the system, the following subjects are equally important.

> --Labor rates outweigh material cost; various designs within a fitting, unusual fittings; nesting and combining fittings; specialty items and components available from manufacturers.

At first these rules or standards might be disliked by certain employees because nobody wants to change the current ways; but after a short time, everyone becomes used to doing it the new way and it becomes the only accepted practice.

Whether large or small, in order to have a well coordinated operation, it is absolutely necessary that each person is aware of what his specific responsibilities are within the company. Once this is clearly defined, it makes it easier for everyone since no time has to be devoted to arriving at a certain decision each time that particular question might arise.

Helpful Fabrication Information 308.

Summary

We cannot over-emphasize the importance of time spent thinking, studying, and planning when determining a required fitting or designing a fitting to solve a ductrun problem.

If you are open-minded and flexible, you are ready to seriously evaluate newer developments and trends and to accept changes whenever practical. Having this ability helps keep you ahead and in a better competitive position than the many people who are much slower to recognize the advantages of making such changes.

#2 - Listing And Sketching HVAC Ductwork

The primary purpose of this section is a reminder that substantial savings in time and money can be attained by taking advantage of simplified sketching and listing practices. The suggestions that are discussed and illustrated in this section are modern and efficient methods which can be used to sketch and list ductwork. They do not require a complete change in current method of listing or require any investment. Rather, they are practical suggestions that can help to reduce the amount of time spent on these duties, thus improve the efficiency of your work.

In this section, we use the term "lister" to include a person who is a draftsman or sketcher or both. One of the important functions of a lister's job is thinking; his drawings or sketches express his thoughts and decisions. The more economy in drawing or sketching that he can employ, the more time he will have available for the real productive effort of creative thinking, which includes determining the most efficient drawing or sketch, avoiding unnecessary details.

The lister uses the shop ticket to sketch or draw and list the fittings and duct so that they can be made in the shop. He should be familiar with methods and techniques of shop fabrication and field installation, as well as material sizes available in your shop. His ability to visualize is a critical asset when he draws, designs or redesigns the system, and makes shop tickets. Ability to quickly form a mental picture of what kind of fitting or combination of fittings is needed can save shop times as well as field time.

Helpful Fabrication Information

A lister should be trained or taught to think in terms of drafting or sketching simplification and to consciously apply these principles.

The object of listing, drafting, and sketching is fabrication, erection and operation--not fancy art work. What is required is that all information be complete, concise, accurate--and on time.

Simplified sketching and listing is not a new idea. To varying extents, it is practiced every day in drafting rooms, shops and job sites throughout the sheet metal industry. For example, it is no longer considered necessary to draw a piece of duct or pipe on a shop ticket; we simply list its dimensions. This is also true of an end cap--either flush end or sunk end. We have all become so accustomed to seeing and using this method of listing duct or pipe that we may forget that it is actually a simplification.

Eliminating Unnecessary Work

The easiest and most effective way of achieving economy in our drafting or sketching work is to eliminate unnecessary work. Actually this only means minimizing the amount of drafting and sketching you do--leaving off those things which add nothing to the accuracy, completeness, or clarity of a shop drawing, working drawing, or shop ticket. See Fig. 1.

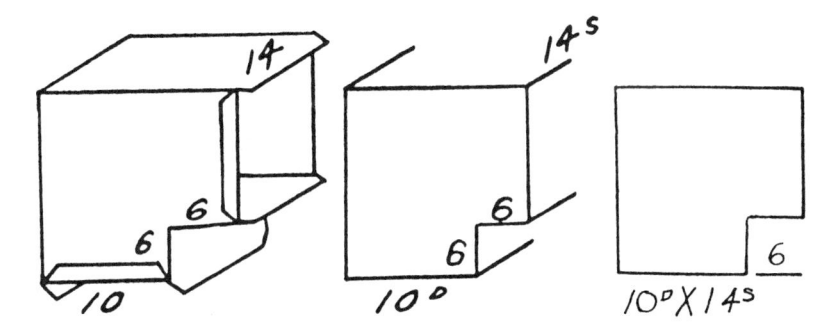

Fig. 1 - These are the three methods used to draw or sketch ductwork on shop tickets. The figure on the right takes the least amount of time. However, if your employees are not skilled or experienced in interpreting working drawings or sketches, one of the first two methods will have to be used. It is obvious that they take more time to draw.

Helpful Fabrication Information

The lister's job is to convey information and issue instructions; he accomplishes this by drawings or sketches and other information. Since the direct and simple way is usually the best way of giving instructions, the lister must recognize the difference between the necessary and the unnecessary. Fussy detail, elaboration, extra views, repetition, or too many lines contribute nothing to a sketch and often confuse the user.

Number of Views

The lister, therefore, should not strictly adhere to a rule that a specific number of views are always necessary. The correct number is the fewest views needed to supply the required information completely and clearly. For a majority of fittings only one view is needed.

Some Items Need No Drawings Or Sketches

The fact that all duct or pipe can be listed without making drawings seems too obvious to mention. But in many sheet metal companies, you will find them sketched repeatedly on shop tickets. The same applies to the following: round pipe, S and drive cleats, all variations of end caps--both sunk end and flush end, access doors, a piece of sheet metal, etc.

More Than One View

Certainly there are items which require more than one view. But the same principle applies: no matter how many views are required, anything more than the minimum is wasteful. Drawing more views than necessary is common for a variety of reasons.

Most draftsmen or sketchers are shop or field men who believe that it is easier for a person to visualize the fitting (or other item) if he has more than one view; consequently, this is the way most people learn to do their sketching on shop tickets--because they lack blueprint reading experience or back-ground. They do not realize that usually, fewer views would be adequate. See Figs. 2 and 3.

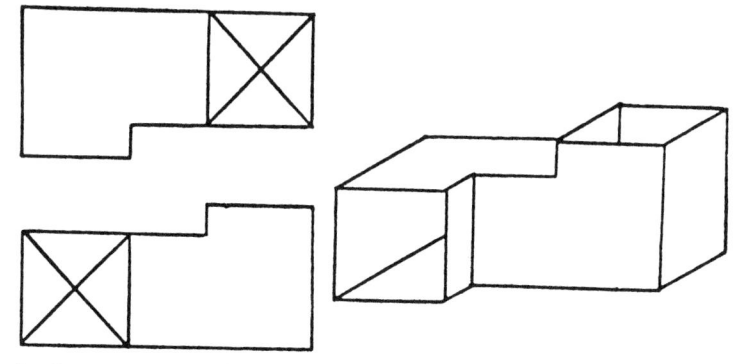

Fig. 2 - In some instances, a perspective drawing or sketch, as shown to the right, is more helpful when drawing a fitting or equipment item than using two or three views by the method of orthographic projection. An example would be an unusual type of fitting or unusual plenum.

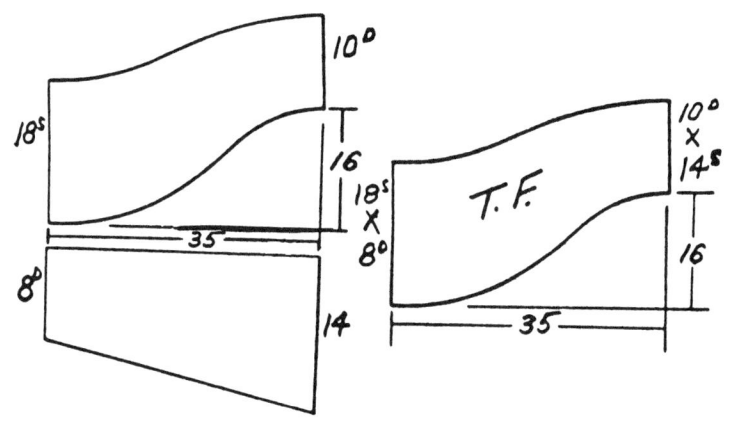

Fig. 3 - No matter how many views are required, anything more than the minimum is wasteful, as shown on the left. The visualization ability of your employees helps determine whether to draw more than one view.

Selection of Views

Poor selection of views can cause confusion and unnecessary drafting or sketching. Remember this basic principle --- the most important view should be selected as the front view. The most important view is always the one that can conveniently indicate the greatest amount of required information; in this case, it is the shape of the fitting that is most important. See Fig. 4.

Helpful Fabrication Information 312.

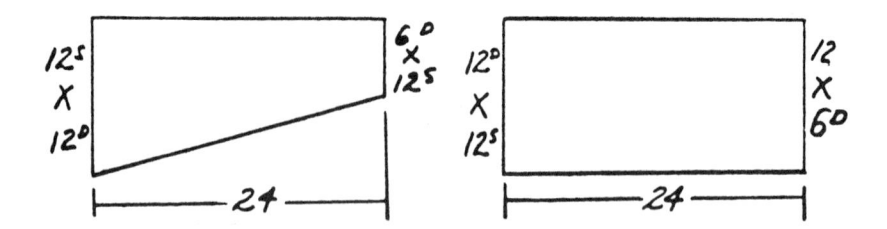

Fig. 4 - Always sketch or draw the view that best illustrates the shape of the item. In this example, it is obviously better to use the view shown at left.

Unnecessary Lines

An excellent motto for a lister: "An unnecessary line is a waste of time." Any line is not necessary if it is more than the minimum needed to make a sketch which can be understood easily and which can be interpreted in only one way. Lines are not on drawings for the sake of beauty or to demonstrate a draftsman's knowledge. Their sole purpose is to spell out to the person making the item a picture he can easily and thoroughly understand or visualize.

Example: A fitting that requires cross-braking does not need this detail drawn; just spell it out or list it on the shop ticket near the fitting, because drawing these cross brake lines on the fitting would only add confusion and take considerable time. See Figs. 5 and 6.

The amount of line work that may be eliminated can generally be determined by considering the people who will be making the items in the shop. Shop workers are familiar with items they make frequently; these sketches should obviously lend themselves more readily to line economy (eliminating unnecessary lines).

Always draw, sketch or list with this thought in mind:

Will the person making the item be able to fully interpret the information you have given him without verbal instructions?

Occasionally verbal instructions are necessary, but this should be kept to a minimum unless they can save considerable drafting time.

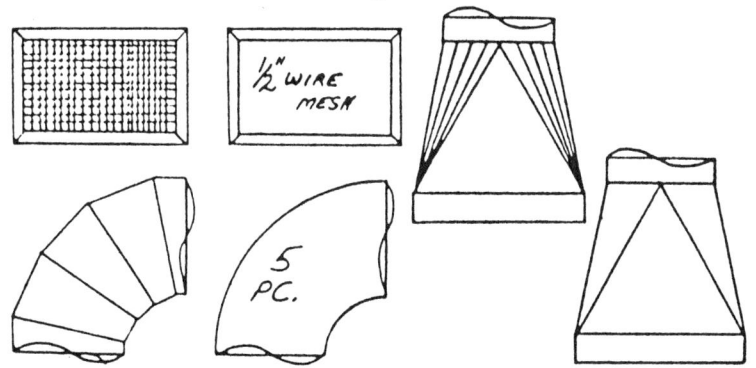

Fig. 5 - Lines should not be drawn to convey beauty or artistry. Their sole purpose is to spell out to the person making the item a mental picture he can easily visualize. The examples above are comparisons of adequate and excessive lines.

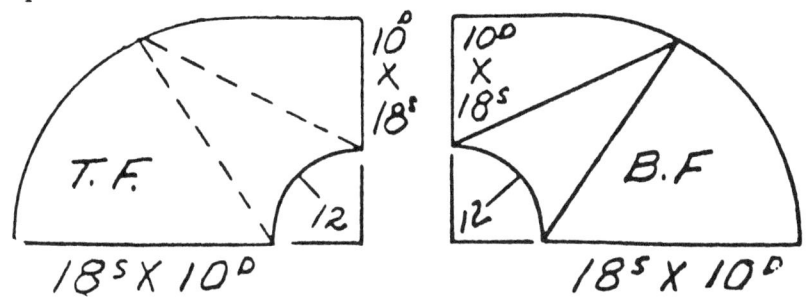

Fig. 6 - Avoid using hidden lines whenever possible. In this case, drawing the fitting in the opposite position (bottom flat rather than top flat) was all that was needed.

Unnecessary Details

There is no excuse for elaboration or fussy detail on working drawings or shop tickets. Taking pride in one's sketching is understandable and commendable. A good drawing or sketch, however, is recognized by clear views and readable dimensioning. for example, see all the drawings in this section.

Dimension

In addition to useless elaboration, an abundance of dimensions should also be avoided. The rule to follow here is: Dimension only what is

Helpful Fabrication Information

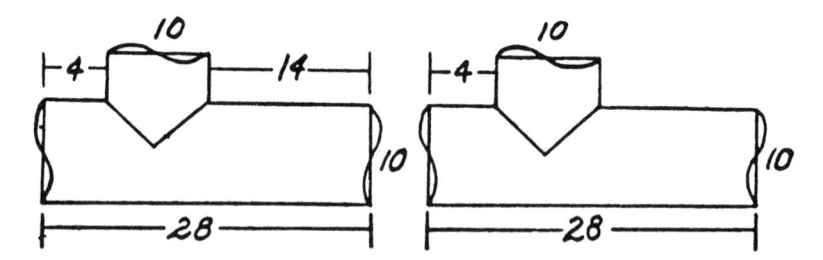

Fig. 7 - Dimension only what is necessary. Do not over-dimension, as shown to the left, since this often results in confusion and mistakes.

necessary. Thought given to the proper dimensioning will not only reduce drafting effort but will make the drawing much easier to understand. See Fig. 7.

The words "same", "alike" and "as shown" are very convenient and can be used to avoid repetition. Such notes as "all corners alike" or "make 1-right and 1-left" are easily understood.

Using Dimensional Schedules

Unless one or two shop men are going to make up all the items for an entire job, do not try to utilize all the space on each shop ticket. It is usually advantageous for several people to be working on the same job. In this way, you can divide the work up more evenly and complete it more quickly. However, if one person is going to make several of the same fitting, but in different sizes, be sure to use a dimension schedule to save time. See Fig. 8.

Size of Drawings

The sheet metal worker does not establish size by taking measurements from a working drawing or shop ticket; he uses the written dimensions on the sketch. The size of the drawing or sketch should be determined by the amount of information that it must give, not by the physical size of the item to be made.

This should not require an explanation. However, an examination of many shop tickets shows that many draftsmen or listers have the

315.   **Helpful Fabrication Information**

DIMENSION SCHEDULE					
FLOOR	SEC.	A	B	C	NO. REQ
6TH	NORTH	10	8	6	2
7TH	SOUTH	12	10	8	3
8TH	EAST	18	12	10	5
9TH	WEST	24	18	12	8

Fig. 8 - Dimension schedules can be advantageous, as shown in the lower half of this illustration. But they may not be convenient if more than one person is going to be making the fittings or items.

mistaken idea that "large items must be drawn large and small items must be drawn small." Space and paper are wasted when drawings are made larger than necessary. Larger sketches usually take more time.

Dimensions Without Arrows

A drafting simplification that has been increasing in use in recent years is marking dimensions without arrows. In addition to saving time, it frequently avoids some confusion by reducing the number of lines on the drawing. In this way, the only lines are those of the item itself plus the short extension lines that indicate the dimension, as illustrated in the figures in this section.

Abbreviations, Symbols and Word Descriptions

The use of a symbol is not new. The rule governing the application of signs or symbols to drafting, listing or sketching can be simply stated: any object that is repeatedly drafted, ordered, specified, or manufactured can be represented by an abbreviation, symbol, or word description. This sign can then be used in place of its full description of drawing.

The lister should be encouraged to analyze his job in an effort to make the greatest possible use of abbreviations, symbols or word descriptions. He will relieve himself of much unnecessary routine work.

Helpful Fabrication Information

The lister should be alert for opportunities to design and apply new symbols for any objects or shapes used frequently in his work and covered by no existing standard symbol.

The use of such symbols on sketches and in written instructions will be of immediate benefit not only to the person who makes the drawings but also to everyone who uses it. It should result in a general saving in time and materials, all translated into reduced costs. When you first start using a new abbreviation or symbol or possibly a word description, inform all people who use your drawings what it means. Keep a permanent list of these to show to new employees.

In the last 20 years, the HVAC industry has adopted the use of many symbols and abbreviations; however some may not be standardized. The use of these abbreviations can mean real savings in time and space without loss of understanding. These basic principles should serve as a guide in establishing your own abbreviations, symbols and word descriptions for office, shop and field use.

1. They are intended as a means of saving time and space. Only use abbreviations which accomplish these purposes.

2. Shop drawings and shop tickets are used by a wide variety of individuals with various backgrounds and training. Due to possible misunderstandings, the time required by all people involved must be considered when determining the time saved by the use of a particular abbreviation, symbol or word description.

It has been argued that abbreviations save only a fraction of the sketcher's time. Taken individually, this is more or less true. Yet any saving, however small, is worth making if repeated often. The use of symbols and word descriptions are also in this classification. Each is a small saving in itself, but the total amount is appreciable each day, week or month when you take an overall view. The lister should welcome any such device which minimizes the "clerical" portion of his work and allows him to devote more time to creative efforts.

Everything Is Relative

Saving a small contractor four hours is comparable to saving a larger contractor as much as 24 or 48 hours. This points out the fact that

Helpful Fabrication Information

everything is relative. Each time a lister saves a few minutes, he is showing his employer and co-workers that he is conscientious. As a sketcher becomes accustomed to these various "time economies," they will gradually become automatic to him and he will save more and more time. As he uses more economies in sketching, he becomes more confident of his judgment, and these procedures become a habit.

Amount of Sketching

The amount of sketching and drafting the residential and light commercial contractor does varies from the operations performed by the contractor who does heavy commercial and industrial work. However, they both use drafting, sketching and listing to some degree--even though the contractor doing residential and light commercial work does not make a scale drawing as often as his industrial heavy commercial counterpart.

Regardless of whether you are in residential, commercial or industrial sheet metal work, many of the suggestions in this section can save you time and money--even if you never make a scale drawing using drafting instruments--even if you freehand-sketch everything from ductruns to shop tickets.

Shop Ticket

A shop ticket or working drawing is usually a freehand sketch; a sheet metal shop drawing is drawn with instruments to be an exact layout of the ductrun system. Many of us at one time or another have used a torn piece of paper to sketch a fitting or two in an emergency; but in most cases, we use some standard type of paper.

Listing Form

Some shops use a "Listing Form" for indicating all the fittings and various items that make up a ductrun system that is going to be made in the shop. Some have space provided for listing the cut sizes of metal required for the specific fittings and/or other items that make up the ductrun system. They are sometimes referred to as Listing Forms, Listing Tickets or Shop Tickets. We use the term "Shop Ticket" in this book. These forms are frequently made and used in triplicate by

Helpful Fabrication Information 318.

shops doing a larger volume of sheet metal shop work, and used in this manner:

- One for the shop worker so that he can make the fitting.
- One for the office for reference.
- One sent to the job site.

Freehand Sketching

When really in a hurry, you have probably made sketches (or have seen sketches made by others) which contained the minimum of lines and explanation. And the fittings were probably made correctly. It should be possible to use sketches that are equally simplified in all of our work, not just when time is limited.

Using A Template

To demonstrate the time and money that can be saved when making up shop tickets, I drew up several fittings using drafting instruments. If I would have sketched them freehand, much time would have been saved.

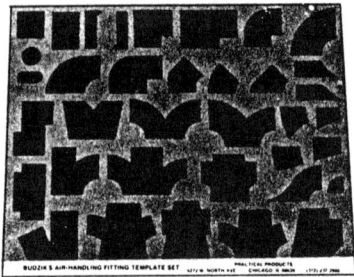

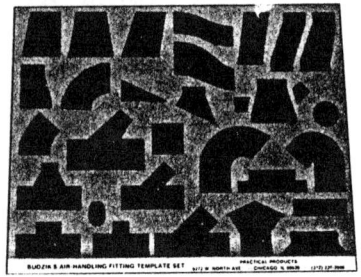

ACTUAL SIZE IS 8¼" x 10¾"

Fig. 9 - Air Handling Fitting Template - Information regarding purchasing this item is at the back of this handbook.

Furthermore, much more time would have been saved if I had used my fitting template. The only reason I did not use it first was to clearly illustrate the timesaving device of the fitting template.

If a fitting template is not going to be used, have the shop tickets made out by sketching rather than meticulously drafting the fittings and other items. Any person who has had some practice and experience in drafting can adapt himself to sketches, which is also referred to as freehand drawing. He has already gained the ability to visualize what the item should look like and how to make a clearly-understood drawing of it. Now, he merely discontinues using the drafting instruments and does not worry about the extreme preciseness of the drawing.

Accuracy Vs. Preciseness

An accurate drawing is free of mistakes; a precise drawing is perfect in appearance. Precision is not an aid to accuracy. Lines that are exactly straight or do not have exact curves do not detract from the shop person's ability to interpret them and make the fitting correctly. Whenever a lister makes an exact scale drawing of a fitting or other item rather than sketching it, he is increasing the cost of preparing the shop ticket without improving it.

Practical Suggestions

An aid when first learning to sketch is to use either graph paper or isometric paper if you must make perspective views.

When it is necessary to make some shop tickets at a job site, it is much easier to sketch them than to draw them with appropriate drafting instruments; or better yet, use a template.

After a little practice, sketching or freehand drawing can be much quicker than drafting; but, using a drafting fitting template is by far the fastest and provides neater drawings of the fittings. Tests have proven that sketching over using drafting instruments can reduce the actual time for the lister as much as 80 percent. Using a template can reduce this time even more.

Helpful Fabrication Information 320.

A template, like the one shown in this section, can save a considerable amount of time and provide very consistent drawings on shop tickets. The fittings on this template comprise just about all the fittings used in a majority of the ductrun systems being designed and drawn today. In addition, it provides a convenient guide to the fittings that can be made most economically. As much as possible, limit the fittings in all ductrun systems you design to the ones on this template---and you will also save in shop fabrication time.

Design Affects Labor Costs

The way a system is designed certainly does affect overall labor costs. Engineer and architects have realized that the first step in construction simplification is design simplification. They have become increasingly concerned with this factor in recent years---and have realized that many designs of fittings that are highly efficient are very costly to fabricate, and that in many cases some design simplification does not greatly affect proper air flow or velocity. Whether designing large or small systems, these suggestions are equally important. Whenever possible:

- Use standard sized fittings and specialty items that can be purchased.
- Avoid hand operations.
- Simplify fittings.
- Use the same fitting more than once in a system.
- Keep up with new developments in the sheet metal trade.

Two factors to consider when re-designing ductwork are the maintenance of proper air flow and velocity. If the fitting has to be installed in a limited or tight space, adhere to the principles of proper air flow. Sometimes this is very difficult due to changes that have taken place during the building's construction.

Unusual fittings are limited only by the imagination of the person planning the ductrun system. In most cases, they are a result of a lack of adequate planning, particularly in new work. In a smaller shop, the person doing this planning is a sheet metal worker. He, therefore, has the knowledge and experience to plan practical fittings in the ductrun system.

Helpful Fabrication Information

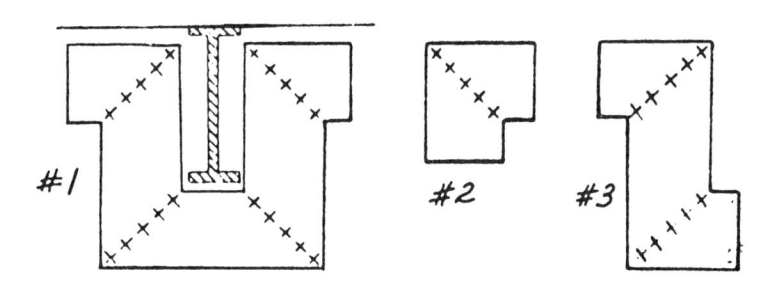

Fig. 10 - When it becomes necessary to get around an obstruction such as an I-Beam or column, select whichever solution is best for you:
    Solution 1: One fitting combining two offset elbows.
    Solution 2: Four 90° square throat and heel elbows.
    Solution 3: Two offset elbows with square throat and heel.

Larger contractors usually hire sheet metal draftsmen who are experienced sheet metal workers in the field as well as in the shop. In this way, they also have the knowledge and experience to draw upon so they, in turn, can plan economical and practical fittings in the ductrun systems. See Figs. 10-13.

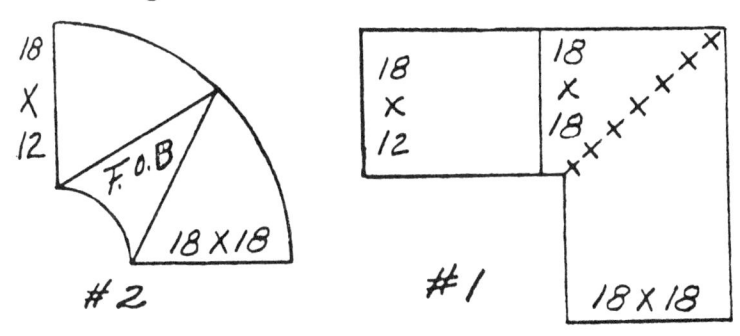

Fig. 11 - To avoid making a complex fitting, it is often possible to combine two common fittings, as shown here:

Solution 1: The two common fittings on the right are a plain change joint, three sides straight, and a square throat and heel elbow.

Solution 2: The fitting on the left is a transition elbow which is considered complex compared to the fittings in Solution 1.

Helpful Fabrication Information 322.

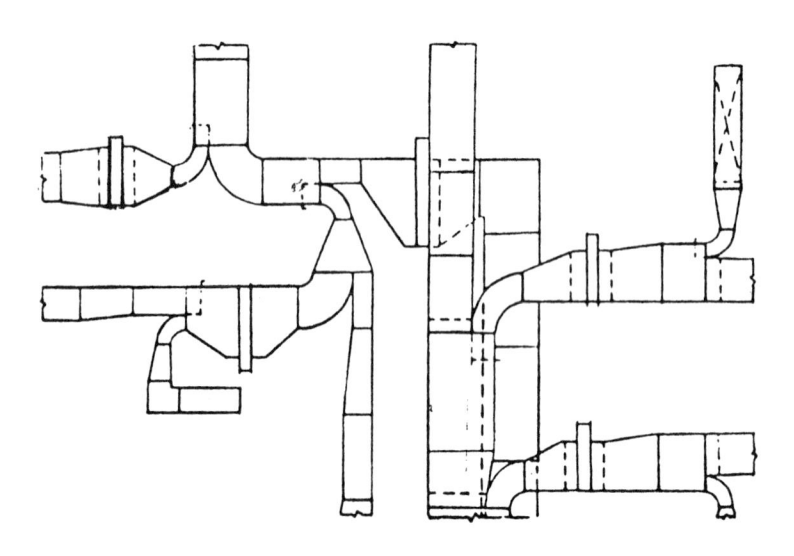

Fig. 12 - This is a good typical example of a partial commercial ductrun system showing several examples of combining and nesting common fittings.

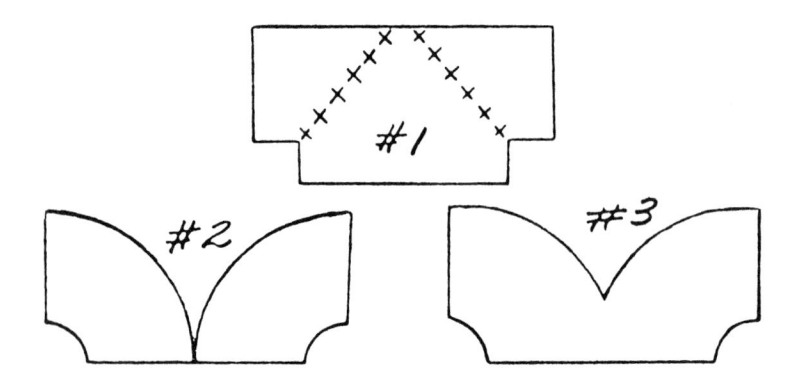

Fig. 13 - When a Y-Branch fitting is needed, here are three solutions available:

Solution 1: Y-Branch with square throat and square heel using manufactured duct turns.

Solution 2: Two 90° elbows.

Solution 3: One Y-Branch.

323.   **Helpful Fabrication Information**

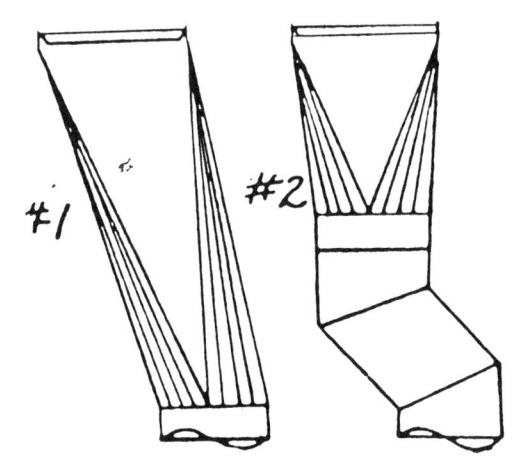

Fig. 14 -The drawing on the left shows how to combine two common fittings to avoid making one complex fitting.

>Solution 1: an offset square to round
>Solution 2: a plain square-to-round and an offset

Nesting Fittings

Many contractors prefer nesting over combining fittings to make one fitting. Reasons:

- Layout is simplified.
- Standard fittings can sometimes be purchased from a local supply house or made inexpensively.
- If there are any changes in the field or job site, you can take care of them more easily; but if it is one combined fitting, it is more difficult to change, if not sometimes next to impossible.
- Skilled shop manpower is not always available to layout the more complex combined fittings.

Many contractors would rather use one fitting than nest several fittings, but they do not have the skilled shop manpower to layout the combined fittings which can be more complex. When nesting fittings, extra field time is required in hooking the fittings together and reinforcing them. Some contractors who do heavy commercial and industrial work join and reinforce them in the shop. This is particularly true when high pressure systems are being installed.

Helpful Fabrication Information

Nesting and Combining Fittings

Both nesting and combining fittings can be advantageously used in solving ductrun problems. In some instances, they simply save time; in others, there is no other method that could be used.

The terms "nesting" fittings and "combining" fittings are often used interchangably. Years ago the term "nesting" was used when referring to fittings that nest exactly against each other. Now this term "combining" fittings refers to using one fitting in the place of two or more fittings.

Remember that combining patterns within a fitting is different than combining fittings, although their purposes are all the same: to use practical efficiencies when possible to save time or labor in the shop or in the field. Both nesting and combining fittings provide a neat, compact appearance as well as a streamlined look. Also they are often necessary due to space limitations. There are countless numbers of ways to combine or nest fittings, as well as to combine patterns. See Figs. 14 and 15 for several examples.

Combined Fittings

Using a combined fitting does have advantages, which are explained in the following paragraphs . . .

Economies are advantageous when working on a housing development or apartment complex with identical heating or air conditioning systems since many of the same fitting will be used.

When nesting fittings, extra field time is required in hooking the fittings together and reinforcing them, which is greatly reduced when combining fittings.

Sometimes purchasing the individual fittings from a supply house is less costly than making the one combined fitting in the shop.

The total cost of all these fittings is sometimes less than the total cost to make the one fitting because of the high hourly wage of sheet metal workers in some parts of the country. Here again, material cost is far less than labor cost. Another consideration is the amount of time it will take to join or tie the fittings together and reinforce them.

325. **Helpful Fabrication Information**

Fig. 15 - These drawings illustrate some of the most common arrangements of nested regular fittings. There are countless numbers of ways to nest common fittings to avoid making a combined fitting.

Also, many people are reluctant to plan combined fittings because the field measuring must be more exact for the fitting to be usable. Here again, the time it takes to do an adequate job of field measuring is certainly worthwhile if the person knows there will be no changes or modifications that would affect the fitting.

If a housing development or apartment complex with identical heating or air conditioning systems is to be built and many of the same fittings will be used, one fitting should be used rather than several fittings. This is also true of commercial jobs where all floors are typical.

Due to the wide range of different labor rates throughout the country, one method is not always advantageous over the other. When considering this along with the other factors mentioned here, the contractor will be able to determine which is best for him. Sometimes it is not possible to plan ahead; and, depending on your location, ordering time does not always allow you to purchase manufactured fittings.

Helpful Fabrication Information

Design Manual and Specifications Manual

Usually it is not necessary for the residential contractor to make a scaled drawing for a majority of the residential systems that he installs, regardless of whether they are various types of perimeter system, crawl space plenum, extended plenum, graduated trunk systems or other types of systems. This is usually true whether he is doing alterations, additions, modernizations or new work. However, he usually does make some type of rough drawing or sketch of the system for himself or his employee who will be either installing the system or making up or ordering the required stock-manufactured fittings.

Some residential, commercial and industrial drawings are done in the one-line method, which is usually dependent on the architect. Naturally this is done for economic purposes and is to his advantage. The Design Manual for HVAC and Specifications Manual are very valuable for commercial and industrial sheet metal contractors, as well as any architect or engineer who designs and writes specifications for heating, ventilating, air conditioning or plumbing systems. Basically, they reduce drafting time considerably as well as avoiding repetition in monotonous specification writing.

The express purpose of this manual and use of the standard design details is to save many valuable man-hours in the preparation of working drawings as well as to present more clearly the required components of a mechanical system as designed and recommended by the engineer. The complete and accurate interchange of information between the builder, the engineering design team, and the installing contractor is greatly facilitated and standardized.

Adequate detailing of components for heating, ventilating and air conditioning systems is a very necessary step toward obtaining the best end result in the construction of the system. Far too often these details are left until the end of the design stage, thereby resulting in skimpy, if any, details of the components. Frequently, components are not detailed at all, but left to the written word of the specifications.

Coordination between the architect-engineer and contractor can go much smoother since both parties know exactly what is expected. Lack of adequate information results in misunderstanding of exactly what is required and often requires considerable time in verbal explanations or the need for additional clarification on drawings. This working manual will considerably reduce the number of man-hours required to produce these drawings. The tedious task of tracing details and the frequent mistakes in transcribing can be eliminated by the use of the Capitoline Trans-A-Plates available for each detail.

The preparation of architectural and engineering specifications demands accuracy, clarity, and completeness in relation to all project designs. The reproduction of specifications is a highly repetitive process where only slight changes occur from project to project that are mainly attributable to equipment changes. In order to facilitate and to economize in the preparation and reproduction process, the full page method has been developed and is based on the premise that all variations can be easily incorporated in relation to specific design drawings.

The Specifications Manual for Heating, Ventilating and Air Conditioning and Plumbing was designed to eliminate writing and typing of job specifications and consists of approximately 500 8 1/2 x 11" pages furnished in a durable loose leaf binder. Each paragraph of the specification descriptions is a full page in length or multiples of a full page. These pages are the masters from which job specifications are assembled and multiple reproductions are made. You will find that following the easy steps are a welcome time and money saving approach to solving your problems in preparing job specifications for any of your heating, ventilating, air conditioning or plumbing projects.

How to Keep Abreast

In residential, commercial, and industrial work, it is generally more economical to purchase fittings and many sheet metal specialty items rather than to make them in your shop. It is usually more economical if you make rectangular pipe or duct in your shop; but it is usually more economical to purchase round pipe than to make it, particularly due to long lengths available.

Compiling a sheet metal library of manufacturers' and suppliers' catalogs which feature the variety of items available is helpful when planning and/or drawing the ductrun systems economically. Be sure you have an up-to-date set of catalogs illustrating the various fittings, duct, supplies, and equipment that are available to you.

Helpful Fabrication Information 328.

A good source for the various listings of catalogs is through the advertisers in trade magazine. Request a new catalog and price list from the manufacturers or distributors every year or two so you have the current prices and learn of any new or different items they have introduced.

It is also advantageous to keep up on the newer developments and ideas; you can do this by reading the trade journals, manuals provided by the associations, and books written for the trade. Remember that association membership and attendance at the seminars, meetings and conventions can all help you to keep up-to-date on newer developments.

If at all possible, observe and study the shop and field procedures of a larger sheet metal contractor who has kept up with the trade changes in methods and techniques of doing sheet metal work. These contractors have become very efficient since their volume of work is great enough that they can take advantage of specialization, having each employee do only specific operations such as one of the following: shop work, field work, estimating, drafting and/or designing, and balancing. Further specialization within shop work includes layout, fabrication, insulating, assembly.

Smaller contractors can take a lesson from larger contractors by following some parts of their operations.

The aspects of planning and organizing are always important. Getting into the habit of constantly looking ahead in planning any system will definitely be helpful. By planning ahead, you will be on the "look-out" for situations where you can save time and labor whether in shop or field.

#3 - Using The Cutting List System
(with over 60 sample fittings and their solutions)

A majority of items made in the sheet metal shop today are simple to layout and fabricate. It is the purpose of this section to have the person who works in the sheet metal shop CONSIDER various factors so he can work as efficiently as possible. By constantly being aware of these various factors when making duct, fittings and miscellaneous items, the person will begin to automatically work with a definite and positive system. Most people do work with a system although they might not realize it. The suggestions in this section can improve the system you already have.

Working in the sheet metal shop with a system can be described as follows: using the machinery and equipment available so that the quickest and best methods and techniques of handling the work most directly are employed, with the thought of coordination so that there is a constant and even work flow.

The person must know what he is doing, do it in a systematic manner, and make every step and motion count. This systematic shop procedure can be followed regardless of whether the person is working in a large or small shop. In most cases, when working in a large shop, many of the decisions will be made for you by someone else, such as determining the gage required or the cutting list. In a small shop, the sheet metal layout man generally does this himself.

It must be realized that applying these "Working with a System" techniques may have to be varied due to the differences between large fully-equipped shops and smaller shops with a limited amount of equipment. Lack of equipment should not affect the layout man's basic systematic working procedure.

If the most desirable piece of equipment is not available, the person should select the next fastest means of doing the job. It is up to the layout man to apply his own ingenuity, knowledge, and experience in selecting alternate methods.

The systematic shop procedures presented here should be followed according to the numerical sequence. They might vary depending on the conditions which exist in your shop; but for all practical purposes, first consider them in this sequence. The following is the list of correct/systematic shop procedures.

1. Study the working drawing or sketch.
2. Determine the method of fabrication.
3. Make up a cutting or shear list.
4. Cut the material required.
5. Do the layout.

Helpful Fabrication Information

   6. Cut and notch.
   7. Mark patterns.
   8. Punch and drill the holes.
   9. Do the forming.
   10. Insulate.
   11. Assemble.

1. Study the Working Drawing or Sketch

Whenever you receive a Work Order or Worksheet or several sheets, you should always begin by designating a number for each fitting, duct, or miscellaneous items. To make necessary revisions, always use a pencil. Follow this same procedure if you are given a drawing of part of a ductrun system or a complete system. Numbering each item provides the following advantages:

a. As the fittings or items move through the different processes in the shop, the location and status of the work in progress can more easily be determined.
b. This eliminates any confusion when the items are being assembled.
c. When the worksheet goes to the field, the fittings or items can be more readily identified.

If the fitting is shipped KD, this number should be placed on all pieces of material that are blanked out consistently on either the outside or inside of the fitting. Marking to the outside is sometimes easier because the inside of the fitting has to be lined. However, even if the fitting is lined, some shops want all marking to be placed in the inside, including:

- size of fitting
- fitting number
- forming information
- information regarding location of fitting, such as Zone #1 S.W.

Be sure that all the necessary dimensions and information are given. Sometimes a fitting has a dimension or other important information missing. By glancing over the worksheet at the very start, you will immediately know if you have to go to somebody for the information; he in turn might have to go to someone else for the answer. While this is being done, you can continue following the other steps of the systematic shop procedures.

Helpful Fabrication Information

Usually, the required gage of each fitting, duct or misc. item is marked. For general purposes, the following chart is usually acceptable:

Dimension of longest side	Gage
12" or less	26 ga.
13-30"	24 ga.
31-47"	22 ga.
48-60"	20 ga.
61 and over	18 ga.

Gages 28 and 30 are used in many residential systems and the sizes vary in different shops as well as in different parts of the country. If cross-breaking is going to be performed on the ductwork, the gage chart would not have to be so closely followed. Also when doing round work, the chart above is appropriate. In addition, the gage of material can vary depending on the purpose of the system, such as a blow pipe system.

The type of material to use might appear as something very obvious, particularly for people who are usually working with galvanized steel. But always check the specifications so you do not start a job using the wrong material.

If a band saw is available, the blanked pieces can be clamped together using special clamps that are designed for use with the band saw.

Always determine the number required of the same fitting. If more than one, after the first pattern or patterns are laid out, they merely need to be reproduced by tracing and cutting them out. If there are many and a band saw is available, you can cut them out.

If you work in a shop with a shear man, he will cut the material from the cutting list he receives. When he has started cutting your pieces from your cutting list, there might be some items you can work on while he is doing this. The following items could possibly be on the work sheet or sheets:

- canvas connections
- dampers
- ductruns for a fitting
- sunk ends/flush ends
- access doors
- S and drive cleats

2. Determine the Method of Fabrication

The following are several factors that determine the method of fabrication which are frequently dependent on one another.

A. Machinery Available

Generally speaking, the more machinery a shop has, the quicker and easier it is to perform the various operations in the least amount of time. An example is as follows: a shop is doing a job that requires a round duct system with the seams all absolutely airtight, with 22 or 20 gage. If welding facilities are available in the shop, the best thing to do would be to make all fittings out of 18 gage, then butt weld all the seams, rather than using riveted lap seams with solder after they have been formed and riveted.

An important factor to remember is that the material usually costs much less than labor. As in this case, 18 gage is more pounds of metal but welding makes it much easier as well as one operation, all saving labor.

B. Size of the Fitting

Small fittings are sometimes laid out combining all patterns. Doing this reduces labor by reducing the following operations to a minimum:

1. cutting
2. notching
3. seaming

However, in some cases the layout of combining all the patterns is complicated if it is a fitting that is not frequently encountered; then the layout might take up the time that would be saved in fabrication and assembly. But, if there are many required of the same fitting, it could be worthwhile to spend the extra time in laying out the combined patterns.

For a large fitting, it might be awkward to handle one combined pattern and might require extra time while fabricating it. Therefore, the factors that generally determine when to combine patterns are as follows:

Helpful Fabrication Information

1. size of fitting
2. quantity required
3. location of seams
4. will fitting or duct be lined or insulated on the inside?

C. Size of Material Available

Quite often when a large fitting is required, standing seams must be used to fasten the various pieces of a pattern together, depending on the width and length of metal available. This can sometimes be eliminated if you are aware of the various sizes of stock available and plan carefully before starting the layout. Remember that it is easier to layout a pattern on one sheet rather than placing several sheets together.

If you need to add angle iron to the fitting for rigidity, this can be done quickly. Using standing seams saves as much time as attaching the necessary angle iron to the patterns.

However, the fact must be considered that the large size of a complete pattern might be too awkward to work with and would require extra time handling. This would defeat the purpose of making one complete pattern from a sheet rather than using several patterns to make up the complete pattern. Again, you must judge each condition separately.

D. Quantity Required

If there are many of the same fitting required, it could be worthwhile to spend the extra time in combining several or all of the patterns. The size of the fittings or items also play an important role when making this decision.

E. Gage of Material Required

Using the specified gage of material is an important factor since some jobs are checked by a government inspector, architect or engineer.

But sometimes it is more economical to use a heavier gage due to the method of fabrication. Consider the example previously cited in paragraph A regarding the possible use of heavier gage and butt welding.

Helpful Fabrication Information 334.

Another example is to consider using a lighter gage if the shop is out of the specified gage; then you could crossbrake all fittings and pipe. But you must remember the general principle----heavier material is less expensive than additional labor hours.

F. Lining the Fittings and Pipe

The factor that has to be determined here is what method will be used to attach the lining to the inside of the fitting or pipe. This might help determine the number of patterns to use to layout a particular fitting. For example, when lining them, the pipe might have to be made up in L sections; transitions, depending on type and size, will need separate patterns.

G. Where They are to be Assembled

Different methods of assembly can be used if they are going to be assembled in the shop than if they are marked K.D. to be assembled on the job site.

3. Make Up a Cutting or Shear List

If at all possible, the person should determine the exact cut size of all patterns that he is to develop. The main reason for this is that the minimum amount of time is then spent in layout.

Some of the factors you want to consider when determining cut sizes of patterns are:

a. On some fittings, only one of the patterns cannot have the exact cut size determined. But much time can still be saved by determining the exact cut sizes of all the patterns possible.

b. Frequently determining exact cut sizes of the various fittings or items appear more difficult than they actually are. Many of these fittings are shown in the section "Using the Labor-Saving Cutting List System."

c. The stretchouts and true lengths for elbows, angles, offsets and transitions can be determined by using a book of charts and layout tables. Or it can be done using a circumference rule and a square for many fittings, except for heel patterns for offsets.

All that is really needed is being familiar with basic math---adding and subtracting whole numbers and common fractions. But, many people are reluctant to use this cutting system to the fullest extent.

Often a person thinks that by working directly off a sheet of metal, he is saving time since he is developing the stretchout and true length of the patterns as he is going along. But the time it takes to determine the exact cut sizes will be time well spent.

4. Cut the Material Required

When cutting the material for various items that are listed on your worksheet, cut the material and mark the size and number of the item or fitting on the material. Doing it this way makes it very easy to select the various pieces for each item or fitting you are laying out. If the shear man is cutting the material for the layout man, quite often he can work on something while waiting, which could be one or more of the following items:

- making or cutting up turning vanes
- dampers
- canvas connections
- cleats
- end caps

5. Do the Layout

In shops where the material is figured out by one person and cut by someone else, the layout man should check each piece of metal against the cut list before starting his layout. In doing so, he will also check to see if the right allowances were made before beginning the layout. Each shop has its own system and seaming allowances will vary slightly. Speed of layout is only acquired with experience, after the layout man first gains accuracy. If any pattern of the layout is wrong, it will have to be laid out again creating double the time, work and material, adding to the cost of the ductrun or system.

Helpful Fabrication Information

6. Cut and Notch the Patterns

Cutting out the patterns is done mostly by hand---some shops having notching dies for the corners, with step gages set for singles and Pittsburg notching. Pipe of standard lengths is generally notched by a hydraulic machine set by the operator.

7. Mark the Patterns

Care should be taken in marking the patterns properly for ease of assembly, especially in fittings that are shipped knocked down (K.D.). To match seams of adjoining pieces, some use a system of letters or numbers along with the fitting number and job number.

Some shops have computer printed stickers to paste on fittings and pipe that indicate the number, sizes, and zone. Others show a color code system of colored dots that is used in the field for designating area and floor for easy distribution to the correct area.

8. Punch and Drill the Holes

Punching of holes is best done while the sheet is still flat with prick marks as a guide for the punch to center on. Gang punching of angle iron for companion frames is best done in a press brake set up with a spring loaded punch and die set, so all holes in the angle are punched at once.

9. Do the Forming

The forming of fittings, pipe, and housing is very systematic to allow ease of forming and a neat and clean looking finished product. Crossbreaking and beading to make the metal more rigid should be first with the seaming to follow.

In some instances an opening has to be cut in a piece of metal; but, due to forming procedure, is best to first dor the forming to eliminate distortion. This procedure is especially true for copper or stainless steel work that is to be installed and exposed to view.

10. Insulate the Pipe and Fittings

Insulation of pipe and fittings for sound is quite common and creates a considerable amount of work in our shops. This facet of fabrication is also done in special order for safety as well as production. All fittings and pipe requiring insulating pins to hold the insulation are left knocked down, as well as those which are insulated without pins. Then the mastic (glue) is sprayed on and insulation added.

When pins are used, retaining clips are added to hold insulation even better for medium and high pressure air supply systems. After insulation is added, the fittings are assembled.

11. Assemble the Pipe and Fittings

When assembling the fittings, any errors in layout, cutting, notching and marking of the various pieces show up. After tacking (knocking over the Pittsburg in spots) the fitting together to check for alignment, squareness and accuracy, the final assembly can proceed. After tacking the fitting together for a Pittsburg seam, an air hammer is used for speed of assembly.

When checking off the fitting on your listing ticket, you should verify that the fitting is properly marked for shipping with job number, name, fitting number, or whatever coding system is used in your particular shop.

Number of Pieces for Pipe

The size and length of a pipe determine the number of pieces to use, which include:

1. one-piece wrap-around
2. two pieces, each L-shaped
3. two pieces, U-shaped
4. four separate pieces

Helpful Fabrication Information

Sample Cut Sizes

The cutting list for the fittings and pipe have been determined, using the following for seam and edge allowances. In some cases, patterns were combined, but not on all of them.

Seam or Edge	Allowance
1. Single edge (duct and straight edge)	1/4"
2. All radius edges (using Easy Edger)	1/4"
3. Clinch Edge	5/8+5/8+5/8=1-7/8
4. Tapins (machine)	1-3/4"
5. Flush end	Add 2" to width and length: 1" + W or L + 1"
6. Sunk end	Add 3-3/4" to width and length: 1 + 7/8 + W or L + L + 7/8
7. Pittsburg (machine)	15/16" (1-3/8" for large ductwork)

Using this system provides the following advantages:

- assures accuracy
- reduces errors
- simplifies layout
- reduces layout time

Housings

Using the cutting list system is extremely labor-saving when making housings. This is due to the fact that the seams are located so no access door panels have to be cut out---the seams are located in a manner to eliminate cutting the access door openings.

339.   **Helpful Fabrication Information**

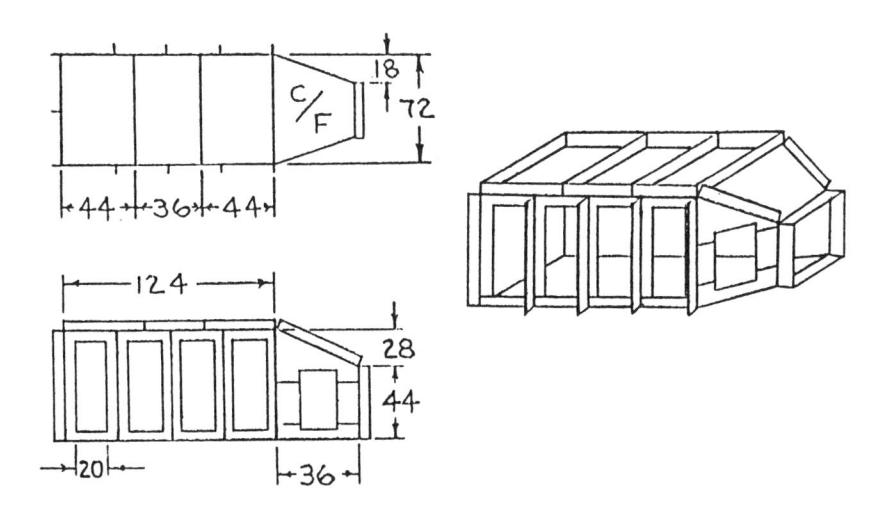

Housing with Access Door Openings Shown

Helpful Fabrication Information 340.

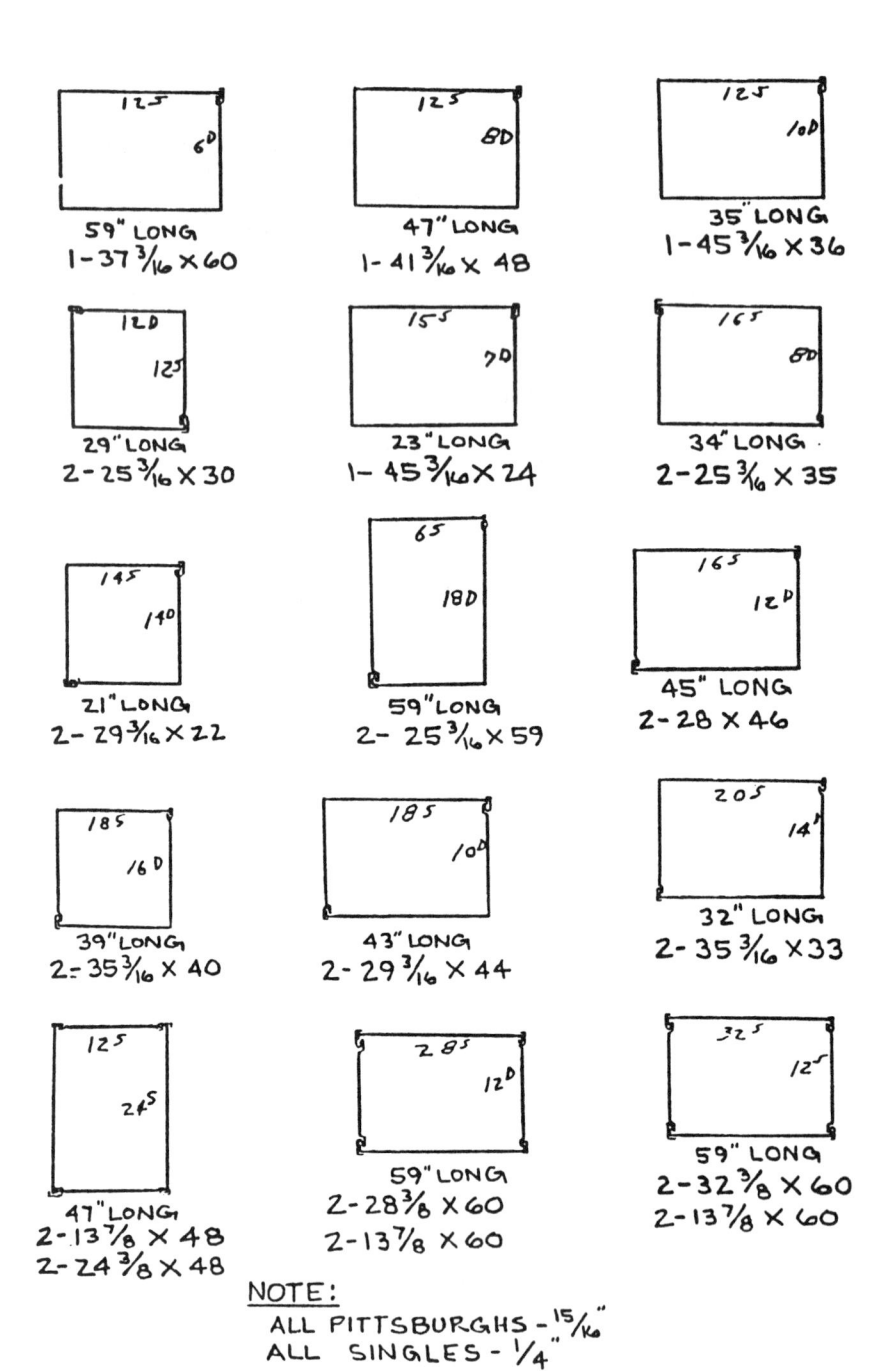

59" LONG
12S / 6D
1 - 37 3/16 × 60

47" LONG
12S / 8D
1 - 41 3/16 × 48

35" LONG
12S / 10D
1 - 45 3/16 × 36

29" LONG
12D / 12S
2 - 25 3/16 × 30

23" LONG
15S / 7D
1 - 45 3/16 × 24

34" LONG
16S / 8D
2 - 25 3/16 × 35

21" LONG
14S / 14D
2 - 29 3/16 × 22

59" LONG
6S / 18D
2 - 25 3/16 × 59

45" LONG
16S / 12D
2 - 28 × 46

39" LONG
18S / 16D
2 - 35 3/16 × 40

43" LONG
18S / 10D
2 - 29 3/16 × 44

32" LONG
20S / 14"
2 - 35 3/16 × 33

47" LONG
12S / 24S
2 - 13 7/8 × 48
2 - 24 3/8 × 48

59" LONG
28S / 12D
2 - 28 3/8 × 60
2 - 13 7/8 × 60

59" LONG
32S / 12S
2 - 32 3/8 × 60
2 - 13 7/8 × 60

<u>NOTE:</u>
ALL PITTSBURGHS - 15/16"
ALL SINGLES - 1/4"

Helpful Fabrication Information

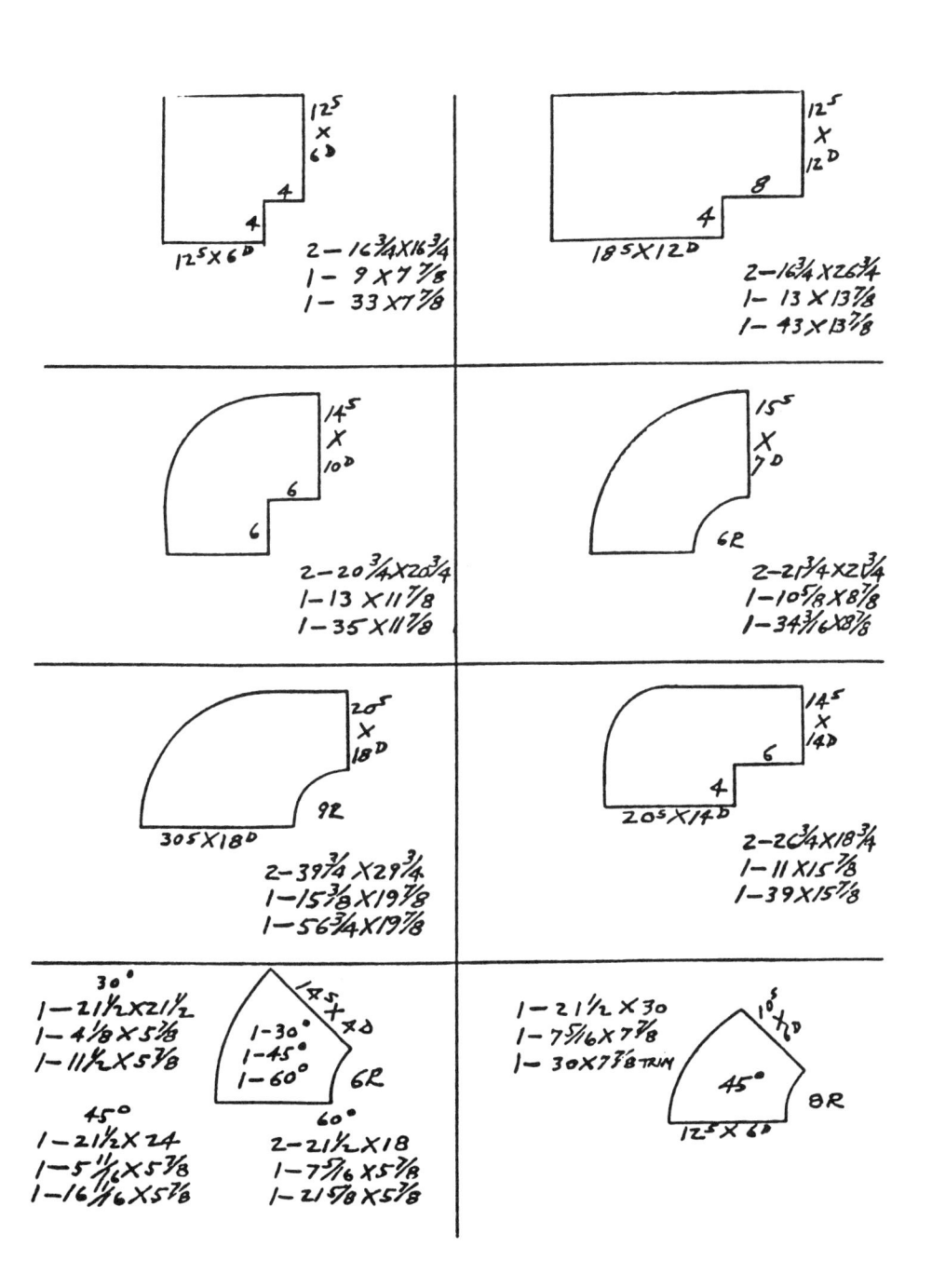

$12^S \times 6^D$ — $12^S \times 6^D$, 4, 4
2 — $16\frac{3}{4} \times 16\frac{3}{4}$
1 — $9 \times 7\frac{7}{8}$
1 — $33 \times 7\frac{7}{8}$

$18^S \times 12^D$ — $12^S \times 12^D$, 8, 4
2 — $16\frac{3}{4} \times 26\frac{3}{4}$
1 — $13 \times 13\frac{7}{8}$
1 — $43 \times 13\frac{7}{8}$

$14^S \times 10^D$, 6, 6
2 — $20\frac{3}{4} \times 20\frac{3}{4}$
1 — $13 \times 11\frac{7}{8}$
1 — $35 \times 11\frac{7}{8}$

$15^S \times 7^D$, 6R
2 — $21\frac{3}{4} \times 21\frac{3}{4}$
1 — $10\frac{5}{8} \times 8\frac{7}{8}$
1 — $34\frac{3}{16} \times 8\frac{7}{8}$

$30^S \times 18^D$ — $20^S \times 18^D$, 9R
2 — $39\frac{3}{4} \times 29\frac{3}{4}$
1 — $15\frac{3}{8} \times 19\frac{7}{8}$
1 — $56\frac{3}{4} \times 19\frac{7}{8}$

$20^S \times 14^D$ — $14^S \times 14^D$, 6, 4
2 — $26\frac{3}{4} \times 18\frac{3}{4}$
1 — $11 \times 15\frac{7}{8}$
1 — $39 \times 15\frac{7}{8}$

30°
1 — $21\frac{1}{2} \times 21\frac{1}{2}$
1 — $4\frac{1}{8} \times 5\frac{1}{8}$
1 — $11\frac{1}{2} \times 5\frac{7}{8}$

45°
1 — $21\frac{1}{2} \times 24$
1 — $5\frac{11}{16} \times 5\frac{7}{8}$
1 — $16\frac{11}{16} \times 5\frac{7}{8}$

$14^S \times ?^D$, 6R
1 — 30°
1 — 45°
1 — 60°

60°
2 — $21\frac{1}{2} \times 18$
1 — $7\frac{7}{16} \times 5\frac{7}{8}$
1 — $21\frac{5}{8} \times 5\frac{7}{8}$

1 — $21\frac{1}{2} \times 30$
1 — $7\frac{5}{16} \times 7\frac{7}{8}$
1 — $30 \times 7\frac{7}{8}$ TRIM

45°, $12^S \times 6^D$, $10^S \times 7^D$, 8R

Helpful Fabrication Information 342.

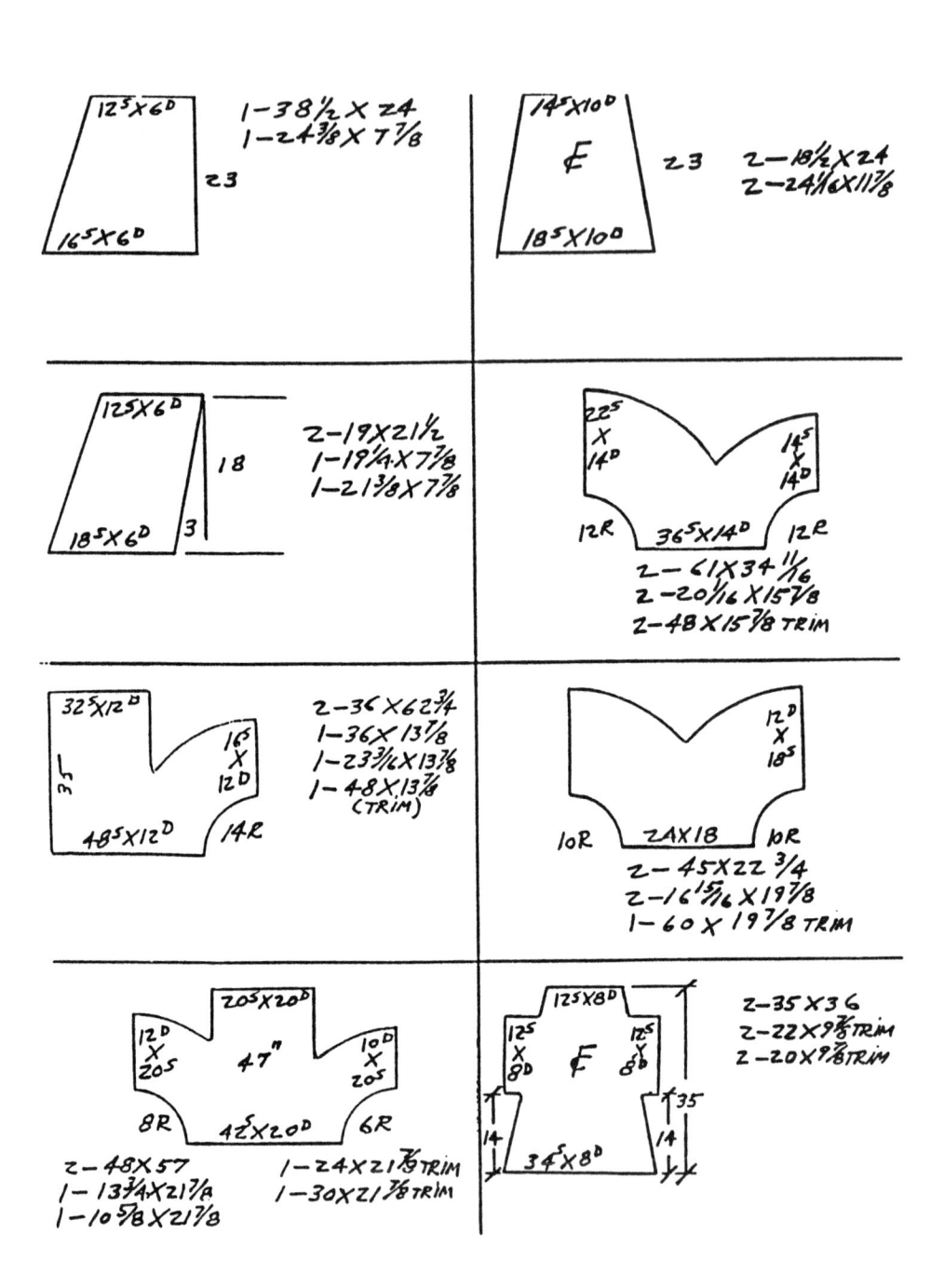

Panel 1 (top left)
12⁵ × 6ᴰ
16⁵ × 6ᴰ
z3
1 − 38½ × 24
1 − 24⅜ × 7⅞

Panel 2 (top right)
14⁵ × 10ᴰ
18⁵ × 10ᴰ
F
z3
2 − 18½ × 24
2 − 24⁴⁄₁₆ × 11⅞

Panel 3
12⁵ × 6ᴰ
18⁵ × 6ᴰ
18
3
2 − 19 × 21½
1 − 19¼ × 7⅞
1 − 21⅜ × 7⅞

Panel 4
22⁵ × 14ᴰ
14⁵ × 14ᴰ
12R 36⁵ × 14ᴰ 12R
2 − 61 × 34 ¹¹⁄₁₆
2 − 20¹⁄₁₆ × 15⅞
2 − 48 × 15⅞ TRIM

Panel 5
32⁵ × 12ᴰ
48⁵ × 12ᴰ
35
16⁵ × 12ᴰ
14R
2 − 36 × 62¾
1 − 36 × 13⅞
1 − 23³⁄₁₆ × 13⅞
1 − 48 × 13⅞ (TRIM)

Panel 6
12ᴰ × 18⁵
10R 24 × 18 10R
2 − 45 × 22¾
2 − 16¹⁵⁄₁₆ × 19⅞
1 − 60 × 19⅞ TRIM

Panel 7
20⁵ × 20ᴰ
12ᴰ × 20⁵   10ᴰ × 20⁵
47"
8R 42⁵ × 20ᴰ 6R
2 − 48 × 57
1 − 13¾ × 21⅞
1 − 10⅝ × 21⅞
1 − 24 × 21⅞ TRIM
1 − 30 × 21⅞ TRIM

Panel 8
12⁵ × 8ᴰ
12⁵ × 8ᴰ   12⁵ × 8ᴰ
F
34⁵ × 8ᴰ
14   14   35
2 − 35 × 36
2 − 22 × 9⅞ TRIM
2 − 20 × 9⅞ TRIM

Helpful Fabrication Information

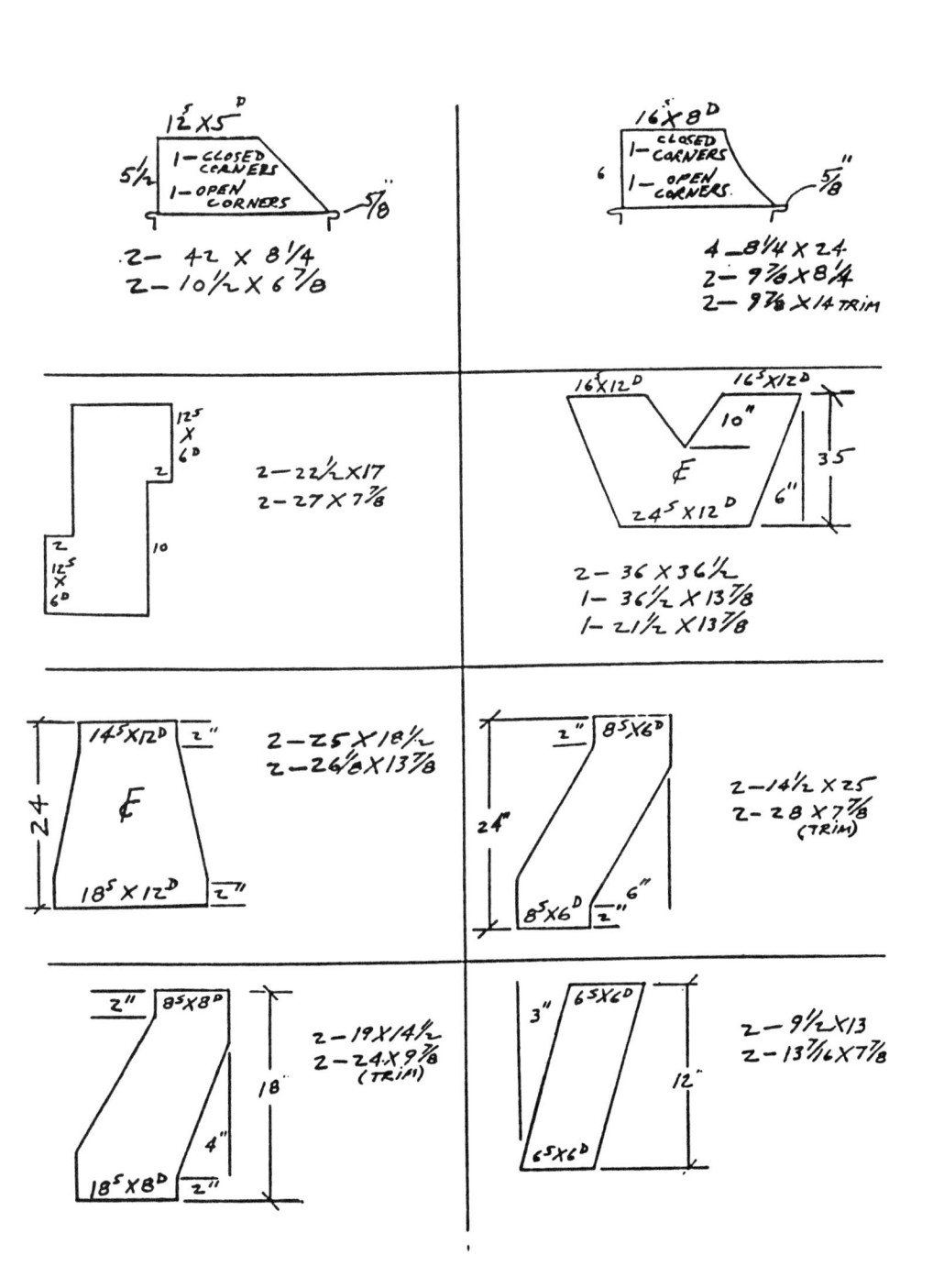

343.

Helpful Fabrication Information

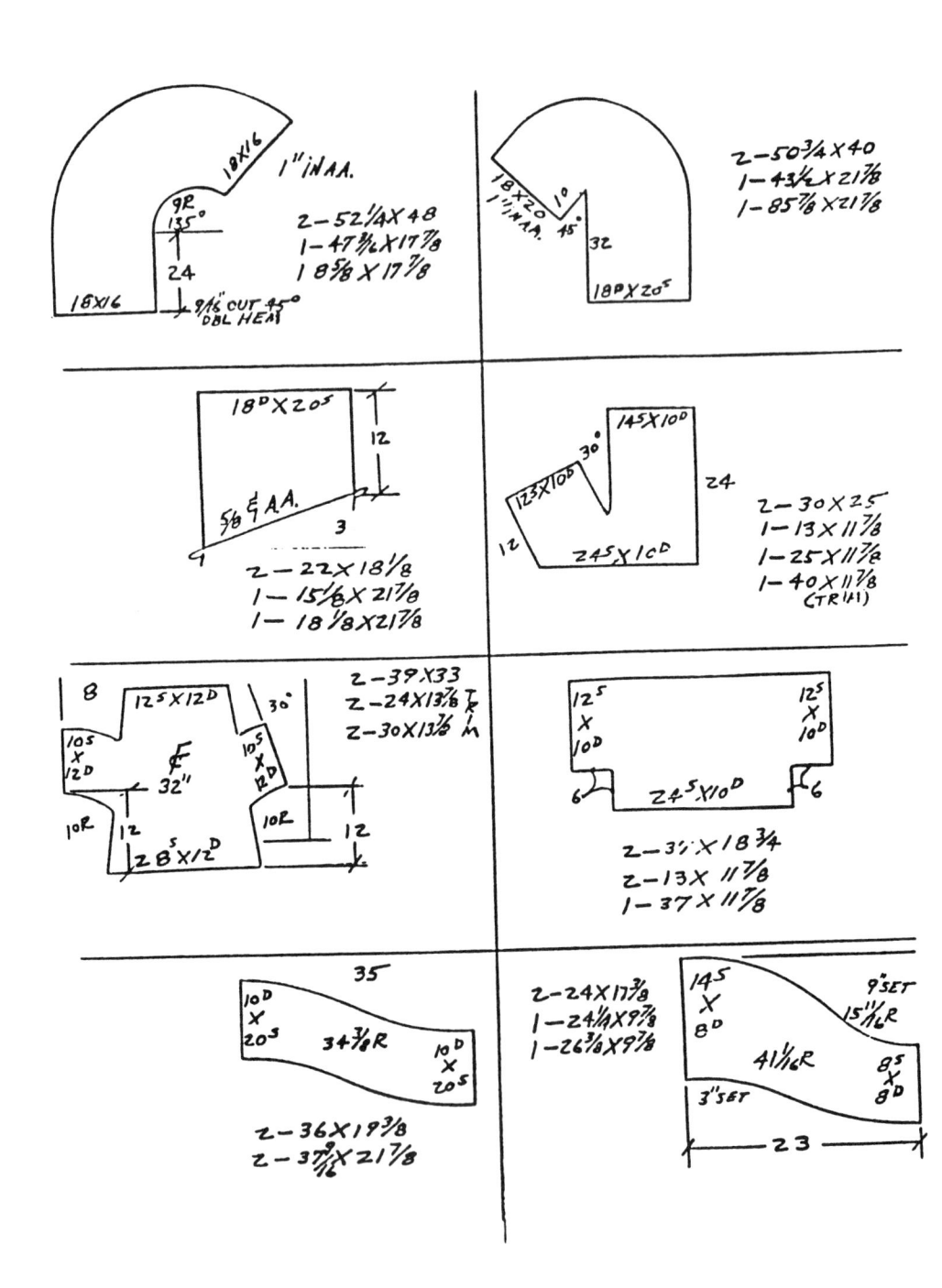

344.

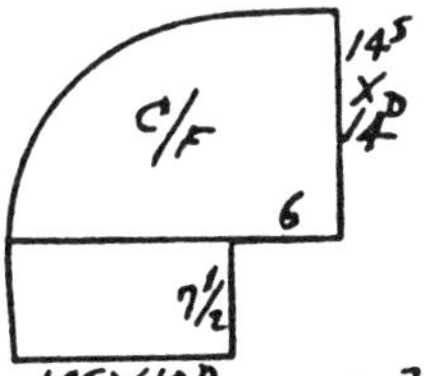
C/F
14S X 14D
6
7 1/2
14S X 10D

2-20 3/4X23 3/8
1-14 1/2X15 7/8
1-36 1/2X15 7/8

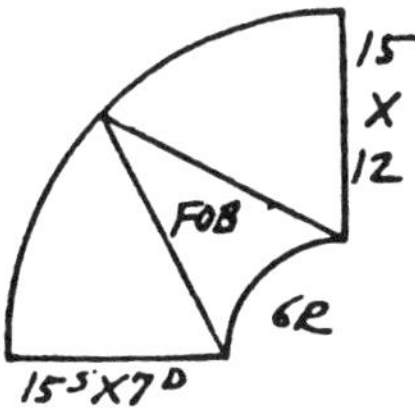
15S
X
12
FOB
6R
15SX7D

1-21 3/4X21 3/4
1-24X24
1-10 5/8X13 7/8
1-34 3/16X13 7/8

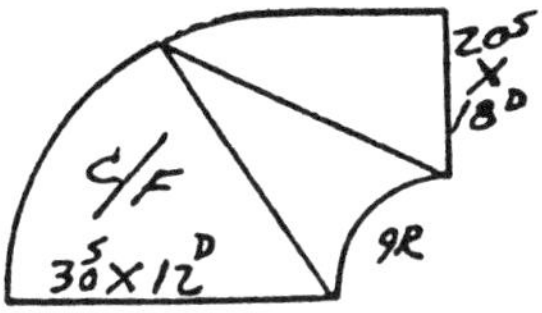
20S
X
18D
C/F
9R
30SX12D

2-39 3/4X29 3/4
1-15 3/8X19 7/8
1-56 3/4X19 7/8

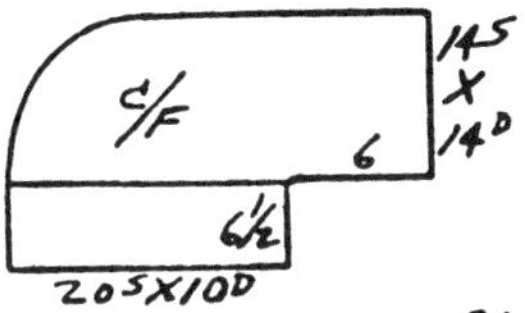
C/F
14S
X
14D
6
6 1/2
20SX10D

2-26 3/4X21 3/8
1-13 1/2X15 7/8
1-41 1/2X15 7/8

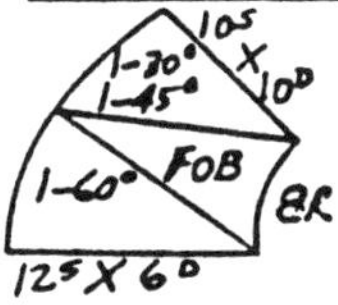
10S X 10D
1-30°
1-45°
1-60°
FOB
8R
12SX6D

1-30°
1-20 1/4X20
1-22X22
1-13 1/16X11 7/8
1-5 15/16X11 7/8

1-45°
1-20 1/4X20
1-24X24
1-17 3/4X11 7/8
1-7 7/8X11 7/8

1-60°
1-20 1/4X20
1-24X24
1-22 3/8X11 7/8
1-9 13/16X11 7/8

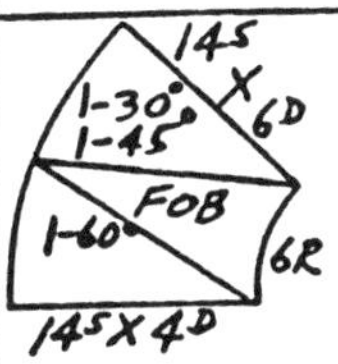
14S X 6D
1-30°
1-45
1-60°
FOB
6R
14SX4D

1-30°
1-20 1/4X20
1-24X24
1-4 7/8X7 7/8
1-12 1/8X7 7/8

1-45°
1-20 1/4X20
1-24X24
1-6 5/16X7 7/8
1-17 5/16X7 7/8

1-60°
1-20 1/4X20
1-24X24
1-7 3/4X7 7/8
1-22 1/4X7 7/8

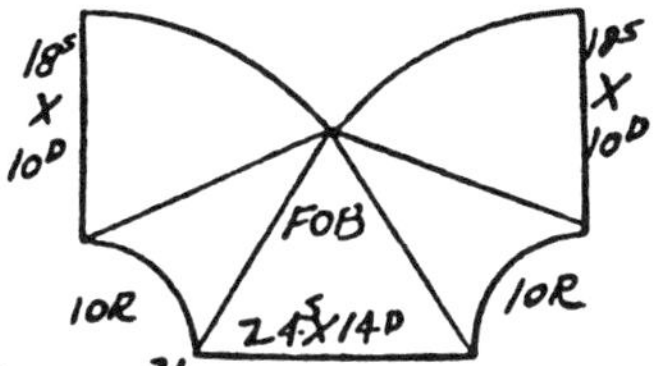
18S
X
10D
18S
X
10D
FOB
10R
10R
24SX14D

1-45X28 3/4
1-48X30
2-16 15/16X15 7/8
2-30X15 7/8 TRIM

1-24X26 3/4
1-24X28
1-24X13 7/8
1-13 3/4X13 7/8
1-13 7/8X36
TRIM

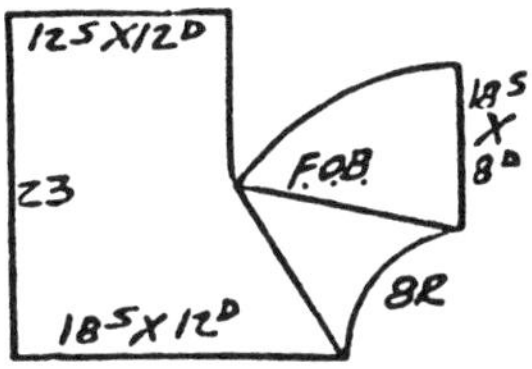
12SX12D
23
F.O.B.
18S
X
8D
8R
18SX12D

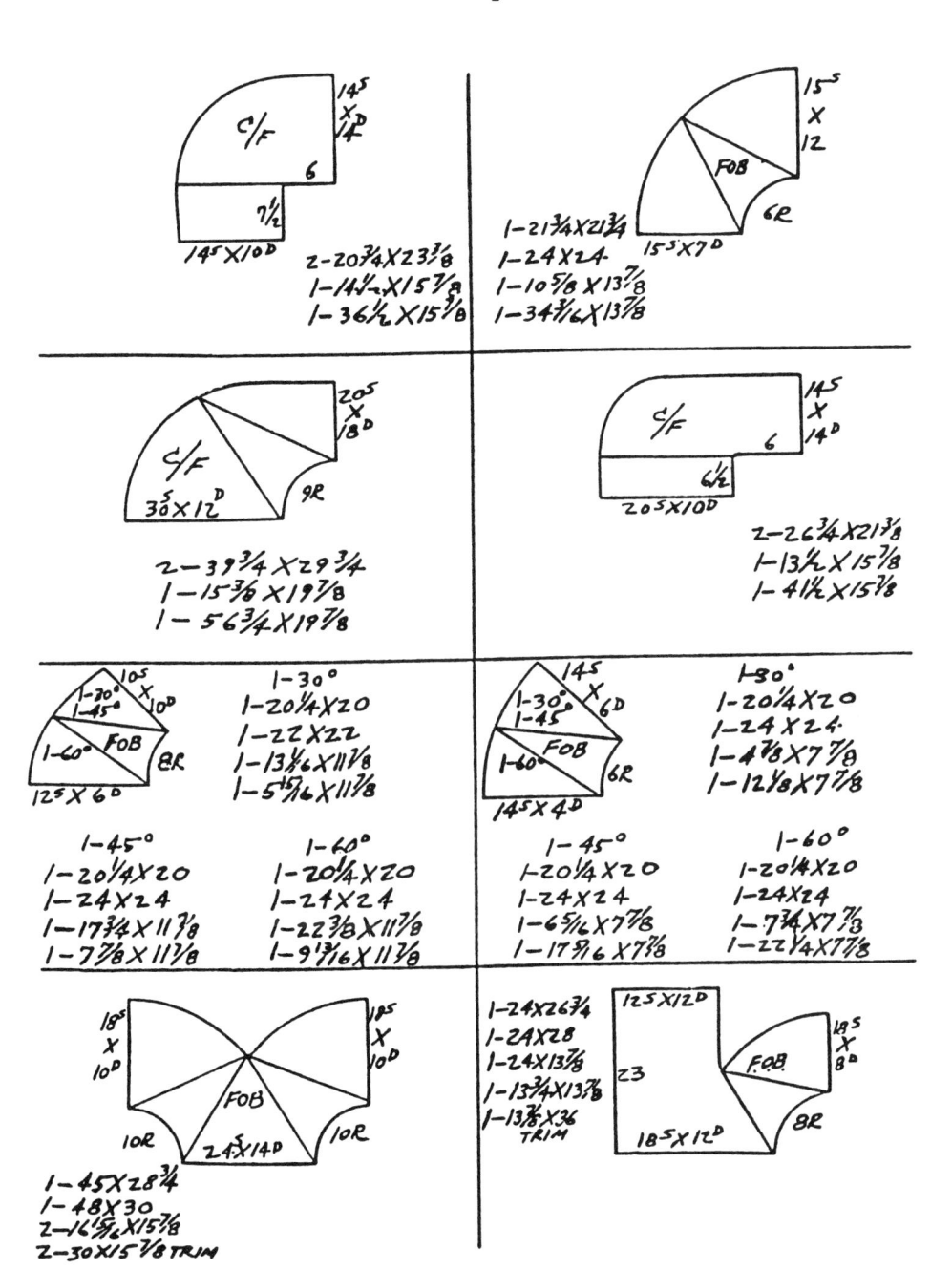

Helpful Fabrication Information 346.

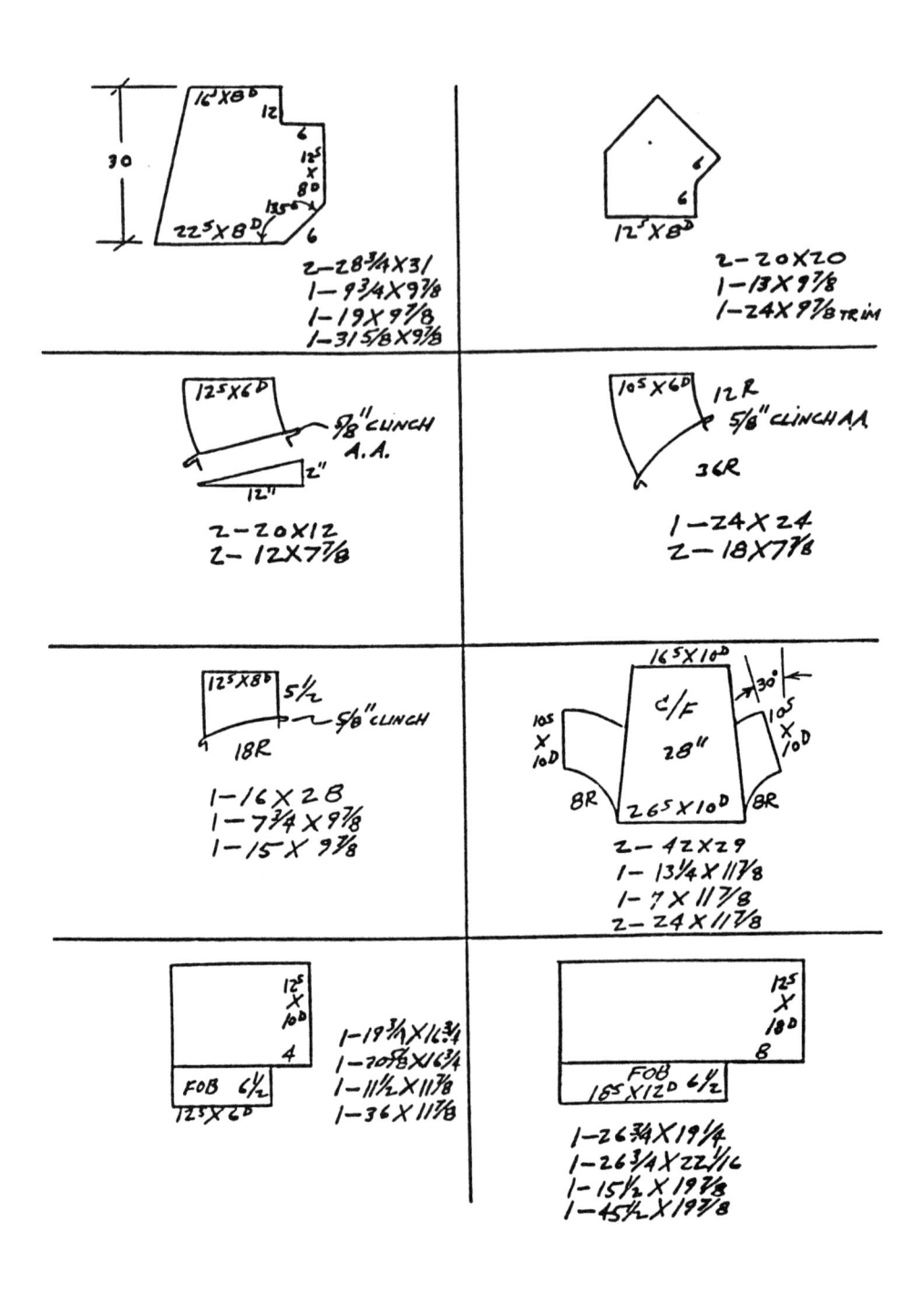

Helpful Fabrication Information

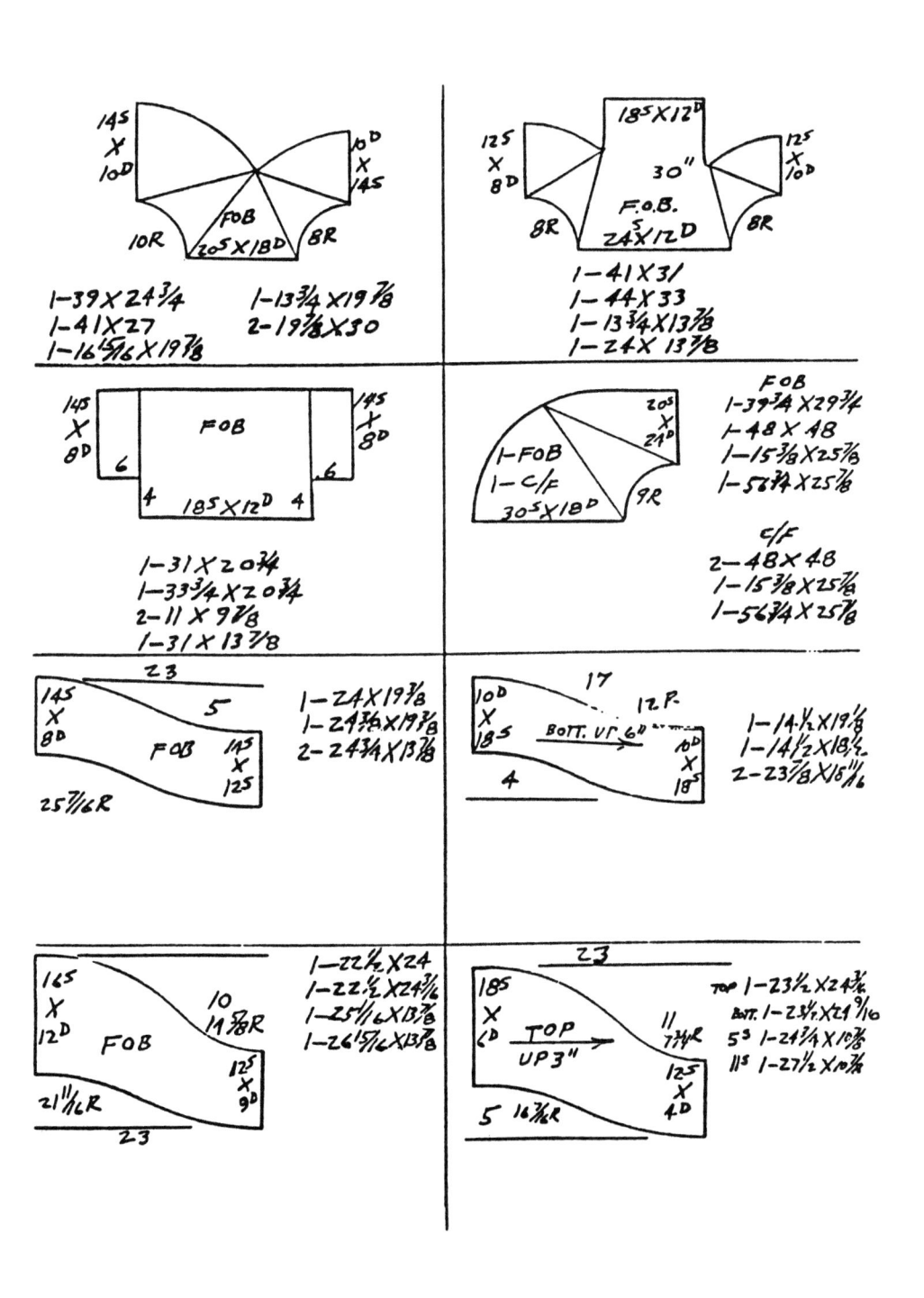

[Page of hand-drawn fabrication sketches with dimensions]

Sketch 1 (top left):
14S × 10D, 10D, 14S, 10R, 8R, FOB, 20S×18D
1—39 × 24¾
1—41 × 27
1—16¹⁵⁄₁₆ × 19⅞
1—13¾ × 19⅞
2—19⅞ × 30

Sketch 2 (top right):
18S × 12D, 12S × 8D, 12S × 10D, 30", F.O.B., 8R, 8R, 24S × 12D
1—41 × 31
1—44 × 33
1—13¾ × 13⅞
1—24 × 13⅞

Sketch 3:
14S × 8D, 14S × 8D, FOB, 6, 6, 4, 4, 18S × 12D
1—31 × 20¾
1—33¾ × 20¾
2—11 × 9⅞
1—31 × 13⅞

Sketch 4:
20S × 21D, FOB, C/F, 30S × 18D, 9R
FOB
1—39¾ × 29¾
1—48 × 48
1—15⅜ × 25⅞
1—56¾ × 25⅞

C/F
2—48 × 48
1—15⅜ × 25⅞
1—56¾ × 25⅞

Sketch 5:
14S × 8D, 23, 5, FOB, 14S × 12S, 25⁷⁄₁₆R
1—24 × 19⅞
1—24⅞ × 19⅞
2—24¾ × 13⅞

Sketch 6:
10D × 18S, 17, 12P, BOTT. UP 6", 10D × 18S, 4
1—14½ × 19⅛
1—14½ × 18½
2—23⅞ × 15¹¹⁄₁₆

Sketch 7:
16S × 12D, FOB, 10, 14⅞R, 12S × 9D, 21¹¹⁄₁₆R, 23
1—22½ × 24
1—22½ × 24⁷⁄₁₆
1—25¹¹⁄₁₆ × 13⅞
1—26¹⁵⁄₁₆ × 13⅞

Sketch 8:
18S × 6D, TOP UP 3", 11, 7¼R, 12S × 4D, 5, 16¾R, 23
TOP 1—23½ × 24¾
BOTT. 1—23½ × 24⁹⁄₁₆
5S 1—24¾ × 10⅞
11S 1—27½ × 10⅞

Helpful Fabrication Information

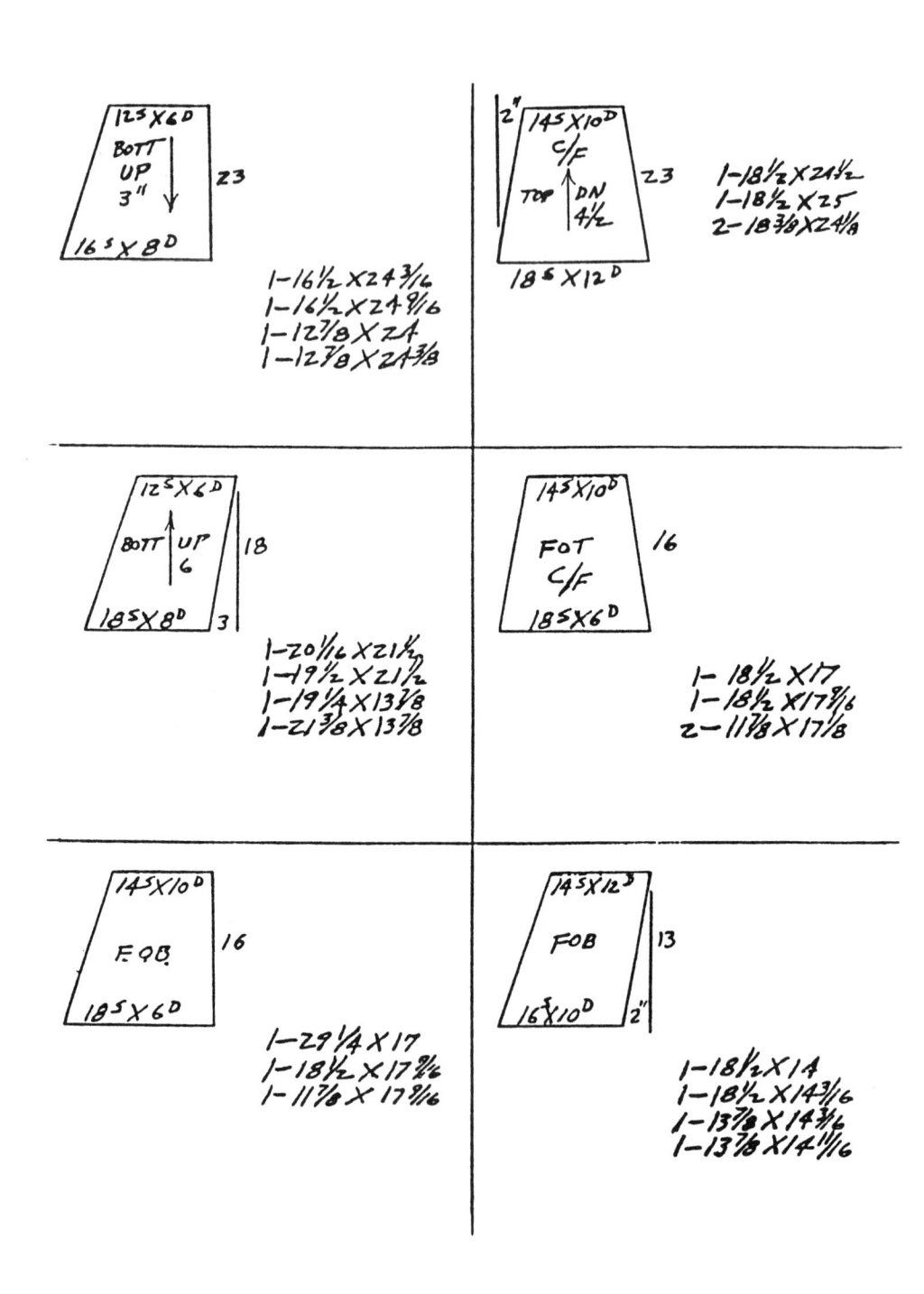

348.

```
 12ˢ X 6ᴰ
 BOTT
 UP    ↓   23
 3"
 16ˢ X 8ᴰ
```
1—16½ X 24 3/16
1—16½ X 24 9/16
1—12 7/8 X 24
1—12 7/8 X 24 3/8

```
2" | 14ˢ X 10ᴰ
    C/F
    TOP ↑ DN    23
        4½
 18ˢ X 12ᴰ
```
1—18½ X 21½
1—18½ X 25
2—18 3/8 X 24 1/8

```
 12ˢ X 6ᴰ
 BOTT | UP    18
        6
 18ˢ X 8ᴰ  3
```
1—20 1/16 X 21½
1—19½ X 21½
1—19¼ X 13 7/8
1—21 3/8 X 13 7/8

```
 14ˢ X 10ᴰ
  FOT
  C/F       16
 18ˢ X 6ᴰ
```
1—18½ X 17
1—18½ X 17 9/16
2—11 7/8 X 17 7/8

```
 14ˢ X 10ᴰ
  F.O.B.     16
 18ˢ X 6ᴰ
```
1—29¼ X 17
1—18½ X 17 9/16
1—11 7/8 X 17 9/16

```
 14ˢ X 12ᴰ
  FOB         13
 16ˢ X 10ᴰ  2"
```
1—18½ X 14
1—18½ X 14 3/16
1—13 7/8 X 14 3/16
1—13 7/8 X 14 11/16

Helpful Fabrication Information

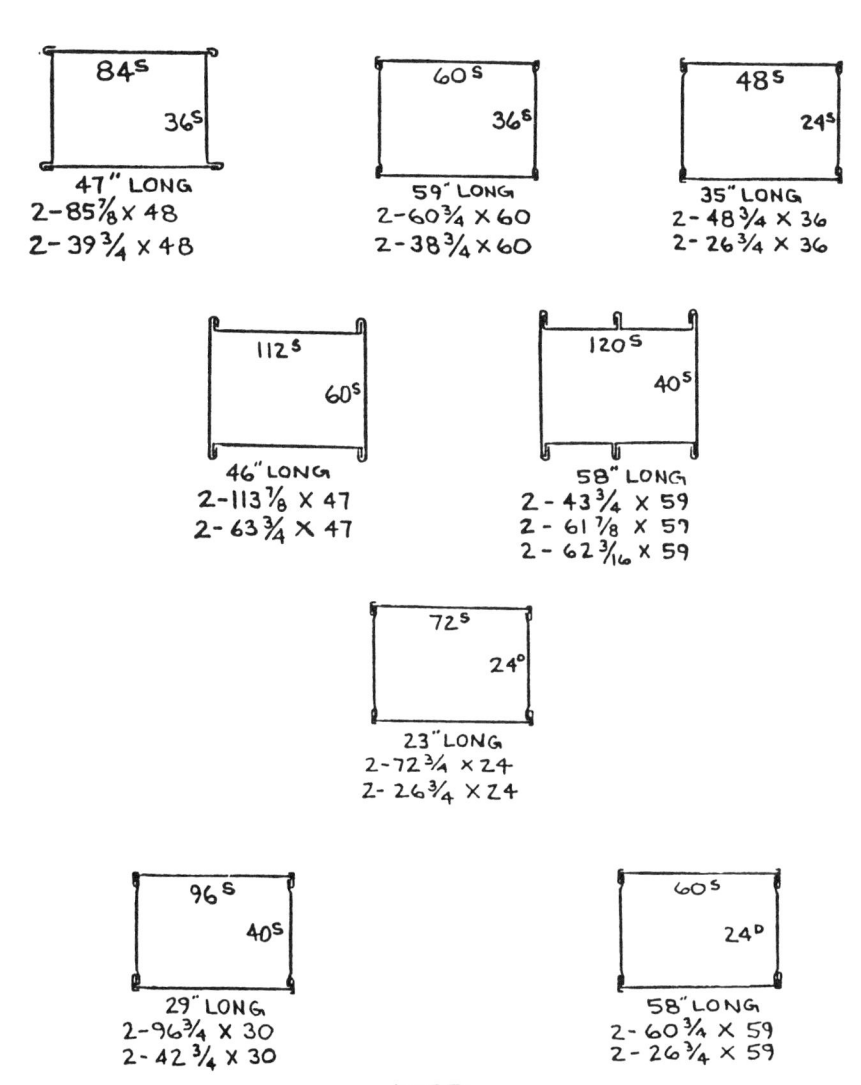

```
   84 S
      36 S
  47" LONG
2 - 85 7/8 x 48
2 - 39 3/4 x 48
```

```
   60 S
      36 S
  59" LONG
2 - 60 3/4 x 60
2 - 38 3/4 x 60
```

```
   48 S
      24 S
  35" LONG
2 - 48 3/4 x 36
2 - 26 3/4 x 36
```

```
   112 S
      60 S
  46" LONG
2 - 113 7/8 x 47
2 - 63 3/4 x 47
```

```
   120 S
      40 S
  58" LONG
2 - 43 3/4 x 59
2 - 61 7/8 x 59
2 - 62 3/16 x 59
```

```
   72 S
      24 D
  23" LONG
2 - 72 3/4 x 24
2 - 26 3/4 x 24
```

```
   96 S
      40 S
  29" LONG
2 - 96 3/4 x 30
2 - 42 3/4 x 30
```

```
   60 S
      24 D
  58" LONG
2 - 60 3/4 x 59
2 - 26 3/4 x 59
```

NOTE:
ALL PITTSBURGHS - 1 3/8"
ALL SINGLES - 3/8

Helpful Fabrication Information 350.

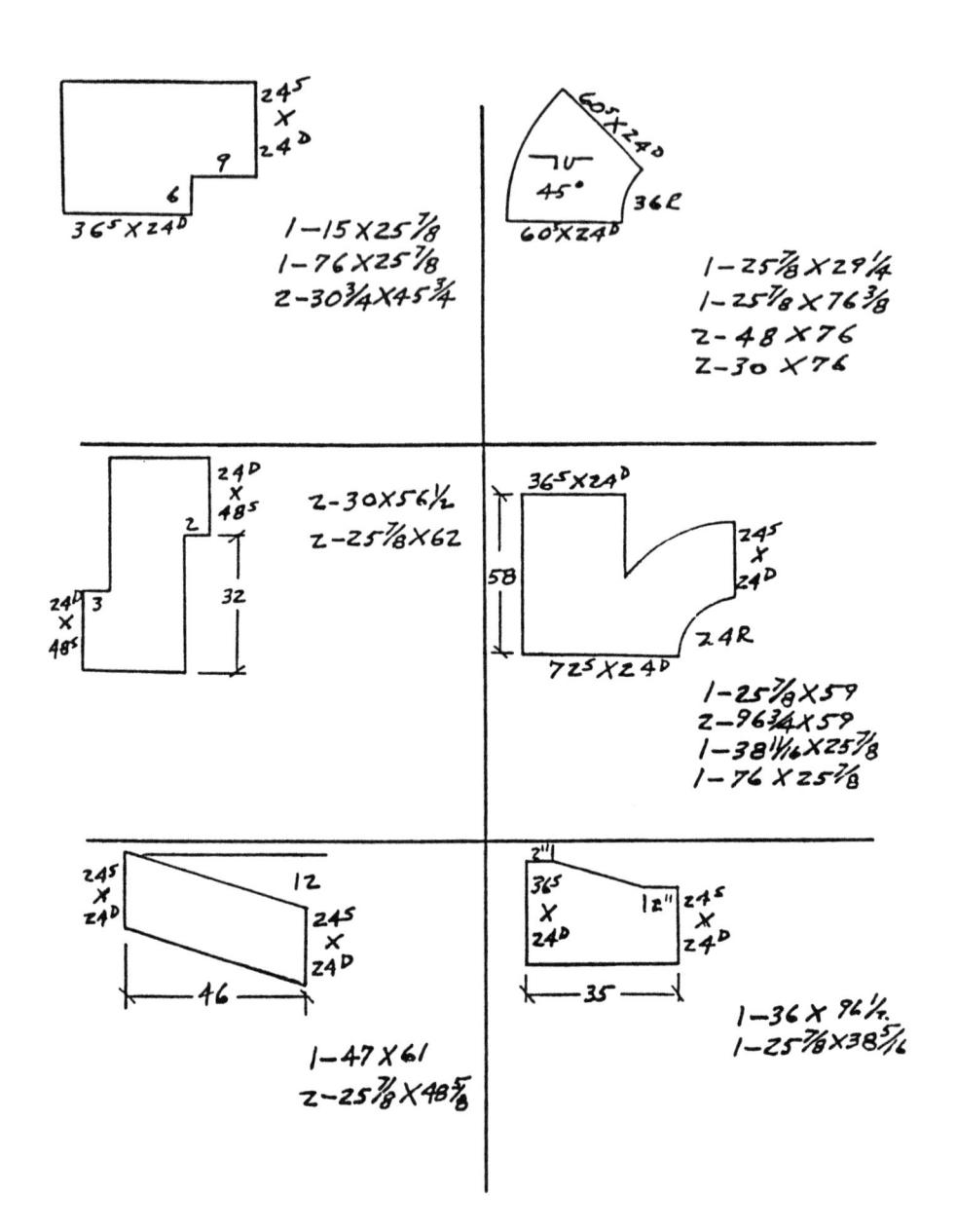

Shape 1 (upper left): $36^S \times 24^D$, with notches labeled 9, 6, and $24^S \times 24^D$
1—15 × 25⅞
1—76 × 25⅞
2—30¾ × 45¾

Shape 2 (upper right): 45° wedge, $60^S \times 24^D$, $60^S \times 24^D$, $36R$
1—25⅞ × 29¼
1—25⅞ × 76⅜
2—48 × 76
2—30 × 76

Shape 3 (middle left): $24^D \times 48^S$, $24^D \times 48^S$, with dimensions 2, 3, 32
2—30 × 56½
2—25⅞ × 62

Shape 4 (middle right): $36^S \times 24^D$, $24^S \times 24^D$, $24R$, $72^S \times 24^D$, dimension 58
1—25⅞ × 59
2—96¾ × 59
1—38 11/16 × 25⅞
1—76 × 25⅞

Shape 5 (lower left): parallelogram $24^S \times 24^D$, $24^S \times 24^D$, 12, 46
1—47 × 61
2—25⅞ × 48⅝

Shape 6 (lower right): trapezoid, 2", $36^S \times 24^D$, 12", $24^S \times 24^D$, 35
1—36 × 96½
1—25⅞ × 38 5/16

Helpful Fabrication Information

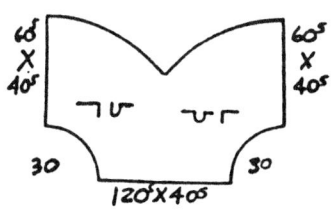

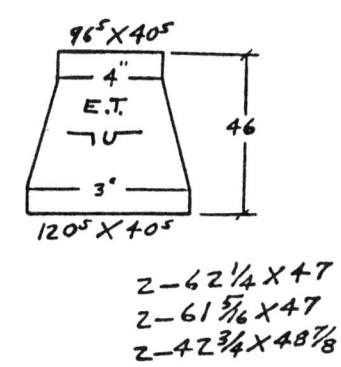

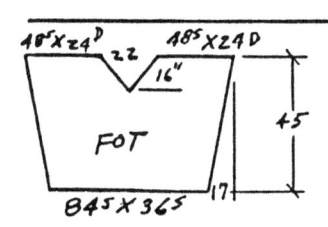

351.

$60^5 \times 40^5$ ... $60^5 \times 40^5$
30 ... 30
120×40^5

TH 2 - 49 9/16 × 42 3/4
H 2 - 76 × 42 3/4
CK 4 - 90 7/8 × 61 7/16
2 - 90 7/8 × 63 3/4

$96^5 \times 40^5$
4"
E.T.
46
3"
$120^5 \times 40^5$

2 - 62 1/4 × 47
2 - 61 5/16 × 47
2 - 42 3/4 × 48 7/8

$48^5 \times 24^D$ ... $48^5 \times 24^D$
22
16"
45
FOT
17
$84^5 \times 36^5$

1 - 118 3/4 × 46
1 - 118 3/4 × 47 5/8
1 - 26 3/4 × 41 1/4
2 - 26 3/4 × 49 1/4

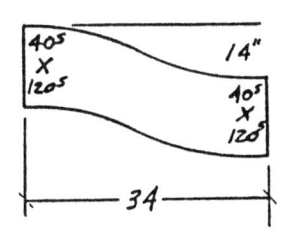

$40^5 \times 120^5$ ... $40^5 \times 120^5$
14"
34

2 - 35 × 54 3/4
2 - 37 15/16 × 122 3/4

Helpful Fabrication Information

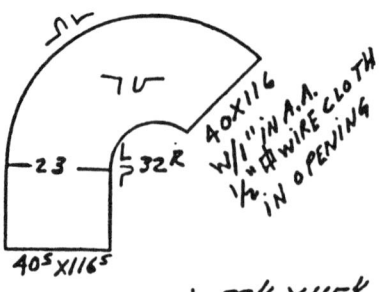

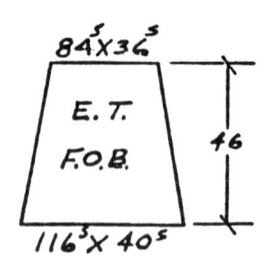

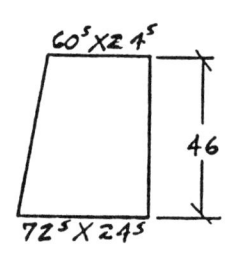

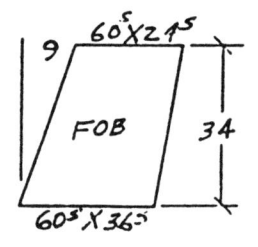

40×116
w/1" in A.A.
1/4 # wire cloth
1/2" in opening

$-23-$ $\quad$ $\overset{L}{\vdash} 32^R$

$40^5 \times 116^5$

$1 - 39\frac{1}{2} \times 115\frac{1}{2}$
(WIRE CLOTH)
H $2 - 58\frac{11}{16} \times 118\frac{3}{4}$
T $1 - 25\frac{3}{8} \times 118\frac{3}{4}$
$1 - 52\frac{11}{16} \times 118\frac{3}{4}$
d $2 - 95\frac{7}{8} \times 60$
$2 - 60 \times 50$

$84^5 \times 36^5$
E.T.
F.O.B.
46
$116^5 \times 40^5$

$1 - 47 \times 116\frac{3}{4}$
$1 - 47\frac{3}{16} \times 116\frac{3}{4}$
$2 - 49\frac{13}{16} \times 42\frac{3}{4}$

$60^5 \times 24^5$
46
$72^5 \times 24^5$

$2 - 72\frac{3}{4} \times 47$
$1 - 26\frac{3}{4} \times 47$
$1 - 48\frac{5}{8} \times 26\frac{3}{4}$

9 $\quad 60^5 \times 24^5$
FOB $\quad$ 34
$60^5 \times 36^5$

$1 - 69\frac{3}{4} \times 35$
$1 - 69\frac{3}{4} \times 37\frac{3}{16}$
$2 - 36\frac{1}{4} \times 38\frac{3}{4}$

352.

#4 - Transitions: Laying Out, Marking and Forming

One of the most commonly used fittings in residential, commercial and industrial ductrun systems is the transition (or change fitting), often referred to as a change joint.

Transitions can be a bottleneck and often cause field slowdowns. These fittings cause the most problems to sheet metal contractors and workers due to mistakes in the original field measuring and sketching of the working drawings, or because of mistakes in laying out, marking, forming and assembling them in the shop.

Due to the many variations in their design and size, very seldom can these transitions be purchased. See Fig. 1.

The purpose of this section is to give suggestions for a systematic approach to field measuring, laying out, checking, marking, forming and assembling transitions.

The more difficult types of transitions are required when doing alterations, additions and modernization work which call for unit replacements, installing air conditioning cooling coils, installing electronic air filters, connecting new ductwork to existing ductwork, etc. The reason this type of work calls for the more difficult transitions is that it might be necessary for all or most sides to pitch. This is due to the fact that you are usually connecting two already permanently-positioned ductrun sections or a unit and a ductrun section.

When doing new work, you frequently have the opportunity to carefully plan the location of the units and ductwork so that the necessary transitions can be those with a minimum number of sides pitching.

In commercial and industrial work where larger fittings are required, transitions are used to connect ductwork to ductwork, and ductwork to blowers, coils, mixing boxes, etc. Large transitions are frequently used in fan rooms.

Since there are many variations in designs and sizes of transitions, some are very easy fittings to field measure and sketch, layout, mark, form and assemble. This is very difficult with other transitions because they are not required as frequently, although they are sometimes

Helpful Fabrication Information 354.

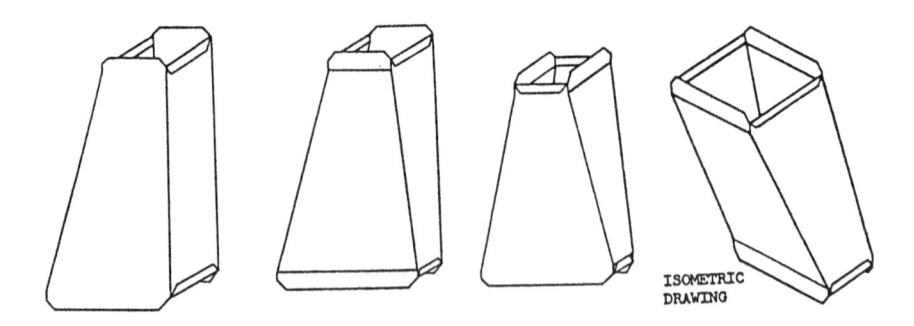

Fig. 1 - Isometric Drawings of Transitions (from left):
- transition with 1 side pitching
- transition with 2 sides pitching
- transition with 3 sides pitching
- transition with 4 sides pitching

necessary. A further difficulty arises since the mistakes in laying out these fittings are not usually realized until the fittings are being assembled. This is especially true when there are several sides of the fitting pitching, dropping or offsetting.

To avoid making these mistakes, extreme caution must be taken in doing the field measuring and sketching, layout, marking and forming. Extra caution must also be taken when making very large transitions in heavy commercial and industrial work since the patterns have to be made in several pieces.

Field Measuring and Sketching

The term "working drawing" usually refers to the dimensioned sketch or drawing the person makes or is given for making the fitting. The term "working view" refers to what is usually drawn on metal to help determine the pattern layout. The Front View is a view that shows the overall shape of the fitting and can be dimensioned and marked so that technically all information required for making the fitting can be shown. The Front View is often referred to as the "Elevation View." The Top View is often referred to as the "Plan View."

Helpful Fabrication Information

When sketching and dimensioning working drawings, you must provide enough information so that the person making the fitting will have no questions or doubts as to exactly what is required. Do not use any abbreviations that the other person might not readily understand. Abbreviations are used to save time; however, the time saved in using an abbreviation might be lost many times over in work stoppage in shop or field.

To aid in field measuring and sketching as well as shop layout, try to plan and locate the units and/or ductwork being connected so that two sides of each opening are in line with each other. A relatively easy transition can then be used--one with only one or two sides pitching.

When measuring the required length of the transition, the working drawing should be stated with finished dimensions (from drive to drive). However, sometimes either one end or both ends of the transition must be "raw". In such a case, be sure you state the overall dimension and mark it accordingly on the working drawing.

Technically, two views are not needed to provide all the necessary information and dimensions unless it is a twisted transition. However, the person who is going to make the transition must be able to sketch or visualize another view in order to determine other necessary dimensions often referred to as "unstated dimensions." This is actually the pitch, drop or offset sometimes marked on a one-view drawing. By drawing an additional view, the process is easier for the person who is going to make the transition.

If the unit and/or ducts are stationary and are located with a tight or limited working space, the transition will often have to be made in four pieces and assembled when it is being installed. This is true regardless of how many sides are pitching. Be sure to mark the working drawing as "K.D." (knock down), which means not to be assembled.

Suggestions When Field Measuring and Sketching:

1. Try to plan and draw transitions that have a minimum number of sides pitching, keeping as many sides straight or flat as possible.

2. Graph paper and isometric paper are an aid in sketching proportionately, especially when making isometric drawings.

Helpful Fabrication Information

3. Do not hesitate to draw more than one view to give a clearer understanding to the person who is going to make the fitting.

4. First draw the Front View (elevation view) then draw the Top View (Plan View). For a person who does not have an understanding of the principles of blueprint reading, you might want to draw an isometric view of the fitting, which is a perspective view showing what the fitting looks like.

5. If the fitting is to be assembled when it is being installed, be sure to mark the drawing "K.D." (knock down).

6. The terms "pitch,""drop" and "offset" are used interchangably because they all refer to a change in direction.

Visualizing Transitions

In order to determine the true lengths when laying out the patterns, it is important to be able to visualize the overall shape of the fitting. As an aid in your field sketching or layout work, it is often helpful to sketch an additional view so you will be able to determine the pitch, drop or offset correctly.

The amount the pattern or patterns pitch is needed to determine the true lengths for the fitting. This is equally true with either of the two methods you use to determine the true lengths. The short time it takes you to determine this view will give you a better understanding of the fitting which will, in turn, reduce mistakes. See Fig. 2.

The sketch is particularly helpful if you have difficulty visualizing the required fitting. It is also an aid when planning how each pattern is to be laid out so that all layout lines and forming information are to the inside of each pattern. If this rule is consistently followed, many forming mistakes will be eliminated.

Number of Pieces for Transitions

Transitions can be made in 1, 2, 3, or 4 pieces. To a large extent, this is determined by how many sides pitch. Generally, the transition is made in 2 pieces if one side pitches; the 2 cheeks and 1 heel pattern are

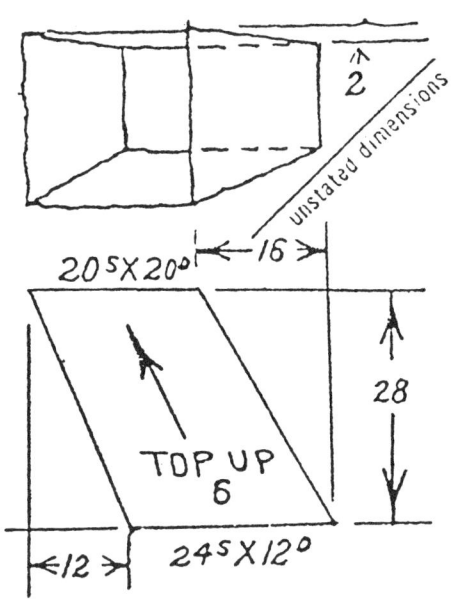

Fig. 2 - Transition fittings with Top View sketched or visualized from the dimensions on Front View.

combined making it U-shaped after it is formed. It is made in 3 pieces if two sides pitch; 1 cheek and 1 heel pattern are combined making it L-shaped when formed, with the other cheek pattern and heel pattern separate. It is generally made in 4 separate pieces if three or four sides pitch.

These principles usually apply also to transitions that are C/F (center flare) one way or both ways. However, if some of these patterns can be combined without consuming too much layout time, it will reduce the cutting, notching, forming, and seaming operations.

Although transitions with 1, 2, 3, or 4 sides pitching are sometimes made in one piece, this is not the general practice in many shops---since they are usually small, are used in residential work, and are developed because they are used as standard fittings to be used in many residential installations.

Laying Out Transitions

When making transitions, triangulation is necessary. Some of the fittings that require triangulation only need it for one pattern, while

Helpful Fabrication Information 358.

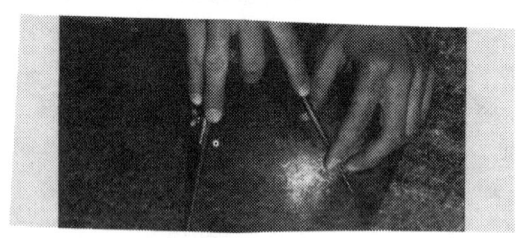

Fig. 3 - Using dividers to set up a true length triangle.

others need it for more than one pattern or for all patterns. Triangulation is the sheet metal layout method which uses right angles (or triangles) to determine true lengths. Stating it another way, triangulation is using true lengths. The basic steps include:

1. Layout the Working View (usually Top View or Plan View).
2. Determine the necessary true length or lengths.
3. Develop the pattern or patterns.

On many transitions, the true length or lengths come out automatically from the flat cheek or heel pattern. However, when all sides pitch, it is necessary to determine the true lengths.

The two most common methods for determining true lengths of patterns of transitions with 3 or 4 sides pitching, all basically using the triangulation principle, are:

1. Using dividers to layout the true length triangles using the two known dimensions and measuring the third dimension with the dividers. Frequently the lines are not drawn and the dividers are just used to locate the points and mark the arcs. See Fig. 3.

2. Using a square and rule to measure the two known dimensions and then measuring the third dimension. This is used when you want to determine blank sizes of all the patterns before doing any layout. See Fig. 4.

Fig. 4 - Using square and rule to measure 2 known dimensions and then measure the third dimension.

Helpful Fabrication Information

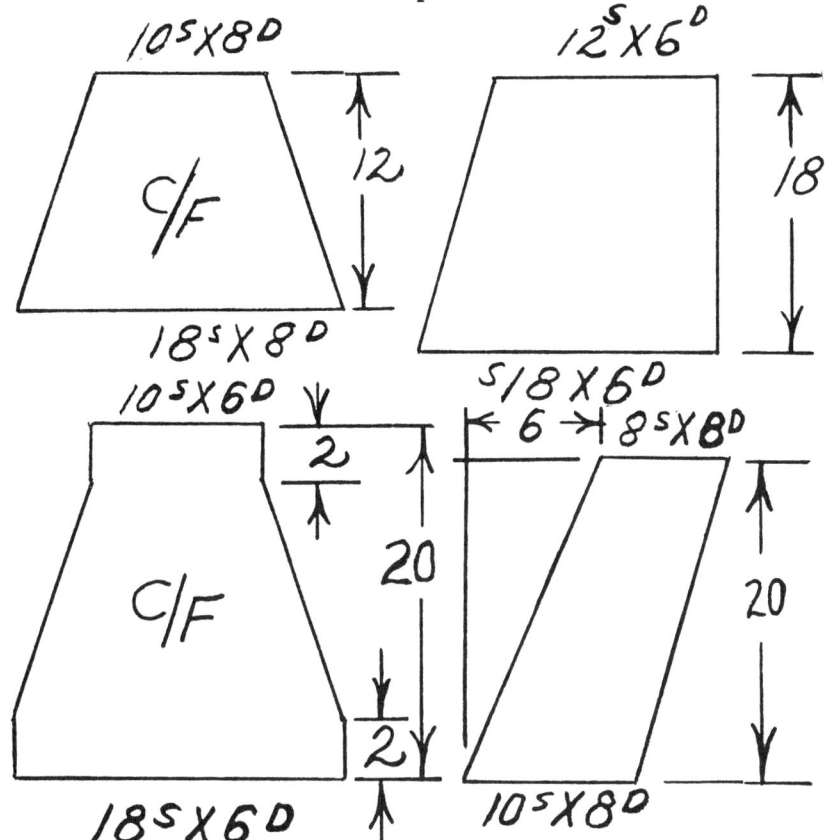

Fig. 5 (above) and **Fig. 6** (next page) - Transitions whose true length or lengths are determined automatically from the flat cheek or heel pattern.

The fittings shown in Fig. 5 are very frequently used fittings. Their true lengths are developed automatically from the flat cheek or heel pattern.

The fittings shown in Fig. 6 are slightly more difficult since they require either the top or bottom cheek pattern to be developed. Again, the true lengths are developed automatically from the flat cheek or heel pattern.

The fittings shown in Fig. 7 are more difficult because all sides are pitching. They require true lengths to be determined for all patterns.

The only difficulty in developing the patterns for these transitions that have all sides pitching is determining the true lengths, which is actually not as difficult as it appears. Sometimes the difficulty arises in a

Helpful Fabrication Information   360.

Fig. 6 - Transitions whose true length or lengths are determined automatically from the flat cheek or heel pattern.

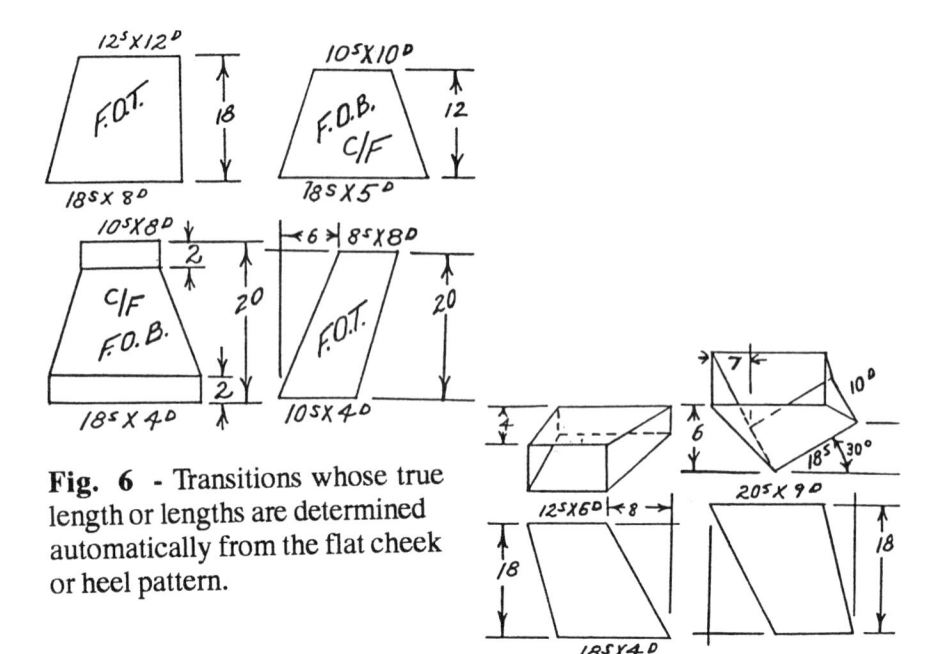

Fig. 7 - Transitions that require true lengths to be determined for all the patterns.

wrong mathematical calculation of the offset (pitch or drop) necessary for the true length triangle or triangles. This is merely adding and subtracting the numbers that represent the dimensions of the fitting such as wrapper or cheek size, pitch or drop, and determining unstated offsets. Such an error can cause a pattern to be too long or too short. However, this might not be noticed while developing the patterns because they would still be the correct basic shape.

When using dividers to determine true lengths, determine each true length as it is needed rather than laying out all the true lengths at once. This avoids confusion especially when numerous true lengths are needed.

The number of true lengths required generally depends on whether or not the fitting is C/F both ways, one way, or not at all. When laying out the working view, be sure to number or letter all points.

Determining Exact Cut Sizes of Patterns for Transitions

If you are determining the exact cut sizes for the patterns before laying them out, you can use a square and rule to determine the true length or true lengths. Determining the cut sizes greatly reduces the layout time required.

Although this method may at first seem difficult to understand, once it is mastered for determining exact cut sizes, it will pay in time saved over and over again. There is a reluctance by some people to use this method, mainly because it involves dealing with math, although it is only addition and subtraction of whole numbers and fractions.

When laying out the patterns, all layout lines and forming information should be kept to the inside of the fitting. Therefore, it is sometimes difficult to visualize the position of a pattern as it should be laid out from the inside. Like anything else, the more you do something, the easier it becomes. This system is used by many contractors that have a large volume of shop work each day.

As you know, the layout of transitions is not as complicated as some people think. After determining the true lengths of one or more dimensions, the traditional pattern development methods are used. The mistakes made are usually not due to a lack of layout ability or understanding. Rather, they are usually due to not taking enough time to properly visualize the plan and the layout of the patterns so they are consistently to the inside of the fitting when it is formed and assembled.

Marking, Forming and Assembling Patterns

When marking transitions, mark the opening or duct sizes to the outside or inside of each piece so that the fitting is assembled correctly.

Determining the Amount to Kink Cheek and Heel Patterns for Transitions: When marking and forming transition patterns, a good practice is to mark the amount the ends of the patterns should be kinked up or down, using inches to designate the amount of kink. The amount of kink is the same as the pitch, drop or offset.

Helpful Fabrication Information 362.

To determine the amount of kink on the transition with three sides straight in Fig. 8, observe the side to which the pattern is to be attached; the difference between the openings is the amount of kink.

Heel Pattern Kink:

12" size of opening
- 8" size of opening

4" amount of kink

8ˢ X 6ᴰ

18

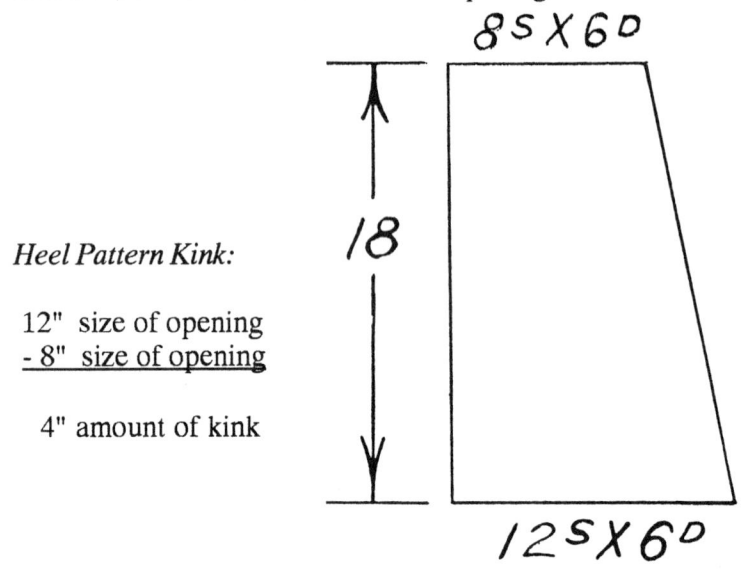

12ˢ X 6ᴰ

Fig. 8 - Transition with 3 sides straight--with forming calculation.

Heel Pattern Kink:

12" size of opening
-10" size of opening
2" amount of kink

Developed Top Cheek Kink:

8" size of opening
- 5" size of opening
3" amount of kink

10ˢ X 8ᴰ

18

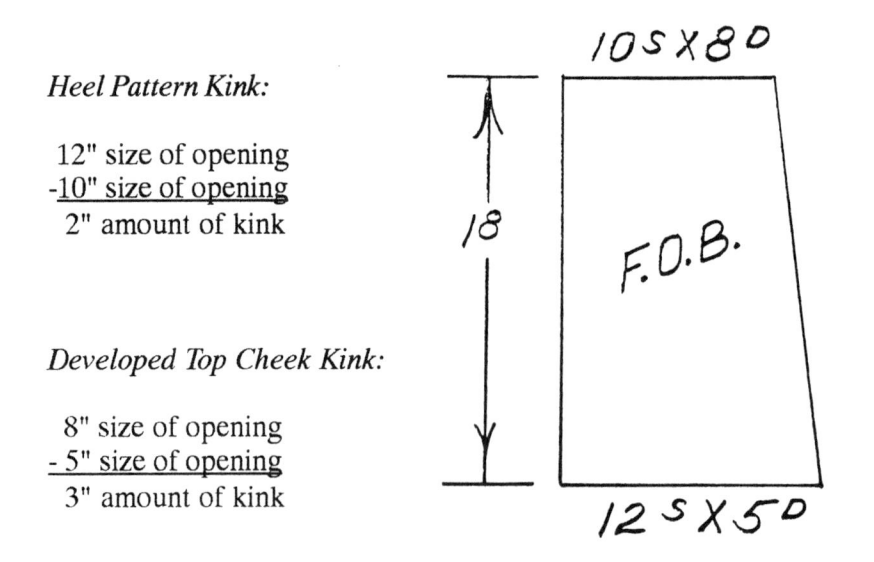

F.O.B.

12ˢ X 5ᴰ

Fig. 9 - Transition with 2 sides straight--with forming calculations.

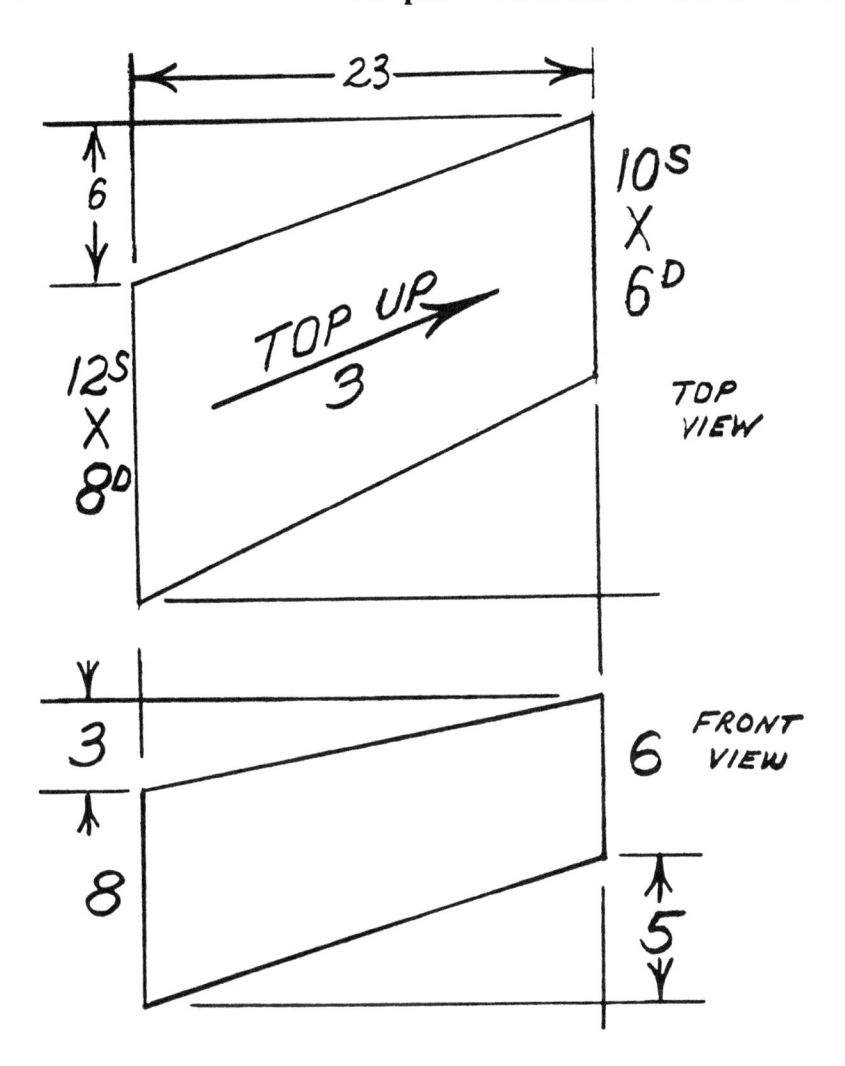

363.   **Helpful Fabrication Information**

[Top view: 23 wide, 6 offset at left, left end 12^S × 8^D, right end 10^S × 6^D, TOP UP 3]

[Front view: left end 8, right end 6, with 3 offset at top left and 5 at bottom right]

Bottom Cheek Kink:

  3" top cheek pitch
 +8" size of opening
 11"
 - 6" opposite opening
  5" amount of kink

Other heel pattern kink:

  6" offset
+12" size of opening
 18"
-10" opposite opening
  8" amount of kink

Fig. 10 - Transition with all sides pitching--with forming calculations.

Helpful Fabrication Information

To determine the amount of kink on the heel pattern and the developed cheek pattern for the transition with two sides straight in Fig. 9, find the difference between the opening sizes.

The amount of kink on the bottom cheek on the transition with all sides tapering shown in Fig. 10 is determined in the front view by adding the amount the top cheek drops or pitches to the size of the opening, and then subtracting the opposite opening.

Using the Hand Brake to Kink for Transitions: The common method for kinking patterns of transitions is to form them by eye on the hand brake. However, to be exact, and especially when using heavy gauge metal, you can measure from the floor. First measure from the lower jaw of the brake where the metal rests against the floor. Then measure from the other end of the formed pattern at the 1" line where the bend will be to the floor.

When kinked the correct amount, the difference in these two measurements will be the required amount of kink as shown in Fig. 11. When kinking the other end of the pattern, measure in the same manner.

When forming the single edges on cheeks of transitions that have a great amount of pitch, drop or offset in relation to the overall height of the transition, it might be necessary to form the single edge less or more than 90°, depending on the fitting, so that it will fit into the Pittsburgh seam properly.

Making a Twisted Transition: Although this fitting is seldom made today, it is occasionally necessary. Twisted transition fittings, as shown in Fig. 12, are considered the most complex type of transition to layout because:

1. Often it is difficult to visualize what it looks like, as well as to field measure and draw it.
2. Many different true lengths are needed to develop the patterns.
3. The position of all the patterns is determined from the inside since all layout lines are usually to the inside of the fitting.
4. Determining the auxiliary kink lines is difficult since they are often not shown on the working drawing.
5. Often diagonal lines from the corners are drawn on the Working Drawing to designate the openings, causing confusion.

365.   **Helpful Fabrication Information**

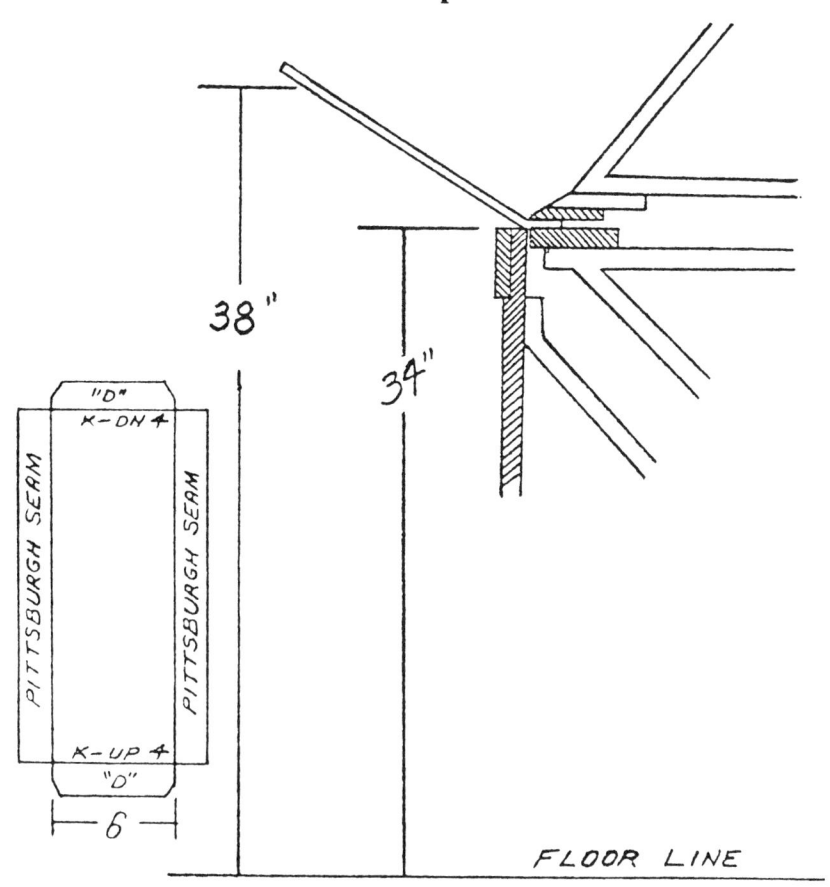

Fig. 11 - Using the hand brake to kink a pattern exactly. The pattern that is being formed is to be kinked 6". Since the distance from the lower jaw of the brake to the floor is 34" in this case, then the distance from the other end of the pattern must be 38" as shown.

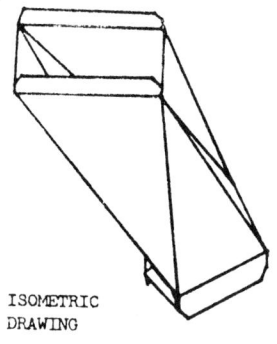

ISOMETRIC DRAWING

Fig. 12 - Twisted transition. Although this fitting is very seldom made today, it is occasionally necessary. They are considered the most complex type of layout.

Helpful Fabrication Information 366.

If you are required to make a twisted transition and it is difficult for you to visualize the patterns from the inside, a good suggestion is to make all the patterns to the outside. In this way, you will have consistency. Never make one pattern to the outside and another to the inside. Remember to mark the patterns correctly.

Determining Auxiliary Kink Lines and the Amount to be Kinked: When making transitions that are radical, use additional or auxiliary (extra) kink lines on the patterns to facilitate assembly.

Doing this successfully is a matter of experience. One aid in learning where to use auxiliary kink lines is to draw miniature or scaled drawings of the patterns on a sheet of paper, cut them out, and crease them where you think the kink lines should be. This can be a great aid, especially until you have gained some experience in doing this type of fitting.

A common method used to determine the amount of kink is to line up the pattern being kinked with the appropriate opening on the Top View, which was used to determine the true lengths. The first time you kink the pattern, it is better to kink it less than the amount required and then gradually kink it more until you get the correct amount.

Although this is a "trial-and-error" method, it is the most commonly used method.

How to Avoid Mistakes

Before doing any layout, be sure you can sketch or visualize the type of transition required.

When determining the unstated pitch, drop or offset, re-check your math calculations so that all dimensions add up correctly before laying out, cutting or forming the patterns.

Complete all the layout on all patterns of the transition. Before cutting them out or forming them, check the lengths of the sides that will be attached to each other to see that they are exactly the same length.

All layout lines and marking information should be consistently placed on the inside of the patterns. In this way, all lines and marking information will be to the inside of the fitting when the patterns are formed and assembled.

When assembling a transition, follow the opening or duct sizes that have been marked on the inside or outside of each piece so the fitting is assembled correctly. If the Working Drawing is marked "K.D.", temporarily tack the fitting together in the corners so that no confusion will arise on the job site.

Summary

Remember that our mistakes when making transitions are usually not due to a lack of layout ability or understanding. They are usually due to not taking enough time to properly visualize and plan the layout of the patterns so they are consistently to the inside of the fitting when it is formed and assembled. Therefore, we see that taking a little time to plan will save a lot of time later.

#5 - Combining Patters to Save Time

When laying out fittings, combining patterns is considered a shortcut because it eliminates some of the cutting, notching and seaming operations. This reduces the time required to fabricate the fittings.

Just as we have learned to use a minimum of layout lines, we should also get into the habit of combining patterns whenever practical and possible. When making pipe or duct, we are all aware of the different ways in which the pieces can be laid out: one piece, L-shaped, U-shaped, 4 pieces, or many pieces due to extra large pipe or duct. Making the decision of which way to make the pipe becomes second-nature to us due to the frequency of the operation. We know that the size and length of the pipe determine the number of pieces to use.

When most people are first learning to layout fittings, their sole concern is to layout each pattern accurately so that all patterns fit together correctly when they are formed. Frequently, little or no

Helpful Fabrication Information

emphasis is placed upon the idea of combining patterns. It is naturally difficult to change our habits. However, if we remember to consider the possibility of combining patterns before starting to layout each fitting, this process will also become "second nature" to us.

When we consider the amount of time saved by eliminating some of the cutting, notching and seaming operations, we see that the short time it takes to plan to combine patterns is very worthwhile.

As you look at the fittings illustrated in this section, you can see that they are fittings that are frequently-used today. As you examine their patterns, you can see the amount of time that can be saved by combining patterns.

Whether Or Not to Combine Patterns

First, consider whether or not it is possible to combine patterns of the fitting to be made. For example, the fittings illustrated in this section comprise a majority of the frequently-used fittings where combining patterns is possible.

Second, consider whether or not it is practical to combine patterns of the fitting to be made. Although there are fittings not illustrated in this section that can have their patterns combined, they are not practical due to the extensive amount of layout time.

FACTORS TO CONSIDER WHEN COMBINING PATTERNS:

1. Size of the fitting
2. Time saved
3. Quantity required
4. Lined (insulated) fitting
5. Wasted material

Size of the Fitting: When making small and medium-sized fittings used in residential work and some commercial and industrial work, you should be able to combine the pattern of the fittings illustrated in this section.

When making large fittings, the amount of time saved in reducing the cutting, notching and seaming operations is lost. This is due to the difficulty in handling the large patterns; it might require the assistance of another person to help in the handling while it is being formed.

When a fitting is to be welded, it is usually the general practice to combine patterns as much as possible, regardless of their size. The time it would take to weld additional seams outweighs the extra time in handling large patterns.

Time Saved: Compare the extra time required to layout the combined pattern to the time saved in reduced cutting, notching and seaming operations. If the amount of time to be saved is greater, it is worthwhile to combine patterns. Then if more than one of the same fitting is needed, it becomes even more advantageous to combine patterns.

When making some fittings, it is not economical to combine patterns but when making several of the same fitting, it becomes economical.

Quantity Required: Combining patterns is particularly helpful and saves time and labor if you are doing residential or commercial work that justifies developing master patterns because the same size and type of fitting will be used many times. This is possible where all houses or apartments will have identical systems; or in commercial work where all floors are typical, which is often the case today. Here again, taking a little time to plan ahead by examining the blueprints or shop drawings will more than pay for itself.

Lined (Insulated) Fittings: When the fittings are to be lined (insulated), several factors must be considered if you combine patterns. Unless you have a press brake, the pins or grip nails that hold the insulation to the fitting must be far enough away from the bend lines of the fitting so they do not interfere with the upper beam of the hand brake.

If a press brake is used, no problems arise because the pins or grip nails that hold the lining to the inside of the fitting do not interfere with the press brake dies unless they are very close to the bend lines of the pattern.

When lining is required, seldom is the fitting made in one pattern due to the extra amount of time that would be necessary to attach the insulation before or after forming the bend lines. If the lining is attached by gluing alone, these forming problems do not arise.

Helpful Fabrication Information 370.

Considering Wasted Material: Some people are hesitant about combining patterns because material is wasted due to the shape of the combined pattern. Usually, the amount of wasted material is small in comparison to the time saved in reducing the cutting, notching, and seaming operations. Today's labor rates outweigh the cost of the wasted material.

Getting Into the Habit of Combing Patterns

Some people are reluctant to combine patterns. They lack confidence because of insufficient layout knowledge and experience. In most cases, this layout is not very difficult, as you can see in the illustrations with this section.

The first time you combine patterns on a more difficult fitting, you might find it helpful to check in a sheet metal layout book to determine how a certain point is obtained.

Until you get used to combining patterns, it might seem easier to make separate patterns because you are familiar with this method. However, it is important to consider combining patterns since these fittings are used so frequently.

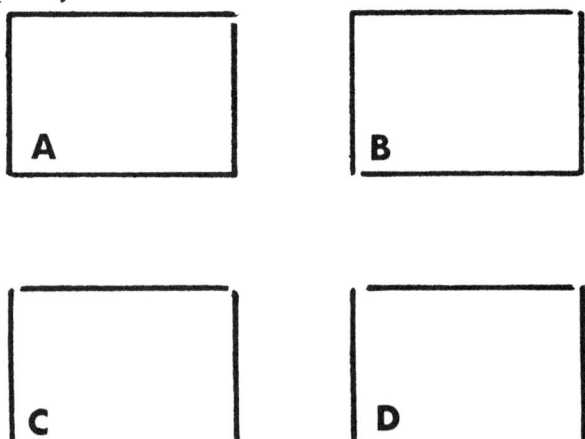

Fig. 1 - The size and length of a pipe determine the number of pieces to use:
      A) one piece wrap around
      B) two pieces L-shaped
      C) two piece U-shaped
      D) four pieces

371.   **Helpful Fabrication Information**

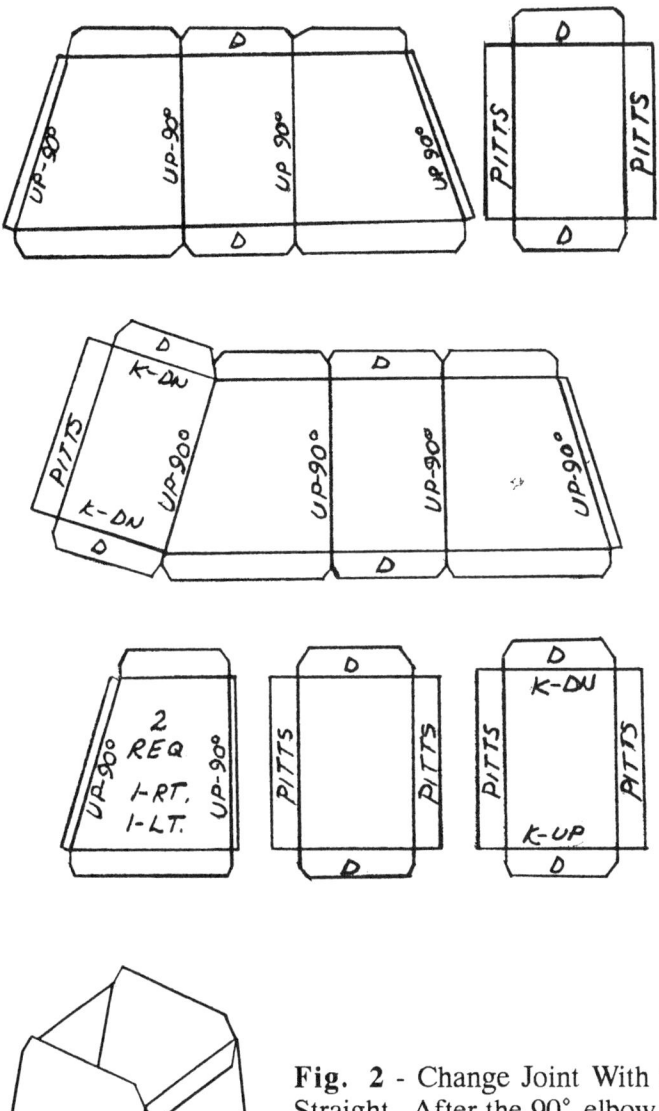

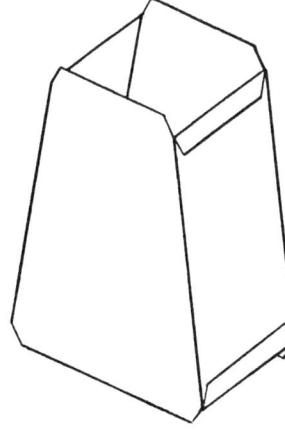

Fig. 2 - Change Joint With 3 Sides Straight. After the 90° elbow, this is the most commonly used fitting. Combining the patterns minimizes cutting, notching and seaming. This change joint is shown with partially combined patterns (cheeks and heel pattern); one-piece pattern; separate patterns.

Helpful Fabrication Information 372.

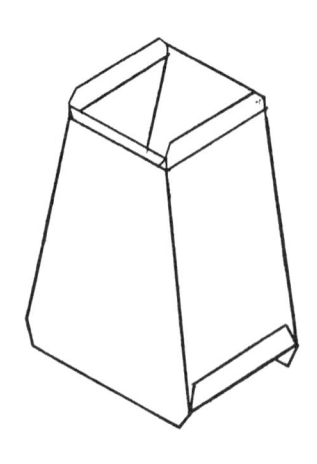

Fig. 3 - Change Joint Center Flare With 2 Sides Straight. The pattern or patterns for this change joint with partially combined patterns (cheek and heels pattern); one-piece pattern; and separate patterns, can be similar to the patterns for the change joint in Fig. 2.

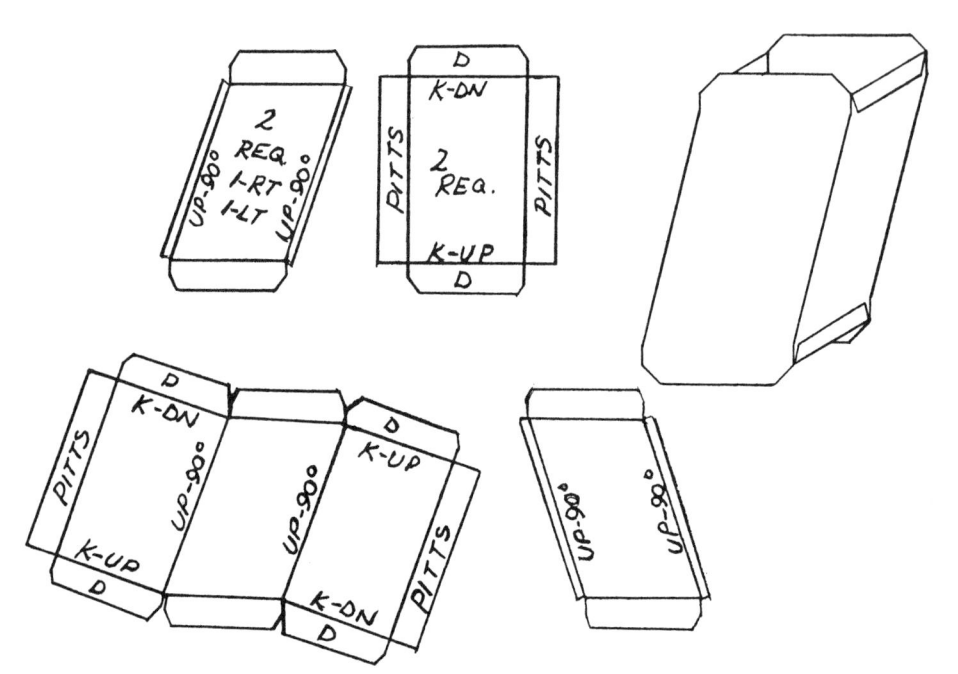

Fig. 4 - Offset With Straight Heels. Combining the patterns minimizes cutting, notching and seaming. This offset is shown with separate patterns and partially combined patterns (cheek and heels pattern). It can be made as a one-piece pattern (not shown).

373.   Helpful Fabrication Information

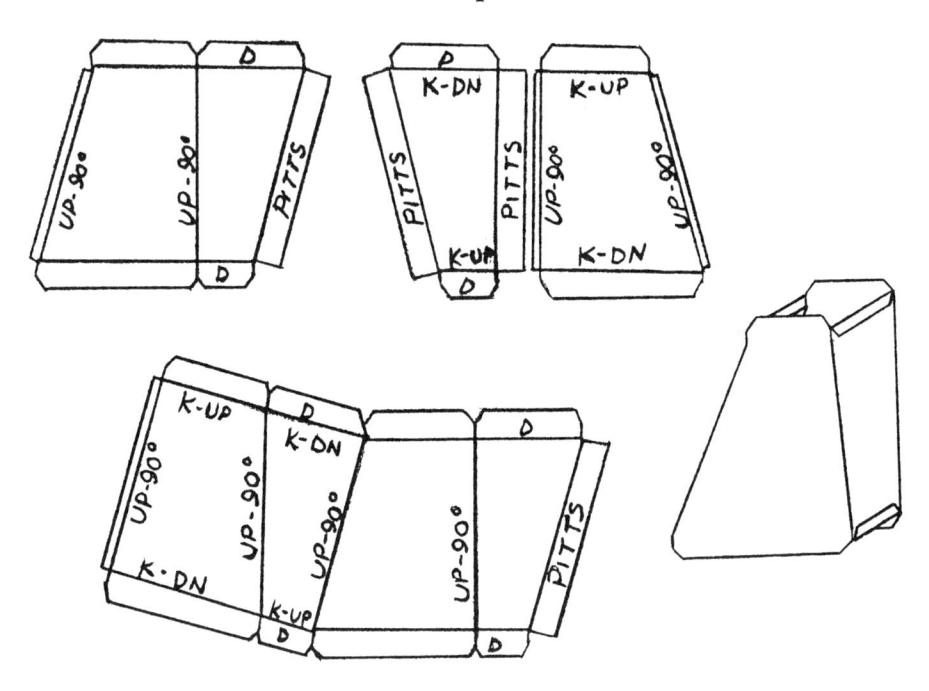

Fig. 5 - Transition Change Joint With 2 Sides Straight. Combining the patterns minimizes cutting, notching and seaming. This change joint is shown with partially combined patterns (cheek and heel pattern) and one piece pattern. If this fitting is large, it might be made as four separate patterns (not shown).

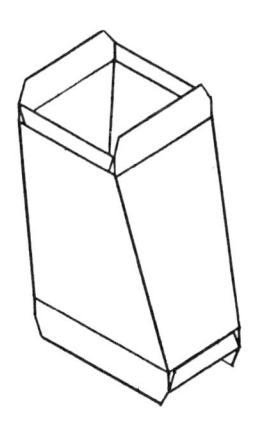

Fig. 6 - Transition change Joint Center Flare With 1 Side Straight. The pattern or patterns for this transition joint can be similar to the patterns for the transition change joint shown in Fig. 5 with partially combined patterns and one piece pattern.

Helpful Fabrication Information 374.

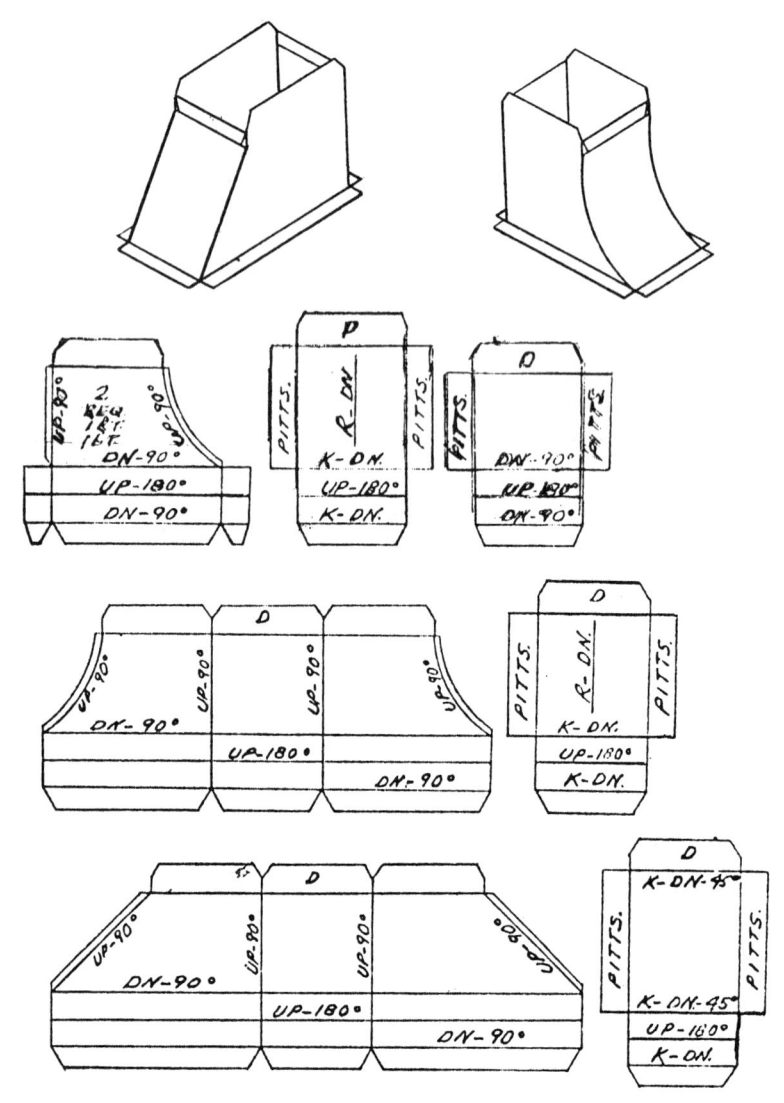

Fig. 7 - 90° Clinch Tees - one with curved throat and straight back and one with straight throat and back. Considerable time can be saved in the cutting, notching and seaming when a combined pattern can be made. Even more time can be saved by combining patterns if the clinch tees must be lined or insulated. Patterns can be combined if open corners are permitted, or if the corners as shown above are attached. This clinch tee is shown with separate patterns (curved throat); partially combined patterns (curved throat) with combined cheeks and heel pattern; and partially combined patterns (straight throat) with combined cheeks and heel pattern. Using straight throat at 45° angle is increasing in use today.

375.   **Helpful Fabrication Information**

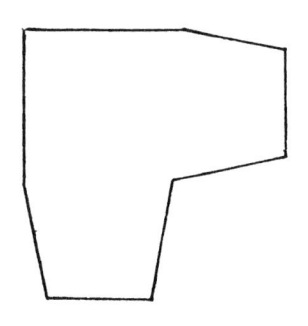

Fig. 8 - Corners For Clinch Tees. When closed corners are required on clinch tees, you can save much time by making them with open corners, thereby letting you combine the patterns. Then attach corners like the one shown. They can be made in large quantity and used as needed. They can be attached by riveting or welding. If closed corners are required, a little time spent on perfecting this small operation will pay for itself in a short time.

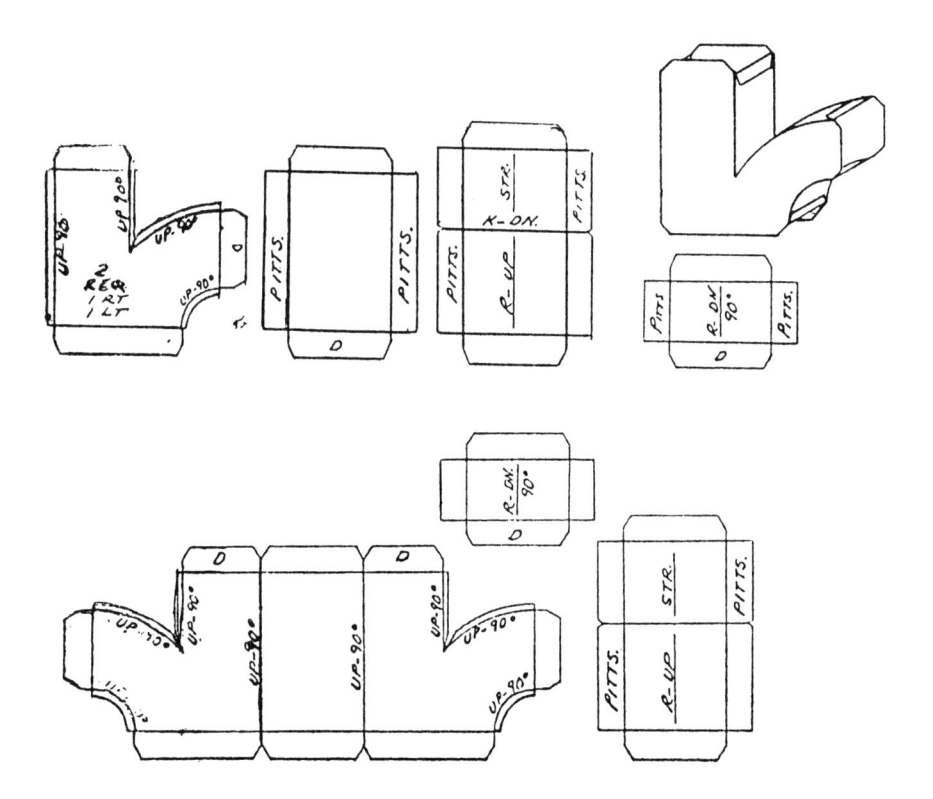

Fig. 9 - 90° One-Way Y-Branch With Curved Throat and Combined Straight and Curved Heel. This Y-Branch is shown with five separate patterns and partially combined patterns (cheeks and heel pattern). If this fitting is large, it is usually made in five separate patterns due to the difficulty in turning the single edges on the cheek patterns.

Helpful Fabrication Information

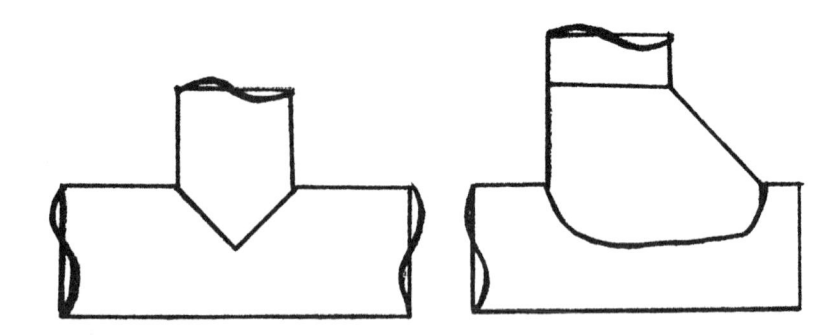

376.

Fig. 10 - Comparison Of Whether Or Not To Combine Patterns. When making round fittings, it is occasionally better to not make a one-piece pattern, such as the boot tee on the right. In this case, two half patterns are just as quick due to extra layout time required if it were to be made in one piece. When making a plain tee, such as the tee on the left, one complete pattern does not require any more layout time than a half pattern.

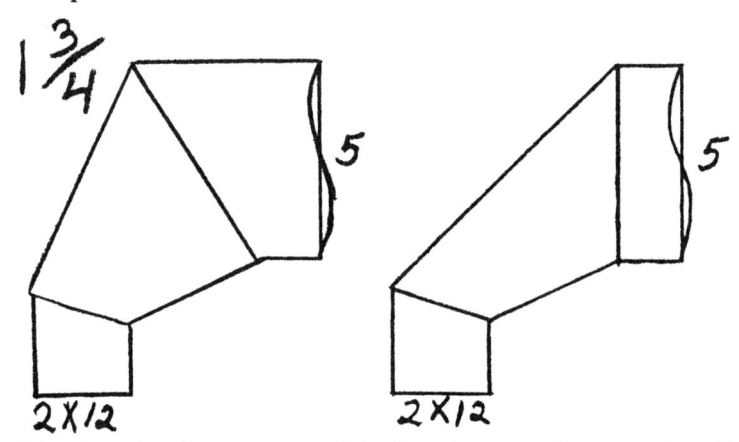

Fig. 11 - Another factor to consider is to keep each separate pattern in a fitting as easy to layout as possible. For example, the fitting on the right requires development for only two patterns with the third pattern being a plain collar. It can be made as just one developed pattern plus the collar. However, on this fitting, the heel on the bottom pattern must be made high enough that the air will still flow properly so the air is not "choked." A fitting like this is seldom made today because it can be purchased in stock sizes for residential work. However, the principle of keeping patterns as simple to layout as possible can certainly be kept in mind when some types of sheet metal fittings have to be made, as well as when some specialty items have to be made.

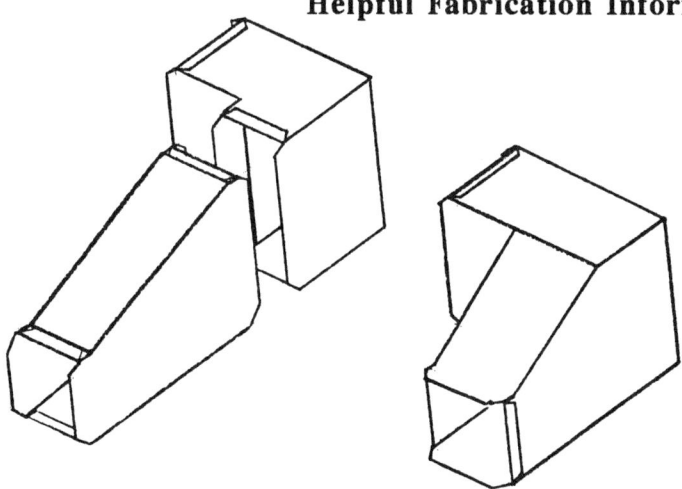

Fig. 12 - Combining patterns to use one fitting rather than two fittings is also a factor to consider whenever practical. Keep in mind that the extra amount of layout time will reduce field connection time, as well as eliminating much of the cutting, notching, forming, and seaming operations. Although the fitting on the right might appear difficult to layout, it is comparably easy. A transition change elbow with curved heel and throat can also be used but requires more layout knowledge than the one fitting shown on the right. Here again, you must use your own judgement.

#6 - Making Large Ductwork Economically

Design for Appearance or Economy

By glancing through the section *"Large Fittings Used Today,"* you can see the various alternatives you can use within certain types of fittings. Basically the two different alternatives show one method for economy of material and use of scrap, and the other method for design appearance.

When making large fittings, it is necessary to do some initial planning in regard to the method of seaming, seam location, and the number of pieces for each pattern. An excellent method is to first sketch the primary view (which in many cases is the cheek) on scrap paper, and determine how many pieces you will need to make up the complete wrapper or wrappers pattern.

Helpful Fabrication Information 378.

Economical Pattern Layouts

A factor to consider when determining design appearance or economy of material is: will it be necessary to attach angle iron on the fitting in the field after assembly, or would it be more economical to have the seams located equal to distribute the rigidity evenly. See Figs. 1-2.

Depending on the size of the fitting required, you can sometimes develop the patterns so the actual kink lines are placed where the standing seam is placed. This not only provides better appearance; but it is also much stronger. If you are going to kink it across the standing seam, the seam must be sliced in order to permit kinking and then reinforced with band iron.

Also, depending on the amount of drop or pitch (difference between wrapper sizes), you can make the developed cheek pattern in several gores or pieces and not need any kink lines except for the ends. The amount of drop or pitch (difference in wrapper sizes) in relationship to the amount of throat radius determines whether or not it is possible to fabricate easily. When forming the seams, the single and double seams should not be formed.

Plan for Usable Scrap

Being thoroughly familiar with all available sheet sizes, widths and lengths in your shop can prove to be helpful in planning the most economical use of material. It can also save some labor due to providing a minimum amount of seaming and cutting. However, sometimes design appearance takes precedence. Depending on the type you are making, the scrap is still frequently usable.

Marking Patterns

When planning the number of pieces within a completed pattern or part, marking all patterns and their seam locations is very important. Frequently, the pieces of patterns are assembled while out in the field. When it takes many pieces to make up one cheek or wrapper, having the pieces marked can certainly save time, confusion and mistakes.

379.   **Helpful Fabrication Information**

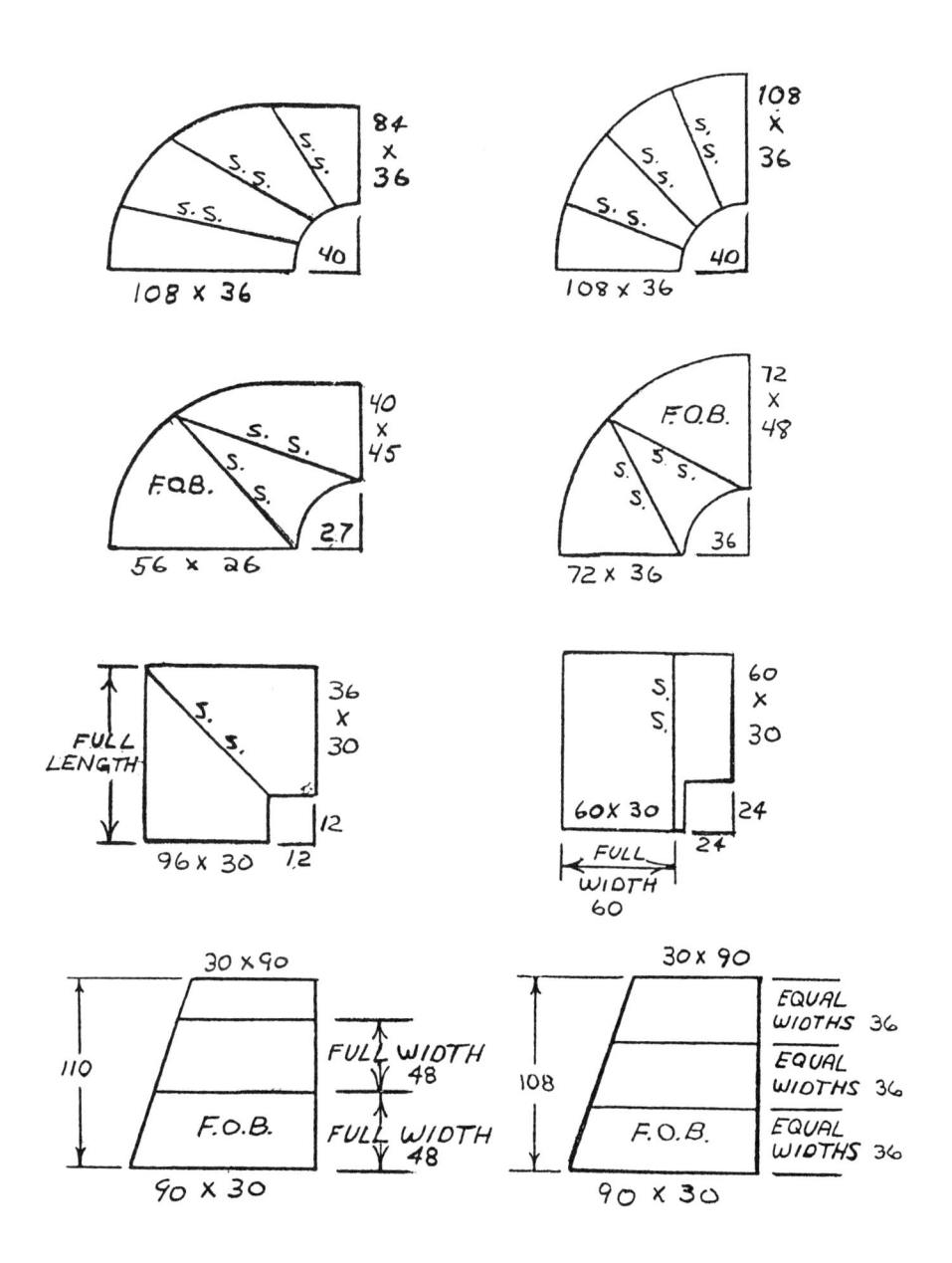

Fig. 1 - Examples of the Most Economical Pattern Layouts
(to best utilize full sheets of metal)

Helpful Fabrication Information 380.

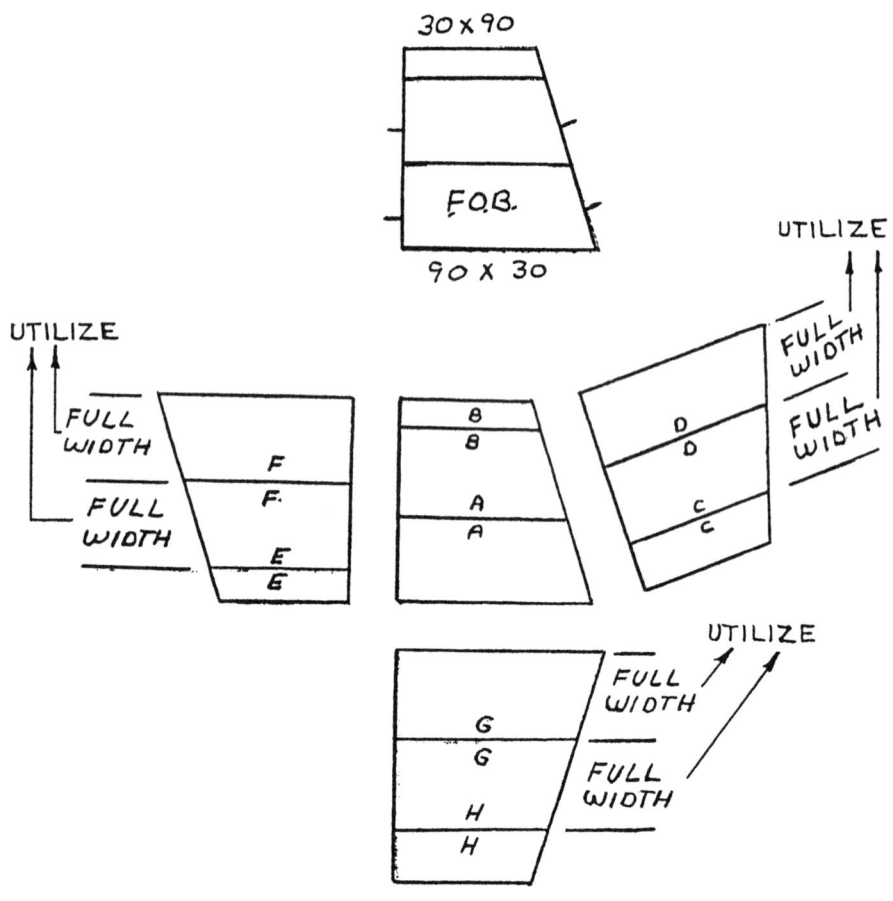

Fig. 2 - Determining Seam Locations to Best Utilize the Full Width of Each Sheet of Metal

Reduced Scale Drawings

On some types of large fittings, it is necessary or helpful to layout a reduced scale of the pattern which is usually a cheek pattern. This reduced scale drawing is often made directly on a piece of sheet metal. If it is a plain radius 90° elbow, the scale drawn can help you determine the miter line that can be laid out from a standard sheet using dimensions you can take off your scale drawing and multiply by the appropriate number. This can provide a big saving in time and labor since it can be done at the shear. The important point when making the shearing list is to draw the seams on the working sketch or drawing and number the pieces.

Helpful Fabrication Information

When making a curved change elbow or curved transition change elbow, due to size it is often necessary to make a scale drawing to determine true lengths as well as the positions of seams.

Working Off a Sheet

In some cases by positioning a square on the outside of the sheet and at the correct angle, it becomes possible to layout an elbow or angle cheek utilizing the width of the cheek so well that the radius is drawn off the sheet. The following are two practical methods you can use to determine if this method is possible:

1. If you are working on a standard 4' x 10' bench, you can lay the square on part of the bench, line up two straight edges along the blades of the square, and measure it off. If the sheets are larger or smaller than the bench you have available, you can still use the approximation method.

2. A more exact method is to make a reduced scale pattern and place it on top of a reduced scale of the standard sheet you have available.

Always consider this method of layout due to the labor cost that can be saved by eliminating much of the cutting, notching, and seaming operations. The only disadvantage is that the scrap is frequently unusable.

Types of Seams

There are a variety of different types of seams that you can use to assemble large fittings, such as an acme lock, grooved lock, hammer lock and riveted lap seam. However, today these are seldom used. The most frequently used seam is the standing seam, since it is easy to fabricate in the shop or field and adds rigidity to the overall fitting.

Seam Allowances

When using standing seams in making a complete pattern, you have to notch 1/8" into the actual section of the pattern; this allows for the growth or thickness of the standing seam from 18 to 24 ga. To better

Helpful Fabrication Information 382.

understand this, look at the large rectangular duct in the section "Large Fittings Most Frequently Used". Add the dimensions, omitting seaming dimensions. You will find that for each standing seam, the overall pieces when added are 1/8" short; when seams are formed and put together, they make up the additional 1/8" that is needed.

Material Sizes Available

For overall material economy, you should try to utilize the full widths and lengths of sheets that are in stock---36", 48" or 60" wide. If the shop has a coil line set-up, you can use any length so long as you have the machinery available for forming it.

Positioning of Sheets for Layout

Positioning of the sheets of metal is very important to the overall layout of the fitting with regard to where to have the standing seams for strength and appearance. When laying out the fittings on the bench, the sheets can be overlapping each other so that two or more pieces can be laid out and marked in proper sequence. Allow 3" within the sheet for the standing seam. See Figs. 3-4.

Housings

When planning the seam locations of a housing, marking the information on the patterns is very important, particularly due to the number of similar types of patterns. The little extra time it takes for planning will more than pay for the time that will be saved when it comes to assemble the housing in the field. For appearance, the marking of sizes and seams should be to the inside of the patterns. However, if the fitting is going to be lined or insulated, all markings except forming information should be to the outside.

Many people are reluctant to make elbows and angles in equal degree gore pieces. Like anything else, when you are not familiar with certain principles, the job or task seems much more difficult than it actually is. One of the best methods for developing confidence in making gore patterns in equal degree is to sketch a fitting on paper and mark it with large dimensions. Then make the fitting on paper 1/8 actual size and

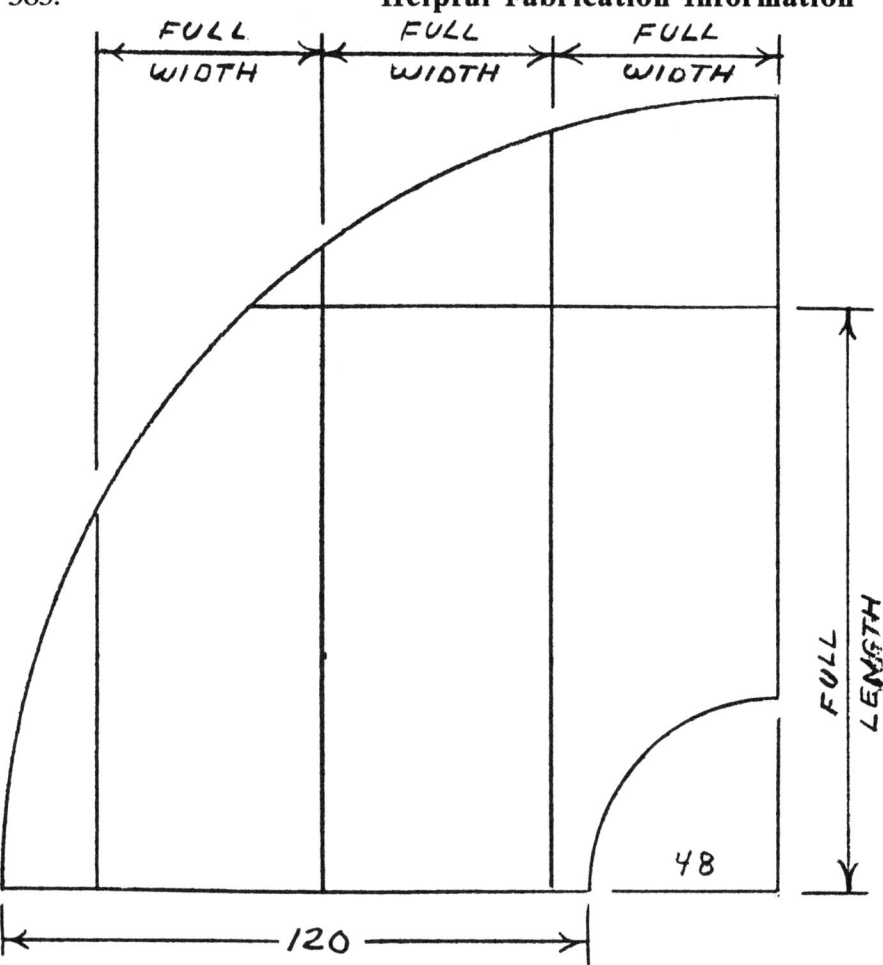

Fig. 3 - Utilizing the Full Length and Width of as Many Sheets as Possible

develop the gore patterns just as you would if you were making the actual full-size fitting in the shop.

Reinforcing Large Ductwork

Large ductwork requires additional reinforcing due to its weight and the volume of air flow. Check with state and local building codes pertaining to the heating and ventilating standards. When reinforcing is required on all four sides, it must be tied together at each corner by riveting, bolting or welding. When reinforcing is required on only two

Helpful Fabrication Information 384.

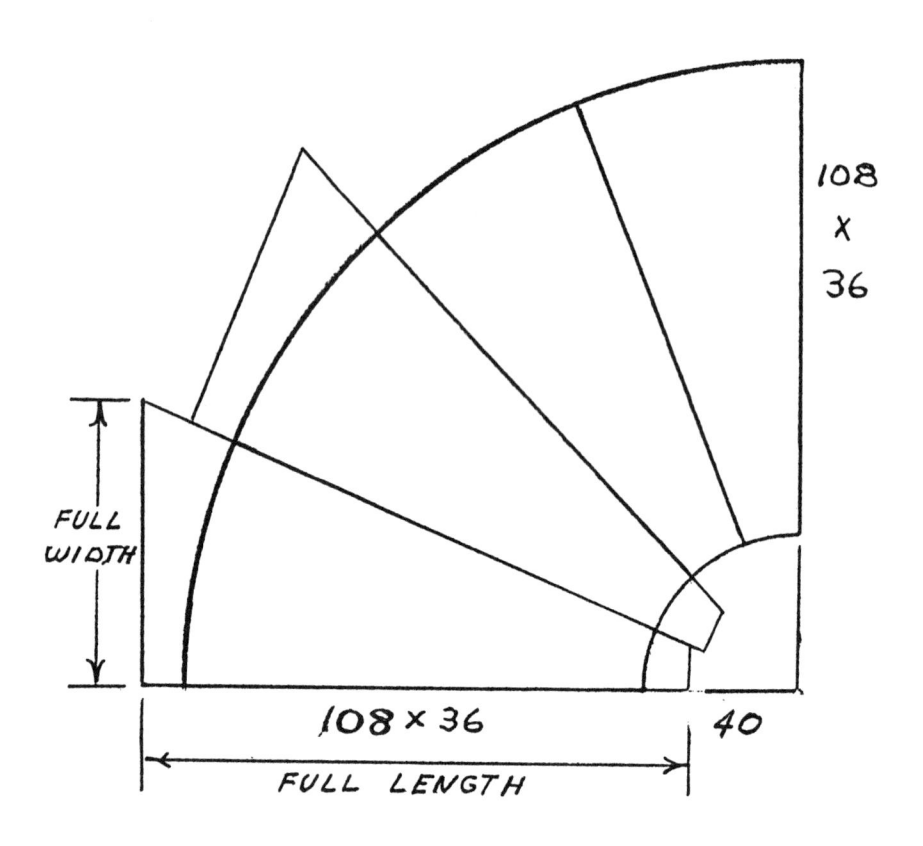

(Figure showing gore pattern layout with dimensions: 108 x 36 marked on upper right, FULL WIDTH on left side, 108 x 36 and 40 along the bottom, with FULL LENGTH indicated.)

Fig. 4 - Layout Patterns Using a Separate Sheet of Metal for Each Gore Pattern

sides, it must be tied together with either tie rods or angles at the ends. The reinforcing size is determined by the dimension of the side of which the angle is applied. Angle sizes are based on mild steel. Reinforcing made in other shapes or of other materials must be equivalent in strength and rigidity. There is no restriction on the length of duct sections between joints. Ducts are normally made in sections 4', 5', 8' and 10' in length.

Tie rods up to 36" long should be a minimum of 1/4" diameter. Tie rods 37" long and over should be a minimum of 3/8" diameter. When 2 tie rods are required, install them at each 1/3 point across the duct.

#7 - *Nesting and Combining Fittings*

When first looking at the drawing or drawings for a ductrun system, whether it is residential, commercial or industrial, it appears to be a complex system that is made up of unusual or complicated fittings. However, we know that the majority of these fittings are common basic fittings that have been nested or combined to make up the complete system. This is true regardless of the size of the rectangular system being installed.

Both "nesting" and "combining" fittings are advantageously used in solving some ductrun problems. In some instances, they simply save time; in others, there is no other method that could be used.

The terms "nesting" fittings and "combining" fittings are often used interchangably today. Years ago the term "nesting" was used when referring to fittings that fit exactly against each other, as illustrated in Fig. 1. Now this term is also used when fittings are partially nested, as shown in Fig. 2. The term "combining" fittings refers to using one fitting in the place of two or more fittings, as shown in fig. 3.

Remember that combining patterns within a fitting is different than combining fittings, although their purposes are all the same; to use practical efficiencies when possible to save time or labor in the shop or in the field.

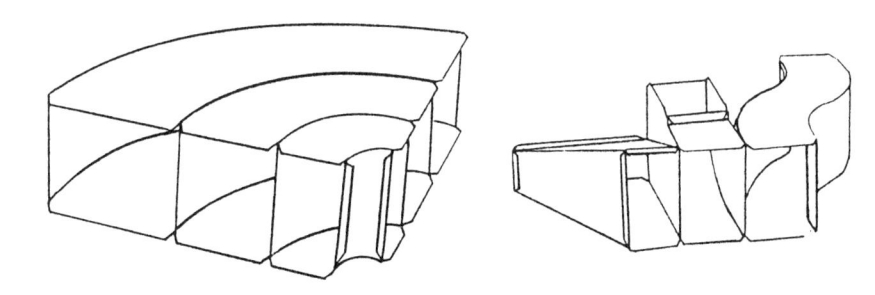

Fig. 1 - Nested fittings that fit exactly against each other

Fig. 2 - Partially nested fittings

Helpful Fabrication Information

Both nesting and combining patterns provide a neat, compact appearance as well as a streamlined look. Also they are often necessary due to space limitations. There are countless ways to combine or nest fittings, as well as to combine patterns. Those illustrated in this section are just a few of the more common ones used. See Figs. 4-6.

Fig. 3 - One combined fitting

Fig. 4 - Common arrangements of nested rectangular fittings.

387. **Helpful Fabrication Information**

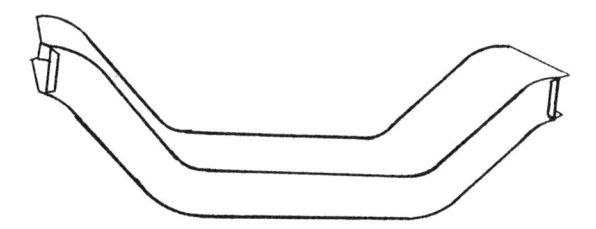

Fig. 5 - Consider the problem above and various solutions available:

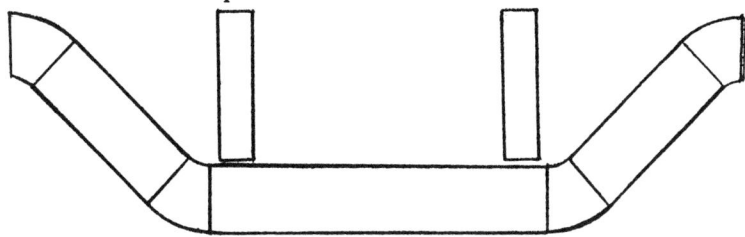

Solution #1 - Takes three pieces of pipe and four angle fittings, plus 12 S cleats and drive cleats. Consider all the time spent cutting the pipe. It certainly adds up to more time than making one fitting.

Solution #2 - Uses One combined fitting to solve ductrun problem.

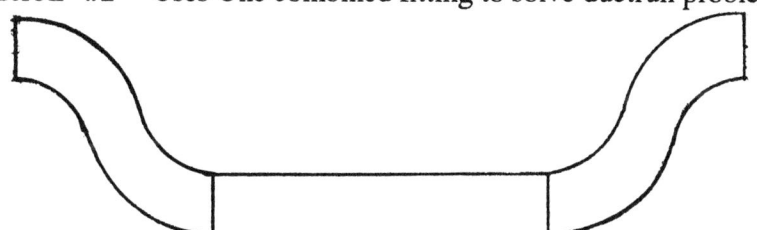

Solution #3 - Uses two offsets and one piece of pipe.

Solution #4 - Uses two offset elbows and one piece of pipe. This solution would probably cause too much resistance in the ductrun system.

Helpful Fabrication Information

Whether Or Not to Nest Or Combine Fittings

It is advantageous to use nesting rather than combining fittings to make one fitting for these reasons:

1. Layout is simplified.
2. Standard fittings can sometimes be purchased or made inexpensively.
3. If there are any changes in the field or job site, you can take care of them more easily; but if it is one combined fitting, it is more difficult to change, if not impossible.

It is frequently better to use one fitting than nest several fittings, but this requires more skilled shop manpower to layout the combined fittings which can be more complex. When nesting fittings, extra field time is required in hooking the fittings together and reinforcing them with heavy commercial and industrial work, it is a good idea to join and reinforce them in the shop. This is particularly true when high pressure systems are being installed.

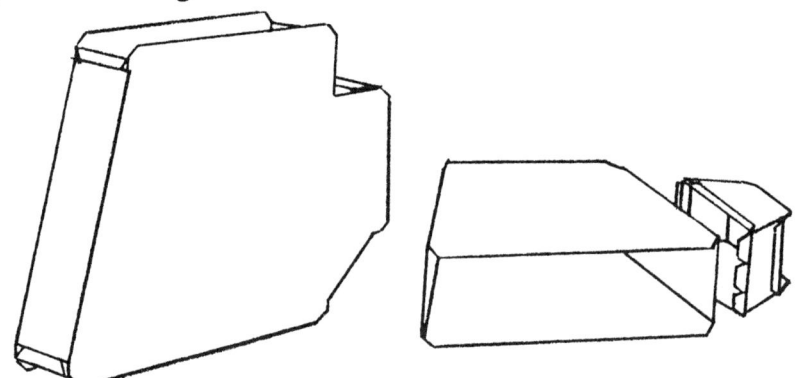

Fig. 6 - When combining fittings, both shop and field time can be saved (this example). However, this cannot be used too often since the heel or wrapper size of the transition would have to be the same as the heel or wrapper size of the take-offs. A disadvantage is that it reduces flexibility when field changes occur. Shop time saved:
1) total of less layout time;
2) less fabrication time because one fitting has fewer pieces than two;
3) less assembly time because of fewer seams; and
4) more time saved when fitting is to be lined or insulated. Field time is saved because it eliminates any measuring or cutting the tee or take-off openings.

Helpful Fabrication Information

Sometimes purchasing the individual fittings from a supply house is less costly than making the one combined fitting in the shop. The total cost of all these fittings is sometimes less than the total cost to make the one fitting because of the high hourly wage rate of sheet metal workers in some parts of the country. Here again, material cost is far less than labor cost. Another consideration is the amount of time it will take to join or tie the fittings together and reinforce them.

Also, many people are reluctant to plan combined fittings because the field measuring must be exact for the fitting to be usable. Here again, the time it takes to do an adequate job of field measuring is certainly worthwhile if the person knows there will be no changes or modifications that would affect the fitting.

If a housing development or apartment complex with identical heating or air conditioning systems is to be built and many of the same fittings will be used, one fitting should be used rather than several fittings. This is also true of commercial jobs where all floors are typical.

Due to the wide range of different labor rates throughout the country, one method is not always advantageous over the other. Sometimes it is not possible to plan ahead. Depending on your geographic location, ordering time does not allow you to purchase manufactured fittings.

Avoid Gaps Between Nested Fittings

When designing or planning a system, one of the most important factors to keep in mind is that the fittings be designed and arranged so it is possible to nest them together. Sometimes this is not anticipated. Then a gap between the fittings will exist, making the overall fittings plus the gap larger than the opening duct or fitting to which you must connect it.

Proportioning Area in Take-Offs

The area for each branch or take-off must be properly proportioned when planning or designing both nested and combined fittings. On some large jobs this has been designated by the architect or engineer; but on some drawings, only the dimension of the main line and the other end of the branches are designated.

Helpful Fabrication Information

To calculate this accurately, compare the total area of the other end of all branches to the area of the main line. Generally, the area of the main line is less and must be divided in proportion to the areas of the branches. This usually is true in ductruns, since making the duct larger slows down the air velocity near the register.

Follow these general steps to proportion the area in the branches (as shown in Fig. 7):

1. Calculate the area of the main line and the total area of the branches.

2. Calculate the percent that the main line area is, compared to the total area of the branches. To do this, divide the main line area by the total of the branches.

3. Multiply this percent by the area of each branch.

4. Divide this number by the depth of the main line to determine the amount of space to be allocated to each branch.

5. Round off these answers either to the nearest inch or 1/2 inch.

Due to the answers being rounded off to the nearest inch or 1/2 inch, the resulting dimensions are not completely accurate. Therefore dampers will be needed.

Other considerations should also be taken into account when determining these dimensions. For example, a short or straight branch might be allocated slightly less than the calculations indicate, while a long or not straight branch (such as 90° turns) might be allocated more than the calculations indicate.

Selection and Location of Dampers

It is necessary to use dampers to help guide and control the air when making most branch fittings, including nested and combined fittings. When take-offs are proportioned exactly, as explained above, fewer dampers are needed since the air is already divided into the correct proportions. However, we usually round off the dimensions to the nearest even inch, so it is usually impossible to balance the system correctly without using dampers.

Helpful Fabrication Information

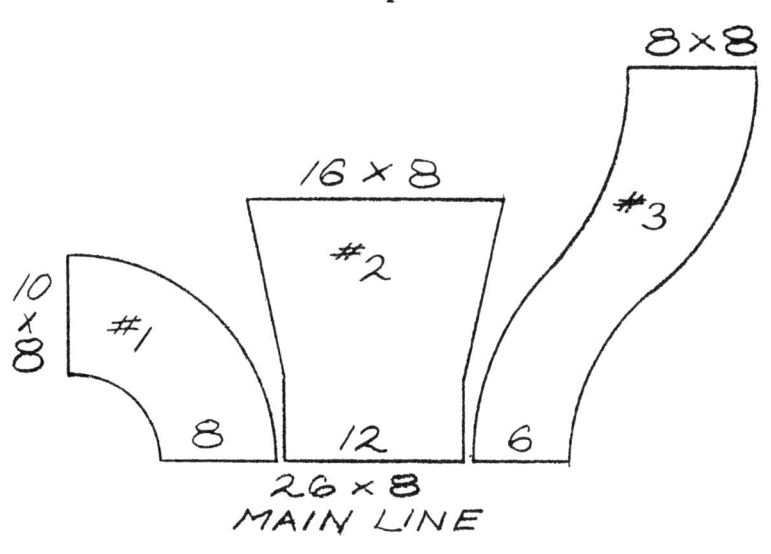

Fig. 7 - Proportioning Area In Take-Offs

Step 1: Main Line Area = 26"x8" = 208 sq. in.
Branch Areas = #1-- 10"x8" = 80 sq. in.
                 #2-- 16"x8" = 128 sq. in.
                 #3-- 8"x8" = 64 sq. in.
                 Total   = 272 sq. in.

Step 2: 208 ÷ 272 = .76   **Step 3:** #1-- 80x.76 = 60.80 sq, in.
                                                      #2--128x.76 = 97.28 sq. in.
                                                      #3-- 64x.76 = 48.64 sq. in.

Step 4:   #1-- 60.80 ÷ 8 = 7.6"
               #2-- 97.28 ÷ 8 = 12.16"   **Step 5:** (nearest inch)
               #3-- 48.64 ÷ 8 = 6.08"   #1 = 8"
                                                                                 #2 = 12"
                                                                                  #3 = 6"
                                                                            Total = 26"

Four common types of dampers are used in rectangualr ductrun systems. They include the splitter damper, the poke damper, the volume-control damper, and the slide damper, along with their numerous variations with different names.

Helpful Fabrication Information

Joining, Tying, and Reinforcing

There are a variety of methods and techniques used for joining, tying and reinforcing nested fittings. They are all similar in the fact that they all serve the same purpose. Most contractors are thoroughly familiar with a majority of these methods, which might vary somewhat in different parts of the country.

To join portions of the fittings together, you merely use a turned drive which is slipped under a trimmed raw edge of the adjoining fitting. These fittings are held in place by nuts and bolts after punching or drilling holes through the heel or cheek patterns, or sometimes by using a button punch. If you trimmed both adjoining edges, simply use an S cleat to avoid air leakage.

Another common method is to notch and turn over part of the hemmed portion with a hammer or dolly. This eliminates having to use an electric drill or hand punch for making bolt holes.

In some parts of the country, a government lock is used to tie the fittings together in heavy commercial and industrial work. The method most commonly used in residential and light commercial work is the flat S cleat or bar cleat.

After the heels or cheeks of the fittings are joined and tied together, it is often necessary to reinforce the fittings depending on their size and arrangement. It is frequently necessary to use a band iron strap. In residential work, a drive cleat or an S cleat is frequently used. If the work is very large, an angle iron is used. Sometimes this is done while in the shop so that when it is being erected in the field, much installation time can be saved. In this way, the men in the field do not have the added problem of combatting flexibility while erecting or installing the fittings. Reinforcing adds rigidity to the nested fittings.

Importance of Visualization

Being able to visualize is an asset to the person who plans, draws or designs the system. To be able to quickly form a mental picture of what kink of fitting or combination of fittings is needed can save shop time as well as field time.

In residential work, it is usually not necessary to make a scaled drawing, regardless of whether they are various types of perimeter systems, crawl space plenums, extended plenums, graduated trunk systems or other types of systems. This is true whether doing alterations, additions, modernization or new work. Some type of rough drawing or sketch of the system is made for the employee who will be either installing the system or making up or ordering the required fittings.

Unusual fittings are limited only by the imagination of the person planning the ductrun system. In most cases, they are a result of a lack of adequate planning, particularly in new work. In a smaller shop, the person doing this planning is a sheet metal worker. Therefore, he has the knowledge and experience to plan practical fittings in the ductrun system. Large sheet metal contractors usually hire sheet metal draftsmen who are experienced workers in the field as well as in the shop. They have the knowledge and experience to draw upon so they can plan economical and practical fittings in the ductrun system.

Two more factors to consider when redesigning ductwork are the maintenance of proper air flow and velocity, and the necessity of putting the fitting into a limited or tight space. Proper air flow should never be sacrificed.

Planning Insures Success

The aspects of planning and organizing are always important. The problem here is that, in most cases, some things are not anticipated until while on the job. Then, rather than drawing or phoning in a fitting to be made, it is easier to phone in or pick up some stock items. Here again, the ability to visualize quickly and anticipate possible problems can certainly save you a lot of time.

Getting in the habit of constantly looking ahead in planning any system will definitely be helpful. By planning ahead, you will be on the "look-out" for situations where you can nest or combine fittings to save time and labor whether in the shop or field.

#8 - Determining Blank Sizes for Elbows and Angles

When laying out elbows and angles in the shop, many people do not determine blank sizes first. They work from a standard size sheet of metal--laying out the cheek patterns first, then cutting them out and forming the single edges of the cheek. Then they measure the formed single edges to get the overall stretchouts and make the throat and heel wrappers. This method is often referred to as "strapping an edge."

Several other methods can be used that have the advantage of being able to determine the exact cut sizes of the heel and throat wrappers before doing any pattern layout. These methods include using a math formula, using a circumference rule and using a chart. However, using the math formula is not practical, as will be explained later. Using the circumference rule and using the chart are the practical methods since they provide the following advantages:

1. Save Time--you eliminate the operation of measuring the single edges, selecting a piece of metal, and going back to the shear to cut the required pieces, and then return back to the bench to notch out corners or use the notching machine.

2. Minimize Layout Time--Less measuring is required.

3. Reduced Scrap or Waste--Since you know the exact size you require, you can plan your shearing operations to reduce waste.

Also, it is economical to use drop offs or smaller pieces.

Quite often, people think there is some special "magic" or mystery in determining exact blank sizes of patterns of fittings. This is not the case at all. When a person is not familiar with this method, it often appears much more difficult than it really is. After going through the examples in this section, you will see how easy it is.

Helpful Fabrication Information

Practical Sheet Metal Math For Shop and Field

When doing shop work or field work, there are several charts and formulas that can be used in sheet metal work to save time, labor, and material. There is often a reluctance of some people to make use of these charts and formulas, mainly because they are not familiar with them and lack an understanding of how they are used. This is partly due to the fact that you are unable to determine what formula was used to obtain the answers on the chart.

This reluctance to using charts and formulas is also partly due to the fact that when first learning a specific method or operation, we learned another way. It could be longer; but since it was the first method learned, it appears to be the easier and faster method because we understood it thoroughly and had performed the operation many times. When a formula or chart must be used because there is no other way to do the job, you become quite familiar and comfortable using it. For example, think of the formula for making a mitered pipe or duct in the field and the frequency of using this formula.

Strapping An Edge

You can form the single edge on the cheek pattern of an elbow or angle and use a flexible steel rule or measuring tape to measure the distance along the outer edge of the formed single edge. This is sometimes referred to as "strapping an edge" and is the most frequently used method for determining heel and throat wrapper stretchouts of elbows and angles. See Figs. 1 and 2.

Although this method may not appear to take much time, consider the many times you must do this due to how frequently you make elbows and angles. Consider the many times you must go back and forth to the material rack and to the shear, not forgetting the time it takes to measure the turned single edge of the throat and heel, all resulting in many wasted footsteps.

Using A Formula

If a person were to use the math formula for a 90° elbow (1.57 x Radius) to determine the wrapper stretchout for throat and heel patterns,

Helpful Fabrication Information

396.

Fig. 1 - Forming the single edge on the cheek pattern of a 90° elbow.

Fig. 2 - Using measuring tape to measure the distance along the outer edge of the formed single edge on the cheek pattern of a 90° elbow. This can be eliminated when making elbows and angles by using the Elbow and Angle Stretchout Chart or using a Circumference Rule.

you would then have to use 1/3 of this for a 30° angle, or 1/2 for a 45° angle, or 2/3 for a 60° angle. See Fig. 3. It really would not be practical for these reasons:

1. Chance of error each time you multiply.
2. You must convert the decimal answer to a fraction.

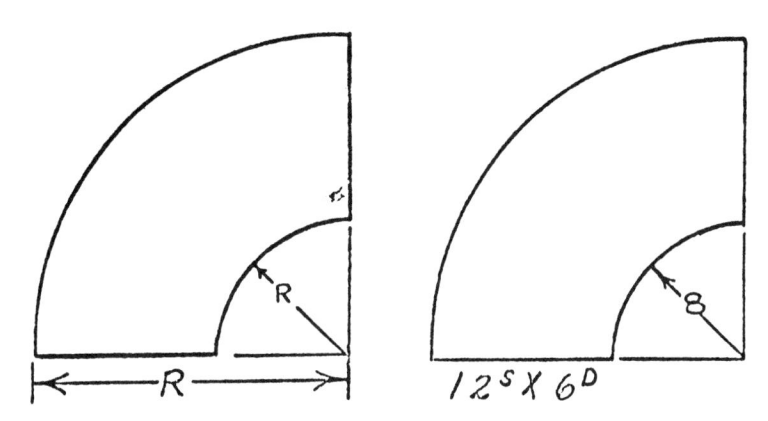

90° elbow with curved throat and heel (working from the 1/2" line)

Throat Stretchout: 1.57 x R   1.57
                          1.57 x 8   x 8
                                               12.56

            12.56
            12-9/16"+1" cleat allowance
            13-9/16" overall stretchout

Heel Stretchout: 1.57 x R   1.57
                          1.57 x 20   x 20
                                               31.40

            31.40
            31-7/16" + 1" cleat allowance
            32-7/16" overall stretchout

Fig. 3 - Using a Formula for a 90° Elbow.

Helpful Fabrication Information 398.

Using a Circumference Rule

Using a circumference rule is a much better method than using the math formula. See Fig. 4. For a 90° elbow, find 1/2 of the given radius on the standard scale at the top of the rule, and read the corresponding stretchout directly below. After obtaining the stretchout dimension for a 90° elbow, then use 1/3 of this for a 30° angle, or 1/2 for a 45° angle, or 2/3 for a 60° angle.

To avoid this calculation, look up the fractional part of the required radius, as shown in Fig. 5.

Fig. 4 - Circumference Rule

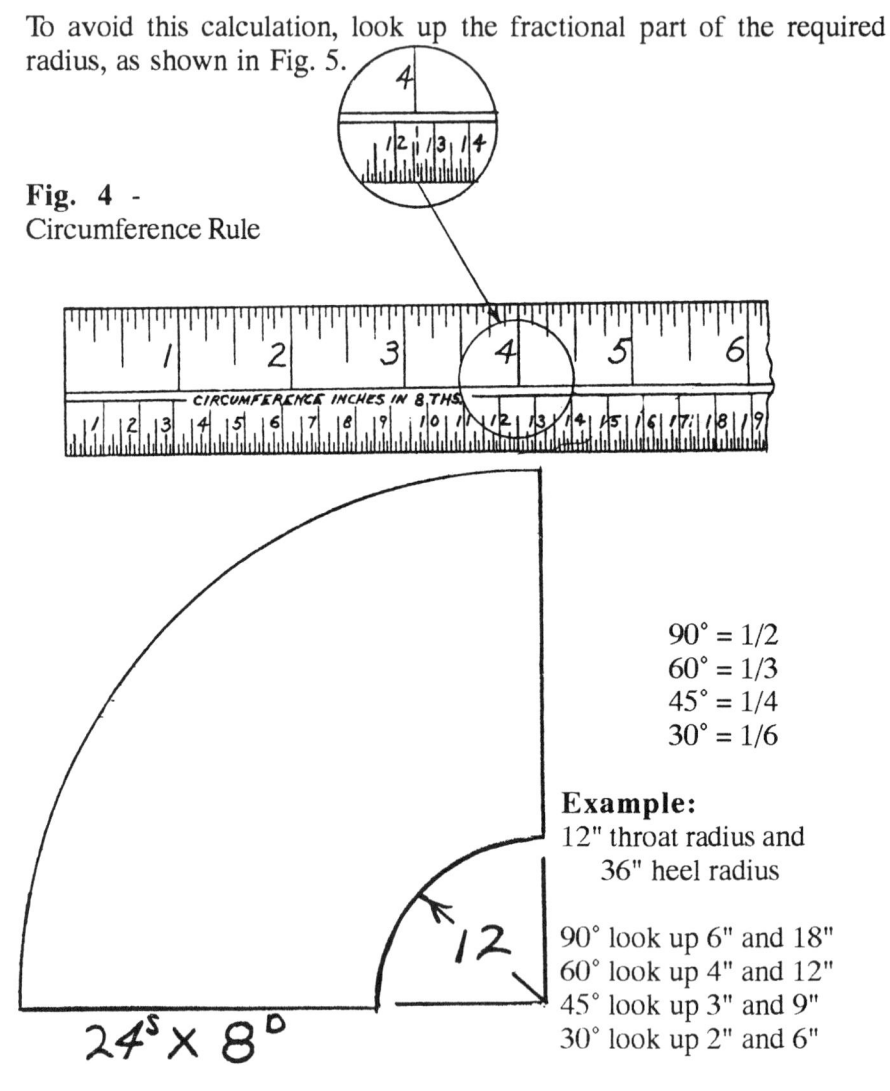

90° = 1/2
60° = 1/3
45° = 1/4
30° = 1/6

Example:
12" throat radius and
36" heel radius

90° look up 6" and 18"
60° look up 4" and 12"
45° look up 3" and 9"
30° look up 2" and 6"

24^s × 8^D

Fig. 5 - Fractional Dimensions for 30°, 45°, and 60° Angles.

399.   Helpful Fabrication Information

Follow these steps when using the circumference rule (and see Fig. 6):

Throat Pattern:
a. Since you are working from the 1/2" line, use the required throat radius. (If you were working from the 1" line, you would subtract 1/2" from the throat radius.)
b. Divide this number in half and look up the resulting number on the top portion of the circumference rule.
c. The corresponding number at the bottom of the circumference rule is the stretchout of the radius.
d. Add 1" to this answer due to the necessary 1/2" line at each end of the fitting.

Heel Pattern:
a. Begin with the throat radius, as above.
b. Add the cheek size to this dimension.
c. Divide this number in half and look up the resulting number on the top portion of the circumference rule.
d. The corresponding number at the bottom of the circumference rule is the stretchout of the radius.
e. Add 1" to this answer due to the necessary 1/2" line at each end of the fitting.

Throat Pattern Calculation:
1. 8 ÷ 2 = 4
2. 4" circumference = 12-9/16" (from chart)
3. 12-9/16" + 1 = 13-9/16" overall stretchout

Heel Pattern Calculation:
1. 20 ÷ 2 = 10
2. 10" circumference = 31-7/16" (from chart)
3. 31-7/16" + 1 = 32-7/16" overall stretchout

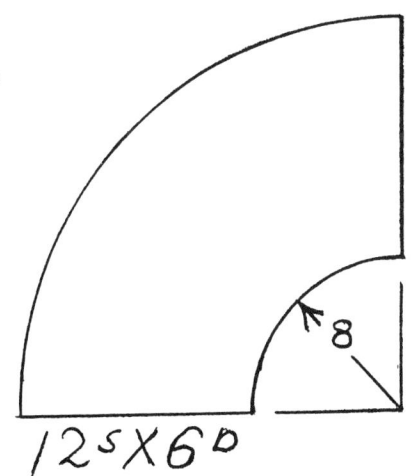

Fig. 6 - Calculations when using circumference rule to determine stretchouts for elbows and angles.

Helpful Fabrication Information

Using a circumference rule is accurate to 1/8". If the reading falls between two divisions, it is read as a 1/16th. For example, the stretchout of an 8" radius, since you look up 4" (1/2 of the required radius), is between 12 1/2" and 12 5/8" so is read as 12 9/16" as shown in Fig. 4.

Using An Elbow And Angle Stretchout Chart

The chart shown in Figs. 7 and 8 (3 digit) gives the stretchouts for 90° elbows ranging from a radius dimension of 2" to 120". Like using the circumference rule, using this chart provides the advantages of:

1. Saving time
2. Minimizing layout
3. Reducing scrap or waste

However, using the chart provides added advantages over using a circumference rule. It eliminates the need to calculate the answer for the 30°, 45°, and 60° angle after obtaining the 90° dimension. These are stated on the chart.

The dimensions on the chart were calculated using the formula and rounding off the answers to the nearest 1/16" since this is the smallest measurement generally used in this type of sheet metal work.

It is a good idea to put the chart in a plastic cover so it lasts longer and is protected from getting dirty or torn. To eliminate any wasted time, keep the chart in a convenient place, such as:

1. Punch a hole at the top of the chart and hang it on a wall or post near your bench.
2. Keep it on a clip board.

Points to Remember When Using This Chart

1. It does not include cleat allowances.
2. It assumes all dimensions on working drawings are finished dimensions.
3. Since some people work from the 1/2" line and others work from the 1" line, the dimensions for each are on separate sides of the chart.
4. When working from the 1" line; subtract 1/2" from the required radius and look up this number as R on the chart.

401.   **Helpful Fabrication Information**

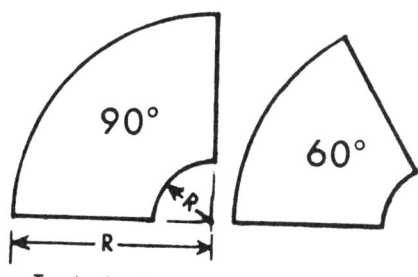

To obtain the throat and heel stretchouts, look up the appropriate dimension R on the Chart.

BUDZIK'S

ELBOW AND ANGLE STRETCHOUT CHART

STRETCHOUTS FOR HEEL AND THROAT WRAPPERS WORKING FROM THE 1" LINE
(See reverse side for working from the 1/2" Line)

R = RADIUS — NOTE: FIGURES GIVEN ARE TO THE NEAREST 1/16". THEY **DO NOT** INCLUDE CLEAT ALLOWANCES.

© Copyright 1972 - by Practical Publications

R = RADIUS

STR. = STRAIGHT

Fig. 7 - Stretchout Chart for Elbows and Angles (con't. on next page)

R	90°	60°	45°	30°	R	90°	60°	45°	30°	R	90°	60°	45°	30°
1½	2-3/8	1-9/16	1-3/16	13/16	41½	65-3/16	43-7/16	32-5/8	21-3/4	81½	128	85-5/16	64	42-11/16
2½	3-15/16	2-5/8	1-15/16	1-5/16	42½	66-3/4	44-1/2	33-3/8	22-1/4	82½	129-9/16	86-3/8	64-13/16	43-3/16
3½	5-1/2	3-11/16	2-3/4	1-13/16	43½	68-5/16	45-9/16	34-3/16	22-3/4	83½	131-1/8	87-7/16	65-9/16	43-11/16
4½	7-1/16	4-11/16	3-9/16	2-3/8	44½	69-7/8	46-9/16	34-15/16	23-5/16	84½	132-11/16	88-1/2	66-3/8	44-1/4
5½	8-5/8	5-3/4	4-5/16	2-7/8	45½	71-7/16	47-5/8	35-3/4	23-13/16	85½	134-1/4	89-1/2	67-1/8	44-3/4
6½	10-3/16	6-13/16	5-1/8	3-3/8	46½	73	48-11/16	36-1/2	24-5/16	86½	135-7/8	90-9/16	67-15/16	45-5/16
7½	11-3/4	7-13/16	5-7/8	3-15/16	47½	74-5/8	49-3/4	37-5/16	24-7/8	87½	137-7/16	91-5/8	68-3/4	45-13/16
8½	13-3/8	8-15/16	6-11/16	4-7/16	48½	76-3/16	50-13/16	38-1/8	25-3/8	88½	139	92-11/16	69-1/2	46-5/16
9½	14-15/16	9-15/16	7-1/2	5	49½	77-3/4	51-3/4	38-7/8	25-15/16	89½	140-9/16	93-11/16	70-1/4	46-7/8
10½	16-1/2	11	8-1/4	5-1/2	50½	79-5/16	52-7/8	39-11/16	26-7/16	90½	142-3/16	94-3/4	71-1/16	47-3/8
11½	18-1/16	12-1/16	9-1/16	6	51½	80-7/8	53-15/16	40-7/16	26-15/16	91½	143-11/16	95-13/16	71-7/8	47-7/8
12½	19-5/8	13-1/16	9-13/16	6-9/16	52½	82-7/16	54-15/16	41-1/4	27-1/2	92½	145-1/4	96-7/8	72-5/8	48-7/16
13½	21-3/16	14-1/8	10-5/8	7-1/16	53½	84	56	42	28	93½	146-13/16	97-7/8	73-7/16	48-15/16
14½	22-3/4	15-3/16	11-3/8	7-9/16	54½	85-5/8	57-1/16	42-13/16	28-9/16	94½	148-7/16	98-15/16	74-1/4	49-1/2
15½	24-3/8	16-1/4	12-3/16	8-1/8	55½	87-3/16	58-1/8	43-5/8	29-1/16	95½	150	100	75	50
16½	25-15/16	17-5/16	13	8-5/8	56½	88-3/4	59-3/16	44-3/8	29-9/16	96½	151-9/16	101-1/16	75-13/16	50-1/2
17½	27-1/2	18-5/16	13-3/4	9-3/16	57½	90-5/16	60-3/16	45-3/16	30-1/8	97½	153-1/8	102-1/16	76-9/16	51-1/16
18½	29-1/16	19-3/8	14-9/16	9-11/16	58½	91-7/8	61-1/4	45-15/16	30-5/8	98½	154-11/16	103-1/8	77-3/8	51-9/16
19½	30-5/8	20-7/16	15-5/16	10-3/16	59½	93-7/16	62-5/16	46-3/4	31-1/8	99½	156-1/4	104-3/16	78-1/8	52-1/16
20½	32-3/16	21-7/16	16-1/8	10-3/4	60½	95	63-5/16	47-1/2	31-11/16	100½	157-13/16	105-1/4	78-15/16	52-5/8
21½	33-3/4	22-1/2	16-7/8	11-1/4	61½	96-9/16	64-3/8	48-5/16	32-3/16	101½	159-3/8	106-1/4	79-11/16	53-1/8
22½	35-5/16	23-9/16	17-11/16	11-3/4	62½	98-3/16	65-7/16	49-1/8	32-3/4	102½	161	107-5/16	80-1/2	53-11/16
23½	36-15/16	24-5/8	18-1/2	12-5/16	63½	99-3/4	66-1/2	49-7/8	33-1/4	103½	162-9/16	108-3/8	81-5/16	54-3/16
24½	38-1/2	25-11/16	19-1/4	12-13/16	64½	101-5/16	67-9/16	50-11/16	33-3/4	104½	164-1/8	109-7/16	82-1/16	54-11/16
25½	40-1/16	26-11/16	20-1/16	13-3/8	65½	102-7/8	68-9/16	51-7/16	34-5/16	105½	165-11/16	110-7/16	82-7/8	55-1/4
26½	41-5/8	27-3/4	20-13/16	13-7/8	66½	104-7/16	69-5/8	52-1/4	34-13/16	106½	167-1/4	111-1/2	83-5/8	55-3/4
27½	43-3/16	28-13/16	21-5/8	14-3/8	67½	106	70-11/16	53	35-5/16	107½	168-13/16	112-9/16	84-7/16	56-1/4
28½	44-3/4	29-13/16	22-3/8	14-15/16	68½	107-9/16	71-3/4	53-13/16	35-7/8	108½	170-3/8	113-5/8	85-3/16	56-13/16
29½	46-5/16	30-7/8	23-3/16	15-7/16	69½	109-1/8	72-3/4	54-9/16	36-3/8	109½	172	114-11/16	86	57-5/16
30½	47-7/8	31-15/16	23-15/16	15-15/16	70½	110-3/4	73-13/16	55-3/8	36-15/16	110½	173-9/16	115-11/16	86-13/16	57-7/8
31½	49-1/2	33	24-3/4	16-1/2	71½	112-5/16	74-7/8	56-3/16	37-7/16	111½	175-1/8	116-3/4	87-9/16	58-3/8
32½	51-1/16	34-1/16	25-9/16	17	72½	113-7/8	75-15/16	56-15/16	37-15/16	112½	176-11/16	117-13/16	88-3/8	58-7/8
33½	52-5/8	35-1/16	26-5/16	17-9/16	73½	115-7/16	76-15/16	57-3/4	38-1/2	113½	178-1/4	118-13/16	89-1/8	59-7/16
34½	54-3/16	36-1/8	27-1/8	18-1/16	74½	117	78	58-1/2	39	114½	179-13/16	119-7/8	89-15/16	59-15/16
35½	55-3/4	37-3/16	27-7/8	18-9/16	75½	118-9/16	79-1/16	59-5/16	39-1/2	115½	181-3/8	120-15/16	90-11/16	60-7/16
36½	57-5/16	38-3/16	28-11/16	19-1/8	76½	120-1/8	80-1/8	60-1/16	40-1/16	116½	182-15/16	122	91-1/2	61
37½	58-7/8	39-1/4	29-7/16	19-5/8	77½	121-11/16	81-1/8	60-7/8	40-9/16	117½	184-9/16	123-1/16	92-5/16	61-1/2
38½	60-7/16	40-5/16	30-1/4	20-1/8	78½	123-5/16	82-3/16	61-11/16	41-1/8	118½	186-1/8	124-1/16	93-1/16	62-1/16
39½	62-1/16	41-3/8	31-1/16	20-11/16	79½	124-7/8	83-1/4	62-7/16	41-5/8	119½	187-11/16	125-1/8	93-7/8	62-9/16
40½	63-5/8	42-7/16	31-13/16	21-3/16	80½	126-7/16	84-5/16	63-1/4	42-1/8					

Wrapper stretchouts for these fittings can also be determined using the chart. Determine the radius dimension as labeled on the drawings below. Determine and add the straight dimension or dimensions marked on the drawings below. Remember that cleat allowances are not included.

Fig. 7 - (contd. from previous page)

403. **Helpful Fabrication Information**

BUDZIK'S
ELBOW AND ANGLE STRETCHOUT CHART

STRETCHOUTS FOR HEEL AND THROAT WRAPPERS
WORKING FROM THE 1/2" LINE
(See reverse side for working from the 1" Line)

R = RADIUS — NOTE: FIGURES GIVEN ARE TO THE NEAREST 1/16".
THEY **DO NOT** INCLUDE CLEAT ALLOWANCES.

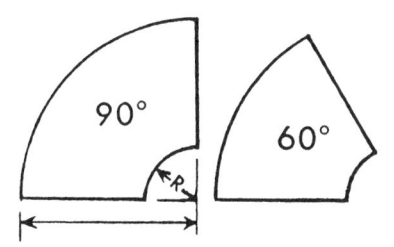

© Copyright 1972 - by Practical Publications

45°   30°

90°   60°

To obtain the throat and heel stretchouts, look up the appropriate dimension R on the Chart.

Fig. 8 - continuation of Fig. 7 - chart on next page.

Helpful Fabrication Information

404.

Fig. 8 - continued from previous page

Helpful Fabrication Information

Step 4 continued from page 191 . . . .

See the samples in Figs. 9, 10, 11 and 12.

For example: When the throat radius is 6" and heel radius is 18", look up 5 1/2" (6" - 1/2) and 17 1/2" (18" - 1/2"). The throat stretchout indicated on the chart is 8 5/8" and the heel stretchout is 27 1/2". Then add 2" to each dimension since you are working from the 1" line. So, the overall throat stretchout is 10 5/8" and the overall heel stretchout is 29 1/2".

5. When working from the 1/2" line: look up the required radius as R on the chart.

For Example: When the throat radius is 6" and heel radius is 18", look up 6" and 18". The throat stretchout indicated on the chart is 9 7/16" and the heel stretchout is 28 1/4". Then add 1" to each dimension since you are working from the 1/2" line. So, the overall throat stretchout is 10 7/16" and the overall heel stretchout is 29 1/4".

6. The method of determining the stretchout is still the same when an elbow or angle is C/F (center flare), when it is flat on one side, or when both cheeks are offsetting.

90° ELBOW
When working from the 1" line:

1. 6" radius-1/2"=5 1/2"
2. 5 1/2" stretchout = 8 5/8" (from chart)
3. 8 5/8"+2=10 5/8" overall stretchout

1. 18" radius - 1/2" = 17 1/2"
2. 17 1/2" stretchout = 27 1/2" (from chart)
3. 27 1/2" + 2 = 29 1/2" overall stretchout

When working from the 1/2" line:

1. 6" radius stretchout = 9-7/16" (from chart)
2. 9-7/16"+1"=10-7/16" overall stretchout

1. 18" radius stretchout = 28 1/4" (from chart)
2. 28 1/4" + 1" = 29 1/4" overall stretchout

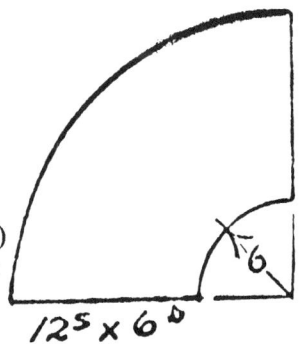

Helpful Fabrication Information

ELBOW WITH CURVED HEEL AND STRAIGHT THROAT

Heel Pattern Calculation:

1. 12" stretchout = 18-7/8" (from chart)
2. 18-7/8"+2+6"+1"=27-7/8" overall stretchout

CHANGE ELBOW WITH CURVED HEEL AND STRAIGHT THROAT

Heel Pattern Calculation:

1. 15" stretchout = 23-9/16" (from chart)
2. 23-9/16"+4"+13"* +1"=41-9/16" overall stretchout

*This 13" dimension was derived by calculating:
Large cheek size plus straight throat dimension minus small cheek size (24+4-15=13")

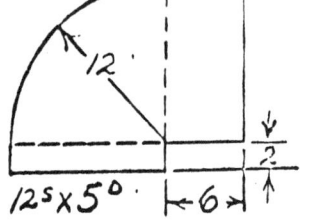

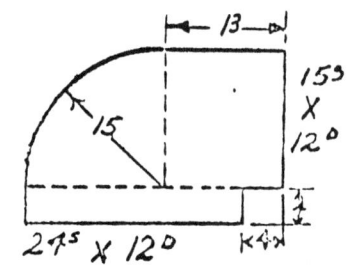

CHANGE ELBOW

Heel Pattern Calculation:
(working from the 1/2" line)

1. 8"+12"=20"
2. 20" stretchout=31-7/16" (from chart)
3. 31-7/16"+6"* +1"=38-7/16" overall stretchout

*This 6" dimension was derived by adding 18"+8"=26" and then subtracting the sum of 12"+8"=20" (26-20=6")

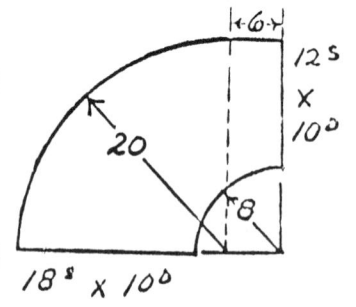

Fig. 9 - Simple Stretchout Calculations Using the Chart.

Helpful Fabrication Information

Points to Remember When Using This Chart

1. It does not include cleat allowances.

2. It assumes all dimensions on working drawings are finished dimensions.

3. Since some people work from the 1/2" line and others work from the 1" line, the dimensions for each are on separate sides of the chart.

4. When working from the 1" line, subtract 1/2" from the required radius and look up this number as R on the chart.

Factors To Consider

Some people feel that when a single edge is formed on an easy edger or power easy edger, it is not exactly uniform throughout the single edge. However, this difference would be so slight that it would not affect the overall fitting.

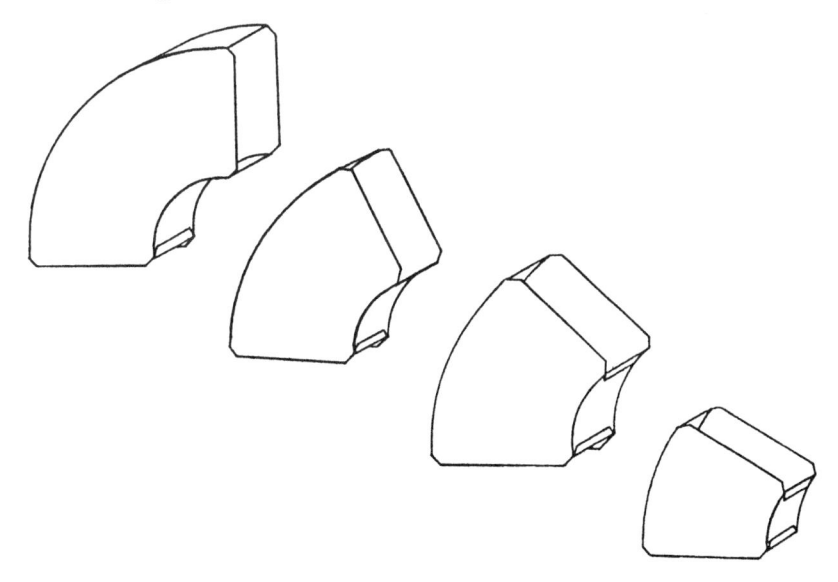

Fig. 10 - Elbows and angles whose heel and throat stretchouts can be determined using the Circumference Rule or using the chart which is quicker.

Helpful Fabrication Information   408.

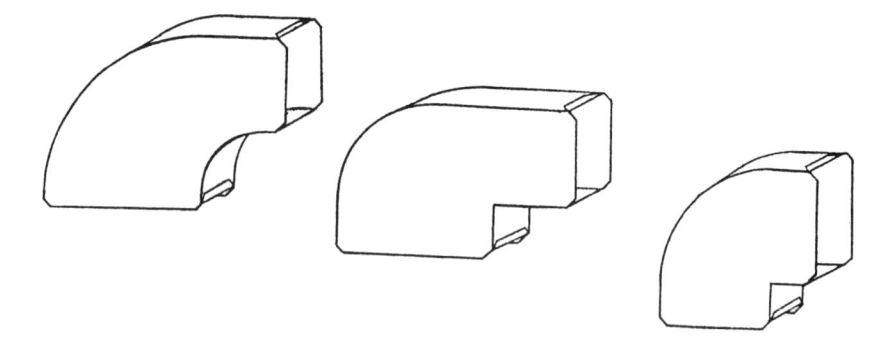

Fig. 11 - Other types of elbows whose heel and throat stretchouts can be determined using the Circumference Rule or the chart. They are (left to right): change elbow, change elbow with curved heel and straight throat, and elbow with curved heel and straight throat.

If you must make a fitting that has an uneven throat or heel radius, you will have to use the circumference rule or the math formula rather than using the chart, or you can use the strapping method.

When making large fittings that require standing seams within a cheek pattern, the size is not changed as long as you allow for the thickness of the standing seams in your cheek patterns. The same is true if you have to make the throat or heel wrappers in more than one piece using standing seams.

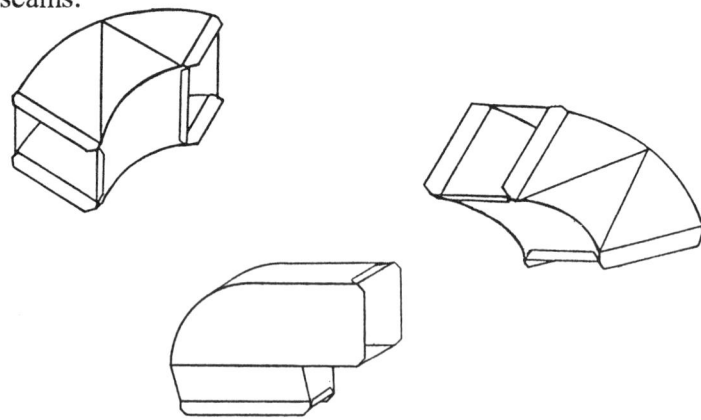

Fig. 12 - Other types of transition elbows whose heel and throat stretchouts can be determined using the circumference rule or chart.

Helpful Fabrication Information

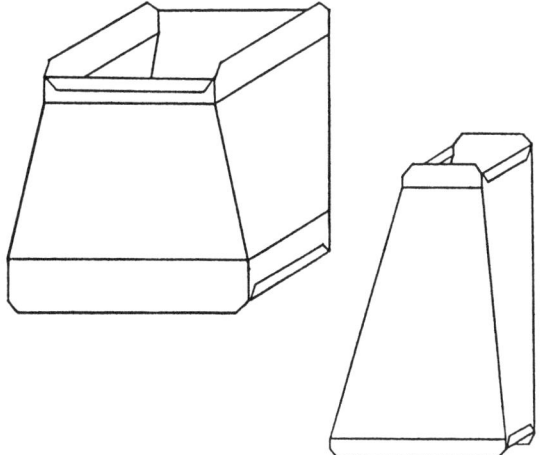

Fig. 13 - Transitions (change joints) whose blank sizes for the patterns can be determined using a rule or square.

Determining exact blank sizes of patterns with a rule and square can also be used when making almost any type of transition (change joint) except a twisted transition since its openings are not parallel to each other. See Fig. 13. This topic will be thoroughly covered in a separate chapter. The reason elbows and angles are illustrated in this chapter is that they are the most frequently used fittings, followed by transitions.

Summary

When an error occurs in the wrong overall stretchout for a heel or throat wrapper, you will usually find that you added or subtracted wrong-- especially when making change elbows or elbows and angles that require straight at one or both ends. When calculating the cut size as working from the 1" line, you might forget and do the layout from the 1/2" line, and vice-versa.

Although these mistakes are not frequently made, many times they are not realized until the fitting is being assembled. Time is lost since you have spent time forming the heel or throat pattern; lost time is greater if the elbows or angles are to be insulated.

Since these mistakes are usually due to a lack of care and not because of a lack of ability, the important point to remember is to be careful when adding or subtracting. This caution can save you time.

Helpful Fabrication Information

Remember that using this chart enables you to determine all blank sizes of the patterns for the fittings shown here. Not only does this save considerable time, it also minimizes layout and reduces scrap or waste.

Footsteps are movements, and movements require time. The strapping method takes extra footsteps which are actually wasted time--since it can be done in a much faster way.

The more elbows and angles you make, the more time you will save when using this chart. Once you get used to this method, you will not want to use the other methods again.

#9 - Determining Blank Sizes (Cut Sizes) for Transitions

After elbow and angle fittings, the transition fitting is the next most common. Although a variety of elbows and angles can be purchased, very few transition fittings can be purchased in standard sizes other than in small standard stack sizes.

This section explains and demonstrates a real labor saving method for making transitions--using a square and rule when laying out transitions in the shop.

Many people don't determine blank sizes first. They work from a standard size sheet of metal, a piece of scrap or drop off. They lay out each pattern using the measured distance to continue laying out the other pattern or patterns, which could be a two-piece, three-piece, or four-piece transition.

Usually in small or medium sized work, the more separate pieces required, the more difficult the layout; consequently, this method can take much time on many transitions. A real timesaving method is to determine all blank sizes first, cut them to size, and lay the patterns out as they should be.

Helpful Fabrication Information

Visualization and Knowledge

Two of the skills you develop through experience in doing sheet metal layout are very important when determining blank sizes. These skills are visualization and knowledge of layout.

Visualizing simply means being able to form a mental image or picture of the required fitting. This helps in your layout work by letting you know exactly what the completed fitting is to look like, the general shape and position of each pattern, and how they fit together to form the complete fitting.

With your experience and knowledge of layout, you know exactly what the patterns should look like and when it's advantageous to combine patterns.

The more skill you've developed in layout and visualization, the easier it is to adapt yourself to this method. This is due to the fact that the procedure is much more meaningful, since you already thoroughly understand the conventional layout method--which is actually the long method.

The method of determining blank sizes is considered a shorter method, eliminating some of the steps, which is not a mystery to you as you understand the whole concept.

A further aid in visualizing a transition fitting is to sketch what the top view would look like. You're usually working from a front view, with all the necessary dimensions on it; this view gives you the overall shape of the fitting. All of the transitions illustrated in this section show the front view, with one also showing the top view since it doesn't have enough information on the front view.

The top view clarifies the amount that the patterns pitch or drop, which is necessary when using a square and rule to determine the blank sizes of patterns.

Large Fittings

When making large fittings, you can also use the system of determining blank sizes even though they require several or many pieces for each

Helpful Fabrication Information

pattern. The time spent in determining the blank sizes is much less than the time saved when laying out the pieces.

Housing

When making housing, you can also use the system of determining blank sizes. You first figure the sizes around the door openings, which greatly reduces scrap and eliminates cutting the opening out of a piece of metal. The more access doors you have in a housing, the more time you save using this method. Here again you must spend a little time in planning, but it will save a lot of time and hard work.

Determining Blank Sizes

Determining blank sizes of patterns for fittings before doing any layout provides the following time saving advantages:

1. Reduces layout time drastically (a minimum of measuring is required).

2. Saves time as you eliminate the extra operations of measuring a side or both sides of a pattern that is necessary to continue laying out the other patterns.

3. Reduces scrap to a minimum. Since you know the exact size required for each pattern, you can plan your shearing operations to reduce waste to a minimum. It becomes very economical to use drop-offs or smaller pieces rather than working from a large sheet.

Quite often people think there's some special magic or mystery in determining exact blank sizes of patterns. This is not the case at all. When a person isn't familiar with this method, it often appears much more difficult than it really is. Understandably so, since there are countless numbers of sizes in each type of transition fitting. However, this method is used for determining all sizes of all the various types of transition fittings, with the exception of a twisted transition since the openings are not parallel with each other.

Helpful Fabrication Information

Blank Sizes of Transitions

After following the step-by-step explanation along with the illustration in Fig. 1 and trying a few yourself, you will soon see how easily this method is mastered. To show that this can be done with almost every transition used today, notice the four transition drawings in Fig. 1. They include virtually every type of transition encountered today, both in new and in old work, from the most simple to the most complex. All the patterns have had all their blank sizes determined using a square and rule.

Blank Size Methods

There are two methods for determining blank sizes of transitions:

1. Using a square and rule.
2. Using a book of layout tables.

Using a square and rule is the most popular of the two methods because it's very meaningful and easier to understand how the answers are obtained. Once you've mastered this method, however, you might want to use a book of layout tables because it eliminates having to use the square and rule and saves even more time.

Using a Listing Sheet

Many shops design their own listing sheets, with space provided for indicating the cutting list blank sizes. These blank sizes are determined either by one specific person in the shop, such as the foreman, or by the individual layout men.

Some shops that have a huge volume of work each day utilize this system, because they wouldn't be able to handle the work in any other way. A different person performs each of the following operations:

1. Determine the blank sizes (lister or shop foreman)
2. Cut the pieces to size (shear man)
3. Layout the patterns (layout man or cutter)
4. Form the patterns (fabricator)
5. Insulate or line them (insulation department)
6. Assemble the fittings (fabricator or assembler)

Helpful Fabrication Information 414.

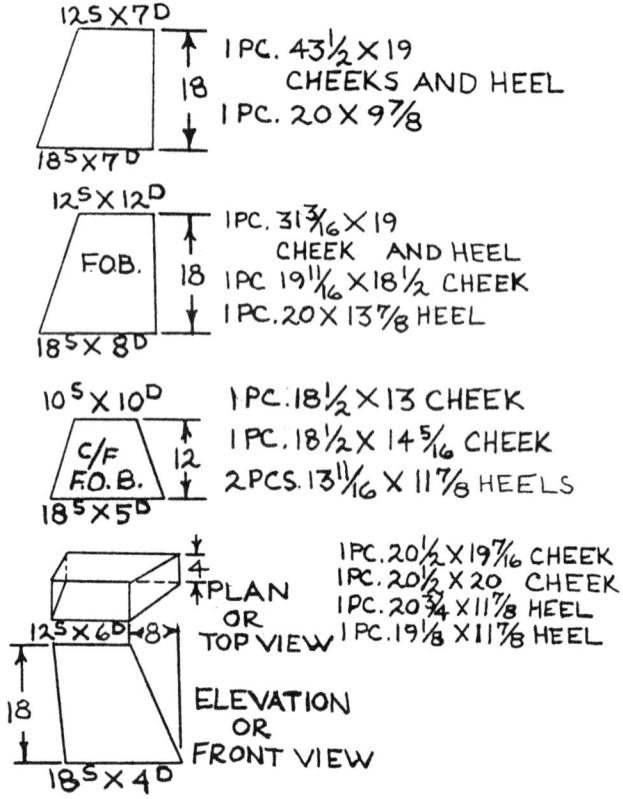

```
12.5 X 7D
   /|     ↑    1 PC. 43½ X 19
  / |   18       CHEEKS AND HEEL
 /  |    ↓    1 PC. 20 X 9⅞
/___|
18S X 7D

12S X 12D
   /|     ↑    1 PC. 31³⁄₁₆ X 19
  /F.O.B.| 18     CHEEK AND HEEL
 /       |    1 PC 19¹¹⁄₁₆ X 18½ CHEEK
/_____|    1 PC. 20 X 13⅞ HEEL
18S X 8D

10S X 10D     1 PC. 18½ X 13 CHEEK
  /|    ↑     1 PC. 18½ X 14⁵⁄₁₆ CHEEK
 /C/F | 12    2 PCS. 13¹¹⁄₁₆ X 11⅞ HEELS
/F.O.B.| ↓
18S X 5D
```

Fig. 1 - The four transitions illustrated above comprise virtually every type of transition that's encountered, from the most simple to the most complex. All of their patterns have had their blank sizes determined by using a square and rule. Seam allowances used were 1/4" single edge 15/16" Pittsburgh seam.

Several books of layout tables are available. They eliminate the need to use a square and rule to determine the correct dimensions for blank sizes of transitions. In addition to transitions, they generally include the blank sizes (stretchouts) for a variety of elbows, plain offsets and change offsets.

In addition to being helpful to the sheet metal worker, these tables are particularly helpful to a lister or sheet metal draftsman who is making the shop drawing. It enables the draftsman to plan the length of the fittings within the standard sheet size widths as much as possible. Sometimes making the fittings a few inches shorter enables each pattern of the fitting to be made from one sheet.

Avoiding Mistakes

When an error occurs in the wrong blank size of a pattern, you will usually find that you added or subtracted wrong. This is sometimes done when you must determine an unstated offset, pitch or drop. Although these mistakes are not frequently made, they are generally not discovered until the fitting is being assembled.

To avoid this, simply follow these two suggestions:

1. When determining the unstated pitch, drop or offset, check your math calculations so that all dimensions add up correctly before laying out, cutting or forming the patterns.
2. Complete all the layout on all patterns of the transition before cutting them out or forming them. Check the lengths of the sides that will be attached to each other to see that they are exactly the same length.

It only takes a few minutes to follow the above two steps on every transition. Not doing so can result in the loss of much time, since you have spent time forming patterns before you realize there is a mistake. The time lost is much greater if the fitting is to be insulated or lined, is very large, or if the fitting is to be sent out from the shop unassembled and to be assembled in the field.

Since these mistakes are usually due to carelessness and not because of a lack of ability, the important point to remember is to be careful when adding or subtracting. This caution will eliminate mistakes.

Remember that using this method of a square and rule to determine blank sizes not only saves considerable time, it also minimizes the layout time and reduces scrap or waste to a minimum.

The next time you are making a transition, consider this suggestion. Before laying it out in the conventional way, determine the blank sizes. After completing the patterns by the conventional method, check the overall pattern sizes before cutting them out to see if you've determined the blank sizes correctly. After they come out correctly for you a few times, then try this with the less complex transitions where only one or two sides are pitching. Then the next time you're making a transition, try this method eliminating the conventional way.

You'll soon see that once you get used to this method and actually see how much time you can save, you'll never want to use the conventional method again.

Part 11
The Role of the Computer in the Sheet Metal Industry
--
With Actual Shop Examples

With newer developments and computers being used in the sheet metal industry, this section will provide information regarding basic terminology, basic uses, and sample applications. Much of this information is available in the reprints of the "Computer News" columns from SNIPS Magazine.* This section is organized as follows:

1. Introductory explanations and definitions.

2. Applications from manufacturers/suppliers of computer hardware and/or software.

3. "Computer News" columns from SNIPS.*

The physical equipment in a computer system is referred to as *hardware*. The computer can receive data (information) from many different hardware input devices such as the keyboard, a digitizer tablet, a light pen or a mouse. This data is processed in the *CPU (Central Processing Unit)* and is stored for future use on a magnetic tape, floppy or hard disk. It may also be graphically displayed on several output devices such as a *monitor screen*, which is also called a *CRT (cathode ray tube)*. Dot matrix printers and flatbed or drum-type pen plotters (high speed computer controlled drafting machines) are used to create hard copy drawings on paper or drafting film.

The instructions or commands that the operator uses to tell the computer what to do and how to do it are known as software programs.

Computer-Aided-Drafting (CAD) or computer graphics is the process of creating drawings with the aid of a computer and its component parts.

---
* A complete page of information about this publication (SNIPS Magazine) and their Book Department is on page 255.

These instructions are often displayed on the screen in the form of a menu and assist the CAD drafter in manipulating the cursor (crosshairs used to draw with) to create a drawing.

The designer/drafter, interacting with a computer, can now produce a drawing with complex calculations and images, faster and much more cost effectively than ever before. Most CAD software utilizes XYZ coordinate systems that allow each point or line particle to be digitized and stored in memory. This permits the use of previously unknown design techniques such as the ability to visually display on the monitor screen an object rotating 360° in any direction, to show its many complex sides.

CAD frees the draftsman of tiring repetitious tasks of manual methods.

Similar to CAD, CAM refers to Computer-Aided Manufacturing, and has many applications.

CYBERMATION: COMPUTER-CONTROLLED PLASMA CUTTING SYSTEMS

Cybermation software programs were specifically developed to make Computer Aided Design and Computer Aided Manufacturing of sheet metal fittings an easy task for nontechnical personnel. Here are the programs that are now available to users of various Cybermation fitting cutting systems.

Two-Dimensional Parts Library

This Advanced Geometric parts library contains over 50 pre-programmed shapes plus customized programs for gore pieces, gears and similar repetitive shaped parts. A single part program can be used to cut an infinite variety of configurations by simply entering the appropriate dimensions for points shown on the primary drawing in this illustration.

Three-Dimensional Parts Libraries

These extensive and unique libraries include rectangular and round/oval fittings, cone sections, large round elbows and special shapes for

The Role of the Computer

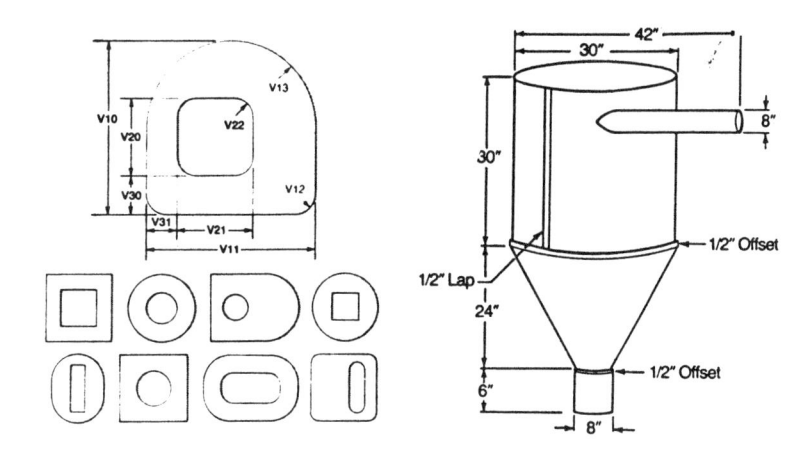

Parts of this stainless steel dust collector were developed in 9 minutes using Cybermation English-language libraries. Cutting time was 3 minutes.

specific applications. When used in combinations, these programs can produce a wide variety of complex assemblies.

Rectangular Fittings

This three-dimensional library covers over 36 different fittings including dropped cheek, rectangular-to-round transitions, and even access door cutouts.

Round/Oval Fitting, Level 1

This library covers the 9 most commonly used round/oval duct fittings.

Round/Oval Fittings, Level 2

This library has a total of 68 different configurations including Level 1 fittings. It represents the industry's most advanced and comprehensive round/oval fitting program available.

CHOP Program for Oversize Parts

If, during job take-off, the operator enters dimensions for a fitting that has parts too large to fit on the sheet, the computer will inform the

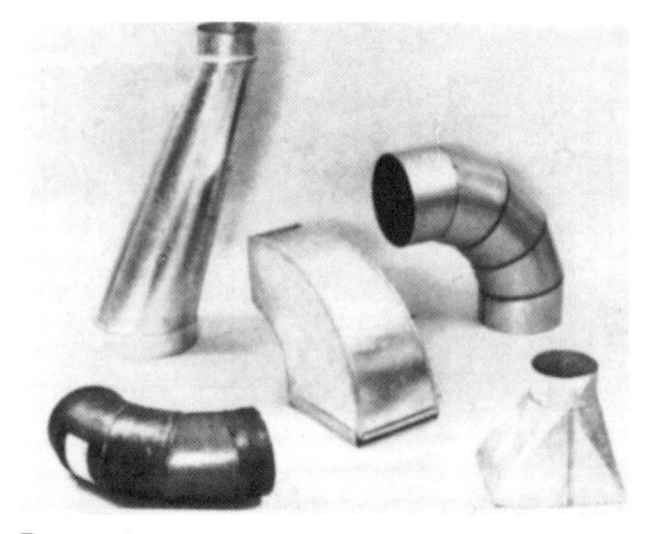

Typical Round/Oval, Level I fittings.

Typical Round/Oval, Level II fittings.

operator and continue with the rest of the job layout. Cybermation's unique CHOP program is then used to reduce or "chop" the large parts into smaller pieces. This CHOP program automatically adds the appropriate standing seam allowances to these chopped pieces and generates full nesting and label documentation that is incorporated into the original job layout program.

The Role of the Computer

Finished oversize part that was programmed by CHOP to fit standard size sheet.

Rotational Nesting Programs Optimize Material Usage

Cybermation SUPERNEST and Rotational Next programs automatically rotate certain shaped parts during the job layout process to obtain a tighter grouping of parts on the sheet.

These exclusive Cybermation programs are made possible by the greater computer power that is inherent in all Cybermation duct cutting systems. The Rotational Next program is basic to small-shop systems, and SUPERNEST is supplied with higher production systems. Savings range from 10% to 20% in material used when compared to sheet layouts produced by conventional "blank" nesting of rectangles.

NC AUTOPROGRAM is a Unique Design-as-you-go Program

Cybermations NC AUTOPROGRAM is an easy-to-use, question/answer CAD/CAM program that is ideal for designing and cutting one-of-a-kind short-run parts and complex shapes. It's an available option that greatly increases the versatility of Cybermations systems. The person planning the job simply answers multiple choice questions that appear

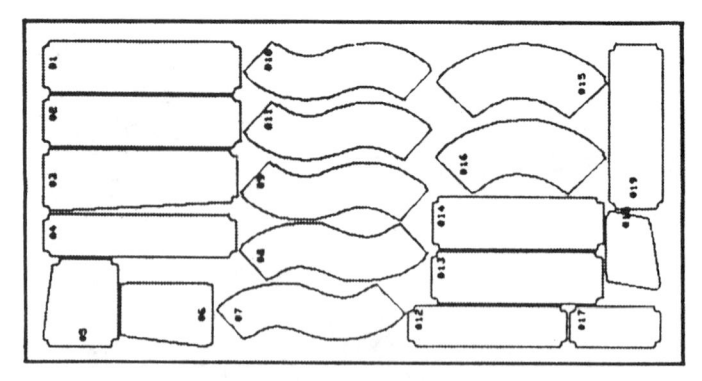

Typical sheet layout showing how rotational nesting of certain parts optimizes sheet utilization.

on the CRT screen with keyboard entries that are mostly numeric. The part being developed is drawn on the NC AUTOPROGRAM plotter as data input is received by the computer, and any mistakes that occur are immediately seen and readily corrected.

CFC 110 System

The CFC 110 System was specially designed to give small-shop duct fabricators the benefits and advantages of advanced Cybermation computer-controlled fitting cutting at a reasonable price. The economically priced CFC 110 small-shop system is the first to put "big system" performance within reach of modest budgets.

CFC 150 System

Specifically engineered for high-production cutting of sheet metal fittings, the Cybermation CFC 150 was the industry's first totally integrated computer-controlled fitting cutting system. Introduced in 1982, the CFC 150 revolutionized the state-of-the-art in sheet metal cutting.

CFC 260 System

Running at speeds up to 500/IPM, the CFC 260 System outproduces all other fitting cutting systems, with as many as 400 fittings per shift.

The Role of the Computer

Construction Technology, Inc. • Cybermation

570 Taxter Road
Elmsford, NY 10523
(914) 592-5906

377 Putnam Avenue
Cambridge, MA 02139
(617) 492-8810

Highly stable machine design assures cutting accuracy. Rigidly mounted on Thompson bars and moving on anti-friction roller bearings, the torch holder glides smoothly through programmed contours with no skewing or mechanical play. Low rail on operator's side of the cutting tables provides unrestricted access to work areas for fast setup and unloading.

AUTO PLAN/CYBERDRAFT

This CAD/CAM system with duct fabrication transfer has these trade features:

- A trade knowledgeable computer designed for use by the trade without computer knowledge.
- A self-directing design that permits use within 7-10 hours following delivery and set-up without formal CAD training.
- An operational plug-in voice command that takes only minutes for recognition which reduces all operator commands to approximately a dozen replies.
- A direct downloading capability - without manual takeoff - for use with fabrication cutting systems.
- And direct control of both plasma and laser cutting systems.

SUPER-DUCT ESTIMATING SOFTWARE by WENDES (WECS)

Galvanized Program

The galvanized program covers estimating labor and material for the following items:

- Rectangular Galvanized
    - Low, Medium and High Pressure
    - Eight Different Fittings and Straight Duct
- Round Galvanized
- Flexible Tubing
- Lining and External Insulation
- Duct Accessories
    - Turning Vanes   Cleats
    - Splitter Dampers   Reinforcing Angles
    - Canvas Connections
- Equipment
    - Multiblade Dampers   Louvers
    - Fire Dampers   VAV Boxes
    - Grilles, Registers, Diffusers

The program covers all types of connections and automatically generates the required materials, including:

- Cleats   - Angle Flanges
- Ductmate   - TDC
- Low, Medium and High Pressure Connections

The Role of the Computer

It already has user-adjustable price and labor files, loaded and ready to go. They include:

- Shop Labor
- Fittings
- Field Labor
- Plasma Arc Cutting Machines
- Straight Duct
- Lining
- Coil Line Fabrication

Takeoff of all items can be made sequentially from drawings and entered directly into the computer. Takeoff audit trail appears on screen and is printed out.

Grand Totals Program

The Grand Totals program finalizes the bidding process of the SUPER-DUCT estimating system and generates a bottom line bid price which includes everything.

The Grand Totals recaps all ductwork totals first. It then allows you to input . . .

- Equipment quotations
- Sub-contractor quotations
- Special items
- Markups (A formula is included for automatic calculation of markups)
- Cost factors

. . . and then it automatically generates the . . .

- Grand Totals summary
- Bottom line bidding price

It is a powerful tool for "what if?" strategic bidding. For example:

1. With the Grand Totals program you can test out different markups for overhead and profit.

2. You can analyze and project different company sales and cost scenarios for the forthcoming year.

Opening Menu's and Takeoffs

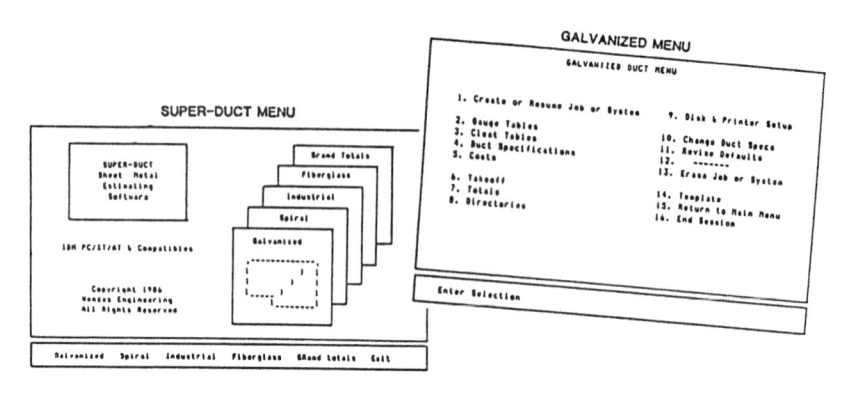

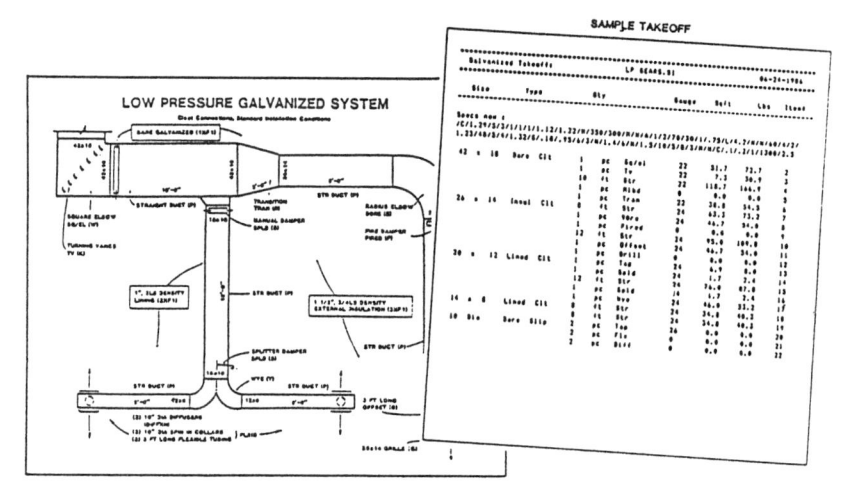

3. You can test out the effect on the final bidding price of different quotations quickly and easily. You can look at what your bid will be with different wage rates and material costs.

The Grand Totals program works with all the SUPER-DUCT estimating modules, galvanized, spiral, fiberglass ductboard and industrial exhaust ductwork.

It's truly easy to use and self-explanatory on the screen.

The Role of the Computer

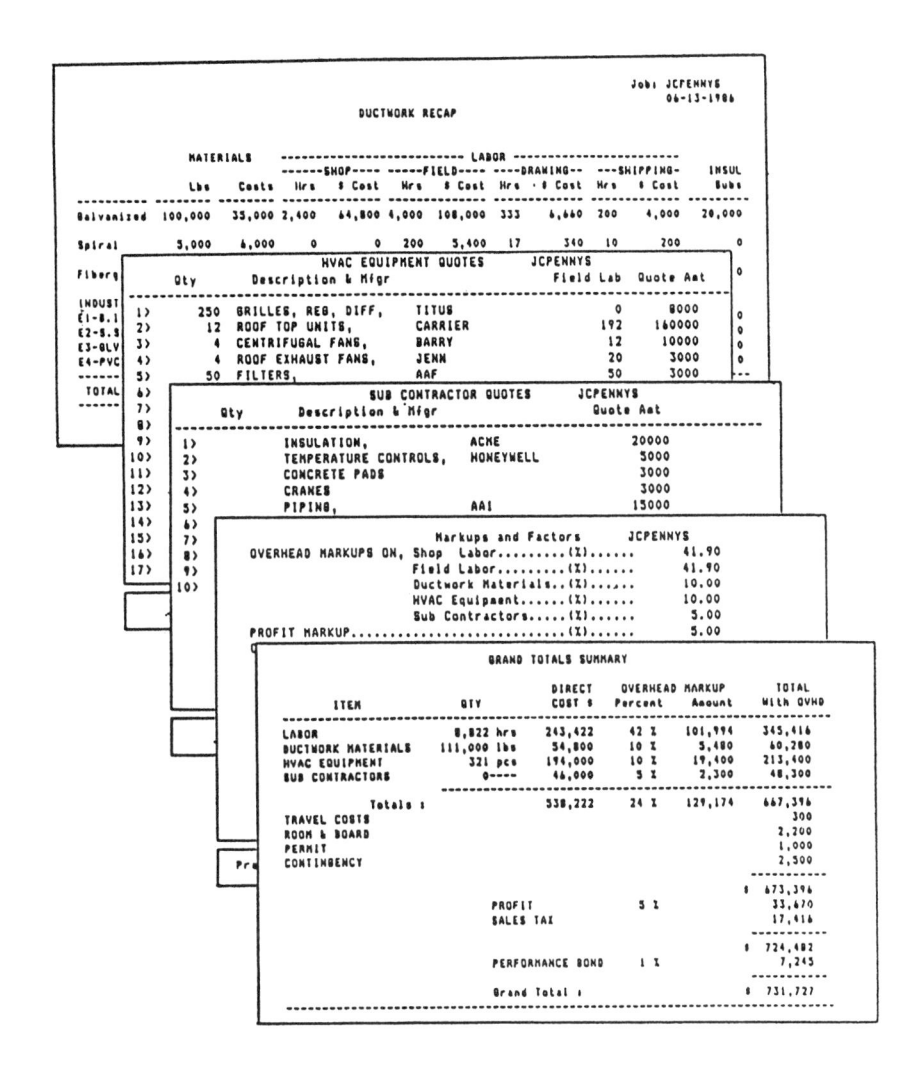

427.

The Grand Totals program recaps ductwork totals, allows you to input equipment and sub-contractor quotations, special items, markups, cost factors and then automatically produces a grand totals summary.

Free 4-hour training sessions are available at Wendes Engineering and are scheduled once or twice a month. Also, special half day training sessions are available at your facilities if you are outside a 75 mile radius from Wendes Engineering, for a fee. If computer hardware is purchased, this half day is required. Full support and service are provided for a full year.

428. The Role of the Computer

SUPER-DUCT
Software

DIGITIZER PEN OR KEYBOARD ENTRY

This Remarkable System Calculates Labor and Material for Complete Sheet Metal Estimates

- All Types of Ductwork
- Duct Accessories
- Lining and Insulation
- Equipment
- Special Items
- Quotations
- Sub-Contractors
- Markups

Automatically Generates Bottom Line Price

Runs On: IBM PC/XT/AT • IBM Compatibles • TRS II/12/16/4 • Tandy 1000/1200/2000/3000
Standard Units and Metric

Please send more information on WECS Super-Duct
Name_____Company_____
Address_____
City_____State_____Zip_____

WECS WENDES ENGINEERING AND CONTRACTING SERVICES
95 Gaylord Street • Elk Grove Village, Illinois 60007 • (312) 593-2178

Quick Pen for Sheet Metal and Air Conditioning Contractors
Computer Aided Estimating

The QuickPen TouchMenu and electronic pen make continuous take-off possible. You never need to touch the computer keyboard, change hands or fumble with different data entry or measuring devices. You no longer need to clutter your work area with numerous pens, counting probes, linear measuring devices and computer terminals. One data entry device does it all.

The First Complete Program for Sheet Metal, Ventilation and Air Conditioning Contractors

Sheet metal, ventilation and air conditioning contractors including blow pipe and industrial contractors can estimate:

- Galvanized, stainless steel, aluminum, PVC coated, fiberglass ductboard and other specified materials.
- Full pressure ranges from .5 inch W.C. to 10 inch W.C. User can define and change construction standards to meet their requirements.
- Round or oval pipe and fittings; single or acoustical double wall construction.
  . may be taken off as shop fabricated or purchased items.
  . will handle round pipe from 3 inch to 90 inch.
  . will handle a full library of round and oval fittings.
  . will handle all oval sizes.
  . will handle snap lock, low and high pressure spiral pipe.
  . will handle welded seam pipe down to ten gauge.
- All equipment and miscellaneous items.
- Double wall housings and plenums
  . areas can be calculated with the touch of the pen.
  . can be handled as fabricated or purchased items.
- Louvers, hand dampers, barometric dampers, duct access doors, control dampers, fire or smoke damper sleeves may be estimated as fabricated or purchased items.

Use Any Specification You Want

The user has complete control over all construction standards. ASHRE, SMACNA, new SMACNA, or any other standard. The QuickPen has the ability to recognize and conform to project specifications, automatically adjusting to user defined material by gauge, size and pressure. Hangers, transverse connectors, and reinforcing may be specified by the user to provide the most economical configuration.

A Unique Comprehensive Project Preview

The QuickPen project preview is a unique, comprehensive program where the estimator can enter all pertinent data for the job. All job specifications, information and notes can be stored in the project preview. Chief estimators, project managers, superintendents, foremen, detailers and management will all save valuable hours of thumbing through plans and specifications in search of this information.

Some of the key features of the project preview are lists of bidders by categories, user changeable check lists, correction factors, and exclusions. Shotgun or budget estimates are provided for estimate comparisons or for negotiating work, and are updated with each estimate.

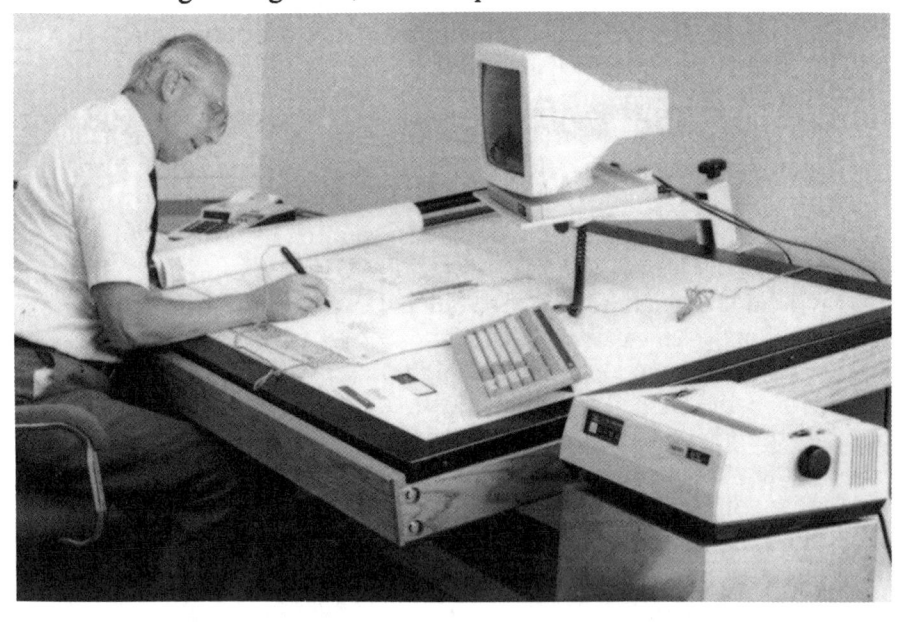

QuickPen
Computer Aided Estimating Inc.

7338 South Alton Way, Suite J
Englewood, Colorado 80112

The Role of the Computer

Detailed Labor Estimates

QuickPen allows labor correction factors to be changed at any time during takeoff. Computer Aided Estimating provides the option of calculating 5 labor categories: shop, field, drawing/detailing, insulating and service. Field and fabrication labor can be calculated by the conventional per pound method using single or multiple factors. Labor may also be calculated by duct size, square foot, pound, linear feet, and gauge of metal or by piece.

QuickPen automatically conforms to your method. The program can break down materials, fabrication and installation labor to the finest degree for estimating or managing the project. The system can give reports by plan number, floor or zones, or system. The contractor has complete control over the type and quantity of information he gets from the system. He can get as little or as much information as he needs at any time.

A Comprehensive Understandable Summary

Individual detailed summaries are furnished for each important cost category---equipment and materials, fabrication, labor, service, sub-contractors and special items. Individual item recaps of all equipment, materials, fabrication and labor down to the smallest item can also be furnished. With detailed estimate information made available, the stage is set for tight, accurate control over the project.

The QuickPen estimating system combined with the QuickPen work in place or labor tracking program gives contractors total control over every job they build. The work in place program provides contractors with almost instant access to a list of all items actually completed along with the associated labor costs and hours originally estimated for those items. This information combined with job cost information provides contractors the first complete system for tracking actual productivity.

QuickPen is Setting the Standard for Estimating Software

State of the art technology, built in help screens, easy to read user manuals, professional training and customer support make QuickPen easy to learn and easy to use. Contractors can use the tables that come

The Role of the Computer

QuickPen Sheet Metal Estimating System
Makes estimating easier than 1-2-3!

Touch 1 and 2 and you automatically get:

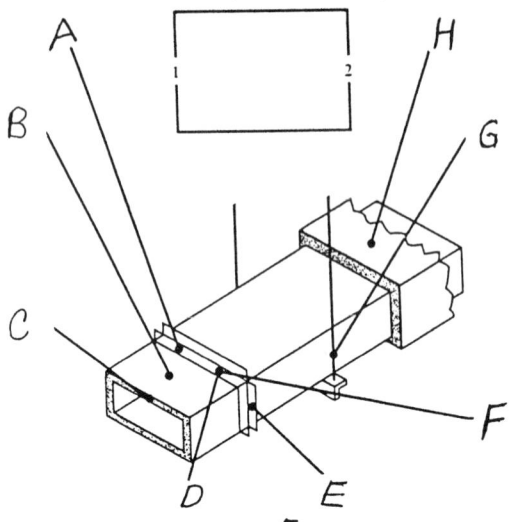

A — Duct Connection Sealer
User specifies systems to seal
Seals only joints where required
Type of material
Quantity
Unit and total costs
Labor

B — Duct Material
Material and gauge as specified
Number of full lengths
Number of pieces
Percentage straight duct/fittings
Quantity in square feet or pounds
Waste calculated
Unit and total costs

C — Line.
Oversized duct if required
Type and thickness of material
Quantity
Waste calculated
Unit and total cost
Adhesive and pins: quantity & cost
Labor

D — Joint Sealer
User can specify systems to seal
Quantity Labor •
Labor   All labor
           Shop fabrication
           Field/erection labor
           Odd length production rates
           Labor factor
           Correction factors for work condition
           Hours
           Hourly wage rates
           Cost of labor
           Detailing labor
           Material handling labor
           Supervisory labor

E — Reinforcing for Connectors and Intermediates
Project standards used automatically
Type
Quantity: linear feet and pounds
Waste calculated
Unit and total costs
Labor

F — Joint Connectors
Type and material
Gasket material, corners, etc.
Quantity: linear feet or pounds
Waste calculated
Unit and total costs
Labor

G — Hangers
Project standards used automatically
Type
Quantity: linear feet and pounds
Can calculate waste
Unit and total costs
Labor
Hanger supports:
  Type and size
  Quantity
  Unit and total costs

H — Duct Wrap/Insulation
Type and thickness of material
Quantity
Overlap calculated
Waste calculated
Unit and total costs
Labor

The Role of the Computer   433.

Above - Touchmenu strip in use.
Below - Touchmenu split into sections to fit on page in this book.
Bottom - Touchmenu's QuickPen in use.

with QuickPen or take advantage of the flexibility of the system and customize the tables to utilize their own data.

Several man years of development by some of the industry's leading HVAC estimators and a team of software engineers have made Quick-Pen the most comprehensive estimating system on the market. That fact combined with Computer Aided Estimating's attention to detail will make QuickPen the standard of excellence for many years to come.

The L-TEC Duct Cutting Systems

- . . . A fully integrated system for cutting sheet metal fittings. Designed and manufactured by L-TEC Welding & Cutting systems based on continuous cutting machine manufacturing experience since 1923.

- . . . A family of economical, automatic duct cutting systems to meet individual production requirements. Cut from 30 to 10 gauge sheet metal and up to 1" plate with optional high current plasma units.

- . . . Cut galvanized and black iron as well as stainless, aluminum and virtually any metal by selecting from the broadest family of plasma cutting packages available.

- . . . Easy-to-use software packages written by sheet metal fabricators for sheet metal fabricators. All new, improved generation of software based on years of duct cutter field experience.

- . . . The clearest, easiest-to-read shop labeling system in the industry eliminates assembly and shipping errors common to other shop practices.

- . . . Systems are supported by the nationwide L-TEC distributor network, and backed by the L-TEC field service organization.

The Hardware

- . . . A family of machine models manufactured by L-TEC with speeds up to 550 in/min.

The Role of the Computer

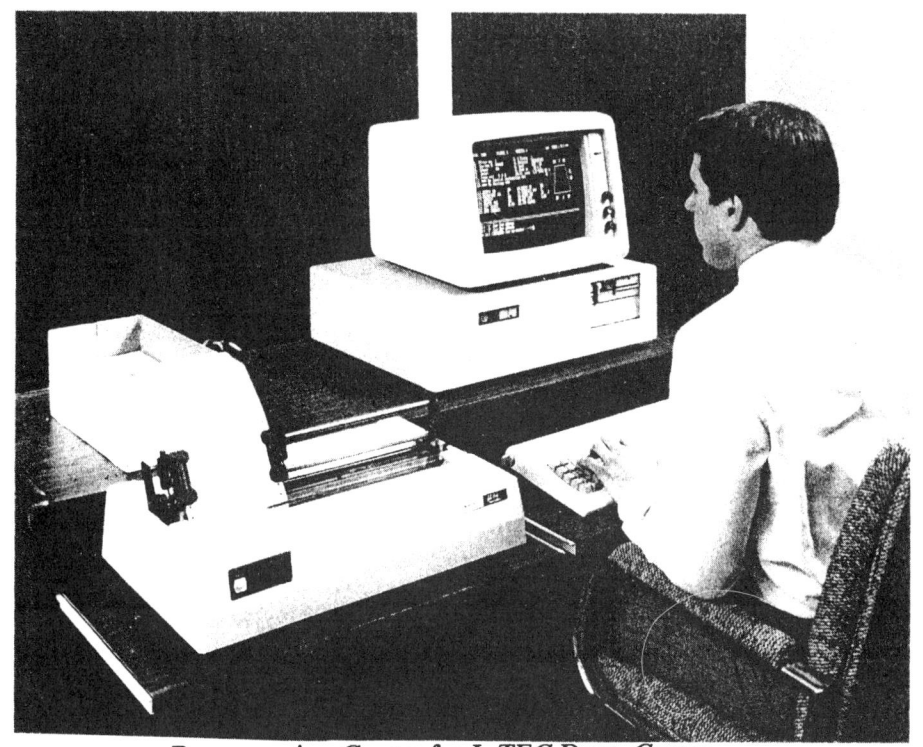

Programming Center for L-TEC Duct-Cutter

- . . . Gantry designs make most efficient use of floor space. Expand your output without expanding the size of your shop.

- . . . Positive drive systems minimize slippage at high speeds even in corners resulting in improved fitting accuracy and greater overall production.

- . . . A family of plasma cutting systems to suit individual production needs from L-TEC, the inventor of the plasma cutting process. Our systems are proven in thousands of installations.

- . . . L-TEC is the most integrated of all the duct cutter suppliers -- cutting machine, control and plasma. This means greater dependability for our customers and the high quality support they have come to expect.

- . . . L-TEC and your local L-TEC Welding distributor is your single source for complete plasma cutting systems, as well as oxy/fuel and MIG welding systems -- torches, power supplies and welding wire.

L-TEC Microprocessor Controls

. . . L-TEC microprocessors efficiently control duct cutting operations and in addition can provide many performance features found only on larger steel fabrication systems. These include:

Program Edit at the keyboard (for part changes)
Variable Part Programming (for families of parts)
Step and Repeat (for automatic quantities)
Trace/Record/Cut (teach mode option)
English/metric dimensions
Scaling (enlarge or reduce programmed part size)
Corner Pause (for square corners)
Jog Off Line and Return (for ease of torch maintenance)
Part Rotate
Down load up to 100 sheets of fittings
Onboard diagnostics

The Software

. . . Software programs are the result of continual development since 1974 by East Coast Sheet Metal Fabricating Corporation.

. . . Complete libraries are available for rectangular, round and oval fittings and for estimating.

. . . Unique program creates unlimited fitting varieties from simple menu-driven screens. Unlike other systems which use a limited library of numbered fittings, the L-TEC Duct Cutting System can produce virtually thousands of fitting variations without reference materials of any kind. Fittings are actually developed on the screen.

. . . Dozens of operator selected defaults reduce fitting take off time to a matter of seconds.

. . . Computer calculates many dimensions based on operator input and fitting inlets are automatic based on outlet of previous fitting.

The Role of the Computer

- Operator selects whether fittings are made in two, three or four pieces to conserve material and make assembly easier.

- Correction mode brings up and changes any fitting dimension or specification in a matter of seconds.

- Take-off operators learn the system in as little as two days and require no previous computer experience.

- Hard disk systems can combine rectangular, round and oval fittings in same nest to conserve material and greatly reduce production time.

- Fitting pieces are rotated as they are nested to maximize material usage.

- Choice of nest routine permits all pieces of same fitting to be nested on same sheet for ease of sorting or on multiple sheets to conserve material.

- Software completely compatible with East Coast Sheet Metal CAD system to eliminate the need for manual takeoff and greatly increase productivity.

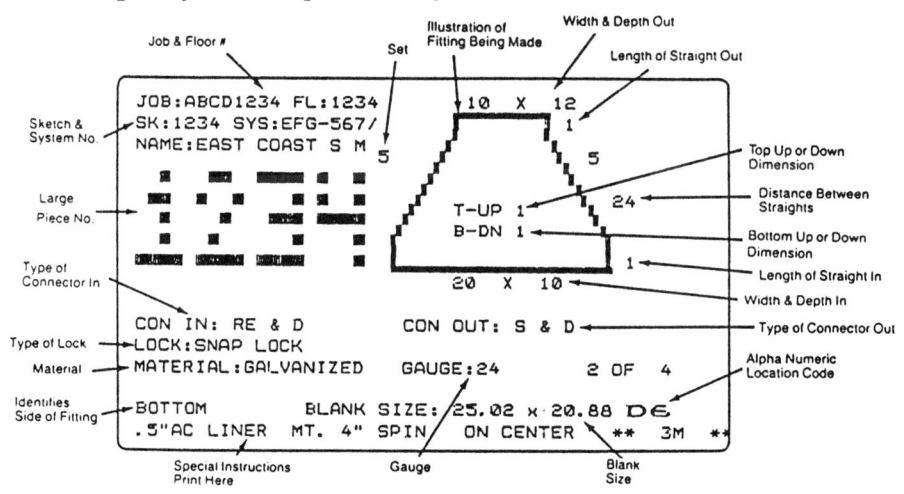

A color-coded label to reduce or eliminate assembly and shipping errors.

- ... Estimating program provides step-by-step procedure to determine your true manufacturing and installation costs based on labor and materials. Over 350 line items for labor alone are provided and these can be customized based on actual user experience.

IBM Computers

- ... L-TEC Duct cutting Systems can be supplied with enhanced IBM "XT" or IBM "AT" computers and hard disk drives depending on selected system.

- ... Color monitor (optional) reduces eye strain.

- ... Authorized dealers for sales and service are widely available.

- ... Compact system can be conveniently installed in any office area.

- ... High speed bi-directional printer produces management reports, color-coded labels and accurate estimates.

Cutting Table

- ... Large cutting tables can be extended for more flexibility, higher productivity.

- ... On two-table systems sheet sizes up to 240" long can be used for greatest reduction of scrap.

- ... Manual dampers permit alternate air exhaust from each table during cutting for maximum down-draft.

- ... Alpha-numeric grid around perimeter quickly locates pieces from code on label. This feature eliminates the time consuming task of interpreting nesting diagrams.

L-TEC DUCTLING

- ... With two employees or two hundred, L-TEC's new Ductling can dramatically increase your productivity and lower your

The Role of the Computer

L-TEC Ductling provides a 72" x 120" cutting area as a newer economical way to cut sheet metal fittings.

   manufacturing costs. If you have been waiting for a high performance system at the right price, your wait is over.

. . . L-TEC's cutting machine experience combined with East Coast Sheet Metal know-how brings the sheet metal industry an economical tool with many proven features of the larger L-TEC Duct Cutting System.

. . . The Ductling provides a 72 in. x 120 in. cutting area that can be expanded to meet greater demands. The unique standalone operator console with 9 inch display screen and fingertip controls keeps the operator fully informed about system status, program execution and even diagnostics.

. . . Ease of installation, positive drive system and high performance air plasma are important features in the design of the Ductling. At speeds up to 250 inches-per-minute without needing corner slowdown, high productivity is assured. L-TEC's 30 amp air plasma system and feathertouch plate riding head mean consistently high quality cutting of galvanized, carbon and stainless steels as well as most other metals.

. . . Choose from a library of East Coast Sheet Metal fittings that have been developed from years of sheet metal and software experience. Created by sheet metal contractors for sheet metal contractors, this software was designed with a sole purpose -- to make take off and fabrication as simple and efficient as possible. A computer to suit your individual needs may be selected from several types.

ORCA Sheet Metal Layout System

Computer Assisted Sheet Metal Layout

The ORCA Sheet Metal Layout System guarantees increased productivity by providing a simple, consistent, and organized method of duct and fitting production. Every phase of your manufacturing process is consolidated into a single step.

Detailing is done in an instant. By selecting a fitting from the menu, the drawing is produced automatically. Select connectors for each end and they appear on the drawing instantly. You simply enter the desired fitting dimensions.

Once you enter the fitting, a complete detail sheet is printed that includes the detail drawing, shear list, materials and labor (based on your rates), and layout.

You need only configure the system once for seam and connector allowances. When you select a seam or connector for a particular fitting your allowances are automatically added to the shear size.

With the material/labor feature of the ORCA Layout System you'll never spend another minute tallying up materials for job costing. The ORCA Layout System gives you the bottom line on costs even before the job is done!

SAMPLE PRINTOUT

The Role of the Computer

Right on each detail sheet is the square footage of lining and labor (based on your man hours per square foot rate). And total metal poundage and labor (based on your man hours per pound rate for rectangular and round duct by gauge). The ORCA Layout System also accumulates materials and labor as fittings are input so you can print out a bottom line job cost summary. This feature also makes a great tool for estimating when you want accurate, piece-by-piece costs.

Pattern dimensions are given to make layout a snap. A recent survey of shops using the ORCA Layout system reports an average time savings of 35%. Some shops were as high as 50%.

Layouts are designed to be done directly on the metal with maximum efficiency. For round fittings, lengths are given to be measured at equal intervals. You can select the number of intervals you want for either greater speed or greater accuracy.

Metal thickness is allowed for on all round layouts so you get an accurate pattern in up to 1 inch plate.

You save additional shop time with the fitting label feature. The ORCA Layout System eliminates the time spent writing job information and assembly instructions on fitting pieces. After detailing fittings for a job using the ORCA Layout System, load tractor fed labels into your printer and select the Labels option from the menu. The program will print a label for each piece of each fitting in the job. Each label has a picture showing how to position it on the piece along with complete job information and assembly instructions.

FEATURES

Full graphic detailing.
Automatic shear lists.
Automatic layout.
Material/Labor computation.

Fitting Labels
User-defined layout intervals.
Allows for metal thickness.
User defined allowances.

BENEFITS

- Details are always neat and complete.
- Save shop time. All necessary details are on the label.
- Accurate shear lists reduce waste.
- You can select greater speed or greater accuracy.

442.   **The Role of the Computer**

RECTANGULAR

TEE · STRAIGHT DUCT · TAP IN · TAPER

ELBOW · SQUARE THROAT RADIUS ELBOW · GOOSE NECK · SQUARE THROAT GOOSE NECK

MITERED OFFSET · RADIUS OFFSET · RADIUS ELBOW/DROP CHEEK · RADIUS TEE

ROUND

CENTERLINE TAPER · OFFSET TAPER · MITERED TAPER

ROUND MITER · ROUND OFFSET · TEE-WYE · WYE-BRANCH

GORED ELBOW · SQUARE-TO-ROUND · SADDLE · TAPERED SADDLE

OTHER

BELT GUARD · HOOD MITER

ORCA SYSTEMS

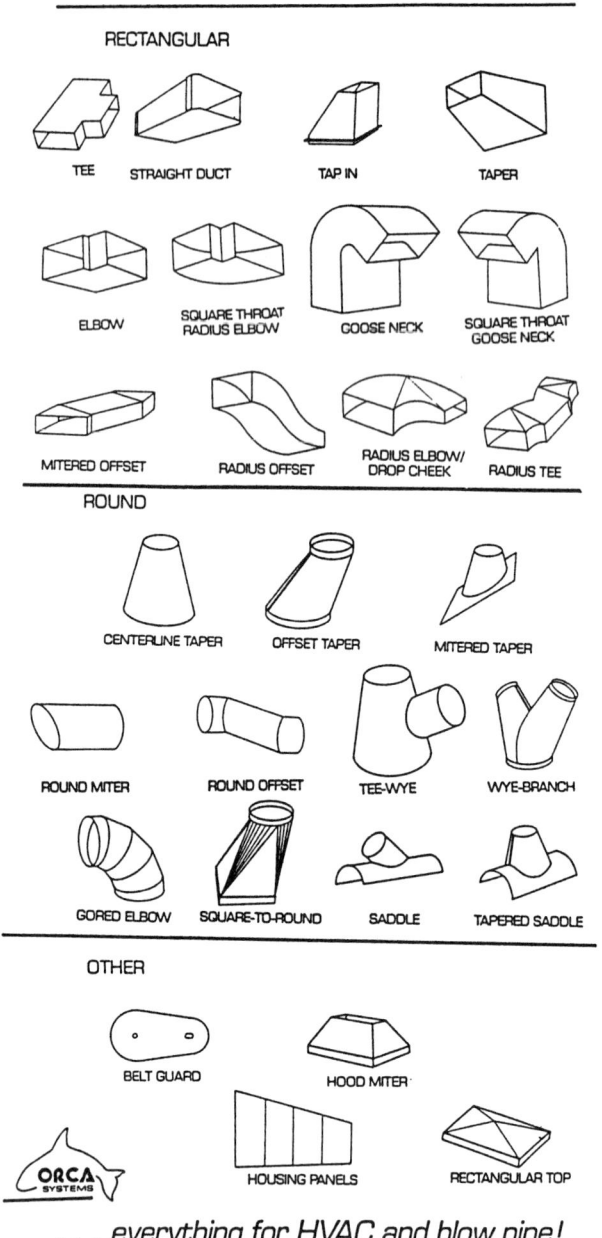

HOUSING PANELS · RECTANGULAR TOP

. . . everything for HVAC and blow pipe!

The Role of the Computer

443.

PAGE FROM MANUAL

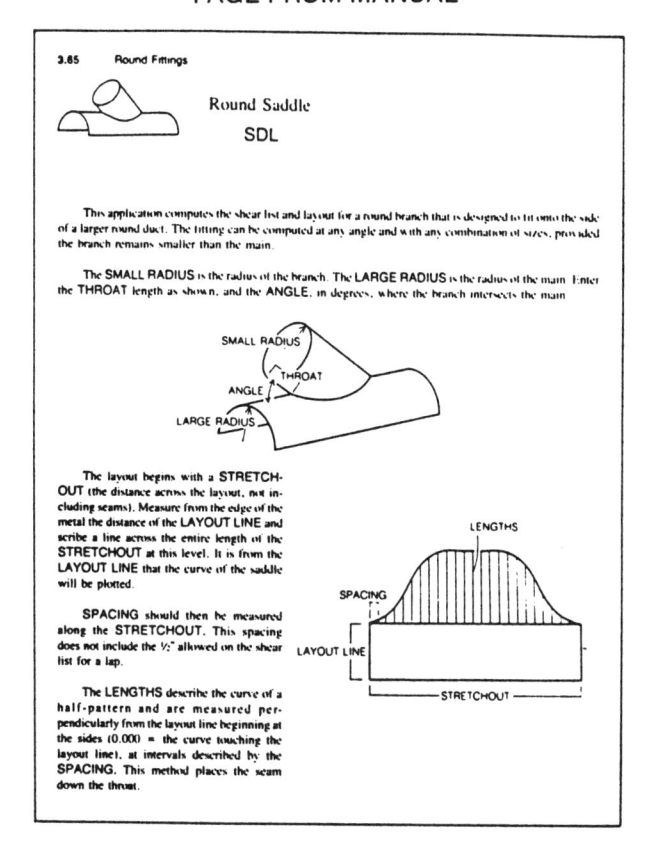

3.85 Round Fittings

Round Saddle
SDL

This application computes the shear list and layout for a round branch that is designed to fit onto the side of a larger round duct. The fitting can be computed at any angle and with any combination of sizes, provided the branch remains smaller than the main.

The SMALL RADIUS is the radius of the branch. The LARGE RADIUS is the radius of the main. Enter the THROAT length as shown, and the ANGLE, in degrees, where the branch intersects the main.

The layout begins with a STRETCH-OUT (the distance across the layout, not including seams). Measure from the edge of the metal the distance of the LAYOUT LINE and scribe a line across the entire length of the STRETCHOUT at this level. It is from the LAYOUT LINE that the curve of the saddle will be plotted.

SPACING should then be measured along the STRETCHOUT. This spacing does not include the ½" allowed on the shear list for a lap.

The LENGTHS describe the curve of a half-pattern and are measured perpendicularly from the layout line beginning at the sides (0.000 = the curve touching the layout line), at intervals described by the SPACING. This method places the seam down the throat.

ORCA Systems

- Layout is consistently quick and simple. All fittings can be laid out fast.
- Get an accurate pattern even in heavy gauge plate.
- Fits your shop--your equipment, your way of doing things.
- Keep on top of costs. Job costings are done instantly.

PRO-DUCT
Hand-Held Computer Systems

PRO/DUCT serves the needs of the HVAC industry. . .featuring hand-held computers, programs that have been developed for fitting layout, engineering and estimating.

At last, computerized duct fabrication that is easy to use and affordable by any contractor or individual sheet metal worker.

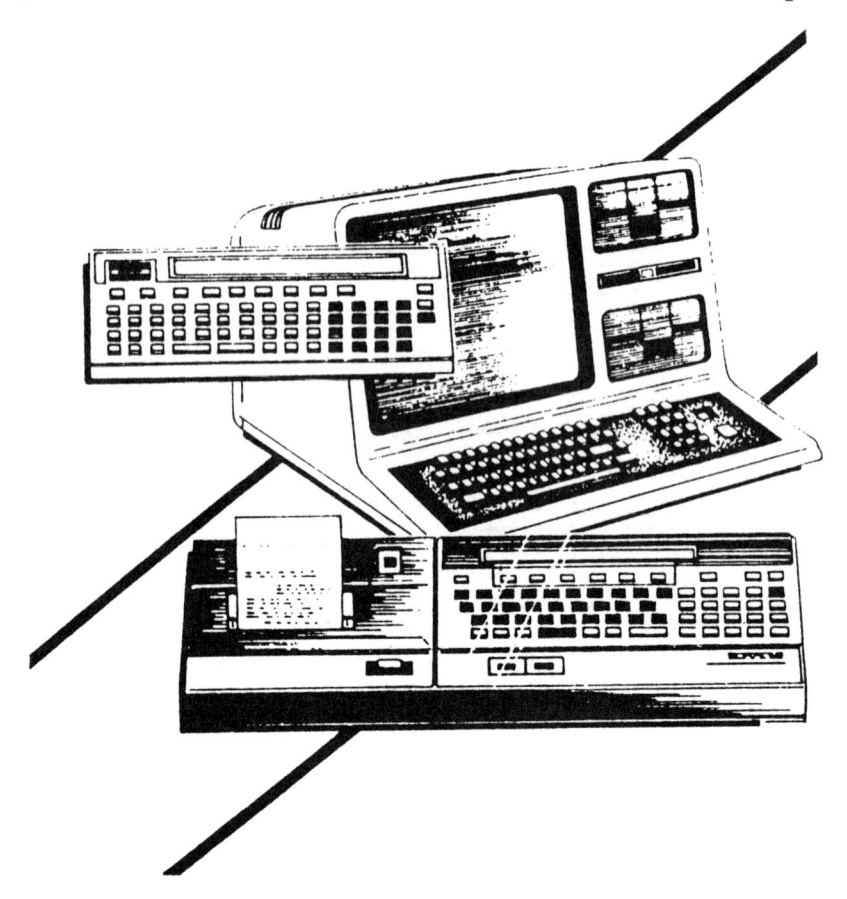

NOTE: Most PRO/DUCT programs are also available to run on all popular personal computers.

This is the world's smallest CAD/CAM computer with a 4-color built-in plotter that draws ductwork! Do no confuse this computer with older technology programmable pocket calculators.

Performs many of the same functions as systems costing $100,000. Cut sheets, templates and triangulation tables are eliminated. In the shop, at job-sites or while traveling, drawings and cut lists can be prepared automatically.

Merely select a fitting picture from the computer screen graphics and enter duct size, etc. The computer prepares the fitting ticket in seconds.

The estimating program helps you bid the job. Auto-Detailer fitting layout program helps you fabricate the job.

The Role of the Computer

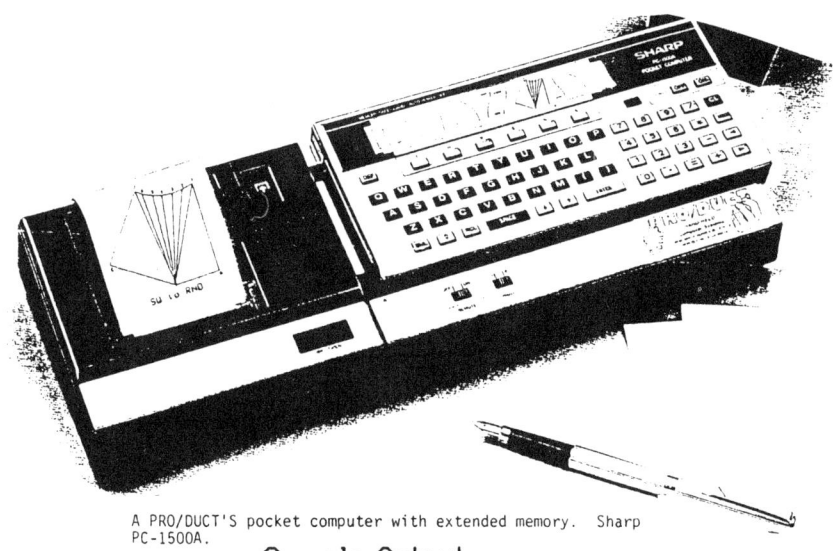

445.

A PRO/DUCT'S pocket computer with extended memory. Sharp PC-1500A.

Sample Output

Estimating

Layout

Energy Calcs

PRO/DUCT HAND-HELD COMPUTER SYSTEMS
9348 SANTA MONICA BL., STE 101
BEVERLY HILLS, CA 90210
(213) 271-9224

PRO/DUCT system reflects 20 years experience in engineering, contracting and duct manufacturing. The system has been used by hundreds of contractors to bid and fabricate projects worth billions of dollars.

PRO/DUCT was formed in 1982 by Carl Sheriff, P.E., holder of an advanced engineering degree, two Professional Engineering registrations and a college teaching credential. Carl Sheriff also authors the "Computer News" column in SNIPS.

Bidmaster Estimating Programs

Estimating Programs for Your Trade

Each contracting trade is unique in its terminology, materials and take-off methods. So each BIDMASTER program is trade specific, addressing the needs of your particular field. You'll find BIDMASTER estimating software written for:

Electrical	General
Mechanical	Concrete/Excavation
HVAC	Drywall

BIDMASTER programs are flexible. Adapting the programs to fit your requirements (for instance, your material and labor costs, or the type of job you're working on) requires no programming; just follow simple file maintenance procedures. RX4000 estimating follows a series of easy steps, beginning with takeoff.

Completely Automatic Takeoff

A traditional takeoff entails many hours of counting, measuring, calculating, and checking for errors. RX4000 takeoff gets the job done

BIDMASTER ESTIMATING PROGRAMS

The Role of the Computer

in about one-fourth the time, with almost 100% accuracy! It's simple - just touch the count probe to each item and trace the length probe along each linear area you wish to measure on the blueprint. The measurements are entered directly into the system. Each item is then extended for material cost and labor, including all byproducts. No calculating is necessary. BIDMASTER software does it for you.

One Entry - One Keystroke

Keyboards are a problem area on many computers, requiring the user to make a series of keystrokes for each entry, often in a complex code.

The RX4000 estimating keyboard allows you to make a one-keystroke entry for most takeoff items. And these items are printed right on the keyboard overlay in the terminology of your trade. You don't need to learn any computer codes or languages. For maximum flexibility, blank overlays are provided so you can write in your material choices for each particular job.

Nothing Left Out

Accidental omission of takeoff steps or items is a major source of error in many bids. BIDMASTER estimating programs guide you through takeoff with a series of prompts that appear on the CRT display. You can hand in your final bid with complete confidence that every item on the blueprint is included in the estimate.

You'll Have Plenty of Time to Adjust the Bid

You can now apply discounts to material costs and adjustment factors to labor hours, obtaining a more accurate job analysis on costs and hours. The RX4000 then prints out a Labor Category breakdown with a phase-by-phase overview of the adjusted totals. Your experience comes into play as you analyze the bid, making further adjustments as necessary to fine tune the estimate.

Bid Summary - Bringing It All Together

The Bid summary printout brings together the adjusted material and labor costs with quoted items, direct job expenses, nonproductive labor hours, sub-contractor and other costs, and lets you apply your profit percentage, hourly rate, overhead, sales tax, and bond rates to obtain the total bid price. Because BIDMASTER software functions so quickly, you can make several estimates, varying factors and discounts to judge their impact.

The Winning Bid

And that's how the RX4000 system and BIDMASTER estimating software work - step by step - to help you generate winning bids quickly and easily. The RX4000 serves as a tool, built to do the job as simply as possible. It's a tool that works the way you do, with the adaptability to meet your needs, allowing you to fine tune each bid with your experience. Speed, accuracy, flexibility, ease of use. These are the keys to the RX4000 system of generating profitable bids - every time!

Estimation Incorporated
805-L Barkwood Court
Linthicum Heights,
Maryland 21090

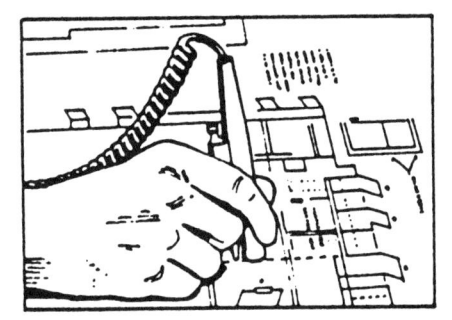

The Role of the Computer
SNIPS   June, 1989

Computer News

Anaheim Technologies Releases New Bid Pricing Software

Anaheim Technologies, Inc., 320 Fifth Ave., Troy, N.Y., 12182, has just released Anaheim Bid, a new software for pricing bids, proposals and quotations. The program also provides added insight into bid analysis.

The Anaheim Bid software balances profit with the chance of winning, to find the optimum price for every bid. An advanced

Expert System recommends selling tactics, an adjustment for risk, and whether not to bid. A "What-if" analysis provides quick revised recommendations. The program asks questions about costs, competition and the customer and generates a strategy report from the information. The entire analysis can be completed in under 20 minutes.

The program runs on IBM PC, XT, AT, PS/2 and compatible computers and requires a 640K RAM, a hard disk and DOS of 2.1 or higher.

ACCA To Hold "How To Computerize Your Business" Seminar and Trade Show, Oct. 20-21

The Air Conditioning Contractors of America (ACCA) has announced its 4th annual seminar and trade show on computers. It is titled, "How to Computerize Your Business", and will be held Oct. 20-21, in Arlington, Va.

This seminar and trade show will give participants an opportunity to view the latest in HVAC related software. Additional information can be obtained from Christie Higgins at ACCA, 1512-16th St., N.W., Washington, D.C., 20036.

Harper Offers New Residential, Commercial and Refrigeration Heat Loss/Gain Programs

A new type of heat loss and heat gain program has recently been announced by Glen M. Harper. It will run residential, commercial and refrigeration heat loss/heat gain calculations and is very simple to use, according to Harper.

Residential Section Formatted After ACCA Manual J

The residential section is formatted after ACCA's Manual J and prints out each room and the total on a standard 8½x11" sheet of paper, or on the computer screen. It has built-in Manual J factors, or the user can enter his own factors on the full screen input.

It will edit, save and load calculations, both rooms and totals. It has a special program to enter one's own personalized set of factors. The program automatically figures the cfm for each room and the total. Latent and sensible heat is shown and it calculates both heat loss and heat gain as one runs the calculation.

Commercial Section Follows ACCA Manual N

The commercial section follows ACCA's Manual N exactly and calculations can be edited, saved, loaded, and the worksheet printed out on three sheets of plain paper or on the computer screen.

The full screen worksheet allows one to fill in the blanks on all calculations and figures the calculation as you progress.

Refrigeration Section Follows Dunham-Bush Format

The refrigeration heat gain section follows the Dunham-Bush format and uses ASHRAE factors. It is a very large program, according to Harper, and will handle most any size or condition needed to calculate.

It too, uses full screen input (fill in the blanks) and calculates the totals as you progress. This program can also edit, save, load and print out the calculation on the screen or on paper. It uses the short and long form calculation.

This Master HLHG program will only work on a hard disk and takes up 610K of space. To install, simply type INSTALLC and follow the instructions on the screen.

Free information and Demodisk sets are available from Glen M. Harper, P.O. Box 369, Avondale Estates, Ga., 30002.

Reprinted with permission from SNIPS Magazine.

450.

Elite Announces AutoCAD Compatibility For FIRE Program

Elite Software Development, Inc., P.O. Drawer 1194, Bryan, Texas, 77806, announces AutoCAD compatibility for FIRE, a computer program for fire sprinkler hydraulic calculations.

The FIRE program performs hydraulic calculations in exact accordance with the latest standards set by the NFPA. FIRE handles tree, grid, and hybrid systems with up to 250 sprinklers.

Through a joint effort between Elite Software and the CaddLINK Corp., the program can now fully utilize data generated from AutoCAD drawing files created by the CaddLINK Fire Protection Drawing System. A complete fire sprinkler system can be designed, drawn, and completed for submittals and shop fabrication. All fire protection symbols used in the AutoCAD interface are NFPA 172 standards.

Data-Basics Introduces Enhanced Version of Construction Master Accounting System

Data-Basics, 11100 Cedar Rd., Cleveland, Ohio, 44106, has recently introduced an enhanced version of its Construction Master Accounting System (CMAS) computer software.

The new software, CMAS Plus+, offers many new features, including a window-based system for multiple menu/screen access, compatibility with the Novell Network, expanded journal entries, and enhanced system security to limit access to specific software functions.

Endorsed by the National Ass'n of Plumbing-Heating-Cooling Contractors (NAPHCC), CMAS Plus+ runs on IBM, PC, XT, AT, and IBM compatible computer systems. It is available on DOS, XENIX, and Novell Networks, and can be interfaced with word processing and spreadsheet software.

U. of Wisconsin to Hold Computer Correspondence Course

The University of Wisconsin-Madison will be offering an independent study course on programming the 8086 family of microprocessors with 10 correspondence lessons which may be submitted on a diskette or using Textlink with computer modem.

The 8086 family of microprocessors is at the heart of the IBM-PC and other computers that run MS-DOS, UNIX, XENIX, and other widely used operating systems. One may need to program his microprocessor in assembly language to get at otherwise inaccessible machine and operating system functions. Programming the 8086

The Role of the Computer

family of microprocessors covers assembly language programming for this family of processors, using the Microsoft Macro Assembler.

Most importantly, those participating will learn practical, realistic assembler programming. In this course, the examples illustrating various techniques are designed to be extensive, realistic, and useful.

For further details, contact Prof. Don Gritymacher of the Dept. of Engineering, University of Wisconsin-Madison, 432 N. Lake St., Madison, Wis., 53706.

SNIPS September, 1989

Computer News

Sheriff Discusses Portable and Lap-Top Computers

Presented here, is another column, authored by Carl Sheriff, who has contributed many articles for this department over the past couple of years. He is president of Pro/Duct Computer Systems.

This month, Carl Sheriff discusses portable and lap-top computers. His comments follow:

Those reading this column regularly know that I am a proponent of the portable and laptop computer. Those reading ads in this and non-trade publications also know that the portable computer has come out of the closet. The portable computer had been considered no more than sophisticated calculators.

Recent significant improvements in processor and storage technology have changed the pocket computer into a legitimate business tool. In my shirt pocket, I carry the equivalent of an IBM PC, albeit without a full size screen and printer.

Any Computer Is Portable If It Can Be Used Without Plugging Into Outlet

I consider any computer portable if it can be used without being plugged into an electrical outlet and can be carried onto an airplane. This eliminates the "luggables" and "transportables" that are really reworked desk-top computers built into a case.

Among the truly portable computers are the pocket and lap-tops. The primary distinction is that the lap-tops have full size QWERTY (named for the first six letters on the top line of the keyboard) keyboards. Small, non-standard keyboards simply do not allow effective typing.

The Role of the Computer

About Lap-Top Failures

Lap-top computers have had their failures. I just saw the ill-fated IBM-convertible lap-top computer being sold at discount on television's Home Shopping Club. IBM has never been known for over-whelming technology, and with lap-tops, IBM was "out-teched" by Japanese competition.

The front runners in the lap-top world are not the same as those in the desk-top market. Apple is about to introduce its machine. Compaq has only recently done so. The major players are Zenith, Toshiba and NEC. Tandy, however, with its Model 100 has sold more of the portable computers than anyone else.

Lightweight notebook systems, two to six pounds, are aimed at those who want to write, maintain small databases, or use the portable computer to communicate with the computer at home-base. The Radio Shack (Tandy Model 100/102) satisfies these needs with built-in programs and modem. Few of the notebook sized portables are DOS compatible, although they can easily transfer files to DOS or MacIntosh desk-top computers.

About the Newest Lap-Top Computers

The newest lap-top computers compromise full functionality for lightweight and long battery life. These "ultralites" feature solid state disk ram modules instead of floppy disk drives for program and data storage.

Disk drives are still mechanical mechanisms in an electronic environment. Disk drives consume energy and are subject to motion shock, undesirable characteristics in a portable system.

General purpose lap-top computers that essentially perform as well as desk-top units weigh 10-20 pounds and are typically "clam-shell design." They contain floppy and hard disks, up to four megabytes of memory and use the fast 80386 processors.

Displays are exotic gas plasma. The shortcomings: $7,000-$9,000 price and two to three hour battery life.

What to Look For

Look for at least a supertwist LCD display and preferably a backlit supertwist. Black letters on paper-white background is best. Gas plasma and illuminesant displays offer high resolution, but are expensive, power consuming and are orange, or off color.

Portable printers are available, but don't depend on them to give letter quality output. They usually use thermal paper, have limited graphic capabilities and have a short battery life.

For the ultimate portable computer — the Seiko wrist computer. It attaches to an interface and transfers information to or from your desk-top computer, has a four line screen and full, although necessarily small, keyboard.

Carl Sheriff would be glad to answer questions on any type of computer or application. He may be reached at Pro/Duct Computer Systems, 9348 Civic Center Dr., #101, Beverly Hills, Cal., 90210.

Elite Software Offers New Version of Psychart Program

Elite Software, P.O. Drawer 1194, Bryan, Texas, 77806, is now offering a powerful new version of its psychrometric analysis (Psychart) computer program.

Said to be the only software of its kind, Psychart displays the psychrometric chart on a computer screen and allows a designer to perform all operations and analysis normally done using a conventional psychrometric chart.

The new, faster version of Psychart features AutoCad compatibility by creating DXF files for Psychart results and reports. The program's DXF files contain complete Psycharts with full points and processes shown. Psychart follows exact procedures from the 1985 ASHRAE Handbook.

Psychart displays numerical values for all properties for any selected point on the Psychart. Points on the chart can be labeled for future reference, and reports of their properties can be displayed on the screen, printed, or stored in a file. Lines for all standard psychrometric processes such as heating, cooling, humidification, mixing, etc., are displayed on the chart with simple user commands.

Harper Heatloss and Heatgain Programs Now Automatically Calculate Duct Size

Glen M. Harper, who has developed the Master Heatloss and Heatgain computer program has announced recent improvements.

Harper reports that both of his residential Heatloss and Heatgain programs will now automatically calculate the duct size of both rooms and totals. The calculation is based on ACCA's Manual D and ASHRAE's formulas.

All prior purchasers of the Harper program can get the new version free if requested before the end of 1989. Contact Glen M. Harper, P.O. Box 369, Avondale Estates, Ga., 30002.

Construction Industry Show Covers Management and Computer Systems

MCS '89 - the Management & Computer Systems Show for the Construction Industry takes place, Nov. 14-17, at the Rosemont O'Hare Exposition Center, Rosemont, Ill. Three days of trade show exhibits and four days of seminars and conferences will be featured.

Information on MCS '89 is available from David Hanchette, Fails Management Institute (FMI), P.O. Box 31108, Raleigh, N.C., 27622.

452.
Red Wing Unveils New Business Inventory System #2.0

Red Wing Business Systems, Inc., 610 Main St., Red Wing, Minn., 55006, is now marketing their new Business Inventory System, Version 2.0. The system allows contractors to easily modify it as need be throughout a series of screen prompts. The inventory system is designed to handle a very simple inventory system, keeping only a minimum amount of information; or a very complete system, with a wide selection of in-depth information.

Contractors, having from three to 30 employees and under 25,000 inventory items, can use Red Wing's Business Inventory System for tracking various items, keeping stocking information, recording multiple prices for each item and tracking inventory at multiple locations. The system is ideally suited for HVAC, plumbing and electrical contractors, according to Lyle Warrington, president.

SNIPS   November, 1989

Computer News

Sheriff Discusses Computer Generated Plans and Bills Of Material

Presented here, is another column, authored by Carl Sheriff, who has contributed many articles for this department over the past couple of years. He is president of Pro/Duct Computer Systems.

This month Carl Sheriff discusses computer generated plans and bills of materials. His comments follow:

Application of computers in the HVAC and sheet metal industry was slow to start but has progressed geometrically with the advent of affordable systems and sophisticated software, bolstered by the "I've gotta have one, too" mentality of contractors. Computers have eased the estimating and drafting chores, but have not caused a fundamental change in the bidding process.

Those in the construction industry cannot be oblivious to the redundancy and waste of human resources involved in dozens of contractors taking off the same job. It's just the way it has always been done. Never mind that the lowest bidder is often so only because he forgot something.

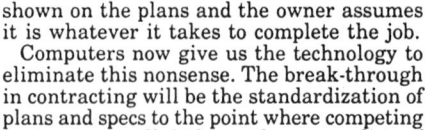

The Role of the Computer

Other Industries Do Not Depend On Each Bidder

Other industries building multi-million dollar projects, such as in aerospace, do not depend on each bidder to figure the quantities of items to be furnished. In such a case, nobody knows exactly what is included in a bid. The bidder assumes it is whatever is shown on the plans and the owner assumes it is whatever it takes to complete the job.

Computers now give us the technology to eliminate this nonsense. The break-through in contracting will be the standardization of plans and specs to the point where competing contractors will bid on the same list of materials. The list will be generated by the architect or consulting engineer through a database integrated with the designer's CAD system.

Such Computer Systems Available Now

Such computer systems are available now, although expensive and with steep learning curves. Each and every object in a CAD drawing, be they walls, ceiling tiles, or ducts, have associated attributes such as size, color, unit cost and location.

Any of the popular CAD programs has the ability to generate a bill of materials directly from the drawing. This capability is little used except to print room finish or equipment schedules. The technology is here. The resistance to change is what must be overcome.

Complete Bill of Materials and Drawings Can Be Stored

A complete bill of materials and drawings for even the most complex building project can be stored on CD_ROM optical disks and be distributed to contractors. These disks are similar to audio compact disks. They can hold 550 megabytes of information and cost less than one blue-print to reproduce. No more lugging a load of plans.

The information on an optical disk is equivalent to 25,000 pounds of blueprints. CD_ROM devices are now in the $5,000 range, but can be below $500 if mass produced. Photographs, 3D views and an audio track can be incorporated into the CD as part of the construction documents.

Computer generated plan and specification information distributed electronically can be used not only for bidding, but for actual fabrication. Plasma machines can cut fittings directly read from mechanical engineer's plans.

Benefits Are Lower Overall Costs

The benefits of designer supplied bill of materials are lower overall costs to owners and increased profitability to contractors with less litigation. The burden, however, on the architect/engineer would increase.

The Role of the Computer

The designer would have to be clearer and accurate in conveying his intent. Items inadvertently left off a plan, however, would at least have established unit costs. Extras and deducts would no longer be the subject of dispute.

I propose that organizations such as SMACNA and ASHRAE form a standard for computer generated bills of materials.

Bidding, based on standard, computer generated drawings and bills of materials would change the nature of the construction business — for the better!

Carl Sheriff would be glad to answer questions on any type of computer or application. He may be reached at Pro/Duct Computer Systems, 9348 Civic Center Dr., #101, Beverly Hills, Cal., 90210.

Software Shop Introduces Job Costing Package

Software Shop Systems, Inc., P.O. Box 728, Farmingdale, N.J., 07727, has announced the introduction of ConTrak II Version 5.0, an integrated accounting and job costing package for specialty contractors.

ConTrak II operates on IBM's PS/2 family, PC/ATs, and compatibles. The system consists of eight modules: job cost; payroll; accounts payable; purchase orders; accounts receivable; general ledger; service billing; and inventory.

Trump's Software Services Markets AIA Billing Computer Software

SNIPS readers with IBM computers and compatibles are reminded of the availability of a computer program which will help relieve a lot of tedious paper work. We refer to Trump's Software Services, Inc.'s AIA Billing Software.

This program, which prints the 702 and 703 forms, accomplishes error-free calculations, including retentions, in minutes instead of hours. The program allows quick access to revise figures or do next Draw Request.

Write Trump's Software Services, Inc., 209 S. Main St., Crown Point, Ind., 46307, for more information.

Microcomputer Technology Introduces New Automatic Profile Nesting Software

Microcomputer Technology Consultants Ltd., P.O. Box 467, Lockport, N.Y., 14094, has announced the introduction of a new profile nesting software package for the flame-cutting industry.

Entitled ProNest, the new program automatically positions each part on the nest following rotation, grain restraint, and priority requirements to obtain maximum yield.

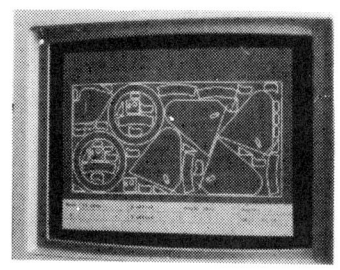

The program also determines an optimized cutting order and generates plate utilization reports, cutting sequence, plots, and other pertinent manufacturing data.

ProNest is designed for the IBM AT, PS/2, or true compatible running at 12 MHz or faster, with a math co-processor.

Complete technical specifications and a free demo disk are available.

Computer Spending on the Rise In the Construction Industry

With the proliferation of the computer into all corners of the industry, its growth in the construction field is expected to balloon in the next five years, according to a new study by the Sweet's Group, the construction product information arm of McGraw-Hill Information Services Co.

For the first time since Sweet's began its study a decade ago, individual office's average spending-to-date for hardware and software increased substantially. At this time last year, offices spent an average of $34,000 for equipment in the course of their buying life. Comparative spending for similar equipment within the past year alone has increased this cumlative total 71% to $58,000

Heuristics Int'l Offers Pattern Cutting Software

Heuristics International, 32 River Rd., Cos Cob, Conn., 06807, is now offering Shortcut, a software program for pattern cutting on metal sheets. Program operation is easy to learn and will save up to 15% in metal waste.

The software also includes programs for inventory management and order book processing, and is available on a 30-day trial basis.

New Scheduling/Machine Loading Module Featured In Kenetek Management Software

Kenetek, Inc., 5033 Winton Rd., Cincinnati, Ohio, 45232, has announced that Bottom Line, the business management software system written especially for job shops and small manufacturers, now includes Scheduling/Machine Loading functions.

Developed by Kenetek, Inc., Bottom Line handles job costing, routing/estimating, inventory management, purchasing, accounts receivable/payable, order entry, general ledger, and now scheduling/machine loading.

Bottom Line is IBM PC compatible, menu-driven, and has built-in networking and multi-user functions supporting Novell, PC-MOS/386, etc.

FHP and Elite Software Announce Marketing Agreement

Florida Heat Pump Mfg. (FHP) and Elite Software Development, Inc., Bryan, Texas, have announced a new software marketing agreement.

Under the agreement, FHP will provide Elite Software's Earth-Coupled Pipe Loop Sizing program (ECA) to its customers through its nationwide distributor network. ECA is designed to quickly calculate the loop pipe length necessary for heating and cooling a building with a given heat pump, soil, and weather conditions.

In April, 1990, FHP will conduct software training seminars at its headquarters. For further information, contact FHP, 601 N.W. 65th Ct., Fort Lauderdale, Fla., 33309.

SNIPS   March, 1990

Computer News

Sheriff of Pro/Duct Asks, "Are Computers Worth It?"

Presented here, is another column, authored by Carl Sheriff, who has contributed many articles for this department over the past couple of years. He is president of Pro/Duct Computer Systems.

Sheriff's article this month, asks the question, "Are Computers Worth It?" His comments follow:

Every time one of Peat, Marwick's 15,000 auditors heads out for a job, a personal computer is toted along. Calculations which once took hours, are now done on an Excel spreadsheet. But, ask the firm if the computers are worth it and even the big eight accounting firm can't say.

Determining Cost Benefit Is Difficult

Peat, Marwick isn't alone. Although computers can enable substantial time savings which are of obvious economic benefit, determining precisely the cost benefit of a computer system is inherently difficult, if not impossible.

The Role of the Computer

The problem is in attaching a dollar value to information. There are no hard and fast rules to setting value to something as nebulous as information. Just too many variables exist to quantify the time or dollar value of information. With most firms, it is simply a management call on investment in computers.

Most businesses like to work out some sort of cost/benefit analysis to justify the expense before purchasing a computer. How does one place a value on a lost bid or proposal that could have been obtained with the use of a computer? It is one of those things that don't happen because you don't have a computer that are costing the most.

Costs Easily Determined

Costs of hardware, software and peripherals are easily determined. The costs of training and retraining are far more than the system hardware itself. However, not only are training costs more difficult to determine, those costs are often completely neglected by management in selecting a system.

Macintosh computers, far more expensive than IBM clones, are justified by their short learning curve. The learning curve of the Mac is not only shorter, but does not have the learning curve. The learning curve of the Mac is not only shorter, but does not have the learning curve "wall" that prevents MSDOS computer users from fully taking advantage of the power of their systems.

Survey Computer Users In Your Firm

One method of evaluating computer use is to survey those in your firm using computers by asking how the computer effects their job, the degree to which it provides a competitive edge, and its effectiveness as a revenue generating tool. The survey may be a formal quarterly questionnaire, but for a small firm will most likely be just user feedback to the boss.

The survey results may not so much yield specifics, but will give management an insight on how computers better enable people to do their jobs. User feedback often gives management ideas not even imagined when first contemplating a computer system.

If you are still asking: "What do I need a computer for?", then you are the one most in need.

Carl Sheriff would be glad to answer questions on any type of computer or application. He may be reached at Pro/Duct Computer Systems, 9348 Civic Center Dr., #101, Beverly Hills, Cal., 90210.

Elite Software Announces Improvement To Its Commercial HVAC Loads Calculation Program

Elite Software Development, Inc., P. O. Drawer 1194, Bryan, Texas, 77806, has introduced a major new improvement to its commercial HVAC loads calculation program (CHVAC 4.0). CHVAC 4.0 quickly calculates peak heating and cooling loads, as well as cfm air quantity requirements with complete psychrometrics.

The Role of the Computer

This program is based on exact table values and procedures described in the 1989 ASHRAE Handbook. Improvements include greater power and ease of use with much faster calculation speed. A new option is a zone data overview screen designed to ease the organization of zones under air handler systems.

Additional copy features have been introduced for the easier replication of common data such as air handlers, plenums and zones. In addition, the number of master construction types for roofs, walls, partitions, glass sections and shading configurations have been increased. The CHVAC 4.0 provides comprehensive reports, listing detailed zone loads, air handler summary loads, total building loads and tonnage requirements. Prices start at $295.

Lennox Introduces Two New Computer Programs

Lennox Industries, Inc., has recently announced the introduction of two new computer programs that contractors and engineers can use for applications with Lennox heating or cooling products.

The company has developed Lennox product templates compatible with "AutoCAD", and advanced computer-aided design software.

Lennox' AutoCAD package contains drawings for all residential or commercial Lennox products, including the company's new GCS16 and CHA/CHP16 2-ton to 5-ton units.

According to Bill Dickson of Lennox' LOGIC Software Group, "The program allows users to easily access drawings of Lennox units when designing residential or commercial product installations."

Lennox' second software introduction is an equipment selection program that, like the AutoCAD program, features all Lennox equipment and accessories. It can run on any IBM PC or compatible DOS 2.x, 3.x, or 4.x with 512K RAM, two floppy disk drives or a hard disk, and an 80-column printer.

Lennox' equipment selection program is divided into sections for listing heating and cooling equipment specifications and ratings, product features, options, thermostats, and controls.

For additional information on either of the two new programs, contact Lennox, LOGIC Software Group, P.O. Box 809000, Dallas, Texas, 75380.

SNIPS   May, 1990

Computer News

Sheriff of Pro/Duct Discusses "Working At Home — Telecommuting"

Presented here, is another column, authored by Carl Sheriff, who has contributed many articles for this department over the past several years. He is the president of Pro/Duct Computer Systems.

Sheriff's article this month covers the subject of, "Working At Home — Telecommuting". His comments follow:

A project estimator spreads a set of plans out on his dining room table and performs a take-off without the interruptions common at the office. His portable computer compiles the estimate and automatically transmits the data to the office.

A mechanical engineer, instead of driving an hour to work, rolls out of bed, checks his electronic mail, FAX's a reply and starts work on drawings on his affordable CAD system — all in his bathrobe.

A contractor with projects spread over several states is able to resolve job site problems by phone from his home in the mountains. He also has a hand held cellular phone to keep in touch at all times.

Above Is Called Telecommuting

These above three examples are what 10 million Americans are doing: telecommuting. Telecommuting or telecomputing is defined as working either at home, or at a remote office.

In the last 10 years, with the advent of affordable computers, FAX machines and cellular telephones, telecommuting has become a popular alternative to the conventional work week.

Employee Advantages

The advantages for the employees include:

* Less time spent in commuting. This can amount to 2 to 3 hours a day — not to mention the associated nervous tension and energy waste.

* Flexible work hours. Nine to five is a thing of the past. Telecommuters can work when it suits them.

* More comfortable work environment. It's hard to beat pajamas and your favorite arm chair.
* Savings on clothes, restaurant and automobile expenses.
* Improved family ties. Telecommuters have more time with their families and often are able to live where their families want to.

Employer Benefits

Employer benefits of telecommuting are listed as follows:

* Lower fixed payroll costs. Free-lancers or independent contractors can be retained as needed.
* Improved productivity. Telecommuters, for a number of reasons, usually tackle their jobs with extra vigor. Surprisingly, it is easier to track their job performance than that of office workers.
* Higher employee morale. Working at home gives telecommuters a feeling of having control over their personal and family lives.
* Less office space required. This is especially advantageous in metropolitan areas where rents can be several hundred dollars per square foot.
* Less absenteeism and tardiness. How can you be late to your home office? Mental health sick days are reduced. Telecommuters feeling under the weather are more likely to work anyway.

Successful Telecommuter Usually A Self-Motivating Individual

Telecommuters fall into two broad categories: salaried; and self-employed. Most employers still have not come to grips with the notion of off-site workers. The typical successful telecommuter is also a self-motivating individual.

The advantages of working at home: higher productivity; less stress; time and energy savings; and lower overhead, are perhaps more obvious than the latent disadvantages.

Problem number one is isolation. It is harder for the home office worker to keep their fingers on the pulse of what's going on. Some people miss the "shmooze" and gossip around the office water cooler.

You don't have the guy in the next office to bounce ideas off of. The office football pools are a thing of the past.

Telecommuters report that the gang at the office forget about them when it comes time for parties. Working at home also means that the boss may not know what a fine job you are doing when it comes time for a raise or promotion. If you're into office politics, telecommuting is not for you.

Distraction Problems

Distraction can be a problem. The television, refrigerator, or the kids are just a few feet away. For procrastinators, there are all kinds of excuses for goofing around. Some will spend their day running meaningless errands or doing house work.

The Role of the Computer

On the other hand, many people find themselves becoming electronic workaholics. Because you are responsible for bringing in the bucks, guilt for not sitting behind the computer develops.

Telecommuting Requires Self-Discipline

The solution, in either case, is to establish a work schedule, just as if you worked in the office. Take breaks. Have lunch meetings. Reward yourself with raids to the refrigerator only after completing a task.

Telecommuting requires self-discipline. When you work at home, nobody is looking over your shoulder to make sure you get the job done. Dagwood Bumpstead had it easy. Mr. Dithers would give him a kick. When you are a telecommuter, the motivation has to come from within.

Carl Sheriff would be glad to answer questions on any type of computer or application. He may be reached at Pro/Duct Computer Systems, 9348 Civic Center Dr., #101, Beverly Hills, Cal., 90210.

Elite Software Offers New HVAC Component Parts Program

Elite Software Development, Inc., P.O. Drawer 1194, Bryan, Texas, 77806, is now offering Parts, a new computer program for the rapid and optimal selection of HVAC component items and parts.

Parts computerizes the look-up and pricing of component parts used in the HVAC industry. The software is designed to work with many different parts lists including ones from HVAC manufacturers and supply houses.

By entering an item description or part number, or even partial number and description, users can quickly view part numbers, descriptions and prices. The Parts program can inform the user that a part has been discontinued and recommend the best possible replacement.

Harper Offers Free Update On FuelCost Estimator Program

Glen M. Harper, originator of the FuelCost Estimator program advises that several important changes have been made to this program.

In addition to estimating the operating cost of air conditioners and furnaces using natural gas, LP-gas, fuel oil or electricity and for air-to-air heat pumps and water-to-air heat pumps, and the cost of auxiliary heat using the same four different types of fuels on heat pumps, the new version of the FuelCost Estimator incorporates the recently ARI suggested blower cost on all appropriate units, plus a number of other improvements.

A copy of this new update will be sent free to any original purchaser of this program, since its origination in 1980. Contact Glen M. Harper, P.O. Box 369, Avondale Estates, Ga., 30002.

The Role of the Computer
SNIPS   July, 1990

Computer News

Sheriff of Pro/Duct Discusses "Computers As Appliances"

Presented here, is another column, authored by Carl Sheriff, who has contributed many articles for this department over the past several years. He is the president of Pro/Duct Computer Systems.

Sheriff's article this month covers the subject of, "Computers As Appliances". His comments follow:

I plug in my toaster and it works. I turn on the blender and it works. The TV, microwave and telephone all work. Those of you that have gone out and bought a MSDOS computer have discovered that nothing works.

At least nothing remotely complicated. Programs don't install. All kinds of weird files have to be created for a program to run. Most software conflicts with other software. Good luck getting a color monitor to display properly.

Good luck in having enough memory to run that fat program. No wonder contractors seek to buy cheap clones. Saving on the initial cost is the only way they can justify the after purchase expense of setting up the system.

Sorry, I Don't Do Windows

An example of what doesn't work on MSDOS machines is Microsoft Windows 8.0. Recently released with much fanfare, this is Microsoft's latest attempt to bring to the land of DOS the Graphical User Interface (GUI) popularized by the Apple Macintosh.

Microsoft's first version of Windows prompted a lawsuit by Apple Computer over rights to the graphic interface. Trouble is, even without the lawsuit, the earlier version of Windows was doomed. Though it tried to be better than MSDOS, it was slow and awkward. It was plain ugly.

Windows Needs Fast Medicine

Windows has inherently sticky problems. Unlike the Mac's operating system, Windows is an overlay to MSDOS and as such has a lot of overhead to support. Windows needs a fast machine (an 80386 at 20 Mhz) and huge amount of memory (6 megabytes) to work acceptably. The attractiveness of cheap clones soon fades when you need to spend $8,000 for a computer that can handle Windows.

Simply installing windows does not guarantee full benefit of the graphic user interface. Software publishers have to go through the time and expense of modifying their software to accommodate Windows. This has to happen in a market with thousands of programs, hundreds of vendors and a resistance to concede to Microsoft who already is the market leader.

The consistent user interface that Macintosh users take for granted exists entirely because Apple alone controls the Mac. From the beginning, Apple has dictated how Macs were to interact with the people who use them.

That is why every Mac program runs on every model Mac, why every font is available at any time and why any type printer can be connected without fumbling with DIP switch settings. The consistent "look-and-feel" does more than cut training time.

It allows millions of Mac users, who thought they just wanted to do spreadsheets, discover that they have the capability to create drawings, publish newsletters and communicate with other computers.

What ever happened to OS-2, IBM's version of a graphic user interface? That operating system never materialized because it was written by attorneys, not programmers. The system received little support among software developers.

Unfortunately we are still in the age of computers where many of the hardware and software designers emerged from the main frame world where they never had to deal with computer users that were contractors, not computer nerds.

I resent IBM considering me a DUMB TERMINAL!

Carl Sheriff would be glad to answer questions on any type of computer or application. He may be reached at Pro/Duct Computer Systems, 9348 Civic Center Dr., #101, Beverly Hills, Cal., 90210.

ESAB Automation Offers Video On FastCAM Parts Programming

ESAB Automation, Inc., P.O. Box 2286, Fort Collins, Colo., 80522, just released a new video presentation of the FastCAM Parts Program System. The video demonstrates the ease of programming, blocking, nesting, digitizing, copying, plotting and many other features of the FastCAM system designed for use in the metal working industry. It also demonstrates several automated X-Y cutting applications including spindle, oxyfuel, plasma and waterjet cutting.

FastCAM is a PC based system that communicates with CAD systems, so CAD files can be used for the production process without having to be redrawn. All mathematical calculations are performed automatically saving programmers hours of time preparing a file for production.

Elite Software Announces "Mouse" Support For Engineering Programs

Elite Software Development, Inc., P.O. Drawer 1194, Bryan, Texas, 77806, has announced "Mouse" support for all of its 34 engineering programs. Elite's integration of the computer mouse significantly improves the efficiency, accuracy and operational speed of its programs.

The mouse greatly reduces manual typing through fast cursor placement and easy access menu items. The mouse can eliminate 30 or more key strokes with simple movements of the cursor on the computer screen. Elite's programs work with the Microsoft mouse and various compatibles.

C-U-C Software Systems Offers Management Computer Program For HVAC Contractors

Steve Vannoy, C-U-C Software Systems, P.O. Box 21455, Billings, Mont., 59104, has announced the availability of a new Executive Support System (ESS) management software package.

Vannoy describes ESS as a comprehensive, affordable management system designed specifically for HVAC contractors. It features fully integrated job costing, payroll, accounts payable, accounts receivable, general ledger, inventory control and service management modules. The system, adaptable to plumbing, roofing and general contracting applications, is PC based and network capable.

Compusource Offers New Software for Service Contractors

Compusource Corp., 21735 S. Western Ave., Torrance, Cal., 90501, is now offering Contrac2, a complete computer system for the service contractor engaged in HVAC, electrical and plumbing work that includes accounting, job costing and service management.

The system provides instant information on all service calls including: scheduled service calls and mechanic assigned; calls needing service in specific zones; calls in wide areas sorted by service time; all calls in the system sorted by time sequence received; mechanics assigned to calls and those who are available for calls; schedule of future calls; and high priority calls.

By pressing the appropriate function key, the dispatcher can determine if a mechanic is currently in that zone and when one will be available. Personal customer information such as service and payment history, along with credit references can also be verified.

Computer News

ACCA Reschedules Computer Seminar and Show

The Air Conditioning Contractors of America's (ACCA) "How to Computerize Your Business" trade show and seminar, which was scheduled for Nov. 5-6, in Atlantic City, N.J., was cancelled.

The exhibitions have been rescheduled for Feb. 20, to be held in conjunction with ACCA's 23rd Annual Meeting, Feb. 20-23, in Tarpon Springs, Fla. The workshops have not been rescheduled.

For complete computer trade show and annual meeting information, contact Christie Kenney, ACCA, 1513 - 16th St., N.W., Washington, D.C., 20036.

Carrier and Climatic Sign Agreement To Market Business Software For HVAC Distributors

Carrier Corp., P.O. Box 4808, Syracuse, N.Y., 13221, and its South Carolina distributor, Climatic Corp., have signed an agreement authorizing Climatic to market business management software for Carrier, Bryant, Day & Night, and Payne wholesaling distributors.

Climatic Software Systems (CSS), an arm of Climatic Corp., 2270 LeGrande Rd., Columbia, S.C., 29224, grew from efforts by both companies to develop software packages for day-to-day business operations such as inventory and receivables, and long-range forecasting. Professionals with expertise in computerized information systems and HVAC distribution in both organizations shared their knowledge to develop programs customized for the wholesaling business.

"This alliance between the leading industry manufacturer and one of the top HVAC distributors not only benefits both companies, but all distributors of United Technologies HVAC equipment," said John Bailey, founder and CEO of Climatic.

The Role of the Computer

Elite Software Introduces New Energy Analysis Program

Elite Software, P.O. Drawer 1194, Bryan, Texas, 77806, has introduced EZ-LCCID, a new energy economic analysis program for calculation of life cycle costs for building systems design.

EZ-LCCID computes life cycle costs, presents worth values, savings to investment ratios and discounted payback periods. The EZ-LCCID offers a full screen "fill-in-the-blank" data entry, mouse support, built-in help and greatly improved ease of use. Comprehensive reports show year-by-year breakdown of economic costs, total life cycle costs, baseline comparisons and detailed payback analysis.

The new program is IBM-PC compatible and fully operational demos are available.

InteliCAD Computers Unveils New Low Cost CAD Systems At SMACNA Convention

InteliCAD Computers, Inc., introduced the Colt, a new low-cost, full-featured CAD system for the sheet metal industry at the recent SMACNA convention in Kansas City, Mo.

The Colt is a turn-key system featuring a microcomputer, printer, an A-D size plotter, color graphics and InteliCAD software. The system is built around AutoCAD, a leading industrial CAD system, and offers built-in data-base including a complete library of sheet metal fittings, SMACNA tables for rectangular and round duct and trade knowledge based on its developers' 35 years of experience in the sheet metal industry. The system also accepts individual shop standards as part of its library.

A special feature of the system is AutoRUN, which automatically draws straight duct runs with a single command. Real-time checking for collision avoidance with obstacles is also a standard feature of the system. The Colt has also been engineered for expansion into larger systems offered by InteliCAD.

For further information on the Colt, contact InteliCAD Computers, Inc., 1807 N. 105th Ave., E., Tulsa, Okla., 74116.

Elite Software Announces Metric Version Of Its Commercial HVAC Loads Computer Program

Elite Software has introduced a metric version of its commercial HVAC loads calculation program (CHVAC 4.0). CHVAC 4.0 quickly calculates peak heating and cooling loads as well as cfm air quantity requirements with complete psychrometrics. This widely used program is based on exact table values and procedures described in the 1989 ASHRAE Handbook.

This new metric version means that CHVAC is now useful to much of the world's HVAC design community. Because it calculates loads in both northern and southern hemispheres, it can be used on any project, domestic and foreign. All input and output procedures fully conform to European metric conventions.

Other new options include a zone data overview screen designed to ease the organization of zones under air handler systems. Copy features allow easier replication of common data such as air handlers, plenums, and zones. Ample report options allow users to tailor and customize reports. Graphic reports include bar chart and exploded pie charts.

CHVAC provides comprehensive reports listing detailed zone loads, air handler summary loads, load summary, total building loads and tonnage requirements. CHVAC is IBM-PC compatible and offers complete mouse support. For more information and demos contact Elite Software, P.O. Drawer 1194, Bryan, Texas, 77806.

Cornerstones-Wright Issues New HVAC Software Catalog

Cornerstones-Wright, Inc., P.O. Box 4904, Portland, Me., 04112, has released the 7th edition of its HVAC software catalog with computer software tailored for HVAC dealer-contractors and engineers. It is available free.

Included in this edition are Cornerstone's HVAC sizing programs and the recently enhanced version 4.0 of residential operating costs, a software program which helps dealer-contractors estimate energy costs and show their customers the benefits of high efficiency equipment. All programs will run on IBM PC and compatibles.

Computer News

New Load Calculation Program Available From Glen M. Harper

The "Boss" is the name of Glen M. Harper's latest program combination. It consists of three Master type programs with their 17 individual HVAC programs all combined to make one menu-driven, user-friendly program.

The Master Heatloss/Heatgain Program will run a residential (ACCA's Manual J), a commercial (ACCA's Manual N), or a refrigeration (ASHRAE factors) calculation. All programs are "fill-in-the-blanks" type, save on disk, printout on screen or blank paper, and offer full edit functions.

The Master HVAC module is made up of six integrated HVAC type programs that will keep up with customer invoicing, statements, service calls, equipment, and serial numbers.

The Master Estimator module consists of eight programs useful in the HVAC industry. No special equipment is needed to draw floor plans with the computer and printer. Besides complete estimating capabilities, the module will produce a complete bill of materials, showing quantities needed and local prices to build a new small or large building.

For additional information, contact Glen M. Harper, P.O. Box 369, Avondale Estates, Ga., 30002.

Sheriff Says, "First There Was Fast Food, Now There's Fast Information"

Presented here, is another column, authored by Carl Sheriff, who has contributed many articles for this department over the years. He is president of Pro/Duct Computer Systems.

Sheriff's article this month covers the business application of on-line information technology and provides some definitions to ease HVAC dealer-contractors into telecommunications. He says, that first there was fast food ... now there is fast information. His comments follow:

On-Line Information Technology

The business application of on-line information technology is generally ignored by HVAC dealer-contractors. In this, the information age, few contractors have the information edge.

The Role of the Computer

I am writing about simply connecting your computer, via a modem, to one of the many Bulletin Board Systems (BBS), or on-line information. Such systems enable anyone to tap the true power of computer technology: the dissemination of information.

A Few Definitions

A word of relief: connecting "on-line" is not expensive. A couple of hundred dollars buys a 2400 Baud modem with telecommunications software. To further ease you into telecommunications, here are a few definitions.

* Baud: The rate at which data is transmitted. Generally, 1200 or 2400 Baud, about 120 or 240 characters per second.

* Connect Time: The amount of time your computer is connected, via the modem and telephone lines to the host computer. You are usually charged a nominal hourly rate (typically $5-$100/hr.) for connect time, even if you go for coffee while connected.

* Down-Loading: Retrieving information from a data base and simultaneously saving it onto your own computer.

* Electric Mail (E-Mail): The use of a central computer to facilitate the sending or receiving of messages between two other computers.

* Log On and Log Off: Electronically connecting or disconnecting from a host computer. Logging on usually requires an ID number and pass word.

* Modem: Technically a modulator/demodulator. Simply an internal device that allows your computer to communicate with another computer via telephone lines.

* On-Line: An active two-way electronic link between computers.

What Opens Door to Information Supermarket

A computer, a 1200 or 2400 Baud modem and any commercially available communication software package opens the door to the information supermarket. A supermarket in that there is a wide selection and the product is the freshest available.

The largest and best known vendors of information are H & R Block's Compuserve and GE's GEnie. These are basically consumer oriented information utilities that do, however, serve as a gateway to more business and technically oriented data bases. Such data bases are accessed at a premium connect charge, by paid subscription, or on a per inquiry basis.

Other Data Bases Available

Dialog is one of the biggest business information vendors with over 370 data bases, holding 210,000,000 references to over 100,000 publications. Dow Jones, Dun & Bradstreet, and McGraw-Hill offer data bases, sometimes only through one of the major vendors, that may appeal to those of us in the construction industry.

The Role of the Computer

For those looking for a job, there's Corporate Jobs Outlook. Employers are especially impressed with applicants showing their computer proficiency by applying on-line.

Major HVAC equipment suppliers maintain product information data bases for use by their sales force and customers. FAX is wonderful, but one-way. The computer allows instant two-way data communication, an exchange of information.

Going on-line can also mean joining a Special Interest Group (SIG). For those interested in starting a HVAC Contractor's User's Group, please leave an E-Mail message for Carl Sheriff or Pro/Duct at GEnie Information Services.

Carl Sheriff would be glad to answer questions on any type of computer or application. He may be reached at Pro/Duct Computer Systems, 9348 Civic Center Dr., #101, Beverly Hills, Cal., 90210.

Horgan Introduces New HVAC Computer Program

Horgan Vertical Applications Co., RD #9, Box 273-C, Coatesville, Pa., 19320, has introduced a new computer program for the HVAC industry. It is called Auto/Npro which is an IBM/PC and compatible program for calculating heat loss and heat gain for commercial buildings.

Horgan says that the program provides an implementation of ACCA Manual N. There are 124 programs stored on disk and the program features pull-down menus, pop-up windows, and a pop-up calculator. Requirements are an IBM compatible computer with MS DOS 2.0 or higher, a 448K memory, and at least one single disk drive.

Elite Offers New EZ-DOE Energy Analysis Program

Elite Software, P.O. Drawer 1194, Bryan, Texas, 77806, has announced EZ-DOE, an IBM-PC version of the U.S. Dept. of Energy main frame computer program, DOE-2.1D.

DOE-2.1D is the approved program of the California Energy Commission and is fully endorsed for Title 24 use on California buildings.

EZ-DOE is designed to accurately calculate the hourly, monthly, and annual energy use of a building and its life cycle cost of operation. With all the advanced features of the full main frame version, EZ-DOE's windows, user-friendly menus, electronic mouse support, full screen editing, and dynamic error checking make EZ-DOE a state-of-the-art program for the HVAC professional.

EZ-DOE offers many sophisticated analysis techniques and accurately simulates the operation of all types of heating and cooling plants, including ice water thermal storage and cogeneration systems. Up to 22 different air handling systems, each with multiple control options, are supported.

SNIPS   **March, 1991**   461.

Computer News

Sheriff Discusses Project Management Software

Presented here is another column written by Carl Sheriff, who has contributed many articles for this department over the years. He is president of Pro/Duct Computer Systems.

Sheriff's article this month discusses project management software. His comments follow:

Project Management Software

Project management, whether constructing a building or installing a production line, requires goals, and each goal breaks down into milestones that must be performed in sequence. If you want to install an air conditioning system, you first need to get draw plans, obtain permits, order the equipment and fabricate the duct work.

Each milestone in a project breaks down into steps of its own. You can't draw plans until you've hired a draftsman. You can't obtain a permit until you've performed energy calculations.

Helps Keep Track of Tasks

Project management computer programs are designed to help you keep track of all those steps, called tasks. Project management software, or project managers, can also allocate resources such as the people that will perform the tasks. Most importantly, project managers super-impose the tasks and resources on a calendar to make sure things happen when they're supposed to.

Project management techniques and software date from the Polaris Missile submarine development program where PERT, Program Evaluation and Review Technique, was used. The more common technique recognized by many construction contractors is CPM, or the Critical Path Method.

Promise of Project Management Software Is Appealing

The promise of project management software is appealing. Just type in a list of tasks, resources and dates, and the computer generates an elaborate chart that depicts a project's steps and schedule. Unfortunately, project management software is especially susceptible to the old computer maxim: "garbage in, garbage out".

Charts and graphs won't help you meet a deadline if the dates and data you originally entered were unrealistic. Further, project managers impose restrictions and require updating that many contractors find too much trouble. Project managers are not for everyone, but are often required on government or major building projects.

What Project Mangers Software Is

Project managers are part spreadsheet, part database and part graphics programs. Like a database program, data, the tasks, times and resources involved can be stored and retrieved. Like a spreadsheet program, project management software lets you play "what if" by entering different numbers and seeing the effect on the entire schedule.

For example, what if the crew size was five, instead of eight, causing the duct work to be hung in nine days instead of six. Would this cause a domino effect on other trades and ultimately cause a delay in the entire project?

Or, would the finish ceiling work have to wait on the electricians anyway? Like a graphics program, the project manager can generate quality scheduling bar charts (Gnatt charts), flow diagrams and graphs that can be used to control, or even sell a job!

A Variety of Programs Exist

A variety of programs exist for the MSDOS and Macintosh platforms. Prices range from $295 to $4,000. What's the difference? The high end software has the ability to manage multiple projects consisting of thousands of tasks.

They have more analytical features and can generate more types of reports and charts. You'll have to weigh the program's price and sophistication with the level of your needs and experience.

If you are new to project managers, you may get better results from a $295 package. The $4,000 program's features won't help you if you find the program too intimidating. Many of the more expensive programs come with video or personal training.

Starting with one program may not limit you from upgrading in the future. Many of the programs, as with data base and spreadsheets, read each other's data. If you can get over your management-on-the-fly attitude, then try project management software. Ask for a demonstration version that includes a work book, videotape and software.

Carl Sheriff would be glad to answer questions about any type of computer applications. He may be reached at Pro/Duct Computer Systems, 9348 Civic Center Dr., #101, Beverly Hills, Cal., 90210.

AAA Enterprises Markets Sharp Energy/Financial System For Residential/Commercial Use

AAA Enterprises, P.O. Box 450733, Atlanta, Ga., 30345, utilizes the Sharp PC-1270 battery-powered pocket computer/printer interface for several complete energy/financial programs for calculating residential and commercial loads.

The Role of the Computer

Every measurable factor affecting energy efficiency is considered including: indoor/outdoor temperature (by season); air changes; humidity; type; length and height of walls; windows; doors; ceiling; and floors. Other factors covered: ventilation; kitchens; people; duct gain and loss; and summer/winter infiltration.

Five separate programs, each with special features to meet specific needs are offered. The compact and portable computer is ideal for on-the-job or for the meeting with a prospective client.

Elite Software Introduces New Load Calculation Program For Macintosh Computers

Elite Software Development, Inc., P.O. Drawer 1194, Bryan, Texas, 77806, has introduced RHVAC, a heating and cooling load calculation program for residential and small commercial buildings that works on Apple Computer's Macintosh line.

RHVAC features the complete "look and feel" of Macintosh software and runs under Finder and Multi-Finder System 6. Design weather data for 150 cities listed in Manual J are part of RHVAC and are automatically used as required. Design weather data can be revised and additional weather data for another 350 cities can be added.

Significant features of the new software include the ability to rotate the entire building or individual rooms, provisions for exterior glass shading and mechanical ventilation, automatic calculations and the ability to work with up to 1,000 rooms per project.

Comprehensive reports list general product data, equipment sizing information, detail room load calculations and room load summaries complete with cfm quantities.

Pro-Mation Markets Software For Estimating and Job Costs

Pro-Mation, a division of The Flagship Group, Inc., P.O. Box 279, Midvale, Utah, 84047, specializes in marketing computer software for the construction industry.

Pro-Bid estimating software enables the user to make the right bids and win more contracts by analyzing costs more efficiently.

Job-Cost With Contract Changes software keeps costs low by controlling the daily job costs of any size or type of contracting business. Every expense item is automatically tracked.

Information on these programs and other available software is available from Pro-Mation at the above address.

ARW Announces Release of New Financial Planning Software

The Air-conditioning & Refrigeration Wholesalers Ass'n (ARW) has released "Profit Advisor," a new software program designed to help any company increase profitability.

The Role of the Computer

The program is designed to help management develop a detailed financial plan quickly and easily, set realistic profits targets and forecast sales. It also aids in planning expenses and product mix, determining cash needs and assigning sales quotas.

For more information about "Profit Advisor," contact ARW Research & Education Foundation, 6360 N.W. 5th Way, Suite 202, Fort Lauderdale, Fla., 33309.

Caddylak Systems Offers New Software On Job Descriptions

Caddylak Systems, Inc., 131 Heartland Blvd., Brentwood, N.Y., 11717, is now offering a new software program entitled, "The Complete Portfolio of Prewritten Job Descriptions Plus Disk."

The program contains 150 ready-to-print, professionally-written job descriptions from entry level positions to corporate managers. The descriptions may be used "as is," or altered to reflect the job as it exists within your company.

The program comes with a book, "The Complete Portfolio of Prewritten Job Descriptions," which includes guidelines that explain various job description formats and EEOC rules affecting employee records.

The program is available for either IBM or Macintosh computers.

Wendes Mechanical Consulting Services Offers New Updated Programs and Manuals

Wendes Mechanical Consulting Services, Inc., 95 Gaylord St., Elk Grove Village, Ill., 60007, is now offering new 1991 upgraded computer programs and manuals.

The computer programs include Super-Duct Upgrade V5.0 sheet metal estimating software, which provides duct pressure tables; gauge, connection and reinforcing tables; automatic selection of Ductmate, TDC and cleats; expanded grille, diffuser and louver damper selections; expanded selections of lining and ductwrap; pricing per gauge; optional digitizer pen or keyboard entry; and automatic editing, duplications and price comparisons.

Another revision includes Super-Pipe Upgrade V4.0, which covers estimating of all types of piping; valves and fittings; connections; speciality items; equipment; connections, hanger sets and couplings; insulation and trenching; automatic assemblies and price comparisons; digitizer pen or keyboard entry; adjustable price and labor tables; pricing service for automatic updating; and automatic editing, duplication and price comparisons.

Other updated manuals available from Wendes include the 1991 update of the Sheet Metal Estimating Manual and a sheet metal estimating Home Study Course.

Elite Software's Ductsize Program Now AutoCAD Compatible

Elite Software Development, Inc., P.O. Drawer 1194, Bryan, Texas, 77806, has announced that its Ductsize program is now fully compatible when integrated with a new AutoCAD accessory program from DAC Software, Inc.

Ductsize is based upon the 1989 ASHRAE Handbook of Fundamentals and the SMACNA HVAC Duct Systems Design Manual and calculates optimal duct sizes using static regain, equal friction or constant velocity methods. Ductsize allows up to 500 duct sections and is suitable for both constant volume and VAV systems.

DAC Software's Auto-Architect HVAC Module, when used with AutoCAD, greatly simplifies drawing duct work, HVAC equipment, fittings and controls. The HVAC module can readily extract duct system layout data from the AutoCAD drawing file allowing Ductsize to automatically size the duct system. After sizing the duct system, the module can read the Ductsize output sizes and automatically create a double-line and three dimensional duct drawing from the original shaded line.

Ductsize has recently been upgraded and now provides for diversified air cfm flows and feature electronic mouse support.

SNIPS April, 1991

Computer News

Software: Do You Get What You Pay For?, Asks Smith of Elite Computer Software

William W. Smith, shown here, is president of Elite Software Development, Inc., P.O. Drawer 1194, Bryan, Texas, 77806. His firm, established in 1979, is one of the oldest independent engineering software companies providing HVAC programs to contractors and engineers around the

country.

Elite Software offers over 30 computer programs, including duct sizing, commercial and residential HVAC loads, commercial and residential energy analysis, refrigeration box loads and glass shading.

This month, Smith discusses, "Software: Do You Get What You Pay For?" His comments on this subject follows:

Software Prices Offen Differ By Magnitudes of 10 or More

Unlike hard, physical items like sheet metal, condensing units, and evaporator coils, software does not have a consistent, narrow range of prices for a given type of program. Sure, sheet metal prices vary slightly from source to source, but the percentage difference in prices available is actually quite small.

In the software world, prices for a given type of program often differ by magnitudes of 10 or more. For example, there are legitimate service management programs for customer record keeping and dispatching that range in price from $99 to over $10,000. If hardware costs are included, the price differential is even greater. With such tremendous disparity in software prices, do you really get what you pay for?

Sometimes, But Not Always

The answer to the above question is sometimes, but not always. Back in the early 80's a company called Borland International started a revolution in software pricing. In a gutsy move for a fledgling company, Phillipe Kahn, founder of Borland, introduced a super high quality software language called Turbo PASCAL at the bargain basement price of $49.00. Existing competitive software was priced at $495.00, and many computer users were skeptical.

Once Turbo PASCAL was reviewed by the computer magazines and given high marks, the skeptics were quieted. Not only was the product considered well worth $49.00, many thought it the best computer language available at any price. As a result, unheard of numbers of computer users bought Turbo PASCAL.

Traditionally, only computer professionals bought computer languages, especially given their relatively high prices. But, the price of the Turbo PASCAL was so low and the quality so high, that an unexpectedly high number of people bought the product, thus insuring the survival of upstart Borland International.

Although now a giant in the software industry, Borland to this day remains committed to the low price, high volume, and high quality product strategy. With a Borland product, you always get more than you pay for and higher priced comparable programs are by no means automatically better.

The Role of the Computer

Many HVAC Contractors Aware of Borland

Many people, including lots of HVAC contractors, are aware of the amazing success of Borland International. All these consumers, no matter what their profession, continue to look for the Borland type software supplier in their field. Doctors want low cost, high quality medical records keeping software.

And HVAC contractors want this high volume concept for load calculations, estimating, accounting, and service management software. Is there a Borland type software vendor for every application? Unfortunately, no, but there is a good reason for that.

Most computer marketing experts believe that Borland's concept of very low prices only works in markets of very high volume. Every program ever developed by Borland is aimed at a wide range of users, not just doctors, lawyers, or contractors, but everybody who uses a computer for any reason. That wide appeal constitutes a vast market where sales volumes are potentially so large that even with low prices, revenues are sufficient to insure adequate profits for survival and growth.

Although a close equivalent of Borland can almost never be found for such specific application software as HVAC and contracting markets, that does not mean that low priced application software itself cannot be found. There are always small companies in a given field that would like to become the Borland of their industry.

Those companies offer very low cost software in the $49.00 to $99.00 range like Borland, but unlike Borland, the programs offered are usually not state of the art with extensive user manuals.

As all contractors know, it is easy to offer low price, but altogether more difficult to offer low price with premium quality. It's not impossible to do this in the software world as a look at Borland reveals, but it does require a large market for success.

About Market For HVAC Software

The market for HVAC related software is not tiny, as there are thousands of contractors, engineers and owners who can use some type of HVAC software.

However, it is definitely not large enough to attract the attention of Borland, Microsoft, Ashton-Tate or Lotus. The largest software companies only write programs for applications where there are millions of potential buyers.

Market size and software pricing are not difficult concepts to understand. It is obvious that large markets make it easier for software companies to lower prices, but what about low cost software in small markets like HVAC? Is such software worth considering, and does it offer good value?

The Role of the Computer

When Shopping For Software Consider Every Program Offered

When shopping for software for a given task, it is always worthwhile to consider every program offered on the market, no matter what its cost. After all, it makes sense to purchase the lowest cost program that meets the desired requirements. Depending on the desired features, a very low cost program may offer the best value for the job.

Unlike the general computer market, where it is actually possible for a low cost program to be the very best in its field, such an occurrence is unlikely in specialty markets like HVAC. As concerns low cost software in specialty markets, some generalizations can be made.

On the positive side, most low cost software is simpler, and thus easier to learn than comparable expensive software. Another benefit of low cost software is that computer hardware requirements are typically not so great.

Common Draw-Back to Low Cost Software

Perhaps the most common draw-back to low cost software is that it simply doesn't offer some critical desired feature. For example, some contractors want a sheet metal estimating program that can provide fabrication information to a plasma cutter along with estimating costs.

A low cost estimating program is highly unlikely to provide a link to plasma cutting machines. Another example occurs with duct sizing programs. Low cost duct sizing programs do not have links to CAD programs like AutoCAD.

Other Draw-Backs

Besides the lack of advanced features, the other draw-back to low cost software usually occurs with the user interface. Low cost programs usually have simple data entry procedures based around questions that appear one after another on the screen.

More expensive programs typically use a full screen, "fill in the blank" style of input and work with an electronic mouse as well. Low cost programs typically have limited built-in help information while some expensive programs have a unique help screen for every input item.

In the specialty software markets, the old adage, you get what you pay for, has more meaning than in the general software market of business utilities, word processors and spread-sheets. However, even in specialty markets like HVAC, low cost programs serve the legitimate purpose of providing basic functions at a very fair price.

Low cost software, as long as it provides a certain minimum level of user friendliness, is a good way to start with computers.

William Smith will welcome comments on his remarks from readers. Readers can communicate with him at P.O. Drawer 1194, Bryan, Texas, 77806.

"Palmtop" Handheld Computer Offers Heat Loss/Gain Calculation Energy/Financial Analysis

AAA Enterprises, P.O. Box 450733, Atlanta, Ga., 30345, has programmed the Sharp PC-1270 battery-powered handheld computer and printer to calculate and print out residential and commercial heat load/gain loads, residential energy comparisons and financial analysis.

Local weather data is included internally to calculate heating and/or cooling energy estimates.

Extremely simple to use, the 16 character screen asks simple "yes" or "no" questions about the construction and R values and dimensions are entered from the key-pad to the calculator.

Manufactured by Sharp Electronics, the equipment is programmed and distributed by AAA Enterprises at the above address.

Estimation Offers New Line Of Hardware For Contractors

Estimation, Inc., 805-L Barkwood Ct., Linthicum Heights, Md., 21090, has unveiled two new additions to their hardware line for 1991.

466.

Heading the line up is the all-new System VI, which features the first 80486 microprocessor in an estimating system. The 80486 is designed for demanding multi-user applications and features an advanced level of data storage and high processing speeds. The system uses 8 MB of single in-line memory (SIMM) module technology and has an uninterruptible power supply to prevent loss of data during power outages. A 14" monitor is also included with the System VI as are a 120 MB mini cartridge tape back-up unit and a 100 MB hard disk drive, which can be upgraded to 330 MB.

Estimation has also introduced an enhanced version of their standard Bidmaster PLUS System III featuring a 80386 microprocessor, a 14" monitor and a 44 MB hard disk drive which is expandable to 330 MB for increased data storage. The system is available in single and multi-user configurations to meet varying needs.

Timesaver Systems Offers Software On Maintenance Management

Timesaver Systems, Inc. P. O. Box 4688, Portland, Ore., 97208, is marketing a new IBM PC based CMMS/Phase 1 computerized maintenance management software package. All aspects of maintenance, repair and improvements for buildings, machinery, equipment and grounds are computerized.

CMMS/Phase 1 saves typing by common tasks being entered once and accessed by a single code. Master jobs are defined once and used over and over again. Automatic preventive maintenance scheduling, equipment history, task descriptions, down-time causes, parts used, crafts, crews and accounting cross reference are provided by the software.

SNIPS June, 1991

Computer News

Trane Command-Aire and Elite Software Announce Joint Marketing Agreement

Trane Command-Aire and Elite Software Development, Inc. have announced a new joint marketing agreement. Under the agreement, Trane Command-Aire will provide Elite's powerful HVAC design software to its dealers through its nationwide distributor network.

The programs include Elite's RHVAC for Manual J residential HVAC loads calculations, AUDIT for HVAC operating cost and equipment selection and ECA, for ground source heat pump analysis. RHVAC and AUDIT are fully compatible and use the same project data files to minimize redundant data input.

The Role of the Computer

Elite Software produces over 30 programs for mechanical, electrical and plumbing engineers. For more information contact Elite Software, P.O. Drawer 1194, Bryan, Texas, 77806.

SNIPS September, 1991

Computer News

Sheriff Comments On "Personal Computers: 10 Years Old"

Presented here is another column written by Carl Sheriff, who has contributed many interesting articles for this department over the years. He is president of Pro/Duct Computer Systems.

This month, Sheriff comments on the 10th anniversary of the personal computer, as follows:

Personal Computers: 10 Years Old

The IBM Personal Computer has turned 10 years old and IBM and Apple Computer have agreed to share technologies.

"So what!" It's not like IBM invented the personal computer. IBM's entry into the market just "legitimized" it. Now, the IBM/Apple joint venture will legitimize the Macintosh operating system and finally lay to rest the objection that no software is available for the Mac. Macintosh and IBM will soon be fully compatible.

What Everybody Was Talking About When Personal Computer Was New

Ten years ago, when the personal computer was still new on the scene, everybody was talking about it. There was a feeling in the air that these things were going to change the world. Analysts predicted that before long, every home and small business in America would have a computer.

The PC was going to change the way we live. There were TV commercials showing kids being left behind in school because their parents didn't buy them a computer. Today, however, people still think of the personal computer as some weird machine used by weird people.

Now that we have computers, little is different. We now do more heat load calculations or at least recalculations; do more automated take-offs, but have fewer successful bids and do more revisions of word processing documents.

Business productivity is no higher now than it was 30 years ago. The paperless office was a pipe dream. Teleconferencing, picture phones, smart buildings, and electronic mail have been bombs.

The Role of the Computer

About Lack of Dramatic Change In the HVAC Industry

I suppose the lack of dramatic change in the HVAC industry is easily explained by the immaturity of the computer age. Ten years is an incredibly short period of time in the life of an invention. Computers today are 12 to 20 times faster than the old clunkers we marveled at in Radio Shack stores.

PC's have gone from 64,000 characters of memory to 4,000,000. Yet, the computer is still in its infancy and will surely become more useful and intuitive as years go by. Even so, 55 million computers have already been sold in the United States, and 110 million throughout the world.

About the Near Future

Soon, we'll have computer chips many more times powerful than the ones we have today. Soon, the nation will be wired wall to wall with fiber-optic cable, which can carry hundreds of times more data than copper wire.

Construction plans, for example, will be transmitted through these networks or be supplied on optical disk. Computers will have the capability of voice and hand writing recognition. The key board, the major obstacle in using computers, will be obsolete.

Disk crashes, confusing documentation, incompatible software and other nightmares have discouraged many users from using computers to their fullest. Many contractors still think computers are useless.

It's not that I think contractors innately shy away from computers. It's just that computer vendors have not given our industry what it wants: a tool to increase productivity and make life more enjoyable.

The most incredible computer system, with slam bang graphics and multi-megahertz speed, cannot compare with a real human being in real three dimensions, resolving a problem of a duct and a pipe in the same place.

Carl Sheriff would be glad to answer questions about any type of computer applications. He may be reached at Pro/Duct Computer Systems, 9348 Civic Center Dr., #101, Beverly Hills, Cal., 90210.

Mitchell Instruments and Elite Software Announce Joint Marketing Agreement

Mitchell Instruments Co. and Elite Software Development, Inc. have announced a new joint marketing agreement. Under the agreement, Mitchell Instruments Co. will provide 10 of Elite's HVAC and electrical design software through its nationwide distribution network.

The programs include Elite's CHVAC for commercial HVAC loads, DUCTSIZE for automated duct sizing, HVAC TOOLS (software utilities), DPIPE for waste drainage pipe sizing, FIRE for fire sprinkler hydraulic calculations, LIGHT for zonal cavity lighting calculations, FLUDWARE for lighting design, PSYCHART for psychrometric analysis, COORD for fuse and breaker coordination and SHORT for short circuit calculations.

Mitchell is a major supplier of industrial instrumentation. Elite Software produces over 34 programs for mechanical, electrical and plumbing engineers. For more information contact Elite Software, P.O. Drawer 1194, Bryan, Texas, 77806.

Estimation, Inc., Releases New Project Manager Program

Estimation, Inc., 809-L Barkwood Ct., Linthicum Heights, Md., 21090, has announced the release of a new Project Manager program designed specifically for the construction contractor. Project Manager lets contractors capture information needed for efficient analysis of labor and material costs on a job as it progresses, as well as maintain historical data once the project is completed.

The program automatically generates reports for each cost center of the job, including labor and materials, providing feedback on the accuracy of the labor units being used and allowing contractors to identify potential cost overruns early.

Project Manager also produces detailed management reports on job profitability and billing amounts. Reports can be generated for individual jobs or selected categories, such as all open jobs, or jobs with current period entries. Individual parts of a job can also be broken out for detailed analysis and then recombined for a complete job over-view.

A module of Estimation's Manager PLUS software series, the program can be used as a stand-alone package, or in conjunction with Estimation's Bidmaster PLUS or A.L.E.C. estimating systems.

Custom Software Offers Updated Easy Sheet Metal Estimator

Custom Plumbing Software, 488 N. Main St., Suite 201, Wilkes-Barre, Pa., 18705, is now offering an updated version of the Easy Sheet Metal Estimator, a series of spreadsheet worksheets for contractors.

Easy Estimator offers Lotus 1-2-3 compatible worksheets that do not require Lotus 1-2-3 to run. Instead of proprietary formats that claim "spreadsheet like" features, Easy Estimator uses the "standard" format. Unlike other software with complex, multiple level screens, Easy Estimator is a single-page worksheet that closely resembles paper worksheets, and it provides the contractor with knowledge that may be used for other applications.

Easy Estimator may be used as is, or Custom Plumbing Software will perform customizing free of charge. Or, you may use Lotus 1-2-3 or any other Lotus compatible spreadsheet to customize the template to further duplicate individual styles and methodology of estimating.

Computer News

Smith of Elite Software Says, "DOS 5.0 — Good To Go!"

William W. Smith, shown here, is president of Elite Software Development, Inc., P.O. Drawer 1194, Bryan, Texas, 77806. His firm, established in 1979, is one of the oldest independent engineering software companies providing HVAC programs to contractors and engineers around the country.

Elite Software offers over 30 computer programs, including duct sizing, commercial and residential HVAC loads, commercial and residential energy analysis, refrigeration box loads and glass shading.

This month, Smith discusses the use of the newly released Microsoft DOS 5.0, pointing out how its benefits are immediate and significant. He says, "DOS 5.0 — Good to Go!", and his comments follow:

Microsoft just recently released DOS 5.0 and many IBM compatible PC users are wondering whether it's worth the trouble to upgrade. Most companies are now using DOS 3.3 or DOS 4.01 and they remember the problems encountered from previous upgrades. Microsoft has historically had significant problems with initial releases of new versions of DOS.

Usually these problems are swiftly corrected with a flurry of minor updates. But many of the companies who quickly implemented DOS 3.0 and DOS 4.0 wish they had waited for others to test the new DOS releases before they had. Are the new enhancements to DOS 5.0 worth upgrading to and is it safe to do so right now? The answer is yes on both counts.

New DOS 5.0 Relatively Bug Free

Unlike previous releases of DOS, DOS 5.0 is relatively bug free. To date, no major problems have been reported and there are only a few anomalies to be aware of. The most common problem a program might have with DOS 5.0 involves the use of memory.

Some programs, like Borland's SideKick 2.0, make certain assumptions about the amount of memory available. Since DOS 5.0 can make a great deal of system memory available to application programs, SideKick 2.0 does not work when it encounters free memory where it does not expect any to be free.

The Role of the Computer

Making more memory is not the fault of DOS 5.0. Consequently, software vendors are scrambling to correct such faults in their programs. To make those few offending programs useable in the interim, a utility program called LOADFIX is provided with DOS 5.0 that lets the software operate normally.

Memory Use Problems Easily Solved

Other memory use problems can arise between DOS 5.0 and certain programs. However, there are usually work around solutions for most of these problems as well. The typical solution usually involves adjusting the computer's CONFIG.SYS or AUTOEXEC.BAT file.

Another sure-fire way to remove memory conflicts with DOS 5.0 and certain programs is to use QuarterDeck's QEMM memory management utility program. QUEMM is a commercial program that retails for $99.

Besides memory conflicts, some programs do not provide support for keyboards containing 101-or 102 keys. Such programs include Lotus Metro, Lotus Express, and Borland Turbo Lightning.

As with the memory problems, DOS 5.0 provides a work-around solution for these keyboard problems as well. Fortunately, DOS 5.0 to make adjustments allowing over 25 programs to operate normally.

On the surface, it may seem like a lot of trouble to use DOS 5.0 with some programs. However, it is important to note that only a very small percentage of existing software requires adjustments. Most software runs directly as is. In addition, DOS 5.0 is currently so popular that all software vendors are updating their programs to make better use of the enhanced capabilities of DOS 5.0.

About the Greatest Benefit of DOS 5.0

Perhaps the greatest benefit of DOS 5.0 is that it can make an additional 40K of memory available to application programs. This means that larger projects and jobs can be analyzed by application software. In addition, many programs can operate faster since less disk accessed is required with more internal memory available.

Since DOS 5.0 can make more memory available, does this mean that DOS 5.0 is smaller in size than previous versions of DOS? No. DOS 5.0 is actually larger in file size than previous versions of DOS, but it can now load most of itself into extended memory (beyond the first 640K) so that more memory is available to programs using the first 640K of standard memory.

So the point is that your computer must be equipped with extended memory beyond 640K for DOS 5.0 to make more of the standard 640K memory available to programs. Since the majority of IBM compatible computers are sold with extended memory, most PC users experience an automatic increase in available standard memory with DOS 5.0.

The Role of the Computer

DOS 5.0 Improves Use of Memory

DOS 5.0 further improves the use of memory by enabling expanded memory where desired and allowing the loading of device drivers into high memory locations. This kind of memory management is accomplished with commands and files like HIMEM.SYS, LOADHIGH, and EMM386.EXE. However, this capability is advanced and novice users cannot typically make use of it without aid from a knowledgeable computer user.

Besides vastly improved memory management, DOS 5.0 was also given numerous new commands and system utility programs. For example, DOS 5.0 can now unerase a file that may have been accidentally deleted.

DOS 5.0 even provides a command called MIRROR that saves the names of deleted files so that file recovery is made easier. In some cases, DOS 5.0 can even unformat a disk that was mistakenly formatted.

Other Major Features

Other major new features include the provision of a new, easy to use full screen editor called EDIT. This replaces the infamous EDLIN program that was supplied with DOS for years. Another replacement involves the BASIC language.

DOS 5.0 is now provided with QBASIC which is the interpretative portion of Microsoft's popular Quick BASIC. Although QBASIC is not the full Quick BASIC package, it is very close and much improved over previous versions of BASIC provided with DOS.

Another nice feature added was the ability to print CGA, EGA, and VGA level graphic screens to high resolution laser and ink jet printers. In the past, DOS could only print CGA level graphic screens to Epson and IBM graphics printers using the "PrtSe" key. DOS 5.0 now supports graphic screen printing to all these printers.

Use of DOS Improved

The ease of use of DOS has also been improved. The DOSSHELL command is a graphical program and file manager that makes selecting and manipulating files much easier than typing long commands. A new feature of DOSSHELL is "task switching" or the ability to start one program and then start another program without exiting from the first program.

There are actually many more minor enhancements to DOS 5.0 than can be mentioned here. Some of the enhancements are beneficial only to advanced DOS users, but all in all, the enhancements are well worth the cost to users at any level. Existing users of DOS need only pay $59 to upgrade to DOS 5.0, while purchasers of most new IBM compatible computers automatically get DOS 5.0 included.

Problems with DOS 5.0 are few and minor. And the benefits are immediate and significant. Without a doubt, DOS 5.0 is "Good to Go!"

William Smith will welcome comments on his remarks from readers. Readers can communicate with him at P.O. Drawer 1194, Bryan, Texas, 77806.

New ARW Program Offers Members Discounts on Computer Supplies and Business Forms

The Air-conditioning & Refrigeration Wholesalers Ass'n (ARW) recently introduced a new program, through Moore Business Forms, which offers significant discounts on Moore's complete line of stock computer paper, business forms and computer supplies to ARW wholesaler and associate member firms in the continental U.S.

According to ARW's executive director, David Kellough, "These items have become a substantial expense for wholesaler and supplier firms in recent years. This program, in many cases, can reduce a company's annual expenditure for these products by thousands of dollars."

For further details on the Moore Discount Program, or information on ARW membership, contact ARW, 6360 N.W. 5th Way, Suite 202, Ft. Lauderdale, Fla., 33309

Nordyne Offers CertiDuct Duct Layout Computer Software

Nordyne, 1801 Park 270 Dr., St. Louis, Mo., 63146, parent company of Intertherm and Miller heating and cooling equipment, offers CertiDuct, an innovative software program which calculates duct capacity. Available in magnetic disk form, CertiDuct calculates the cfm of air and the Btu capacity of the duct systems being described.

CertiDuct software uses "prompts" to ask questions about specific air duct layout on a program which adapts to IBM-type hardware.

ContrAcct Systems Corp.'s Contractor Accounting Software Offers Job Costing-Collections

ContrAcct Systems Corp., 208 N. Washington St., Naperville, Ill., 60540, offers accounting software designed for contractors. Designed to save time doing routine paper work functions, as well as to provide management information to owners, ContrAcct runs on single user DOS, networks and UNIX/XENIX/AIX multi-user operating systems.

The program's single entry accounting eliminates costly duplications and errors. Hand posting is eliminated to job cost, general ledger and payroll.

The system keeps track of original estimates, change orders, current estimates, actual job-to-date and balance-to-complete.

The software is designed to reduce clerical

The Role of the Computer

expenses and paper work in processing invoices, AIA documents, lien waivers and other financial documents.

Payroll checks are accurately prepared, including seven types of payroll overhead. Government and union payroll reports are also prepared.

Sandy Beaches Software Introduces Personnel Management System

Sandy Beaches Software, 1265 W. Broadway, Hewlett, N.Y., 11557, has announced a powerful, new, low-cost personnel management system called "The Employee Record-Keeping System."

The new system allows the user to organize, store and retrieve information on past, present and even potential employees instantly. There are more than 60 fields that cover personal data, job description, salary status and history, insurance, pension and union information, and attendance and vacation time. Multi-level password protection keeps data secure and private.

"The Employee Record-Keeping System" requires 512K of memory and runs on IBM computers or compatibles. It imports and exports to other packages and is network aware. Free technical support is available.

Coastal Computer Offers Wide Line of Computer Programs

Coastal Computer Corp., 6120 Winkler Rd., Suite J, Fort Myers, Fla., 33919, offers a full line of computers and integrated programs along with video tape presentations.

Among the programs available from the firm are: service management; service agreements; service dispatch and scheduling; service and equipment history; job cost control; inventory control; general ledger; accounts payable; accounts receivable; payroll; and sales lead generation.

Data-Basics Announces New 1.3 Version of CMAS Plus

Data-Basics, Inc., 11000 Cedar Rd., Suite 110, Cleveland, Ohio, 44106, has announced the release of version 1.3 Construction Master Accounting System (CMAS) Plus software. CMAS Plus is an integrated accounting/job costing/ service dispatch and billing system designed specifically for plumbing, HVAC, mechanical and electrical contractors.

The CMAS Plus dispatch board has been revised to provide new flexibility in sorting and utilization of information. The dispatcher can look at all unassigned calls or only pending calls. Dispatches can be sorted by priority, date entered, zone or job-site name, while customer history is accessed.

Job Costing report capabilities have been expanded to show complete at job, phase and "as budgeted" levels. A new Project Analysis Report has been added.

Shop Data Systems Offers New Software That Lays Out and Cuts Kitchen Patterns

Shop Data Systems, Inc., has announced its new "Kitchen Works" software package. The new package will be marketed to custom stainless steel commercial kitchen fabricators.

The new "Kitchen Works" package comes with 50 standard shapes, including: sink assemblies; drain-boards; tubs; drawers; shelves; and tables. The software handles all the layouts for back-splashes, corners and front edges common to kitchen fabrication. The software uses standard industry terms to prompt the operator for dimensional information.

The "Kitchen Works" package can be combined with Shop Data Systems' CAD drawing system for ultimate part design flexibility. The system is compatible with plasma and laser cutting systems.

More information can be obtained from Kenn Horn, Shop Data Systems, Inc., 712 W. Walnut St., Garland, Texas, 75040.

Compusource Offers Business Management System For Contractors

Compusource Corp., 20 Centerpointe Dr., Suite 105, La Palma, Cal., 90623, is now offering Contrac2, a complete business management computer system specifically designed for plumbing, heating, air conditioning and electrical contractors with special emphasis on service dispatch, job cost and accounting.

Contrac2 tracks all job costs including labor, materials and equipment from the time they are committed until the job is closed. Other features include automated purchasing, payroll inventory control, contract billing and completely integrated accounting which automatically updates general ledger for complete financial reporting.

Customer information such as service calls, payment history and credit references can also be verified with the system.

Contrac2 runs on 286, 386 and 486 based microcomputers supporting form one to six terminals.

Elite Software Introduces New Metric Version Of Its HVAC Tools Program For 11 Design Tasks

Elite Software has introduced a metric version of its popular HVAC software tools program called HVAC Tools. HVAC Tools allows the quick calculation of 11 common HVAC

The Role of the Computer

design tasks.

These tasks include duct sizing, wire sizing, three way coil interpolation, mixed air and state point psychrometrics, fan curve and cost analysis, U-Factor calculations, refrigeration line sizing, and the quick look-up of common HVAC formulas. Tools also performs fan curve/cost analysis and three way interpolation of HVAC units.

This new metric version means that HVAC Tools is now useful to much of the world's HVAC community. All data entry and output procedures fully conform to European metric conventions. Values computed by Tools can be returned to other programs. HVAC Tools follows ASHRAE and NEC procedures.

For more information and demonstration software, contact Elite Software, P.O. Drawer 1194, Bryan, Texas, 77806.

SNIPS   October, 1992

Computer News

Software Shop Systems Offers New Job Estimating Software

Software Shop Systems, 1340 Campus Parkway, Wall, N.J., 07719, is now offering specialized data bases to enhance the utilization of the company's ACE CSI estimating software.

The individualized data bases are sold separately and include Heavy Construction, Sitework and Landscape, Residential, Light Commercial, Repair and Remodel, Mechanical, Concrete, Electrical, Plumbing and Interior.

Titus Implements New Order Processing Software

Titus, 990 Security Row, Richardson, Texas, 75081, has implemented the new "Titus Order Processing Software" (TOPS) for its sales representatives. The software is designed to simplify order procedures, quotes, pricing and specifications for Titus grilles, registers, diffusers and terminal units.

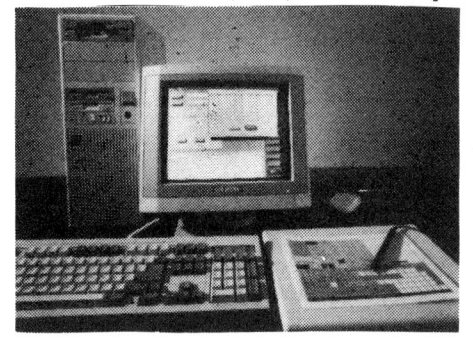

TOPS is the Titus module for Chorus Line, a product of QuickPen International, Englewood, Colo. The program is specifically designed to meet the needs of the Titus manufacturers reps. All take-off information is entered only once, which begins the preparation for electronic order entry.

SNIPS   November, 1992

Computer News

Detroit ACCA Chapter Members Surveyed on Computer Attitudes Lack Enthusiasm Over Technology

Fifteen years after buying their first computer, some of almost 30 Detroit-area HVACR dealer-contractors taking part in a pilot-study for an intended statewide survey made it clear that they are less than enthusiastic about computers. The contractors acknowledge, though, there have been benefits of having "gone computer."

Of about 30 respondents, only one company still has not bought its first computer. Of that number, only two computer users were really "Gung Ho" about computers.

Long Learning Curve Inhibits Utilization

Fewer than one-third of the respondents use computerized dispatching; about one-third use computers for system design; almost all of them use computers for general accounting and for word processing.

The "excessively" long learning curve which almost everyone mentioned, coupled with the fact that "not every company has a computer-nut in-house" means that most computers are under utilized, several contractors commented.

Several Personal Computers Favored Over Minicomputer

"Our experience would suggest that most of us who have gone the mini-computer route would have been better served with several personal computers, some networked, some not," was a comment which reflected a frequent opinion.

"A necessary evil;" "Generate too much paper;" "The owner can never justify spending the time to learn application software, so he has to find other ways to be sure he isn't being cheated by his computer-knowledge staff," were other typical comments.

Editor's Note: Metro Detroit Chapter of Air Conditioning Contractors of America (ACCA) is located at 16341 Canterbury Ct., Mt. Clemens, Mich., 48044.

472.

Elite Software Adds Sharp As New Computer Programmer

Elite Software Development, Inc., Bryan, Texas, has announced the addition of Mickial Sharp to its staff of computer programmers.

Sharp has joined Elite's staff as a programmer and technical writer. In his new position, Sharp will work in new product development and product enhancement within Elite's line of HVAC software programs.

Merry Mechanization Releases Nesting Software For Shears

Merry Mechanization, Inc., 1068 S. Lake St., Suite 5, Forest Lake, Minn., 55025, has announced the release of Shear Nesting, a new software package for nesting of fittings using a straight-cut shear.

The program operates by entering part numbers, widths, lengths, quantities and sheet sizes desired. The program will automatically nest the parts in the most efficient manner possible, display the sheets on the screen and sequentially list a set of loading instructions. The square inches of scrap and reusable scrap are also displayed. Any reusable scrap pieces are numerically marked and can be inventoried for later use.

SNIPS December, 1992

Computer News

HVAC Wholesaler Uses Load Calculation Software As Marketing Tool

William W. Smith, shown here, is president of Elite Software Development, Inc., P.O. Drawer 1194, Bryan, Texas, 77806. His firm, established in 1979, is one of the oldest independent engineering software companies providing HVAC programs to contractors and engineers around the country.

Smith contributes columns periodically to this news section. This month, Smith tells how an aggressive HVAC wholesaler has used his load calculation software as a vital marketing tool. His comments follow:

The Role of the Computer

How Benoist Bros. Supply, Mt. Vernon, Ill., Uses Computer to Competitive Advantage

In a time of increasing competition and shrinking profit margins, many HVAC equipment wholesalers have had to find new ways, and tools, for not only maintaining but growing their businesses.

One company currently experiencing rapid and healthy growth is Benoist Bros. Supply Co., Mt. Vernon, Ill. The firm is a wholesale distributor of HVAC products serving the southern areas of Illinois, Indiana and Missouri, northern Kentucky and St. Louis. The company has 41 employees and specializes in supplying HVAC equipment for residential and light commercial buildings.

Computerized Load Calculations Provide Important Competitive Advantage

In their continuing efforts to become more competitive and responsive to its customers, Benoist Bros. has increasingly turned to computers and software. Jack Benoist, CEO, has found, at least for his business, that computerized load calculations have provided important competitive advantages for his company.

Although he doesn't perform large system design work, he does provide small system sizing and "design" help to his dealers and contractors as an extra "value added" service to help them win more jobs.

He explains "For example, I might have an owner who is putting up a $100,000 building, like a body shop or dentist's office. He won't hire a engineer to do the job when he can get his dealer to do it for him. Using QHVAC, I show his dealer how much tonnage the job requires and prove that it will work for him. This is a value added service we provide to our customers so they can get the job."

Benoist notes it was not always this way in the past. "In the old days, we couldn't help our dealers like this because of the prohibitive amount of time it took to do manual load calculations.

"As a result, we were limited to smaller and less profitable projects. Now, we can handle those larger projects because we can do the load calculations on a computer in very little time."

Elite QHVAC Program Handles Small and Medium Sized Building Very Well

Benoist was introduced to computerized load calculations with Elite Software's QHVAC program in the mid-1980s. "Because most of our jobs are residential and light commercial buildings," he explains, "they don't require formal engineering design. QHVAC handles the small to medium size buildings very well.

"Our dealers and contractors now look to us to provide engineering expertise and recommendations for them to bid their jobs. QHVAC paid for itself on itself on its first job," he recalls.

The Role of the Computer

An example of the importance of this new capability occurred recently when one of his dealer's jobs required a "make-up" air solution for a small factory in Mt. Vernon. "The dealer asked us to perform the load calculations necessary for the air changes. Because the program's reports were so professional and persuasive, our dealer had no competitors after we made the initial presentation using QHVAC. Needless to say, he ended up with a $50,000 job."

At another project, a dealer presented a negative pressure problem in a large building requiring a large amount of "make-up" air. Benoist remembers, "The owner didn't want to complete the entire make up project at once but rather wanted to do it in stages.

"With QHVAC we helped our dealer and easily provided the loads for each step and show the owner exactly what each step would provide him in additional temperature and negative pressure reduction. The program allowed us to adapt easily to many design changes from the client and provide all new loads. QHVAC enabled us to do this unusual job quickly and accurately — the versatility of program was essential for this job."

Computer Generated Reports Critical To Selling Process

Benoist admits that the program's computer generated reports are critical to the selling process. "One of the major benefits is that we can provide solid and precise documentation of the design process for my dealers to use a sales tool to their customer. We provide nice cover pages, and all the figures the program used to calculate the loads, locations, weather data, specifics of the buildings, operation times, maximum peak loads for the summer and winter and the hours those get generated.

"They can see everything right in front of them — it's impressive. And because these reports came out of the computer they're also more believable and persuasive."

"When a customer compares a competitor's rudimentary rule of thumb handwritten calculations side-by-side to our guy's comprehensive and professional-looking computer produced reports there is no doubt our guy will get the job every time."

He notes another impressive, and unexpected, benefit in the program's psychrometric analysis report. "Our customers are used to seeing psychrometrics only on large jobs. It's another service we provide to help our customers."

Using Program As Value Added Service

Benoist notes that using the program as value added service has helped increase his commercial business 10% to 20%. "It makes us more competitive and helps put us in a strong leadership position in our area. Believe me, if I didn't use QHVAC to help my dealers, they would take their business to some other wholesaler who gave them that service. It's that important."

Benoist says they have never had a problem with a design using QHVAC. "None of our customers or dealers have told us later that the equipment is not properly heating or cooling the building. This says a lot for the program and gives us tremendous confidence in our judgement.

"We also have a sense of pride in the job that's not been excessively designed. For us, it's not reassuring that your customer could have paid 30% more than necessary. It will catch up with you when you are seen as an expensive supplier. Believe it or not, we still have significant competitors who do not provide computerized load calculations and they are being hurt — no question about it."

He adds that his competitors who still use antiquated rule of thumb methods are not considering new energy-efficient materials, better insulation, tighter buildings and higher efficiency equipment.

"In today's market, customers are much more intelligent and knowledgeable; they simply will not pay excessive amounts for equipment like they used to. Although my less sophisticated competitors are still making money, they are not taking care of their customers and their profit margins are shrinking."

Small Wholesalers Not Computerized Becoming Dinosaurs

"Small wholesalers who are not computerized and not providing this kind of service are becoming dinosaurs. They're going out of business right now and will continue to drop off. The National Ass'n of Wholesalers has estimated that a great many simply will not exist in only a few years."

Lap-Top and Personal Computers To Be Added By Benoist

For Benoist however, the company's plans for further computerization include supplying small lap-top computers for all of its salesmen and personal desk-top computers for at least 80% its staff. He adds, "We'll also connect all of our computers to our new mini-computer for increased efficiency and productivity gains. And we'll load QHVAC into our salesmen's laptops so that they can perform load calculations right at the customer's location."

Jack Benoist concludes, "QHVAC has been an outstanding program for us; it's a very useful tool that we use every week. The world has changed and marketing and productivity will determine the future of wholesalers. QHVAC is, in the end, a powerful marketing tool that makes us very competitive and allows us to make more money because we can access a much larger market."

William Smith will welcome comments on his remarks from readers. Readers can communicate with him at P.O. Drawer 1194, Bryan, Texas, 77806.

474.

Custom Control Panels Offered By Upstate Electrical Technologies

Upstate Electrical Technologies, Inc., 7635 Main St., Fishers, N.Y., 14453, designers of custom computer controlled monitoring and control systems, now offers a custom control panel service. Upstate will now build a custom panel to customer specifications or provide a complete design, manufacturing and installation service.

Upstate offers a broad range of design and manufacturing experience applicable to process control, refrigeration control and panels for monitoring and control of nearly any endeavor.

Compusource Corp. Announces New Enhanced CONTRAC2 Release 6.0 Software

Compusource Corp., 20 Centerpointe Dr., Suite 105, LaPalma, Cal., 90623, is now marketing its CONTRAC2 Release 6.0 an enhanced version of its CONTRAC2 business application software for HVAC, plumbing and electrical contractors.

Using the system, maintenance contracts can be scheduled on a specific day, and a given job site can have multiple calls under the same contract in any month. All service calls can be estimated relative to the number of hours they take, allowing dispatchers to provide customers with more information.

CONTRAC2's new QUICK TURN-IN permits technicians to call in from field, report the task name, and the entire parts list is automatically relieved from inventory. An invoice, complete with parts and labor sub-totals is printed and ready when the technician returns to the shop.

Federal Construction Criteria On Compact Disc Adds Product Information, CCB for Windows

Construction product information and CCB for Windows have now been included in the Fourth Quarter release of Construction Criteria Base (CCB), the compact disc system published since 1987 by the National Institute of

The Role of the Computer

Building Sciences, 1201 L St., N.W., Suite 400, Washington, D.C., 20005.

Contact Layne Evans, manager of information systems for NIBS, at the above address for information.

STAFDA Issues 1993 Computer Software Guide to Members

The Specialty Tools & Fasteners Distributors Ass'n (STAFDA), Box 44, Elm Grove, Wis., 53122, has issued its 34-page 1993 Computer Software Guide to its membership. The guide is intended to help members research any upgrade of their present computer system.

The software guide consists of a section which provides a summary of each participating software vendor, contact information and a brief description of the system.

Next, is an objective matrix of features which provides a means of comparing the vendors on a head-to-head basis. Each of the software vendors had their software reviewed with a User Group consultant in the fall of 1992 to ensure that all the questions were answered accurately.

Siebe Environmental Controls/IBM Collaborate on SiteManager Services

Siebe Environmental Controls, 1354 Clifford Ave., Loves Park, Ill., 61132, and International Business Machines (IBM) Customized Operational Services Business Unit have jointly developed a data center service offering called IBM Systemview SiteManager Services.

SiteManager protects and enhances data center operations by monitoring information systems processing and environmental conditions.

Trouble conditions are immediately reported by SiteManager locally as well as remotely to an IBM Monitoring Center. The result is early detection of potentially disastrous outages of operations. In parallel, SiteManager protects data processing by initiating an orderly shutdown and restart, when necessary.

Elite Software Announces New Program for Analyzing Energy Usage and Cost in Buildings

Elite Software Development, Inc., P.O. Drawer 1192, Bryan, Texas, 77806, has introduced EZ-DOE, a new program that calculates hourly, monthly and annual energy use of a building and its life cycle costs of operation. EZ-DOE simulates operation of all types of heating/cooling plants, including ice water thermal storage and cogeneration systems.

EZ-DOE is IBM-PC compatible and based on the Dept. of Energy's main-frame program, "DOE-2,.1D", the standard for the California Energy Commission and Title 24 work. Up to 24 different air handling system types, such as dual-duct, VAV, packaged unit, etc., each with multiple control options are supported.

Computer News

Estimation Appoints Goodwin National Sales Mgr.

Estimation, Inc., Linthicum Heights, Md., has announced the appointment of Robert Goodwin to the position of national sales manager. He has been with the firm for 11 years.

In his new position, Goodwin will be responsible for sales and managing Estimation's national sales force. He is also Estimation's top selling sales rep of all time.

Upstate Electrical Brochure Covers Refrigeration Computer Control System

Upstate Electrical Technologies, Inc., P.O. Box J, Fishers, N.Y., 14453, is offering a new free brochure describing its Refrigeration Executive computer control system.

The system provides continuous monitoring and control of refrigeration systems from a single control center and provides information on temperature, humidity, pressure, equipment status, alarm conditions and energy usage. All real time functions can be accessed from off-site locations via telecommunications.

Midwest Computer Show To Be Held May 19-21, Rosemont, Ill.

The 1993 Midwest Computer Show will be held at the Rosemont Convention Center, Rosemont, Ill., May 19-21.

The show will feature exhibits addressing operating systems, desktop publishing, networking, windows, graphics, mainframes and executive information systems, along with exhibits of major software developers. Educational sessions will also be held covering a wide variety of computer topics.

For further show information, contact the CPA Society, 222 S. Riverside Dr., 16th Floor, Chicago, Ill., 60606.

ABC Announces Purchasing Agreement With Xerox

The Associated Builders & Contractors (ABC), has announced a purchasing agreement with the Xerox Corp. which guarantees ABC members discounts on a wide range of Xerox products and services. Under terms of the agreement, ABC members will receive preferred pricing on Xerox copiers, printers, engineering document products and other equipment.

The agreement also extends to training, systems management, network and professional services.

ABC has launched an informational campaign to alert members to the discount opportunities available under the agreement. Xerox has also developed an advertising and marketing program aimed directly at builders and contractors.

Load Controller for Demand Rates Marketed By Dencor

The new Series 200C Demand Computer for commercial applications by Dencor, Inc., reduces electric utility bills by shifting energy use to off-peak periods and controlling demand peaks. It provides a variety of control strategies for individual loads including priority, duty-cycling, and alternating.

The Demand Computer helps the user visualize the impact of individual electric loads on energy use by continuously showing the rate of energy consumption. As each load is turned on or off, the display will change showing the consumption of that load. Current transformers or KYZ pulses may be used to monitor power.

The Demand Computer accommodates demand rates with split on-peak periods and a separate schedule for weekends. The memory provides automatic adjustments for holidays, daylight saving time changes and seasonal changes in on-peak periods. Power-line carrier modules are available to control hard-to-reach loads.

For further information, contact Dencor Energy Cost Controls, Inc., 1450 W. Evans, Denver, Colo.. 80223.

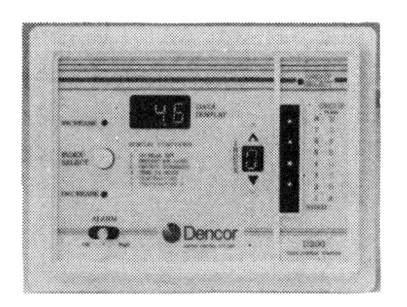

Elite Software Offers New Earth Coupled Analysis Program

Elite Software Development, Inc., P.O. Drawer 1194, Bryan, Texas, 77806, is now offering ECA 3.0, a new and more powerful version of its earth coupled analysis program. ECA calculates optimal required loop pipe lengths necessary for heating and cooling a building with a given heat pump, soil and weather conditions.

The program can compute pressure losses through the equipment room, heat pump, header pipe and the earth coil and can analyze any vertical and horizontal system. ECA provides extensive "built-in" data of most pipe types including polyethylene, polybutylene, copper, iron and others. This data can be easily revised and additional pipe types can be entered.

Additional new features include updated heat pump adjustment calculations and equipment performance data to match the newest Florida Heat Pump equipment. The program also includes expanded weather data for 220 cities.

SNIPS   April, 1993

Computer News

OSHA-Soft Releases New Version Of Regulation Software

OSHA-Soft, Inc., P.O. Box 668, Amherst, N.H., 03031, has released a new 2.0 version of their FastRegs software. This regulation scanning program provides quick referencing, searching and printing of relevant OSHA and EPA regulations.

The software can be used on any IBM PC, XT, AT, PS/2 or compatible computer with 512K RAM and hard disk. Options for the software include a subscription to either a monthly or quarterly update to the regulations. Each update is sent on a single diskette and includes a newsletter to further explain the regulation changes.

Data-Basics Offers Updated Version Of CMAS Plus Software

Data-Basics, 11000 Cedar Rd., Suite 110, Cleveland, Ohio, 44106, has just released Version 1.5 of its CMAS Plus software. CMAS Plus is an integrated accounting/job costing/service management software for specialty contractors.

New in Version 1.5 is Work In Process, which allows the user to recognize unbilled earnings, or more specifically, the value of unbilled labor and other expenses. Revenue values are calculated and updated to general ledger and job costings as entries are recorded into the system. Work In Process is cleared when sales journal entries are recorded in accounts receivable.

The Role of the Computer

Another new feature of Version 1.5 allows users to maintain multiple billing addresses for a single customer, and finally, a New Maintenance Contract Report will show profitability by contract item.

Elite Software Releases A New Version Of Its Residential HVAC Loads Calculations Program

Elite Software Development is now distributing a new version of its residential HVAC loads calculations program, RHVAC 4.0. RHVAC accurately calculates peak heating and cooling loads for residential and small commercial buildings. New features include attractive graphic reports which show total building loss and heat-gain loads in easy-to-understand pie charts and bar graphs.

In addition, RHVAC now works with an electronic "mouse" for a substantial improvement in efficiency, accuracy and operation speed. A mouse greatly reduces manual typing through fast cursor placement and easy access to menu items and can often save over a thousand keystrokes in a typical computing session.

RHVAC works in full accordance with the methods described in the seventh edition of ACCA's Manual J. Although HTM values are taken from Manual J, the user has the option of entering his own U-Value for each wall, roof, or glass section. Design weather data for 156 cities listed in Manual J are part of RHVAC and automatically used as required.

RHVAC allows the user to rotate the entire building or individual rooms and has the ability to work with up 1,000 rooms per project. RHVAC 4.0 is priced at $395. For more information, demos and updates contact Elite Software, P.O. Drawer 1194, Bryan, Texas, 77806.

Elite Software, Bryan, Texas, Expands Operations

Elite Software, P.O. 1194, Bryan, Texas, 77806, is expanding its operations. The company has doubled its office space and hired additional staff. The newest addition to the Elite staff is software engineer Ashok Velayudham, who will be working on new product development in Elite's electrical software programs.

Elite Software produces over 30 software programs for mechanical, electrical and plumbing engineers and contractors.

ASG Estimator Integrates CAD Drawing Process with Timberline Estimating and Means Pricing

ASG, 4000 Bridgeway, Suite 309, Sausilito, Cal., 94965, which develops integrated software for contractors who use AutoCAD has introduced the ASG Estimator. The new CAD

The Role of the Computer

estimating system uses R.S. Means pricing and Timberline Software CAD integration technology.

This automated CAD-estimating technology gives users a greater ability to evaluate design/cost alternatives. It also produces integration of the design/build cycle, easier customization of plans and more realistic budgets.

New Easi-Est S.M. Estimating Program Includes Alternate Bid

A new wrinkle in sheet metal estimating by computer is offered by Easi-Est Software, Inc., P.O. Box 463, Huntington, N.Y., 11743. The program includes two bids: the bid following specifications and an alternate bid and redesign with material substitutions.

The alternate bid may include a changed aspect ratio, squared off duct or conversion from rectangular to round to reduce costs by almost 40% without entering the entire take-off.

The program assembles all zone or job worksheets automatically. The Subcontractor Tracking feature allows the estimator to keep track of subcontractor bids as they come in, sorts them and selects the lowest in each category, adds mark-ups, sales tax, bonds and totals for the bid assembly in minutes rather than hours.

Information and free sheet metal tutorial disk is available from Easi-Est at the above address.

Part 12

Materials for Making Your Shop Layout

-- Factors to Consider --

1. These cut-out templates represent average sizes of the various types and styles of each particular machine.

2. Included in the cut-out templates are several additional templates with various sizes for the purpose of modifying to your custom needs in regard to special machinery and equipment.

3. In many cases, you many require more than the one cut-out template that is included, such as Layout Benches, Cleat Benders, Pittsburgh Machines, Squaring Shears, Hand Brakes and Press Brakes. Simply cut out the required template and trace as many as you require on the additional colored paper included at the back of this handbook.

4. If you have a larger shop than graph paper available, simply make several photocopies and tape them from underneath.

5. Secure cut-out templates with thumb tacks, which makes it quick and easy to change or move them around.

6. If you use flat bed, band or movable tables to carry raw or finished items to various places throughout the plant, use the correct size cut-out template checking that it fits between all other templates on the plan layout.

7. Sometimes due to limited space, you might want to have some of the machines or equipment on casters so they can be "locked" into a stationary position and unlocked whenever necessary.

8. The amount of storage area required should be determined to include all material and supplies that you currently use, such as the various types, sizes, and gages of metal.

9. Open yard area can sometimes be utilized for storage of materials; sometimes a disregarded truck or bus is used for this.

10. You might want to sacrifice an excellent location for some particular machine and equipment, and use it for something more important, such as the Foreman's or superintendent's office or area. You alone must make this decision - - what is most important in regard to overall profit.

11. Sometimes a wall can be removed if it is non-bearing. However, many times it can be a bearing wall that cannot be removed. If this exists in your shop, you should give careful considera-tion to making an opening in the wall or walls so that it is possible to see into the other area when necessary.

12. The sample layouts in this handbook did not allow space for offices which would have rooms or areas designated for Estimating, Drafting, etc. However, this can be on the same level of the shop or on a second floor, if available, directly above the shop.

If at all possible, the office area should be off to itself as well as away from any noises in the shop, since most thinking and planning time is done here.

Also the sample shop layouts did not include any washroom facilities, lockers, showers, coffee machines, storage areas, welding area, bins, foremen's office or area, and inspection area.

Materials for Making Your Shop Layout

Machinery and Equipment Lists

ANGLE IRON & CLEAT CUTTER - 36" X 12"

ANGLE IRON & CLEAT RACK - 168" X 60"

ANGLE IRON & CLEAT RACK - 120" X 36"

ANGLE IRON MACHINE - 24" X 24"

ARC WELDER - 66" X 36"

BAND SAW (HORIZONTAL) - 44" X 24"

BAND SAW (VERTICAL) - 42" X 24"

BAR CLEAT MACHINE - 58" X 24"

BAR FOLDER - 50" X 30"

4' - 0" BOX BRAKE - 100" X 48"

BUTTON PUNCH SNAP LOCK FLANGER - 24" X 24"

CHEEK BENDER (BENCH FRAME) - 24" X 18"

CLEAT BENDER (FLOOR STAND) - 37" X 20"

COIL STORAGE - 60" X 60"

COIL STORAGE - 60" X 48"

COMBINATION BUTTON PUNCH CHEEK BENDER
   & NOTCHER - 36" X 24"

COPER NOTCHER - 18" X 17"

DRILL PRESS - 44" X 21"

DROP-OF RACK - 48" X 36"

DUCT BOARD CUTTER - 130" X 30"

EASY EDGER (HAND) - 12" X 12"

EASY EDGER (POWER) - 24" X 24"

FABRI-DUCT - 51" X 18"

FABRI-DUCT - 65" X 18"

FOOT SHEAR - 50" X 31"

INSUL-PIN WELDING MACHINE - 24" X 12"

INSULATION CUTTER & BENCH - 168" X 60"

INSULATION CUTTER & BENCH - 168" X 48"

BENCH - 120" X 48"

HAND TRUCKS - 120" X 48"

HAND TRUCKS - 96" X 36"

HARDWARE BIN - 48" X 18"

HARDWARE STORAGE (ROUND STYLE) - 36" DIA.

4' HAND BRAKE - 100" X 48"

8' HAND BRAKE - 134" X 52"

LARGE POWER ROLLER - 72" X 36"

LAYOUT BENCH - 120" X 48"

CABINET HAND TOOL - 36" X 18"

POWER CLEAT TURNER - 58" X 24"

ADDITIONAL TEMPLATES FOR MODIFYING:
   144" X 24"   192" X 36"
   240" X 48"   288" X 60"

CABINET WITH ROTARY MACHINES - 24" X 24"

MATERIAL RACK - 102" X 42"

MATERIAL RACK - 126" X 54"

MATERIAL RACK - 126" X 66"

Materials for Making Your Shop Layout

MOVEABLE TABLE - 96" X 36"

MOVEABLE TABLE - 120" X 48"

NIBBLER MACHINE - 39" X 26"

PEDESTAL GRINDER - 18" X 12"

6' POWER BRAKE - 89" X 64"

8' POWER BRAKE - 113" X 64"

10' POWER BRAKE - 137" X 64"

12' POWER BRAKE - 161" X 64"

16' POWER BRAKE - 185" X 64"

POWER CLEAT MACHINE - 58" X 24"

POWER EASY EDGER - 24" X 24"

PITTSBURGH MACHINE - 58" X 24"

POWER NOTCHER - 18" X 12"

4' POWER SHEAR - 123" X 104"

6' POWER SHEAR - 147" X 104"

8' POWER SHEAR - 171" X 104"

10' POWER SHEAR - 195" X 104"

12' POWER SHEAR - 220" X 104"

POWER ROLLER - 72" X 42"

RAIL MACHINE - 48" X 24"

"S" & "D" MACHINE - 58" X 24"

SLIP ROLLER - 61" X 11"

SNAP LOCK MACHINE - 58" X 24"

SPEEDIBENDER - 157" X 70 1/2"

SPEEDINOTCHER - 133" X 24"

SPOT PIN WELDER - 21" X 14"

SPOT WELDER - 36" X 18"

STANDING SEAM MACHINE - 58" X 24"

STEEL IRON WORKER - 66" X 24"

STONE SAW - 58" X 53"

TURRET PUNCH PRESS - 31" X 25"

VANE COIL STORAGE

VANE STORAGE

VISE - 16" X 7"

WELDING MACHINES - 60" X 30"

ASSEMBLY & INSULATION BENCH 102" X 42"

MOVEABLE TABLE - 36" X 36"

MOVEABLE TABLE - 48" X 48"

Materials for Making Your Shop Layout

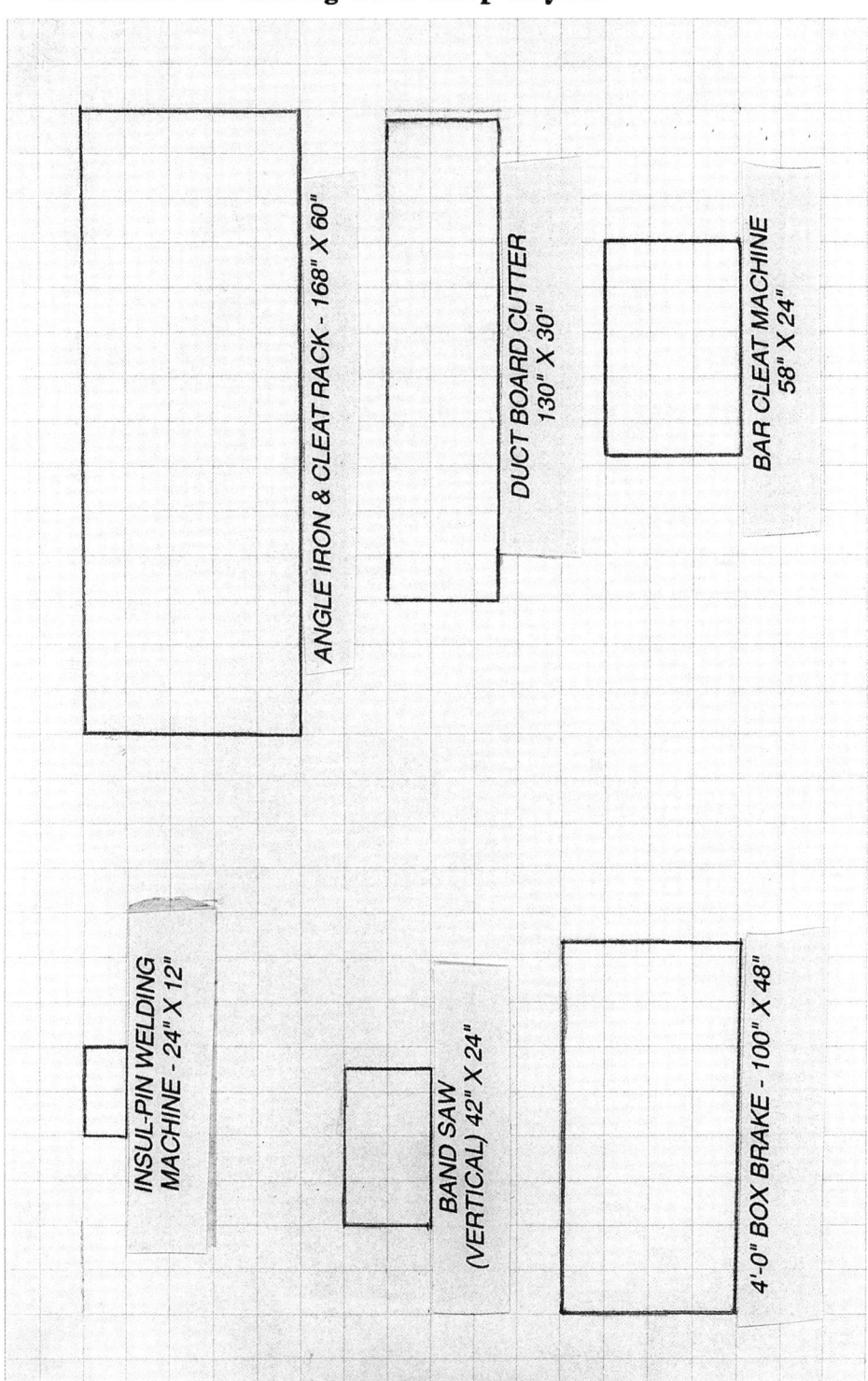

Materials for Making Your Shop Layout 487.

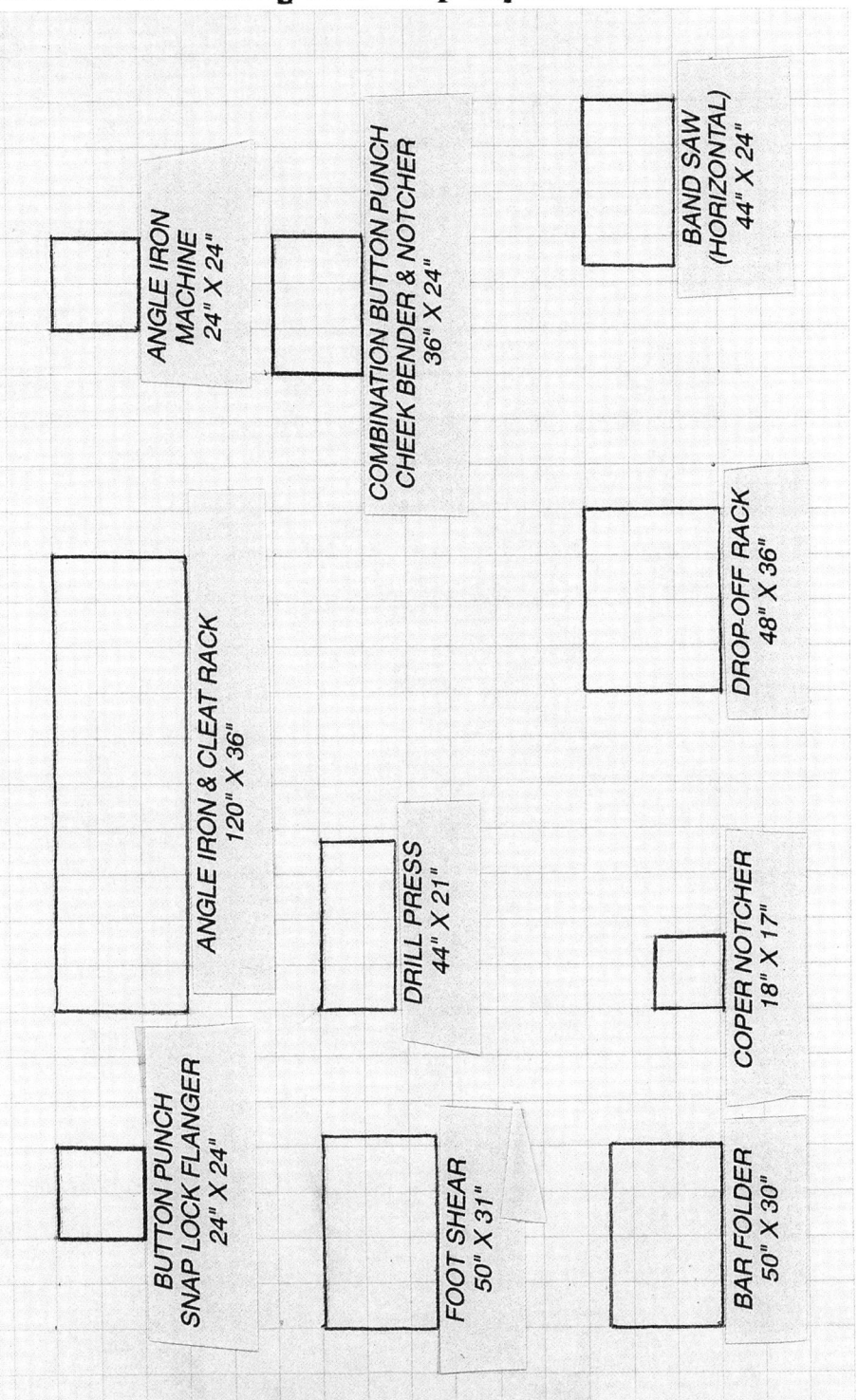

- ANGLE IRON MACHINE 24" X 24"
- COMBINATION BUTTON PUNCH CHEEK BENDER & NOTCHER 36" X 24"
- BAND SAW (HORIZONTAL) 44" X 24"
- ANGLE IRON & CLEAT RACK 120" X 36"
- DROP-OFF RACK 48" X 36"
- DRILL PRESS 44" X 21"
- COPER NOTCHER 18" X 17"
- BUTTON PUNCH SNAP LOCK FLANGER 24" X 24"
- FOOT SHEAR 50" X 31"
- BAR FOLDER 50" X 30"

Materials for Making Your Shop Layout 489.

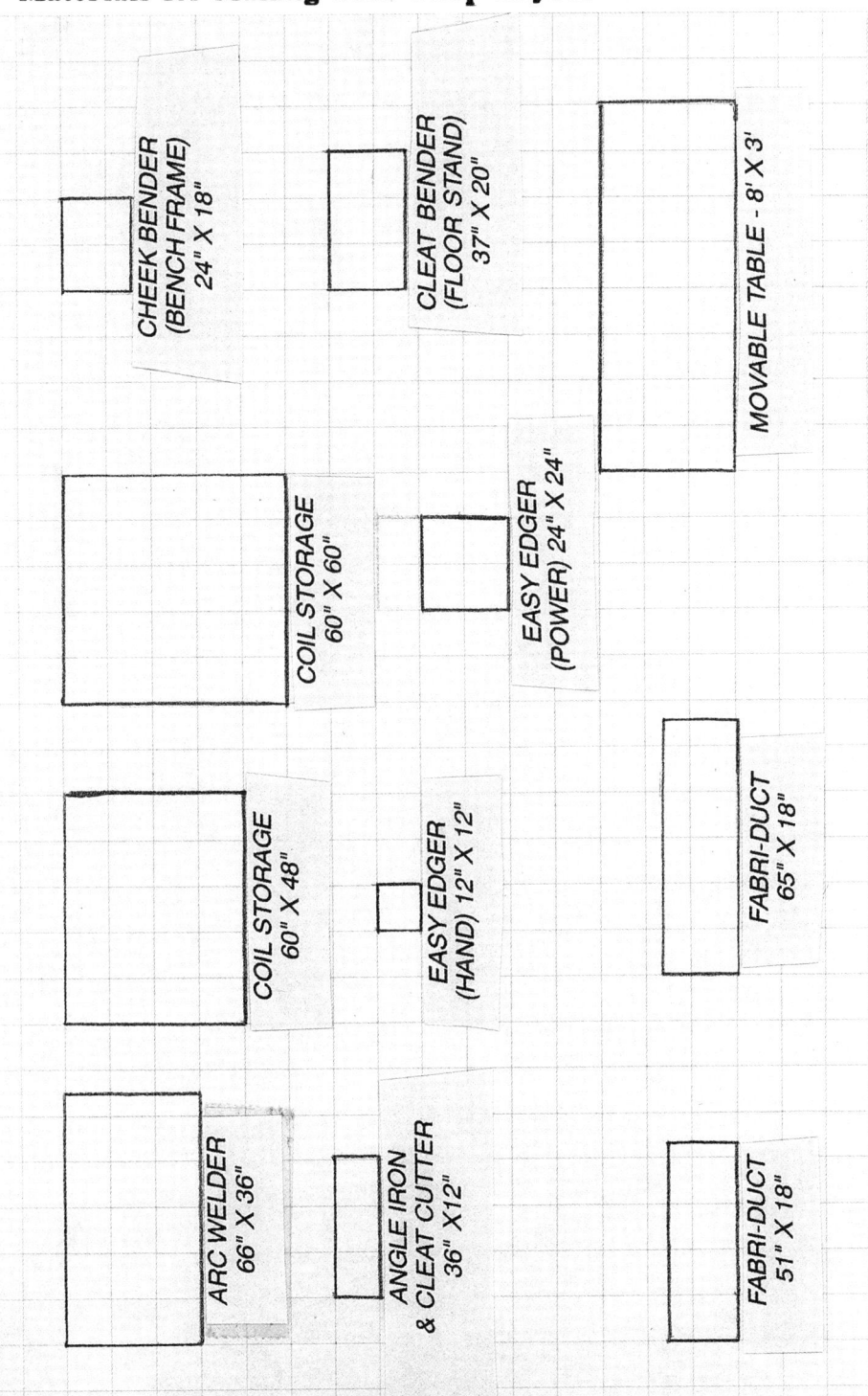

- CHEEK BENDER (BENCH FRAME) 24" X 18"
- CLEAT BENDER (FLOOR STAND) 37" X 20"
- MOVABLE TABLE - 8' X 3'
- COIL STORAGE 60" X 60"
- EASY EDGER (POWER) 24" X 24"
- FABRI-DUCT 65" X 18"
- COIL STORAGE 60" X 48"
- EASY EDGER (HAND) 12" X 12"
- ARC WELDER 66" X 36"
- ANGLE IRON & CLEAT CUTTER 36" X 12"
- FABRI-DUCT 51" X 18"

Materials for Making Your Shop Layout 491.

12' POWER BRAKE - 161" X 64"

LAYOUT BENCH - 10' X 4'

HAND TRUCKS - 10' X 4'

10' POWER BRAKE - 137" X 64"

Materials for Making Your Shop Layout 493.

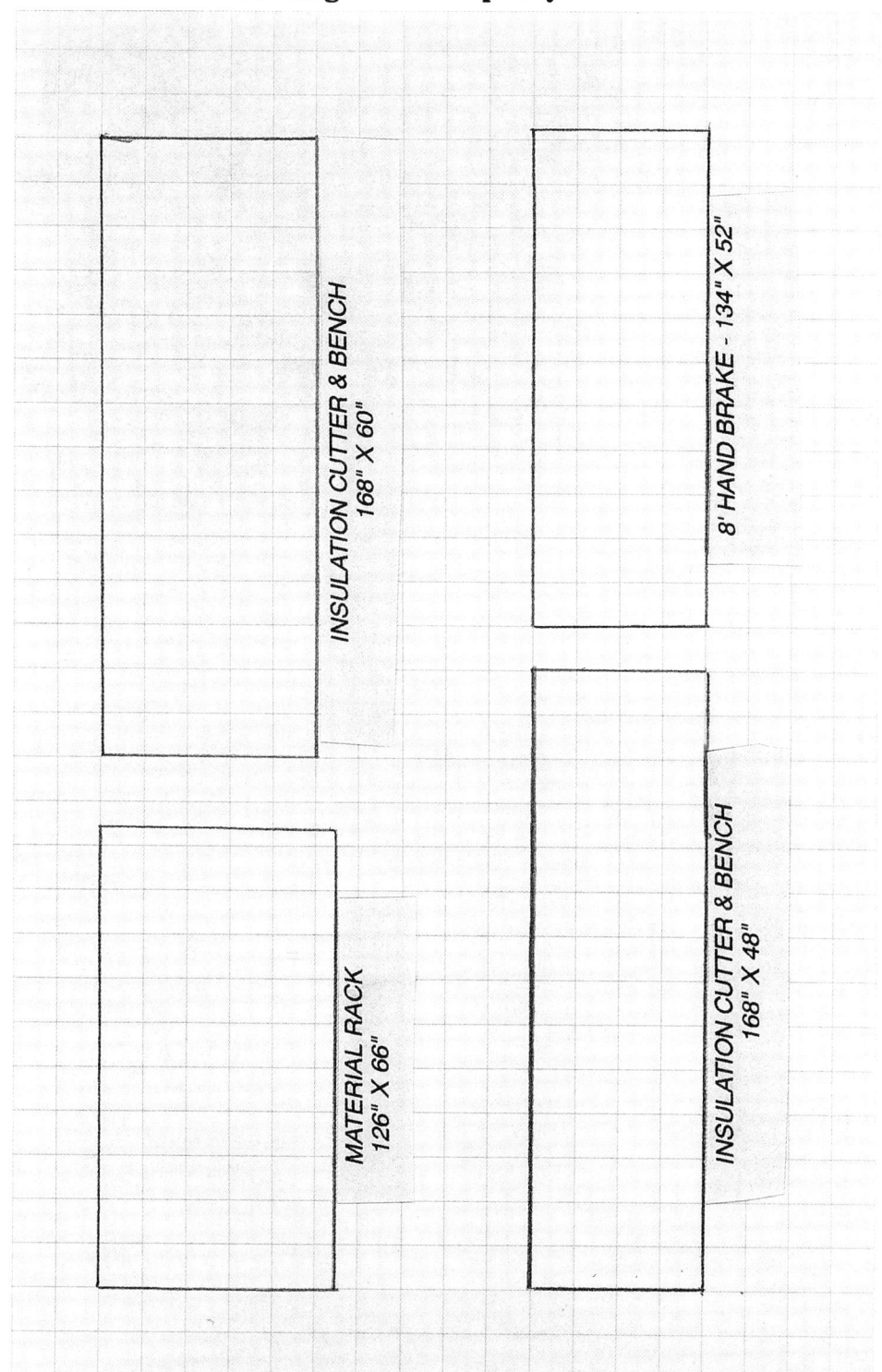

INSULATION CUTTER & BENCH
168" X 60"

8' HAND BRAKE - 134" X 52"

MATERIAL RACK
126" X 66"

INSULATION CUTTER & BENCH
168" X 48"

Materials for Making Your Shop Layout 495.

- 4' HAND BRAKE - 100" X 48"
- HARDWARE BIN 48" X 18"
- CABINET WITH ROTARY MACHINES - 24" X 24"
- PEDESTAL GRINDER 18" X 12"
- HARDWARE STORAGE (ROUND STYLE) - 36" DIA.
- BENCH - 10' X 4'
- LARGE POWER ROLLER 72" X 36"
- POWER CLEAT MACHINE 58" X 24"

Materials for Making Your Shop Layout 497.

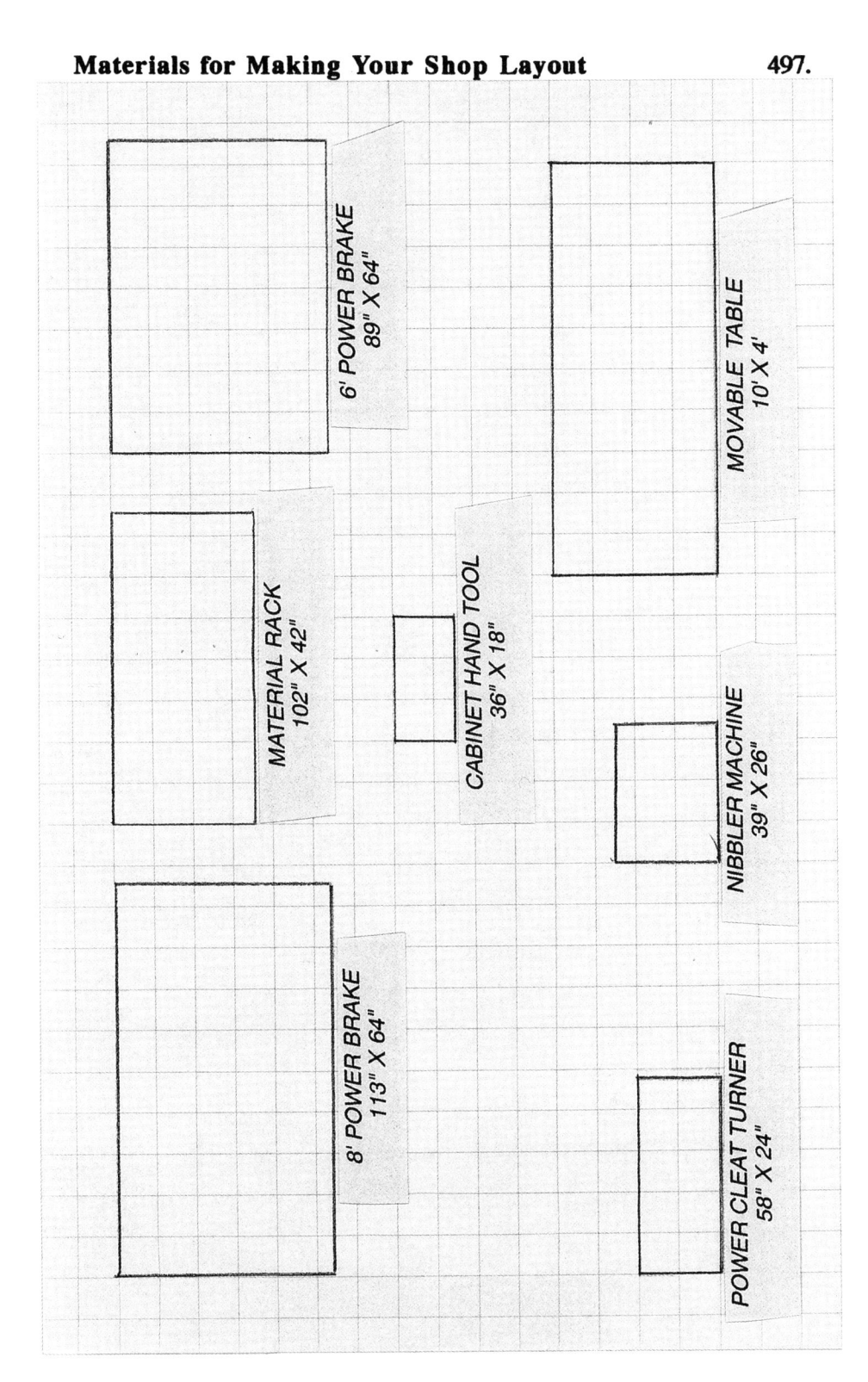

- 6' POWER BRAKE 89" X 64"
- MOVABLE TABLE 10' X 4'
- MATERIAL RACK 102" X 42"
- CABINET HAND TOOL 36" X 18"
- NIBBLER MACHINE 39" X 26"
- 8' POWER BRAKE 113" X 64"
- POWER CLEAT TURNER 58" X 24"

Materials for Making Your Shop Layout 499.

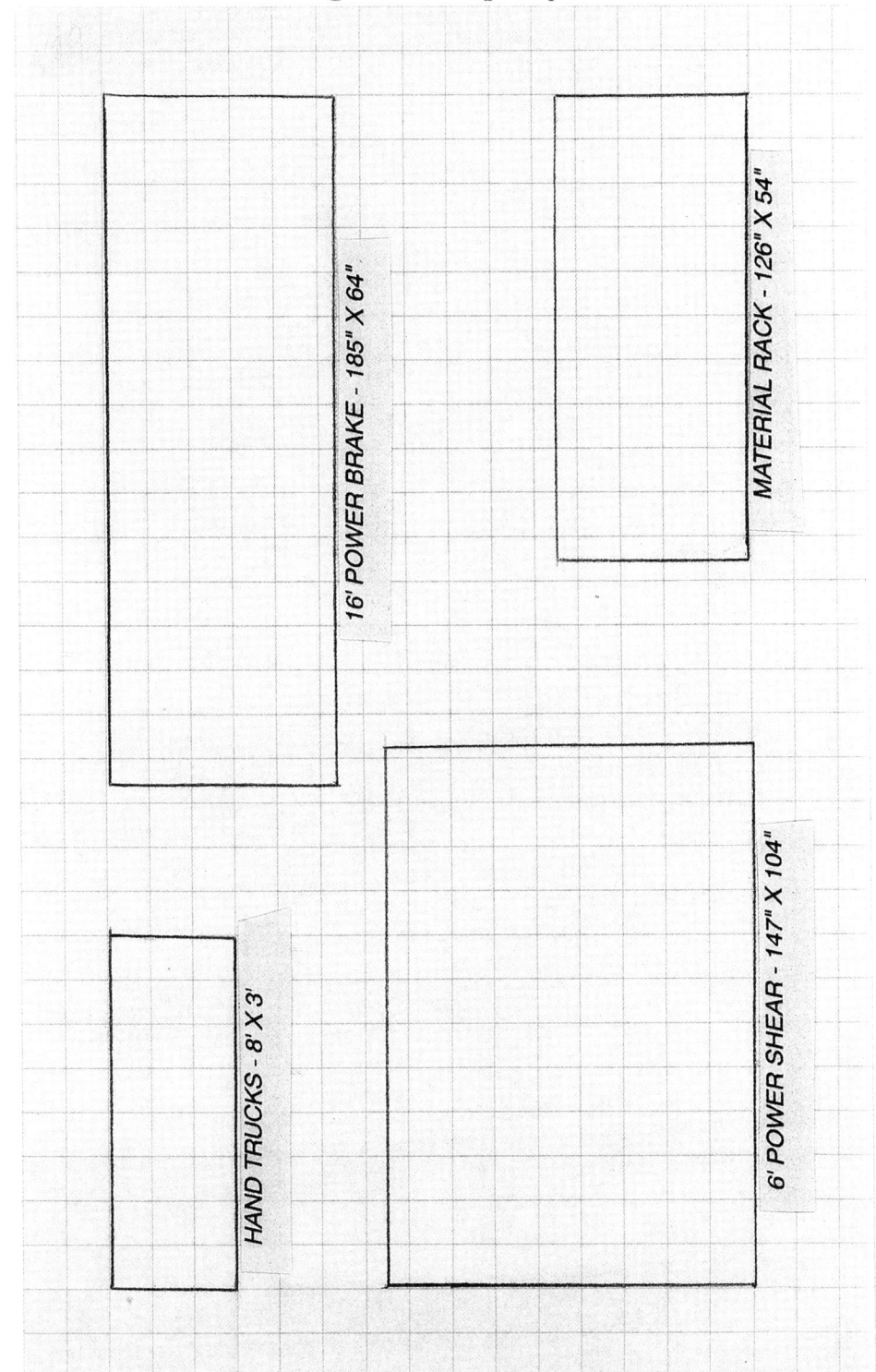

- 16' POWER BRAKE - 185" X 64"
- MATERIAL RACK - 126" X 54"
- HAND TRUCKS - 8' X 3'
- 6' POWER SHEAR - 147" X 104"

Materials for Making Your Shop Layout 501.

- POWER ROLLER - 72" X 42"
- PITTSBURGH MACHINE - 58" X 24"
- WELDING MACHINE - 60" X 30"
- SPOT WELDER - 36" X 18"
- TURRET PUNCH PRESS - 31" X 25"
- VANE COIL STORAGE / VANE STORAGE VISE - 16" X 7"
- 4' POWER SHEAR - 123" X 104"
- STEEL IRON WORKER - 66" X 24"
- STANDING SEAM MACHINE - 58" X 24"

Materials for Making Your Shop Layout 503.

MOVABLE TABLE 48" X 48"

STONE SAW 58" X 53"

12' POWER SHAFT - 220" X 104"

"S" & "D" MACHINE 58" X 24"

POWER EASY EDGER - 24" X 24"

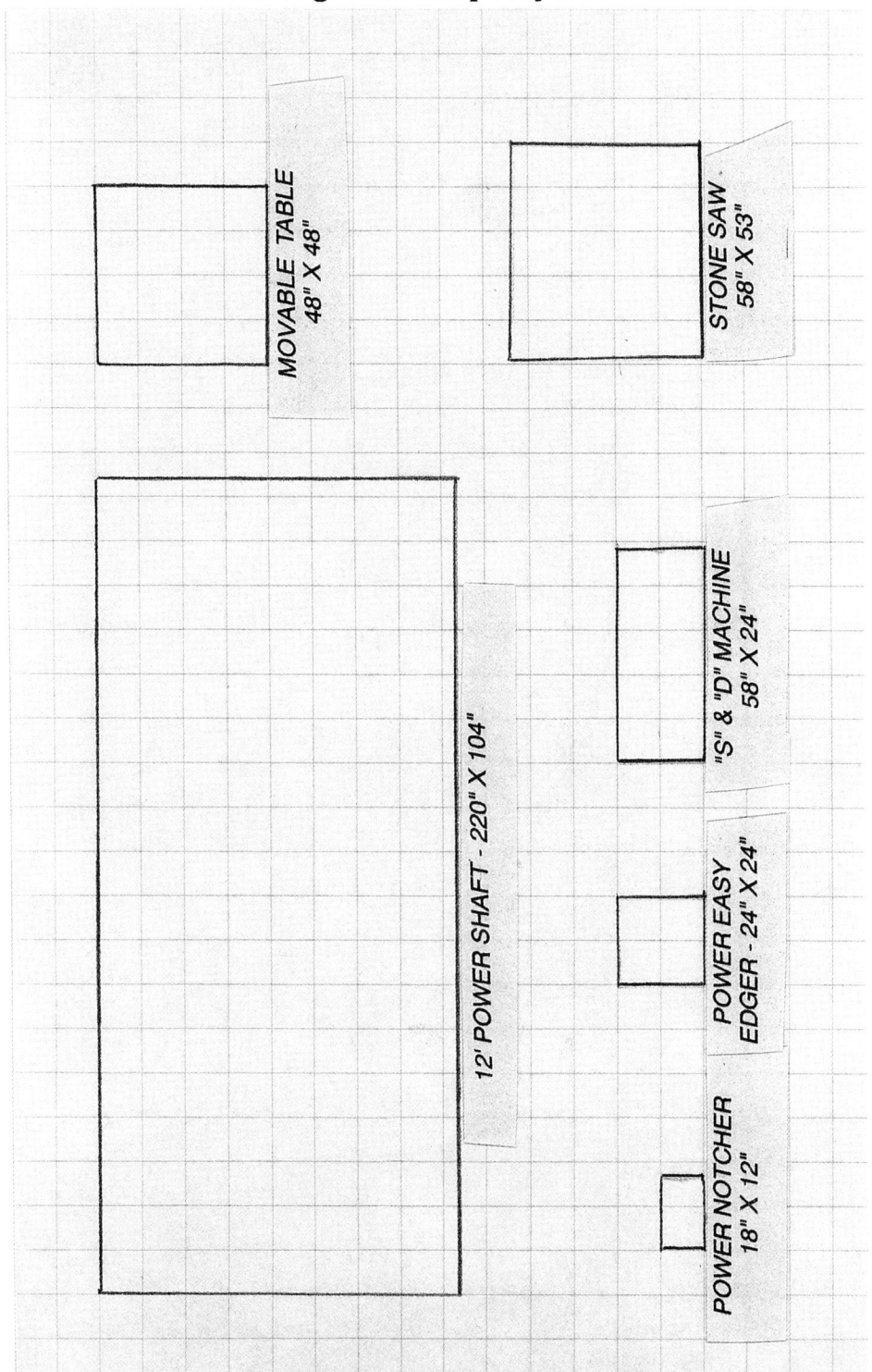

POWER NOTCHER 18" X 12"

Materials for Making Your Shop Layout 505.

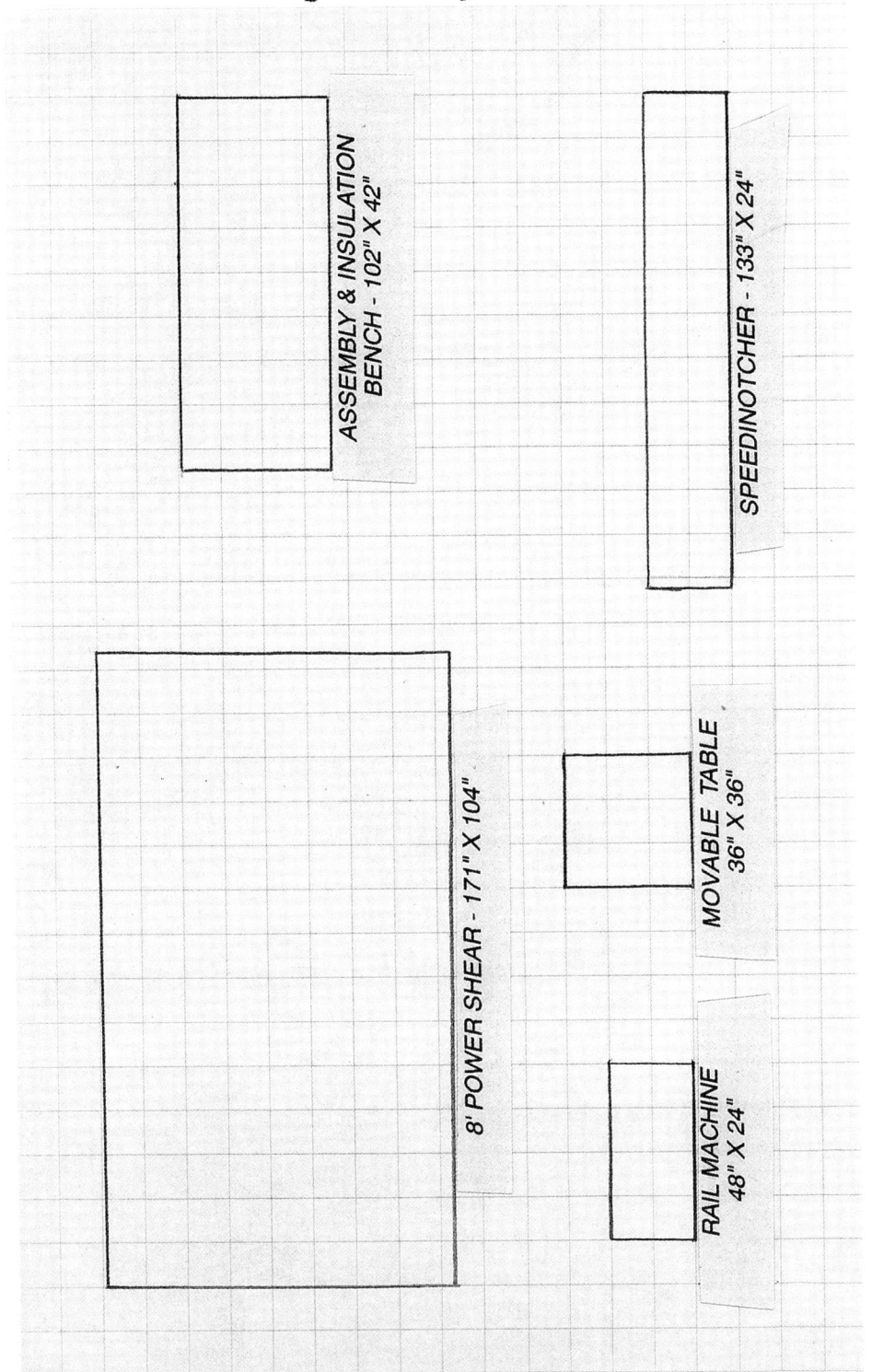

ASSEMBLY & INSULATION BENCH - 102" X 42"

SPEEDINOTCHER - 133" X 24"

8' POWER SHEAR - 171" X 104"

MOVABLE TABLE 36" X 36"

RAIL MACHINE 48" X 24"

Materials for Making Your Shop Layout

SPEEDIBENDER - 157" X 70 1/2"

10' POWER SHEAR - 195" X 104"

SPOT PIN WELDER 21" X 14"

Materials for Making Your Shop Layout 509.

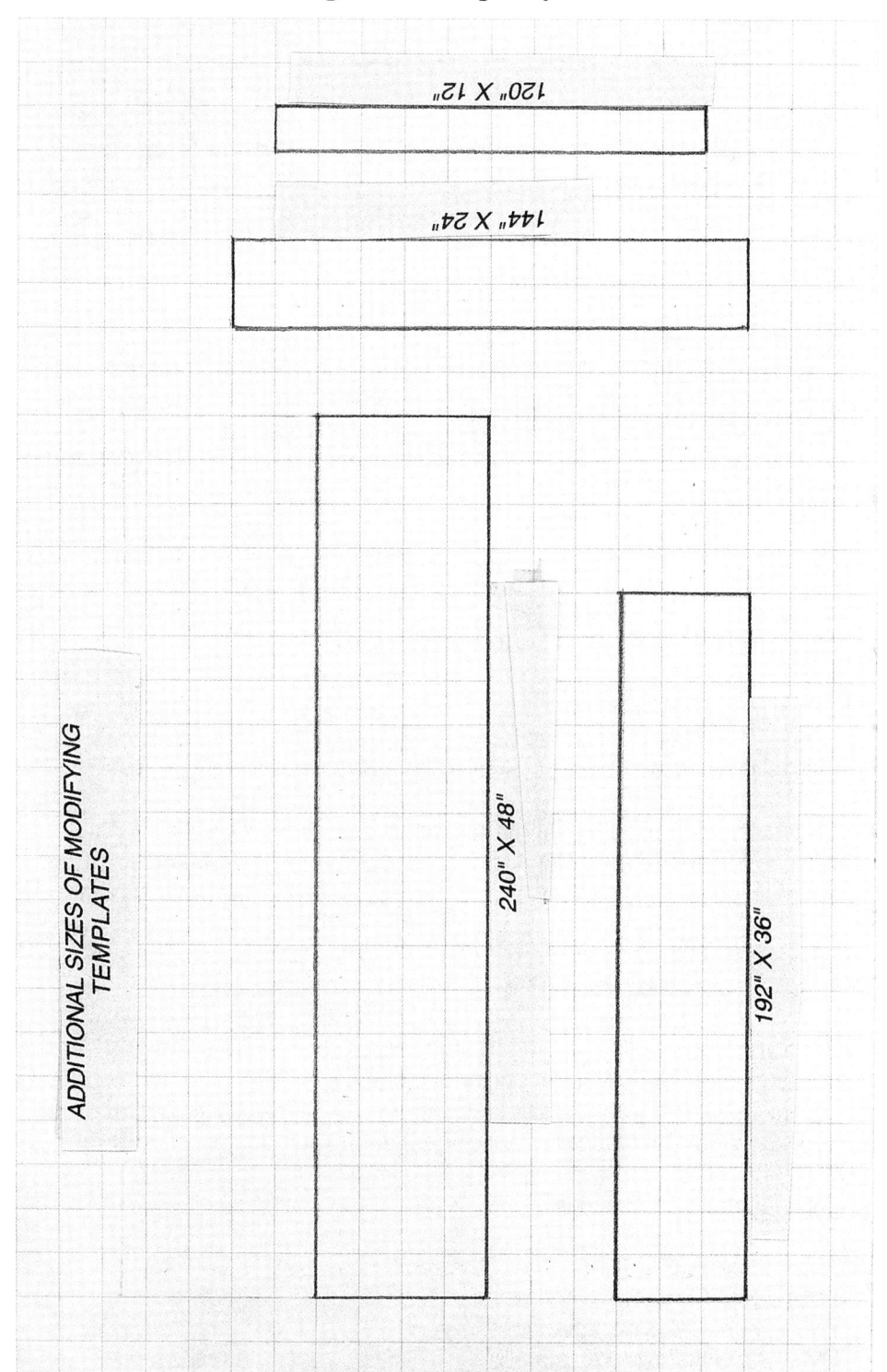

120" X 12"

144" X 24"

ADDITIONAL SIZES OF MODIFYING TEMPLATES

240" X 48"

192" X 36"

FMA and THE FABRICATOR®

When you need reliable technical information on today's most productive metal forming and fabricating processes, join the Fabricators & Manufacturers Association, International (FMA). This not-for-profit organization serves industry as a resource for metal forming and fabricating technology, as well as management information. FMA serves members in over 25 countries on five continents.

The most important reason to join FMA or one of its technology associations is to receive vital technical and management information that will improve the productivity of your operations. When you join FMA, you automatically receive many informative publications that will keep you up-to-date on the newest techniques, equipment and industry activities.

As a member of FMA, you also have access to the most complete technical library in the fabricating industry. This library is your premier source for useful information that can help you work with suppliers, distributors and potential customers worldwide.

These pages tell you more about FMA's educational benefits and membership services. To receive more information or to join FMA, call the FMA Membership Department at (815) 399-8700.

The FMA staff and educational resources are ready to help you achieve your goals for high quality and productivity in your manufacturing operations.

TECHNICAL DIVISIONS/TECHNOLOGY ASSOCIATIONS

FMA membership allows you to enroll in either the Technical Division or Technology Association of your choice. This member benefit allows FMA to serve your interests more effectively by providing you with specialized technical information in your specific area of activity:

FMA Technical Divisions . . .

FMA Sheet Metal Fabricating Division
FMA Roll Forming Division
FMA Technical Divisions (contd.) . . .
FMA Pressworking Division   (contd.)

FMA and THE FABRICATOR®

FMA Coil Processing Division
FMA Plate and Structural Fabricating Division

FMA Technology Associations . . .

1. American Tube Association/FMA
2. Tube & Pipe Fabricators Association, International/FMA
3. Society for Computer-Aided Engineering/FMA

Educational benefits include:

1. Technical Information Center
2. Technology Conferences, Seminars and Workshops

EXPOSITIONS include:

1. FABTECH Expositions and Conferences
2. PRESSTECH Expositions and Conferences
3. Tube & Pipe International Expositions

PUBLICATIONS include:

1. The **FABRICATOR®**
2. **STAMPING Quarterly®**
3. **TPQ--The Tube & Pipe Quarterly**
4. Quarterly Technology Updates
5. FMA News
6. Member Resource Directory

The **FABRICATOR®** is published 10 times a year. Subscriptions are free to anyone in the metal forming and fabricating industry, and may be obtained by calling the Circulation Department, phone below. You may also write or call for details regarding membership and services available.

Fabricators & Manufacturers Association, Intl.
833 Featherstone Road
Rockford, IL 61107-6302

Phone 815-399-8700   FAX 815-399-7279

METAL *Fabricating* INSTITUTE

Metal Fabricating Institute was founded in the late 1960's as a full-time educational and service organization for the metal fabricating industry. The educational arm of the Institute was established as "a self-sustaining educational program devoted to basic education and new techniques in metal fabricating ... and is recognized for its practical approach to everyday fabricating problems."

The Institute sponsored its first fabricating seminar in June, 1968, at Rockford College, Rockford, Illinois. That seminar, which drew 230 attendees, marked a notable beginning of higher education in the metal fabricating industry. Since that first seminar, the Institute has sponsored well-over 100 fabricating, manufacturing, and management seminars all over the continental United States and Canada.

Seminars are conducted at various universities throughout the country and only through the permission of the engineering departments of the cooperating universities. Some of the colleges and universities utilized as training centers, past and present, have included Rockford College (Illinois), Purdue University, University of Cincinnati, California State College at Long Beach, San Jose State College, Texas Christian University, Southern Methodist University, Texas A & M University, University of South Florida at Tampa, North Carolina State University, Spring Garden College (Philadelphia), and McMasters University in Ontario, Canada. With an "alumni association" exceeding six thousand in number, Metal Fabricating Institute attracts attendees from a broad cross-section of both the metal fabricating industry as well as geographical regions. From the small job shops to the Fortune 500's, participants come from all over the United States, as well as from many parts of Canada and Europe. A typical seminar averages a representation of thirty-three states and one or two foreign countries.

If you would like more information about our seminars, please write to:

                        Metal Fabricating Institute
                        710 South Main Street
                        Rockford, Illinois 61101

SNIPS MAGAZINE

SNIPS is published monthly and is a journal of constructive help for the air conditioning, warm air heating, sheet metal and ventilation trades, and those who do roofing work in connection.

SNIPS is a friendly, close-to-the-reader, newsy periodical, long established as the "Bible" of the industry. Stories feature work done by readers, plus numerous new product reviews and reports of local, state and national trade association activities on an almost exclusive basis.

In addition to the feature articles, **SNIPS** regular "Department News" sections include:

Advertisers Index	Market Matters
Book News	National Association News
Coming Conventions	Obituaries
Computer News	Rambling With Reps
Editor's Page	Refrigeration News
Estimating, Credits and Collections	Roofing, Siding and Insulation News
HVACR Service Information	Solar Heating News
Heating Problem Discussions	Solid Fuel Heating News
Hydronics News	Successful Sales Ideas
Industry Educational News	Supply Trade and New Product News
Insurance and Safety Matters	
Letters From Readers	Supply Trade Personnel News
Little Journeys to Interesting Places	Truck News
	Ventilation News
Machine, Tool and Shop News	Want Ads
Management Matters	

SNIPS features local and regional events in the "Sectional News" including the US in 14 sections, Canada and other foreign countries.

A special service provided by **SNIPS** is its Book Department which carries a wide selection of trade and related books.

Write for subscription information and for a Book Catalog:

SNIPS Magazine
1949 Cornell
Melrose Park, IL 60160   FAX 708-544-3884

INDEX

3D drawings 133
Bidmaster estimating program 446-448
Blank sizes for fittings 395, 410
Buy equipment 30

CAD/CAM 101, 110, 116, 119, 129, 235-253
Capacity 40
Coil handling 287
Coil processing 124
Combining fittings 385
Combining patterns of fittings 367
Community relations 45
Complete change 5
Computer, hand-held 443-446
Computers 96
Computers in HVAC sheet metal 417-477
Continuous flow line 11
Cut sizes for fittings 395, 410
Cutting list system (HVAC) 328
Cybermation 418-424

Depreciation 32
Design steps 50
Duct cutting system 434-440
Duct estimating 424-428, 446-448
Duct fabrication, custom 260
Ductwork 308
Ductwork, large 377

Economics of costs 63
Efficiency 4, 7
Employees 14
Equipment considerations 20-35
Equipment, maximum returns 87
Expansion 44, 169

Fabrication information 297-415
FABRICATOR®, articles 86-234
FABRICATOR®, description 84
Factors to consider 36-45, 46-59
Flexibility 42, 46
Flow of work 36
Flow patterns 54-56

Implementation of layout 17
Inspection tour 10
Inventory and storage system 260

JIT (just-in-time) 145
Job costing system 150

L-tec duct cutting system 434-440
Layout principles 11
Layout problems 4
Leasing equipment 30, 32, 94
Listing and sketching (HVAC) 308
Lot size, economic 79

Machine maintenance record 25
Machinery considerations 20-35
Machinery, versatile 271
Maintenance 39
Manufacturing process 70-82
MAPI system 64-69
Material handling 37, 46, 57-59
Merry Mechanization, Inc. 235-253

NC controls 119
Nesting fittings 385

O.S.H.A. 16
ORCA sheet metal layout system 440-443

Part inspection 74
Partial change 5
Plans, long-range and short-range 43
Plasma cutting system 418
Practical shop layout 6
Price quotes 29
PRO-DUCT hand-held computer 443-446
Problems, typical layout 48
Production 70-82
Productivity, measuring 154
Public relations 45

Quality of products 39
Quick pen touch-menu estimating 429-433

Rent equipment 30
Replacement of machinery 26, 60-69

Safety 38
Security 41
Shearing, short run 136
Sheet metal layout system 440-443
Shop layouts 256-288, 479
Short-run process 161
Snips Magazine, articles 254-296
Snips Magazine, computer columns 449-477
Snips Magazine, description 255
Software 96, 99
Space requirements 79
Storage 40
Stretchout charts, elbow and angle 401-404
Supervision 38

Templates for shop layouts 485-509
Theft 41
Transition fittings 353, 410

Used equipment 29

Wendes estimating software 424-428
Work-in-progress 47

PRACTICAL PUBLICATIONS
DIVISION OF PRACTICAL PRODUCTS — ESTABLISHED 1969

PRECISION SHEET METAL — 2nd Edition
Shop Theory (Text) - 736 pages - $49.95
Student's Workbook - 206 pages - $21.95
Instructor's Guide - 206 pages - $29.95

PRECISION SHEET METAL
Shop Practice (Text) - 88 pages - $15.95
Student's Workbook - 86 pages - $21.95
Instructor's Guide - 86 pages - $29.95

SHEET METAL TECHNOLOGY
3rd Edition
360 Pages 7" x 9" - $19.95

SPECIALTY ITEMS USED TODAY
2nd Edition
Including Methods of Design
and Fabrication and
Important Trade Topics
670 pages
407 pages of trade information
$54.95

**INSTRUCTOR'S ANSWERS
GUIDE FOR PRACTICAL
SHEET METAL LAYOUT SERIES**
$24.95

**SHEET METAL SHOP
FABRICATION PROBLEMS**
Including Over 350
Graded Parts
136 Pages - $19.95

PRACTICAL SHEET METAL PROJECTS
130 Graded Projects
with Drawings, Forming
Information and Sequences
50 Basic Projects
35 Intermediate Projects
20 Advanced Projects
25 Mini Projects
SECOND EDITION
RICHARD S. BUDZIK

**PRACTICAL SHEET METAL
PROJECTS**
2nd Edition
130 Graded Projects
With Drawings, Forming
Information and Sequences
213 Pages - $26.95

**SHEET METAL LAYOUT TABLES
FOR THE HEATING, VENTILATING
AND AIR CONDITIONING INDUSTRY**
Over 205 Pages Consisting of
Over 31,000 Mathematical
Solutions - $29.95

**PRACTICAL GUIDE FOR
IMPROVING YOUR
SHEET METAL SHOP LAYOUT**
With Easy-To-Use
Suggestions and Aids
212 pages - $29.95

THE WORLD'S LARGEST AND MOST COMPLETE SHEET METAL PUBLISHER

PRECISION SHEET METAL — 2nd Edition
Blueprint Reading (Text) - 124 pages - $18.95
Student's Workbook - 184 pages - $21.95
Instructor's Guide - 201 pages - $29.95

PRECISION SHEET METAL — 2nd Edition
Mathematics (Text) - 349 pages - $21.95
Student's Workbook - 254 pages - $21.95
Instructor's Guide - 254 pages - $29.95

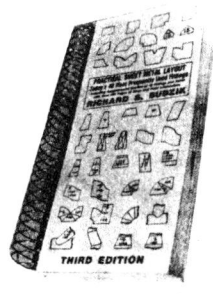

TODAY'S 40 MOST FREQUENTLY USED FITTINGS — VOLUME 1
Including Supplemental Section of 48 Fittings and Items.
(4th Edition) - 296 pages - $24.95

TODAY'S 40 MOST FREQUENTLY USED FITTINGS — VOLUME 2
Over 425 Pages of Shop and Field Information (4th Edition)
$39.95

ROUND FITTINGS USED TODAY
2nd Edition
Including Methods and Techniques of Fabricating Round Work
255 pages
97 pages of trade information
$21.95

FITTINGS USED TODAY THAT REQUIRE TRIANGULATION
2nd Edition
Including the Theory of Triangulation
224 pages
62 pages of trade information
$21.95

PRACTICAL COST ESTIMATING FOR METAL FABRICATIONS
8½" x 11" - 300 pages - $49.95

*OPPORTUNITIES IN REFRIGERATION AND AIR CONDITIONING

CONTRACTOR'S BUSINESS HANDBOOK
by our author, Richard S. Budzik, and his wife, Janet K. Budzik.

ORDER FORM
PLEASE PRINT

We Use
United Parcel Service

ORDER BY: _____
Date

_____
Name

_____
Address

_____
City

_____
State   Zip

Phone Number (in the event of any problem with your order)

_____ - _____ - _____
Area Code

SHIP TO: (If Different Than Ordered By)

_____
Name

_____
Address

_____
City

_____
State   Zip

☐ **Payment Enclosed**
(we pay postage and handling)

☐ **Bill School**
(includes postage and small fee for packaging)

*10% Educational Discount — School, Union or Association letterhead or invoice must accompany order.

Qty.	Title	Price
_____	Practical Sheet Metal Projects	29.95
_____	Sheet Metal Shop Fabrication Problems including over 350 Graded Parts	21.95
_____	Today's 40 Most Frequently-Used Fittings ---Volume 1 ----------	29.95
	---Volume 2 ----------	39.95
_____	Round Fittings Used Today including Methods and Techniques of Fabricating Round Work 3rd Edn.	21.95
_____	Fittings Used Today that Require Triangulation including the Theory of Triangulation 3rd Edn.	21.95
_____	Specialty Items Used Today including Methods of Design and Fabrication and Important Trade Topics 3rd Edn.	54.95
_____	Instructor's Answer Guide For Practical Sheet Metal Layout Series	29.95
_____	Today's Practical Guide To Increasing Profits For Contractors	49.95
_____	Sheet Metal Layout Tables for the Heating, Ventilation and Air Conditioning Industry including over 31,000 Practical, Usable, Accurate Mathematical Solutions	29.95
_____	Practical Guide For Improving Your Sheet Metal Shop Layout with easy to use Suggestions and Aids	29.95
_____	Precision Sheet Metal Shop Theory textbook	21.95
_____	Student's Workbook	21.95
_____	Instructor's Guide	26.95
_____	Precision Sheet Metal Blueprint Reading textbook	18.95
_____	Student's Workbook	21.95
_____	Instructor's Guide	26.95
_____	Precision Sheet Metal Mathematics textbook	21.95
_____	Student's Workbook	21.95
_____	Instructor's Guide	26.95
_____	Precision Sheet Metal Shop Practice textbook	15.95
_____	Student's Workbook	21.95
_____	Instructor's Guide	26.95
_____	Sheet Metal Technology textbook 3RD Edn.	24.95
_____	Student's Workbook	9.95
	Instructor's Guide	9.95
_____	Opportunities in Refrigeration and Air Conditioning (order from VGM Career Horizons, 8259 Niles Center Road, Skokie, IL 60077)	Hard 9.95 Soft 7.95

PRACTICAL PUBLICATIONS
DIVISION OF PRACTICAL PRODUCTS — ESTABLISHED 1969
6272 W. North Avenue • Chicago, Illinois 60639-9990 • (312) 237-2986

_____ Practical Cost Estimating for Metal Fabrication $64.95

ORDER FORM
PLEASE PRINT

We Use United Parcel Service

ORDER BY: _____
Date

_____
Name

_____
Address

_____
City

_____
State   Zip

Phone Number (in the event of any problem with your order)

___ ___ - _____
Area Code

SHIP TO: (If Different Than Ordered By)

_____
Name

_____
Address

_____
City

_____
State   Zip

☐ **Payment Enclosed**
(we pay postage and handling)

☐ **Bill School**
(includes postage and small fee for packaging)

*10% Educational Discount — School, Union or Association letterhead or invoice must accompany order.

Qty.	Title	Price
_____	Practical Sheet Metal Projects	29.95
_____	Sheet Metal Shop Fabrication Problems including over 350 Graded Parts	21.95
_____	Today's 40 Most Frequently-Used Fittings	
	---Volume 1 ----------	29.95
	---Volume 2 ----------	39.95
_____	Round Fittings Used Today including Methods and Techniques of Fabricating Round Work 3rd Edn.	21.95
_____	Fittings Used Today that Require Triangulation including the Theory of Triangulation 3rd Edn.	21.95
_____	Specialty Items Used Today including Methods of Design and Fabrication and Important Trade Topics 3rd Edn.	54.95
_____	Instructor's Answer Guide For Practical Sheet Metal Layout Series	29.95
_____	Today's Practical Guide To Increasing Profits For Contractors	49.95
_____	Sheet Metal Layout Tables for the Heating, Ventilation and Air Conditioning Industry including over 31,000 Practical, Usable, Accurate Mathematical Solutions	29.95
_____	Practical Guide For Improving Your Sheet Metal Shop Layout with easy to use Suggestions and Aids	29.95
_____	Precision Sheet Metal Shop Theory textbook	21.95
_____	Student's Workbook	21.95
_____	Instructor's Guide	26.95
_____	Precision Sheet Metal Blueprint Reading textbook	18.95
_____	Student's Workbook	21.95
_____	Instructor's Guide	26.95
_____	Precision Sheet Metal Mathematics textbook	21.95
_____	Student's Workbook	21.95
_____	Instructor's Guide	26.95
_____	Precision Sheet Metal Shop Practice textbook	15.95
_____	Student's Workbook	21.95
_____	Instructor's Guide	26.95
_____	Sheet Metal Technology 3RD Edn. textbook	24.95
_____	Student's Workbook	9.95
_____	Instructor's Guide	9.95
_____	Opportunities in Refrigeration and Air Conditioning (order from VGM Career Horizons, 8259 Niles Center Road, Skokie, IL 60077)	Hard 9.95 Soft 7.95

PRACTICAL PUBLICATIONS
DIVISION OF PRACTICAL PRODUCTS — ESTABLISHED 1969
6272 W. North Avenue • Chicago, Illinois 60639-9990 • (312) 237-2986

_____ Practical Cost Estimating for Metal Fabrication $64.95